WORKING
WITH WOOD

3/4" dowel holes

5 3/4"

5 1/2"

McKNIGHT
PUBLISHING COMPANY
BLOOMINGTON, ILLINOIS

GILBERT R. HUTCHINGS
Professor
Industrial Technology and Education
Western Michigan University
Kalamazoo, Michigan

G. EUGENE MARTIN
Professor and Chairman
Department of Industrial Arts
Southwest Texas State University
San Marcos, Texas

J. MARIO COLEMAN
Associate Professor
Industrial Education and Technology
West Texas State University
Canyon, Texas

WORKING WITH WOOD

FIRST EDITION

Lithographed in U.S.A.

Library of Congress Catalog Card Number: 81-82309

SBN: 87345-084-1

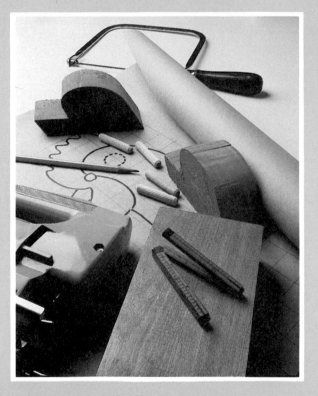

Editor: Robert W. Todd

Copy Editing: Robert Cassel
Layout: Elizabeth Purcell
Production: Sandy Savage
            Sandy Baker
Production Assistance: Mary E. Williams
Design: Forward Productions
Art: Howard Davis
Project Art: Aldren Watson
Photography: Lawrence E. Funk
            Jim Driscoll
            Michael Jenkins
            Barry Moline
            Kanti Sandhu and John Provancher
            Western Michigan University

Woodland photograph on page i by David Cavagnaro
Photographs on pages i, iv, v, vi, viii, 4, 7, and 10
reprinted with permission from the
ORTHO Book, **Wood Projects For The Home**
Copyright © 1980, Chevron Chemical Company

10   9   8   7   6   5   4   3   2   1

The authors of **Working With Wood** have endeavored to introduce beginning students to wood. To teach woodworking and keep motivation high, the text has been written in a "hands-on" manner. The student is addressed directly throughout the text to help ensure *his* or *her* participation.

The text is organized to get the student working on a project right away. It is written *for* the student, to be used *by* the student. Procedures and explanations are written so they are easy to understand and follow. After all, the best way to learn about wood is to work with wood.

Section I introduces the subject of woodworking, then quickly involves the student with project design, planning, material selection, layout, and safety.

Section II takes the students a step further, explaining how to identify and use all types of hand tools. The material is written to guide the students, step by step, through the hand cutting and shaping of their project.

Section III introduces and describes the various techniques and methods of joining pieces of wood. Both the how and the why are discussed in an easy-to-understand fashion.

Section IV instructs students about materials and techniques used to smooth project surfaces for finishing. Organizing this information into a separate section helps to emphasize the importance of this often overlooked step.

Section V describes in detail the materials and procedures used to finish a project. Information is provided to help students select the right finishes for their projects.

Section VI contains detailed information about the power tools and machines used by woodworkers. Each tool is described with reference to its uses, operation, and safety. Power tool information is placed at this point in the text so it will not interfere with "basic" woodworking skills. However, this information can easily be referenced at any point during the course.

Section VII contains selected topics related to woodworking. A chapter on cabinetmaking provides necessary information on making tables, shelves, drawers, cabinet doors, and many other cabinet parts. A chapter on upholstery includes procedures for making foam, cane, and splint seats for stools and chairs. A career chapter explores many woodworking careers. This chapter also contains tips for evaluating and selecting careers.

Section VIII discusses trees and forestry. This section provides valuable information about how trees grow and are harvested for use. This section also contains a unique wood species unit with full-color photographs. These photos show the variety of wood and provide a practical reference for indentifying unknown woods.

The wood species unit also contains over 30 color pictures of wood products. These products serve as examples of quality design and construction. These may also encourage students to create their own designs.

Section IX contains 42 original and motivating woodworking projects. Most of these project plans contain complete working drawings and a photo of the finished project. The projects range from easy to difficult, providing suitable projects for just about any woodworking student. All projects were selected for their quality of design and appropriateness. They can all be made using the processes and techniques presented in this text.

Where there is woodworking, there must also be *safety.* This textbook handles safety as comprehensively as possible. Safety information is provided in two separate safety chapters: chapter 7, "Safety," and chapter 31, "Power Tool Safety." Safety information is also interspersed throughout the other chapters in the text.

Metrics are included in the text to help students associate, and later replace, customary with metric measurements. Metrics are not included where they would needlessly confuse the student, or where there have been no conversions to date. For instance, a 3/8-inch dowel rod is not converted to metrics since metric dowel rods are not yet available.

FOREWORD

Section I

Planning your Work

Section II

Hand Tool Woodworking

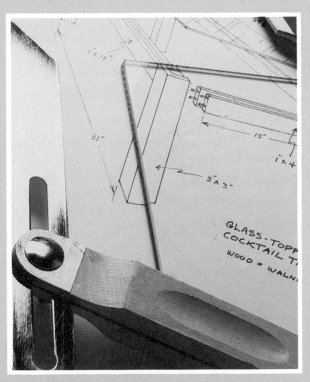

Section

III

Joining Stock

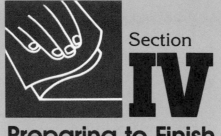

Section

IV

Preparing to Finish

CONTENTS

Section V

Wood Finishing

Section VI

Power Tools

Section VII

Selected Woodworking Topics

Section VIII

Wood Technology

Section

IX

Projects

PLANNING
YOUR WORK

Chapter

1

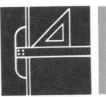

Working with Wood

Art Gallery of Ontario, Toronto

Fig. 1-1. This is an Indian camp in the 1850s. To make a canoe, the Indians cut birch bark, wrapped it around a bent cedar frame, and sealed it with pine gum.

Fig. 1-2. The mahogany table in the center of this old woodworking shop was made more than 200 years ago. Do you recognize any of the tools used to cut and shape the table?

The Henry Francis du Pont Winterthur Museum

It is difficult to imagine a world without wood. For thousands of years — almost forever — people have worked with wood. They have used wood to build objects for protection, shelter, transportation, comfort, amusement, and even inspiration. Bows and arrows, rooftops, canoes, tables, chairs, baseball bats, and guitars — all have been made from wood. Why do you think this is so? Why has wood been such an important resource?

Woodworking — An Old Craft

So many things were built from wood because most places had such a large supply. While other materials were scarce or far away, there was usually plenty of wood close by. The supply is still plentiful where trees grew back and people replanted them.

Wood was also used so much because it was easy to work with. Remember, up until a hundred years ago there were no power tools or machines. Wood was easy to carve and shape by hand, and thin pieces bent easily without breaking. Wood is light and that made it easy to handle. It also floats, and, when properly treated, is waterproof.

As people found more uses for wood, they learned to identify the different kinds. Colorful woods with beautiful grain patterns were used by cabinetmakers to make fine furniture. Attractive woods were also used by artists to make beautiful works of art. Strong woods for building homes and bridges were identified and used by builders. Hard, shock-resistant woods were discovered by toolmakers. Water-resistant woods for ships, barrels, and shingles, were found by shipbuilders and manufacturers.

At first no one knew which woods were strong and which were water resistant. It took hundreds of years of trial and error to find the best uses of wood. For example, the first hammer handles probably broke after only a few blows. Toolmakers tried various woods for these handles, however, and found stronger, more shock-resistant woods. Later toolmakers found even stronger woods.

The search for better wood materials and uses is by no means over. It goes on even today. Wood still offers the potential for discovery. Because wood is versatile and beautiful, its possibilities are almost endless. Building a project with wood provides as much satisfaction today as it did hundreds of years ago.

Learning About Wood

Think for a moment — what do you know about wood? You probably learned as a child that wood comes from trees. You know that trees grow, producing more and more wood. You might know a few kinds of wood by name. Perhaps you can even identify a few by sight, although this is often much easier when the

wood is still part of the tree. Now, as you begin this course, you will want to learn much more — as much as possible — about wood.

There are actually hundreds of kinds of wood. Each kind has its own qualities. See Fig. 1-5. You will learn which woods are best for making certain objects. You will learn the

Philadelphia Maritime Museum

Fig. 1-4. This fishing vessel is made of Portuguese pine. The boat first set sail in the North Atlantic in 1883 and is still in sailing condition today.

Fig. 1-5. The woodworker selected ash wood for this table. The qualities of ash make it ideal for bending into various shapes.

Kingsley Chapin Brooks

Fig. 1-3. More than five kinds of wood were used to construct this grand piano. Notice the differences in grain patterns from wood to wood.

Bannister Harpsichords, Hopewell, NJ

different ways of handling the different woods. You will see how project designs affect your choice of wood. You will also learn how to emphasize the natural beauty of wood.

Color photographs of the most-used woods are shown in section VIII. You can also increase your knowledge of woods by reading chapter 4. You will want to refer to this information frequently as you design and build your project.

The best way to learn about wood is to work with it. Using hand tools to cut and shape your project, you will notice how soft or hard the wood is. You will discover the best ways to cut with and against the grain. You will quickly notice how color, grain pattern, strength, and weight differ from one wood to the next.

You can build your project more quickly and efficiently with power tools. It would be a mistake, however, for a beginning woodworker to overlook the advantages of using hand tools skillfully. Using hand tools is more than a way to learn about wood. Much of the finest furniture ever made was made only with hand tools.

Fig. 1-6. Using hand tools is an important part of woodworking. Here a skilled woodworker is carving a decorative sunburst. Woodcraft Supply Corporation

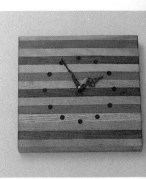

Oak, walnut, mahogany, maple

Pine

Walnut

Redwood

Fig. 1-7. Each kind of wood has its own special appearance. Consider how the wood will add to your project's beauty.

The Beauty of Wood

One of the great pleasures in working with wood is creating objects that enhance its beauty. See Fig. 1-7. Turn a piece of wood over in your hands. Carefully inspect its grain and color before deciding how to use it. Look for an imaginative way of contrasting wood colors or combining different woods. Also learn about the countless ways of finishing your project so it is protected and attractive.

Compare the many woods and finishes in a furniture store. Look closely at a piece of fine furniture. You will see the beauty of different wood colors and figures. You will see how woodworkers use their imagination and skill to enhance the natural beauty of wood.

As you learn to create beautiful wood pieces, you will develop respect for wood. Wood is a natural material that takes decades to produce. Use it wisely. Learn to be as careful with common woods as you would be with expensive woods. This will help you conserve material and keep costs at a minimum. By working carefully you can make a project that will last for many years.

Planning a Project

"If a thing is worth doing, it's worth doing well." It is difficult, if not impossible, to disagree with this expression. The expression is especially important in this course. Make your project the very best it can be. It should work as you intend it to work. It should also be as attractive as possible. Use the minimum amount of material and make the best use of your time. Learn all that you can. When your project is finished, you want to be able to say, "It was worth doing well."

The first step in making the best possible project is to make a plan. Your plan actually begins when you choose your project. Deciding what to make does not sound difficult. However, it is an important decision. Do not make it hastily. Making a sailboat may sound great, but would it really be a good choice? Do you have the space and necessary materials? Do you know enough about woodworking to take on such a big project? Reading chapter 2 will help you determine the best project for your present skills, time, and needs. Someday you may be able to design and construct your own sailboat — but probably not yet.

The Henry Francis du Pont Winterthur Museum

Fig. 1-8. Shaker furniture combines simplicity with quality construction. The furniture shown here was made in the early 1800s. It is as attractive and strong now as it was when it was made.

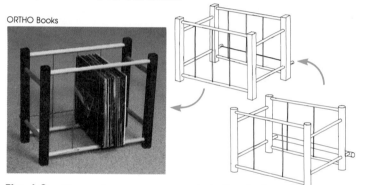
ORTHO Books

Fig. 1-9. Many changes were made in the design of this record rack. The changes made the rack easier to build and more functional. To build this record rack, see the project section of this text.

As you read chapter 2, you will begin to realize that **design** is a big part of your project plan. There is much more to designing a project than deciding its size and shape. The complete design of any project includes a collection of answers to important questions. How much weight will it support? Where will it be used? Who will use it? In your shop and in industry these questions are called **stating the problem**. Once you have stated the problem, it will be much easier to identify a solution. Sketches and models will help you select the best ones. See Fig. 1-9.

You may complete two or three project designs before you start cutting any wood. Be patient. Most beautiful wood products started with a pencil and paper, not a saw. The sawing, planing, and gluing will come soon enough. They should never precede a final design.

Safety First

You will be reminded over and over of safety rules for the woodworking shop. You may start to think that safety is the most important part of this course. Well, it is. Any enjoyment and satisfaction you get from making your project, depends on safety. You will not enjoy making your project if you seriously injure yourself or someone else.

So many of the tools and materials used in woodworking can be dangerous. You must know how to use the tools. You must concentrate on what you are doing every second. It only takes a momentary distraction to cause an accident. That accident might result in a minor scratch, or it could cause a serious, painful injury.

All accidents — whether they be minor or serious — are caused by people. They are caused by people who are not being careful, who are not thinking ahead. No accident is excusable. They can all be avoided if people know and use safety.

We must all work together to eliminate accidents. Everybody in the woodworking shop must have a **safety attitude**. Everybody must **listen** to and **follow** instructions. Everybody must **learn** the safety rules of the shop, and everybody must **use** those safety rules.

Each person must stop and think about what he or she is doing. Each person must work carefully and safely. This way there will be no accidents, and no one will be injured. Woodworking is too much fun to lose even one day due to an accident that should never have happened. Everyone will enjoy woodworking if EVERYONE THINKS SAFETY.

Study Questions

1. Name one wooden object used for each of the following purposes: shelter, transportation, comfort, sports, music.
2. Give two reasons that wood has been such an important, useful resource.
3. Through the years, how have woodworkers been able to find the best uses for different kinds of wood?
4. What do you know about wood? List as many kinds of wood as you can think of. Put a check next to each kind that you can identify.
5. What is the first step in making the best possible wood project?
6. Think of something you might like to build with wood. Can you think of two questions you would need to answer in designing this project?
7. How important is safety in woodworking?
8. How can accidents be eliminated?
9. To eliminate accidents, **who** must practice safety?

Project Design

Chapter

2

An important part of any project is its design. The design determines the project's type, size, shape, function and appearance. Careful planning at the design stage can help you avoid construction problems before they occur.

In industry many people work on the design of a product. These designers and engineers make sure the product is easy to make, and is the right size and shape. They also make sure that it will work properly when completed. In the woodworking shop, **you** will be responsible for the design of your project.

Project Selection

The first step in designing a project is deciding what to make. Try to make something you can use. Bookcases, hat racks, bread boxes and picture frames are possibilities. You may already know what you want to make. If not, you must think of a good project idea. You will find many good resources for project ideas in the following paragraphs.

Finding Ideas. One good source of project ideas is the project section, section IX, in this text. Other sources include magazines, project books, and furniture catalogs. A visit to your school or community library could be very helpful. You may even get an idea by browsing through a furniture store or gift shop.

Your teacher may be a good source of project ideas. He or she may have a special project already designed to fit your abilities and time limitations.

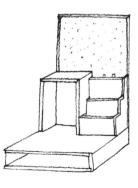
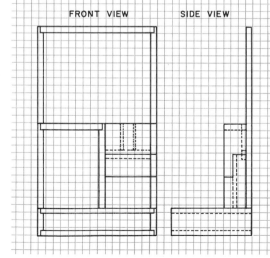

ORTHO Books

Fig. 2-1. Many design questions were asked before this telephone caddy was built. How much space is needed for the telephone? Will the telephone book fit in the slot? How much space is needed for notes and pencils?

7

Fig. 2-2. These are design sketches for an ordinary step stool. They show how you can create new and different designs by using your imagination.

One of the best sources of project ideas is your own imagination. Imagination is that mental quality that allows you to invent new and different ideas. Producing new ideas is also called creative thinking. By using your imagination and creativity you can create a unique (original) project idea. See Fig. 2-2.

Choosing a Project. List several project ideas that interest you. Then select the one that best suits your needs. Remember to select a project that you can use.

You should consider several other factors before selecting a project.

- your ability
- time available
- equipment available
- cost of project

If you are a beginner, do not attempt an advanced project, such as a grandfather clock. As you gain experience, you can select projects of greater difficulty. Help yourself be successful. Pick an easy project for your first try.

Design Considerations

After you have selected the type of project, start thinking about its design. Good designs are not developed by chance. They are the result of careful planning around three major considerations. These considerations are function, appearance, and the selection of material.

Function. All products are designed for a particular use, or function. For instance, a bookcase is designed to hold books. That is its function. A sailboat, on the other hand, has transportation as its main function.

It is important that a project do what it is intended to do. A bookshelf designed so that books slip off the shelves would be of little use. See Fig. 2-3. A sailboat designed without a sail would be poorly designed. You must design your project carefully to make it work. The better the functional design, the better your project will work for you.

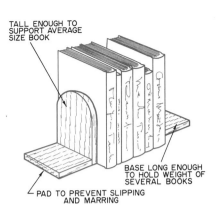

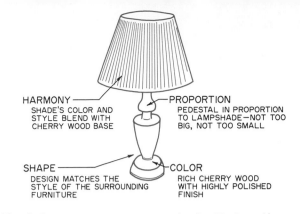

Fig. 2-4. APPEARANCE. You are the final judge of how well the elements of your project blend together.

Fig. 2-3. FUNCTION. Will your project work the way it should?

Appearance. Besides being useful, your project should be attractive in appearance. Appearance refers to the way your project looks — beautiful, ugly, or in between.

The appearance depends on many design elements. A few of these are shape, color, proportion, balance, and harmony. See Fig. 2-4. The test of whether these elements are used successfully is the overall appearance of your project. If it is attractive, the design is good from the standpoint of appearance.

It is important to understand that what is attractive to you may not be attractive to someone else. You may not be able to satisfy everyone with the appearance of your design. Be open to helpful comments, but design your project so **you** will be happy with its appearance.

Selection of Materials. An important factor in the overall design is the selection of materials. The wood you choose affects the project's appearance, strength, durability, and cost. It also affects the ease with which it can be constructed. See Fig. 2-5.

Poor selection of materials can ruin an otherwise good design. For example, a mallet (wooden hammer) made of soft wood, such as pine, would not be very strong or durable. A hard wood, such as maple, would be better. A wall plaque, however, need not be strong. A soft wood could be used. Using pine would make it easy to cut letters into the plaque. A

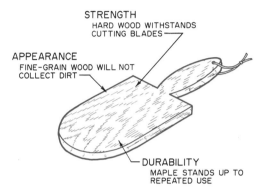

Fig. 2-5. MATERIALS. An important part of design is selecting the best type of wood for your project. Pine, for example, would not provide the strength and durability needed for a cutting board.

wood such as hickory would be more difficult to work and more expensive.

Read chapter 4, "Material Selection," and study the wood species described in section VIII. This will help you decide what materials best fit the design of your project.

Design Procedure

A successful design is usually the result of being organized. Professional designers develop their design faster and easier by following a plan, or procedure. Dividing the procedure into steps helps the designer concentrate his or her efforts on the design problem. Similar steps should be followed when designing a wood project. These steps include stating the problem and making sketches. When necessary, making a mock-up is also included.

Stating the Problem. A successful design is really a solution to a problem. For instance, a

Fig. 2-6. This firewood tower is functional: it holds more wood in less floor space than a box does. It is made of mahogany because the wood is both attractive and durable.

Fig. 2-7. This designer stated the problem by saying: "I'd like a chest big enough to hold all my indoor games. It should be attractive enough to put in the family room. It should also be sturdy enough to use as a game table or coffee table."

square, open box is one solution to the problem of storing record albums. Storing the albums is the main design problem. Looking more closely, you may see other problems. You may want the box to be attractive. You may want it to hold a certain number of records. Listing all the problems you can think of is called stating the problem. See Fig. 2-7.

Stating the problem requires gathering information on the use and purpose of a project. The more information, the easier it is to develop a good design. With all the facts, you will not waste time designing an unsatisfactory project.

Making Sketches. Once the design problem is clearly stated, you need to make sketches. Sketches are freehand drawings of possible solutions to a design problem. Sketch all of your design ideas, even if they seem unimportant. An unimportant or unusual idea may lead to a good design. It is through sketching that most designs take shape.

Your first sketches do not need to be detailed. As you improve your ideas, add detail to them. The wooden chest in Fig. 2-8 is a simple design. It shows how an idea can progress from a sketch to a detailed design. It also shows how the designer improved on the idea. Try to improve your ideas as you design your project.

Fig. 2-8. The detailed final drawing of the game chest was developed from simple sketches.

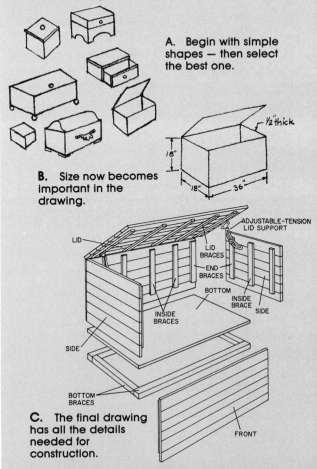

A. Begin with simple shapes — then select the best one.

B. Size now becomes important in the drawing.

C. The final drawing has all the details needed for construction.

To make sketches, you will need a sketch pad, a pencil, and an eraser. First, draw lines to show the project's shape. Next, add lines to show the thickness of materials. Then add general dimensions. This gives a picture of the overall size and shape.

Do not be afraid to change your ideas or erase a sketch. Even finished sketches may need changing. Good designers often make many changes before they decide on a final sketch. These changes are part of the designing process.

The final sketch will later be made into a working drawing. This drawing will guide you through the construction of the project.

Mock-up. A model built from a sketch is called a mock-up. A mock-up lets you actually see the project's height, width, and depth. It also lets you see how the parts fit together. The mock-up gives you a clear picture of the project before it is built. Any changes in design can be made on the mock-up. This helps you decide on the best design. It also helps you pick the best construction methods.

Not all designs require a mock-up. Complicated or hard-to-sketch designs may need one. Sometimes you will make a mock-up of the whole project. Other times you will make one for only part of the project.

Fig. 2-9. The mock-up is scaled to be the same shape as the final product. One inch in the small cardboard chest equals 4 inches in the real chest.

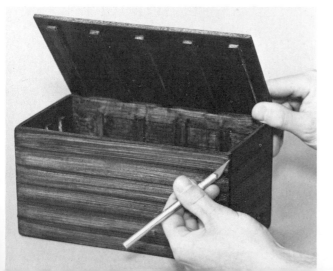

Mock-ups can be smaller or larger than the project. However, they are usually built to **scale.** This means all the dimensions of the sketch are increased or decreased by the same amount.

A mock-up may be made with many types of materials. Paper, cardboard, plastic (such as polystyrene foam and Plexiglas), clay, and wood are examples. The material chosen should be easy to cut and shape. You do not want to spend a lot of time building the mock-up. Generally a mock-up is made out of material that is cheaper than the material selected for the actual project. Mock-ups need not be sturdy or workable. Their only purpose is to show the appearance of the finished project. See Fig. 2-9.

New Terms

1. designers
2. engineers
3. function
4. material selection
5. mock-up
6. scale
7. sketching
8. stating the problem

Study Questions

1. What is the first step in designing a project?
2. Identify some examples of project resources.
3. What are the three major considerations in developing your design?
4. What part does imagination play in designing your project?
5. What kinds of information do you need before stating the problems?
6. Give two reasons why it is important to sketch the designs of a wood project.
7. How do the first sketches differ from later sketches?
8. Why should you make a mock-up of your project before you start to build it?
9. What does it mean to build a mock-up to scale?

Chapter 3

Parts of a Plan

Before you get out the wood and start to saw, you should make a plan. A plan will help the job go smoothly, with little waste and few mistakes. Taking the time to make a complete project plan will save you extra work and frustration during construction.

A detailed plan for a woodworking project looks like the one shown in Fig. 3-1. Notice that it contains three basic parts: drawings, a bill of materials, and a plan of procedure. These parts work together, showing what the project will look like and how it will fit together. They also show you the project's dimensions, how much material the project needs, and how to build it.

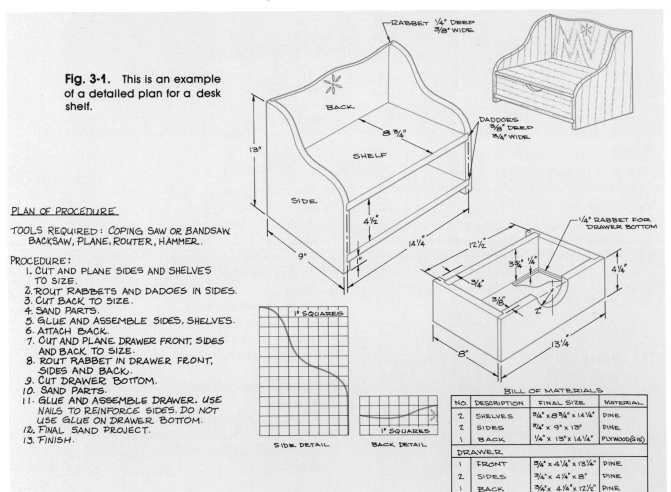

Fig. 3-1. This is an example of a detailed plan for a desk shelf.

RABBET 1/4" DEEP 3/8" WIDE

BACK

DADDOES 3/8" DEEP 3/4" WIDE

8 3/4"

SHELF

13"

SIDE

4 1/2"

14 1/4"

12 1/2"

9"

1"

1/4" RABBET FOR DRAWER BOTTOM

3 3/4" 1/4"

3/4"

3/8"

2"

4 1/4"

8"

13 1/4"

1" SQUARES

SIDE DETAIL

1" SQUARES

BACK DETAIL

PLAN OF PROCEDURE

TOOLS REQUIRED: COPING SAW OR BANDSAW, BACKSAW, PLANE, ROUTER, HAMMER.

PROCEDURE:
1. CUT AND PLANE SIDES AND SHELVES TO SIZE.
2. ROUT RABBETS AND DADOES IN SIDES.
3. CUT BACK TO SIZE.
4. SAND PARTS.
5. GLUE AND ASSEMBLE SIDES, SHELVES.
6. ATTACH BACK.
7. CUT AND PLANE DRAWER FRONT, SIDES AND BACK TO SIZE.
8. ROUT RABBET IN DRAWER FRONT, SIDES AND BACK.
9. CUT DRAWER BOTTOM.
10. SAND PARTS.
11. GLUE AND ASSEMBLE DRAWER. USE NAILS TO REINFORCE SIDES. DO NOT USE GLUE ON DRAWER BOTTOM.
12. FINAL SAND PROJECT.
13. FINISH.

NO.	DESCRIPTION	FINAL SIZE	MATERIAL
2	SHELVES	3/4" x 8 3/4" x 14 1/4"	PINE
2	SIDES	3/4" x 9" x 13"	PINE
1	BACK	1/4" x 13" x 14 1/4"	PLYWOOD (GIS)
DRAWER			
1	FRONT	3/4" x 4 1/4" x 13 1/4"	PINE
2	SIDES	3/4" x 4 1/4" x 8"	PINE
1	BACK	3/4" x 4 1/4" x 12 1/2"	PINE
1	BOTTOM	1/4" x 6 3/4" x 12 1/4"	PLYWOOD (GIS)

BILL OF MATERIALS

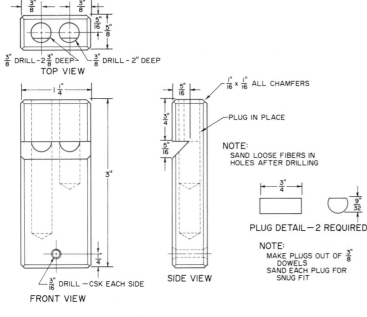

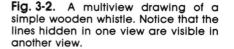

Fig. 3-2. A multiview drawing of a simple wooden whistle. Notice that the lines hidden in one view are visible in another view.

A project plan generally starts with simple drawings. These drawings are usually quickly drawn sketches. They show only the rough appearance of the project. They can be, and usually are, changed and redrawn until the final project design is determined. The final sketch is then made into a precise working drawing.

Working Drawings

Working drawings show **in detail** the size and shape of the project and its parts. They include dimensions that show you where to cut and shape stock. They also show you how the project will fit together. Two general kinds of drawings are used in woodworking plans. They are multiview drawings (orthographic projections), and pictorial drawings. Many woodworking plans use both kinds of drawings. This makes the project easy to visualize and still provides all the needed information.

Multiview Drawing. Three separate drawings are usually contained in a multiview drawing. Each drawing shows a different view — front, top, side — of the project. See Fig. 3-2. These three views will usually show every detail on the project. For complex projects extra views may be needed to show unusual parts or assembly details.

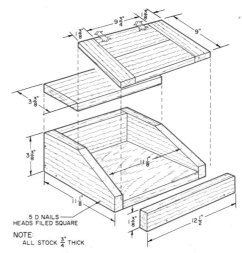

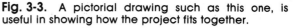

Fig. 3-3. A pictorial drawing such as this one, is useful in showing how the project fits together.

Pictorial Drawing. As the name implies, a pictorial drawing is like a picture of the project. It shows three views of a project, all in one drawing. It shows the project at an angle, as in Fig. 3-3.

Pictorial drawings are harder to draw than multiview drawings. They are more lifelike and are usually easier to read, however. Details are sometimes harder to show in pictorial drawings.

Drawing to Scale. Working drawings should be drawn to scale. All dimensions should be

Fig. 3-4. This plan for a bed frame should have been drawn to a smaller scale. A huge drawing like this would not only be hard to read, but hard to make. Drawings made too small will cause similar problems.

Fig. 3-5. Scales are instruments used to reduce or enlarge the dimensions of a project without changing its proportions. Scales are provided on each of the instrument's three sides.

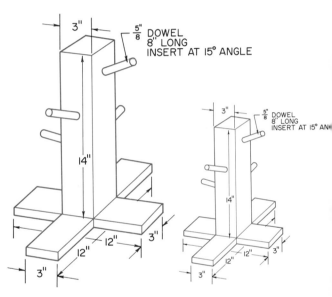

Fig. 3-6. The two scale drawings above will produce the same size mug tree.

increased or decreased by the same amount (in proportion) when drawn. This means you can make your drawing either smaller or larger than the finished project without changing its appearance. You then have a working drawing that is easy to use. Can you imagine trying to use a full-size drawing of a bed frame, as shown in Fig. 3-4? It would be very unhandy, if not impossible.

Most projects need to be drawn smaller than their actual sizes. You can do this easily with a scale. See Fig. 3-5. A typical scale has measuring units for full size, half-size, quarter-size, and eighth-size drawings. A quarter-size drawing, for example, would be only one-fourth the project's final size. A 1-inch (25 mm) measurement on the project would be 1/4 inch (6 mm) on the drawing.

Determine the most convenient scale reduction by comparing the size of the project to the size of the drawing paper. Architectural drafters, for instance, use scales in which 1 inch equals 1 foot. Their projects are houses and buildings so they must reduce dimensions a great deal. You may need to scale your project up or down. Your drawing must show enough detail and still fit on the paper. See Fig. 3-6.

Drawing Lines. To make or read a working drawing, you must know the meaning of several lines. You also need to know how to make these lines. Study Fig. 3-7 and the following information to learn about these lines.

Object lines (also called visible lines) are bold and dark. They show the visible outline of the project.

Hidden lines are drawn as short, even dashes. They show the location of parts not seen in a particular view.

Center lines are thin, light lines. They are drawn with alternating short and long dashes.

They indicate the center of project parts or holes.

Extension lines are thin lines used with dimension lines to show the size of project parts. Extension lines extend beyond the edges of a project to help show dimensions.

Dimension lines have arrowheads at each end. They are drawn between two extension lines to show dimensions.

Making Working Drawings

You must be patient and accurate to make working drawings correctly. Working drawings determine how good the project looks and how well it fits together. If the drawing has mistakes, so will the project.

Use the final sketch of the project to determine the scale of the working drawing. The scale should allow the project to be drawn on regular-size paper. Use the scale to draw each line on the project. For most beginners it is much easier to make a multiview drawing than a pictorial drawing. See Fig. 3-8. The sketch will serve as a pictorial drawing.

Draw the dimensions carefully. The lines can be off a little, but the dimensions must be correct. They must show the exact length, width, and thickness of each part.

They should also show the sizes of holes, grooves, angles, and hardware.

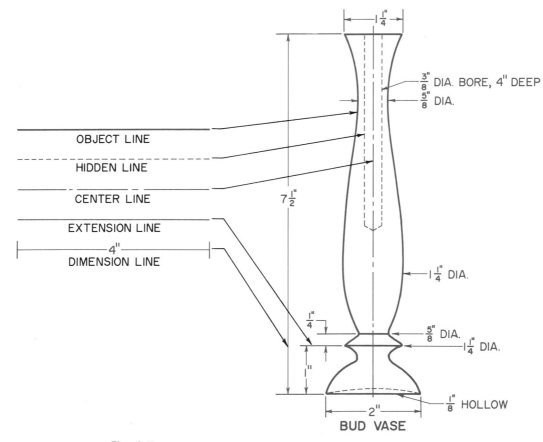

Fig. 3-7. Several types of lines are used in working drawings.

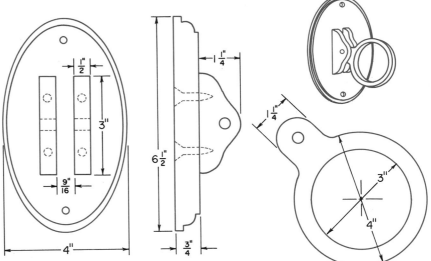

Fig. 3-8. This multiview drawing is made from a sketch of a towel ring.

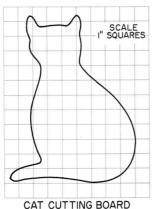

CAT CUTTING BOARD

Fig. 3-9. An irregular design, such as this cat, should be drawn on a grid. This will help you make an accurate layout later.

Drawings with irregular designs and curves should be drawn on a grid, as shown in Fig. 3-9. Draw the grid to the same scale as the rest of the drawing. Then draw the design within the grid.

When laying out the design on the stock, make a full-size grid on a large piece of paper. Then transfer the design to the full-size grid and cut it out. This becomes your pattern for the layout. For more information see page 40.

Bill of Materials

A bill of materials is a complete list of the materials (wood, hardware, and finishing materials) required to make a project. A detailed bill of materials, as shown in Fig. 3-11, provides space for the following information.

- number and description of each part.
- kind of material (oak, brass, varnish, etc.).

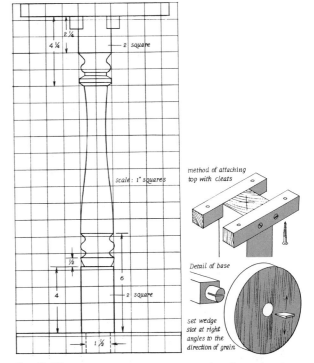

Fig. 3-10. This is what a working drawing of a fern stand might look like. See section IX.

- size and amount of each material.
- cost of each material.

Not all bills of materials are this detailed. Some are called "materials list," or simply "materials." If you are using a bill of materials that is not complete, add the necessary information.

Use the working drawings as a guide to fill out the bill of materials. The working drawings show the dimensions of each part. They also help you determine the kinds of materials needed. Chapter 4, "Material Selection," will also help you choose materials. You may need to do some checking to find out the material costs. Costs vary depending on where you buy the materials.

When the bill of materials is completed, you should know how much lumber to buy and how much it will cost. You should also know what part of the project each material will be used for.

Allowing for Waste. There is always waste when you cut and shape wood. You must allow for this waste when you plan your lumber needs. This is normally done by slightly increasing the finish sizes of each project part.

Finish sizes are the sizes given on the working drawing. Each part must be cut to its finish size for the project to fit together properly.

Rough sizes are determined by slightly increasing the finish sizes. Using rough sizes allows for the waste in cutting and shaping. Remember, it is always better to have too much stock than not enough. However, you want just a **little** too much. Ordering more lumber than you need will increase the cost of your project. Use the following general rules to determine rough sizes.

- Add 1/2 inch *(13mm)* to 1 inch *(25 mm)* to the length of each part.
- Add 1/4 inch *(6 mm)* to 3/8 inch *(9 mm)* to the width of each part.
- Specify standard lumber 1/16 inch *(2 mm)* to 3/16 inch *(5 mm)* thicker than the thickness of each part.
- Small parts do not need as much extra material as large parts.

Rough sizes are not always included on a bill of materials. If yours does not include rough sizes, be sure to make the additions before ordering your lumber. This step is important because ordering too little lumber will delay your project's construction.

Measuring Lumber. Lumber is measured and sold by the board foot, square foot, and

Fig. 3-11. A complete bill of materials for the fern stand pictured in Fig. 3-10 would contain these items.

Name: Janet Brown   Starting date Sept. 20

Project: Fern Stand   Completion date Dec. 12

No. of parts	Description	Finish size	Rough size	Material	Bd. Ft. or Sq. Ft.	Unit cost	Total cost
1	Top	3/4" × 9" DIA	1" × 9-1/2" × 9-1/2"	Cherry	.63	**1.60**	1.01
1	Base	1-1/4" × 10" DIA	1-1/2" × 10-1/2" × 10-1/2"	Cherry	1.15	**1.65**	1.90
2	Cleats	3/4" × 3/4" × 5"	1" × 7/8" × 5-1/2"	Cherry	.04	**1.60**	.06
1	Spindle	2" × 2" × 20-1/4"	2-1/8" × 2-1/8" × 20-3/4"	Cherry	.65	**1.70**	1.10
1	Wedge	1/8" × 1" × 1-1/4"	1/8" × 1-1/16" × 1-5/16"	Walnut	Scrap	—	—

Other Materials

No.	Description	Size	Unit cost	Total cost
8	Screws	1-1/2" × 8" Flathead	.10	.80
	Finish			.50
			Total Cost	$5.37

lineal foot. You will use these units to measure lumber for your project.

Board feet (bd. ft.) is the measurement used to buy all solid lumber. A board foot measures 1 inch thick, 12 inches wide, and 12 inches long. Notice that a board foot contains 144 cubic inches. See Fig. 3-12. Wood less than 1 inch thick is considered a full inch when computing board feet. Stock over 1 inch is figured by the next greater quarter inch. For example, a piece of oak 1-3/8 inch thick would be considered 1-1/2 inches thick.

Woodworkers determine board feet by measuring the thickness, width, and length of a board. The measurements are then put into one of the following formulas. If the length is in feet, use the first formula. If all the dimensions are in inches, use the second.

$$(1) \text{ board feet } = \frac{\text{Thickness (}''\text{)} \times \text{Width (}''\text{)} \times \text{Length (}'\text{)}}{12}$$

Example: A board measuring 1″ × 12″ × 18′ contains 18 board feet.

$$\frac{1 \times 12 \times 18}{12} = 18 \text{ bd. ft.}$$

$$(2) \text{ board feet } = \frac{\text{Thickness (}''\text{)} \times \text{Width (}''\text{)} \times \text{Length (}''\text{)}}{144}$$

Example: A board measuring 1″ × 12″ × 18″ contains 1-1/2 board feet.

$$\frac{1 \times 12 \times 18}{144} = 1\text{-}1/2 \text{ bd. ft.}$$

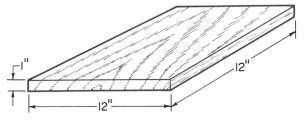

Fig. 3-12. The standard measurement for solid lumber is the **board foot**. A board foot measures 1 inch thick, by 12 inches wide, by 12 inches long.

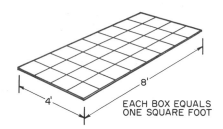

Fig. 3-13. The standard size for sheet stock (plywood, particle board, hardboard) is 4 feet by 8 feet. One standard sheet has 32 square feet.

Square feet (sq. ft.) is the measurement used to buy plywood, particle board, and hardboard. A square foot is 12 inches wide and 12 inches long. See Fig. 3-13. The thickness of the board is not considered when determining square feet. A piece of plywood measuring 4 feet wide and 8 feet long contains 32 square feet.

Lineal feet (lin. ft.) is the measurement used for moldings and pre-shaped wood. A lineal foot is 12 inches long. See Fig. 3-14. Thickness and width are not considered when determining lineal, also called running, feet.

Cost. Project plans seldom include the cost of materials. This is because materials are priced differently, depending on where you buy them. However, when making your own bill of materials, you should include cost information. Cost of materials often determines whether you will build a project or not.

Plan of Procedure

A plan of procedure lists the necessary steps for building the project. As you can see in Fig. 3-15, the plan should also include a list of the necessary tools and machines. You may find it necessary to alter your plan because you lack a particular tool. This kind of problem is best solved before you begin construction.

The purpose of the plan of procedure is to keep you "on track" during construction. Without a plan it is too easy to make mistakes

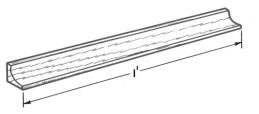

Fig. 3-14. Specially shaped wood and moldings are sold by the lineal foot. This illustration shows one lineal foot of decorative cove molding.

Plan of Procedure

Project: Fern Stand

Tools Required: Coping or bandsaw, backsaw, plane, lathe, drill.

Procedure:
1. Cut top and base to rough sizes.
2. Cut and plane top and base to finish size.
3. Sand edges of top and base.
4. Cut spindle to rough size. (Glue up stock if necessary.)
5. Turn spindle to desired shape.
6. Cut and shape cleats and wedge.
7. Cut slot in spindle for wedge.
8. Sand all parts.
9. Assemble base to spindle with glue and wedge.
10. Assemble cleats and top to spindle with screws.
11. Final sand.
12. Finish.

Fig. 3-15. A carefully prepared plan of procedure for building the fern stand would include these steps.

or forget steps. Without a plan it is also easy to waste precious shop time wondering what to do next. Making a plan of procedure is easy and will actually save you time.

Make a plan of procedure by simply thinking your project through the building process. Study the parts to determine how each is made. Then determine the order in which the parts will fit together. This will help you identify the order in which each part should be made. With this information you should be able to make an organized plan of procedure.

As you list each step, you need not be too detailed. Complex steps, however, may need some special notes. You know the steps are clear and complete if someone else can follow the plan to make the project.

New Terms

1. bill of materials
2. board feet
3. center lines
4. dimension lines
5. extension lines
6. finish sizes
7. hidden lines
8. lineal feet
9. multiview drawings
10. object lines
11. pictorial drawings
12. plan of procedure
13. rough sizes
14. square feet
15. working drawings

Study Questions

1. List the three parts of a project plan.
2. There are two types of working drawings. Name them.
3. Give two advantages and two disadvantages of pictorial drawings.
4. Why do woodworkers usually make their working drawing to scale?
5. On a working drawing, is accuracy more important in drawing lines or in drawing dimensions?
6. What types of information are found on a bill of materials? Give at least three examples.
7. Why are materials ordered in rough sizes?
8. How are rough sizes determined for length?
9. Lumber is sold by three different measurements. What are they?
10. How many board feet are there in a board measuring 2″ x 6″ x 12″?
11. What dimension — length, width, or thickness — is not considered when determining square feet?
12. What materials are purchased by the square foot?
13. What is the only dimension considered in determining lineal feet?
14. What materials are purchased in lineal feet?
15. Give two advantages to making a plan of procedure.
16. Explain how you would go about making a plan of procedure.

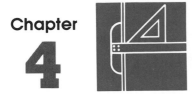

Material Selection

To build your project, you can choose from a variety of materials. Depending on the project, you can select solid woods such as oak and pine. You can choose materials such as moldings, veneers, plastic laminates, and hardware. Manufactured lumber, such as plywood, hardboard, and particle board, is also used in building projects.

Whichever materials you choose, they will affect the strength and beauty of your project. You must carefully consider both the type of material and the quality. A chair cannot be strong if it is made from a weak wood. A project cannot be attractive if it is made with unattractive materials.

Cost is also an important consideration. For example, a chest of drawers made entirely of walnut would be expensive. Not all parts of a chest need to be walnut. A back panel of hardboard would be cheap and easy to make. It would serve the purpose as well as a walnut panel. Since the back panel does not show, the hardboard would not affect the appearance of the chest. In this case, the cost of the materials would be the important consideration.

Your project may require one or more of these materials. The following information will help you select the best ones. As you choose the materials, note them on your bill of materials.

Solid Lumber

Solid wood offers a variety of qualities unmatched by any other material. The many different kinds of solid wood are divided into two basic types: hardwood and softwood. See Fig. 4-2. **Hardwood** is cut from trees that bear

leaves. Some examples of hardwood are maple, walnut, cherry, willow, and yellow poplar. **Softwood** is cut from trees that bear needles and cones. Examples of softwoods are pine, redwood, and red cedar.

Hardwoods generally offer a wider variety of grain patterns and colors than do softwoods. Hardwoods also tend to be harder, although a few are softer than some softwoods. Hardwoods, however, are usually more expensive and harder to work than softwoods. They also have larger pores, which can be attractive, but often need to be filled.

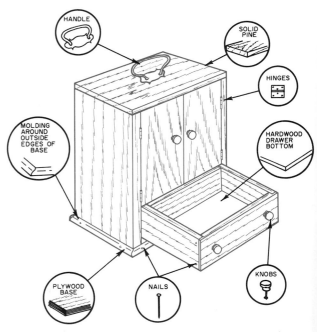

Fig. 4-1. A typical wood project contains materials other than wood. This jewelry box was made with just a few of the many materials available to the woodworker.

You will usually select a certain wood for its appearance (color and grain pattern), and the way it suits its intended use. Before choosing, you should decide which qualities you need for your project. Some woods are very colorful (cherry, walnut, red cedar). Some are nearly white in color (maple, pine, basswood). Some are hard (oak, ash, hickory), and some are soft (pine, redwood, willow). If you want a natural, reddish color, for example, you might select cherry, mahogany, or cedar. You should review section VIII before selecting wood for your project. It contains color photographs and descriptions of many types of wood that you will be using.

How Lumber Is Made

From the time a tree is cut until it is sold as lumber, it goes through several processes. Understanding these processes will help you select the right lumber for your needs.

Since lumber comes from trees, the first step in making lumber is to cut down the trees. The trees are then taken to sawmills where they are sawed into boards.

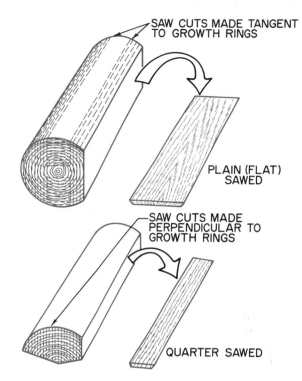

Fig. 4-3. Quarter sawing and plain sawing are the two methods of sawing lumber.

Fig. 4-2. The major difference between hardwood and softwood is the type of tree from which they are cut. Although different in composition and appearance, they are both useful in making projects.

Sawing Lumber. There are two methods of sawing wood into boards. See Fig. 4-3. The most common method is called plain, or flat, sawing. In **plain sawing** the wood is cut tangent to the annual growth rings. Although boards cut in this manner have attractive, curved grain patterns, they have a tendency to warp.

The other method of sawing wood into boards is called quarter sawing. In **quarter sawing** the wood is cut perpendicular to the annual growth rings. These boards have more resistance to warp than plain sawed wood, but have straight grain patterns.

Whether they are plain or quarter sawed, most boards are cut in a variety of widths and thicknesses. Generally they are cut as wide as the log will permit. Thicknesses are made in 1/4-inch graduations, usually from 1 inch to 4 inches thick. It is not uncommon to order the thickness of hardwood by quarters of an inch.

For example, 5/4 (five-quarter) thick hardwood would be 1-1/4 inch thick.

Drying Lumber. After the boards are sawed, they are sorted (according to quality) and made ready for drying. Wood must be dried to remove excess moisture, which could later cause cracking and splitting. There are two ways of drying lumber: air drying (AD) and kiln drying (KD). In **air drying** the wood is dried naturally by the sun and wind. This takes a year or more and is suitable for wood that will be used outdoors. In **kiln drying** the wood is dried in large ovens. This method removes enough moisture to allow the wood to be used indoors.

Surfacing Lumber. After the wood is dried, it is often **surfaced** (planed smooth). Most softwood lumber can be purchased **S4S**. This means that all four sides of the board have been planed smooth. Most hardwood lumber is sold either **rough** (no surfacing), or **S2S** (surfaced on two sides — top and bottom). If you do not have access to a planer or jointer, you should buy S2S or S4S lumber. Although surfaced lumber costs more, it will save you time.

You should realize that all boards are sized for sale before they are surfaced. For example, a S2S board 1 inch thick will only be 3/4 inch thick after it is surfaced. This board will still be sold, however, as a 1 inch-thick board. You must remember to take this into account when you order your wood.

Lumber Defects

Because wood is a living material, it is subject to several types of defects. In fact, almost every board has at least a few. See Fig. 4-4. As you learn more about woodworking, you will learn how to work around and correct the defects in wood. The most common defects are explained below.

Knots occur whenever limbs and branches are located on a tree. Knots are made of hard wood and are usually dark in color. They are difficult to work with tools.

Shakes and *checks* are cracks on the ends of boards. Shakes are located between the annual rings. Checks are located across the annual rings.

Pitch pockets are small cavities in the surface of a board. They often contain sap (pitch) or bark.

Wane is a rounded edge on a board. Wane is actually a small part of the round surface of a log.

Warp is the general term used to describe a board that is not straight and flat. There are four types of warp: crook, bow, twist, and cup. See Fig. 4-5.

Grades of Lumber

When strength and appearance are considerations, make your project from a good grade of wood. If these qualities are not important, use a lower grade, which will be cheaper.

Grade refers to the quality of the wood. It is determined by two factors. One is the size of the board. The other is the number and seriousness of defects. See Fig. 4-4. These factors determine the percentages of clear wood (no defects) on a board. The higher the percentage

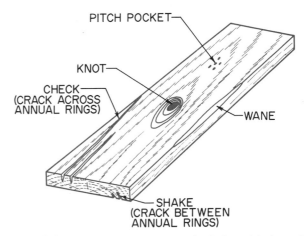

Fig. 4-4. The most common defects found in wood are pictured here. The number and seriousness of defects compared to the amount of clear wood determines the grade of lumber.

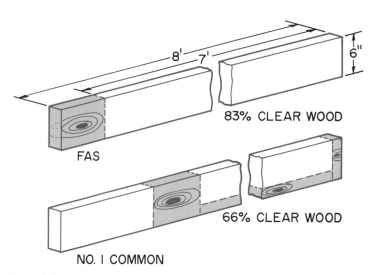

Fig. 4-6. These hardwood boards are identical except for the number and seriousness of their defects. The defects determine how the boards are graded.

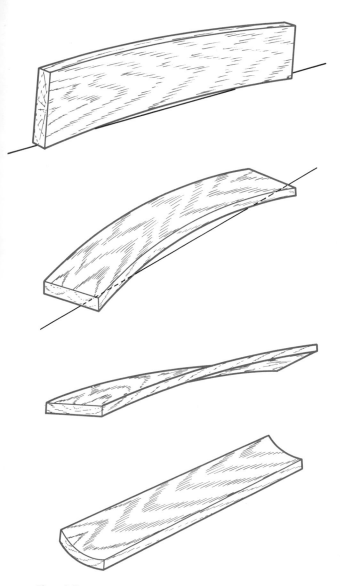

Fig. 4-5. Boards can warp in several different ways.

of clear wood, the better the grade. A good grade contains few knots, shakes, checks, and pitch pockets.

Many projects contain different grades of lumber. All visible parts should be made from good grades of wood. For example, you should use the best grades of hardwood for a desk top.

Parts of the desk that do not show may be made from lower grade woods. The hidden framework of the desk may be made of No. 1 Common hardwood, for example. This lower grade wood is less expensive than other grades but still provides adequate support.

Hardwood Grades. There are several grades of hardwood lumber. The three commonly used for wood projects are Firsts and Seconds, Select, and No. 1 Common.

First and Seconds, or *FAS* is actually a combination of the two best grades: **Firsts** and **Seconds.** A board graded FAS must be at least 6 inches wide and 8 feet long. The bad side of the board yields about 83% clear wood. See Fig. 4-6.

Select wood must be at least 4 inches wide and 6 feet long. Its bad side has more defects than the bad side of a FAS board. Its good side, however, is as good as a FAS board.

No. 1 Common is the poorest grade of hardwood used in woodworking projects. This grade must be at least 4 inches wide and 2 feet long, or 3 inches wide and 3 feet long. It yields about 66% clear wood on the bad side. Lumber

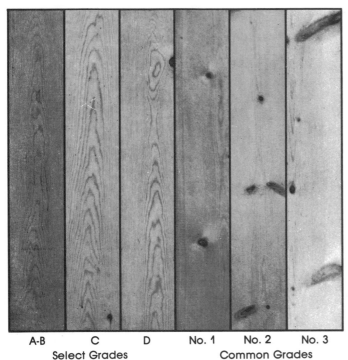

A-B	C	D	No. 1	No. 2	No. 3
Select Grades			Common Grades		

Fig. 4-7. Notice how the grades of softwood lumber improve as you look from right to left.

Fig. 4-8. This Early American magazine rack was made with No. 1 Common cedar lumber. The defects contribute to the desired appearance and style.

yards sometimes refer to this grade as **shorts.** See Fig. 4-6.

Softwood Grades. There are three grades of softwood lumber suitable for woodworking projects. They are Select, Common, and Factory and Shop Lumber. See Fig. 4-7.

Select grades are marked A, B, C, and D. Grades **A** and **B** are the best grades. They are usually combined and called **B and better.** B and better is used when a clear, smooth surface is needed.

Common grades range from No. 1 to No. 5. The higher the number, the more defects the grade has. No. 1 and No. 2 are the best common grades. Common lumber is used on structural members (2″ × 4″ studs).

Factory and shop lumber is softwood lumber that has been shaped. This means a design has been shaped into the boards. Exam-

ples of this grade are tongue-and-groove boards.

Selection of Lumber

You already know that many factors must be considered when selecting lumber. An order for solid lumber should contain the following information.

- kind of wood
- grade
- thickness, width, and length
- number of board feet
- sawing method (plain or quarter sawed)
- kiln-dried or air-dried
- surfacing (rough, S2S, S4S)

For most woodworking projects you will want to choose a good grade of plain sawed, kiln-dried lumber. You should use lumber surfaced on at least two sides (S2S) if a planer is unavailable in your shop.

Plywood

Plywood is a construction material made by gluing together thin layers of wood. These

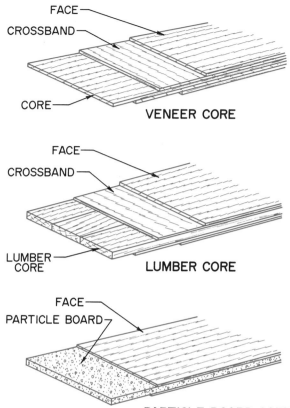

FACE

CROSSBAND

CORE

VENEER CORE

FACE

CROSSBAND

LUMBER CORE

LUMBER CORE

FACE

PARTICLE BOARD

PARTICLE BOARD CORE

Fig. 4-9. Different materials are used to make the center of a plywood sheet. Notice how each layer of the sheet is at a right angle to the previous one.

layers are called **veneers.** Each veneer (ply) is glued at a right angle to the previous one. This placement of veneers makes the plywood strong in every direction. It also makes the plywood **dimensionally stable.** This means that the plywood does not expand or contract as the humidity and other conditions change. Solid lumber does not have uniform strength in all directions. Solid lumber also tends to change dimensions as the humidity and temperature change.

Most plywood consists of three basic parts. The **core** is the center of the plywood sheet. It is usually made of veneer (veneer core) or solid wood (lumber core). Some plywoods have particle board or hardboard cores. See Fig. 4-9.

On either side of the core are sheets of veneer called **crossbands.** Crossbands increase the strength and thickness of the plywood. There may be two, four, or even six crossbands in a sheet of plywood. The number of crossbands depends on the total number of plies. Three-ply plywood has no crossbands. It has only a core and two face veneers.

Face veneers are the outside veneers of plywood. They are sometimes called face (front) and back veneers. The two basic kinds of face veneers are softwood and hardwood.

The kind of face veneer determines the type of plywood. Softwood plywood has face veneers of softwood, such as fir or pine. Hardwood plywood has face veneers of hardwoods, such as oak, cherry and birch. Generally hardwood plywood is of better quality and more expensive than softwood plywood. Softwood plywood is used in the construction industry more than the furniture industry.

Grades of Plywood

Plywood is available in many grades. The grade of plywood is determined by the quality of the face veneers. The better the grade of face veneer, the more expensive the plywood.

The two faces on a sheet of plywood are often different grades. If only one side of the plywood will show, be economical. Choose a plywood with only one good side. Carpenters commonly identify plywood as G1S (good one side) and G2S (good two sides).

The best grade of softwood plywood is marked by the letter **N.** Lower grades range from A to D. See Fig. 4-10. Plywood graded **N-A** has one face of the best veneer (N). The other face is a lower quality veneer (A). The grade is usually marked on the face or edge of the sheet.

Numbers are used to grade hardwood plywood. The grades range from 1 to 4. The best grade is **1,** the poorest grade is **4.** See Fig. 4-11. Grade 1 has few defects. It may have either a premium or good face veneer. The wood grains of the **premium** veneers are matched to form a

N	Smooth-surface designed for a natural finish. Free of open defects. Allows not more than six well-made repairs per 4 × 8 panel.
A	Smooth, paintable. Not more than eighteen neatly made repairs. May be used for natural finish in less demanding applications.
B	Solid surface. Shims, circular repair plugs and tight knots to 1″ permitted. Wood or synthetic patching material may be used. Some minor splits permitted.
C (Plugged)	Improved C veneer with splits limited to ⅛″ width and knotholes and borer holes limited to ¼″ × ½″. Admits some broken grain. Synthetic repairs permitted.
C	Tight knots to 1½″. Knotholes to 1″. Synthetic or wood repairs. Discoloration and minor sanding defects permitted. Limited splits allowed.
D	Knots and knotholes to 2½″. Limited splits are permitted.

Fig. 4-10. Grades of Softwood Plywood

Grade	Face Veneer	Allowable Defects
1	PREMIUM — Book or slip matched for pleasing effect.	Burls, pin knots, slight color streaks and inconspicuous small patches in limited amounts.
1	GOOD — Unmatched, but sharp contrasts in color, grain and figure not permitted.	Burls, pin knots, slight color streaks and inconspicuous small patches in limited amounts.
2	SOUND — Free from open defects; a painting grade.	All appearance defects permitted so long as smooth and sound. Smooth patches permitted.
3	UTILITY	All natural defects; including open knots, wormholes and splits, maximum size of which are defined.
4	BACKING	Defects practically unlimited; only strength and serviceability are considered.

Fig. 4-11. Grades of Hardwood Plywood

pattern. **Good** veneers are not matched. Grades 2, 3, and 4 have more and larger defects as the grade number increases. A sheet graded "1-3" has one good side and one poor side.

Selection of Plywood

Plywood is widely used for making projects. Because it is expensive, it is important to select it wisely. When you select plywood, determine the needed:

- thickness (strength)
- core material
- moisture resistance, and
- quality.

Some general guidelines are as follows:

1) Use the minimum thickness that supplies enough strength.
2) Use lumber-core plywood when edges will show or require special shaping. Lumber-core plywood is more attractive than other types. It is also more expensive.
3) Use exterior-type plywood for projects to be used outdoors. Exterior-type plywood has been glued with a special moisture-resistant glue.
4) Use the lowest grade of plywood that meets your needs.

Hardboard

Hardboard consists of exploded wood fibers. These fibers are pressed together to form thin sheets (usually 1/8, 3/16, and 1/4 inch). The sheets are hard, moisture resistant and mold-proof. Hardboard will not split or splinter like plywood. However, it is not as strong or rigid.

Hardboard is sold in two grades: Untempered (Standard) and Tempered. **Untempered** hardboard is lightweight, strong, and smooth on one side. **Tempered** hardboard has been soaked with special oils and baked. It is stronger, darker, and more water resistant than Untempered hardboard. Tempered hardboard is available with either one (S1S) or two (S2S) smooth

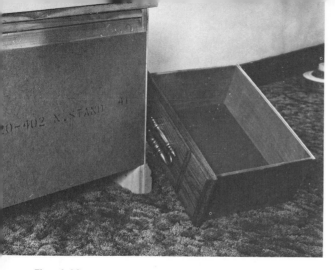

Fig. 4-12. Because hardboard is inexpensive, it is used where strength and appearance are not important. The back and the drawer bottom of this project were made of hardboard.

sides. It is available with special patterns (wood grains) and perforations (pegboard).

Hardboard has various uses. It is used for house siding and paneling. It is also used for furniture parts such as back panels and drawer bottoms. It is even used in automobiles, television sets, radios and many other manufactured goods.

You may find a good use for hardboard on your project. If so, you will find it an easy material to work with. Hardboard is easy to cut with power tools. It is also easy to glue and screw to wood.

Particle Board

Particle board consists of wood wastes (chips, flakes, and shavings), vegetable fibers, petroleum wax, and adhesive. Sheets of particle board are made by combining these materials under pressure. See Fig. 4-13. Particle board is often used as a base for wood veneers and plastic laminates. It is also used as a core for hardwood plywood.

Particle board is sold in three grades: A, B, and C. The grades are determined by the amount of material in a sheet. This is called **density.** A has a high density, B a medium density, and C a low density. High-density particle board contains large amounts of wood material. Low-density particle board contains less

wood material than the other grades. The higher the density, the harder and heavier the particle board is.

Particle board is made with either an interior or exterior adhesive. Make sure you use the exterior type for projects to be used outdoors. It will withstand heat and moisture better than the interior type.

Veneers

Veneers are thin (1/16-1/10 inch thick) sheets of wood. See Fig. 4-14. They are glued over solid wood, plywood, and particle board.

The major advantage to using veneers is the cost. They are less expensive than solid wood. You can use an inexpensive core material but still have an attractive wood veneer surface. Besides being as attractive as solid wood, veneer-covered plywood is more dimensionally stable. This is especially true for large surfaces. You can glue veneers only to smooth, solid surfaces, however.

Most veneers used for furniture and projects are made of hardwood. Many exotic woods are available in veneers. Because they are scarce or expensive, or both, they are difficult to obtain in solid wood. Some examples are ebony, rosewood, and zebra wood.

Veneers are easy to work with because they are so thin. They can be easily shaped around

Fig. 4-13. A sheet of particle board is produced by placing wood chips under great amounts of pressure.

Fig. 4-14. Veneers are made from a wide variety of woods. They are used to cover unattractive wood surfaces.

Fig. 4-15. This project has been veneered to produce an attractive design on the surface.

gentle curves. They can also be arranged in patterns. This is done to enhance the beauty of the grain. See Fig. 4-15. You may want to create your own pattern. For more information on veneers see chapter 46.

Plastic Laminates

Plastic laminates are sheets of base materials, such as cellulose, cotton, and fiberglass, covered with a resin glue. Pressure and heat are applied to these materials. This produces a hard, plastic sheet (usually 1/16 inch thick). See Fig. 4-16.

Plastic laminate sheets come in many colors and textures. They resist abrasions, heat, and stains. They are also waterproof. They are, however, brittle and hard to work with.

They are used primarily for surfaces that must withstand water and heavy wear. Kitchen counter tops and tabletops are examples.

Plastic laminates are glued only to smooth surfaces free of defects. If there are defects in the surface, fill them with wood filler. Then apply contact cement to both the surface and the laminate. Wait until the cement is dry to the touch. Then press the surfaces together to form a permanent bond. For more information see chapter 46.

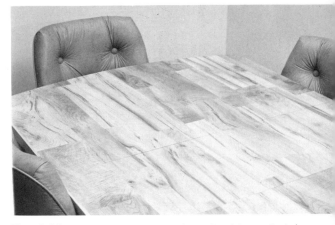

Fig. 4-16. Plastic laminate is thin, durable material used to cover objects such as this kitchen table.

Moldings

Molding provides furniture with decoration and design. It is also used to cover edge and end grain.

Wood moldings are available in many sizes and shapes. See Fig. 4-17. They are made from the best grades of softwoods and hardwoods. Softwood molding is more common. It is readily available at lumber yards. Hardwood molding, however, is not readily available. It is usually made by the woodworker with a shaper or router (chapters 42 and 43).

Hardware

Many different types of hardware are used on wood projects. Hinges, pulls, locks, latches, and drawer slides are a few examples. See Figs. 4-18 - 4-21.

Select the hardware that most closely matches the project design. For example, some hinges are surface mounted (visible), and others are not. Use the surface-mounted hinges if they add to your project's appearance. You should use the same style of hardware on all parts of the project. Identify the type of hardware for your project as you complete the bill of materials. For more information on hardware, see chapter 45.

Fig. 4-17. You can purchase wood moldings ready made (usually pine), or make your own with a router or shaper.

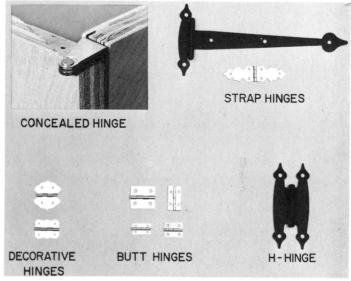
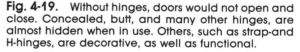

Fig. 4-19. Without hinges, doors would not open and close. Concealed, butt, and many other hinges, are almost hidden when in use. Others, such as strap-and H-hinges, are decorative, as well as functional.

Fig. 4-18. An almost endless variety of knobs and handles are available for the doors and drawers on your project.

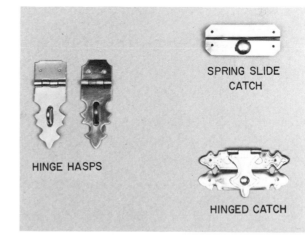

Fig. 4-20. Catches like these are used to hold wooden boxes closed.

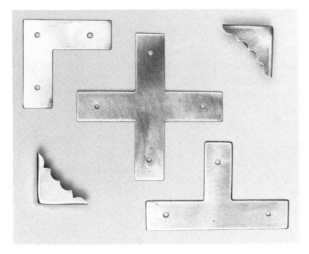

Fig. 4-21. Many other types of hardware are used primarily for decoration.

New Terms

1. air drying
2. checks
3. core
4. crossbands
5. density
6. dimensionally stable
7. face veneer
8. grade
9. hardboard
10. hardwood
11. kiln drying
12. molding
13. molding
14. particle board
15. pitch pockets
16. plain sawing
17. plastic laminate
18. plywood
19. quarter sawing
20. shakes
21. softwood
22. surfaced
23. veneer
24. wane
25. warp

Study Questions

1. What are three considerations you must make in selecting materials for your project?
2. What are two differences between plain- and quarter-sawed wood?
3. Give one reason for buying S2S lumber rather than the less expensive rough lumber.
4. In selecting the right grade of solid wood for your project, you must consider what two factors?
5. Explain why you might use different grades of lumber on the same project.
6. What are the four grades of hardwood lumber? Which two are usually combined?
7. What are the three grades of softwood lumber? Which of these grades would you select for the studs to frame a house?
8. Is kiln-dried or air-dried lumber used for most woodworking projects?
9. What are two advantages of plywood, as compared to solid wood?
10. Name the three basic parts of a sheet of plywood.
11. Which type of plywood would you select for constructing a piece of furniture?
12. How are plywood grades determined?
13. Grade 1 hardwood plywood is of two types: premium and good. Explain the difference between the two.
14. When should you use the more expensive lumber-core plywood? Why?
15. What special feature makes exterior-type plywood desirable for outdoor use?
16. What are the advantages of hardboard compared to plywood? What are the disadvantages?
17. List three differences between Tempered and Untempered hardboard.
18. Why are many exotic woods available only as veneers?
19. Give two advantages of veneers compared to solid wood.
20. What is the major use of plastic laminates?
21. What is the function of moldings?
22. Give two considerations in selecting hardware for a project.

Measuring

Measuring is like a second language to the woodworker. Making and reading measurements provide the woodworker with necessary information. Measurements tell how much stock is needed and the size of the project. They tell where cuts should be made and where to drill. Almost every step in making a project requires measurement. Precise and careful measurements are a must for quality construction. The more accurate the measurements, the better the project fits together. See Fig. 5-2.

Customary vs. Metric Measurement

Two systems of measurement are presently used in the United States. They are the customary system and the metric system. The metric system is known as the **International System of Units,** abbreviated **SI.** The customary system has been used in the United States for a long time. It is not used by any other country. The metric system is the standard system of measurement throughout the world. For this reason the United States is converting (changing) to the metric system.

Conversion from the customary to the metric system has been slow and irregular. Many industries, such as the automotive and machine tool industries, have already changed to metrics. Other industries are in the process of converting. The lumber industry, however, has not started its change to metrics. Until the lumber industry does change, it is important that the woodworker know how to use both systems of measurement.

Fig. 5-1. Manufacturing furniture requires many measurements. For the assembly operations to go quickly and smoothly, all measurements must be exact.

White Furniture Company

Fig. 5-2. Almost every step of constructing a project includes careful measurement. Here a student uses a tape measure to accurately lay out holes.

The Customary System

You may use the customary system with your project. Woodworkers use it to measure length, weight, and volume.

The woodworker measures length in **feet** and **inches.** Sometimes length is measured in parts of an inch (1/16, 1/8, 1/4, 1/2). See Fig. 5-3. It is important to determine all length measurements before you start building.

Bench rules, try squares, tape measures, folding rules, and steel squares all measure length. These woodworking tools are marked in inches and parts of an inch. Some are marked in feet.

The woodworker uses **ounces** and **pounds** to measure weight. Some fasteners (brads, pins, nails) are sold in pounds and ounces. Some finishes (water stain, pumice) are sold in ounces. You may need to measure other supplies for your project in ounces and pounds. You will measure weight with a scale.

Liquids are measured by volume. In the customary system, volume is measured in **fluid ounces, pints, quarts,** and **gallons.** Woodworkers buy paint, varnish, and glue in these quantities.

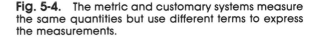

Measurement	Metric Units	Customary Units
Length	millimeter centimeter meter kilometer	inch foot yard mile
Weight	gram kilogram metric ton	ounce pound ton
Volume	millileter liter	ounce cup pint quart gallon

Area	square
	  millimeters
	square
	  meters
		square
		  inches
		square feet
		square
		  yards

Temperature	degree Celsius	degree Fahrenheit

Speed	kilometer
	  per hour
		miles
		  per hour

Fig. 5-4. The metric and customary systems measure the same quantities but use different terms to express the measurements.

The Metric System

The metric system serves the same purpose as the customary system. It measures quantities — length, weight, and volume, for example. The metric system simply uses different terms to express these quantities. See Fig. 5-4. Length is measured by the meter, volume by the liter, and weight by the gram. Figure 5-5 shows how metric and customary units compare.

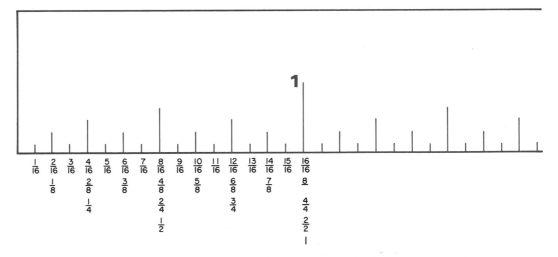

Fig. 5-3. The lines between the inch marks represent fractions of an inch. The enlarged section of this rule is marked in 16ths of an inch. The fractions in black have been calculated to the lowest common denominator.

The metric system is easy to learn. It has fewer base units than the customary system. There are 50 units of measurement in the customary system. There are only 7 in the metric system. For example, in the customary system, length is expressed in base units of inches, feet, yards, and miles. The one base unit for length in the metric system is the **meter.** This is possible because the metric system uses prefixes with the base units. These prefixes are used to indicate quantities smaller or larger than the base unit. Just three prefixes — milli, centi, and kilo — are used to express most measurements. See Fig. 5-6.

The metric system is also easy to use. It is easy to use because it is a decimal system. In a **decimal system** all of the units and prefixes are multiples of the number 10. This means all metric measurements can be easily multiplied and divided by 10. It is as simple as moving a decimal point to the left or right. Our money system is a decimal system you already know and use. Notice in the following examples how the metric and money systems are similar.

- A dollar divided by 100 is one **cent.** A meter divided by 100 is one **cent**imeter.
- To multiply $5 by 10, simply add a 0 to get $50. To multiply 5 meters by 10, simply add a 0 to get 50 meters.

An example using the meter shows how prefixes and units are combined in the metric system. The prefix **milli** means 1/1,000, so a **millimeter** is 1/1000 (.001) of a meter. The prefix **centi** means 1/100, so a **centimeter** is 1/100 (.01) of a meter. The prefix **kilo** means 1,000, so a **kilometer** is 1,000 meters. See Fig. 5-6. With just three prefixes and the base unit

I METER

I YARD

A. LENGTH: A meter is a little longer than a yard (about 1.1 yards).

I LITER

I QUART

B. VOLUME: A liter is a little larger than a quart.

I OUNCE

I GRAM

C. WEIGHT: A gram is a little more than the weight of a paper clip, about the weight of a dollar bill. It takes about 28 dollar bills to equal an ounce.

Fig. 5-5. Compare the metric measurements with the customary sizes that you know.

Prefix +	Base Unit =	Metric terms for measurement	Meaning
Milli (m)	+ meter (m) liter (l) gram (g)	millimeter (mm) = milliliter (ml) milligram (mg)	1/1000th
Centi (c)	+ meter liter gram	centimeter (cm) = centiliter (cl) centigram (cg)	1/100th
Kilo (k)	+ meter liter gram	kilometer (km) = kiloliter (kl) kilogram (kg)	1000

Fig. 5-6. Learning three prefixes and three base units, you can express almost all of the measurements needed in woodworking.

(meter), you can express any metric length. If you can multiply and divide by 10, you can easily work with those measurements.

Woodworking tools with metric units are available. Bench rules, tape measures, try squares, and steel squares measure length in metric units. Some even have both metric and customary units of measurement. See Fig. 5-7. The metric units are often expressed in symbols (abbreviations), just as customary units are. Be sure to study the metric units and their symbols before measuring.

Many woodworking supplies are also available in metric measurements. Most weights are labeled in both ounce/pound and gram/kilogram units. Containers of liquid finishes are labeled in both liters and quarts/gallons.

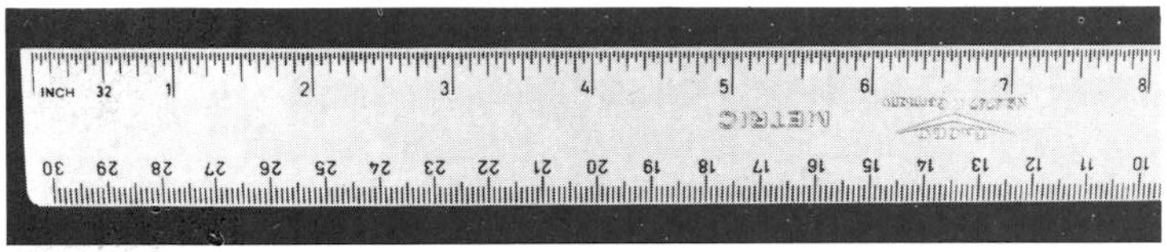

Fig. 5-7. For each project, use either metric or customary measurements. Switching back and forth can easily cause inaccurate measurements.

New Terms

1. centi
2. customary system
3. decimal system
4. gram
5. kilo
6. meter
7. metric system
8. milli

Study Questions

1. What two systems of measurement are presently used in the United States?
2. Why is the United States changing measuring systems?
3. What are the customary units of weight? Give an example of how woodworkers might use these measurements?
4. Explain why the metric system is easy to learn.
5. What are the three most commonly used prefixes in the metric system?
6. How many millimeters are there in one meter?
7. How many centimeters are there in 3.7 meters?
8. Give the symbols (abbreviations) for millimeter, centimeter, milliliter, and kilogram.

Fig. 5-8. Metric — Customary Conversion Chart

	Approximate Conversions to Metric Measures			Approximate Conversions from Metric Measures		
	When You Know	Multiply By	To Find	When You Know	Multiply By	To Find
Length	inches	2.5	centimeters	millimeters	0.04	inches
	feet	30	centimeters	centimeters	0.4	inches
	yards	0.9	meters	meters	3.3	feet
	miles	1.6	kilometers	meters	1.1	yards
				kilometers	0.6	miles
Area	square inches	6.5	square centimeters	square centimeters	0.16	square inches
	square feet	0.09	square meters	square meters	1.2	square yards
	square yards	0.8	square meters	square kilometers	0.4	square miles
	square miles	2.6	square kilometers	(10,000 m²)		
Mass	ounces	28	grams	grams	0.035	ounces
	pounds	0.45	kilograms	kilograms	2.2	pounds
	short tons	0.9	metric ton	metric ton	1.1	short tons
	(2000 lb)			(1000 kg)		
Volume	teaspoons	5	milliliters	milliliters	0.03	fluid ounces
	tablespoons	15	milliliters	milliliters	0.06	cubic inches
	cubic inches	16	milliliters	liters	2.1	pints
	fluid ounces	30	milliliters	liters	1.06	quarts
	cups	0.24	liters	liters	0.26	gallons
	pints	0.47	liters	cubic meters	35	cubic feet
	quarts	0.95	liters	cubic meters	1.3	cubic yards
	gallons	3.8	liters			
	cubic feet	0.03	cubic meters			
	cubic yards	0.76	cubic meters			
Temperature	degrees Fahrenheit	5/9 (after subtracting 32)	degrees Celsius	degrees	9/5 (then add 32)	degrees Fahrenheit

Stock Layout

Professional woodworkers get the most out of every board. They select the right wood for the job (see chapter 4) and then lay it out carefully. **Layout** is the measuring and marking of materials that need to be cut and shaped. A poor layout wastes material needlessly, making the project more expensive.

Lay out your stock as professionals do. Use every possible inch of the wood. This will not only save money on materials, but will also make cutting the stock easier.

Layout Tools

You need layout tools to make an accurate layout. Layout tools help you mark dimensions, lines, and shapes, on stock. Some layout tools measure distances, such as length, width, and thickness. Some draw or **scribe** (mark by scratching) lines, circles, and angles. Still others are used to see if parts are level or square (90° angle). The following layout tools are the ones used most frequently in woodworking. Most jobs go much easier when you use the proper tools.

Rulers. Distances are measured and laid out with rulers. See Fig. 6-1. Rulers are usually made of wood or steel. Some are made of aluminum and some of plastic. Markings (called graduations) are usually in inches divided into 16ths, 8ths, 4ths, and halves. Some are marked with metric measurements (chapter 5). Many rulers have metric graduations on one side and customary graduations on the other. Use one or the other. Never switch back and forth. Also avoid using a damaged ruler that could affect the accuracy of your measurements.

Bench rules are the most commonly used rulers for cabinetmaking. Bench rules are sold in 1-, 2-, and 3-foot lengths. They are used to measure short distances. See Fig. 6-2. They frequently have brass inserts on each end to prevent damage and wear. It is a good idea to measure from the 1-inch mark. This way wear on the ends of the ruler will not affect the accuracy of your measurements.

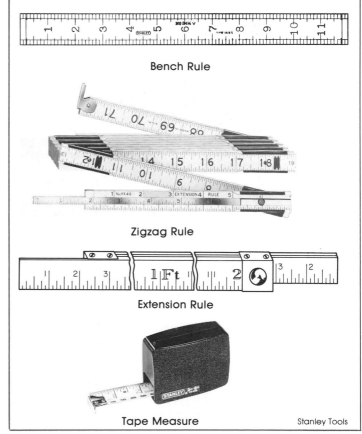

Bench Rule

Zigzag Rule

Extension Rule

Tape Measure

Stanley Tools

Fig. 6-1. Rulers used in woodworking

Fig. 6-2. Turn the bench rule on edge to get the most accurate measurements.

Bench rules are also used as straightedges. A **straightedge** can be any tool that has at least one straight edge. This edge is used to make straight lines between measured points.

Zigzag, or folding, rules are used frequently by carpenters for rough layouts. See Fig. 6-1. They usually come in 4-, 6-, and 8-foot lengths. The zigzag rule gets its name from the back and forth motion used to fold and unfold it. Too much use and wear can reduce the accuracy of this rule.

Some zigzag rules have a small, sliding ruler called an **extension rule** at one end. The extension rule slides into position to measure inside distances. The measurement on the extension rule must be added to the measurement on the zigzag rule.

Tape measures consist of a flexible steel blade coiled in a protective case. They are available in lengths from 6 to 100 feet and in both customary and metric graduations. They measure long distances accurately. See Fig. 6-3. Because they are flexible, they can also measure around curved surfaces.

Squares. To draw lines perpendicular (at right angles) to edges, you will often use squares. See Fig. 6-4. Squares are used to check squareness and measure distances. They are also used to draw straight lines and angles. They are made of metal and are very accurate. Handle squares carefully to maintain this accuracy.

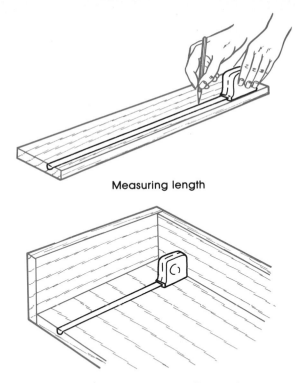

Measuring length

Measuring inside distances. (Be sure to add the length of the protective case to the total measurement.)

Fig. 6-3. Tape measures are especially useful for measuring long distances.

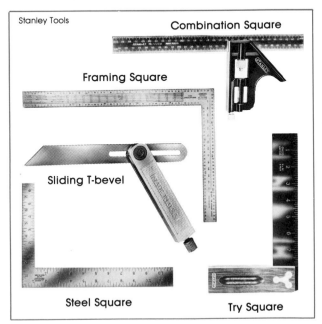

Stanley Tools

Combination Square

Framing Square

Sliding T-bevel

Steel Square

Try Square

Fig. 6-4. Squares used in woodworking

Fig. 6-5. Try squares are used to measure and square small stock.

Fig. 6-6. Steel squares are used to square the ends of wide boards. Notice that the square is tipped so it will hook on the edges of the stock.

Try squares are the most common squares found in woodworking shops. They consist of a handle and a blade. The handle is often made of wood. The blades are graduated in 1/8- and 1/16-inch divisions and are from 6 to 12 inches long.

Try squares have many uses. They are used to make lines perpendicular to an edge. They are used to measure and lay out the width of stock. They are also used to check cuts for squareness. See Fig. 6-5.

Steel squares, like try squares, are L-shaped. Most steel squares are much bigger than try squares. They also have two steel blades instead of one. The longer blade is called the **body.** The shorter blade is called the **tongue.** Steel squares are used to lay out lines and angles. See Fig. 6-6. They are also used to check squareness.

Framing, or carpenter's, squares are large steel squares. They have helpful tables and scales for carpenters and cabinetmakers. See Fig. 6-4.

Combination squares have an adjustable head that slides along the blade. Blades are commonly 8 to 12 inches long. The combination square is really many tools in one. It can be used to draw lines and angles, check squareness, and measure distances. See Fig. 6-7.

Sliding T-bevels are not actually squares, although they are used in much the same way. Their primary use is to check and transfer angles on wood. Their adjustable blades can be set with a protractor or steel square at any angle from 0 to 180°. See Fig. 6-8.

MARKING WIDTH. SLIDE THE SQUARE ALONG THE EDGE WHILE HOLDING THE PENCIL AT THE END OF THE BLADE

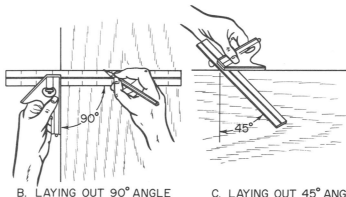

B. LAYING OUT 90° ANGLE

C. LAYING OUT 45° ANGLE

Fig. 6-7. Uses of the combination square

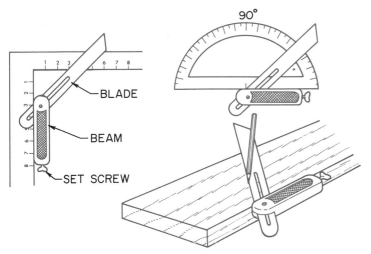

Fig. 6-8. Uses of the T-bevel

Marking Tools. Clear, sharp, layout lines are just as important as accurate measurements. These lines serve as guides for sawing and shaping stock. A wide or hard-to-see line can result in an inaccurate cut. Most of the tools used to mark wood are shown in Fig. 6-9.

Pencils are the most common marking tools. A sharp, no. 2 pencil will make a dark, clear, easy-to-follow line. Another advantage of pencils is that marks can be erased without staining or damaging the wood. Sharpen the pencil regularly during layout.

Scratch awls consist of a sharp, metal point attached to a wooden handle. The scratch awl makes a light scratch on wood, metal, and plastic surfaces. It is used most often to mark locations for holes. See Fig. 6-10.

Sloyd and utility knives are also used to scribe lines on wood. See Fig. 6-9. Either type of knife can be used to make fine, accurate layout lines. If you use a knife, be sure of the layout before marking the line. Knife marks are hard to remove.

Marking gauges are used to scribe lines parallel to edges. They have an adjustable head that slides along an 8-inch beam. At one end of the beam is a sharp metal pin. The pin makes a thin mark as the gauge is moved along an edge.

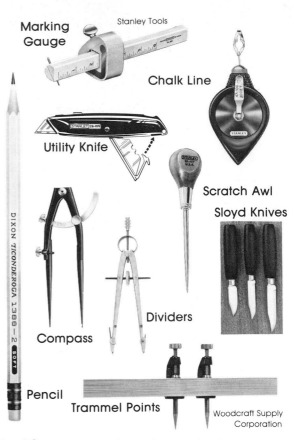

Fig. 6-9. Marking tools used in woodworking

Fig. 6-10. A scratch awl can be used to mark the location of holes to be drilled.

Fig. 6-11. Marking gauges are used to mark lines parallel to an edge.

MARKING GAUGE

MAPLE BLOCK 1½" x 2" x 3"
(3.7 cm x 5.0 cm x 7.6 cm)

½" DOWEL,
7" (17.5 cm) LONG

CARRIAGE BOLT

NAIL TIP

½" (1.2 cm) DRILL

¼" (6 mm)

SAW KERF

FRONT VIEW

Fig. 6-12. Plan for making a marking gauge

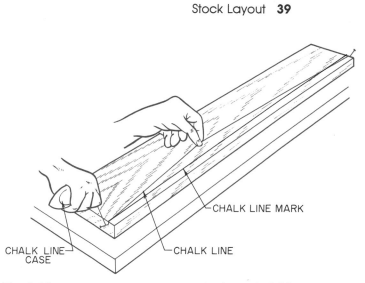

CHALK LINE MARK

CHALK LINE CASE

CHALK LINE

Fig. 6-13. A chalk line is used to mark a long, straight line on a board.

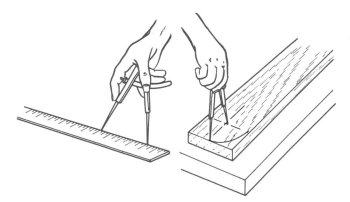

Fig. 6-14. A divider can be used to scribe a circle.

See Fig. 6-11. Marking gauges are extremely useful for marking the thickness of stock. Figure 6-12 shows a simple plan for making your own marking gauge.

Chalk lines are used to lay out long, straight lines. A line coated with chalk is stretched between two points as shown in Fig. 6-13. When the line is snapped, the chalk marks the wood where the line hits it. You can purchase chalk lines in easy-to-use reels.

Many chalk line reels can also be used as **plumb bobs.** The plumb bob consists of a weight on the end of a string. It tells whether or not something stands truly vertical (straight up and down).

Dividers have two long, adjustable legs joined at a pivot point. See Fig. 6-9. Usually there is a sharp metal point at the end of each leg. Dividers with a pencil at the end of one leg are called **compasses.** Dividers and compasses are used most often to mark perfect arcs and circles. See Fig. 6-14. They are also used to divide lines into equal parts and mark off equal spaces.

Trammel points consist of two sharp points attached to a bar. See Fig. 6-9. The points can

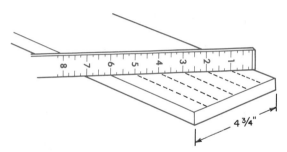

Fig. 6-16. You can easily divide a board into equal parts by laying a rule diagonally across the board. This board has been divided into six equal parts.

Fig. 6-15. You can easily make trammel points in the shop. Simply cut a strip of wood longer than the desired radius. Then drill two holes, one for a pencil and one for a pivot point.

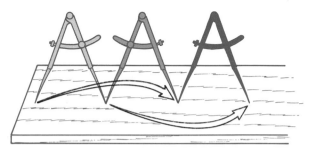

Fig. 6-17. You can divide a board into equal parts with a divider. "Walk" the divider across the board, "stepping" alternately to the left and right.

be placed anywhere on the bar. Circles and arcs too large for dividers are marked with trammel points. You can make your own trammel points as shown in Fig. 6-15.

Special Layout Techniques

Most woodworking layouts consist of simple tasks such as marking straight lines and perfect circles. Many layouts require special techniques, however. The following information explains how to do many special layouts. For layouts not included here, ask your instructor to suggest or supply a drafting textbook.

Equal Parts. A special technique helps you easily divide a board into equal parts. Place a bench rule on edge across the stock's surface. See Fig. 6-16. Position the rule so the diagonal distance divides evenly by the number of desired parts. For example, you need to divide a board 4-3/4 inches wide into six equal parts. Place the rule diagonally across the wood surface. The distance from one edge to the other should measure 6 inches. At each inch graduation, mark a point with a pencil or awl. Through these points, draw lines parallel to the edges of

the board. A marking gauge is a helpful tool for this procedure.

You can divide a board into equal parts very easily if metrics are used. Simply divide the number of millimeters by the number of divisions desired. Mark off the amount with a metric rule.

Dividers can also be used to layout equal divisions. See Fig. 6-17. Determine the distance of each part. Set the divider to this distance and walk it along the stock. Place a mark wherever the points of the divider touch the stock.

Irregular Designs. You may need to transfer an irregular design from a drawing to wood. Irregular designs are usually drawn on a grid in the working drawings. The **grid** is made up of equal-size squares drawn to scale. To transfer the design, you must draw the grid full size on a piece of paper. Draw the grid lines lightly. Then draw the design on the grid with dark lines. This makes the design easy to see over the grid. See Fig. 6-18.

Draw the design on the large grid exactly as it appears in the working drawing. Locate the curved lines where they intersect the grid. Connect these lines freehand or with a French curve. Make sure the lines are smooth and the curves are even and flowing.

Cut out the design with a pair of scissors. Then tape the design to the wood with masking tape. Trace around the design with a pencil to transfer it to the wood.

If the design is symmetrical (the same on each side of center), you can make a **half pattern.** This saves time because you need to draw only one side of the design. See Fig. 6-19.

Duplicate Parts. Some projects include several parts of the same design and size. You can save time by laying out all identical parts at once. Clamp the pieces together in a vise. Make a single layout as shown in Fig. 6-20. Be sure all pieces are in the same position before marking.

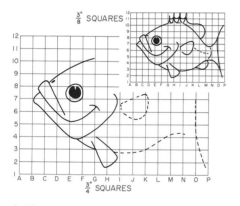

Fig. 6-18. To transfer a design from the working drawing to the wood, draw the grid and design to full scale on a sheet of paper. Then lay the design on the wood and mark around it.

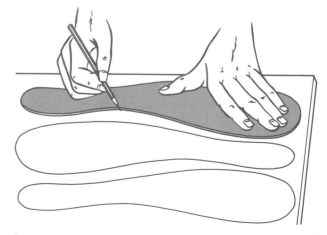

Fig. 6-20. To lay out identical parts quickly and accurately, clamp the parts together and mark them.

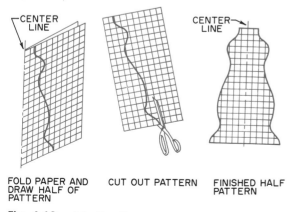

FOLD PAPER AND DRAW HALF OF PATTERN   CUT OUT PATTERN   FINISHED HALF PATTERN

Fig. 6-19. A half pattern is a drawing of one-half of a symmetrical design. A half pattern is drawn on folded paper. After the half pattern is cut and unfolded, the complete design can be transferred to the wood.

Fig. 6-21. Use a template to lay out identical curved parts.

To make many identical curved parts, use a template to save time. **Templates** are patterns made from cardboard, sheet metal, or thin wood. See Fig. 6-21. After making the template, place it on the stock and trace around it. You can even show the location of drilling holes by cutting holes in the template.

Ellipses. Tabletops are often in the shape of an ellipse, or oval. The easiest way to lay out an ellipse is shown in Fig. 6-22.

1. Lay out the length (AC) and width (BD) of the ellipse. The lines should be perpendicular and meet at center X.
2. Set a compass at half the distance of AC. Use B as a center point to draw arcs intersecting AC at points 1 and 2.
3. Insert a small pin at points 1, 2, and B. Fasten a string tightly around the three pins.

4. Remove the pin at point B. Replace it with a sharp pencil.
5. Keep the string tight as you draw the line forming the ellipse.

Hexagons. A six-sided figure with equal sides and equal angles is called a hexagon. To lay out a hexagon, see Fig. 6-23.

1. Draw a circle. The circle's diameter should be equal to the maximum width of the hexagon.
2. Set the compass to half the circle's diameter (radius). Choose any point on the circle as your center point and strike an arc on the circle.
3. Using the arc as your center point, strike another arc. Continue this way until you have made six equally spaced points.
4. To complete the hexagon, connect the six points with straight lines.

Octagons. An eight-sided figure with equal sides and equal angles is called an octagon. To lay out an octagon, see Fig. 6-24.

1. Square the stock to required dimensions.
2. Draw two diagonal lines (AC and BD).
3. Set a compass at a distance equal to AX. Use A as a center point to draw an arc through AB and AD. Repeat this process with B, C, and D as center points.

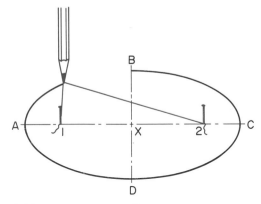

Fig. 6-22. Laying out an ellipse

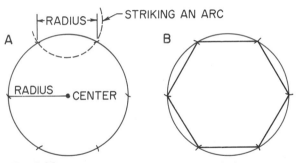

Fig. 6-23. Laying out a hexagon in a circle

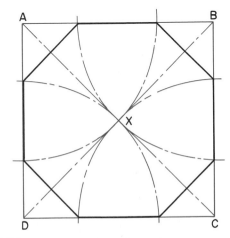

Fig. 6-24. Laying out an octagon in a square

4. Connect the arc points across the corners with a straight line. This completes the octagon.

Layout Considerations

Almost every layout is different than the next. This is due to differences in wood, design, and the required tools. The wood itself, however, is the most important factor in the layout.

Since the wood seldom grows in the exact size needed, you must measure, mark, and cut it to shape. In doing so, you must consider grain direction, defects in the wood, and waste resulting from cutting and shaping.

Grain Direction. The alignment of pores in wood is referred to as grain direction. When you look at wood closely, you can easily see these pores. The grain provides wood with attractive patterns. The grain also indicates the wood's strength. Wood is strongest when resisting pressure applied **across** the grain. The same wood is weakest when resisting pressure applied **with** the grain. It is important to keep this in mind during the layout. A mistake with grain direction will weaken the finished project. See Fig. 6-25.

Defective Lumber. Almost all rough lumber contains defects. Defects such as knots, checks, pin holes, and warp can detract from the appearance of your project. They can also reduce the wood's strength and workability. When you lay out your project, try to avoid the defects without wasting wood. See Fig. 6-26.

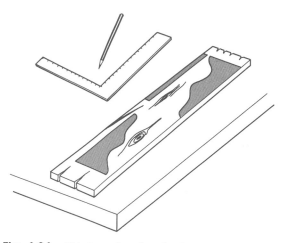

Fig. 6-26. This layout makes the best use of the clear wood. Defects such as knots and pitch pockets are attractive on some projects and should be laid out accordingly.

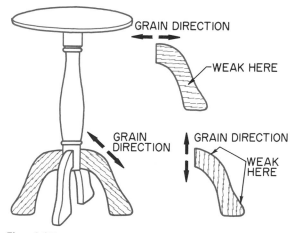

Fig. 6-25. The legs of this small table were laid out properly. Wood is strongest when resisting pressure applied **across** the grain.

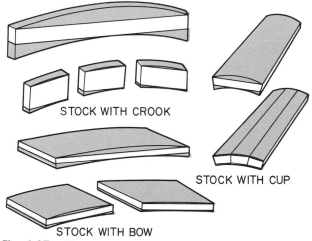

Fig. 6-27. Warped boards are most efficiently used as small pieces.

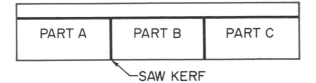

Fig. 6-28. If you must lay out all the parts at once, be sure to add the width of the saw kerf.

You may need to reposition some parts so you can cut out the defects.

For long or wide pieces, try to use the wood with the least amount of warp. **Warp** refers to unwanted bend or twist in a board. Use warped stock for smaller parts of the project. The seriousness of warp is reduced when the board is cut into smaller lengths. See Fig. 6-27. In smaller sizes the warp is much easier to remove without wasting stock.

Sheet Stock. Plywood, hardboard, particle board, and other sheet stock, come in accurately sized sheets. The edges of these sheets have been cut straight and square at the factory. These edges are called **factory edges.** Factory edges are good starting places for all layout measurements. Be careful not to damage them.

Kerf Allowance. On some layouts you need to keep waste to an absolute minimum. Sometimes this means figuring in the **kerf** (groove made by the saw) during layout. Do this by cutting a kerf in a scrap piece of stock. Measure the distance across the kerf. Add this distance between the parts to be cut out. See Fig. 6-28. If done correctly, each cut will form the sides of two parts.

Figuring in the kerf is a difficult layout process. It is easier to allow plenty of space between layout lines. This way each piece can be measured and cut separately.

New Terms

1. bench rule
2. chalk line
3. combination square
4. divider
5. extension rule
6. factory edge
7. framing square
8. grid
9. half pattern
10. kerf allowance
11. layout
12. marking gauge
13. plumb bob
14. scratch awl
15. scribe
16. sliding T-bevel
17. sloyd knife
18. steel square
19. straightedge
20. tape measure
21. template
22. trammel points
23. try square
24. utility knife
25. warp
26. zigzag rule

Study Questions

1. Name four layout tools used to measure length.
2. Give three uses of squares.
3. Which square can be used in place of several different tools?
4. Name two layout tools used to draw circles and arcs.
5. Give two possible results of a poor layout.
6. List three general uses of layout tools.
7. Why should you **not** use a damaged ruler?
8. Why should you measure from the 1-inch mark when using a bench rule?
9. When you mark wood, what is one advantage to using a pencil?
10. Describe one method of dividing a board 6¾ inches wide into three equal parts.
11. What three factors concerning the wood must you consider during layout?
12. Is wood stronger **with** or **across** the grain?
13. List three problems caused by defects in lumber.
14. How can you reduce the amount of waste when working with warped lumber?
15. Describe the method for reducing waste that involves saw kerfs.

Try to remember the last time you injured yourself. Maybe you cut a finger, scraped an arm, or bruised a knee. Do you remember the first thought to cross your mind after the accident? Was it anything like:

"I knew I shouldn't have been in such a hurry."

"I should have followed the directions."

"Why didn't I put that in a vise?"

If thoughts like these crossed your mind, you probably could have avoided your accident. By slowing down or by following directions you could have prevented an injury. In thinking ahead you would have been using **safety** to prevent accidents and injuries.

Thinking Ahead

Anyone can learn and use safety. By turning the "I should have" **after** the accident into a safety rule **before** the accident, you can prevent accidents. By thinking ahead, you can anticipate and avoid most unsafe conditions. Visualize every detail of how you will perform a job **before** you begin. Ask yourself "What will happen if. . .?" Ask as many "What if. . ." questions as you can think of. For example, examine the cutting method used in Fig. 7-1. Ask yourself:

"What will happen if the wood splits?"

"What will happen if the wood cuts too fast?"

"What will happen if the blade breaks?"

These questions help you identify unsafe conditions and anticipate injuries. By answering any one of these questions you can anticipate an injury in Fig. 7-1. The worker's thumb is in direct line with the saw blade. The worker has not thought ahead, and he could easily be injured.

Using Safety

There is more to safety than finding unsafe conditions. You must also change the unsafe conditions. Safety requires **doing** as well as **knowing.** After anticipating an injury to his thumb, the worker in Fig. 7-2 changed the positioning of his hands. This seems obvious. How-

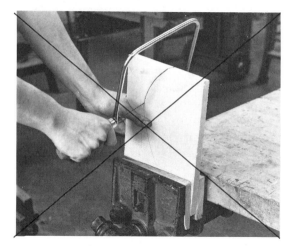

Fig. 7-1. This set up is not safe. The worker's thumb is in direct line with the saw blade. The worker has not thought ahead.

Fig. 7-2. This set up is much safer than the one in Fig. 7-1. The wood is clamped more securely and the worker's hand is not in the path of the saw blade.

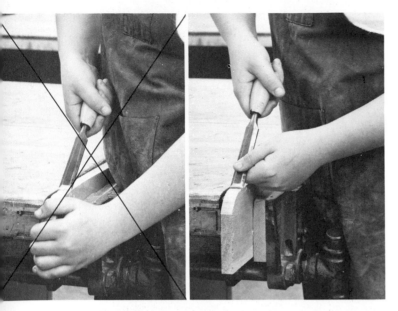

Fig. 7-3. When using cutting tools, cut away from your body. Keep your eyes on your work at all times. Even a minor distraction can cause a severe injury.

ever, many workers fail to change conditions they know to be unsafe. They think that recognizing dangerous situations is enough. Too often this faulty thinking results in accidents.

Safety must be used constantly. One unsafe condition left unchanged can result in a serious injury. Those who know safety, but do not use it, are the ones who end up thinking "I knew I shouldn't have done that." Knowing what went wrong does not ease the pain.

You will find unsafe conditions in every woodshop. Many of these conditions have already been identified for you. Someone else has already asked the "What if...?" questions and anticipated possible injuries. Woodworking instructors have developed proven methods for preventing those injuries. These methods are called **safety rules.** It is necessary that you learn and use these rules. They are divided into three groups: personal safety, general safety, and tool safety. Study and follow these rules carefully. They can and do prevent serious injuries.

Fig. 7-4. Before you try to move a heavy object, think about the proper way to lift it. Bend your knees, not your back, to prevent an injury.

Fig. 7-5. Proper eye protection will prevent flying wood chips and splinters from injuring your eyes.

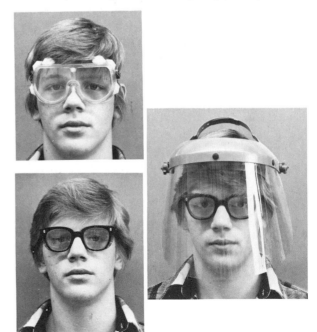

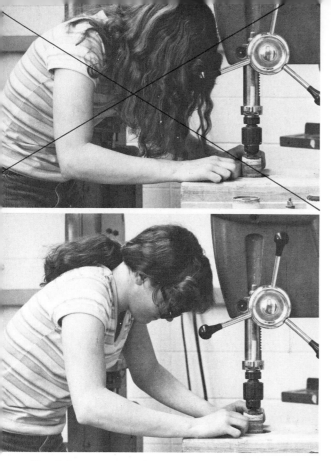

Fig. 7-6. Long hair can cause a serious injury if it gets caught in a machine.

Personal Safety

Body — Cut **away** from your body with all cutting tools. If the tool slips, it will move away from you. Keep your body out of the cutting line of a tool, as shown in Fig 7-3.

Lift heavy materials with your leg and back muscles. Bend your knees, not your back. See Fig. 7-4.

Eyes — Wear eye protection — eyeglasses or goggles — in the woodshop. This will keep wood shavings and sawdust from getting in your eyes. See Fig. 7-5. Be especially careful when using your breath or compressed air to remove dust particles from surfaces.

Hair — All precautions must be taken to keep long hair out of rotating machines such as lathes and drill presses. Tie back long hair or put it into a net. See Fig. 7-6.

Hands and Fingers — Keep fingers away from sharp cutting edges on hand tools and machines.

Use a brush to clean machines and workbenches. You can cut yourself or get a splinter by wiping a surface with your hand.

Never wear gloves while operating machines in the woodshop. Gloves easily catch in moving parts, drawing your hands into cutting edges. See Fig. 7-7.

Ears — Your hearing can be damaged by loud, continuous noise. It is recommended that you wear ear protection in loud, noisy areas. See Fig. 7-8.

Fig. 7-7. Do not wear gloves when working close to the moving parts of a machine.

Fig. 7-8. Wear ear protection when you work with extremely noisy machines.

Jewelry — Remove jewelry such as rings, watches, bracelets, and necklaces when working with tools and machines. These articles can catch in machines, pulling an arm or finger into a cutting edge.

Clothing — Wear clothing secured tightly to your body. Keep shirt sleeves, ties, belts, and apron strings from dangling near moving equipment. Clothing can catch in rotating equipment and pull you into a cutting edge. See Fig. 7-9.

Do not carry tools in your pockets. A sharp point in a pocket can cause a serious injury to you or a classmate.

SAFETY General Safety

— Pay attention to what you are doing. When your attention is drawn away from your work, you can easily hurt yourself or others.
— Listen carefully to all instructions. Not knowing what you are doing is a dangerous situation for everyone.
— Avoid quick movements such as running, shoving, and horseplaying, which are dangerous. The slightest bump could cause an injury.
— Be sure you know where exits and fire extinguishers are located in case of fire. You should also know which is the right extinguisher for putting out a particular fire.

Fig. 7-9. This student is properly dressed for working safely around machinery. Never wear jewelry or loose clothing that could catch in a machine.

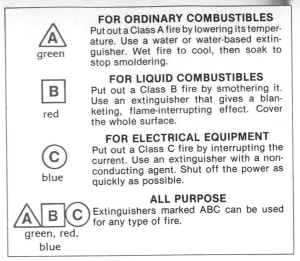

A green	**FOR ORDINARY COMBUSTIBLES** Put out a Class A fire by lowering its temperature. Use a water or water-based extinguisher. Wet fire to cool, then soak to stop smoldering.
B red	**FOR LIQUID COMBUSTIBLES** Put out a Class B fire by smothering it. Use an extinguisher that gives a blanketing, flame-interrupting effect. Cover the whole surface.
C blue	**FOR ELECTRICAL EQUIPMENT** Put out a Class C fire by interrupting the current. Use an extinguisher with a non-conducting agent. Shut off the power as quickly as possible.
A B C green, red, blue	**ALL PURPOSE** Extinguishers marked ABC can be used for any type of fire.

Fig. 7-10. Know where the fire extinguishers are kept in your school shop. Know how to use them. Once the fire has started, you probably will not have time to read the instructions.

Use an extinguisher marked **A** to put out ordinary fires, where no electricity is involved. With burning liquids such as gasoline and oil, use an extinguisher marked **B.** Use an extinguisher marked **C** for electrical fires. **ABC** extinguishers can be used for all fires. See Fig. 7-10.
— Do not leave a sharp object sticking out of a vise. Someone could be cut while walking past the vise.
— Keep the floor around workbenches and machines clear of wood scraps. These scraps could cause a classmate to stumble and fall. See Fig. 7-11.
— Avoid carrying long pieces of wood by yourself. Ask someone to help. This will prevent a swinging board from hurting someone. See Fig. 7-12.

Fig. 7-11. Sweep up chips and sawdust and remove waste material from the shop. Never use your hands to sweep away sawdust. This is an easy way to get splinters.

Fig. 7-12. Many tasks in a woodworking shop require cooperation. To avoid injury and equipment damage, ask for help in handling long pieces.

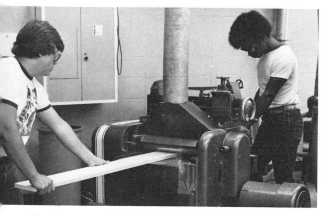

Fig. 7-13. Processing a long piece of stock often requires two people. Give the helper instructions before you begin working.

— Do not turn long pieces of wood vertically (up and down) and allow them to come close to fluorescent lights. Fluorescent tubes break easily and contain toxic (poisonous) materials.
— Be willing to assist a classmate when you see that help is needed. In a woodshop cooperation is a must in order to safely perform many tasks. See Fig. 7-13.
— Place combustible waste material in covered metal containers. Dispose of the material daily.

Tool Safety

— Before using a tool, study the safety rules listed with the individual tools and procedures in this text. These rules are provided for your safety. Follow them.

— Use the right tool for the job. For example, using a wood chisel as a screwdriver is very dangerous. See Fig. 7-14.
— Do not operate tools before you have permission from your teacher.
— Learn how to adjust hand tools before you use them. Using a tool before you are ready is not safe.
— Guards and warnings are placed on tools and machines for everyone's protection. Keep all guards in place and observe all warnings.
— SAFETY ZONES are areas marked on the floor around machines. These zones identify the danger area around a machine. Safety zones are also used to prevent the machine operator from being bothered by classmates. The machine operator should be the only person in a safety zone. See Fig. 7-15.

Fig. 7-14. Using the wrong tool for a job can cause an injury.

Fig. 7-15. The machine operator should be the only person in the safety zone. Unless it is marked otherwise, the safety zone is about an arm's length away from the machine operator.

— When carrying hand tools turn sharp points toward the floor. An injury could result from carrying a tool with its sharp edge pointing out.

— Position hand tools so their cutting edges point toward the center of the workbench. This will help prevent injuries.

— Report any defective (broken) tools to your teacher. Using a defective tool can be dangerous.

First Aid

If someone is injured in your class, quickly report it to the teacher. Most shop injuries are minor. First aid can usually be administered in the shop or nurse's office. See Fig. 7-16. However, serious injuries can occur in a school shop. You should know some basic rules for first aid and be able to assist the teacher if necessary.

OSHA

In 1970 the United States Government passed the Occupational Safety and Health Act (OSHA). The purpose of this act was to make America a safe place to work. This was done by setting safety standards that industries must follow. These standards require industries to protect their workers from injury. Workers must wear protective devices such as safety glasses, hard hats, hearing protectors, and protective shoes when there is a threat to personal safety.

OSHA also requires the manufacturers of equipment and machines to make their products safe. For example, warnings and guards are now required on machines to help protect their operators from injury.

OSHA has affected school shops in an indirect, but positive, way. As previously mentioned, machines purchased since 1970 have warnings and guards to improve their safety. Some even have brakes which stop rotating cutters when the power is turned off.

Fig. 7-16. All accidents and injuries — even minor ones — should be reported to the teacher.

OSHA is attempting to reduce the number of personal injuries. However, it cannot control every action of each person working in a shop. Safety must be practiced by each person while working at home, at school, and in industry. REMEMBER THAT YOUR SAFETY, AND THE SAFETY OF OTHERS, DEPENDS UPON YOUR ACTIONS.

New Terms

1. accident
2. OSHA
3. safety
4. safety zone

Study Questions

1. How do you find out if unsafe conditions exist?
2. What must you do after identifying unsafe conditions?
3. What has already been done to help you use safety in the school woodshop?
4. Why should you remove jewelry when working with power equipment?
5. Name one way you should **not** clean a workbench.
6. Why are fluorescent lights dangerous?
7. What is the first thing you should do if someone is injured in the woodshop?
8. Name four types of protective devices worn by workers since 1970.
9. What is OSHA? What is its purpose?
10. Why should you wear eye protection when cutting wood?

HAND TOOL
WOODWORKING

Sawing

Wood seldom comes in the size you need for your project. Usually you need to saw it to the correct dimensions. Many styles and sizes of handsaws are available for your different sawing needs.

All handsaws, regardless of type, consist of a blade and a handle. Teeth are filed into one edge of the blade. These teeth have sharp points. When the blade is moved back and forth across wood, the points separate the wood fibers.

Saw blades vary in their number of points per inch. Commonly used saws have between 4 and 22 points per inch. The number of points determines how the saw will cut. A saw with few points per inch makes a rough cut quickly. A saw with more points per inch makes a smoother cut, but does not cut as fast.

The number of points per inch is sometimes stamped on the heel of the blade. If it is not given, you can count the points. The number of **points** is always one more than the number of **teeth**. See Fig. 8-1.

All saw teeth are bent alternately (every other one) to the left and right of the blade. This pattern of alternate bends is called the **set** of the teeth. It is this set which makes the groove, or **kerf,** slightly wider than the blade. This prevents the blade from binding (getting stuck) during the cut.

Saws for Making Straight Cuts

The crosscut saw, ripsaw, backsaw, miter saw, and dovetail saw are all designed to make straight cuts in wood. Each saw is designed to make certain kinds of cuts.

Crosscut Saw. Wood is cut to length with a crosscut saw. See Fig. 8-2. A crosscut saw is designed to cut **across** the grain. It can be used to cut **with** the grain, although this can be done more easily with a ripsaw. The crosscut saw is also the best saw for cutting plywood.

The teeth of the crosscut saw have sharp points. These teeth tear the wood fibers as the blade moves across the grain. See Fig. 8-3. This tearing produces sawdust.

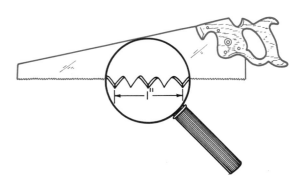

Fig. 8-1. The kind of cut made by a saw is determined by its number of points per inch. Count the number of teeth in an inch and add **1** to find the number of points. This blade has six points per inch.

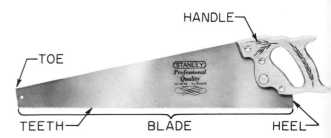

Fig. 8-2. Crosscut saws and ripsaws have the same basic parts and design.

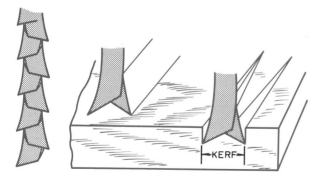

Fig. 8-3. The sharp points on crosscut teeth tear the wood fibers, making a W-shaped kerf.

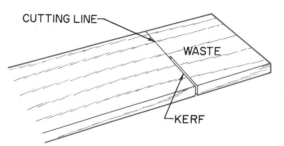

Fig. 8-5. Always make the kerf on the waste side of the layout line.

Fig. 8-4. This is the proper position for using the crosscut saw. Notice that the thumb is being used to guide the blade while starting the cut.

An all-purpose crosscut saw has eight points per inch. The usual blade length is 26 inches from heel to toe. A 20-inch crosscut saw is called a **panel saw.** The panel saw's length makes it easy to carry in a toolbox and easy to use.

Using Crosscut Saws. When cutting with a crosscut saw, use the following procedure.

1. Mark a line across the board at the desired length. Measure the length with a rule or tape measure. Mark it with a pencil and square. For more information on layout, see chapter 6.

2. Place the board on a stool, bench, or sawhorse. A long board may require more than one support. Hold the board with your left knee and left hand (if you are right-handed). See Fig. 8-4. Place boards too short to be held this way, in a vise.

3. Position the blade on the **waste side** (side you do not use) of the cutting line. See Fig. 8-5. Following the middle or inside of the cutting line will make the board too short. Use your left thumb to guide the blade when starting the cut. See again Fig. 8-4. Keep your thumb away from the teeth of the blade. These teeth are sharp and can easily cause an injury.

4. Hold the saw against the board. Start the cut by pulling the saw gently back. Pull back with short strokes until the kerf is started.

5. While making your cut, hold the saw at a 45° angle, as in Fig. 8-6. The saw works best at this cutting angle. Make sure the saw is cutting straight across the board. Also be sure it is cutting perpendicular (at a right angle) to the surface of the

Fig. 8-6. The best cutting angle for crosscutting is about 45°.

Fig. 8-7. You can use a try square to check the angle of the saw blade.

Fig. 8-8. Twisting the blade will often help to get it back on line. Too much twisting can cause the blade to bind in the kerf.

Fig. 8-9. Wood splits easily at the end of a cut. To prevent this, hold the piece being cut off and make short, gentle strokes.

board. This can be checked with a try square. See Fig. 8-7.

6. Use long, even strokes. Quick, jerky strokes produce an uneven cut. Do not force the saw. The weight of the blade should be enough to make the cut.

7. If the saw moves away from the cutting line, twist the saw handle slightly. Continue twisting until back on the right track. See Fig. 8-8.

8. When the cut is nearly complete, shorten your strokes. With your left hand, support the part of the board being cut off. See Fig. 8-9. This will prevent the wood from splitting and falling to the floor. If the board is too long to support alone, ask for help.

9. When you cut plywood, be careful not to split the face veneer. Position the plywood with its best side up. After you start the kerf, reduce the cutting angle. Your strokes should be nearly horizontal. You can sometimes use masking tape to prevent splitting. Put the tape over the cutting line. Then redraw the line if you cannot see through the tape.

Ripsaw. Wood is cut to width with a ripsaw. Ripsaws are designed to cut **with** the grain. Their appearance and parts are the same as the crosscut saw. See again Fig. 8-2. However, the shape of the teeth and the number of points per inch are different.

Ripsaws have large, coarse (rough) teeth with knife-like edges. They do not have sharp points. See Fig. 8-10. Ripsaws are designed to cut, rather than tear, the wood fibers. The cutting action produces small chips instead of sawdust. A ripsaw with 5½ points per inch works best for most ripping cuts.

Using Ripsaws. When cutting with ripsaws, use the following procedure.

1. Mark the board for cutting the desired width. You can use a pencil and a combination square or straightedge. For more information on layout, see chapter 6.

2. Place the board on a stool, bench, or sawhorse. Hold the board with your knee and hand. Be sure the wood is firmly supported. Also be sure you can follow the cutting line without sawing into the support. See Fig. 8-11. On long stock you may need to use more than one support.

3. It is difficult to make a straight, perpendicular cut with a ripsaw. Therefore, leave some material on the waste side of the cutting line. You can plane the edge to the exact size later. When making a

long cut, you can clamp a wooden straightedge to the board. The straightedge serves as a guide, as shown in Fig. 8-12.

4. The steps for using a ripsaw are much the same as steps 3-9 for the crosscut saw. Use the ripsaw, however, at a 60° cutting angle instead of a 45° angle. See again Fig. 8-11.

5. When you rip a board, the kerf may close. This will bind the saw blade. If this happens, push a wedge into the kerf, as shown in Fig. 8-13. This frees the blade and makes cutting easier.

Fig. 8-11. Hold the ripsaw at a 60° angle to the work. Be careful not to cut into your support.

Fig. 8-12. It is much easier to cut a straight line using a straightedge. Keep the blade flat against the straightedge as you cut.

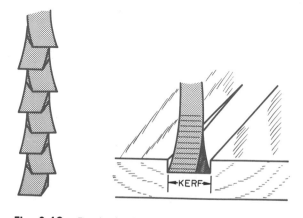

Fig. 8-10. The knife-like edges of ripsaw teeth cut the wood fibers. Ripsaws make flat-bottomed kerfs, unlike the W-shaped kerfs made by crosscut saws.

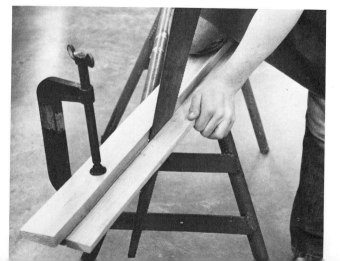

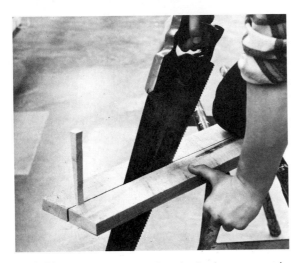

Fig. 8-13. If the blade binds in the kerf, use a wooden wedge to spread the kerf.

Fig. 8-14. Backsaws are used to make fine, accurate cuts for wood joints.

Backsaw. Accurate cuts for wood joints are made with backsaws. The backsaw has a thin blade. This blade is stiffened with a heavy metal back called a **spine**. See Fig. 8-14. The metal "back" gives the saw its name.

Backsaws are commonly 14 inches long and have 13 points per inch. Backsaw blades have fine, crosscut teeth with very little set. Because of this, the backsaw cuts a narrow, smooth kerf. These kerfs help ensure the accuracy needed for wood joints.

Using Backsaws. When cutting with a backsaw, use the following procedure.

1. Lay out the cutting line. For the most accurate cuts, mark the wood with a knife rather than a pencil. Additional layout information is given in chapter 6.
2. One way to hold the wood is to use a **bench hook.** See Fig. 8-15. A bench hook can save you time and it is easy to make. A plan for making a simple bench hook is shown in Fig. 8-16.

   To use the bench hook, simply hook the lower lip on the edge of the workbench. Then place the wood to be cut in front of the stop. The waste side of the cutting line should be even with the edge of the stop.

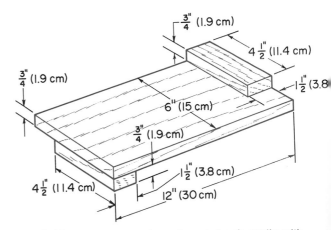

Fig. 8-15. A simple bench hook holds the stock in place while you make the cut.

Fig. 8-16. You can make a bench hook easily with scrap lumber. Attach the stop and lower lip to the frame with glue and screws.

Fig. 8-17. When you use a bench hook, line up the waste side of the line with the edge of the stop. This will help you make a straight cut.

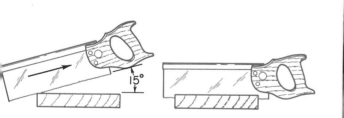

Fig. 8-18. Start a cut with a backsaw by pulling the saw **back** at a 15° angle. After the kerf has been started, lower each stroke until your strokes are parallel to the board.

Fig. 8-19. You can make a depth gauge for a backsaw by clamping a board to the blade. The bottom of the blade should extend below the board the same depth you want the finished cut.

Fig. 8-20. You can use a backsaw in a wooden miter box to make angled cuts for miter joints. This worker is making a picture frame.

The stop will help guide the saw to make a straight cut. See Fig. 8-17.

Hold the saw with your right hand (if you are right-handed). Hold the wood and the bench hook with your left hand. Be sure to keep the bench hook snug against the workbench. If a bench hook is not available, hold the stock in a vise.

3. Start the cut by gently pulling the saw toward you. The saw should be at a 15° angle to the work. Repeat this stroke until the kerf is started. When the kerf is about 1/4 inch *(6 mm)* deep, start back-and-forth strokes. The strokes should go the full length of the saw blade. As the cut deepens, slowly reduce the cutting angle of the saw. Reduce the angle until the blade is parallel to the surface of the board. See Fig. 8-18. Do not rush the cut. Backsaws cut slowly. If the saw starts to bind, clean the sawdust from the kerf.

4. When you make cuts that do not go completely through the wood, use a depth gauge, as shown in Fig. 8-19. This ensures that all cuts are made to the same depth.

Miter Box. Backsaws are often used with miter boxes to make miter (angle) cuts. See Fig. 8-20. These U-shaped boxes hold the stock while the backsaw makes an accurate cut. You can make your own wooden miter box by following the plan in Fig. 8-21.

To use the wooden miter box, clamp it in a vise. If no vise is available, hook it on the bench as you would a bench hook. Mark the piece to be cut and place it inside the miter box. Line up the cutting line with the desired kerf. Hold the piece tightly against one side of the miter box. With a backsaw, saw through the piece. See Fig. 8-20. Do not use a crosscut saw with a wooden miter box. It will ruin the accuracy of the box.

Miter Box and Saw. A miter saw is basically a large backsaw. It is made to be used in an adjustable miter box. See Fig. 8-22. A metal miter box and saw make accurate angle cuts from 30° to 90°. They can also be used to make accurate straight cuts. Sliding in adjustable tracks, the blade stays straight up and down. It also stays at the desired angle.

Using Miter Boxes and Saws. The miter box and saw is easy to use. When cutting with the miter box and saw, use the following procedure.

1. Mark the cutting line on the board. For the most accurate marking, use a knife instead of a pencil. For more information, see chapter 6.

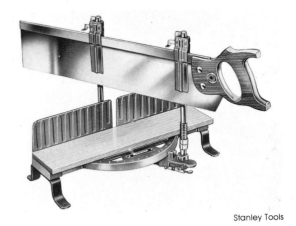

Stanley Tools

Fig. 8-22. An adjustable miter box and saw

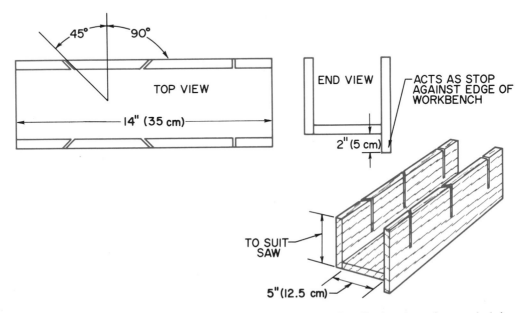

Fig. 8-21. Following this plan you can make a simple miter box from shop material. Be especially careful when making the guide kerfs — any mistake here will be duplicated every time you use the box.

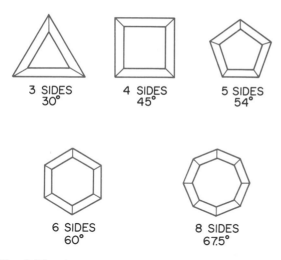

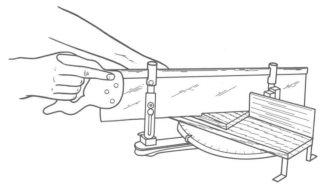

Fig. 8-24. When you use the adjustable miter box and saw, the saw's weight will provide enough downward pressure to make a clean cut.

Fig. 8-23. Angles of miter cuts are determined by the number of sides to the frame. Set the miter box and saw to the given number of degrees.

2. Adjust the miter box to the desired angle. The most common settings are 90° and 45°. See Fig. 8-23.
3. Raise the saw in its guides. Slide the board under the saw. Position it snugly against the fence.
4. Lower the saw onto the board. Align the blade with the cutting line. Be sure the blade is on the waste side of the line.
5. Hold the board securely with one hand. Start the kerf by pushing the blade forward. Keep the blade parallel with the surface. See Fig. 8-24.
6. Some small pieces will move while you saw them. These pieces should be clamped to the frame of the miter box.

Dovetail Saw. Dovetail joints are cut by hand with the specially designed dovetail saw. See Fig. 8-25. A common dovetail blade is 10 inches long and has 15 points per inch. Like the backsaw blade, the dovetail blade is strengthened by a metal spine. The dovetail blade is even thinner than the backsaw blade. This thin blade makes a very thin kerf. Such kerfs are needed for delicate, accurate joints. The dovetail saw is used in the same manner as a backsaw.

Fig. 8-25. Dovetail saws are designed to cut fine, intricate dovetail joints.

Saws for Cutting Curves

The coping, compass, and keyhole saws are used to cut curves. These saws are designed to cut out shapes and make designs in wood.

Coping Saw. Fine, irregular shapes in wood are often cut with a coping saw. The coping saw consists of a thin blade fastened to a metal

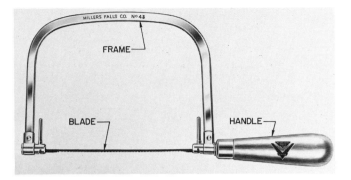

Fig. 8-26. Coping saws are used to cut curves and irregular shapes in thin wood.

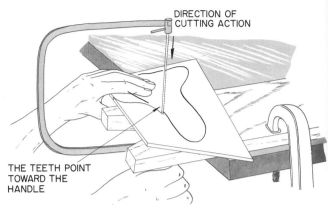

Fig. 8-27. A simple saw bracket provides extra support for work being cut with a coping saw.

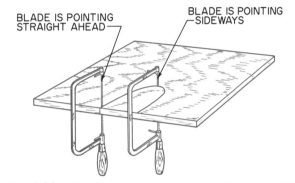

Fig. 8-28. Coping saw blades can be turned to cut in any direction, making it possible to cut curves such as this one.

frame. See Fig. 8-26. This thin blade enables the coping saw to cut intricate, complicated designs. It can also make inside cuts. **Inside cuts** are cuts that cannot be made by starting from the outside of the wood. The coping saw can only cut as far inside the wood as the depth of the frame.

Using Coping Saws. Use the following procedure when cutting with a coping saw.

1. Lay out the cutting line on the board. Use a pattern cut from cardboard or heavy paper. For more information see chapter 6.
2. Clamp the piece in a vise. The cutting line should be close to the vise jaws. To maintain support, you may need to move the piece as you cut. When you use a vise, the teeth of the saw blade should point **away** from the handle. If not inserted properly, the blade should be reversed.
3. During sawing, thin wood tends to vibrate in a vice. Wood less than 3/8 inch *(9 mm)* thick should be held over a saw bracket. See Fig. 8-27. A **saw bracket** is a device that provides extra support for thin pieces. It also gives you better control. It lets you move the piece easily while sawing.
   When you use a saw bracket, point the teeth of the saw blade **toward** the handle. The saw then cuts on the downstroke. This forces the work down on the bracket

as you saw, making it easier to hold the work. See again Fig. 8-27.

4. With a saw bracket, keep the blade within the V-cut of the support. Guide the cut by moving the work piece. Be sure to cut on the waste side of the cutting line. Keep your fingers clear of the cutting path of the blade.
5. Use even, regular strokes. Do not force the saw. Do not try to make sharp turns quickly. Use short, gentle strokes while turning the blade. Turning the blade too quickly may break it. Turn the blade in the frame when the frame cannot follow the cutting line. See Fig. 8-28.

6. Remove most of the waste before cutting sharp and square inside corners. Sometimes several cuts are needed to finish an inside corner.

7. To make an inside cut, drill a hole in the waste part of the design. See Fig. 8-29. Locate the hole so it barely touches the cutting line. Disconnect one end of the blade and put it through the hole. Reattach the blade and begin cutting. When the cut is complete, disconnect the blade and remove it from the wood.

8. A dull coping saw blade can be replaced. On most saws this is easily done. Simply unscrew the handle and unhook the blade pins. Then insert the new blade and tighten the handle. Friction (two surfaces rubbing together) can make a coping saw blade very hot. Do not touch the blade until it has cooled.

Compass and Keyhole Saw. Large curves and irregular shapes are cut with the compass saw and the keyhole saw. Both have narrow blades that taper (get smaller) toward the tip. They are often used for cutting in places that cannot be reached with a coping saw.

The compass saw is larger than the keyhole saw. See Fig. 8-30. Most compass saw blades are 14 inches long with eight points per inch.

They make a fast but fairly rough cut. Compass saws are used when a large (6 inches, 150 mm, or larger) design must be cut. See Fig. 8-31.

The keyhole saw is smaller than the compass saw. It also has a narrower blade. A common keyhole saw is 12 inches long and has ten points per inch. It is used to cut designs too intricate for the compass saw. (A coping saw can be used to make cuts even more intricate or detailed.)

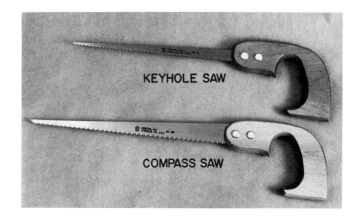

Fig. 8-30. The compass saw is larger than the keyhole saw.

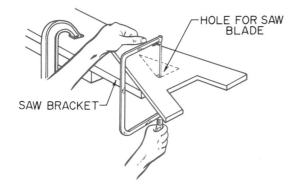

Fig. 8-29. To make an inside cut with a coping saw, first drill a hole in the waste material close to the cutting line. Then insert the coping saw blade through the hole.

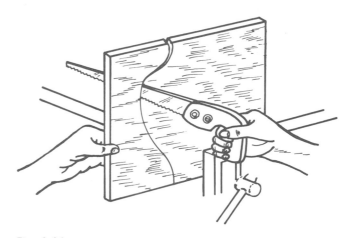

Fig. 8-31. Compass saws are used to cut large, irregular designs. Smaller designs are usually cut with a keyhole or coping saw.

Using Compass and Keyhole Saws. Use the following procedure when cutting with compass and keyhole saws.

1. Lay out the cutting line. Use a pattern cut from cardboard or heavy paper. For more information see chapter 6.
2. Clamp the stock in a vise.
3. When making an inside cut, drill a hole next to the cutting line. The hole should be in the waste part of the stock. It should be larger than the tip of the saw blade. This gives you enough room to start the cut. Use short strokes at first. As the kerf is made longer, use more of the blade in each stroke. See Fig. 8-32.

For outside cuts, saw to the cutting line at a gradual angle. Use long, even strokes. Make sure you stay on the waste side of the line.

Use short strokes when sawing around a corner. Use only the tip of the saw. The tapered toe of the saw will let you cut a fairly sharp curve.

Care and Maintenance of Saws

For saws to work properly and last a long time, you must take care of them. Follow these "do's" and "don'ts," and your saws will last a lifetime.

Coat the blade with wax or light oil. This keeps moisture from touching the blade. Moisture can cause the blade to rust. A rusted blade is hard to push and pull during cutting. Heavy rust can also dull the teeth, and even weaken the blade.

Do not press heavily on the saw when cutting. Too much pressure can cause the blade to kink (bend sharply). This ruins the saw for making accurate cuts.

Never let the saw's teeth touch metal. One stroke against a nail or the jaws of a vise can dull the teeth. It is also important to protect the teeth when storing the saw. See Fig. 8-33. The teeth should rest on a soft surface or the saw should be hung by the handle.

Dull saws should be sharpened by an experienced person. An unskilled person without proper equipment may damage the saw.

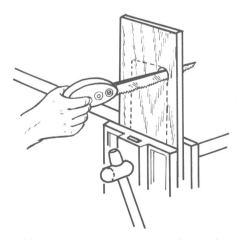

Fig. 8-32. Keyhole saws are used like coping saws to make inside cuts. Notice how the hole was drilled to form one corner of the design.

Fig. 8-33. Keep saws where there is no chance of the teeth being dulled by metal objects.

Sawing Safety

- Wear glasses or goggles to protect your eyes from sawdust and wood chips.
- Keep your hands and legs away from the cutting path of the saw.
- Let saw blades cool before touching them. They sometimes become hot during cutting.

New Terms

1. backsaw
2. bench hook
3. compass saw
4. coping saw
5. crosscut saw
6. dovetail saw
7. inside cut
8. kerf
9. keyhole saw
10. miter box
11. miter cut
12. miter saw
13. panel saw
14. ripsaw
15. saw bracket
16. set
17. waste side

Study Questions

1. What happens as you move the points of a saw blade against a wood surface?
2. Name three parts common to all saws.
3. What determines the cutting traits of a saw?
4. Which saw makes the smoother cut — one with 10 points per inch, or one with 20 points per inch? Which saw will cut faster?
5. How many points are there per inch on a saw blade with 15 teeth per inch?
6. Is a crosscut saw designed to cut wood to width or length?
7. Give two advantages of the panel saw's length.
8. On which side of the cutting line should you usually make a cut?
9. At what angle should you make a cut with a crosscut saw?
10. How does a ripsaw differ from a crosscut saw in design? in purpose?
11. Ripsaws bind easily. How can you solve this problem?
12. What is the one basic difference in the way you use ripsaws and crosscut saws?
13. Why is the backsaw used to make cuts for wood joints?
14. What easily made device holds wood pieces secure while they are cut with a backsaw or dovetail saw?
15. What kind of cuts are made with a backsaw and wooden miter box?
16. What is the major use of dovetail saws?
17. For what types of cuts are coping saws used?
18. What device is used to hold thin pieces while cutting with a coping saw?
19. Compass and keyhole saws are used for what kind of cuts?
20. Name one way of preventing a saw blade from rusting.
21. Why should you apply light pressure as you cut with a saw?

Planing and Scraping

After sawing your wood to rough size, you will probably need to plane it. There are four possible reasons for planing. Any or all could apply to your project.

- **remove mill marks and surface defects** — Mill marks are small arc-shaped marks left by power planing and joining machines. See Fig. 9-1. Planes remove these and other surface blemishes.
- **reduce dimensions** — If a joint fits too tightly, thin shavings can be removed with a plane. Planing can also make a board thinner, narrower, and even slightly shorter.
- **make surfaces true (flat)** — Planes are used to make surfaces smooth and flat.
- **square stock** — The surfaces of most pieces in a project need to be made square. Planes are often used for this purpose.

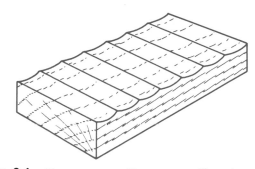

Fig. 9-1. Planes are used to remove mill marks made by machines.

Hand Planes

A hand plane consists of a sharp, chisel-shaped cutting edge in a holding device. This holding device is adjustable so that the cutting edge extends into the surface to be cut. As a plane is pushed along a surface, the cutting edge removes a thin layer of wood.

Depending on classifications, there are ten to fifteen kinds of hand planes. They are divided into two groups: standard (also called bench) planes and specialty planes. All bench planes are similar in design, but they differ in size. Each of the specialty planes has its own design and use.

Jointer Plane

Fore Plane

Jack Plane

Smooth Plane

Stanley Tools   Woodcraft Supply Corporation

Fig. 9-2. The main difference between bench planes is size.

Bench Planes. Most planing is done with a bench plane. See Fig. 9-2. Each bench plane has its cutting blade mounted at a 45° angle. The blades range in width from 1-3/4 to 2-3/8 inches, depending on the type of plane. Frame lengths range from 7 to 24 inches. The long planes are, of course, heavier than the shorter ones. Generally the shorter, lighter planes are used for small pieces. For longer, wider stock, longer planes are used. All of the bench planes require two hands to operate.

Smooth planes are the shortest bench planes. They are available with 8- and 9-inch frames. They are used primarily for final smoothing. They are especially useful for planing and trimming short stock.

Jack planes have 14- and 15-inch frames. **Junior jack** planes have 11-1/2-inch frames, making them easier to operate. Jack planes are all-purpose planes. They are used more frequently than any other type of plane. Because of their intermediate size, they are used for both rough and final smoothing.

Fore planes have 18-inch frames. They are used to plane long boards. They are especially useful in planing edges.

Jointer planes have the longest frames. They are available in 22- and 24-inch models. Jointer planes are used to plane very long surfaces smooth and flat.

Specialty Planes. Fig. 9-3 shows the various specialty planes. Notice that no two are alike in design. They have blades of different shapes and sizes. The blades are mounted at different angles in their special frames. These variations in design make each plane especially suitable for a particular job.

Block planes are probably the most frequently used specialty planes. They are the best planes for planing end grain. They are also used to smooth and fit furniture and interior trim in houses. Block planes range in size from 3-1/2 to 7 inches. The cutting blade on a block plane is set at a smaller angle than the blade of a bench plane. The smaller cutting angle and

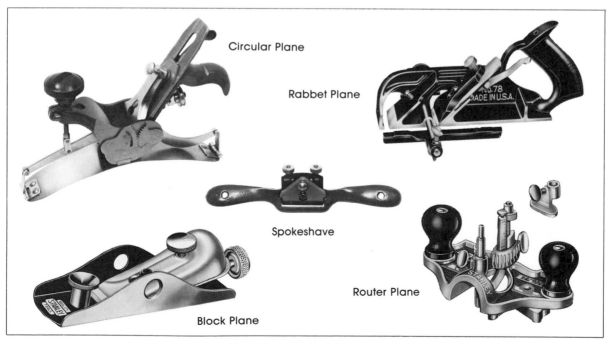

Circular Plane

Rabbet Plane

Spokeshave

Router Plane

Block Plane

Fig. 9-3. Specialty Planes

upturned bevel allow the block plane to easily cut hard wood. Block planes can be operated with one hand.

Rabbet planes are designed to cut rabbet joints. These planes solve the problem of planing accurately in corners. The plane iron in some rabbet planes can be mounted in either the front or back. The front position allows for close cutting in a corner. The rear position makes the plane easier to use in most situations.

Router planes are used to clean out the bottoms of dadoes, grooves, and other recessed areas when making joints. Several sizes of cutters can be inserted to control the width of cut.

Circular planes have flexible frames that allow them to adjust to curves. They are used to smooth both convex (outside) and concave (inside) surfaces.

Spokeshaves were developed to make round, tapered, wagon wheel spokes. They are now used to form and shape irregular designs.

Understanding Planes

Planes are complex tools. They have many parts. You must learn how to assemble and adjust these parts correctly. You cannot do this

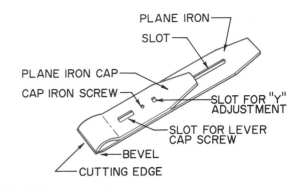

Fig. 9-5. Double Plane Iron Assembly

unless you understand how planes work. The more you understand, the better results you will get when you plane.

Parts of a Plane. The parts of a standard bench plane are shown in Fig. 9-4. The cutting blade is called the **plane iron**. The plane iron and the **plane iron cap** are held to the **frog** by the **lever cap**. The frog supports the plane iron as the plane iron extends through the opening, or **mouth** of the **frame**. On the frog are two adjustments: the adjusting nut and the lateral adjusting lever. The brass **adjusting nut** raises and lowers the plane iron through the mouth. This regulates the depth of the cut. The **lateral adjusting lever** lines up the plane iron, making it parallel with the frame bottom. The bench plane is held and guided with a **knob** and a **handle**.

The plane iron and the plane iron cap are held together with a screw. Together they are called the **double plane iron**. See Fig. 9-5. They fit together with the bevel down and the hump of the cap away from the plane iron.

The plane iron performs the actual cutting. The plane iron cap reinforces and strengthens the plane iron. It also breaks the wood fibers and causes them to curl. See Fig. 9-6. To break the fibers, the cap must fit tightly to the plane iron. If it does not, the fibers will clog between the cap and the plane iron. The fibers will then cover the sharp edge and prevent cutting.

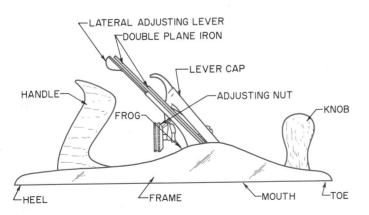

Fig. 9-4. To operate a plane correctly, you must be familiar with the parts.

Assembling a Plane Iron. To assemble the double plane iron, hold the plane iron as shown in Fig. 9-7. The bevel should be facing down. With the humped part up, place the cap on the plane iron at a right angle. This prevents damage to the cutting edge. Put the screw through the large hole and slide the cap away from the cutting edge. Turn the cap parallel to the plane iron and slide it 1/16 inch *(2 mm)* from the cutting edge. Then tighten the screw.

With the bevel down, lower the double plane iron into position over the frog. Be sure the slot in the plane iron cap fits over the fork attached to the brass adjusting nut. See Fig. 9-8. Also be sure the small disk at the base of the lateral adjusting level is inside the long slot of the plane iron. Place the lever cap over the lever cap screw and lock the plane iron in place. Adjust the lever cap screw until the lever cap snaps tightly into place.

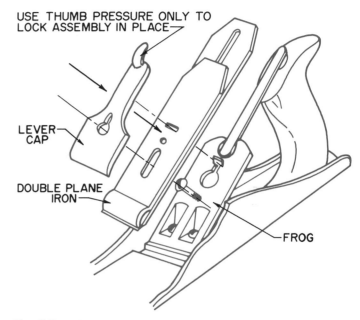

Fig. 9-8. After the plane iron is assembled, it is attached to the frog.

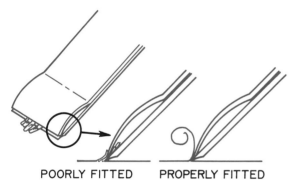

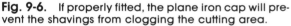

Fig. 9-6. If properly fitted, the plane iron cap will prevent the shavings from clogging the cutting area.

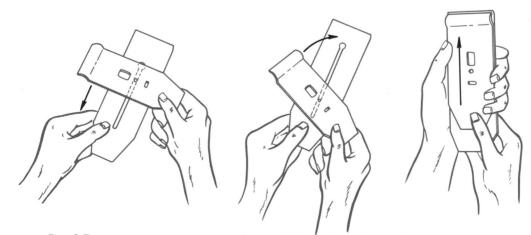

Fig. 9-7. The plane iron cap is usually set 1/16 inch (2 mm) behind the cutting edge. For fine cuts on hard wood and for planing cross grain, the cap should be closer to the edge.

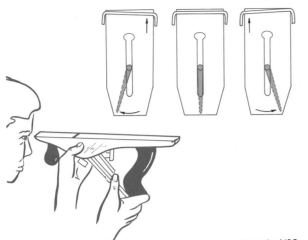

Fig. 9-9. Adjust the plane iron so that it extends 1/32 inch (.8 mm) through the mouth and is parallel to the frame.

Fig. 9-10. Use the largest plane (A) available to get a flat cut. You cannot get a flat cut with a plane that is shorter (B) than the distance between the high spots.

Adjusting a Plane. After locking the double plane iron into place, adjust the cutting edge. Use the following procedure.

1. Turn the plane upside down. If possible, turn the plane toward a lighted area. Turn the adjusting nut until the cutting edge extends through the frame about 1/32 inch *(.8 mm)*.
2. Move the lateral adjusting lever until the cutting edge is parallel to the frame. See Fig. 9-9.
3. Make a trial cut on a piece of scrap. Make sure you cut with the grain, not across it. Do **not** make your trial cut on end or edge grain.

4. Slightly lower or raise the plane iron to get the desired shaving.
5. Readjust the lateral adjusting lever if the plane digs deeper on one side than the other. The plane is adjusted correctly when it pushes easily and produces an even shaving.

Using Planes

All planing operations are basically the same. Whether you are removing mill marks or making a surface flat, you use the same planing stroke. In fact, you can accomplish several planing tasks in one operation. If you must reduce a board to size and square it, you need not do one operation and then the other. You can reduce, square, and smooth all at once.

General Planing Techniques. Use the following procedures for all planing operations.

1. Choose the best surface to plane first. The best surface has the fewest flaws and most interesting grain pattern.
2. Mark high spots with a pencil. Ink and felt pens permanently stain wood. Check for high spots by laying the stock on a level surface to see if it rocks. You can also use a square.
3. Fasten or clamp the stock to the workbench. This frees both hands for controlling the plane.
4. Select the proper plane for the job. For long surfaces use the longest available plane. A shorter plane will follow the irregularities rather than remove them. See Fig. 9-10.
5. Position yourself so that you can easily shift your weight back and forth as you plane.
6. Make sure the bottom of the plane is clean and free of gum (dried sap). Gum deposits make the plane hard to push. They will also dull the plane iron.
7. Always plane WITH the grain. Planing against the grain will produce a rough, torn surface. See Fig. 9-11.

8. Slightly shift downward pressure as you move the plane away from an end or edge. See Fig. 9-12. As you begin, apply pressure to the knob. Through the middle of the stroke, apply equal pressure to the knob and handle. Toward the end of the stroke, shift the pressure to the handle. Failure to shift the pressure results in a tapered (angled) cut.

9. Planing diagonally is often the easiest way to make wide, flat surfaces true. If you do rough plane diagonally, make a light, final cut with the grain.

10. You can achieve an effect similar to planing diagonally. Do this by planing with the grain while holding the plane at a slight angle. Wood fibers are easier to cut at an angle than straight ahead.

11. Be sure to lift the plane from the surface after each stroke. Pulling the plane back across the wood will dull the cutting edge.

12. As you plane, continually check your progress. Use a straightedge or try square. See Fig. 9-13.

13. When you finish with a plane, lay it on its side. This prevents dulling of the cutting edge and damage to surfaces. Store planes in a dry place to prevent rusting, which makes them hard to push.

Fig. 9-13. Carefully check the surface as you plane. Always check for high spots in more than one direction.

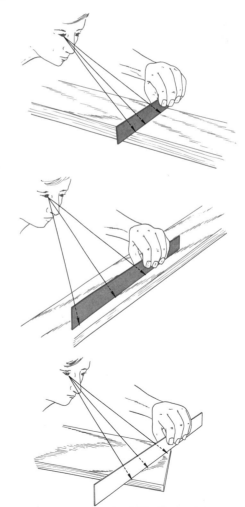

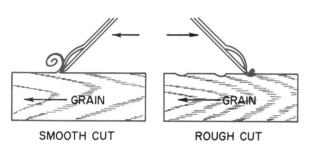

Fig. 9-11. Always plane with the grain. If you are not sure of the grain direction, plane so that the grain does not pull out.

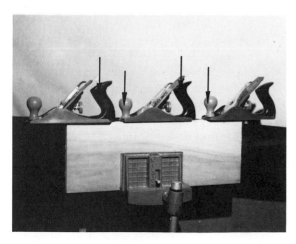

Fig. 9-12. As you plane, apply pressure to the part of the plane that is directly over the board.

Planing Faces. Select the best face to plane first. Plane the minimum amount to make the surface true and smooth. If you need to plane to finish thickness, do so on the second face. Use the bench plane that works best for the size of the surface. Follow the steps below to plane a face.

1. Measure and mark the desired thickness on the board's edges and ends. These lines will serve as guides for squareness and stopping points for thickness.
2. Clamp the stock end to end on a workbench. Use a vise dog and bench stop as in Fig. 9-14. Never clamp the board edge to edge. The clamp pressure will cause the board to cup. This makes it impossible to plane the board flat.
3. Adjust the plane iron to make thin shavings. Make the first stroke. Then determine if you need to make a thinner or deeper cut.
4. Plane across the entire board. If you start in the middle or pull up before the end, you will not produce a flat surface.
5. Frequently check the surface in each of the three ways shown in Fig. 9-13. Mark the high points with a pencil and resume planing.

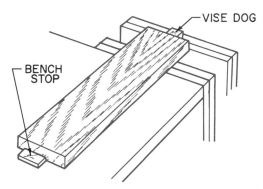

Fig. 9-14. Clamp the stock between a bench stop and vise dog to plane a face. Clamping ends rather than edges will prevent bowing.

Fig. 9-15. You can reduce the width of a board by planing the edges.

Planing Edges. Plane the best edge first. Plane the minimum amount to make the surface smooth and flat. Because only a narrow shaving is removed, edges are the easiest surfaces to plane. The length and width of the edge will determine which bench plane you use. Use the following procedure to plane an edge.

1. Measure and mark the desired width on the board's faces and ends. These lines will serve as guides for squareness and stopping points for width.
2. Mount the board in a bench vise with the edge to be planed up. To ensure accuracy, make the edge parallel to the top of the vise.
3. Adjust the plane iron to the desired depth of cut.
4. Make sure the plane is perpendicular to the face as you cut. This is sometimes difficult with narrow edges. Plane across the entire surface. See Fig. 9-15. Do not start in the middle or pull up before an end.
5. Use a straightedge or try square to be sure the edge is true. If checking shows high spots, mark them and resume planing.
6. Use a try square to check squareness between the edge and the planed face. See Fig. 9-16. These surfaces must be square before you plane another surface.

Fig. 9-16. Use a try square to check that the edge and face are square.

Planing Ends. Board length can be reduced a small amount by planing the ends. The hardness of end grain makes this difficult, however. Block planes are designed specifically to plane end grain. A regular bench plane can also be used. Use the following procedure to plane ends.

1. Measure and mark the desired length on the board's edges and faces. These lines will serve as guides for squareness and stopping points for length.
2. Secure the board in a vise with the end to be planed up. The end should be as close as possible to the vise to reduce vibration.
3. Adjust the block plane to the desired cutting depth.
4. Planing end grain can easily cause splitting. See Fig. 9-17. Special planing methods are used to prevent splitting. One method is to plane from both edges toward the middle. See Fig. 9-18. Another method is to clamp a scrap piece to an edge as shown in Fig. 9-19. The scrap piece supports the edge, preventing it from splitting.
5. Use a straightedge or try square to check that the end is true. Mark the high spots that need further planing.
6. Check that the end is square with both the planed edge and face.

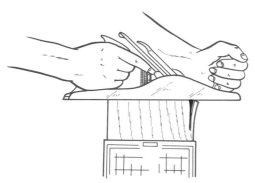

Fig. 9-17. This is the **wrong** way to plane end grain. Never plane toward an unsupported edge. See Figs. 9-18 and 9-19.

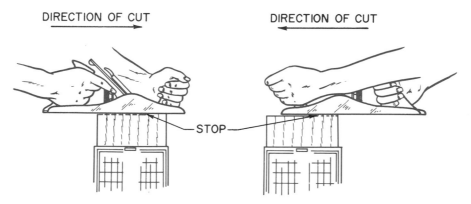

DIRECTION OF CUT →   DIRECTION OF CUT ←

—STOP—

Fig. 9-18. Avoid splitting the end grain by planing in both directions. Do not extend the cuts over either edge.

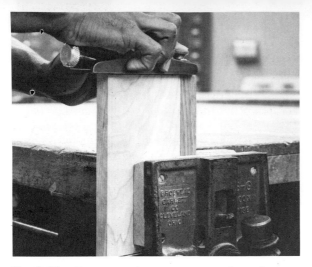

Fig. 9-19. You can clamp a scrap piece to one edge to help prevent end grain from splitting. Always plane toward the scrap piece.

Squaring Boards. To square a board, plane the best face, edge, and end, in that order. Then plane the second end, edge, and face, in that order. See Fig. 9-20. Plane each surface so it is square with its adjoining surfaces. Check the squareness of the surfaces with a try square.

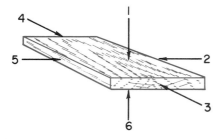

Fig. 9-20. To square a board, plane the surfaces in the order shown. Make each surface square with its adjoining surfaces.

Fig. 9-21. Tapers, chamfers, and bevels are angle cuts often used for decoration.

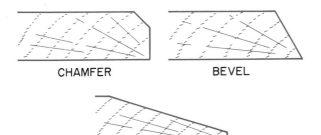

CHAMFER   BEVEL

TAPER

Decorative Cuts. Some angle cuts used primarily for decoration are often made with planes. Three of the more common decorative cuts are bevels, chamfers, and tapers. See Fig. 9-21.

Bevels are angle cuts extending across entire edges or ends. They can be made to any angle. **Chamfers** are angle cuts, usually 45°, extending across only part of a surface (face, end, or edge). One method for laying out chamfers and 45° bevels is shown in Fig. 9-22. Layout techniques for bevels other than 45° are shown in Fig. 9-23.

Hold the stock for bevels and chamfers in a vise as shown in Fig. 9-24. Use the planing procedures for surfaces, edges, and ends, described earlier in this chapter. As you work, frequently check your cuts with a combination square or sliding T-bevel.

Tapers are angle cuts that run along the entire length of a board. See Fig. 9-21. This makes a long piece narrower at one end. Any number of sides can be tapered. Tapers are used to decorate long pieces of furniture, such as table legs.

Square the stock before you lay out a taper cut. With a pencil, mark where the taper starts. Then mark the end to be tapered, showing how much stock is to be removed. Using a straight-

Fig. 9-22. Chamfers can be laid out with a pencil and combination square, or a marking gauge.

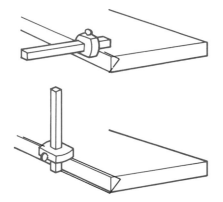

Fig. 9-25. A spokeshave can be used to make chamfers, bevels, and other decorative cuts.

Fig. 9-23. To lay out a bevel or chamfer, use a protractor to set a sliding T-bevel to the desired angle. Lay the T-bevel on the surface and mark the angle with a pencil. Extend the lines with a marking gauge. Use the T-bevel to check the angle as you plane.

Fig. 9-24. It is easier to plane chamfers and bevels if the board is held at an angle. Clamping the stock with a hand screw and then clamping the hand screw in a vise, will make this possible.

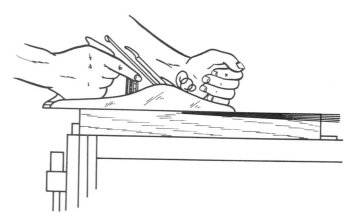

Fig. 9-26. The lines show the lengths of the strokes used to cut a taper on a table leg.

edge, draw a line between the marks. With the stock in a vise, plane toward the tapered end. Make short cuts at first. Gradually increase the length of each stroke. See Fig. 9-26. Check your work frequently with a straightedge and try square. If more than one taper is made on a surface, cut the first before laying out the second. This way your layout lines will not be removed as you shape the stock. If a large amount of stock must be removed, use a saw and then plane the surface smooth and flat.

Sharpening Planes

Successful planing depends on a sharp plane iron. Two operations, honing and grinding, are used to sharpen plane irons. **Honing** (also called whetting) sharpens the tip of the cutting

Stone	Color	Texture	Use
Hard Arkansas	White or black	Very hard & fine	Final polishing
Soft Arkansas	White	Hard, medium fine	General honing
Washita	Pink White	Medium coarse	Initial honing
*India (aluminum oxide)	Brown	Coarse, medium fine	Initial or final honing
*Crystolon (silicon carbide)	Grey or black	Coarse, medium fine	Initial or final honing

*These are artificial stones available with one side coarse and the other side fine.

Fig. 9-27. Oilstone Chart

Fig. 9-28. One side of this Crystolon oilstone is coarse; the other side is fine.

edge. **Grinding** shapes the entire cutting edge. Plane irons are honed whenever they become dull, and after each grinding operation. Grinding is not done as frequently. Only defective cutting edges, such as those with nicks, and deformed or worn bevels, require grinding.

Honing. The oilstones most often used for honing are described in the chart in Fig. 9-27. An artificial stone with a coarse grit on one side and fine grit on the other will serve most purposes. See Fig. 9-28. Mount the oilstone in a holder to keep it stationary. Coat the stone with a light machine oil. This lubrication keeps metal particles from clogging the surface. To sharpen the blade, use the following procedure.

1. Place the beveled portion of the cutting edge flat on a medium or coarse oilstone. Rock the blade slightly up and down until you feel the flat portion of the bevel against the stone. This is the correct position for honing.

2. With both hands on the plane iron, move it in a figure eight or long, oval pattern. See Fig. 9-29. Use the entire surface of the oilstone so it will wear evenly. Hone the blade until the edge is sharp and straight. This may produce a wire edge on the tip of the blade.

3. Remove the wire edge by placing the blade flat against the oilstone with the bevel side up. See Fig. 9-30. Make a few

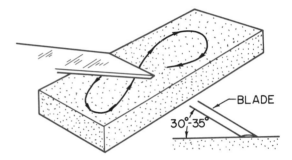

Fig. 9-29. To hone a plane iron, move the blade in a figure-eight pattern. Always keep the bevel flat against the stone.

Fig. 9-30. Remove the wire edge by honing the back side of the plane iron. Make sure you hold the blade flat against the stone.

strokes, rubbing the blade in a circular motion. Be sure the blade is kept flat. Otherwise a bevel will form on the back side. This will cause the blade to cut incorrectly. Hone the bevel side and the flat side alternately until the wire edge comes off. Slicing a sliver from a scrap piece of stock will also help to remove the wire edge.

4. After the wire edge is removed, use a fine oilstone to further hone the edge. Use the same technique as before. Hone just enough to make the edge smooth and clean. This final honing makes the blade sharper.

5. Test the blade for sharpness by making a slicing cut on a scrap board. The blade should cut easily and cleanly. Do **not** rub your finger over the cutting edge or shave hair from your arm to test sharpness. These actions can cause serious cuts.

Grinding. Do not grind a plane iron unless the cutting edge and bevel have been damaged or worn. The less you grind a plane iron, the longer it will last. Careful honing will keep a plane iron sharp and reduce the need for grinding.

Plane irons can be ground freehand. This is difficult and requires practice. If you grind a plane iron freehand, use the plane iron cap as a guide. See Fig. 9-31.

The most accurate way to grind a new bevel is to use a special sharpening attachment on a grinder. See Fig. 9-32. This ensures a straight, even grind, without grinding too much of the blade. Use the following procedure to grind with an attachment.

1. Mount the plane iron in the attachment as shown in Fig. 9-32. Adjust the attachment to the desired angle. This is usually between 25 and 30°.

2. Turn the inward adjusting screw until the cutting edge of the plane iron just touches the grinding wheel.

3. Start the grinder and move the plane iron back and forth across the wheel. Check for the correct angle. Keep the blade cool by dipping it in water or allowing it to air cool after each pass.

Be careful not to let either edge of the plane iron slip off the edge of the wheel. This could easily cause a nick that would mean starting over. Continue grinding

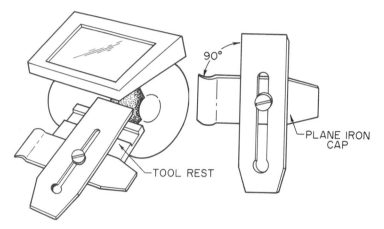

Fig. 9-31. To grind a plane iron freehand, screw the plane iron cap to the plane iron as shown. Adjust the plane iron cap on the tool rest so that the bevel of the plane iron is flat against the grinding wheel. Turn on the grinder and slide the blade back and forth across the wheel. Be sure to keep the plane iron cap snugly against the tool rest as you grind.

Fig. 9-32. A grinding attachment ensures straight, accurate grinding.

Rockwell International

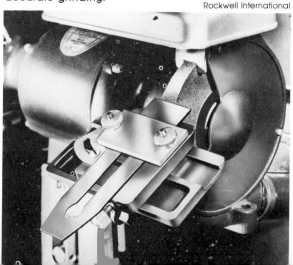

until no metal is being removed and a wire edge has formed completely across the new bevel. If imperfections remain, readjust the inward adjusting screw and resume grinding.

4. When grinding is complete, hone the blade as described earlier.

Scrapers

Scrapers are used to remove mill marks and minor imperfections left by planes. They are also used to smooth wood surfaces with unusual grain patterns. These surfaces tend to chip easily when planed. Careful use of scrapers can greatly reduce the time and effort needed for hand sanding. The various scrapers and their uses are explained in the following paragraphs.

Hand scrapers are simple-looking, usually rectangular tools of high-grade steel. See Fig. 9-33. A small, barely visible hook along the edge of the scraper does the cutting. Hold the scraper in both hands as shown in Fig. 9-34. Whether you push or pull the scraper, move it with the grain. The scraper should cut very thin shavings from the surface of the wood. If you get dust rather than small curls, the scraper needs sharpening.

Cabinet scrapers look like spokeshaves. See Fig. 9-35. They work much like hand scrapers but are easier to hold and use. They are often used in place of rough and intermediate sanding.

To use a cabinet scraper, insert the cutting blade. The inserted edge should be even with the bottom of the frame. Tighten the screws. Then adjust the depth of cut with the adjusting thumbscrew. Push or pull the scraper in the opposite direction of the bevel. See Fig. 9-35. Lift and return the scraper to start a new stroke.

Double-edge scrapers consist of a double-edged blade inserted in the end of a wooden

Woodcraft Supply Corporation

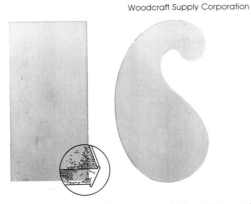

Fig. 9-33. Hand scrapers. The scraper to the left is used to scrape flat stock. The one to the right is used to scrape curved stock.

Fig. 9-34. To use a hand scraper, push or pull it at a 70° angle. A sharp scraper produces tiny shavings. If the scraper makes dust instead of shavings, it needs sharpening.

Stanley Tools

Fig. 9-35. Cabinet scraper. Use a cabinet scraper the same way you would a hand scraper. The frame makes the scraper easy to hold and keeps the blade at the correct angle.

Red Devil Tools

Fig. 9-36. Flat, hooked, and reversible blades are available for double-edge scrapers.

Stanley Tools

Fig. 9-37. Use a fine mill file to draw file the edges of scrapers. Cabinet scrapers should be filed at 45° angles.

Fig. 9-38. Honing a hand scraper

handle. See Fig. 9-36. These scrapers are seldom used to smooth wood. They are used primarily to remove dried glue spots, paint, and old finishes. The blade is usually pulled across surfaces. Dull blades are replaced rather than sharpened.

Stanley Tools

Fig. 9-39. Burnishers are used to form the cutting edges on hand and cabinet scrapers.

Sharpening Scrapers

As with planes, scrapers must have sharp cutting edges to work properly. Scraper blades must be sharpened frequently. Use the following procedure to maintain sharp cutting edges on cabinet and hand scrapers.

1. Mount the blade in a vise with the cutting edge up. Draw file the edge with a fine mill file. Pull the file toward your body with both hands. On a hand scraper make the end of the blade flat and square with the sides. On a cabinet scraper, file the edge to a 45° angle. See Fig. 9-37.
2. Remove the blade from the vise and hone the filed edge. See Fig. 9-38. Remove the wire edge by rubbing the blade flat on the oilstone.
3. Again mount the blade in a vise. Form the new edge by using a burnisher. See Fig. 9-39. Put a couple of drops of oil on the burnisher. Start in the middle of the blade and burnish both ways. Use firm strokes. Pull the burnisher across the edge at a 90° angle on the first stroke. With each new stroke, gradually tilt the burnisher to one side. See Figs. 9-40 and 9-41. You can burnish with a screwdriver blade if a burnisher is not available.

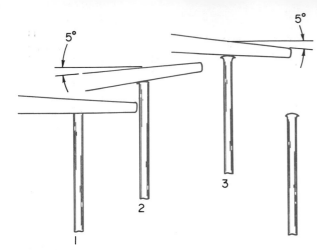

Fig. 9-40. Hand scrapers are burnished to about a 5° angle. They can be burnished on one or both sides of the edge.

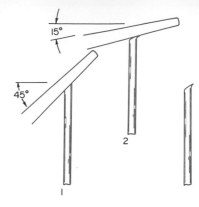

Fig. 9-41. Cabinet scrapers are burnished to a 15° angle on one side only.

SAFETY Planing and Scraping Safety

- Wear safety glasses when planing and scraping.
- Wear goggles or a face shield when grinding plane irons.
- The cutting edges on scrapers and plane irons are sharp. Handle them with care.
- Never test the sharpness of a plane or scraper by rubbing your finger across the cutting edge. You could easily cut your finger.
- Never leave a hand or cabinet scraper mounted in a vise. Someone could bump into it and be injured.

New Terms

1. bevel
2. block plane
3. burnisher
4. cabinet scraper
5. chamfer
6. circular plane
7. double-edge scraper
8. double plane iron
9. draw filing
10. fore plane
11. grinding
12. hand plane
13. hand scraper
14. honing
15. jack plane
16. jointer plane
17. mill marks
18. oilstone
19. rabbet plane
20. router plane
21. smooth plane
22. spokeshave
23. taper
24. wire edge

Study Questions

1. List four reasons for planing.
2. Give one reason why you might need to reduce the dimensions of a board.
3. Describe what happens as a hand plane is pushed along a wood surface?
4. All hand planes belong in one of two groups. Name the two groups.
5. Name the four types of bench planes.
6. All bench planes are alike, except for one difference. What is the difference?
7. Which specialty plane is used most frequently?
8. Why is the block plane the best plane for planing end grain?
9. Why must you be familiar with the parts of a bench plane and how they fit together?
10. What problem results from a loose-fitting plane iron cap?
11. In assembling the double plane iron, why is it necessary to place the cap on the plane iron at a right angle?
12. What do you look for to determine the best surface on a piece of wood?
13. Should you plane WITH or AGAINST the grain?
14. Why must special planing methods be used to plane end grain?
15. Careful scraping will reduce the time and effort needed for what step in preparing for finishing?
16. How can you tell if a hand scraper needs sharpening?

Shaping and Carving

You cannot cut all wood surfaces to their final size and shape with saws and planes. Chisels are often needed to chip and cut material from recessed areas. Files and rasps remove small amounts of material from curves and irregular designs. Various carving tools are used to make decorative designs in wood. These cutting tools and others used to shape and form wood are discussed in this chapter.

Chisels

Chisels are simple cutting tools used for many different jobs. They are often used to trim wood joints so they will fit correctly. They are also used to shape irregular designs and make simple, decorative cuts. Chisels are especially handy for removing stock to make gains (recessed areas) for hinges. Whatever the woodworking project, a chisel will probably be needed. You should become familiar with the common types of chisels and how to use them.

Types of Chisels. The different types and sizes of chisels are quite similar in appearance. Every chisel consists of a heavy steel blade attached to a handle. See Fig. 10-1. The chisels most commonly used in woodworking are firmer, pocket, butt, and mortise chisels. The basic difference between these chisels is their size.

Firmer chisels are considered all-purpose chisels. They range in width from 1/8 inch to 2 inches. The edges of firmer chisels are usually not beveled. See Fig. 10-2.

Pocket chisels are similar to firmer chisels but have shorter blades and beveled edges. See Fig. 10-3. The beveled edges are not as strong as plain edges, but they are easier to use in tight spots. Pocket chisels generally range in width from 1/4 inch to 1-1/2 inches.

Butt chisels are short chisels with beveled edges. See Fig. 10-4. Blade lengths range between 2-1/2 and 3 inches. Widths range from

Buck Brothers

Fig. 10-2. Firmer chisels do not generally have beveled edges. They are all-purpose chisels.

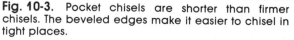

Stanley Tools

Fig. 10-3. Pocket chisels are shorter than firmer chisels. The beveled edges make it easier to chisel in tight places.

Stanley Tools

Fig. 10-4. Butt chisels have short, wide blades. They are used primarily to recess door hinges.

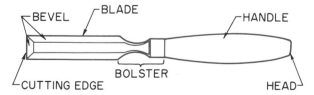

Fig. 10-1. A chisel consists of a handle and a steel blade, with a sharp cutting edge at the end of the blade.

Fig. 10-5. Mortise chisels are heavy and strong. They are used with a mallet to cut mortises for mortise-and-tenon joints.

Fig. 10-7. Always secure the stock with a vise or clamp when you chisel. For accurate cuts guide the chisel with your thumb and forefinger.

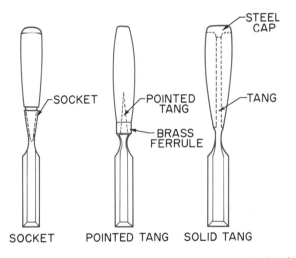

Fig. 10-6. Three methods are used to attach chisel handles and blades.

1/4 inch to 2 inches. Butt chisels are used primarily to cut gains for door hinges.

Mortise chisels are very long and heavy. See Fig. 10-5. They have thick, square edges. Mortise chisels are used with a mallet to cut mortises for mortise-and-tenon joints. Common widths are 1/4, 5/16, 3/8, and 1/2 inch.

Chisel Handles. Plastic and hardwood are used to make chisel handles. Wooden handles often have leather washers to help soften mallet blows. Some have brass ferrules (bands) to prevent the wood from splitting. Plastic handles often have metal caps to prevent splitting.

The way a chisel blade is attached to its handle affects the chisel's use and durability. Three methods are used to attach chisel blades and handles. See Fig. 10-6.

Socket chisels have funnel-shaped holes on their blades. The holes are driven over the matching cone-shaped tips on the handles. Friction holds the two parts together. The socket handle is the most common handle on wood chisels. It can withstand moderate use with a mallet.

Pointed tang chisels have long, narrow points on their blades. The points are driven into the handles, which have metal ferrules to prevent splitting. These handles are not designed to withstand heavy blows from a mallet.

Solid tang chisels have long tangs that extend through the handles and connect to steel caps. The force of a mallet blow passes through the solid tang to the blade. This makes it possible for solid tang handles to withstand heavy mallet blows.

Using Chisels

Be especially careful when you work with chisels. They have sharp cutting edges that can be dangerous. Always keep your hands behind the cutting edges. Cut away from your body whenever possible. Use the following procedures for the various chiseling operations.

1. Select a chisel the same width as the desired cut, or slightly smaller.

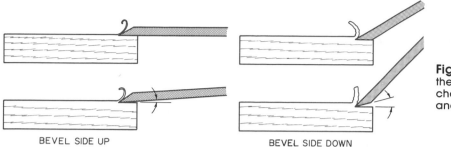

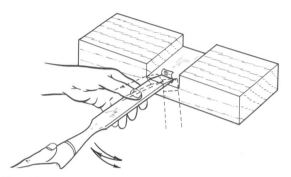

Fig. 10-8. You can alter the depth of a chisel cut by changing the cutting angle and turning the blade over.

BEVEL SIDE UP   BEVEL SIDE DOWN

Fig. 10-9. You can remove large amounts of material by **tapping,** not pounding, the chisel with a mallet. The head of the mallet should be either rubber, wood, or rawhide.

2. Clamp the stock to a workbench or put it in a vise. It should be secure enough to withstand pressure from the chisel.
3. If you are right-handed, hold the chisel in your left hand. Apply pressure with your right hand. Holding the blade between your thumb and forefinger will help you guide the chisel. This is important for thin, accurate cuts. See Fig. 10-7.
4. When possible, cut with the grain. Do not try to cut too much stock at once. You can control the depth of the cuts by altering the cutting angle. See Fig. 10-8. Generally, hold the bevel down to remove large amounts of stock. Hold the bevel up to make finer cuts.

Making Rough Cuts. Remove large amounts of excess material by making rough cuts. Make these cuts with the bevel side of the chisel down. You can remove the material faster by

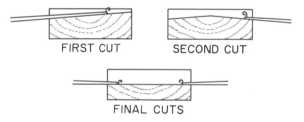

Fig. 10-10. Moving the chisel from side to side keeps the cutting edge at an angle to the wood fibers. This shearing action makes the cutting easier.

FIRST CUT   SECOND CUT

FINAL CUTS

Fig. 10-11. Make cuts across the grain from both sides toward the middle. The bevel should be turned up.

tapping the chisel with a soft-faced mallet. See Fig. 10-9. As you approach the layout lines, turn the chisel so the bevel side is up. This gives you greater control. Back-and-forth shearing cuts make fine cutting easier. See Fig. 10-10.

Cutting Across the Grain. Wood has a tendency to chip and splinter at the outside edges when cut across the grain. To avoid this, always chisel from both sides to the center. See Fig. 10-11. When both sides are deep enough, trim the middle flat.

Cutting Curves. You often need to cut curves with a chisel. Slightly different procedures are used for convex (outside) and concave (inside) curves.

To cut **convex** curves, remove the bulk of the material with a series of straight or slightly angled cuts. See Fig. 10-12. Then trim the stock to the layout line with a back-and-forth, shearing cut. Do all cutting with the bevel up.

To cut **concave** curves, work with the bevel side down. Remove excess stock with straight cuts. Trim to the line with a shallow cut. Tilt the chisel back as you follow the curve. See Fig. 10-13.

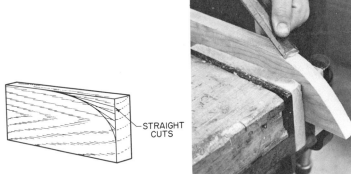

Fig. 10-12. in cutting a curve, first make straight cuts to remove excess material. Then make fine cuts along the layout line for the finished curve.

Fig. 10-13. Cut concave (inside) curves with the bevel down. Cut with the grain whenever possible.

Gouges

Gouges are chisels with curved blades. See Fig. 10-14. They are used to hollow out cavities for projects such as shallow bowls. Two basic types of gouges are available. One type has its cutting edge on the inside of the blade. The other has its cutting edge on the outside of the blade. The outside gouge is the most common. Gouges are basically the same lengths and sizes as chisels. Their handles and blades are also attached with the same methods used for chisels.

Using Gouges

Use an outside gouge to hollow out cavities. See Fig. 10-15. The outside gouge can make

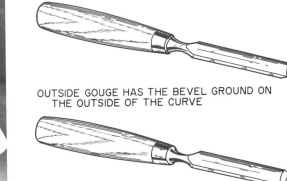

OUTSIDE GOUGE HAS THE BEVEL GROUND ON THE OUTSIDE OF THE CURVE

INSIDE GOUGE HAS THE BEVEL GROUND ON THE INSIDE OF THE CURVE

Fig. 10-14. Gouges are used to make concave cuts.

Fig. 10-15. This worker is starting to make a shallow, hand-carved dish. He is removing excess stock with a gouge. The outside edges will be shaped later.

deep, heavy cuts because the bevel is against the wood. Control the depth by raising or lowering the handle. Use a mallet to drive the gouge for heavy cuts.

Use an inside gouge to smooth a rough cavity. On an inside gouge the bevel is away from the wood. This produces a smoother cut than is possible with an outside gouge. If you must use a mallet with the inside gouge, tap it lightly. To remove the final, thin shavings, apply pressure to the gouge by hand.

Taking Care of Chisels and Gouges

Chisels and gouges are expensive tools. If they are to work properly for a long time, you must maintain them. This means they must be kept in near-new condition.

Preventing Damage. It is much easier to prevent damgage to chisels and gouges than to fix them. Take care of your chisels and gouges by observing the following rules.

- Never use a regular, steel hammer as a mallet to drive chisels and gouges. The hammer will ruin the tool's handle and could damage the blade.
- Never use a chisel or gouge as a screw-driver, scraper, or pry bar. These uses will quickly destroy the cutting tool.
- Do not use chisels and gouges on stock with nails, grit, or other foreign matter on its surface. These materials will dull or nick the blades.
- Store chisels and gouges so their cutting edges are protected. Never store them so their edges touch other hard objects. This will dull the blades.
- Coat the blades of chisels and gouges with oil or wax before storing for a long time. The coating will prevent rust.
- Be sure that all handles fit tightly to their blades. To tighten a loose handle, grip the handle with the blade pointing straight up. Then tap the end of the handle on the top of a bench. This will secure the handle without damaging the cutting edge.

Sharpening Chisels and Gouges. Sharpen dull blades on chisels and gouges by honing them on a lubricated oilstone. Move the cutting edge of the chisel over the oilstone in a figure-eight pattern. Continue this until a wire edge forms. See Fig. 10-16. Gouges are honed in a rocking motion, as shown in Fig. 10-17. Be sure to maintain the original angle of the bevel.

Grind nicked cutting edges on a grinder. It is important to grind the bevel to the angle of the original bevel. This is usually about 25°.

To sharpen chisels, follow the step-by-step grinding and honing instructions for plane irons in chapter 9. Gouges are much harder to sharpen. Do not attempt to grind gouges until you have a great deal of woodworking experience.

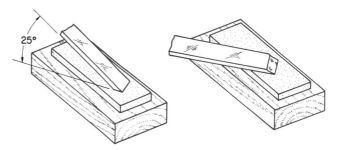

Fig. 10-16. To sharpen a chisel, hone the bevel to a 25° angle. Then remove the wire edge by honing the flat side of the blade.

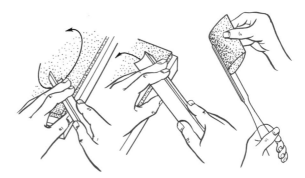

Fig. 10-17. To sharpen a gouge, hone the bevel with an oilstone. Then lightly polish the inside curve with a slipstone.

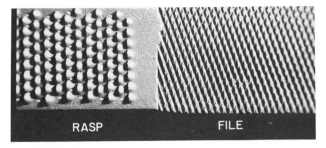

Fig. 10-18. Rasps have individual teeth. Files have rows of teeth.

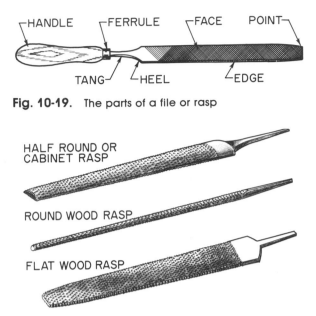

Fig. 10-19. The parts of a file or rasp

Fig. 10-20. Round, half-round, and flat rasps are the three most commonly used rasps.

Files and Rasps

Files and rasps consist of hardened steel blades covered with small cutting edges called teeth. Files and rasps are used to shape and smooth project parts, especially curves, edges, and end grain. They are used only in situations where other cutting tools will not work.

The difference between files and rasps is in the arrangement and shape of the teeth. Files are actually continuous rows of grooves. Rasp teeth, on the other hand, are individual points separated by open spaces. See Fig. 10-18.

Both files and rasps have a sharp tang on one end. See Fig. 10-19. The tang should never be mistaken for a handle. The handle is attached to the tang. Never use a file or rasp without first attaching a handle.

Rasps. Large amounts of stock (1/8 to 1/4 inch, 3 to 6 mm) are removed with a rasp. Rasp teeth are large and widely spaced. They seldom clog, as file teeth do. Rasps cut quickly, but leave a rough surface. The rough surface must then be smoothed with a file and coated abrasives before finishing.

Rasps are commonly available in three shapes: flat, half round (cabinet), and round. See Fig. 10-20. They come in two basic classifications of coarseness: bastard (rough) and smooth. The length of the rasp also affects the coarseness. The longer a rasp is, the coarser it is. For example, a 12-inch smooth rasp has coarser teeth than a 10-inch smooth rasp. The most useful rasps for woodworking are half-round, bastard-cut rasps between 8 and 14 inches long.

Files. Small amounts of stock are removed with files. Files are commonly used to smooth small and irregular wood parts that have been cut to rough size. They are also used to smooth metal and to sharpen many cutting tools.

Files are made in many shapes. The most common shapes used in woodworking are flat, half round, round, and triangular. Two types of **cuts** (shape of teeth) are available. A **single-cut** file has a single row of teeth cut across the face. A **double-cut** file has two rows of teeth, one cut across the other. See Fig. 10-22. Double-cut files cut faster and leave a rougher surface than do single-cut files. Single-cut files are used to remove very little stock and produce a smooth surface.

The coarseness of a file is determined by cut and length. The most common classifications of coarseness are bastard, second cut, and smooth. Like rasps, the longer the file is, the coarser it is.

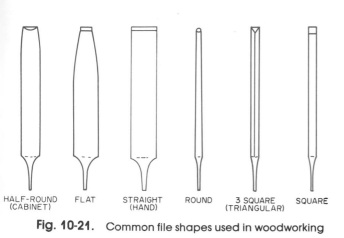

HALF-ROUND (CABINET)　FLAT　STRAIGHT (HAND)　ROUND　3 SQUARE (TRIANGULAR)　SQUARE

Fig. 10-21. Common file shapes used in woodworking

SINGLE CUT　　DOUBLE CUT

Fig. 10-22. A single-cut file will make a smoother, finer cut than a double-cut file of the same length and coarseness.

Using Files and Rasps

Select the file or rasp that best fits the shape of the cut. A half-round blade is a good all-purpose shape. It can cut flat, convex, and concave edges. Use a rasp to remove large amounts of material. Use a file to make smoother cuts. Do not use a file or rasp without a handle. For both filing and rasping, use the following procedure.

1. Secure the stock in a vise. Place the area to be cut as close to the vise jaws as possible. This will reduce vibration as you work.
2. It is a good idea to coat files and rasps with a thin layer of ordinary chalk. This helps keep the teeth from clogging.
3. Hold the handle with your right hand (if right-handed) and the point with your left hand.
4. Make a forward stroke across the surface. Push at an angle and with the grain. See Fig. 10-23. You can control the depth of the cut by the amount of pressure you apply while pushing.

    Cutting will take place on forward strokes only. Lift the file or rasp away from the

Fig. 10-23. Files and rasps cut on the forward stroke. For best results, angle the file slightly as you shape the stock.

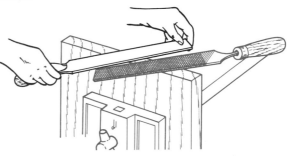

Fig. 10-24. Avoid splintering the outside edges of the stock by filing from both sides toward the center.

Fig. 10-25. Use a file card to remove waste material clogging the file teeth. The file card has wire bristles on one side and softer bristles on the other.

surface on back strokes. This will prevent unnecessary wear on the teeth.

5. Always work from the edges of the stock toward the middle. This will reduce the chances of splintering at the edges. See Fig. 10-24. This is especially important when shaping end grain.
6. Use a file card to clean files and rasps. **File cards** are small, flat brushes. See Fig. 10-25. The file card removes filings from file and rasp teeth. Use the file card as you work. If the teeth become clogged, they will not cut properly.

Taking Care of Files and Rasps

Although files and rasps appear rugged, they need special care to keep them in top condition. The most important part of maintenance is keeping them sharp. Files and rasps cannot be sharpened. When they become dull, they must be replaced. Maintain your files and rasps by observing the following rules.

- Never let files and rasps hit or rub against each other. They are extremely hard and will dull each other's teeth.
- Never use files and rasps as pry bars. They are brittle and prying on them can break them.
- When files and rasps become clogged, clean them with a file card. Do not try to clean the teeth by hitting the file against a bench top. Clean badly clogged files by soaking them in paint thinner.
- Keep file teeth from clogging by coating them with talcum powder or chalk.
- Tighten loose handles by twisting the handle or tapping the end on a bench top.

Surform Tools

The new forming tools, called Surform Tools, are used much like files and rasps. See Fig. 10-26. The Surform frames hold different types of steel blades. The amount of material removed

Stanley Tools

Fig. 10-26. Surform Tools are used for many of the same purposes as files and rasps.

with each stroke depends on the cutting angle. See Fig. 10-27. The holes in the blade allow wood shavings to escape through the blade. This prevents clogging. When the blade becomes dull, you can easily remove it from the frame and replace it.

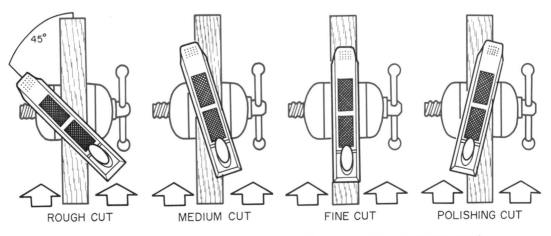

ROUGH CUT   MEDIUM CUT   FINE CUT   POLISHING CUT

Fig. 10-27. The depth of cut on a Surform Tool is regulated by the cutting angle.

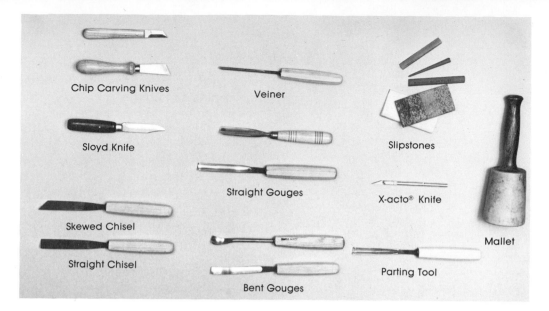

Fig. 10-28. Various carving tools

Carving Tools

Carving is probably the most basic method of shaping wood. With simple carving tools, you can shape wood into very detailed designs. The following tools are the tools most frequently used by wood carvers.

Knives are primarily used for whittling. X-acto, utility, pocket, and sloyd knives are a few of the many types used. Special chip carving knives are often used for finish carving.

Carving chisels are used to make straight cuts. They usually have bevels ground on both sides. They are available with either straight or **skewed** ends.

Carving gouges are curved chisels used to make concave cuts. They are available in various sizes and sweeps. The sweep refers to the amount of curve the blade has. The bevels of carving gouges are cut on the outside of the blade. You can control the depth of a cut by tipping the blade up or down.

Parting tools have narrow, V-shaped blades. They are used to make small, detailed lines and grooves. They are available in different sizes and angles.

Veiners are very small gouges, similar to parting tools. Veiners are used for fine detailed cuts.

Mallets used with carving tools are generally round in shape. They are used to drive carving tools when hand force is not enough. Carving tools and mallets are not designed for heavy pounding, which will quickly ruin both.

Oilstones are used frequently during carving to keep the tools sharp. Sharp tools make carving easier, more enjoyable, and safer. Slipstones are used to sharpen curved and V-shaped blades, such as those on gouges and parting tools. **Slipstones** are small, fine oilstones shaped to fit irregular surfaces.

Wood for Carving

Not all woods can be carved successfully. Knots and defects, irregular grain patterns, and hard wood can cause problems. Most clear woods with straight grain can be used for carving. Beginning carvers should use soft woods. Softwoods such as clear white pine, cedar, and redwood are excellent for carving. They are also available at most lumber yards.

When you become skilled in carving and sharpening techniques, you can use harder woods. Hardwoods such as mahogany, oak, ash, cherry, and walnut make good carving materials. Although these woods are seldom found at lumber yards, they can be purchased from hardwood distributors.

Fig. 10-29. Incise carving is done by making incisions into the surface of the wood. The background stays intact.

Methods of Carving

There are four basic methods of carving wood. They are usually used in combination to create the final design.

Incise carving is the simplest type of carving. It consists of making deep cuts and grooves in wood surfaces. In this way a basic design is carved into the wood. Uncut surfaces become the background for the design. See Fig. 10-29. Shallow U- or V-shaped cuts are made with a gouge, veiner or parting tool. Deeper cuts can be made with a chisel.

Chip carving is a popular type of carving. It involves the removal of triangular chips from the surface. As in incised carving, the background remains on the surface. The designs are often in the form of geometric patterns. Chisels are used to make designs such as those in Fig. 10-30. **Stop cuts,** or deep, vertical slices, are the primary cuts in chip carving. After the stop cut is made, a **slicing cut** allows the chip to be cut free. See Fig. 10-31.

Relief carving is produced by cutting away the background so the design is below the wood's surface. See Fig. 10-32. Stop and slicing cuts are made around the outside of the design. The design is shaped by incise carving. Then the background is removed.

In **low-relief** carving the design is part of the original surface. In **high-relief** carving all parts of the design are carved to give a third dimension. This type of carving, of course, requires more time and skill.

Fig. 10-30. Chip carving is usually used to produce geometric patterns.

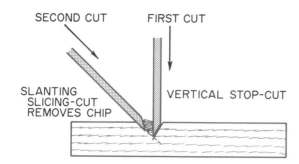

SECOND CUT   FIRST CUT

SLANTING
SLICING-CUT   VERTICAL STOP-CUT
REMOVES CHIP

Fig. 10-31. A slicing cut is made at an angle to the stop cut to allow the chip to be cut free.

Wendall Fuller

Fig. 10-32. Low-relief carving is produced by lowering the background and keeping the design on or near the surface.

Davie Griffith

Fig. 10-33. Whittling cuts were made to give this carving its final shape.

Whittling is done primarily with saws and knives. Whittling produces objects that are completely three-dimensional. See Fig. 10-33. A design is transferred to the wood. Then as much stock as possible is removed with a coping saw, jig saw, or band saw. The design is finished by making slicing cuts with a knife. The stock is usually held in one hand and the knife in the other. Because of this, extreme safety precautions are needed to prevent finger and hand injuries.

Shaping and Carving Safety

SAFETY

Chisels, files, and carving tools have very sharp edges. They can be dangerous if proper safety procedures are not followed. Review the following safety rules before using shaping and forming tools.

- Wear safety glasses. Small wood chips can easily become lodged in your eyes.
- Keep your fingers and hands out of line with cutting edges. A tool could slip and cause a severe injury.
- Whenever possible, secure the stock with a vise or clamp. This will free both hands for holding the tool.
- When you must hold the stock by hand, hold it tightly. Be careful not to cut toward your hand.
- Always cut away from your body.
- Keep cutting edges sharp. It takes more pressure to drive a dull tool. The extra pressure increases the chances of the tool slipping and causing an injury.
- Be careful where you put tools with sharp cutting edges. A falling tool is dangerous. Never position tools so their cutting edges extend over the edge of a bench.
- Never use the tang of a tool as the handle. The tang may not seem sharp or dangerous, but it can easily puncture your hand. Always cover tangs with handles.
- Carry tools with the sharp points toward the floor. This reduces the chances of your accidentally injuring a fellow worker.

Give tools to co-workers handle first.
When you store shaping and forming tools,
make sure the cutting edges are not exposed.

New Terms

1. butt chisel
2. chip carving
3. file
4. file card
5. firmer chisel
6. gouge
7. high-relief carving
8. incised carving
9. low-relief carving
10. mallet
11. pocket chisel
12. rasp
13. slipstone
14. socket handle
15. solid tang
16. sweep
17. Surform Tools
18. tang
19. whittling

Study Questions

1. What are chisels used for?
2. What is the advantage of using chisels with beveled edges rather than square edges?
3. Name two materials from which chisel handles are made.
4. Name the three methods used to attach chisel handles to blades.
5. How are the sizes of chisels usually indicated?
6. Name the four basic kinds of chisels as determined by size.
7. Give the two methods for driving chisels.
8. Describe how a rough cut is made with a chisel.
9. What is usually the best angle for the bevel of a chisel?
10. Describe the basic difference between the two types of gouges.
11. What is the major use of gouges?
12. What is the difference between files and rasps?
13. Which tool — file or rasp — clogs more quickly?
14. Files and rasps are available in different degrees of coarseness. Name the degrees of coarseness for both files and rasps.
15. What shape is a good, all-purpose shape for files and rasps?
16. Describe the cutting stroke for files and rasps.
17. Why should you **not** make back-and-forth strokes with files and rasps?
18. Surform Tools can make cuts similar to what two hand tools?
19. What are two advantages to Surform Tools?
20. How is the depth of the cut regulated with Surform Tools?
21. Name four types of tools used in wood carving.
22. Give three ways that certain woods can cause problems for the beginning wood carver.
23. List two hardwoods and two softwoods that make good carving material.

Drilling and Boring

Drilling and boring are the methods used to make round holes in wood. There is some confusion about the difference between drilling and boring. The cutting principles are the same and the terms are often used interchangeably. However, in this text **drilling** refers to making holes with drills. **Boring** refers to making holes with bits. Both drills and bits are described in this chapter.

Almost every wood project requires the cutting of one or more holes. Holes are cut for dowels used to join stock. Holes are made for decoration and to help remove waste material when shaping wood. Holes are also necessary to fasten wood with screws. The special tools and techniques used for cutting screw holes are explained in chapter 16, "Metal Fasteners."

Drilling Tools

In woodworking, holes 1/4 inch (6 mm), or less, in diameter are usually drilled. The following tools are used to drill these holes by hand.

Hand Drill. Small holes can be easily drilled with a hand drill. See Fig. 11-1. Simply rotate the crank with one hand while bearing down on the handle with the other. As you drill, the three-jaw chuck holds the cutting tool securely. The chuck holds all cutting tools with round shanks, such as twist drills. Twist the outer sleeve of the chuck clockwise to tighten it and counterclockwise to loosen it. Always tighten the chuck with hand pressure; never tighten it with pliers.

There are several different sizes and types of hand drills. The smaller drills have a maximum chuck capacity of 1/4 inch. The larger hand drills have a 3/8-inch chuck capacity. Less expensive hand drills have only one pinion. Good-quality hand drills have two pinions and hollow handles for storing drill points and twist drills.

Twist drills are cutting tools used in hand drills. The use of twist drills is not confined to hand drills, however. Twist drills are especially useful in drill presses and portable electric drills.

Stanley Tools

HANDLE

CRANK AND HANDLE

FRAME

IDLER PINION

SPEED GEAR

PINION

DETACHABLE SIDE HANDLE

CHUCK

Fig. 11-1. Hand drills are useful tools for making small holes.

They can be used to cut holes in materials such as wood, metal, and almost any plastic.

Twist drills come in many sizes. Four classifications are used to size them: inch, letter, number, and metric. Only the inch and metric sizes are used in woodworking. Letter and number sizes are used mainly in metalworking. Regardless of the classification, twist drills are usually sold in indexed sets. See Fig. 11-2.

Automatic (Push) Drill. The small holes used to start screws and nails are often made with automatic drills. See Fig. 11-3. Pushing down on the handle causes the spiral shaft in the drill sleeve to turn the chuck. **Drill points** are the only cutting tools that can be used in an automatic drill. They range in size from 1/16 to 11/64 inch. See Fig. 11-4.

Boring Tools

Holes larger than 1/4 inch are usually bored. They are bored with a bit brace that holds and twists a boring bit into the wood.

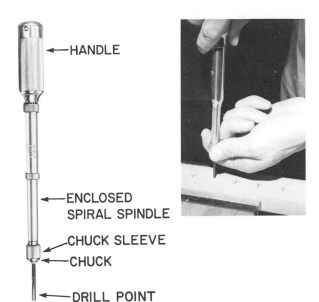

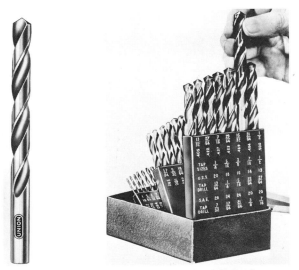

Union Twist Drill Company   Huot Manufacturing Company

Fig. 11-2. Twist drills are usually sold in indexed sets. As soon as you finish with a drill, return it to its proper slot. This way you will always know where to find the drill.

← HANDLE

← ENCLOSED SPIRAL SPINDLE

← CHUCK SLEEVE

← CHUCK

← DRILL POINT

Fig. 11-3. Push drills are operated by pumping the handle up and down. Drill points are the only cutting tools that can be used in push drills. The drill points are usually stored in the handle of the drill.

Stanley Tools

Fig. 11-4. These drill points are used in push drills.

Bit Brace. A bit brace is a tool that looks like a bent piece of rod with a handle. See Fig. 11-5. Use the bit brace like you would a crank. Hold the head stationary while you turn the handle. This causes the chuck, which holds the bit, to turn at the same speed. The chucks on bit braces are designed specifically to hold bits with square, tapered tangs (ends).

Good-quality bit braces have chucks with ratchet mechanisms. With a ratchet mechanism, you can turn the chuck without making a full

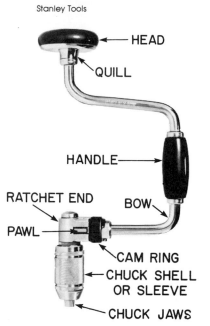

Fig. 11-5. Bit braces with ratchet mechanisms make work in small, confined areas much easier.

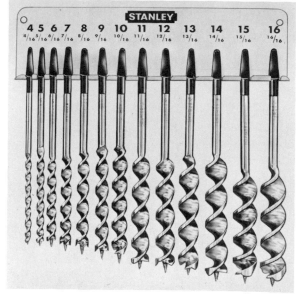

Fig. 11-7. Auger bits are designed specifically for boring holes in wood with a bit brace.

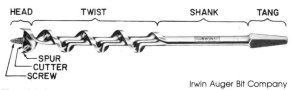

Fig. 11-8. Parts of an auger bit

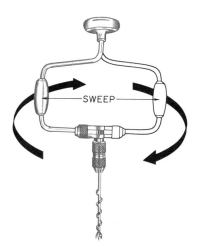

Fig. 11-6. The larger the circle (sweep) made by turning the handle of a bit brace, the more boring force the brace has.

sweep of the handle. This is useful in tight spots, where a complete swing is impossible.

The size of a bit brace is determined by the diameter of its **sweep** (circle made by turning the handle). See Fig. 11-6. The larger the sweep, the greater the twisting force applied to the bit. Smaller sweeps do not have as much leverage,

but turn the bit faster. A bit brace with a 10- to 12-inch sweep is best for most work.

Boring Bits. Several kinds of bits are used to bore holes. They all fit into the bit brace. The type and size of hole you are cutting will determine which bit you need.

Auger bits are the cutting tools designed specifically for bit braces. See Fig. 11-7. They are used only to cut wood. They should not be used in any other tool or for cutting any other material. They are fast and easy to use. They cut clean, accurate holes in all types of wood.

The tang of the auger bit is square and tapered. It fits into the chuck of the bit brace. The head, or cutting portion, of the auger bit consists of three parts: spurs, cutters, and a screw. See Fig. 11-8. As the chuck is turned, the **screw** pulls the bit into the wood. This forces the **spurs** into the wood fibers, where they scribe a circular notch. As the bit is pulled deeper, the **cutters** remove the waste material.

Stanley Tools

Fig. 11-9. Dowel bits are used in bit braces to make accurate dowel holes. They are usually a little shorter than auger bits.

Fig. 11-10. Doweling jigs center the holes and keep them perpendicular. Used with dowel bits, they produce accurate dowel holes.

The **twist** portion of the bit then carries the waste material away from the hole.

The size of an auger bit is indicated by a number on the tang. The number tells how many 16ths of an inch are in the bit's diameter. For example, a bit marked "5" will cut a hole 5/16 inch in diameter. A number 8 auger bit will cut a hole 8/16, or 1/2 inch in diameter. Auger bits are also available in metric sizes.

Dowel bits are used to make dowel holes. See Fig. 11-9. They come in sizes to match the common dowel diameters. They are used with doweling jigs as shown in Fig. 11-10. More information on doweling jigs is provided in chapter 13.

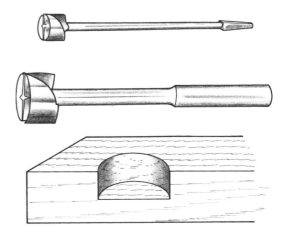

Fig. 11-11. Two types of Forstner bits are used to make flat-bottomed holes. Those with square tangs are used in bit braces. The bits with round shanks are used in drill presses.

Forstner bits are used to make flat-bottomed holes. See Fig. 11-11. Some Forstner bits have square tangs for use in bit braces. Others have round shanks designed for use in drill presses.

Forstner bits are used to make blind holes. **Blind holes** are holes that do not extend completely through the wood. Forstner bits are also used to hollow out large cavities, such as the hand-shaped candy dish in Fig. 11-12. To make such a cavity, remove most of the stock with the Forstner bit. Then smooth the cavity with a chisel or gouge.

Expansive bits are used with bit braces to make large holes. See Fig. 11-13. Expansive bits have two adjustable cutters. With one cutter, you can adjust the bit to make holes from 1/2 inch to 1-1/2 inches *(13 to 38 mm)* in diameter. With the other cutter you can make holes from 7/8 inch to 3 inches *(22 to 75 mm)* in diameter.

Unlike the auger bit, the expansive bit uses only one cutter at a time. Therefore, more twisting force is needed to drive the bit. Use a brace with at least a 12- inch *(300 mm)* sweep.

Depth gauges. It is often necessary to control the depth of blind holes. See Fig. 11-14. Blind holes, such as dowel holes, do not extend completely through the wood. Using a depth

Fig. 11-12. Forstner bits are often used to remove waste material before carving.

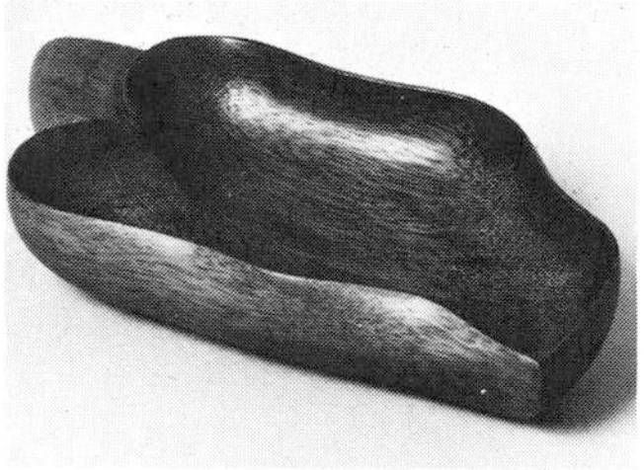

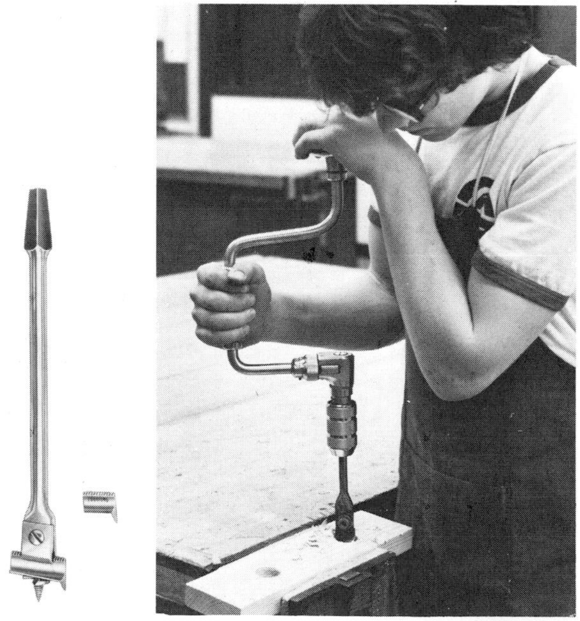

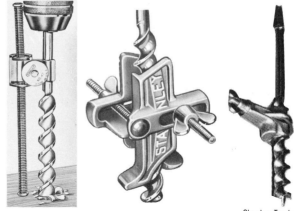

Stanley Tools

Fig. 11-14. Several types of depth gauges are used to make blind holes the correct depth.

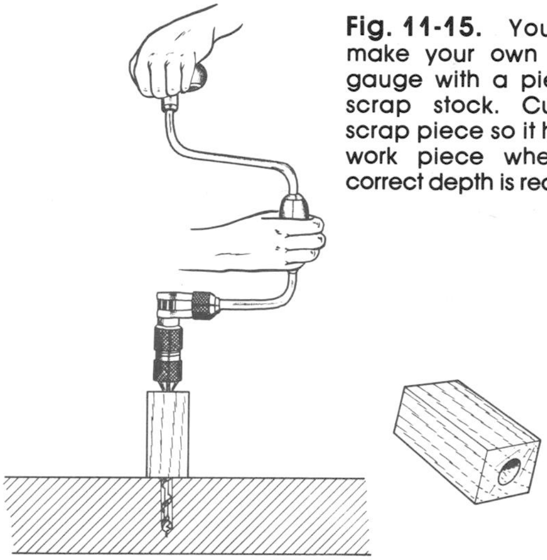

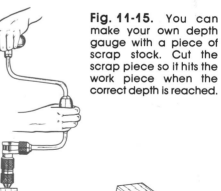

Fig. 11-15. You can make your own depth gauge with a piece of scrap stock. Cut the scrap piece so it hits the work piece when the correct depth is reached.

Stanley Tools

Fig. 11-13. Expansive bits are used to bore large holes in wood.

gauge ensures that all blind holes will be made to the proper depth.

You can make a nonadjustable bit or drill gauge with scrap wood, as shown in Fig. 11-15. A piece of masking tape wrapped around the bit or drill can also serve as a depth gauge. See Fig. 11-16. This method does not stop the drill, as do other gauges. You must be careful to stop cutting when you reach the tape.

Fig. 11-16. Wrapping masking tape around the bit at the proper depth is the simplest way of making a depth gauge. This method is not as accurate as others, however.

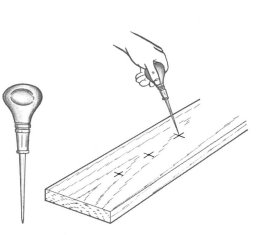

Fig. 11-18. Mark the center point of each hole with a scratch awl. This ensures that the drill or bit will be properly centered.

Laying Out Holes

The layout is the same whether you are drilling or boring a hole. It is important to lay out the position of the hole carefully. A hole in the wrong place is usually worse than no hole at all.

Lay out the location of the hole with a rule and a pencil. Follow your working drawing and measure accurately. Measure and mark the center point from both sides of the surface. See Fig. 11-17. Make an indentation at this point with a scratch awl. Make a hard, deep indentation. This will help you start the drill or bit in the right location. See Fig. 11-18. If you are laying out a series of holes that must line up, assemble and mark the pieces as shown in Fig. 11-19.

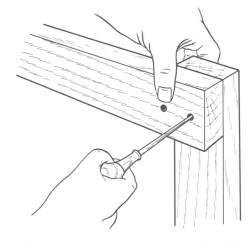

Fig. 11-19. To lay out matching holes, align the parts and mark through the existing holes.

Drilling and Boring Holes

After laying out the holes, you are ready to drill or bore them. Use the following procedure to bore a hole with a bit brace and auger bit. Although different tools are used, drilling procedures are basically the same.

1. When possible, clamp the wood vertically in a vise. This lets you hold the bit brace in a comfortable position. It also lets you apply pressure and keep a close eye on the cutting angle of the bit. See Fig. 11-20.

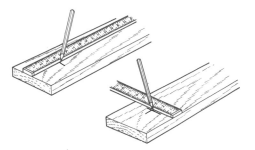

Fig. 11-17. To layout the center of a hole, measure from two directions.

Fig. 11-20. Make sure the stock is clamped securely before you drill or bore a hole. Whenever possible, clamp the stock vertically, as pictured here.

Hole Size	Cutting Tool
1/32"-1/8"	Brad or finish nail
1/16"-11/64"	Drill points
1/16"-1/4"	Twist drills
3/16"-1"	Auger bit, Forstner bits, or dowel bits (depending on use)
5/8"-3"	Expansive bits
1/8"-1/4"	Screw Mate

Fig. 11-21. Guide for Selecting Cutting Tools

Fig. 11-22. Start the hole by placing the tip of the bit in the indentation. While applying some pressure, slowly turn the handle. The screw part of the bit will help pull the bit into the wood.

2. Center the point of the proper-size bit in the indentation made during layout. See Fig. 11-22. This should be the exact center of the hole. Start turning the bit brace clockwise. Turn at a comfortable rate of speed. The screw of the bit will pull the bit into the wood. On bits and drills with no screws, you must apply more pressure.

3. As you bore the hole, constantly check the angle of the bit. Always check in two directions, as shown in Fig. 11-23. You can usually be accurate by checking the angle from the top while a classmate watches from the side. For more accuracy use a try square to check for 90° angles. For angles other than 90°, use a T-bevel set to the proper angle. See Fig. 11-24.

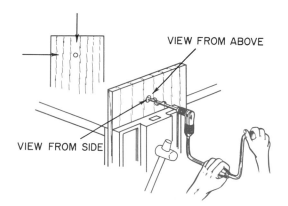

Fig. 11-23. As you bore, check for straightness from two directions. What looks straight from one direction, may not look straight from another.

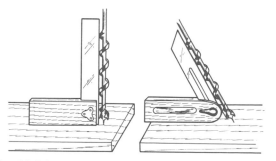

Fig. 11-24. Check 90° holes with a try square. Use a T-bevel to check other angles.

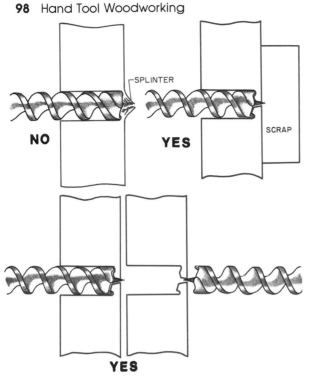

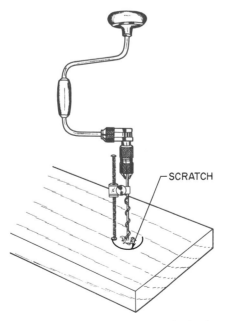

Fig. 11-25. Two methods are used to prevent splintering when you bore or drill completely through a board. Use a back-up board or bore from both sides.

Fig. 11-26. Be careful not to scratch the top of the stock when you use a depth gauge for blind holes.

4. Continue boring until the tip of the screw breaks through the other side. Turn the board around and finish the hole from that side. This prevents the wood from splintering. You can also prevent splintering by placing a back-up board behind the hole. See Fig. 11-25.

5. If you are cutting a blind hole, it is a good idea to use a depth gauge. Clamp and adjust the gauge to the proper depth. Be careful that the gauge does not scratch the surface of the stock as you reach the final depth. See Fig. 11-26.

Drilling and Boring Safety

- Wear safety glasses when drilling and boring. Without the glasses, wood chips can fly up and possibly lodge in your eye.
- Secure stock with a vise or clamp before drilling or boring. As you apply force, an unclamped piece could spin away and hit you or a fellow worker.
- Keep your fingers away from the exposed gears on a hand drill. The gears can easily pinch.
- Remove sharp drill points, twist drills, and auger bits from drills and braces before you carry them across the lab. The sharp points can cause a severe injury.
- Drills and bits become hot when making a hole. Let them cool before touching them.
- Automatic (push) drills are spring operated. Be extra careful not to let them slip and cause an injury.

New Terms

1. auger bit
2. automatic drill
3. bit brace
4. blind hole
5. boring
6. chuck
7. cutters
8. depth gauge
9. dowel bit
10. drilling
11. drill points
12. expansive bit
13. Forstner bit
14. hand drill
15. ratchet mechanism
16. screw
17. shank
18. spur
19. sweep
20. twist
21. twist drill

Study Questions

1. Explain the difference between drilling and boring.
2. Give three reasons why you might need to make holes for a project.
3. Would a hole 1/2 inch in diameter usually be bored or drilled?
4. Name the cutting tool that can be used in a hand drill.
5. List the four classifications used to size twist drills.
6. Describe the major use of automatic drills.
7. What tool is used in every hand boring operation?
8. Describe the shapes of the tangs that fit into bit braces.
9. When is a chuck with a ratchet mechanism especially handy?
10. How is the size of a bit brace determined?
11. What are the standard sizes of bit braces?
12. What size hole will be cut by an auger bit marked "9"?
13. Explain why it is best to use a dowel bit to cut dowel holes.
14. List four types of bits that can be used in a bit brace.
15. Describe a method for checking the depth of blind holes when no depth gauge is available.
16. In laying out holes, why should you mark the center with a deep, hard indentation?
17. How should the stock be clamped for a drilling or boring operation? Give two reasons why it is clamped this way.
18. In how many directions must the angle be checked while drilling or boring a hole? How do you check the angle of a hole bored at an angle other than 90°?
19. Describe a method that will help prevent splintering.

Section
III

JOINING

STOCK

Wood Joints

To construct your project, you must join and fasten pieces of wood. You can do this with a wide variety of wood joints, using glue or metal fasteners. An important decision in designing a project is which type of joint to use. Each type has both advantages and disadvantages.

Selecting the Right Joint

Some joints are strong, but hard to make. Others are attractive, but not very strong. In selecting a joint for your project, you must consider the joint's strength, appearance, and difficulty of construction.

You can often determine which qualities are needed by the project itself. For example, in making a picture frame, you would not be as concerned about strength as you would be about appearance. On the other hand, if you were making a toolbox, strength would be your first concern. In either case you would choose a joint that is not too difficult to make.

Strength. The strength of a joint depends on three factors.

- the amount of glue area
- the materials used
- how well the joint is made

The larger the glue area, the stronger the joint will be. A glue joint with a small gluing surface is often reinforced (strengthened). Dowels and splines are used to increase the glue area.

The part of the board used for a joint also affects the joint's strength. A joint made with edge or face grain will be as strong, or stronger, than the wood itself. However, when the **end** grain is used, the joint will not be this strong. If joints made with end grain will be under stress (pressure), they should be reinforced.

Fig. 12-1. Most projects contain at least one of these common joints.

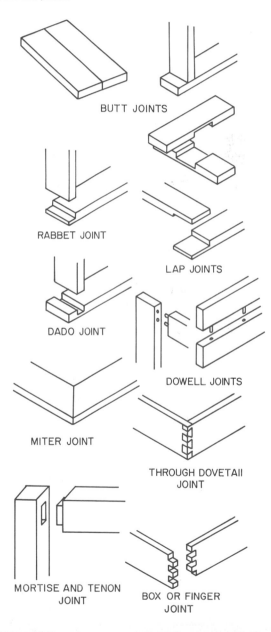

BUTT JOINTS

RABBET JOINT

LAP JOINTS

DADO JOINT

DOWELL JOINTS

MITER JOINT

THROUGH DOVETAIl JOINT

MORTISE AND TENON JOINT

BOX OR FINGER JOINT

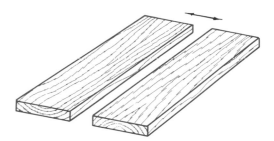

Fig. 12-2. The corners of this chest are joined with dovetail joints. Because the joints are well made, they add to the chest's beauty.

Regardless of the glue area, or the part of board used, a joint must be well made to be strong. You must cut and shape the boards so they fit together snugly. Glue cannot hold together two pieces of wood that do not touch.

Appearance. The appearance of the joints can make the difference between a professional-looking project and a sloppy one. An attractive wood joint fits the design of the project and is well made. Craftsmen do not hide the joints. Instead, they often rely on well-made joints to increase the beauty of their projects. See Fig. 12-2. Designers of fine wood products call this use of joints "honesty in design."

Construction. As you select a joint for appearance, decide whether or not you can construct that joint properly. Some joints are much harder to make and require more skill than others. You should choose a joint that has the features you want and is easy to make. As you become more experienced, you can try more complicated joints. Keep in mind that a poorly made, complicated joint will not be strong or attractive. A well-made, simple joint will be.

Butt Joints

The most common joints used in woodworking are butt joints. Butt joints are easy to make, but must often be reinforced. The five basic types of butt joints are described below.

Edge-to-Edge. Narrow boards are glued together to make a wider board with edge-to-

Fig. 12-3. Edge-to-Edge Joint

edge butt joints. See Fig. 12-3. Tabletops and other large wood surfaces are often made with this type of joint.

Edge-to-Face. Corners of boxes are often made with edge-to-face butt joints. See Fig. 12-4. These joints are also used to attach facing (trim) or molding to a project.

Face-to-Face. Decorative molding is often attached to a project with face-to-face butt joints. See Fig. 12-5. These joints are also used for gluing boards together to make thicker stock. Stock used for carving and turning bowls on a lathe is usually built up using face-to-face joints.

End-to-Edge. Frames for tables and cabinets are often constructed with end-to-edge butt joints. See Fig. 12-6. Because end grain is part of these joints, they are weak and should be reinforced. Dowels, splines, rabbet joints, end lap joints, and metal fasteners are used to strengthen these joints.

End-to-Face. The corners and sides of projects are often made with end-to-face butt joints. See Fig. 12-7. These joints are easy to make. The use of end grain makes them weak, however, and they must be reinforced. Another disadvantage of end-to-face joints is that they show end grain.

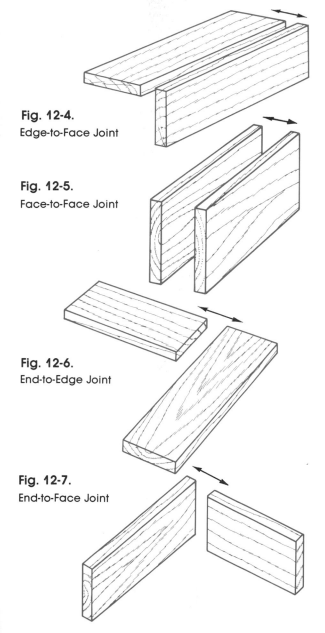

Fig. 12-4.
Edge-to-Face Joint

Fig. 12-5.
Face-to-Face Joint

Fig. 12-6.
End-to-Edge Joint

Fig. 12-7.
End-to-Face Joint

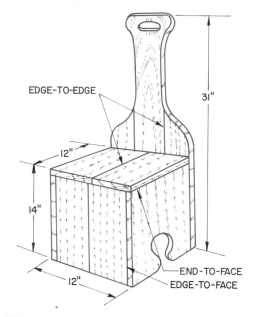

Fig. 12-8. All the joints in this step stool are butt joints.

Dowel Joints

Dowels are cylindrical (rod-shaped) pieces of wood. They are often used to reinforce butt joints. Inserting two or more dowels into a joint produces what is usually called a dowel joint. See Fig. 12-9. These joints are used more than any other type in the construction of furniture. They are strong and easy to make. They also help to align (position) pieces during assembly.

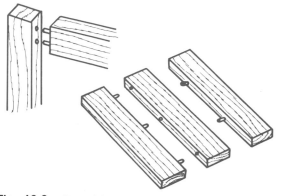

Fig. 12-9. Dowel joints provide extra strength. They are especially useful with joints made from end grain.

Miter Joints

Butt joints which have joining edges and ends cut at angles (usually 45°) are called miter joints. The two basic types of miter joints are the **edge** and the **flat** miter. See Fig. 12-10. Both types of miter joints are used to improve a project's appearance. They do this by hiding the joint and showing a continuous (unbroken) grain pattern. Because they hide the laminations, miter joints are especially helpful in improving the appearance of plywood.

Miter joints are often used for picture frames, boxes, and projects of contemporary design. The major disadvantage of miter joints is that the joining surfaces are usually made of end grain. This creates a weak joint that should be reinforced with splines, dowels, or metal fasteners.

Rabbet Joints

Rabbet joints (Fig. 12-12) are used as corner joints for boxes, cases and drawers. See Fig. 12-13. Sometimes they are used to install bottoms of boxes or backs of cabinets. Rabbet joints are usually reinforced with nails or screws.

Rabbet joints are popular with hand woodworkers. The joints are easy to cut, and they hide some end grain. They are stronger than butt joints because they provide more glue area. They also help to hold parts in place during assembly.

Fig. 12-11. Miter joints hide end grain. This makes the edge grain continuous around corners.

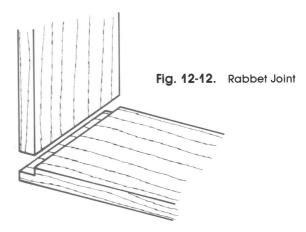

Fig. 12-12. Rabbet Joint

Fig. 12-13. The rabbet joints in this drawer are simple to make. They are made stronger by adding dowels or nails.

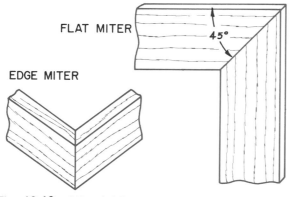

FLAT MITER

45°

EDGE MITER

Fig. 12-10. Miter Joints

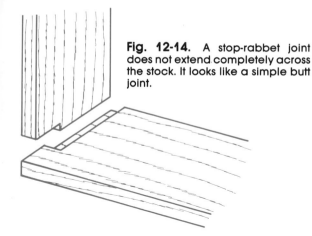

Fig. 12-14. A stop-rabbet joint does not extend completely across the stock. It looks like a simple butt joint.

lap joints are strong because of the large amount of glue area.

The three common half lap joints are the end, middle, and cross laps. See Fig. 12-15. The **end lap** is used to extend the length of a board and to make a right-angle (90°) joint. The **middle lap** is used to make a T-shaped joint. The **cross lap** is used in furniture when two pieces of wood intersect (cross each other). This joint "locks" the pieces together and is the strongest joint for this purpose.

Half Lap Joints

All half lap joints are made by removing one-half the depth of the pieces to be joined. Then the pieces are put together, one over the other. This way two pieces of stock can be joined without increasing thickness at the joint. Half

Dado and Groove Joints

Dado joints and groove joints are very similar. Groove joints are cut in the same direction as the wood grain. See Fig. 12-16. Dado joints are cut across the wood grain. See Fig. 12-17. Both joints are used for strength and alignment in assembly. They are also two of the best joints for installing shelves or dividers in a cabinet. They will hold slightly warped boards (such as shelves) straight.

Fig. 12-15. Half Lap Joints

Fig. 12-16. This serving tray is made with grooves to hold the bottom panel. Notice that the grooves are cut **with** the grain.

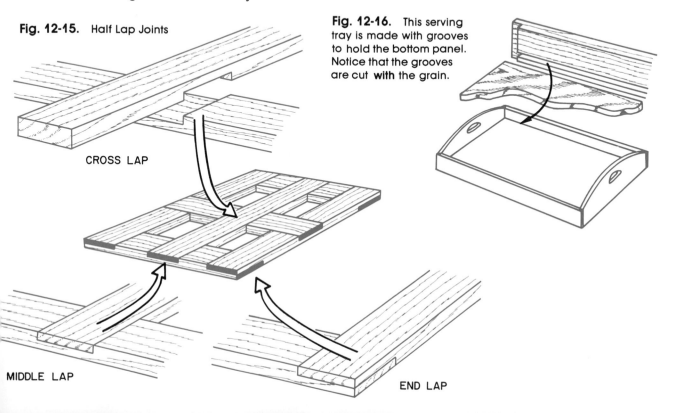

CROSS LAP

MIDDLE LAP

END LAP

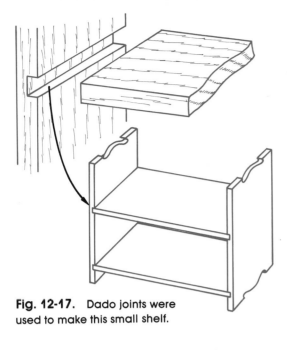

Fig. 12-17. Dado joints were used to make this small shelf.

Fig. 12-18. A blind dado joint stops before it reaches the front edge. Although it looks like a butt joint, the blind dado joint is much stronger.

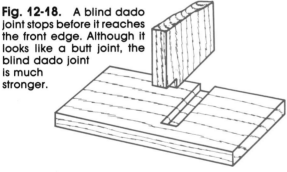

Tongue-and-Groove Joints

The tongue-and-groove joint is used for frame construction and for gluing boards to make wide, flat surfaces. See Fig. 12-19. This joint is stronger than a butt joint because of the additional glue area. It also aligns parts during assembly.

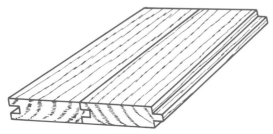

Fig. 12-19. Tongue-and-Groove Joint

Spline Joints

The spline joint is used to join edges and corners of stock. As a variation of the tongue-and-groove joint, it is often used to strengthen miter joints and edge-to-edge butt joints. See Fig. 12-20.

A **spline** is a thin piece of wood, usually one-third the thickness of the boards to be joined. The spline fits into grooves cut in the pieces to be joined. The spline reinforces the joint and also aligns parts during assembly.

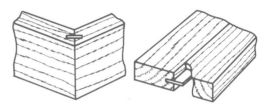
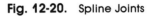

Fig. 12-20. Spline Joints

Rabbet-Dado Joints

The rabbet-dado (Fig. 12-21) joint is used for corner construction on boxes, frames, and drawers. The rabbet-dado joint is a variation of the tongue-and-groove joint. The main difference is that the tongue of the rabbet-dado has only one shoulder. This makes the rabbet-dado easier to cut than the tongue-and-groove joint. This joint also helps align the parts during assembly.

Fig. 12-21. Rabbet-dado joints are often used in drawer construction.

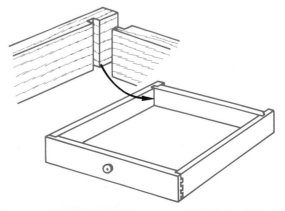

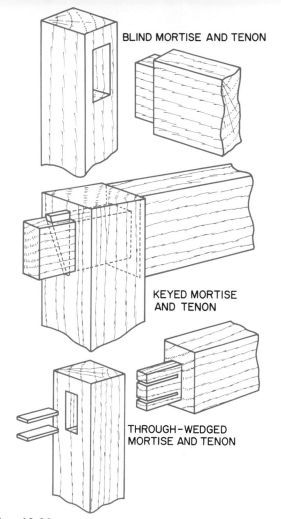

BLIND MORTISE AND TENON

KEYED MORTISE AND TENON

THROUGH–WEDGED MORTISE AND TENON

Fig. 12-22. There are many types of mortise-and-tenon joints.

Fig. 12-23. This small stool was made with a keyed mortise-and-tenon joint.

Mortise-and-Tenon Joints

Mortise-and-tenon joints (Fig. 12-22) are considered the strongest joints. They are used for leg and rail construction in chairs, tables, and stools. See Fig. 12-23.

The construction of a mortise-and-tenon joint is time consuming and complex. Therefore, the dowel joint is replacing many mortise-and-tenon joints in furniture construction. The dowel joint is a strong joint, and more easily made than the mortise-and-tenon.

Dovetail Joints

A dovetail joint is a strong joint because the pieces interlock. See Fig. 12-24. It is commonly

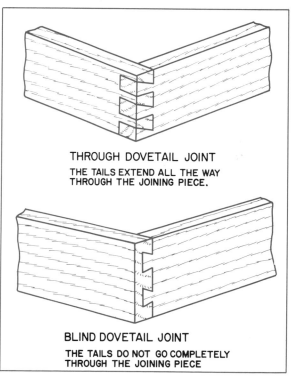

THROUGH DOVETAIL JOINT
THE TAILS EXTEND ALL THE WAY THROUGH THE JOINING PIECE.

BLIND DOVETAIL JOINT
THE TAILS DO NOT GO COMPLETELY THROUGH THE JOINING PIECE

Fig. 12-24. Two types of dovetail joints. The through dovetail is generally used for decorations. The blind dovetail is used on drawer fronts.

Fig. 12-25. Finger joints are used primarily for box construction.

used in drawer construction and is a mark of quality furniture. The joint is sometimes exposed on the corners of cabinets and boxes. This makes the end grain of the tenon portion of the dovetail visible. This is not only a strong construction, but also an attractive one.

Finger Joints

Finger joints, also called box joints, are used mainly to join the corners of boxes. See Fig. 12-25. Finger joints are strong because of their large glue areas. They are also attractive, often adding to a project's beauty.

New Terms

1. butt joint
2. dado joint
3. dovetail joint
4. dowel
5. dowel joint
6. finger joint
7. groove joint
8. half lap joint
9. miter joint
10. mortise-and-tenon joint
11. rabbet-dado joint
12. rabbet joint
13. reinforce
14. spline
15. spline joint
16. tongue-and-groove joint

Study Questions

1. List the three qualities you must consider in selecting the right joint for your project.
2. Give an example of how the project will determine the important considerations in selecting the right joint.
3. What three factors determine the strength of a joint?
4. If you glue together two boards 1 inch thick × 2 inches wide × 10 inches long face-to-face, and two more boards the same size edge-to-edge, which joint is the strongest? Explain.
5. Which surface of a board — face, end, or edge — makes the weakest joints? What is always done to joints made with this surface?
6. List the five kinds of common butt joints. Give one advantage to butt joints. Give one disadvantage.
7. What type of butt joint would you use to frame a table or cabinet?
8. What type of butt joint would you use to build up stock for turning on a lathe?
9. Give two disadvantages to using an end-to-face butt joint.
10. Name the two basic kinds of miter joints.
11. What is the major advantage to using miter joints? How is this done?
12. What is the major disadvantage to using miter joints?
13. What type of joint is used more than any other in the construction of furniture?
14. Why are rabbet joints popular with hand woodworkers?
15. What type of joint is used in furniture construction when two pieces of wood must intersect? Why are these strong joints?
16. Name the two types of joints that work best for installing shelves in a cabinet.
17. Which joint is easier to make — the rabbet-dado or the tongue-and-groove?
18. Although the mortise-and-tenon joint is one of the strongest joints for reinforcing corners, it is not used as frequently as the dowel joint. Why?
19. What is a common use of dovetail joints?
20. Why are finger joints strong?

Cutting Wood Joints by Hand

Making a wood joint by hand is a satisfying experience for both skilled and beginning woodworkers. Working with simple hand tools, you experience every detail of the cutting and shaping process. This helps you develop your skill with tools. It also improves your understanding of wood. A fine, hand-cut joint is a sign of a craftsman. See Fig. 13-1. This chapter discusses the ways of making joints by hand. Cutting joints with power equipment is discussed in section VI.

Accuracy

Strength and neatness in wood joints depends on accurate construction. A well-made joint requires a precise layout. When you lay out the stock, be sure to follow your project plans. They contain the dimensions for each joint. Lay out your work with a knife. A knife

Fig. 13-1. Making the joints in this project by hand was a satisfying experience for the woodworker.

Roland Shackford

will make a sharp line from which to work. If you use a pencil, keep it sharp. A dull pencil will make a thick, inaccurate line. For more layout information, see chapter 6.

Layout should be followed by careful cutting and shaping. When you cut a joint, follow the layout lines carefully. Always cut on the waste side of these lines. The lines themselves should not be removed. Never cut deeper than a layout line, and always cut straight. For more information on cutting and shaping, see chapters 8, 9, and 10.

A properly made joint should fit together snugly without being forced. When glue is applied, the wood will absorb some of it. This will cause the wood parts to swell. If the joint fits too tightly to begin with, it will not fit after the glue is applied.

Use a chisel or plane to trim tight-fitting joints. Do not use coated abrasives or files, which will round the edges. Rounding the edges reduces the joint's contact area and weakens it. All wood surfaces being joined should be flat.

There should be no air gaps or voids (empty spaces) in the joint. The pieces should also line up properly. Remember, it takes patience and hard work to make a tight-fitting joint with hand tools.

Making Common Butt Joints

Common butt joints are the easiest of all joints to lay out and cut. To form a butt joint you simply push the pieces against each other. An accurate fit depends on making the pieces flat and square.

Edge-to-Edge Joints. Narrow boards are joined together to make a wide panel with edge-to-edge butt joints. See Fig. 13-2. These joints are used to make tabletops, doors, and other wide

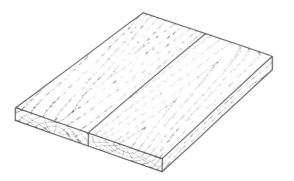

Fig. 13-2. Edge-to-edge joints are used to make tabletops, cabinet doors, drawer fronts, and many other flat surfaces.

Fig. 13-3. Wood tends to warp opposite the rings in the end grain. The warp can be minimized on a panel by alternating the rings.

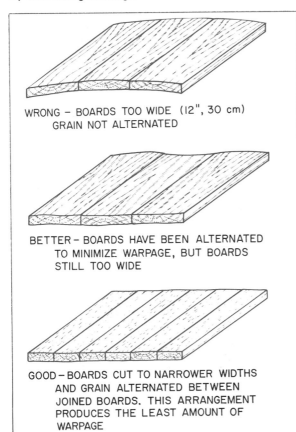

WRONG – BOARDS TOO WIDE (12", 30 cm) GRAIN NOT ALTERNATED

BETTER – BOARDS HAVE BEEN ALTERNATED TO MINIMIZE WARPAGE, BUT BOARDS STILL TOO WIDE

GOOD – BOARDS CUT TO NARROWER WIDTHS AND GRAIN ALTERNATED BETWEEN JOINED BOARDS. THIS ARRANGEMENT PRODUCES THE LEAST AMOUNT OF WARPAGE

pieces. Dowels are sometimes added to strengthen these joints.

1. Lay out the wood and cut it to rough size. It is not a good idea to join pieces more than 6 inches (150 mm) in width. Wider stock tends to warp and ruin the panel. See Fig. 13-3.

2. Alternate the boards so the growth rings of the end grain run in opposite directions. Wood tends to warp opposite the direction of the growth rings. By alternating these rings, you will reduce the chances of the panel warping. See Fig. 13-3. Experienced woodworkers often rip a board into narrow pieces, alternate the growth rings, and glue the board back together. The resulting board is not any wider than the original one. It is less likely to warp, however.

3. After arranging the boards in the proper order, mark them as shown in Fig. 13-4.

4. With a hand plane, plane the edges of each board. Clamp the pieces in a vise. The top faces should be on the outside and opposite one another. Plane the edges until they are flat and smooth. You should try to remove one thin shaving from the entire length and width of the pieces. This ensures that the edges will fit together snugly. See Fig. 13-5.

5. Check each joint by placing the edges together and holding them next to a light. If light shows through the joint, plane the high spots. If no light shows through, the pieces are ready for gluing and clamping.

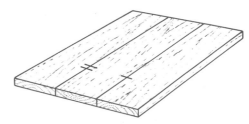

Fig. 13-4. After arranging the boards in the proper order, mark them as shown. This will help you assemble the joint.

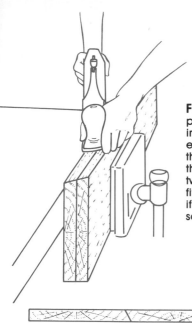

Fig. 13-5. This is the proper method of planing edges for edge-to-edge butt joints. Take a thin, even shaving from the entire surface of the two edges. They will then fit tightly together even if they are not perfectly square.

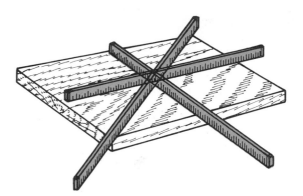

Fig. 13-7. As you plane a face, repeatedly check for flatness. Use a straightedge to check the face in three directions. If any light shows through, plane the high spots.

Fig. 13-8. This bowl was made from a block of wood built up with face-to-face butt joints.

Fig. 13-6. Face-to-face butt joints are often used to build up stock for turning on a lathe. This block of wood will be turned into a small bowl such as the one shown in Fig. 13-8.

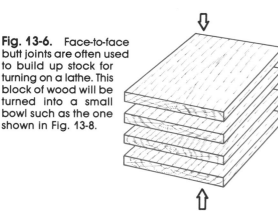

Face-to-Face Joints.

Thick boards are made with face-to-face butt joints. These joints are also used to make large blocks of wood for lathe turning and carving. See Fig. 13-6.

1. Lay out the wood and cut it to rough size.
2. With a hand plane, smooth the faces of the boards. Plane the faces until they are flat. Check for flatness with a straight-edge or a square. See Fig. 13-7.
3. After the pieces are planed, check the fit of the joint. Place the faces together and hold them near a light. If light shows through, plane the high spots. If no light shows through, mark or number each piece. This will identify the order of pieces for gluing and clamping.

End-to-Edge Joints.

The end of one piece joined to the edge of another forms an end-to-edge butt joint. See Fig. 13-9. This joint is used to make frames for cabinets and other furniture. Because end grain is part of this joint, it is very weak. It must be reinforced with dowels or metal fasteners. Mortise-and-tenon joints are stronger and sometimes used in place of end-to-edge butt joints.

1. Lay out the wood and cut it to rough size.
2. With a hand plane, plane the edge that will be used in the joint. It must be flat and square or the end will not fit against it properly. Check for flatness and square-ness with a square and straightedge.

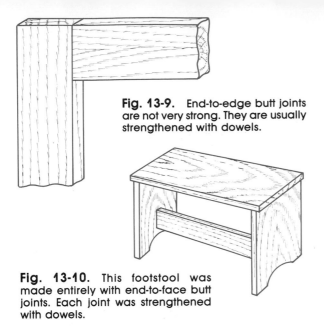

Fig. 13-9. End-to-edge butt joints are not very strong. They are usually strengthened with dowels.

Fig. 13-10. This footstool was made entirely with end-to-face butt joints. Each joint was strengthened with dowels.

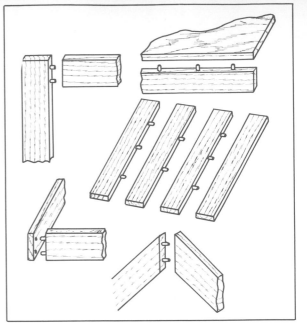

Fig. 13-11. Dowel joints are used primarily to strengthen butt joints. Dowel joints are easy to make and very strong.

3. With a backsaw, cut the end of the second piece. This end must also be flat and square. Then it will fit tightly to the edge of the first piece.
4. Check the fit by putting the end and edge together and holding them near a light. If light shows through the joint, carefully plane the end of the second piece until it fits tightly.
5. Use dowels or metal fasteners to strengthen this joint. For more information see "Making Dowel Joints."

End-to-Face Joints. Carcass and frame construction often make use of end-to-face butt joints. See Fig. 13-10. These joints are often replaced by rabbet or dado joints to increase strength.

With one difference, make end-to-face butt joints like end-to-edge butt joints. Instead of the edge, however, make the face of one piece flat and square. If you use dowels to strengthen this joint, make sure not to drill through to the exposed face.

Making Dowel Joints

Dowel joints are reinforced butt joints. They are similar in strength to mortise-and-tenon joints, but much easier to make. See Fig. 13-11.

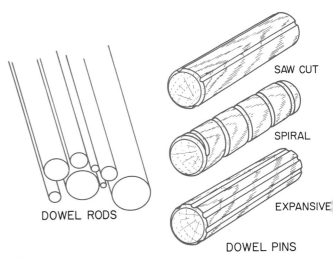

DOWEL RODS

SAW CUT

SPIRAL

EXPANSIVE

DOWEL PINS

Fig. 13-12. Dowel pins are more expensive than pins made from dowel rods. Dowel pins are already grooved and beveled, however.

Dowels. Dowel joints are reinforced with cylindrical (rod-shaped) pieces of wood called dowels. Dowels are usually made of birch or maple. You can purchase them as dowel rods or preshaped dowel pins. See Fig. 13-12.

Dowel rods are 3 feet long. They have diameters ranging from 1/8 to 1 inch. From these rods you can make dowel pins of the desired length and shape. To do this you must cut a rod to length, bevel each end, and cut a groove in the side.

You can buy preshaped dowel pins by the box. They have beveled (slanted) ends and either spiral or straight grooves. They are from 1 to 3 inches long, and 1/4 to 1/2 inch in diameter.

It takes time and effort to cut your own dowel pins. Preshaped dowel pins are easier to use because no cutting or shaping is required. They are, however, more expensive.

Choosing the Right Dowel. You must choose the right dowel for each joint. The diameter of the dowel should be about half the thickness of the stock. It should not be more than half. For example, 3/4 inch *(19 mm)* stock would best be joined by dowels 3/8 inch in diameter.

A dowel should be between 2 and 3 inches long. Two-inch dowels are most common and work well for most projects.

Laying Out and Cutting Dowel Joints. The first step in constructing a dowel joint is to make the appropriate butt joint. Make sure the joint surfaces are cut cleanly and smoothly.

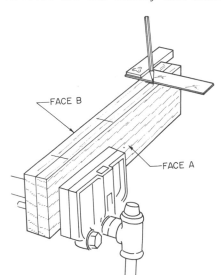

Fig. 13-13. Recommended spacing for dowels along an edge is 4-6 inches (100-150 mm). Always place dowels at least 1 inch (25 mm) from ends and edges.

The joint should have a tight fit. Then the dowel pins can be added. Use the following procedure to add the dowel pins.

1. Place the two pieces to be joined in a vise. The mating (joining) surfaces should face up and align with each other.

2. Lay out the position of the dowels. Using a square, mark lines across both surfaces to indicate positions for dowels. The dowels should not be too close to the edges or to one another. See Fig. 13-13. On edge-to-edge joints, the dowels should be 4-6 inches *(100-150 mm)* apart. Use at least two dowels for end-to-edge and end-to-face joints. See Fig. 13-14.

3. With a marking gauge, mark a line in the center of each board. Place the body of the marking gauge on the marked or exposed surface of each piece. This way the layout lines must match up. See Fig. 13-15.

4. Where the lines intersect, drill holes the same diameter as the dowel pins. See "Doweling Jigs" in this chapter. Drill to a depth of one-half the length of the dowel pin plus 1/16 inch *(1.5 mm)*. The extra 1/16 inch allows space for glue. It will also provide enough room for the joint to close over the dowel.

5. If you are using dowels cut from dowel rod, bevel each end. This helps the pins

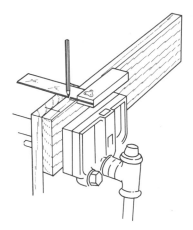

Fig. 13-14. Laying out an end-to-edge dowel joint

start easily in the dowel holes. Also cut or file grooves along the length of the dowel. This lets air escape as you press the dowel into the hole. Without grooves, the dowel will compress the air. Then the air will push the dowel out of the hole.

6. Dry assemble (assemble without glue) the joint and check the fit. The joint should

come together without any gaps. Gaps are usually caused by long dowels or shallow holes.

Doweling Jigs. A jig is a device used to hold pieces of stock and tools during cutting operations. Doweling jigs hold and keep the drill bit perpendicular to the surface being drilled. This simplifies both the layout and drilling of dowel holes. It also increases accuracy. Several styles of doweling jigs are shown in Figs. 13-16, 13-17, and 13-18.

You can use a bit brace and dowel bit for hand work. You can also use a portable electric drill with the correct twist drill in a doweling jig.

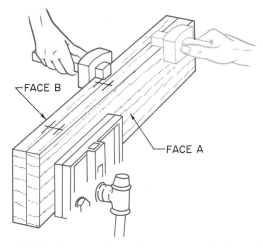

Fig. 13-15. Lay out the centers of dowel holes with a marking gauge. Place the gauge on the outside face of each board to make the intersecting lines.

Fig. 13-16. This doweling jig has interchangeable sleeves. The sleeves are manufactured in sizes to fit the standard dowel rods.

Fig. 13-17. A self-centering doweling jig automatically centers itself. This reduces the number of steps needed for layout.

Fig. 13-18. A turret-type doweling jig allows the proper drill guide to be rotated into position.

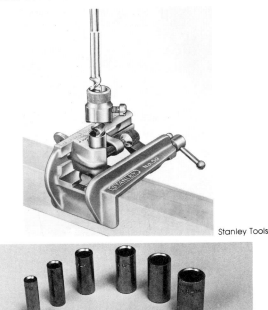

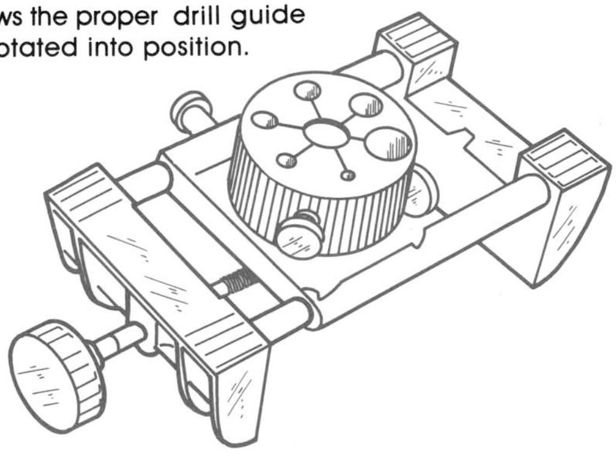

Stanley Tools

Dowel Centers. You can lay out dowel holes accurately and easily with dowel centers. See Fig. 13-19. Dowel centers are available in standard dowel sizes. They are especially useful if the first holes were not accurately placed.

Drill the holes in one of the pieces to be joined. Select dowel centers of the proper size and place them in the drilled holes. Position the two pieces as they will be assembled and then press together. The dowel points will mark the exact centers for the second set of holes.

Making Miter Joints

Miter joints are normally cut at 45° to form 90° corners. However, they can also be cut at other angles. One of the most common uses of the miter joint is in picture frames. See Fig. 13-20. Picture frames are usually made as follows.

1. You can use special picture frame molding for the sides. Otherwise, lay out and cut your stock to the correct width and thickness. Then cut the rabbet for the picture and glass in the back side of the stock. These rabbets are usually 1/2 inch *(12 mm)* wide and 1/2 inch deep.
2. Figure the finish length for each frame member. See Fig. 13-21.
3. Cut the stock to rough lengths. The rough lengths should be about 1 inch *(25 mm)* larger than the finish lengths.
4. Cut a 45° miter on one end of each of the four members. Use an adjustable miter box and saw. You can also use a wooden

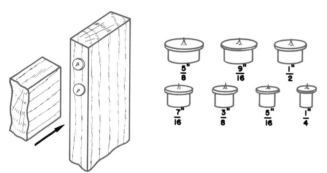

Fig. 13-19. Dowel centers are used to lay out matching dowel holes. The dowel centers make small marks on the wood to indicate the location of the dowel hole.

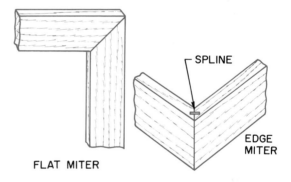

Fig. 13-20. Miter joints are used to hide end grain. They are not very strong and are usually reinforced with dowels or splines.

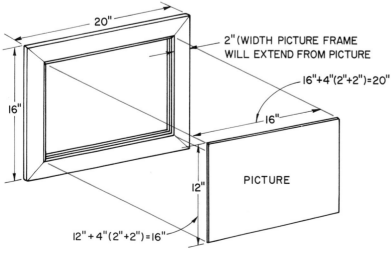

Fig. 13-21. To lay out the cuts for a picture frame, first determine the total outside dimensions. Measure the width from the inside rabbet to the outside of the frame. Double this measurement and add the product to the dimensions of the picture to be framed. This will give you the finish sizes for the frame pieces measured along the outside edges.

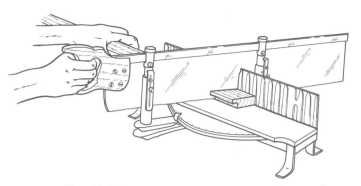

Fig. 13-22. When using a metal miter box and saw, hold the stock firmly against the fence. Notice that the rabbet is turned down and the cut is angled away from the rabbet.

Fig. 13-23. This is the correct method of holding a frame to be nailed. Apply glue before nailing.

miter box and a backsaw. For information on using a miter box and saw see chapter 8. Make sure the short end of the miter is toward the rabbet in the back of the frame. If the miter is cut in the other direction, the joints will not fit. Cut just enough off the long side to produce a complete miter cut. See Fig. 13-22.

5. After making the first miter cut, measure the finish length of each member. Mark this length on the outside edge. Square the mark across the face. Make the cut so that the saw just barely cuts through the layout line at the outside edge. Remember, when making a four-sided project such as a picture frame, the opposite sides must be exactly the same length. If not accurately cut, the joints will not fit tightly and the frame will not be square. You may want to use the length stop on the miter box to ensure equal lengths.

6. After the pieces are cut, check the joints by assembling the frame. All members should make full contact with each other. If the joints do not close tightly, trim the high spots. Use a chisel, block plane, or backsaw. Use a backsaw for large gaps only. With the joint securely clamped in a miter vise, cut along the joint. This will slightly reduce the size of the frame. Do not use coated abrasives and files to trim high spots. Both tools round the edges, causing a poor fit.

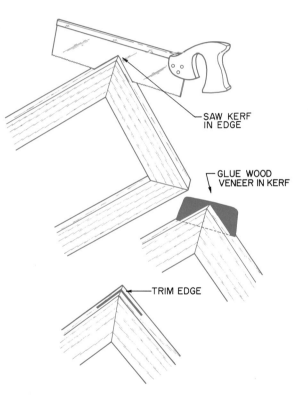

SAW KERF IN EDGE

GLUE WOOD VENEER IN KERF

TRIM EDGE

Fig. 13-24. An edge miter can be reinforced with a feather. The kerf for the feather is made after the frame has been assembled.

When the joints fit properly, mark or number each piece. This will identify the parts that go together for assembly.

7. You can reinforce the joints with metal fasteners, as described in chapter 16. Nails are the most common fasteners for

reinforcement. Fig. 13-23 shows how to clamp a frame for nailing. You can make even stronger joints by inserting dowels, splines, or feathers. See Fig. 13-24.

Making Rabbet Joints

A rabbet joint is easier to make than most joints. This is because only one of the two joining pieces needs to be cut. The second piece is simply cut square and placed in the rabbet. See

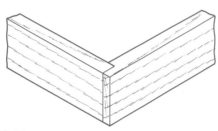

Fig. 13-25. Rabbet joints are often used for the corners of boxes and drawer fronts.

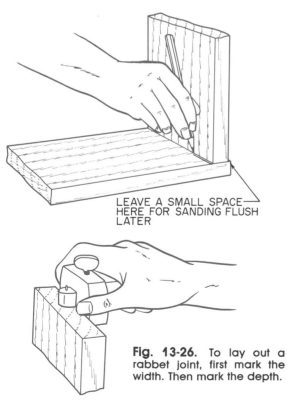

LEAVE A SMALL SPACE HERE FOR SANDING FLUSH LATER

Fig. 13-26. To lay out a rabbet joint, first mark the width. Then mark the depth.

Fig. 13-25. When both members are end grain, rabbet joints should be reinforced with nails, screws, or dowels. Rabbet joints have the advantage of hiding most end grain that normally shows on butt joints. Rabbet joints are used for small cabinets, boxes, and drawer construction. Use the following procedure to make a rabbet joint.

1. Lay out and cut all stock to finish size. The finish size for the second piece should allow extra material to fit into the rabbet.
2. Bring the two members together like they will be in the joint. Leave a small amount of space on the outside edge to allow for sanding. Scribe a line to indicate where the rabbet is to be cut. See Fig. 13-26.
3. Square this line onto each edge.
4. Set the marking gauge and scribe a line on the end for the depth of the rabbet. Extend this line onto each edge. See Fig. 13-26. The depth of the rabbet should be about two-thirds the thickness of the stock.
5. Cut the sides of the rabbet with a backsaw, dovetail saw, or miter box and saw. Make the end cut first. Then cut the shoulder. Be sure to cut along the waste side of each line. See Fig. 13-27.
6. Use a router plane set to the correct depth to trim the rabbet smooth and flat. See Fig. 13-28. Use a chisel if you do not have a router plane.
7. You can use a rabbet plane to cut and trim a rabbet with the grain. See Fig. 13-29. It

Fig. 13-27. For the most accurate rabbet cuts, clamp a block next to the layout lines. Hold the backsaw flush against the block.

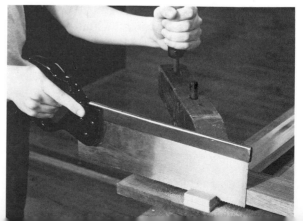

Fig. 13-28. Clean out rabbets with a router plane or chisel. Be careful not to splinter the edge.

Fig. 13-29. You can use a rabbet plane to cut a rabbet **with** the grain. Several strokes will be needed to obtain the correct depth.

is best not to use the rabbet plane on stock less than 7 inches *(175 mm)* long, however. Rabbet planes are difficult to hold steady on short stock.

Rabbet planes eliminate the need for layout. You simply set the depth gauge and fence for the size rabbet desired. You should check the fence and depth gauge settings by making test cuts on scrap stock. Do not try to remove too much stock with a single cut. Make repeated cuts until all the stock is removed.

8. Check the fit of the joint. Hold the two members together to see if the surfaces make full contact. Use a chisel or router plane to trim any high spots causing an uneven fit. When the joint fits properly, number the members with a pencil. This will identify the parts for assembly.

Making Dado and Groove Joints

Both dado and groove joints are similar to rabbet joints. They are not cut at the edges and ends, however. See Fig. 13-30. A second member, such as a shelf or divider in a cabinet, fits into the dado or groove. A **groove** is a recessed area cut WITH the wood grain. A **dado** is a recessed area cut ACROSS the grain. Use the following procedure to make both dado and groove joints.

1. Cut all stock to finish size.
2. Square a line, locating one edge of the joint according to your drawing. Mark an "X" on the side of the line where the joint will be cut. See Fig. 13-31.
3. Place the two joining pieces together as they will fit in the joint.
4. Draw the line marking the other side of the groove or dado.
5. Using a square, extend both lines across the edges.
6. Set the marking gauge for the depth of the cut. The depth should be about one-third to one-half the board's thickness. Scribe lines for the depth along both edges between the lines extended from the face.
7. Cut along the lines on the face with a backsaw, dovetail saw, or miter box and saw. Make these cuts just inside the lines (waste side). See Fig. 13-32. When you have finished making the cuts, the lines should still be there.

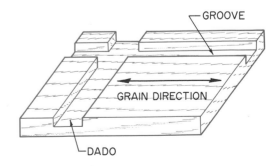

Fig. 13-30. Dadoes are cut **against** the grain. Grooves are cut **with** the grain.

8. Remove the waste material with a chisel narrower than the distance between the two outside cuts. Do not chisel any deeper than the depth lines indicate. See Fig. 13-33. Extra saw cuts between the outside cuts make this removal easier.

9. Set the router plane to the correct depth and clean out the bottom of the cut.

10. Dry assemble the joint to check for fit. It should fit together easily without being loose.

Making Rabbet-Dado Joints

Rabbet-dado joints make strong corners. They are used for box construction and for attaching drawer backs to drawer sides. See Fig. 13-34. A rabbet-dado joint is made by cutting a dado in one piece and a rabbet in the other.

1. Cut and square all stock to finish size.
2. Place the pieces together as for an end-to-face butt joint. Following the other

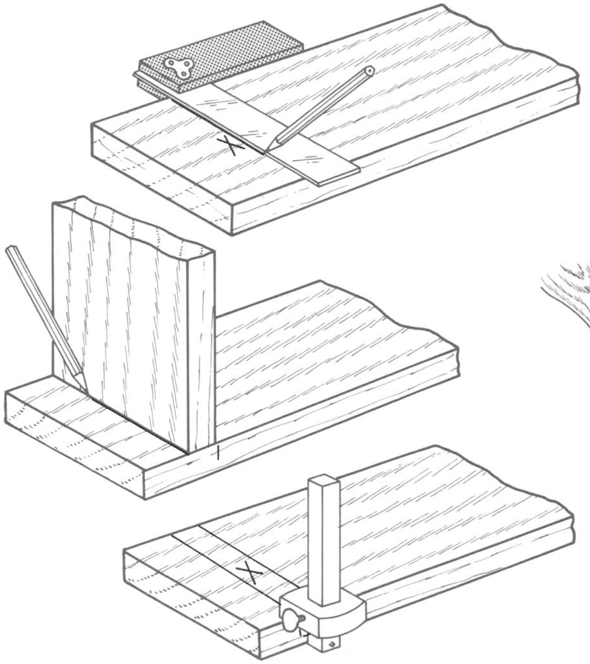

Fig. 13-31. These are the steps for laying out a dado or groove joint. Make all cuts on the side of the layout line closest to the "X."

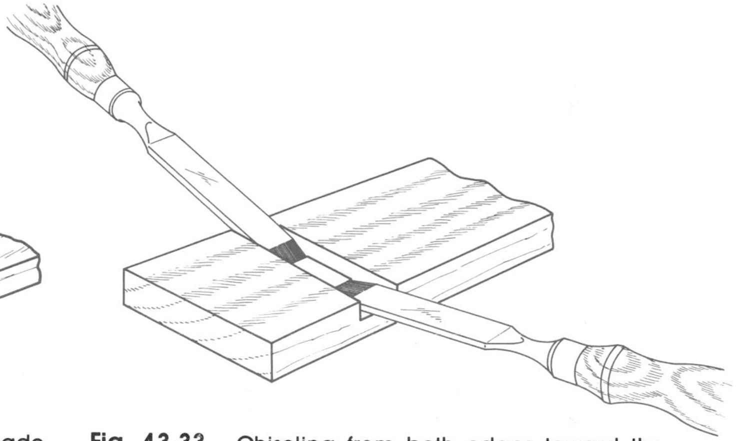

Fig. 13-32. Cut on the waste side of each line. Keep the saw horizontal and do not cut deeper than the depth lines.

Fig. 13-33. Chiseling from both edges toward the middle will help prevent the stock from splintering.

Fig. 13-34. Rabbet-dado joints were used to join the corners of this small box. They are strong, durable joints.

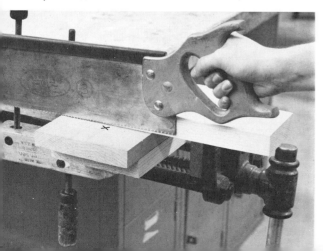

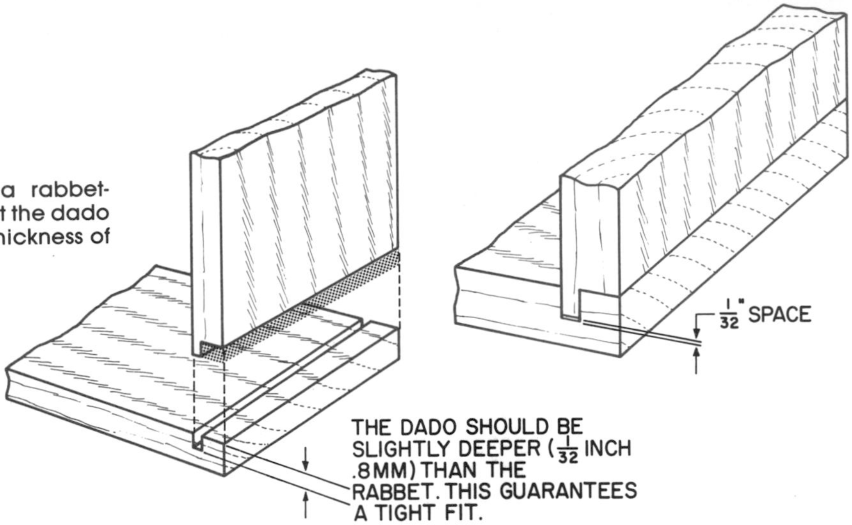

Fig. 13-35. This shows how a rabbet-dado joint is laid out. Notice that the dado should be about 1/3 to 1/4 the thickness of the stock.

$\frac{1}{32}$" SPACE

THE DADO SHOULD BE SLIGHTLY DEEPER ($\frac{1}{32}$ INCH .8MM) THAN THE RABBET. THIS GUARANTEES A TIGHT FIT.

edge, draw a line on the piece in which the dado is to be cut. This line marks the edge of the dado farthest from the end of the board.

3. The width of the dado is usually about one-fourth to one-third the thickness of the piece in which the rabbet is cut. See Fig. 13-35. Measure and mark the width of the dado from the first line. Square the line across the face.

4. Lay out the depth of the dado with a marking gauge. Set the gauge to 1/2 the thickness of the dado piece. Scribe a line on each edge indicating the depth of the dado.

5. Cut out the dado with a saw, chisel, and router plane as described in steps 7, 8, and 9 of the procedure for making dado joints.

6. Lay out and cut the rabbet. Subtract the width of the dado from the thickness of the second piece. With a marking gauge, mark this distance around the edges and the end of the second piece. Then set a depth gauge slightly less than the depth of the dado. Mark this depth across the outside face and the edges of the second piece. Use a backsaw, dovetail saw, or miter box and saw to cut the rabbet. Make the rabbet smooth and flat with a router plane or chisel.

7. Try the joint for fit. If it does not fit tightly, you probably need to remove a small amount of material from the bottom of the dado. Use a router plane or chisel to remove excess material.

Making Half Lap Joints

The several kinds of half lap joints are basically the same. See Fig. 13-36. They differ only by the part of the board on which they are made.

Half lap joints are strong joints. Glue alone provides a strong enough bond if both surfaces are smooth and flat. Hand cutting two large surfaces so they make full contact is difficult, however. Make sure both surfaces are flat. You can use wood screws and nails to eliminate the need for clamping. Use the following procedure to make half lap joints.

1. Place the two members in their exact positions in the joint. Mark cutting lines on each member as shown in Fig. 13-37. You may want to clamp the pieces together to ensure accurate marking. Use a try square to make sure the members are square with one another.

2. Set a marking gauge for one-half the thickness of the stock. Mark the depth of the cut on the edges.

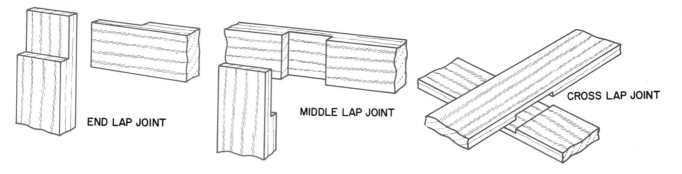

Fig. 13-36. Half lap joints join pieces without increasing the thickness at the joint.

END LAP JOINT

MIDDLE LAP JOINT

CROSS LAP JOINT

3. Cut the joint by sawing just inside the layout lines with a backsaw. Be sure not to saw any deeper than the layout lines. Remove the stock in the middle with a chisel. Make several cuts with the backsaw between the shoulder cuts. This will help remove the waste. See Fig. 13-38.

4. After cutting the joint, check the fit. If it is too tight, plane thin shavings from the edges. This is easier than trying to trim the shoulders of the joint. Continue until the joint fits properly.

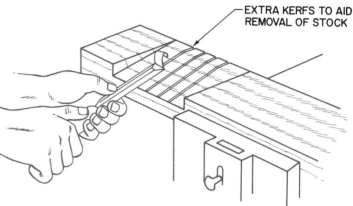

EXTRA KERFS TO AID REMOVAL OF STOCK

Fig. 13-38. Remove waste stock from lap joints with a chisel. Chisel from both edges to the middle to avoid splintering.

Making Mortise-and-Tenon Joints

Mortise-and-tenon joints are the strongest joints used in woodworking. See Fig. 13-39. They are among the hardest joints to make. Hand-cut mortise-and-tenon joints are sure signs of quality. Use the following procedure to cut a mortise-and-tenon joint.

1. Determine the size of the mortise-and-tenon. The tenon is usually one-half the thickness of the piece on which it is cut. The shoulders on each edge of the tenon should be at least 1/4 inch (6 mm) wide. The length of the tenon should be no longer than two-thirds the width of the thicker piece.

2. Use a try square to lay out the shoulder cuts of the tenon. Use either a marking

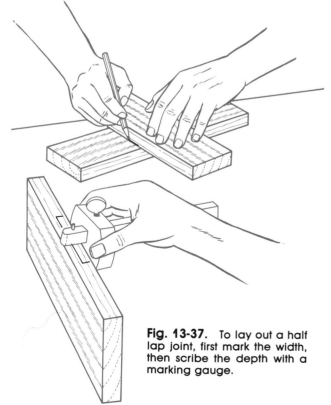

Fig. 13-37. To lay out a half lap joint, first mark the width, then scribe the depth with a marking gauge.

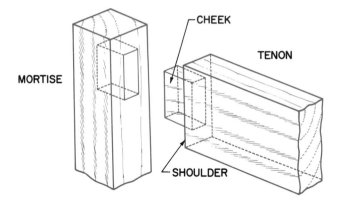

CHEEK

TENON

MORTISE

SHOULDER

Fig. 13-39. Mortise-and-tenon joints are the strongest joints used in woodworking. They are also among the hardest to make.

gauge or a special mortise gauge to lay out the cheek cuts. See Fig. 13-40.

3. Using the tenon size as a guide, lay out the location and size of the mortise. This is usually done with a marking gauge and a try square. You can use a mortise gauge if one is available. See Fig. 13-41.

4. Always cut the mortise first. It is easier to fit the tenon to the mortise than the other way around. Bore a series of holes inside the layout lines. Put a bit gauge on the drill so the holes will be made 1/8 inch *(3 mm)* deeper than the length of the tenon. Then remove the remaining waste material with a chisel. See Fig. 13-42. If you use mortise chisels, it is not necessary to bore holes. Use a mortise chisel that is

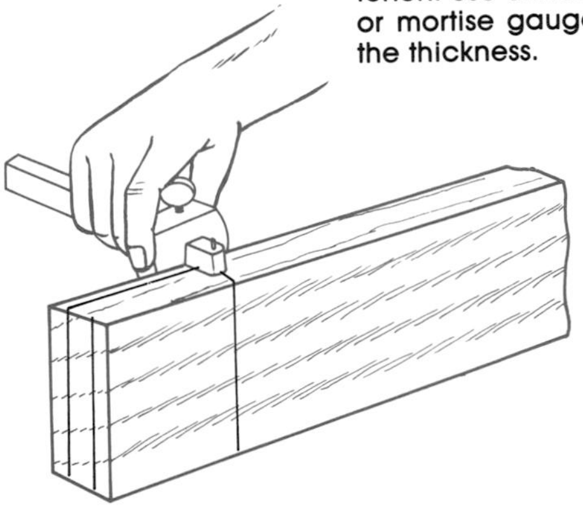

Fig. 13-40. Use a try square to lay out the shoulders of the tenon. Use a marking gauge or mortise gauge to lay out the thickness.

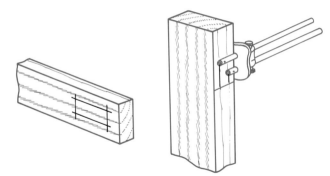

Fig. 13-41. You can use a mortise gauge to lay out a mortise.

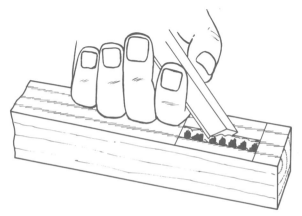

Fig. 13-42. To cut a mortise, first drill a series of holes. Then use a chisel to clear out the waste stock.

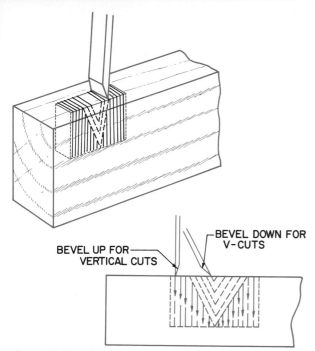

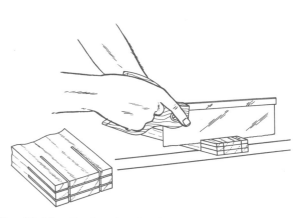

BEVEL UP FOR VERTICAL CUTS

BEVEL DOWN FOR V-CUTS

Fig. 13-43. To cut a mortise with a mortise chisel, make a series of V-cuts. Then make vertical cuts, working from the middle out to the edges.

Fig. 13-44. Cut the cheeks of the tenon first. Then cut the shoulders.

the exact width of the mortise. Fig. 13-43 shows how to clean out a mortise with a mallet and mortise chisel.

5. Cut the tenon to fit the mortise with a backsaw. Cut the cheeks first. Then cut the shoulders. See Fig. 13-44.

6. Assemble the joint. The joint will fit better if you slightly bevel the edges of the tenon. Trim any tight spots. Do this by removing stock from the tenon with a chisel. If the fit is too loose, insert thin pieces of wood until the joint is tight.

New Terms

1. dowel centers
2. doweling jig
3. dowel rod
4. dry assembly

Study Questions

1. Give two ways you benefit as a woodworker by making wood joints by hand.
2. Why should you use a knife in laying out wood joints?
3. What type of joints are the easiest to lay out and cut?
4. An accurate butt joint depends on doing what two things to the pieces making up the joint?
5. What is the advantage to alternating the growth rings when making a panel?
6. Describe the procedure for checking the fit of a butt joint.
7. Name the two types of butt joints most likely to need reinforcing with dowels or metal fasteners.
8. Name two ways in which dowels can be purchased. Give one advantage to each.
9. What is the rule for deciding on the best diameter for a dowel? What is the standard length of a dowel pin?
10. Explain the purpose of grooves along the side of a dowel pin.
11. Give two advantages to using dowel centers.
12. Why must the opposite sides of a picture frame be exactly the same length?
13. Why is the rabbet joint one of the easiest joints to cut?
14. When can you use a rabbet plane to cut a rabbet joint?
15. Which type of woodworking joint is the strongest?
16. Should the mortise, or the tenon, be cut first when making a mortise-and-tenon joint?
17. In making joints, where should all cuts be made with relation to the layout lines?

Chapter 14

Adhesives

Adhesives, commonly called glue, are used to hold wood parts tightly together. Adhesives form durable, almost invisible bonds between pieces of wood. Used properly, they make wood joints stronger than the wood itself.

How Adhesives Work

Adhesives hold wood pieces together by forming a solid, thin layer of glue between the joining surfaces. The glue, while still liquid, conforms to the surfaces. Small amounts even soak into the wood pores, which are similar to holes in a sponge. This gives the glue a firm hold on the wood. When the glue hardens, the bond becomes permanent.

Adhesives harden in two ways. The most common way is through evaporation. Common white glue, for instance, uses water as a solvent. As the water evaporates from the glue, the glue hardens.

Other glues, such as epoxy, harden when a catalyst is added to the glue. A **catalyst** is a chemical that causes a chemical reaction. In the case of epoxy, this reaction causes the glue to harden. This means that no solvent needs to evaporate.

Selecting Adhesives

There is no such thing as a perfect, all-purpose wood glue. Instead, there are different types of adhesives to meet different needs. Each type has its own special qualities. Before you choose an adhesive, determine which qualities your project needs. Important qualities to consider are strength, water resistance, drying time, and expense.

To select the right glue, carefully study the advantages and disadvantages of the common glues. Resorcinol, for example, has the advantages of being waterproof and durable. However, it is expensive, and it stains the wood around the joint. Using this glue, you gain in water resistance and durability, but lose in cost and appearance.

The selection of resorcinol, or any other glue, is a compromise. Since you must compromise, it is important to select the glue with the necessary advantages.

Do not choose a glue that is overqualified for the job. This would waste money and probably not improve the appearance or use of the project. Anticipate how the project will be used and select an adequate glue. The glue chart on page 127 and the following descriptions will help you.

Polyvinyl-Resin Glue. Also called white glue, polyvinyl-resin glue is an excellent glue for most projects. See Fig. 14-3. It dries quickly, is colorless when dry, and is easy to clean up. White glue also retains some flexibility when dry. This lets the joint stay strong even when

Fig. 14-1. There are many types of wood glue. Read the labels carefully to select the proper glue.

Wooden boat — must be waterproof

Cutting board —
must be water resistant

Bookshelf — need not
be water resistant

Fig. 14-2. The glue for each project was selected to fit that particular project.

Fig. 14-3. Common brands of polyvinyl-resin (white) glue

the wood expands and contracts. The disadvantages of white glue are that it is neither waterproof nor heat resistant. It should be used only on indoor projects. White glue should not be used in places where temperatures rise above 150°F (65°C).

Contact Cement. Both natural and synthetic rubbers are combined with solvents to make contact cement. This adhesive is used mainly to bond plastic laminates, veneers, and sheets of metal, to wood.

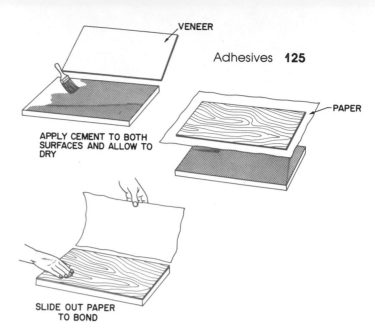

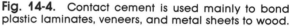

Fig. 14-4. Contact cement is used mainly to bond plastic laminates, veneers, and metal sheets to wood.

Apply contact cement by brushing it on both surfaces to be joined. When the cement is dry to the touch, bring the surfaces together. This forms an instant and permanent bond. See Fig. 14-4.

Clamping is not necessary. The parts must be aligned carefully, however. Once they come together, they cannot be moved. Inserting a piece of paper between the two surfaces will ensure that the parts are properly aligned. The paper will keep the glue surfaces apart while they are positioned. You can then glue the surfaces by simply sliding the paper out and pressing them together.

Hot-Melt Glue. A special heat gun is used to apply hot-melt glue. The heat gun melts and dispenses the glue, as shown in Fig. 14-5. Because it fills small gaps, hot-melt glue will even bond poorly made joints. It is also water resistant. It is used primarily to attach molding and decorative trim to projects.

Hot-melt glue hardens quickly as it cools. You must work fast to assemble the parts before the glue hardens. This makes clamping unnecessary. Be careful when using hot-melt glue. Both the glue and the tip of the gun become very hot. They can easily cause severe burns.

Fig. 14-5. Hot-melt glue must be applied with heat guns. The guns both heat and dispense the glue.

Almost any material — metal, paper, leather, glass, wood, or plastic — can be fastened with hot-melt glue. Its major disadvantages are a lack of strength and shock resistance. Another disadvantage is that lacquer tends to soften it.

Aliphatic-Resin Glue. Creamy yellow in color, aliphatic-resin glue comes ready to use in liquid form. See Fig. 14-6. It is not affected by lacquers, sealers, or solvents. It has some resistance to moisture. It is not waterproof, however, and should not be used for outdoor projects. You can use it at temperatures as low as 50°F (10°C). When dry it will withstand temperatures as high as 248°F (120°C). An added advantage is that you can use aliphatic-resin glue on small parts without clamping.

Spread the glue on the parts to be joined. Rub the parts together to ensure a thin, even spread of glue. The parts will then remain in place without clamping while the glue dries.

Animal (Hide) Glue. Probably the oldest known wood glue is animal glue. It is a natural glue made from hides, bones, tendons, and other parts of cattle. Animal glue is available in either dry or liquid form. See Fig. 14-7. Both forms are strong and durable. However, they do not resist moisture and should not be used for outdoor projects.

To prepare dry animal glue, you must soak it in water until it dissolves. You must then heat the glue in a glue pot. The glue must be applied while it is hot and the wood is warm. If not

applied properly, it will cool and jell before the joint is properly clamped. Because it is so troublesome to apply, dry animal glue is rarely used.

Liquid hide glue comes in liquid form and requires no heating. It has a long drying time compared to polyvinyl and aliphatic glues. This allows extra time for clamping complex assemblies.

Urea-Resin Glue. Also called plastic resin, urea resin is a synthetic glue. It comes as a powder that must be mixed with water before use. See Fig. 14-8. Urea-resin glue has a long drying time, which makes clamping complex assemblies possible. It is also a good choice for projects that need moisture resistance. However, it is not waterproof. A disadvantage of urea resin is that it weakens at temperatures

Fig. 14-6. Common aliphatic-resin glues

Fig. 14-7. Types of animal glue

Fig. 14-8. Urea (plastic)-resin glue is mixed with water to a creamy consistency before it is used.

ADHESIVE	HOW TO MIX	USES	ADVANTAGES	DISADVANTAGES	CLAMPING TIME	COLOR
Liquid Hide	Ready to use	Wood Veneers Plywood Plastic laminates	Strong Cures at room temperature Clamping time allows for complex assemblies	Low moisture resistance	Clamp within 30 minutes. Remove clamps after 2-3 hours.	Tan to brown
Urea Resin (Plastic Resin)	Add water to powder according to directions on container.	Wood Plywood Veneers Use when water resistance is needed. It is not waterproof, however.	Good moisture resistance Cures at room temperature	Not waterproof Low resistance to temperatures above 150° Must be used within 4 hours of mixing Joints must fit well	Clamp within 15 minutes. Remove clamps after 6-8 hours.	Tan
Resorcinol- and Phenol Resorcinol-Resin	Two part mix according to label instructions	Wood Plywood Veneers Boats Outdoor furniture	Waterproof Resists high temperatures	Leaves a dark-colored glue line. Must be applied within 8 hours of mixing Slow drying	Clamp within 20 minutes. Remove clamps after 24 hours.	Dark red
Epoxy Resin	Two part mix (resin & hardener)	All	Fills voids	Expensive Must mix only what you can use	Clamp immediately. Remove clamps after 8-10 hours.	Clear to milky
Polyvinyl Resin (White)	Ready to use	Wood Veneers Plywood Plastic laminates	Strong Fast drying Inexpensive	Low moisture and heat resistance	Clamp within 10 minutes. Remove clamps after 30-40 minutes.	White
Contact Cement	Ready to use	Plastic laminates to wood Veneers	Water resistant Bonds on contact No clamping necessary	Cannot be adjusted after contact is made	None	Tan
Hot Melt	Ready to use	Moldings Carvings Small pieces Patching and repairing wood	Bonds upon cooling Moisture resistant Fills voids	Heavy (thick) glue line Requires heat gun Not as strong as other adhesives	Clamp immediately. Remove clamps after 1-2 minutes.	White
Aliphatic Resin (Carpenter's Glue, or Titebond)	Ready to use	Wood Veneers Plywood Plastic laminates	Strong Heat resistant No clamping needed on small parts	Low moisture resistance	Clamp within 10 minutes. Remove clamps after 20-30 minutes.	Creamy yellow

Fig. 14-9. Adhesive Chart

above 150°F (65°C). Pieces bonded with urea resin must also be clamped very tightly for good results.

Resorcinol-Resin Glues. Resorcinol and phenol resorcinol are dark red, synthetic glues. They are completely waterproof. They are durable but expensive, and show a dark glue line when dry. They are used widely for boat construction and in any situation where moisture is a problem.

Epoxy-Resin Glue. A two-part mix of resin and hardener, epoxy resin dries very quickly. For this reason, it should be prepared only as needed. It is strong, waterproof, and unaffected by gasoline and most other solvents. Epoxy resin is not used often to glue wood because it is so expensive. It is used for special applications. Some examples are gluing other materials to wood and filling voids and cracks in lumber. Because it fills gaps well, it is a good adhesive for poorly made joints.

Gluing Joints

You can apply glue with a brush or directly from the bottle. See Fig. 14-10. Applying glue

Fig. 14-10. You can easily apply glue with a plastic squeeze bottle. You can then spread the glue with a brush.

to large areas is often easier with a notched trowel or paint roller. Spread a wet film of glue evenly on one surface of the joint. It is not necessary to coat both pieces. The glue will transfer to the other piece when clamped.

Apply just enough glue to get some squeeze-out. See Fig. 14-11. **Squeeze-out** is the glue that is squeezed from the joint when pressure is applied. Be careful not to squeeze all the glue from the joint. If there is no squeeze-out, you either need more glue, more pressure, or you have taken too much time for assembly. For more information on proper clamping, see chapter 15, "Clamping Techniques."

Glue Cleanup

Glue is difficult to remove after it has dried on wood. It is much easier to remove while it is still wet. Any glue not properly cleaned from the wood, will prevent stains and finishes from being absorbed. If this happens, glue spots will show through the finish.

Use a damp cloth to wipe away any excess glue during the clamping operation. Be careful to remove glue that could come in contact with the clamps. Glue absorbs iron from clamp parts made of steel. The iron can make dark stains in woods that contain tannic acid. Oak, walnut, and cherry are examples.

New Terms

1. adhesive
2. aliphatic-resin glue
3. animal glue
4. catalyst
5. contact cement
6. epoxy-resin glue
7. hot-melt glue
8. phenol resorcinol-resin glue
9. polyvinyl-resin glue
10. resorcinol-resin glue
11. squeeze-out
12. urea-resin glue

Study Questions

1. Briefly describe how adhesives work to hold pieces of wood together.
2. Explain two ways that adhesives harden.

Fig. 14-11. A small amount of squeeze-out indicates good glue coverage.

3. Give four qualities that are important considerations in selecting the best adhesive for your project.
4. What is the disadvantage in choosing an overqualified glue?
5. Give three advantages of polyvinyl-resin glue. Give two disadvantages.
6. Why is a flexible glue desirable for certain wood joints?
7. What adhesive forms an instant and permanent bond? Describe a method for keeping pieces glued with this adhesive apart while you align them.
8. A special heat gun is needed to apply what type of glue?
9. Give two advantages of aliphatic-resin glue.
10. What is probably the oldest known glue?
11. What is the major disadvantage to dry animal glue?
12. Give one advantage to liquid hide glue, as compared to polyvinyl and aliphatic glues.
13. What is the major disadvantage to urea-resin glue?
14. What types of glue are completely waterproof and strong? What are two disadvantages to these glues?
15. Give three methods of applying glue.
16. Why is it necessary to apply glue to only **one** surface?
17. If there is no squeeze-out when two glued pieces are clamped, one of three mistakes has been made. Explain.
18. Why is it important to remove excess glue while it is wet?

Clamps are devices that hold and apply pressure to stock. There are many sizes and types of clamps. Most pieces needing to be held in place or pushed together can be clamped. For the woodworker, clamps are like extra helping hands.

The most common use of clamps is to hold joints together while they are glued. Joints must stay clamped until the glue dries. Clamping is easy if you prepare properly and choose the right clamps.

Getting Ready to Clamp

Your project should be ready for assembly before you do any clamping and gluing. All parts must fit together and be smooth and clean. Use the following steps to prepare for clamping. Prepare your project carefully and accurately. This will save you time and frustration later.

1. Sand all inside parts and surfaces of the project. Sanding these areas before assembly is easy. It is much harder to sand corners and small areas after assembly. Do not sand the joints. This could make them fit poorly.

2. If you did not mark the pieces earlier, place an identification mark on each piece. Make the marks clearly with a pencil or piece of chalk. Try to place them in areas that will not show after assembly.

   The marks will tell you how the parts fit together during assembly. A part that is not clearly marked could delay the assembly operation. If this happens, the glue might dry before the part is properly clamped.

3. Carefully check the project for smudges, marks, dents, and scratches. If any imperfection (blemish) exists, correct it. See section IV for cures to many common imperfections.

Types of Clamps

Using the right clamp is just as important as preparing the wood. Some clamps are better than others for certain jobs. Read about the following clamps before deciding which clamps you need.

Hand Screws. Probably the most versatile and common clamps in the woodshop are the hand screws. See Fig. 15-1. Hand screws have two wooden jaws controlled by two handles. The wooden jaws protect the stock during clamping. The jaws can be adjusted to a wide range of angles. See Fig. 15-2. This permits clamping of either flat or uneven work.

Fig. 15-1. Hand screws are probably the most versatile clamps in the shop.

Adjustable Clamp Company

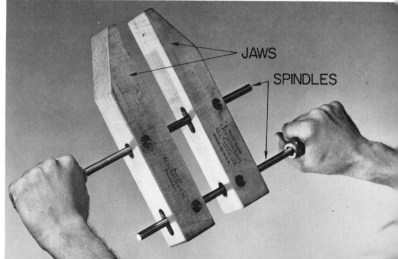

JAWS

SPINDLES

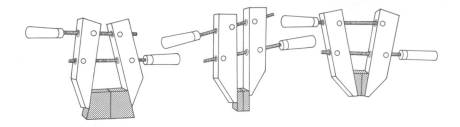

Fig. 15-2. Notice how the jaws of a hand screw can be adjusted to clamp many shapes and angles.

Fig. 15-3. The jaws of hand screws should provide even pressure to the joints. Notice the uneven pressure applied by the clamps in the "wrong" illustration.

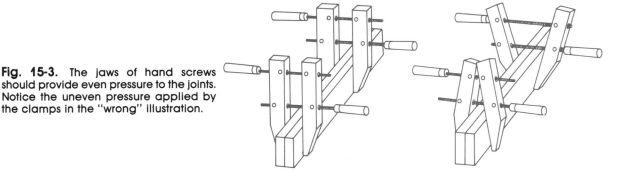

RIGHT   WRONG

To use a hand screw, first make the jaws parallel. Do this by turning one of the handles. Then adjust the clamp in or out by holding a handle in each hand and rotating the clamp. Rotating the clamp in one direction opens it. Reversing the rotation closes it.

After this rough adjustment, place the clamp over the work. Then lightly tighten the handles. Tighten the inside handle first. Then, tighten the outside handle. Be careful that the jaws make flat, square contact with the stock. See Fig. 15-3.

C-Clamps. Small work is most often clamped with C-clamps. See Fig. 15-4. C-clamps come in many different sizes. They are very easy to operate. To use a C-clamp, simply turn the handle until the jaws apply enough pressure. The most common misuse of the C-clamp is applying too much pressure. When more pressure is needed, use a heavy-duty C-clamp or a different type of clamp.

Bar Clamps. There are many sizes and styles of bar clamps. Bar clamps are often used to clamp narrow boards into wide panels. They

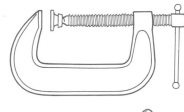

Regular-throat C-clamps are used for general work.

Deep-throat C-clamps reach farther into the center of the stock.

Three-way edging C-clamps are used to clamp edges.

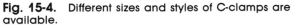

Fig. 15-4. Different sizes and styles of C-clamps are available.

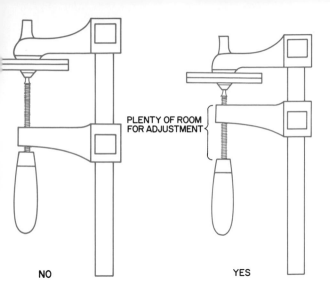

Fig. 15-5. Do not adjust the sliding part of a bar clamp until you have backed off the jaw. After backing it off, you will have enough room to apply the needed pressure.

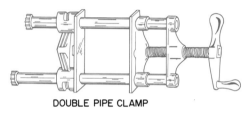

DOUBLE PIPE CLAMP

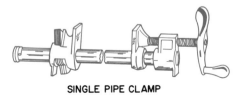

SINGLE PIPE CLAMP

Fig. 15-6. "Clamp fixtures" are pipe clamps without the pipe. Attach the fixtures to common black pipe to use the clamps.

are also used to clamp frames, cabinets, and subassemblies.

To use a bar clamp, turn the handle counterclockwise. This backs off the jaw. See Fig. 15-5. Adjust the slide so the clamp reaches across the stock. Position the clamp on the stock and apply pressure by tightening the handle.

Pipe Clamps. Clamps similar to bar clamps are pipe clamps. Pipe clamps are made with steel pipe rather than bar stock. See Fig. 15-6.

Any length of pipe can be used in a pipe clamp. Use pipe clamps the same way you use bar clamps.

Double pipe clamps use two lengths of pipe. These clamps are very strong. They also apply even pressure to wide and thin panels.

Spring Clamps. For small work needing firm but light pressure, spring clamps are used. These clamps resemble heavy-duty clothespins. See Fig. 15-7. Spring clamps are easy to use. They can be clamped on and removed quickly with one hand.

Band Clamps. Round, square, and oddly shaped objects can be clamped with band clamps. Band clamps consist of a canvas band and a tightening device. See Fig. 15-8. To use a band clamp, place the band around the work. Then tighten the band with the tightening device. Some clamps have a small handle for this. Others need a screwdriver. The canvas

Adjustable Clamp Company

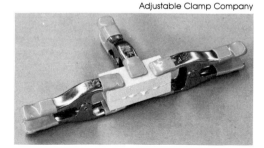

Fig. 15-7. Spring clamps are quick-release clamps used to hold small pieces.

Woodcraft Supply Corporation

Fig. 15-8. Band clamps are ideal for clamping irregular shapes.

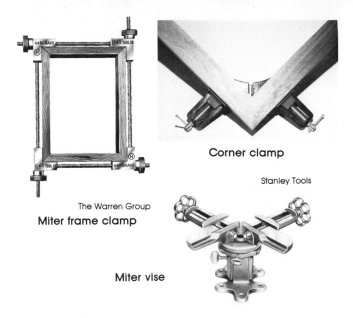

Corner clamp

Stanley Tools

The Warren Group

Miter frame clamp

Miter vise

Fig. 15-9. There are many styles of miter clamps.

band does not mar (spoil) wood surfaces. It is also easy to adjust.

Miter Clamps. The easiest way to hold a miter joint is with a miter clamp. There are many styles of miter clamps. See Fig. 15-9. With some you can clamp all four corners at once. With others, such as corner clamps and miter vises, you can clamp only one corner at a time. Special miter clamps can also be made for assembling frames. See page 116.

General Clamping Procedure

Before you clamp, organize your wood, clamps, and shop area. Everything must be ready when you need it. Once you apply the glue, you have little time to assemble and clamp the joint. If you must hunt for clamps and rearrange pieces, the glue may begin to dry. This could cause a weak, unattractive joint. Avoid problems by using the following procedure.

1. Determine the type and number of clamps needed. It is better to have too many clamps than not enough. Make sure you have enough clamps before you start gluing. Check that you have enough during dry assembly (assembly without glue).

2. Pad the jaws of the clamps so they will not dig into your project. Some clamps have ready-made rubber pads for the jaws. See Fig. 15-10. You can make your own pads with scraps of soft wood. Masking tape will hold these wooden pads on the jaws.

   Hand screws do not usually need pads because the jaws are made of wood. When clamping soft wood, however, the jaws may dig into the project. Use soft, wooden pads for these projects.

3. Cover the work area with old newspapers. This will protect it from dripping glue.

4. Arrange the wood pieces. The identification marks on the joining surfaces should line up.

5. Dry assemble and clamp your project. Handle the clamps carefully. Many are heavy and can easily chip or dent the wood. Use just enough pressure to close the joints. Too much pressure could break the wood.

   Dry assembly gives you a chance to inspect your project. Check for squareness and be sure all joints fit properly. Dry assembly will also help you figure out the correct clamping procedure. Make sure that you have enough of the right clamps. Add clamps to any unclosed joints or unclamped areas.

Fig. 15-10. Pad the metal jaws of your clamps to protect your project. You can use scrap pieces of soft wood as pads.

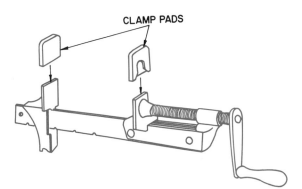

CLAMP PADS

6. Remove the clamps and take the project apart. (Remember to handle the clamps carefully.) Lay the parts in order as you remove them. This way they can be reassembled easily and quickly.

7. Apply glue. See Fig. 15-11. If you are joining many parts at once, use a slow-drying glue. This gives you time to clamp the project before the glue dries. See the glue chart on page 127.

8. Put the project back together and clamp it. Do this the same way you did it during dry assembly. You must clamp the project before the glue dries. There will be plenty of time if you marked the joints and adjusted the clamps beforehand.

When tightening the clamps, apply enough pressure to bring the surfaces together. There should be enough pressure to force air from the joint.

Do not apply too much pressure. Excessive pressure will split the wood. It will also squeeze too much glue from the joint. This causes a **starved** (empty) joint. On the other hand, too little pressure will not bring the surfaces together. This leaves a thick layer of glue, causing a **brittle** joint.

Fig. 15-11. After you have checked the fit, use a brush to apply a thin, even layer of glue.

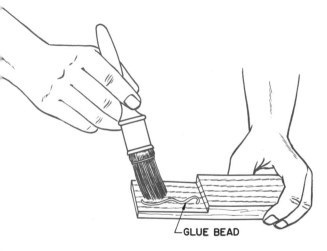
GLUE BEAD

Fig. 15-12. After the glued joints have been clamped, check them for squareness.

Fig. 15-13. Wipe off excess glue with a damp rag. Do not make the rag too wet — too much water could weaken the joint.

9. Carefully check the project for squareness. See Fig. 15-12. Be sure all joints are clamped tightly. All adjoining pieces should be even and properly aligned. Remember, after the glue dries, your project keeps its shape.

10. Use a damp rag to wipe off all excess glue around the joints. See Fig. 15-13. It is much harder to remove glue after it has hardened.

11. With a piece of chalk, write the date and the time on the stock. This tells anyone needing clamps if it is safe to remove them. You can usually remove clamps 24 hours after gluing.

Clamping a Panel

You may need to glue narrow boards together edge to edge. This makes a wide board or panel. If properly assembled, the panel will have strong resistance to warp. Use the following procedure to glue a panel.

1. Prepare the pieces for assembly.
2. Using the identification marks, put the boards in order. They should be faceup, and the growth rings should be alternated. Alternating the growth rings will prevent warping. See Fig. 15-14.
3. Dry assemble the panel. Use either bar or pipe clamps. There should be clamps within 4 inches *(100 mm)* of the panel's ends. The clamps should be about 15 inches *(375 mm)* apart. They should be on alternate sides of the panel. See Fig. 15-15. Tighten the center clamp first. Work toward each end, tightening the clamps until the joint is snug.

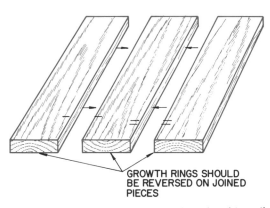

GROWTH RINGS SHOULD
BE REVERSED ON JOINED
PIECES

Fig. 15-14. A small tabletop can be glued together with edge-to-edge joints. The growth rings should be alternated to prevent warpage.

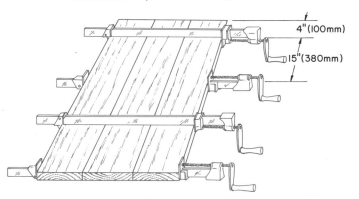

4"(100mm)

15"(380mm)

Fig. 15-15. To clamp a panel properly, space the clamps as shown. Alternate the clamps from side to side. This prevents bowing when pressure is applied.

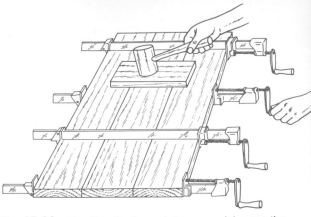

Fig. 15-16. To align the boards in a panel, loosen the clamps and tap the boards with a mallet. Use a scrap piece to protect the boards from the mallet blows.

4. If the joint lines up and fits properly, remove the clamps. Then apply glue to **one** edge of the joint. Rub the edges together to spread the glue. Clamp the boards exactly as you did in dry assembly. Apply enough pressure to close the joint. This pressure should also squeeze out some glue. Wipe off excess glue with a damp rag.
5. The faces of the boards should be even at the joint. If not, slightly loosen the clamps near the uneven spot. Place a piece of scrap wood over the joint. Tap the scrap piece with a hammer or mallet until the joint is flat. See Fig. 15-16. Then retighten the clamps.
6. The panel may buckle when you tighten the clamps. If this happens, clamp a scrap piece to each end of the panel. The scrap piece must have at least one straight edge. See Fig. 15-17. Put a piece of paper between the panel and the scrap piece. This prevents the panel and scrap from being glued together.

Clamping a Miter

Picture frames are examples of projects with miter joints. Miter joints are usually cut at 45° angles. This means that the wood pieces come together at right angles. For this reason, miter joints are difficult to clamp. Special miter clamps are needed to do the job properly. When you glue a miter joint, follow these steps.

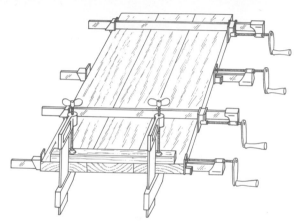

Fig. 15-17. If the panel starts to buckle as you apply pressure, clamp wooden blocks across both ends.

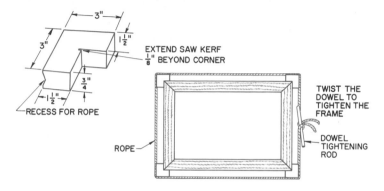

Fig. 15-19. You can make a simple frame clamp by cutting four corner blocks. With a piece of rope and a dowel, you can tighten the blocks around a frame.

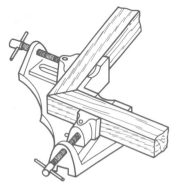

Fig. 15-18. A miter clamp will automatically square each corner.

5. Remove the clamps and apply glue to the joints. Reclamp the boards as before. Apply enough pressure to close the joints. A little glue should squeeze out.
6. Check the frame for squareness with a try square. Another way of checking is to measure the diagonals. See Fig. 15-20.
7. Check the frame for flatness with a straightedge. The straightedge should lie flat on top of the frame.

Clamping Thick Stock

You can make a thin board thicker by gluing boards together face to face. See Fig. 15-21. Woodworkers usually use face-to-face joints to make bowls and table legs on a lathe. To clamp a face-to-face joint, follow the steps below.

1. Prepare the pieces for assembly.
2. Arrange the pieces so the identification marks line up.

1. Prepare the pieces for assembly.
2. Line up the pieces by the identification marks.
3. Select a miter clamp. There are many types. Any one of them can be used with good results. If a miter clamp is not available, you can make your own as shown in Fig. 15-19.
4. Dry assemble and clamp the joints. Be sure that the joints are tight and the frame is square.

Fig. 15-20. Make sure that a frame is square before you clamp it. Use a square or measure across the diagonals. If the diagonals are the same length, the frame is square.

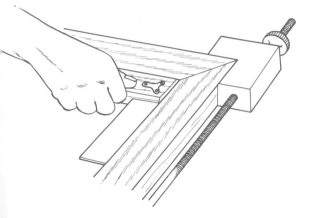

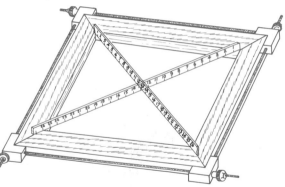

3. Use hand screws, C-clamps, or small bar clamps for face-to-face clamping. Have enough clamps to place one about every 6 inches *(150 mm)*.
4. Dry assemble the stock. Alternate the clamps from side to side. This applies the pressure evenly. Add extra clamps if the joints do not close.
5. If the joints fit correctly, remove the clamps. Then apply glue to **one** surface of each joint. Rub the joining surfaces

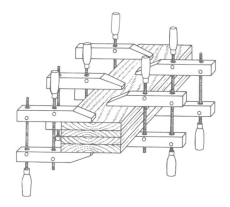

Fig. 15-21. Boards are clamped face-to-face with hand screws, C-clamps, and small bar clamps.

Fig. 15-22. The legs of this table can be glued in subassemblies. First the legs are glued into pairs. Then the two pairs are glued together.

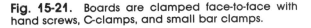

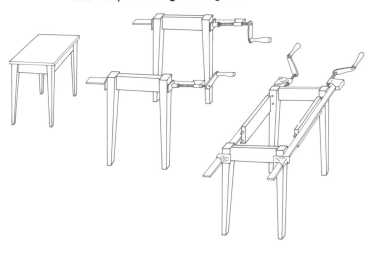

together to spread the glue. Reclamp the stock. Make sure the pieces are properly aligned. Apply pressure until a little glue squeezes out.

Clamping Complex Assemblies

Projects with many parts often cause special problems. For instance, to glue and clamp a footstool, you must glue several parts at once. It is important to think through these procedures carefully. Delays can allow the glue to dry before you apply pressure. Avoid delays by making sure that clamps are adjusted and parts clearly marked beforehand.

Always do a dry assembly before applying the glue. If the assembly is awkward and hard to handle, ask someone to help you. If it still takes over 5 minutes, use a slow-drying glue like liquid hide glue. This gives you more time to arrange and clamp parts. See the adhesive chart on page 127.

It is also important that all parts be properly aligned and square. If one part is out of line, it will affect the alignment of the other parts. Check the alignment of the parts with a square. Make sure you check in several places.

You can often do complex assemblies in small parts called **subassemblies**. For example, you could glue and clamp two legs of a table as a subassembly. You would then glue the other two legs. After each subassembly dried, you could glue and clamp them together. See Fig. 15-22. Subassemblies let you glue and clamp fewer parts at once. This makes the whole assembly process much easier.

Clamping Irregular Surfaces

As a woodworker, you will often need to clamp pieces with irregular shapes. Special attention will be necessary for these jobs. You might even need to invent a new and special clamping method.

For many unusual jobs, the best clamp is the band clamp. Because of the flexible band, you can adjust the band clamp to fit many shapes.

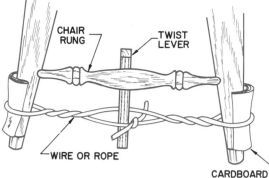

Fig. 15-23. Band clamps are used to clamp irregular shapes, such as this hexagonal nightstand.

CHAIR RUNG

TWIST LEVER

WIRE OR ROPE

CARDBOARD

Fig. 15-24. Windlass clamps are made with rope and either a stick or dowel. These clamps are especially useful for gluing joints on chairs.

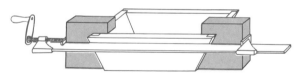

Fig. 15-25. Special clamp blocks can be made to help clamp irregular shapes.

See Fig. 15-23. An easy-to-make variation of the band clamp is the **windlass clamp** shown in Fig. 15-24.

You may need to use hand screws or bar clamps for some pieces with irregular shapes. You can make special **clamp blocks** for these jobs, as shown in Fig. 15-25. Always apply clamping pressure at right angles to the joint when you use clamp blocks.

Safety in the Glue Room

- Always wear approved eye protection when working in the shop.
- Be careful tightening clamps. You can easily pinch a finger in a screw.
- Know where a helper's hands are before tightening a clamp.
- Large bar and pipe clamps are heavy. Be careful when you handle them. You might injure your project, yourself, or another person.
- After handling glue, wash your hands at once. Allowing glue to dry on the skin can cause an infection.
- Wipe up spilled glue at once. Glue is slippery and could cause someone to fall.
- Pick up all scraps. You may prevent a fall.
- Avoid placing long bar clamps so they project into a walkway or aisle. If this cannot be avoided, attach a brightly colored cloth to the ends of long bar clamps. Then the clamps will be easy to see.

New Terms

1. band clamp
2. brittle joint
3. bar clamp
4. C-clamp
5. double pipe clamp
6. hand screw
7. miter clamp
8. pipe clamp
9. spring clamp
10. starved joint
11. subassembly
12. windlass clamp

Study Questions

1. What is the primary use of clamps?
2. Why are the inside parts and surfaces of a project sanded before assembly?
3. List three common clamps.
4. List three clamps used for special purposes. Give the special purpose of each.
5. What damage could result from applying too much pressure with clamps?
6. Explain why a project should be dry assembled before gluing.
7. Why should you write the date and time on glued joints?
8. How far apart should you place the clamps when gluing a panel?
9. Why is it best to glue some projects as subassemblies?
10. What must you remember to always do when clamping irregular shapes with clamp blocks?

Chapter 16

Metal Fasteners

The strength of any project depends on how its parts are fastened together. Many kinds and sizes of fasteners are available. Different nails and screws make up the majority of metal fasteners.

Nails

Sometimes you need to join pieces of wood with nails. By using the right kind and size of nail, you can make your job easier. You can also make your project stronger. The following material will help you select and use nails.

Sizes of Nails. Nails vary in size by length and diameter. Sizes are identified by the term "penny" (abbreviated "d"). Apparently the term once represented the weight in pounds of 1000 nails. For example, when 1000 nails of a certain size weighed 6 pounds, the nails were called "6-penny" nails. Nails are still desig-

nated by penny size. However, the term now indicates length rather than weight.

Nails range in size from 2d to 60d. See Fig. 16-1. Lengths increase 1/4 or 1/2 inch for each additional penny size. The diameters increase as the lengths increase and are designated by **gauge numbers.** The larger the gauge numbers, the smaller the diameters. See Fig. 16-1 again. Wire nails, brads, and escutcheon pins are identified by length and gauge size rather than penny size.

Types of Nails. Nails are made from many materials, including steel, aluminum, and brass. Most nails are made of mild steel. Some are coated to increase their water resistance and holding power. Four types of nails are used most frequently. They are common, box, casing, and finishing nails.

Common nails have large, flat heads. They range in size from 2d to 60d. Common nails

Size	Length	Gauge	Size	Length	Gauge	Size	Length	Gauge
COMMON			BOX			CASING		
2d	1″	15	3d	1-1/4″	14-1/2	4d	1-1/2″	14
3d	1-1/4″	14	4d	1-1/2″	14	6d	2″	12-1/2
4d	1-1/2″	12-1/2	5d	1-3/4″	14	8d	2-1/2″	11-1/2
5d	1-3/4″	12-1/2	6d	2″	12-1/2	10d	3″	10-1/2
6d	2″	11-1/2	7d	2-1/4″	12-1/2	16d	3-1/2″	10
7d	2-1/4″	11-1/2	8d	2-1/2″	11-1/2			
8d	2-1/2″	10-1/4	10d	3″	10-1/2			
9d	2-3/4″	10-1/4	16d	3-1/2″	10			
10d	3″	9	20d	4″	9			
12d	3-1/4″	9						
16d	3-1/2″	8				FINISHING		
20d	4″	6				3d	1-1/4″	15-1/2
30d	4-1/2″	5				4d	1-1/2″	15
40d	5″	4				6d	2″	13
50d	5-1/2″	3				8d	2-1/2″	12-1/2
60d	6″	2				10d	3″	11-1/2

Gauge diameters

15 14 13 12 11 10 9 8 7 6 5 4 3 2

Fig. 16-1. The penny size of a nail indicates the nail's length and diameter (gauge).

larger than 16d are called **spikes.** Common nails and spikes are used primarily for building construction.

Box nails are thinner, lighter, and have wider heads than common nails. They sometimes have cement coatings to increase their holding power. Box nails are used to make boxes and crates. They are also used in light construction work.

Casing nails have cone-shaped heads. These heads provide extra holding power. They also make it possible to set the heads below the wood surface. Casing nails are smaller in diameter than box nails, but larger than finishing nails. They are used for installing windows, door frames, flooring, and trim.

Finishing nails have small heads that can be set below the wood surface. The heads are usually covered with wood putty. Finishing nails are used in any construction where visible nails would not be desirable. Cabinets, furniture, and moldings are some examples.

Besides these four basic kinds, many special nails are manufactured. Wire brads and nails, escutcheon pins, tacks, and staples are just a few. Using different materials, points, heads, shanks (bodies), coatings, lengths, and diameters, manufacturers produce nails for every purpose. Compare the different types and sizes in Fig. 16-2.

Selecting Nails. Choose your nails according to the type of work you are doing. The information earlier in this chapter will help you. Use common nails or box nails if you need holding power. Nails with cement coatings and annular or spiral shanks provide extra holding power. See Fig. 16-3. If you are more concerned with appearance, use casing or finishing nails.

After picking the type of nail, decide on the best length. Whenever possible, the length should be three times the thickness of the first board nailed. Another good rule is that the nail point should not come within 1/8 inch *(3 mm)* of the second surface. Fig. 16-1 gives the lengths for each penny size.

Fastening with Nails

Using nails to join pieces of wood is harder than it looks. Hitting fingers, splitting wood, and bending nails are all common problems. You can eliminate many of these problems by using the right tools and techniques. The following information will help you nail the joints in your project.

Hammers. To drive nails you need a hammer. Not all hammers are alike. Many are designed for a specific purpose, such as shingling a house. The most common, general-purpose hammer is the **claw hammer.** See Fig. 16-4. The claw on one end of the head removes nails.

Claw hammers are available in different sizes. The sizes are determined by the weight of the head. Generally claw hammers range in size from 7 to 20 ounces. A 13- or 16-ounce hammer works well for most purposes. Make sure the hammer is large enough to drive the nails. You should have at least a 16-ounce hammer, for example, to drive a 16d nail. Using

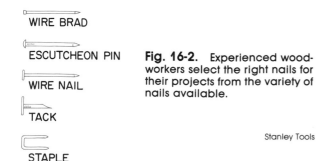

WIRE BRAD

ESCUTCHEON PIN

WIRE NAIL

TACK

STAPLE

Fig. 16-2. Experienced woodworkers select the right nails for their projects from the variety of nails available.

Stanley Tools

Fig. 16-3. Special coatings and different kinds of rings increase the holding power of nails.

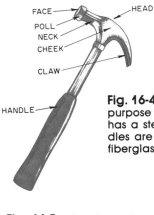

Fig. 16-4. Claw hammers are all-purpose hammers. This hammer has a steel handle. Hammer handles are also made of wood and fiberglass.

Fig. 16-5. Tap the nail until it is started. Then remove your fingers and drive the nail with firm blows. Notice that the handle is gripped near the end.

a smaller hammer would make the job much harder.

Driving Nails. Select a hammer that is comfortable to use. Be sure it is large enough for the job. Hold the hammer near the end of the handle.

Start the nail by holding it upright. Tap it sharply with the hammer. See Fig. 16-5. If the nail bends, remove it and use another. Be sure to keep your eyes on the nail. Do not watch the hammer. You can easily hit your fingers if you do not pay attention.

After two or three taps, the nail should stay upright by itself. Then let go of the nail and drive it with several firm blows. Make the last blows softer to prevent marking the wood.

It is often difficult to start small nails without hitting your fingers. To start small nails, put them through a piece of paper or cardboard.

See Fig. 16-6. You can then drive the nails without hurting your fingers.

Preventing Splits. Driving a nail will often cause wood to split. Splitting is most likely to occur when you nail hardwoods and knotty areas. You can use several methods to avoid splitting.

- Drill a pilot hole for the nail. The diameter of the hole should be about 85% of the nail's diameter. The hole should be drilled to a depth of one-half to two-thirds the nail's length.
- Use nails with blunted (dulled) points. These nails tear, rather than split the wood fibers.
- Space the nails carefully. Do not drive several nails close together along the same grain. See Fig. 16-7.

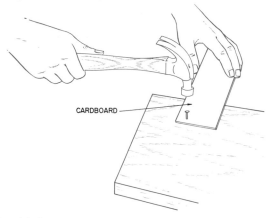

Fig. 16-6. When driving small nails, you can protect your fingers by holding the nail with a piece of paper or cardboard. Once the nail is started, you can tear the paper free.

Fig. 16-7. Driving nails along the same grain will cause splitting. You can avoid this problem by staggering the nails.

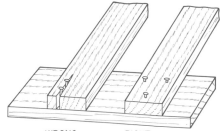

WRONG   RIGHT

Fig. 16-8. Use a nail set to set a nail below the surface. The tip of the nail set should be slightly smaller than the nail head.

Setting Nails. You will usually set finish and casing nails below the wood surface. To do this you need a hammer and a **nail set.** See Fig. 16-8. Select a nail set with a tip slightly smaller than the nail head. Drive the nail until it is almost flush with the surface. Then place the tip of the nail set on top of the nail head. Continue driving the nail until the head is about 1/8 inch *(3 mm)* below the surface. You can then completely cover the nail with wood putty. Never try to set common or box nails.

Toenailing. It is often difficult to nail the end of one board to the face of another. The usual method of doing this is toenailing. To toenail boards, drive the nails at a 30° angle as shown in Fig. 16-9. Always offset the nails to prevent driving them into one another.

Clinching. You can add strength to boards nailed face to face by clinching the nails. To do this the nails must be long enough to go completely through both boards. After driving the nails, bend the points over. See Fig. 16-10.

Removing Nails. You can usually remove nails easily with the claw of a hammer. Slip the claw under the nail head and pull the handle upward. Do not apply too much pressure. This could result in a broken hammer handle.

To protect boards while removing nails, place a wood piece under the hammer head. See Fig. 16-11. The piece of wood will also increase leverage. To remove large nails and nails driven into hard wood, use a **nail claw** or

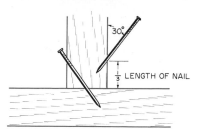

Fig. 16-9. Toenailing makes it possible to nail the end of one board to another board. Drive the nails at 30° angles and stagger them so they do not hit each other.

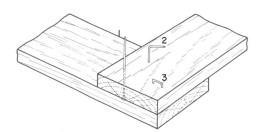

Fig. 16-10. If possible, clinch nails across the grain (see step 3). This provides the greatest amount of holding power.

Fig. 16-11. When removing nails, you can protect the surface and increase leverage by placing a block of wood under the hammer.

Fig. 16-12. Ripping bars and nail claws will help you pull out hard-to-remove nails.

ripping bar. See Fig. 16-12. If the nail head breaks off, use vise-grip pliers to remove the nail.

Wood Screws

Wood screws are useful in fastening wood. They can be retightened and removed without damaging the wood. They also have greater holding power than nails. The one disadvantage to screws is that they are more difficult to install.

Types of Screws. Wood screws are available with flat, round, and oval heads. See Fig. 16-13. Flat heads are used when the screw is set flush with or below the surface. Round and oval heads are used when an exposed head is not a problem. In fact, round and oval heads are often used as decoration.

Most wood screws are available with either **slotted** or **Phillips** heads. See Fig. 16-14. Screws with Phillips heads are easier to drive straight. This is because all the pressure is exerted at the center of the head. Screwdrivers are also less likely to slip off a Phillips head and damage the wood.

Wood screws are usually made of steel or brass. Steel screws are often plated to reduce rusting. Brass screws do not rust and are more decorative. Brass screws are more expensive than steel screws, however.

Sizes of Screws. Wood screw sizes are determined by length and diameter. Most manufacturers make screws from 1/4 inch to 6 inches long. Each length of screw is available in different diameters. The shank diameters are indicated by gauge numbers from 0 to 24. See

Fig. 16-15. Notice that the gauge numbers get larger as the diameters increase.

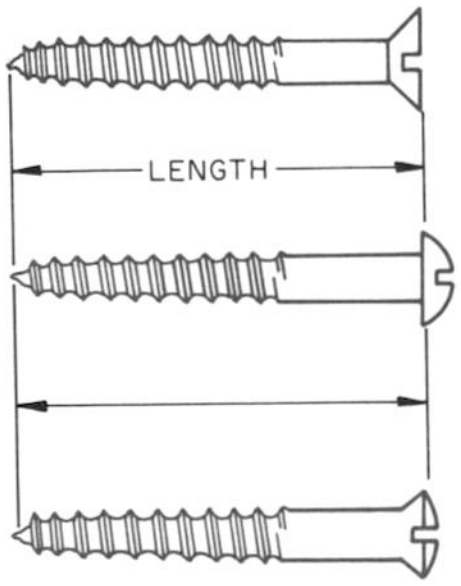

Selecting Screws. You need to consider four factors in selecting screws for your project. They are: type of head, material, length, and diameter. First decide what type of head you need. If the screw should be flush with or below the wood, use flat-head screws. Otherwise, use screws with round or oval heads.

The material the screw is made of is also important. Use brass or plated screws if the screws will be exposed to moisture. Also use brass or plated screws if the screws will be visible. Use less costly, non-plated screws when moisture and appearance are not factors.

For maximum holding power, a screw should go two-thirds of its length into the second piece. This means that all of the threads should go into the second piece. However, the screw point should not come within 1/8 inch (3 mm) of the second surface.

A screw of a certain length is available in different diameters. The larger the diameter, the greater the holding power. Try to use the smallest diameter that provides enough holding power. The chances of splitting the wood increase as the diameter increases.

The best diameter depends on the kind of wood, its thickness, and its grain. The thickness of the wood is usually the most important factor. Thin stock requires screws with small diameters. Thicker stock can take larger screws. Smaller diameters can be used with hard wood than with soft wood. Wood screws will not hold well in end grain. Either the diameter or length should be increased when placing screws in end grain.

Wood screws are usually sold in boxes of 100. When you buy screws, you must specify length, gauge number, type of head, and coating. For example,

"1½ No. 8 F.H. Brass"

means you want a screw 1-1/2 inches long, with an 8-gauge diameter and a flat head, made out of brass.

Fig. 16-13. Most wood screws have either flat, round, or oval heads. Flat heads are set flush. Round and oval heads remain above the surface.

Fig. 16-14. A screw with a Phillips head is easier to drive straight than one with a slotted head. Screwdrivers are also less likely to slip from a Phillips head.

Gauge No. Wire Size	Counterbore for Head Drill Size	Shank-Hole Drill Size	Pilot or Lead Hole Drill Size	
			Hard Wood	Soft Wood
0	.119 (1/8)	1/16	3/64	
1	.146 (9/64)	5/64	1/16	
2	1/4	3/32	1/16	3/64
3	1/4	7/64	1/16	3/64
4	1/4	1/8	3/32	5/64
5	5/16	1/8	3/32	5/64
6	5/16	9/64	3/32	5/64
7	3/8	5/32	1/8	3/32
8	3/8	11/64	1/8	3/32
9	3/8	3/16	1/8	9/64
10	1/2	3/16	5/32	9/64
12	1/2	7/32	3/16	9/64
14	1/2	1/4	3/16	11/64
16	9/16	9/32	15/64	13/64
18	5/8	5/16	17/64	15/64
20	.650 (11/16)	11/32	19/64	17/64
24	.756 (3/4)	3/8	21/64	19/64

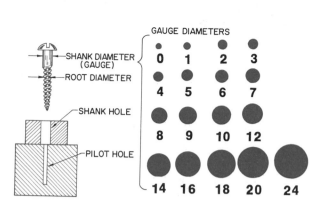

Fig. 16-15. Use this table to find drill and bit sizes for shank and pilot holes. You can find the gauge number of a screw by matching the screw with a circle of equal diameter.

Fastening with Screws

Screws are more difficult to install than nails. Layouts must be more precise. An extra operation — drilling — is needed for screws. Also, a wider range of tools — drills, bits, screwdrivers — is necessary. Do not use screws unless you need the added holding power or will later take your project apart.

Drilling Holes. You must drill two holes to install wood screws. See Fig. 16-15. First drill the **shank hole** through the first piece of stock. The shank hole should be the same diameter as the screw shank. You should be able to easily push the screw into the hole.

Drill the **pilot hole** in the second piece of stock. The pilot hole should be made as deep as the screw will go in the second piece. For hard wood make the diameter slightly less than the screw's root diameter. For soft woods the diameter should be smaller still. The chart in Fig. 16-15 gives bit and drill sizes according to the wood and the screw's diameter. When you put small screws in soft wood, you do not always need a pilot hole.

To align the shank and pilot holes, use the following procedure.

1. Lay out and center punch the location of the shank hole.
2. Drill the shank hole.
3. Place the first piece of wood in position over the second piece. Insert a scratch awl or nail through the shank hole. This will mark the location of the pilot hole on the second piece. See Fig. 16-16.
4. Drill the pilot hole.

Countersinking. If you use screws with flat or oval heads, you must countersink the shank hole. Countersinking is the process of cutting a cone-shaped hole for the screw head. This allows the screw head to be set flush with the surface. Tools called **countersinks** are used for this purpose. See Fig. 16-17. Countersinks can be used in hand drills, bit braces, and power drills. Hand-operated countersinks are also available. If you countersink many holes, put a depth gauge on the countersink.

You can make a shank hole and pilot hole, and countersink in one operation. You can do this with the Screw Mates and Screw Sinks

Fig. 16-16. After you drill the shank hole, put the pieces in position and mark the pilot hole location with a scratch awl.

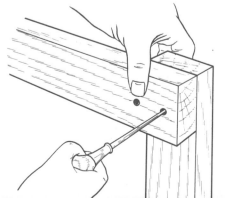

Fig. 16-17. Countersinks are available with different shanks. Use the square shank in a bit brace.

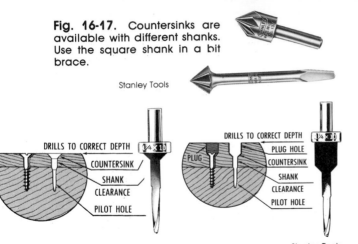

Stanley Tools

DRILLS TO CORRECT DEPTH
¼ X 1
COUNTERSINK
SHANK
CLEARANCE
PILOT HOLE

DRILLS TO CORRECT DEPTH
¼ X 1
PLUG HOLE
PLUG
COUNTERSINK
SHANK
CLEARANCE
PILOT HOLE

Stanley Tools

Fig. 16-18. Screw Mates and Screw Sinks make shank holes and pilot holes, and countersink all in one operation. The Screw Sink also counterbores in the same operation.

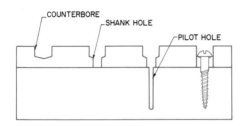

COUNTERBORE
SHANK HOLE
PILOT HOLE

Fig. 16-19. If you set a screw below the surface, counterbore before you drill the shank hole.

shown in Fig. 16-18. Both tools come in several sizes to be used in hand and power drills. Before using these tools, clamp the wood pieces together. Clamp them exactly as they will be fastened.

Counterboring. You can set screws below wood surfaces by counterboring the shank hole. You can then hide the screw to make the surface more attractive. See Fig. 16-19. You can cover the screw with a **wood button**, **plug**, or piece of dowel. See Fig. 16-20.

If you intend to cover counterbored screws with plugs, save your scrap cuttings. Use the scrap pieces to make the plugs. Then the plugs will match the grain and color of the stock. To cut plugs use a plug cutter as shown in Fig. 16-21. If possible, use plug cutters in a drill press.

Always counterbore before you drill the shank hole. This prevents the counterboring

bit from wobbling and cutting an irregular-shaped hole. Use a counterboring bit larger than the diameter of the screw head. The bit should be the same diameter as the plug or button. Drill the shank hole through the center of the counterbored hole. See again Fig. 16-19. Then drill the pilot hole.

Screwdrivers. The most common screwdrivers are **standard** screwdrivers and **Phillips** screwdrivers. See Fig. 16-22. The first is used for ordinary slotted screws. The second is used for the Phillips recessed-head screws. The sizes of standard screwdrivers are determined by the blade length. Phillips screwdrivers are sized by points from 1 to 4, with 1 the smallest. All screwdrivers are available with different sizes of blades and tips.

The spiral rachet screwdriver is a time-saver when installing a large number of screws. You can easily change the blades for either slotted or Phillips-head screws. See Fig. 16-23.

Screwdriver bits for slotted screws or Phillips-head screws are used in a hand brace.

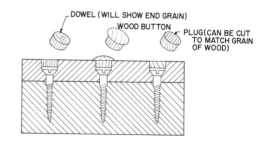

DOWEL (WILL SHOW END GRAIN)
WOOD BUTTON
PLUG (CAN BE CUT TO MATCH GRAIN OF WOOD)

Fig. 16-20. Counterbored holes can be covered with plugs, buttons, or dowels.

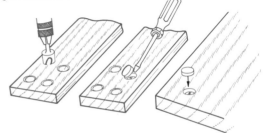

Fig. 16-21. With plug cutters you can easily make attractive plugs for covering screw heads. Plug cutters are available in appropriate sizes.

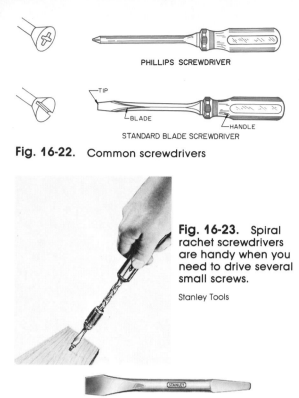

PHILLIPS SCREWDRIVER

TIP

BLADE

HANDLE

STANDARD BLADE SCREWDRIVER

Fig. 16-22. Common screwdrivers

Fig. 16-23. Spiral rachet screwdrivers are handy when you need to drive several small screws.

Stanley Tools

Stanley Tools

Fig. 16-24. Screwdriver bits are manufactured with different shanks for use in bit braces and portable electric drills.

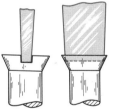

Fig. 16-25. The tip of a standard screwdriver should fit snugly into the slot of the screw head. If the screwdriver slips out, it could damage your project.

See Fig. 16-24. Using a hand brace rather than a screwdriver provides added leverage. This is helpful when installing large screws and screws in hard wood.

Setting Screws. Select the correct screwdriver for the job. Be sure the blade fits snugly in the **full** width of the slot. See Fig. 16-25. Otherwise the blade can slip out and damage the screw slot and your project. To drive slotted screws straight, the tip of the screwdriver should be ground square. Use the longest screwdriver available to provide maximum leverage. Applying soap or wax to the threads makes the screw easier to turn.

Hold the screwdriver in line with the screw. Hold the screw with the other hand. Applying steady pressure, turn the screwdriver slowly to start the screw straight. Do not apply too much pressure. Turn the screw until the head is firmly seated on the surface.

Special Fasteners

Woodworkers use a variety of metal fasteners besides nails and screws. All kinds of special bolts, screws, hooks, plates, and braces, are used to fasten objects togetʰer. Many of the fasteners are designed for usε with metals. However, woodworkers frequently use them in their projects. Many of the special fasteners used by woodworkers are briefly described and pictured here.

Carriage bolts, see Fig. 16-26, have oval heads and are square just below the heads. The square area sinks into the wood. This prevents turning once the bolt is set in a hole. These bolts are used in rough construction and for joints that do not show.

Lag screws usually have square heads. They are driven with a wrench. Like carriage bolts, they provide extra holding power in places that do not show. See Fig. 16-27.

Sheet metal screws, or tapping screws, are threaded the full length of the screw. They are used to attach materials such as plastic and sheet metal to wood. They are especially handy when attaching thin pieces. See Fig. 16-29.

Fig. 16-26. Carriage bolt

Fig. 16-27. Lag screw

Fig. 16-28. Hanger bolt

Fig. 16-29. Sheet metal screws

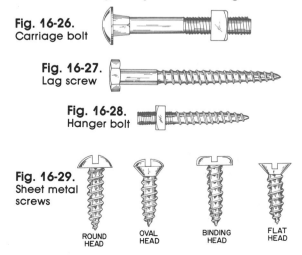

ROUND HEAD

OVAL HEAD

BINDING HEAD

FLAT HEAD

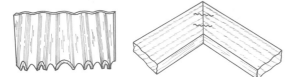

Fig. 16-30. Corrugated fasteners

Fig. 16-31. Mending plates

Stanley Tools

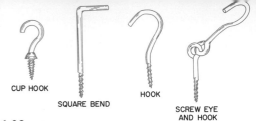

Fig. 16-32. Special screws

Corrugated fasteners are used when appearance is not a factor. See Fig. 16-30. They provide a quick way of joining stock. They will not make joints as strong as those discussed in chapter 12, however. Stagger the fasteners and drive them at an angle to the grain.

Mending plates are flat pieces of steel. They come in several shapes and sizes, as shown in Fig. 16-31. Mending plates are used to reinforce and repair broken and weakened joints. They are usually used in places where they will not show.

New Terms

1. box nail
2. carriage bolt
3. casing nail
4. claw hammer
5. clinching
6. common nail
7. corrugated fastener
8. counterboring
9. countersinking
10. finishing nail
11. gauge number
12. lag screw
13. mending plate
14. nail claw
15. nail set
16. penny
17. Phillips head screw
18. pilot hole
19. ripping bar
20. screwdriver bits
21. Screw Mates
22. Screw Sinks
23. shank hole
24. sheet metal screw
25. spike
26. spiral rachet screwdriver
27. toenailing
28. wood buttons and plugs

Study Questions

1. What two terms are used to identify nail sizes?
2. Most nails are made out of what material?
3. Name the four types of nails used most frequently.
4. Describe the head of a casing nail. What are two advantages to this type of head?
5. Name two ways of increasing the holding power of a nail without increasing its diameter.
6. Give two general rules for selecting the proper length of nail.
7. How are hammer sizes determined? What is a good size for most purposes?
8. In driving a nail with a hammer, how does the last stroke differ from those just before it? Why is this done?
9. Describe the special procedure for driving small nails without hitting your fingers.
10. What problem could result from nailing several nails along the same grain?
11. What can you do to increase leverage when removing nails?
12. Give two advantages of wood screws compared to nails. Give one disadvantage.
13. What are the three most common head shapes on wood screws?
14. Give two advantages of a Phillips head screw compared to a slotted screw.
15. How long should a screw be to achieve maximum holding power?
16. What factor usually determines the proper diameter of a screw?
17. Which hole is drilled first — the shank hole or the pilot hole?
18. What diameter should a shank hole be?
19. Why should you use the longest screwdriver available?
20. What is the advantage to applying soap or wax to screw threads?

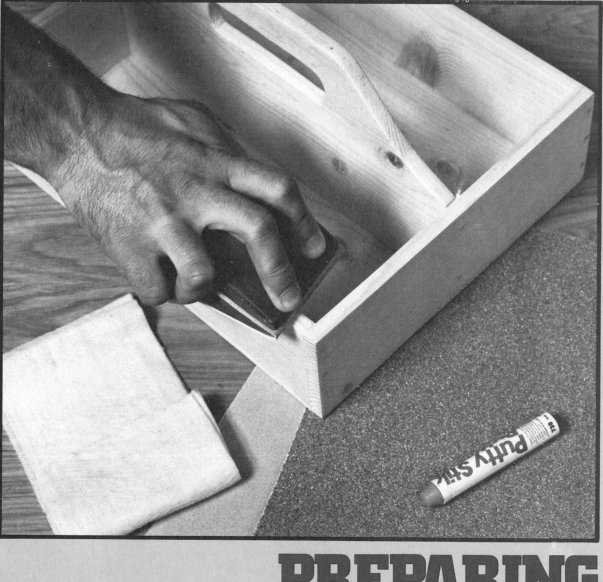

PREPARING
TO FINISH

Chapter 17

Coated Abrasives

Coated abrasives are used most often to smooth and polish wood in preparing for a finish. See Fig. 17-1. They are also used on sanding machines for rough shaping of stock.

A coated abrasive consists of an abrasive (rough) material bonded (glued) to a cloth or paper backing. See Fig. 17-2. The abrasive grains cut the stock much as any other cutting tool would. Each grain acts as a tiny cutting edge. The flexible backing holds the abrasive grains in place. It also lets the rubbing surface bend to fit almost any shape. See Fig. 17-3.

Many types and sizes of coated abrasives are available. The following characteristics determine which coated abrasive you should use.

- kind of abrasive material
- grit size of abrasive
- backing
- bonding
- coating
- size of backing

These characteristics are identified on the back of each coated abrasive.

Fig. 17-1. Coated abrasives are made in a variety of sizes and shapes to fit nearly every smoothing and polishing need.

Kinds of Abrasives

Several kinds of materials are used to make coated abrasives. See the chart in Fig. 17-4. Those commonly used in woodworking are divided into two groups: natural and synthetic.

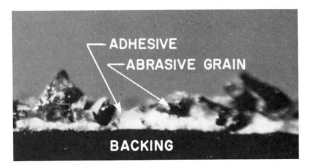

Fig. 17-2. A coated abrasive is made up of thousands of abrasive grains bonded to a backing. Each grain has sharp edges and acts like a tiny cutting tool.

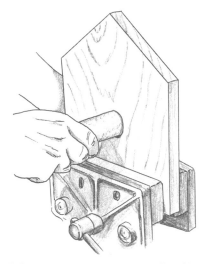

Fig. 17-3. Because of its flexible backing, a coated abrasive can easily be shaped to fit curved or rounded surfaces.

	Abrasive	Color	Durability	Uses
Natural	Flint	White	Low	Hand sanding soft woods or painted woods
	Garnet	Orange or red	Medium	Hand or light machine sanding on all woods
	Emery	Dark brown or black	High	Hand polishing metal
Synthetic	Aluminum Oxide	Gray or tan	Medium high	Hand or machine sanding on all materials
	Silicon Carbide	Black	High	Hand or machine sanding on all materials

Fig. 17-4. Abrasive Materials Chart

Sand is not in either group. To call a coated abrasive "sandpaper," is really incorrect. "Sandpaper" does, however, describe the general appearance and use of coated abrasives.

Natural. Abrasives found in nature are referred to as natural abrasives. Flint (quartz), garnet, and emery are the three most often used in making coated abrasives.

Flint is a white abrasive. It is inexpensive, but not very durable. It is used on gummy materials where the abrasive is likely to clog up before wearing out. Flint is used for light hand sanding, removing loose paint and varnish, and for sanding softwoods.

Garnet is orange-red in color. It is popular with woodworkers because it cuts and polishes quickly. Garnet is more expensive than flint, but stays sharp longer. It is used for most hand sanding and for some light power sanding.

Emery is dark brown or black in color. It is not used to sand wood. Its major use is to polish metal.

Synthetic. Artificial (man-made) abrasives are called synthetic abrasives. These materials are not found in nature. They must be manufactured. This is done by fusing (melting together) several natural materials in an electric furnace.

More than 75% of the coated abrasives used today are synthetic. They last longer than natural abrasives, but are more expensive. They withstand more heat and friction, which makes them ideal for machine sanding. Aluminum oxide and silicon carbide are the primary synthetic abrasives.

Aluminum oxide is gray or tan in color. It is very hard and durable. It is used widely for machine sanding. It also works well for hand sanding.

Silicon carbide is blue-black in color. It is very sharp. It is almost as hard as a diamond, but is very brittle. The abrasive grains break off rather than wear away slowly.

Silicon carbide cuts rapidly with light pressure It works best in sanding soft materials. It is also the primary abrasive for wet-or-dry (waterproof) papers. This makes it an ideal abrasive for finishing. It can be used for sanding between coats of finish. It can also be used, with or without lubricants, to polish the top coat of finish.

Grit Size

On most projects you will do the first sanding with a rough, fast-cutting abrasive. Finer abrasives are used to get the wood ready for finishing. The size of the grit (grain) determines the roughness or fineness of a coated abrasive. The larger the grit, the rougher the abrasive.

Several stages are needed to reduce the abrasive material to the different grit sizes. The abrasives are quarried or manufactured as large rocks, which are crushed into small grains. Then the grains are sorted according to size by passing them over a series of silk screens. See Fig. 17-5. Each screen has a different size **mesh** (openings). A screen with 16 openings per inch, for example, will let large grains drop through. A screen with 100 openings per inch will only let smaller grains drop. The coarsest mesh used for coated abrasives has 12 openings per inch. The finest mesh has 600 openings per inch.

Norton Company

Fig. 17-5. Vibrating silk screens sift and separate abrasive grains into various sizes. Here the crushed grains enter a sifter from the hopper above. They are then sifted through the screen and collected in barrels.

Silicon carbide, aluminum oxide, and garnet are labeled according to mesh size. The older **aught system** of indicating size is also used for aluminum oxide and garnet. The aught system ranges from 10/0 (very fine) to 4 (very coarse). Flint and emery are labeled according to their texture (fine, medium, or coarse). See the chart in Fig. 17-6 for a complete list of grit sizes.

Backings

Abrasive grains are bonded to different backings. Paper and cloth are the most common backings.

The four kinds of paper backings are determined by weight (thickness). The different weights are indicated by the letters A, C, D, and E. "A" weight is a lightweight paper known as **finishing paper.** Finishing paper is used for hand sanding. "C" and "D" weights are medium-weight papers called **cabinet paper.** Cabinet paper is used for hand sanding and on small power sanders. "E" weight is a strong, heavy paper. It is used for machine sanding.

Cloth backings are used for both hand and machine sanding. Cloth backings are more flexible than paper backings. A belt sander, for instance, should have a flexible, cloth backing. Cloth is, however, more expensive.

Fig. 17-6. Abrasive Grit Sizes

General Uses		Grit Texture	Silicon Carbide	Aluminum Oxide Garnet	Flint	Emery
Hand or light machine sanding	Polish sanding or sanding between coats of finish.	Very fine	600			
			500			
	Final sanding prior to finishing.		400	400 (10/0)		
			360			
			320	320 (9/0)		
			280	280 (8/0)		
			240	240 (7/0)		
			220	220 (6/0)		
						Extra fine
	Final sanding prior to painting.	Fine	180	180 (5/0)		
			150	150 (4/0)		Fine
	Intermediate finish sanding.		120	120 (3/0)	Fine	
	Sanding mill marks or machine marks smooth. Sanding rough spots and minor defects.	Medium	100	100 (2/0)		Medium
			80	80 (0)	Medium	
						Coarse
			60	60 (1/2)		
Machine sanding	Rough shaping and leveling. Belt sanding.	Coarse	50	50 (1)		
					Coarse	
			40	40 (1-1/2)		
						Very coarse
			36	36 (2)		
	Rapid removal of stock. Rough shaping. Removal of old finish. Floor finishing.	Very coarse			Extra coarse	
			30	30 (2-1/2)		
			24	24 (3)		
			20	20 (3-1/2)		
			16	16 (4)		
			12			

Backing Weight		Sanding Applications		
Paper	Cloth	Hand	Light Machine	Heavy Machine
A		●		
C		●	●	
D		●	●	●
E				●
	J	●	●	
	×			●

Fig. 17-7. Backing Application Chart

Two weights of cloth are used. "J" weight is lightweight and flexible. It works well in hand sanding curved and irregular-shaped objects. "X" weight is much heavier and stronger. It is used on large sanding machines such as belt and drum sanders. See Fig. 17-7.

Bonds

Two adhesives are used to bond abrasive grains to the backings. The standard adhesive is animal glue. For most woodworking, animal glue is adequate.

Synthetic resin glue is a waterproof adhesive. A waterproof bond is often used during finishing. This lets the finisher use water, or some other liquid, as a lubricant. The lubricants reduce heat, which can spoil a finish. They also help keep the paper clean by carrying away material removed by the abrasive. See. Fig. 17-8.

Fig. 17-8. A fine grit (600) silicon carbide abrasive is used to wet sand a finish. This type of coated abrasive is often called wet-or-dry paper. It can be used with or without a lubricant.

Coatings

Coating refers to how much abrasive is placed on the backing. There are two basic types of coating: closed and open.

Closed. Closed-coated abrasives have no spaces between the abrasive grains. The grains cover the entire backing. Closed-coated abrasives cut rapidly because they have so much abrasive material. They tend to load (clog), however, when sanding some woods, especially softwoods. Softwoods, such as pine, contain a gummy substance called **pitch.** The pitch causes sanding dust to stick to and load the abrasives. Closed-coated abrasives also load quickly when sanding a painted or varnished surface.

Open. On open-coated abrasives only 50 to 75% of the backing is covered with abrasives. This leaves small spaces between the grains. Because of these spaces, the abrasives do not load as quickly. This allows the abrasives to cut longer on gummy surfaces. Although they cut longer, they do not cut as fast as closed-coated abrasives. See Fig. 17-9.

Some abrasives (usually silicon carbide) use a special chemical, **stearate,** to reduce loading.

Fig. 17-9. Notice the difference in spacing between the abrasive grains. Do you know which type would work better on gummy surfaces?

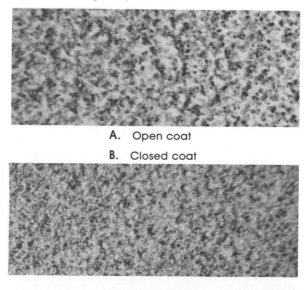

A. Open coat

B. Closed coat

Fig. 17-10. Grit size, weight of backing, and the type of coating are printed on the back of coated abrasives. Can you identify the numbers shown above?

Stearate is a white, slippery material. It helps keep gummy substances from sticking to the abrasives. Stearated abrasives are used mostly for sanding softwoods and wood finishes.

Sizes

Coated abrasives come in many sizes. The most common size is the 9 × 11 inch sheet. This sheet can be cut into smaller sizes to fit sanding blocks and portable sanders. Special abrasive belts, disks, and drums are also available for sanding machines.

New Terms

1. aluminum oxide
2. aught system
3. backing
4. bond
5. closed coat
6. coated abrasives
7. emery
8. flint
9. garnet
10. grit size
11. natural abrasives
12. open coat
13. pitch
14. silicone carbide
15. stearate
16. synthetic abrasives

Study Questions

1. What three basic parts make up a sheet of coated abrasive?
2. What are the two groups into which abrasives are divided?
3. What two natural abrasives are used for woodworking?
4. What abrasive material is used to sand finishes?
5. What is the difference in mesh between a screen that produces a coarse abrasive and one that produces a fine abrasive?
6. What two materials are used for backings?
7. What kind of adhesive is used to make waterproof bonds?
8. Compare closed- and open-coated abrasives. What is the difference in amount of abrasive material?
9. Why would you use an open-coated, rather than a closed-coated, abrasive?
10. What is the standard size of a sheet of coated abrasive?

Sanding is a necessary step in preparing any project for finishing. It removes imperfections in the wood and makes the surface smooth. Without careful sanding, the smallest defects and scratches stand out in the finish. Rough surfaces also absorb finishes unevenly, causing blotchy, spotted finishes. See Fig. 18-1.

Although it is necessary, most woodworkers would agree that sanding is a tiring, time-consuming process. In many finishing schedules it must be repeated several times. The development of power sanding equipment has eliminated much of the time and work. Some sanding, however, should still be done by hand. This chapter explains hand sanding techniques. Chapter 44 explains the use of power sanders.

Selecting Abrasives

All sanding is done with coated abrasives (commonly called "sandpaper" or "abrasive paper"). The first step in getting ready to sand is to select the right abrasive. The two most important considerations are the kind of abrasive and the grit size.

Garnet and aluminum oxide are the best abrasives for wood in most cases. Begin with a coarse or medium grit. Use progressively finer grit sizes as the surface becomes smoother. Generally, for the **rough** (first) sanding, use number 80 (1/0) grit for hardwood, and number 100 (2/0) for softwood. For the **intermediate** (second) sanding, use number 120 (3/0) grit for hardwood and number 150 (4/0) for softwood. For the **final** (last) sanding, use number 180 (5/0) grit for hardwood and number 220 (6/0) for softwoods. The chart on page 150 will help you select the correct abrasive.

Fig. 18-1. Sanding can make the difference between an attractive project and one that looks poorly made.

Fig. 18-2. Using a magnifying glass, you can see the scratches caused by sanding.

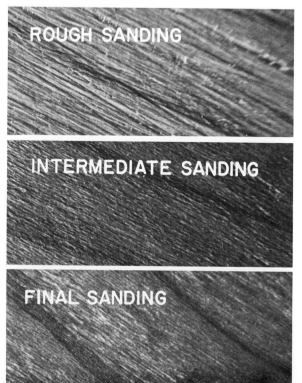

ROUGH SANDING

INTERMEDIATE SANDING

FINAL SANDING

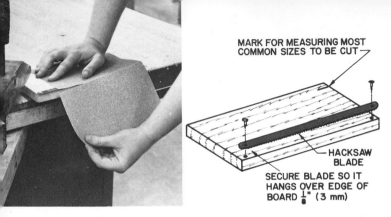

Fig. 18-3. You can use a worn-out hacksaw blade to cut abrasive sheets into smaller pieces.

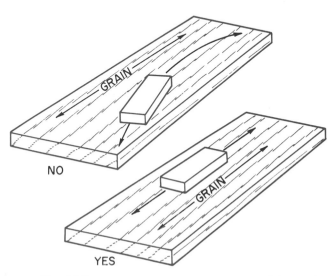

Fig. 18-4. "Break in" abrasive papers by rubbing them abrasive-side-up on the edge of a bench. A flexible paper will last longer and do a better job in hard-to-reach places.

Fig. 18-5. Always sand in the direction of the grain. Begin with coarse and use progressively finer abrasives, moving up one grit size at a time.

Remember, these grit sizes are suggestions for general use. The best grit size for rough sanding depends on the wood, the imperfections, and your reason for sanding. For example, if the surface is free of defects and properly planed and scraped, begin with intermediate sanding. When you are unsure of the proper grit, choose the finest one. An abrasive that is too coarse will scratch the surface needlessly.

For information on appropriate coatings, bonds, and backings, see chapter 17.

Preparing Abrasive Sheets

Standard (9 × 11 inches) sheets of coated abrasives are too large to work with. Divide them into workable pieces. The best size will depend on the type of surface or the size of your sanding block. Divide the sheets by folding and tearing them along a straightedge. Tear the sheets carefully so you do not waste abrasives. A handy jig for tearing sheets of abrasives is shown in Fig. 18-3.

You can make sanding easier and more effective by **breaking in** the abrasive before you begin. See Fig. 18-4. Hold the sheet at two diagonal corners, **abrasive side up.** Pull it back and forth over the edge of a table or bench. Hold the other two corners and again pull the sheet back and forth over the edge. This will make the abrasive sheet more flexible. The abrasive grains will be less likely to peel and chip from the backing. Also, the sheet will be more effective in sanding corners and irregular shapes.

Sanding Techniques

Do not begin sanding until the surface is planed and scraped as smooth as possible. Sand with straight, back-and-forth strokes, using firm, moderate pressure. Whenever possible, sand WITH the grain. Sanding across the grain causes scratches that are very hard to remove. Inspect the surface frequently as you work.

Rough sand until all imperfections (torn grain, dents, and machine marks) are removed.

When the surface is smooth, and only the scratches from the abrasives remain, switch to an intermediate abrasive. Sand with progressively finer abrasives until you obtain the desired smoothness.

After the final sanding, sand the corners with a fine abrasive. Sand lightly, barely "breaking" the corners so they are not sharp. A slightly rounded corner does not chip as easily and allows the finish to build up. This is important because finishes tend to pull back from a sharp edge. After sanding the corners, clean the surface as described later in this chapter.

Sanding Flat Surfaces. Use a sanding block to sand flat surfaces. You can purchase sanding blocks in a variety of sizes and shapes. See Fig. 18-6. However, many woodworkers make their own. A common size (2½ × 4 inches) fits a quarter sheet of the standard size abrasive. See Fig. 18-7. For final sanding the block should have a piece of hard felt, rubber, or cork bonded to the bottom. This provides a slight cushion between the wood block and your work, preventing scratches.

Be especially careful when sanding woods with a hard summer growth and soft spring growth. The soft grain line will sand away faster than the hard grain. Running your fingers over the surface, you will feel the "hills and valleys." This is a common problem with oak, pine, and softwood plywoods. Do not use cushioned sanding blocks for these woods.

When you sand edge grain, be sure to hold the sanding block flat. Edges are usually not very wide, making it easy to tip the block. Sanding with the block tipped at an angle will round the edges. See Fig. 18-8.

To sand end grain, clamp a scrap piece to one edge. Make it flush with the end. Sand in one direction only, toward the scrap piece. The scrap piece will prevent the edge grain from splintering. See Fig. 18-9. On wide boards you can avoid splintering by sanding from each edge toward the center. Keeping the sanding block flat can be difficult on narrow surfaces. Be careful not to tip the block and round the edges.

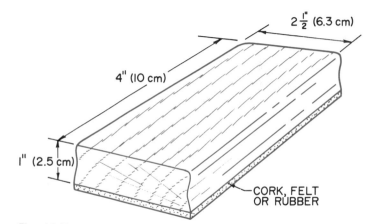

Fig. 18-7. You can make a sanding block like the one above.

CORK, FELT OR RUBBER

4" (10 cm)
2 ½" (6.3 cm)
1" (2.5 cm)

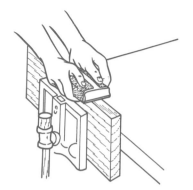

Fig. 18-8. When sanding an edge, be sure to hold the block flat and square. Tilting the block will round the edges.

Fig. 18-6. This manufactured sanding block is made out of hard rubber.

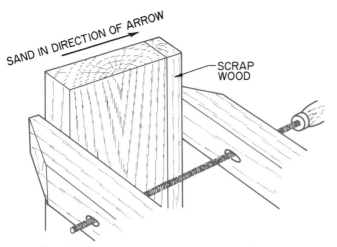

Fig. 18-9. When sanding end grain, clamp a scrap piece flush with one end and sand toward the scrap piece. This will prevent the edge from splintering.

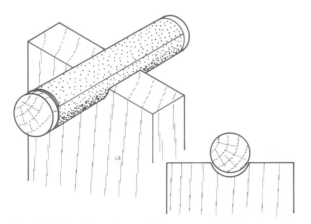

Fig. 18-10. Dowels and other round objects make good sanding blocks for curved surfaces.

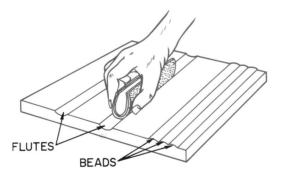

Fig. 18-11. To sand small shapes, such as flutes and beads, roll the abrasive paper to fit the shape.

Sanding Plywood. Special attention is needed to sand plywood surfaces. Be careful not to sand through the veneer. This would expose the glue line, which would be visible through the finish. Checking the edges will give you an estimate of how much you can sand. With most plywood only a final sanding is needed.

Sanding Curved Surfaces. Most curved pieces can be sanded by folding or shaping the abrasive to fit the piece. You can also use objects that match the curve of the surface as sanding blocks. If necessary, you can even cut a special sanding block.

When round stock is long enough, sand with the grain. If you must sand across the grain, use a fine abrasive, 280 (8/0), or finer. Slowly rotate the stock while you sand.

To sand small portions of round stock, tear the abrasive into thin strips. Use the strips as you would a shoeshine cloth, sanding back and forth. A wood lathe makes a good vise for stock that is being sanded. Remember to disconnect the power if you use the lathe.

Sand concave shapes by folding an abrasive around an object that matches the curve of the stock. Such objects as dowels, pencils, cans, and pieces of rubber hose, are a few possibilities. See Fig. 18-10. Sand convex shapes by hand or with a sanding block.

Before sanding beads and flutes, break in the abrasive sheet as described earlier in this chapter. Then fold the abrasive sheet in half. With the grit side out, roll the abrasive into the shape of the flute or bead. See Fig. 18-11.

Sanding Small Parts. A very fine grit is needed to sand carvings and moldings. Use number 220 (6/0) for hardwood and number 280 (8/0) for softwood. Break in the abrasive as described earlier. Then crush it in your hand, rubbing the grit together to dull the edges. Hold the paper loosely and sand lightly. Be careful not to sand away any of the detail on the carving or molding.

To sand small, flat pieces, attach the abrasive sheet to a piece of flat stock. Then clamp the stock to a flat surface, such as a benchtop.

Move the small piece back and forth over the surface. Be sure to move the piece in the direction of the grain. See Fig. 18-12.

To sand confined areas or irregular shapes without a block, make a pad of abrasives. Fold three or four quarter sheets in half, with the abrasive side out. See Fig. 18-13. Stack them together like the pages of a book. This will make a cushion between your hand and the surface. When the outside abrasive wears out, move it to the inside. Repeat this process when the next sheet wears out.

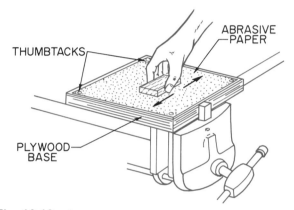

Fig. 18-12. To sand a small, flat piece, attach the abrasive sheet to a flat surface. Then move the piece over the surface.

Fig. 18-13. To sand without a block, make a pad by folding three or four quarter sheets in half and stacking them together.

Raising the Grain

When wood becomes wet, the wood fibers absorb the moisture and swell up. As the fibers swell, they rise above the surface as small, hair-like projections. If this happens after the finish has been applied, it causes a rough, blotchy finish. Many wood finishers guard against this by purposely wetting the wood surface. They can then sand away the wood fibers before finishing. This method of ensuring a smooth, even surface is called raising the grain. Whenever a water stain is to be used, the grain **must** be raised first. See Fig. 18-14. In all other cases, it is not necessary, but recommended.

Raise the grain with hot water and a sponge. Apply just enough water to wet the surface. The grain is usually raised after the project is assembled and the final sanding completed. Sometimes it is done just before the final sanding. This second method is faster because it eliminates one sanding operation. It increases the possibility of removing too much wood, however. To guarantee the best possible finish, final sand, raise the grain, and then repeat the final sanding.

Final Cleanup

After you finish sanding, remove all dust from the surface. Failure to do this can cause a

Fig. 18-14. Raising the grain causes loose wood fibers to raise above the wood surface. They can then be sanded off.

Fig. 18-15. All sanding dust must be removed, or it will cause a gritty, uneven finish.

rough, unattractive finish. Use a clean, dry rag or a vacuum cleaner to remove the dust. When the surface is clean, wipe it with a tack rag.

A **tack rag** is a cloth rag moistened with varnish and turpentine. You can purchase tack rags at paint stores or make your own. To make one, mix 1 part varnish to 4 parts turpentine. Dip a clean cloth (cheesecloth or an old cotton handkerchief) into the mixture. Then wring out the cloth. It should be just moist enough to pick up dust particles without wetting the surface.

Store the tack rag in a clean, tightly sealed jar. If you keep the rag moist, it will last a long time.

Hand Sanding Safety

- Wear approved eye protection. This is especially important if you wear contact lenses. Sanding produces a great amount of dust, which can cause severe eye irritation.
- Wear a filter mask when sanding for a long time. Large amounts of dust can be harmful to your lungs.
- If you use compressed air to dust your project, use an OSHA-approved duster gun at a low pressure. Be extremely careful not to blow dust into your eyes or the eyes of others.
- Use a very light touch when checking a surface with your hand. Be careful of wood splinters. If you get a splinter, tell your teacher immediately.

New Terms

1. breaking in abrasives
2. final sanding
3. intermediate sanding
4. raising the grain
5. rough sanding
6. sanding block
7. tack rag

Study Questions

1. Give two reasons for sanding a wood surface.
2. What are the two most important considerations in selecting the right abrasive?
3. Name the two best abrasives for sanding wood.
4. List the three general steps in a sanding operation. What grit size might you expect to use for each of the three steps?
5. If you are not sure which of two grit sizes to use, should you use the finer or coarser grit?
6. Why is it important to tear the abrasive sheets carefully?
7. Describe the procedure for breaking in a sheet of abrasive. Why should you break in an abrasive sheet?
8. Why should you sand WITH the grain whenever possible?
9. What tool is necessary for sanding flat surfaces?
10. Why must you take special care when sanding wood with hard summer growth and soft spring growth?
11. Describe two methods that prevent splintering when sanding end grain.
12. How can you prevent sanding through the face veneer of plywood?
13. When might a pencil be used as a sanding block?
14. With one exception, you always move the abrasive over the surface to be sanded. When would you move the surface over the abrasive?
15. When is the grain usually raised?
16. You must raise the grain when you use what kind of stain?

Removing Defects from Wood

No finish can be attractive unless the surface is smooth and free of defects. Experienced woodworkers spend a great deal of time removing surface imperfections. With a sharp eye, they try to spot tiny flaws that will show up clearly through the finish. Then they patiently do what is needed to remove these imperfections.

Locating Surface Defects

After the rough and intermediate sanding, carefully inspect the wood surface, looking for defects. Use a floodlight if you have one. See Fig. 19-1. Some defects are difficult to find, even with the best lighting. Unfortunately, the same defects will be easy to see after the finish is applied. If you plan to raise the grain (see page 157), apply water to the surface. This makes defects, such as glue spots, scratches,

dents, and torn grain, show up better. If you are not raising the grain, moisten the surface with V M & P naphtha or alcohol. These liquids will also help you see surface defects. Check and recheck the surface to be sure you have located all the defects.

Removing Glue Spots

You must remove any glue that has dried on the wood surface. Finishes and stains cannot penetrate through the dried glue. If not removed, glue spots will show up as light spots in the finish. See Fig. 19-2. Use a chisel or hand scraper to remove the glue spots. Take special care not to remove the wood. After all the glue is removed, carefully sand with a fine abrasive, (5/0), 180 grit, or (6/0), 220 grit.

Fig. 19-1. Many defects are difficult to find when you are preparing to finish your project. The same defects will be clearly visible after the finish has been applied.

Fig. 19-2. Finishes and stains will not penetrate through glue spots. Be careful not to use excess glue, and remove all spots.

Raising Dents

The easiest way to fix dents is to raise them and sand them flush with the surface. You can use this method if the wood fibers have not been torn. If the fibers have been torn, they must be filled instead. Filling is explained later in this chapter.

To raise small dents, use your finger to place a drop of water on the dent. See Fig. 19-3. Allow it to dry overnight. This should cause the wood cells to swell above the surface. If it does not, apply another drop of water and let it dry. Depending on the size of the dent, this could take up to two or three days.

Fig. 19-3. Small dents can usually be raised by applying a drop of water. After the water dries, sand the wood flush.

Fig. 19-4. Large dents can be raised by steaming them with water and a hot soldering iron.

Using steam is the best and fastest way to raise large dents. Place a damp rag on the dent and heat it. Use an electric soldering copper, a flat iron, or an electric, wood-burning pen. See Fig. 19-4. If the dent does not raise above the surface, pierce it with a fine needle or pin. This allows deeper and faster penetration of the steam. You should pierce dents only if the dent is deep, and steaming has failed. The pierced holes can take extra stain, causing an uneven finish.

Whether you use water or steam, be sure the dent is raised slightly above the surface. The dent will shrink as it dries. It must be above the surface before you begin sanding. Also be sure the dent is completely dry before you sand. If it is not, the fibers will shrink further, leaving a low area on the surface.

Filling Holes

You can fill holes and imperfections at various stages of the building process. The material you use will usually determine when the filling should be done. A few of the more common filling materials are plastic wood, putty, and burn-in sticks. See Fig. 19-5.

Fig. 19-5. A variety of materials are available for filling holes.

Plastic Wood. Several colors of plastic wood are available. Select the color closest to the color of the finish. Plastic wood does not accept stain, so it is important that it match the project's final color. Use a natural color if the surface is to be painted.

Before finishing, build the material up above the surface. Then let it dry completely and sand it flush with the surface. If the defect is large, use several applications. Allow the material to dry between applications. This will prevent shrinking, which causes a low area after sanding. Plastic wood dries quickly. You should apply it rapidly and keep the can covered as much as possible.

Burn-in Sticks. Probably the most permanent method of repairing holes is to use burn-in sticks. The three kinds of sticks are shellac, lacquer, and non-lifting. They are available in about 60 colors. These colors can be mixed to match the finish material exactly. You can apply burn-in sticks to raw wood, between finish coats, and even over the final coat. They are the best method of repair. However, burn-in sticks require special tools and more skill than other methods. Use the following procedure to apply burn-in sticks to unfinished wood.

Fig. 19-7. The burn-in knife is easiest to clean when it is warm. Wipe the blade with a piece of cloth or fine steel wool.

1. Select or mix a color to match the chosen finish. You can use a clear color for small defects.
2. Melt the stick onto the previously heated burn-in knife blade, as shown in Fig. 19-6. If you do not have a burn-in knife, you can use a heated putty knife. If the stick starts to boil, it is too hot. Melt enough of it on the end of the blade so that it drops into the defect.
3. Use a wet finger to press the stick into the defect while the stick is still warm. Build the melted material slightly above the surface.
4. Sand the burn-in stick flush with the surface. Use a very fine abrasive, (8/0), 280 grit. If the surface is flat, mount the abrasive on a sanding block.
5. Clean the knife, let it cool, and store it properly. See Fig. 19-7.

To apply burn-in sticks between coats of finish, follow the procedure above. However, sanding should be done with a special liquid abrasive. This abrasive will cut the burn-in stick but not the finish coat. See Fig. 19-8. After sanding the burn-in material smooth, apply additional finish coats as needed. Restore luster by rubbing and polishing as described in chapter 30.

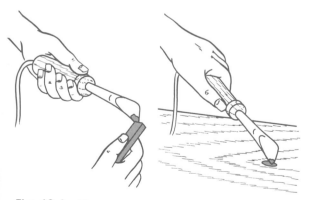

Fig. 19-6. The most permanent way to fill a hole is with a burn-in knife and burn-in stick. You can also use a putty knife heated on an alcohol burner to apply the stick.

Wood Putty. Cracks, knotholes, nail holes, and other small imperfections can be repaired with wood putty. However, wood putty should

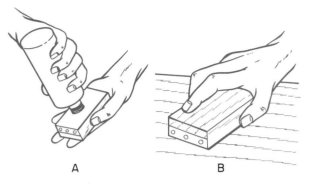

Fig. 19-8. To apply burn-in sticks over coats of finish, you must use liquid abrasives. Apply the liquid abrasive to a felt block (A) and rub it down to a smooth, level surface (B).

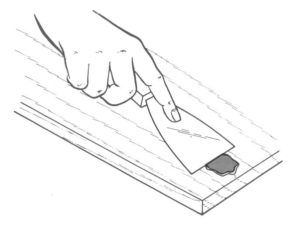

Fig. 19-9. Use a putty knife to apply wood putty. Build the putty slightly above the surface so that it can be sanded smooth.

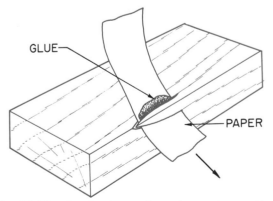

Fig. 19-10. Small splits and cracks can be repaired with glue. Use a piece of paper, as shown above, to work the glue into the crack. Then secure the defect with masking tape until the glue dries.

be used only on bare wood that is to be covered with paint or enamel.

Pack the putty into the defect with a putty knife. See Fig. 19-9. Build it slightly above the wood surface. Let it dry thoroughly (read the label directions). Then sand it flush with the same grit used to final sand.

New Terms

1. burn-in stick
2. plastic wood
3. wood putty

Study Questions

1. If you intend to raise the grain, what can you do to make surface defects show up more clearly?
2. Why is it important to remove even the smallest glue spot from the wood surface?
3. How are most glue spots removed?
4. How would you fix a dent with torn wood fibers?
5. What is the fastest method for fixing large dents? Briefly describe this procedure.
6. Two conditions should exist before you pierce dents. Name them.
7. Why must dents be dry before you sand them?
8. List three materials used to fill holes in wood surfaces.
9. Why should you keep plastic wood containers covered as much as possible?
10. What method of filling holes is the most permanent?
11. Why is a special liquid abrasive needed when applying burn-in stick between coats of finish?
12. You can use wood putty with only one kind of finish and one kind of surface. Explain.

WOOD
FINISHING

Chapter 20

Introduction to Finishing

The last step in building your project is to apply a finish. Finishes are necessary to protect the wood and make it as attractive as possible. Finishing is just as important as design and construction. A poor finishing job can ruin an otherwise well-made project. See Fig. 20-1.

Surface Preparation

The key to a good finish is a properly prepared surface. How much preparation you must do depends on two factors. It depends on the condition of the wood and how careful you were during construction.

All surfaces should be perfectly smooth and clean. A well-prepared surface will absorb 20-30% less finish, saving you time and money. A well-prepared project will finish nicer and keep its attractive appearance longer. The basic steps in preparing a surface for finishing are as follows.

- Rough and intermediate sanding
- Removing surface defects
- Raising the grain
- Final sanding and clean up

If you have not yet completed these steps, see section IV.

How to Select Finishes

There is no perfect finish. They all have advantages and disadvantages. It is up to you to decide which is best for your project. Answering the questions below will help you make that decision.

- How much protection will my project need?
- What sort of appearance do I want my project to have?
- How much time, skill, and experience is needed to apply the finish?

Protection. Wood must be protected from water, dust, wear, temperature changes, and sunlight. How and where you use your project will determine what kind of finish it needs. For example, tabletops and desk tops must be protected against bumps and spills. They need tough, durable, water-resistant finishes, such as varnish or lacquer. Picture frames that hang on walls, however, do not require much protection. In finishing a picture frame you would be more concerned with appearance.

Decide what kind of protection your project should have. Then select the finish that provides that protection and is also attractive.

Fig. 20-1. A fine finishing job will draw attention to good design and quality construction. The plans for this project are given in section IX.

Finish (Solvent)	Protection	Appearance	Application	Summary
Lacquer, Nitrocellulose (lacquer thinner)	Tough, durable Resists — water, alcohol, acid, and heat Does not resist — extreme temperature changes and fingernail polish	CLEAR — deep, rich, darkens less than other clear finishes Various lusters Slight yellowing with age	**Must be sprayed** — dries quickly **Not compatible** with many stains, fillers, and other materials — read labels	Experience and equipment needed for spraying
Brushing Lacquer (lacquer thinner)	Same as above	Same as above	**Brushed** — also dries quickly Must be brushed quickly and skillfully	Has all the advantages of lacquer and can be brushed on Brushing requires skill because of fast drying.
Varnish, natural (turpentine or mineral spirits)	Very tough **Strong resistance** to — water, alcohol, temperature changes, and heat, impact, and chemicals Qualities vary according to oil-resin ratios (see chapter 26)	CLEAR — warm, rich, and beautiful; slight amber color Various lusters	Sprayed or brushed **Extremely slow drying** — (12-48 hours) difficult to keep clean until dry	Being replaced by synthetic varnishes because of its slow drying time
Polyurethane Varnish (turpentine or mineral spirits)	Same as above plus more durable	CLEAR — more transparent than natural varnish Various lusters	Sprayed or brushed easily Dries in about 4 hours **Not compatible** with many stains and fillers — read labels	Good all-purpose finish — Does not add the amber color of natural varnish, shellac, and lacquer
Shellac (denatured alcohol)	Hard, tough Does not resist — water, alcohol Not durable	CLEAR — beautiful, mellow finish Polished to different lusters White used for light woods Orange used for dark woods	Sprayed or brushed — Easy to apply — dries quickly Must be thinned	Beautiful, hard, easy-to-apply finish for pieces that need not withstand wear and will not be subject to alcohol or water
Oil, Watco, Sealacell, etc. (turpentine or mineral spirits)	Durable Resists — water, temperature changes, wear, alcohol, and grease stains	CLEAR — warm, natural No build up, depth, or body, as with shellac, lacquer, and varnish	Rubbed on with cloth or brushed Easiest finish to apply Dries quickly Must be renewed from time-to-time	Easy to apply, dries quickly Gives clear, natural, no build-up finish
Paint (turpentine, water and detergent)	Tough, durable, water-resistant Qualities vary according to mixtures	OPAQUE — hides surface entirely Wide range of colors available Various lusters	Sprayed, brushed, rolled Requires primer coat and sanding between coats Dries quickly	Makes unattractive wood attractive — variety of colors and lusters
Enamel (turpentine)	Slightly tougher and more durable than paint	OPAQUE — much like paint — although tougher and glossier	Same as above	More protection than paint Also glossier and more expensive
Varnish Stains (turpentine)	Little protection Not durable	SEMI-TRANSPARENT — Various colors available	Sprayed or brushed Stains and finishes in one operation	Quick, easy finishes that lack quality

Fig. 20-2. Finishes at a Glance

Appearance. You can create almost any appearance you want for your project. You can use clear finishes to highlight the grain. You can also use clear finishes to bring out the wood's rich beauty. If the wood is unattractive, you can cover it with paint or enamel.

You can make wood lighter or darker with stains and bleaches. You can choose shiny, lusterous finishes, such as varnish. Or, you can choose more natural finishes, such as the penetrating oils. You can also choose from a wide variety of special effects, polishes, and waxes. These materials and methods give your project the desired style and character. The possibilities are limited only by your skill and imagination.

Application. Some finishes are applied quickly and simply. Others are more difficult and take more time to apply. Equipment, drying time, and the number of coats, all vary from finish to finish.

Some finishes, such as penetrating oils, are simply wiped onto the surface with a cloth. Others, like lacquer, require spray equipment. Until you are an experienced finisher, application is an important consideration in selecting a finish. For your first project, choose a finish that is easy to apply.

Finishing Materials

All finishing materials either protect the wood, beautify it, or both. Final finishes (often called top coats) do both. Most of the other finishing supplies add to the appearance of the wood. Materials such as thinners and sealers help with the application process.

Clear Finishes. Natural-looking finishes are produced with clear, transparent top coats. Clear finishes cover and protect wood without hiding it. They bring out and enhance the natural color and grain pattern of wood. See Fig. 20-3.

Shellac produces a beautiful finish that is hard and tough. It goes on easily with a brush and dries quickly. An important disadvantage is that shellac does not protect wood from water or alcohol.

Fig. 20-3. This clear finish highlights the grain pattern, adding to the natural beauty of the wood.

Varnish produces beautiful finishes that resist water and alcohol. Varnish is tougher than shellac and lacquer. It also withstands contractions and expansions of wood better than shellac and lacquer do. Ordinary varnish dries slowly, however. Newer, synthetic varnishes, such as polyurethane, dry much faster. They also have all the advantages of ordinary varnishes.

Lacquer resists heat, alcohol, and water. It is tougher and more durable than shellac. It also produces deep, rich finishes. Because it dries quickly, it should be applied with spray equipment. Special brushing lacquers can be applied with a brush.

Penetrating oil finishes are easily applied and maintained. The oils soak into the wood. There they form a strong, durable, natural-looking finish that resists wear and moisture.

Opaque Finishes. Unattractive woods often need to be covered. This can be done with opaque finishes. Opaque finishes are those that you cannot see through. They hide the wood completely. The most common ones are **paint** and **enamel**. The opaque finishes come in a wide variety of colors. See Fig. 20-4.

Other Finishing Supplies. Many finishing materials besides top coats are used to create the desired appearance. You may use one or several of these materials. It will depend on the wood and the appearance you want.

Fig. 20-4. An opaque finish, such as paint, covers unattractive woods, making projects more attractive.

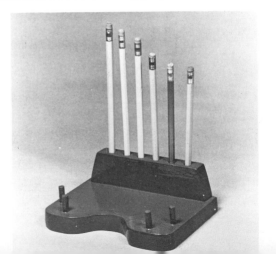

Stains are used to add color to wood without covering the natural grain. See Fig. 20-5. They are applied before the final finish.

Bleaches are used to lighten the color of wood. They are also used to remove sap stains and other blemishes on wood surfaces.

Wood fillers are used to fill wood pores. This makes the wood surface smooth. Fillers are used mostly to fill wood with large pores, such as mahogany, walnut, and oak.

Waxes have two uses in finishing wood. They are used primarily to protect and add luster to the top coat. Some waxes can also be used without top coats. These paste waxes provide natural, mellow finishes.

Polishes are also rubbed over a top coat to beautify and protect it. They are used to produce the brightest, shiniest finishes.

Glazes are used with special finishing techniques to create an antique look. They are easily applied either before or after the first top coat.

Sealers are solutions used to build barriers between finishing materials. They are also used to seal wood pores.

Wash coats are usually sealers that have been thinned. They are used primarily between stains and fillers to prevent bleeding. They also seal the wood pores.

Thinners include materials such as turpentine, naphtha, mineral spirits, and other solvents.

Fig. 20-5. These before-and-after pictures show how stains highlight the color and grain pattern.

Thinners are used for cleanup and for thinning finishes. Each finish has its own thinner.

Developing a Finishing Schedule

Before you finish your project, you should make a finishing schedule. To do this, list all the finish materials and techniques you intend to use. Then put them in the proper order for finishing. The resulting schedule will be your plan while you finish your project.

Fig. 20-6 shows three complete finishing schedules for the most common finishes. Use one of these schedules to develop your own schedule. You may, or may not, do each step in these schedules. For example, two of the schedules contain staining. If you do not want to stain, skip it and go to the next step.

Fig. 20-6. These are complete finishing schedules for the most common types of finishes. You probably will not do all of the steps listed. Skip each undesired step and go to the next one meeting your needs.

Clear, Non-penetrating Finishes (Shellac, varnish, lacquer)	Clear, Penetrating Oil Finishes (Watco, Sealacell, etc.)	Opaque Finishes (Paint, enamel)
1. Prepare the surface	1. Prepare the surface	1. Prepare the surface
2. Physically distress (antique look)	2. Stain (colors wood)	2. Primer
3. Bleach (lightens color)	3. Fill (smooths open-grain wood)	3. First coat of paint or enamel
4. Stain (colors wood)	4. First coat of penetrating finish	4. Surface distress (antique look)
5. Fill (smooths open-grain wood)	5. Additional coats of penetrating finish	5. Additional coats as needed
6. Glaze (antique look)		6. Glaze (antique look)
7. First top coat (shellac, varnish, or lacquer)	6. Wax or polish (to shine)	7. Varnish (for additional protection)
8. Surface distress (antique look)		
9. Additional top coats		
10. Rub and polish (to smooth and shine)		

After you write out your schedule, use it to finish a sample panel. Do each step by carefully following the application procedure in the appropriate chapter. Use the same wood for your sample that you used for your project. Be certain to sand the sample thoroughly.

Finish your sample the same way you plan to finish your project. If it does not suit you, change your finishing schedule. Then make another sample. Sample panels do take time and effort. However, they are the best way to get the finish you want.

Finishing Safety

Finishing safety can be divided into three main areas. Those areas are personal safety, fire safety, and finishing room safety. Before working in the finishing area, learn the safety rules. Once you know the rules, use them.

Personal Safety. Personal safety with finishes means protecting the face, eyes, hands, and body.

- Before using finishing materials, carefully read each label. Follow the directions and warnings on the label. See Fig. 20-7.
- Many solvents for finishing materials are toxic (poisonous). Handle them carefully. Avoid body contact as much as possible.

Fig. 20-7. Carefully read the labels on finishing supplies before using the products. The labels provide information on safety and application.

Fig. 20-8. This finisher is properly dressed for applying bleach and paint and varnish remover.

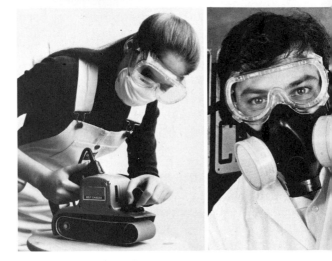

Fig. 20-9. Inhaling toxic materials can be dangerous. Use a filter mask or respirator to prevent this.

- Wear approved eye protection at all times. Be especially careful if you wear contact lenses. Some solvents, such as lacquer thinner, can dissolve soft contact lenses. You should remove soft lenses before working with finishing materials.
- Protect your body from toxic chemicals and acids. Materials such as bleach and varnish remover contain these dangerous materials. Wear face shields, rubber gloves, and rubber aprons. See Fig. 20-8.
- Know the location of the nearest washing facilities. If harmful materials get in your eyes or on your skin, you must clean the area immediately.
- Do not breathe the fumes or dust from toxic finishing materials. Work in a well-ventilated area. Keep materials in tightly covered containers. When necessary, wear a filter mask or respirator. See Fig. 20-9.

Fig. 20-10. Place used finishing rags in a covered container. This decreases the chances of fire.

Fire Safety. Fire safety includes being familiar with materials and practices necessary for the prevention of fire.

- Store flammable liquids in covered metal containers. Cover all containers tightly. As finishing materials evaporate, the fumes can create fire hazards. See Fig. 20-10.
- Know where the fire extinguishers are located. Know which type to use and how to use it. See page 48 for information on using the proper type of extinguisher.
- Fire doors should not be blocked in open positions. The purpose of the doors is to confine fires to the area.
- Store aerosol containers in a cool place.
- Never use an open flame in the finishing area.
- Never use tools that make sparks, such as grinders, close to the finishing area. Unless partitions are used, 20 feet (6 m) is the minimum distance for safety.

Finishing Area Safety. Finishing area safety includes the finishing room, spray booth, and equipment.

- Make sure exits are free of any obstruction.
- Keep the finishing area clean. Wipe up spills immediately to prevent slipping and

falling. Do your part by picking up all debris.
- Use the exhaust system in the finishing area to assure proper ventilation. Fumes from finishing materials will accumulate during application and while the project dries.
- Always use the spray booth when spraying a finish. When filters become dirty, install clean ones.

New Terms

1. clear finishes
2. finishing schedule
3. opaque finishes
4. sample panel

Study Questions

1. What is the last step in building a project?
2. Give the two reasons for finishing your project.
3. List three advantages to preparing your project properly for a finish.
4. Give the three major considerations in selecting the best finish for your project.
5. List five things that damage wood if the wood is not properly protected.
6. What is a common difference in finishes used for attractive woods, as compared to those used on unattractive woods?
7. Name one type of finish that is easy to apply. Name one that requires spray equipment.
8. What is an important disadvantage of shellac?
9. What is the advantage of synthetic varnishes as compared to the natural varnishes?
10. Stains and bleaches are primarily used to change what feature of wood?
11. Name three woods that usually receive an application of paste wood filler.
12. What should you make to help guide you through the finishing process?
13. Why is it important to protect your body when working with many finishing materials?

Chapter 21

Finishing Equipment

Equipment used to apply finishes can be simple or complex. Such finishes as penetrating oils can be applied with rags or brushes. Lacquer, however, is best applied with spray equipment. It is easy to apply a fine finish if you use the right equipment.

Brushes

Almost all finishing materials can be applied with brushes. Brushes come in a variety of shapes and sizes. If they are well cared for, they will last a long time.

A brush consists of **bristles** (hairs or filaments) attached to a wood or plastic handle. See Fig. 21-1. The bristles are attached to the handle with a metal **ferrule** (band). When dipped into a finish, the bristles pick up and retain some of it. The finish can then be spread on the project.

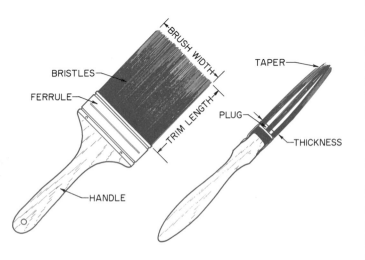

Fig. 21-1. Parts of a brush

Selecting Brushes

It is important to select the right brush for the job. Not all brushes work well with all finishes. The right brush makes the job easier and produces a smoother finish. Using the wrong brush could ruin the brush. When you select a brush, consider the brush's bristles, size, and shape.

Type of Bristles. The quality and use of a brush is largely determined by its bristles. The term "bristle" actually refers to the hair of certain types of hogs. However, the term is used loosely for all kinds of hair and fiber used in brushes.

Bristles hold the finish so that it can be spread on surfaces. The bristles of quality brushes are thicker at the heel than at the tip. This makes the tip of the brush more flexible. Flexibility reduces the number of brush marks left on a surface.

Quality brushes also have bristles with **flagged ends.** This means that the ends of the bristles are split into smaller hairs. Brushes with flagged ends pick up and hold more finishing material than other brushes. See Fig. 21-2. Bristles with flagged ends are also softer and leave fewer brush marks.

Many kinds of bristles are used in brushes. They can be divided into two groups: natural and synthetic.

Natural bristles are made from animal hair. Hog bristles and hair from the tails of skunks are examples. Brushes made with skunk hair are called **fitch** brushes. These are the best brushes for applying brushing lacquer and glazes. Brushes made with hog bristles work best for applying oil-based finishes. Examples

FINISHING MATERIAL

Fig. 21-2. Quality brushes have flagged ends. These ends allow the brush to hold more finish than other brushes do. Flagged ends also leave fewer brush marks.

PPG Industries

Fig. 21-3. Use the brush with the right shape for the job. Flat brushes are best suited for flat surfaces. Oval brushes are the best choice for irregular and curved surfaces.

of oil-based finishes are varnish and oil stains and fillers.

Natural brushes should not be used in water- and latex-based finishes. Natural bristles absorb the water in these finishes. They then become limp and shapeless.

Synthetic bristles are used mainly with water- and latex-based finishes. There are two types of synthetic bristles: nylon and polyester. Nylon bristles are designed for water-based finishes. These bristles are long lasting and produce smooth, even finishes. Polyester bristles are relatively new. They are durable and can be used for both oil- and latex-based finishes. They also work well with lacquer and shellac finishes.

Size of Brushes. Brushes are sized by the length, width, and thickness of the bristles. It is important to select the right size brush. The brush should not be too large or small for the project. A brush wider than the surface will drip finish over the edge. This wastes finish and makes a needless mess. Brushes too small for the job make more work for the finisher.

Shape of Brushes. Brushes come in many shapes. The most common are flat and oval. The flat brush is a general-purpose brush. See Fig. 21-3. The oval brush works well with irregular, curved surfaces. Turned legs and spindles are examples.

Using Brushes

A good brush needs no special preparation. Dip it into the finish gradually. Dip the brush about one-third the length of the bristles. Never dip a brush more than half its length.

After dipping the brush, tap it lightly on the side of the container. This prevents dripping. Do not let the finish drip back to the heel, near the ferrule. It will stay there and dry, making proper cleaning difficult.

Hold the brush handle almost perpendicular with the surface. Apply enough pressure to slightly bend the bristles. Start at the top of the project and work down. When the brush is full, start the stroke on dry wood. Then brush towards the wet area. See Fig. 21-4. Lift the brush gradually as the wet area is lapped. This prevents a thick edge at the end of a stroke.

When you apply finish to inside corners, start with a partially dry brush. Place the tip of the brush in the corner and brush out evenly. Never jab the brush into the corner.

Always brush parallel to edges and grooves on a project. Brushing against edges and grooves

Fig. 21-4. When the brush is full, start the stroke on a dry area. Then brush toward the wet area.

1. Remove excess finish

2. Pour solvent over brush

3. Work solvent through

4. Rinse in solvent

5. Wash in soapy water, then rinse

6. Comb

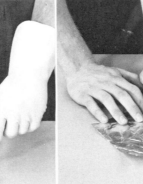
7. Wrap

8. Store properly

Fig. 21-5. Cleaning your brush properly takes a little effort. It also makes your brush last for a long time.

takes extra finish from the brush. This causes runs and sags.

When possible, complete an entire coat at one time. If this is impossible, stop at a corner or edge. Stopping in these places prevents a noticeable lap of new finish over old finish.

Cleaning Brushes

Brushes should be cleaned immediately after use. A properly cleaned and stored brush can be used many times. Brushes are often ruined because they are not properly cleaned and stored. Few wear out from use. To clean a brush, use the following procedure.

1. Wipe the brush on the inside rim of the finish container. This forces excess finish to drip into the container.

2. Rinse the brush by pouring solvent over the brush into a container. A **solvent** is a liquid in which a solid dissolves. See the chart in Fig. 21-6 for the correct solvent.
3. Dip the brush into the solvent. Work out the finish with your fingers. Always wear rubber gloves when you do this.
4. Rinse the brush with clean solvent until the brush is clean.
5. Wash the brush thoroughly in warm, soapy water. Rinse.
6. While the brush is still wet, it is a good idea to comb it. Doing this with a coarse comb straightens and cleans the bristles.
7. Store the brush in its original jacket, in a piece of paper, or in foil. This keeps the brush clean and in its proper shape.
8. Either hang the brush or lay it flat.

FINISHING MATERIAL	SOLVENT
Oil-base materials such as paint, varnish, stains, and paste wood fillers	Turpentine, mineral spirits, paint thinner, and benzine
Glazes	V M & P Naphtha
Shellac	Denatured alcohol
Lacquer	Lacquer thinner
Water-based and latex-based materials such as paint, stains, and varnish	Water and detergent (soap)

Fig. 21-6. Use the correct solvent for each finishing material.

Fig. 21-7. Spraying a project like this is much faster than brushing.

Spray Equipment

Furniture manufacturers usually apply finish with spray equipment. With spray equipment they can apply a smooth finish quickly. Spray finishing is especially useful on projects with large surfaces or many parts. Most lacquers and some stains and varnishes should be sprayed for best results.

A common spray setup includes air compressor, transformer, spray gun, hose, and spray booth. See Fig. 21-8. The **compressor** provides the compressed air needed to operate the spray gun. A motor-driven air pump compresses the air in a large tank. As the air is used, the pump maintains a steady pressure.

Small, portable compressors may not have holding tanks. They supply air directly to the spray gun. These compressors cannot produce high pressures.

Binks Manufacturing Company

Fig. 21-8. A common spraying setup includes air compressor, transformer and spray gun.

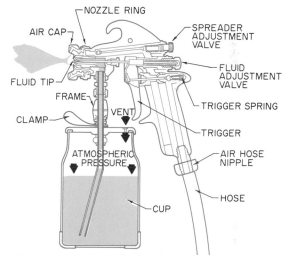

Fig. 21-9. In a suction-feed spray gun, atmospheric pressure pushes the finish from the cup to the fluid tip where it is sprayed on the project.

The **transformer** is located between the compressor and spray gun. It removes water, dirt, and oil from the air before the air enters the hose. The transformer also regulates the air pressure.

The **spray gun** attaches to the air hose from the transformer. A suction-feed spray gun can be used on most projects. The finish is placed in a quart, or smaller, cup. The cup is attached to the spray gun. When the trigger is squeezed, a stream of compressed air reduces the pressure at the fluid tip. See Fig. 21-9. This lets pressure in the cup push the finish up to the fluid tip. The compressed air then breaks the finish into small droplets or mist and carries the finish to the surface.

The **spray booth** is a special enclosed area for spraying finishes. It is well-ventilated to reduce potential fire and health hazards. It removes fumes and overspray (finish that does not stick) from the spray area. This prevents overspray from landing on and sticking to other surfaces.

Using Spray Equipment

Spraying a good finish requires clean and properly adjusted equipment. The project should also be clean and dust free. You can blow loose dust from the project with air from the spray gun. The best way of removing dust, however, is with a tack rag. Follow these steps for setting up and using the spray gun. Study the safety rules for spraying finishes in chapter 20 before you begin.

1. Mix the finish to the proper consistency (thickness or thinness). The correct mixture is usually given on the finish container. Brushing consistency is considered good spraying consistency. If thinning is needed, use the proper solvent. See the chart in Fig. 21-6.

2. Strain the finish into the cup. The strainer (filter) removes particles that could clog the gun. It also removes particles which could cause a rough finish.

3. Connect the air hose between the gun and the transformer. Set the transformer to the correct air pressure. For most applications this will be between 30 and 40 pounds.

4. Adjust the spray pattern with the **spreader adjustment valve.** The normal pattern is 8 inches *(200 mm)* wide. For a small project, reduce the width of the pattern. This is done by turning the spreader adjustment valve clockwise (to the right). Tape a piece of newspaper to a wall to test the spray pattern. See Fig. 21-10.

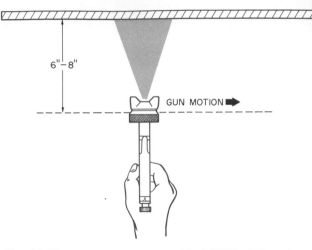

Fig. 21-10. Hold the spray gun 6 to 8 (150 to 200 mm) inches from the project.

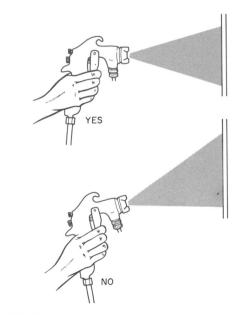

Fig. 21-11. Keep the spray gun at right angles to the surface. Tipping the gun up or down will produce an uneven finish.

5. Adjust the amount of material sprayed on the surface. There are two ways to control this. You control the speed of the gun moving over the surface. You can also change the amount of material sprayed from the gun.

    The amount of material sprayed is controlled by the **fluid adjustment screw.**

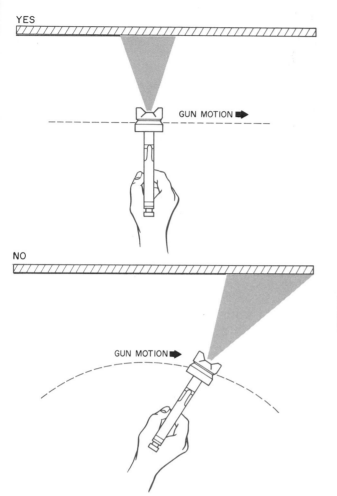

YES

NO

GUN MOTION ➡

GUN MOTION ➡

Fig. 21-12. Move the spray gun in a straight line, parallel to the surface. Moving the gun in an arc, as shown above, will produce an uneven finish.

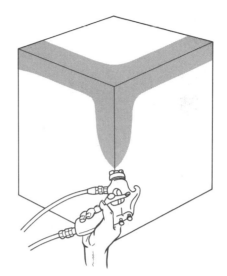

Fig. 21-13. Band the edges and corners before you spray the entire project. Aim the gun so that the sides of the corner receive equal amounts of finish.

Turn the screw clockwise to reduce the amount of material. Turn the screw counterclockwise (to the left) to increase the amount of material.

6. First spray the least visible (back and bottom) parts of the project. Spray the parts that are most visible (top and front) last. This reduces the chances of overspray causing a rough finish on the most visible areas.

7. Hold the gun 6 to 8 inches *(150-200 mm)* from the surface. It should be at a right angle to the surface. See Fig. 21-11. Begin spraying with the gun extended beyond the end of the project. Move the gun along the surface. The nozzle should be the same distance from the surface at all times. See Fig. 21-12. Release the trigger a few inches past the end of the surface.

8. Projects with sharp corners should be banded. **Banding** means making the first spray passes at the corners. See Fig. 21-13. Banding produces extra material buildup on the corners. Extra finish is needed because the corners are hit and marred frequently. Banding also prevents rubbing through the finish during the rubbing and polishing steps.

9. After banding, spray the remaining surface. Overlap each pass 50%. This ensures full coverage.

Follow the preceding steps for a smooth, even finish. If you have problems, check the charts in Figs. 21-14 and 21-15. These charts explain how to solve spray finishing problems.

If your spray pattern looks like:	It is usually caused by:	
	1) Dried material in the side port	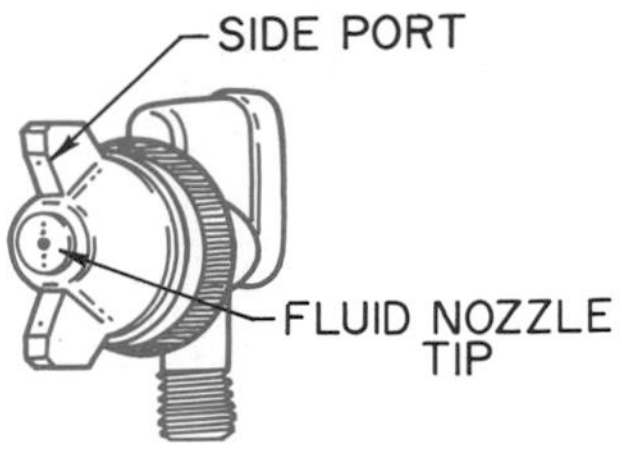 SIDE PORT
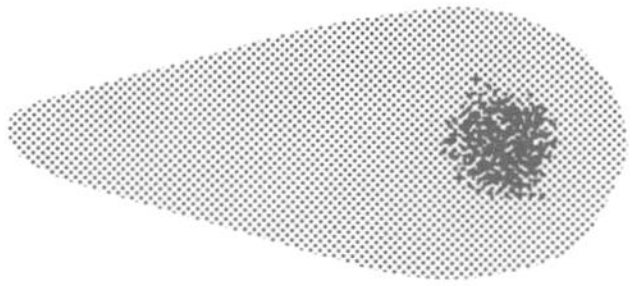	1) Dried material around outside of fluid nozzle tip 2) Loose air nozzle 3) Bent fluid nozzle or needle tip	FLUID NOZZLE TIP
	1) Atomizing air pressure too high 2) Trying for too wide of a spray pattern with thin material 3) Not enough finish available	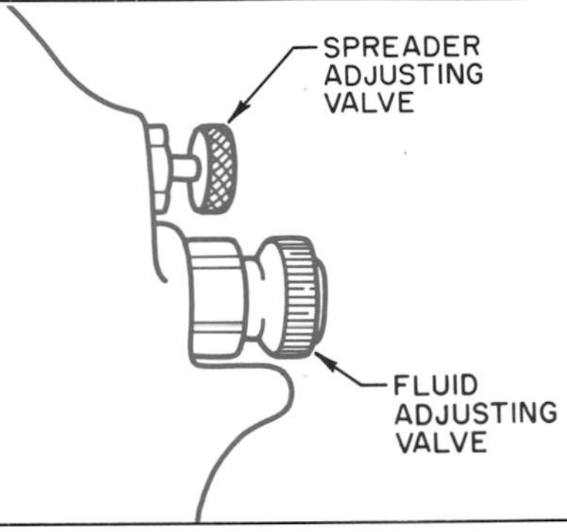 SPREADER ADJUSTING VALVE
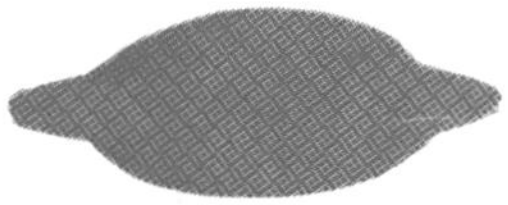	1) Atomizing air pressure not high enough 2) Too much finish going into the gun	FLUID ADJUSTING VALVE

Fig. 21-14. Faulty Spray Patterns and Their Causes

Fig. 21-15. Spraying Problems and Causes

Problem	Causes				
Orange Peel (finish resembles texture of orange)	Not enough or poor quality thinner	Spray gun too far from surface	Spray gun too close, causing film to ripple	Not enough air pressure, especially for synthetics	Too much air pressure, especially for lacquer
Runs and Sags	Finish piled on too heavily	Moving gun too slowly	Finish thinned out too much	Gun not held at right angle to surface	Gun not triggered at end of stroke
Streaks	Distorted spray pattern caused by dirty air cap or fluid tip	Gun not held at right angle to surface	Improper over-lapping		
Blushing (tendency of lacquer to dry with cloudy dis-coloration	Humid conditions				
Dry Finish	Not enough fluid mixed with air	Gun held too far from surface	Wrong air cap or fluid cap	Overspray falling on already sprayed surface	
Sputtering and Fluttering	Loose fluid needle packing nut	Finish too heavy for gun	Loose or damaged fluid tube	Air cap and fluid tip not tightened to spray gun	Clogged air vent in top of suction-feed fluid cup	Not enough material in cup or fluid container

Fig. 21-16. Clean finishing material from a spray gun as shown. Hold a clean cloth over the air cap and pull the trigger. This will force excess finish back into the cup.

Cleaning the Spray Gun

The spray gun must be cleaned immediately after each use. Finishing materials left in the gun will dry and then plug passages. Some finishes can ruin the gun this way. If the gun is cleaned immediately, it is a quick and easy job. The longer you wait, the more difficult the cleaning becomes. Keep the gun clean by following these steps.

1. Loosen the cup from the gun. Leave the fluid tube in the cup. Loosen the air cap. Hold a clean cloth over the air cap and pull the trigger. The compressed air will force the finishing material from the gun back into the cup. See Fig. 21-16.
2. Empty the cup and clean it with the proper solvent. See Fig. 21-6.
3. Pour a small amount (about 1 inch, 25 mm) of clean solvent in the cup. Tighten the air cap. Spray three or four short bursts of clean solvent.
4. Loosen the air cap. Hold a clean cloth over it. Pull the trigger to force the solvent back into the cup. See Fig. 21-16.
5. Dampen a clean rag with clean solvent and wipe the air cap, gun, and cup. Make sure no material is left in the small holes of the air cap. Make sure none is left around the fluid needle. You may need to clean these places with a small brush and clean solvent. If the small openings are

still clogged, use a toothpick or small piece of wood. **Never use metal.** These holes are accurately machined. The gun will not operate properly if the air cap holes are enlarged or damaged.

Aerosol Containers

Aerosol cans of finishing materials are commonly referred to as "spray paints." They provide an easy method for applying a finish. They require little cleaning, and they do a professional job.

Most finishes are available in aerosol containers. Some retail paint stores can fill aerosol containers with finishes. This would include any specially mixed colors of your choice.

Be careful when you select finishes in aerosol containers. They must work well with other materials used in the finishing process. For example, you cannot use a lacquer-based paint over an oil-based paint. Read and follow the instructions on the can.

Using Aerosol Containers

To use an aerosol container properly, you must understand how it works. The aerosol can contains about two-thirds finish and one-third propellant. The propellant is a gas that has been pressurized above the finish. When you press the spray head, the propellant forces the finish through the dip tube to the spray tip. See Fig. 21-17.

To work properly, the container should be at room temperature (70° F, 21° C). A cold can has a low level of pressure. With low pressure the finish does not spray properly. A can that gets too hot may burst. Follow these instructions when using aerosol finish.

1. Shake the can thoroughly. The agitation balls should move and rattle freely inside the can. Swirl the can to loosen finish settled on the bottom. Then shake the can up and down to mix the finish.
2. Hold the can 10-16 inches *(250-400 mm)* from the project while spraying. For

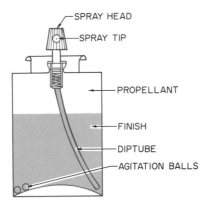

SPRAY HEAD
SPRAY TIP
PROPELLANT
FINISH
DIPTUBE
AGITATION BALLS

Fig. 21-17. Cross section of an aerosol can

more exact distances, follow directions on the container. Do not hold the can too close to the surface. Propellant may become trapped in the finish, causing small bubbles. Sags and runs are also more likely if you hold the can too close.

Do not hold the can too far from the work. The finish may dry before landing on the project. This causes a dry, rough finish.

3. Start spraying beyond the end of the project. Push down on the spray head and move across the project. Keep the spray head the same distance from the project. Release the spray head a short distance past the project. Light, back-and-forth strokes produce a better finish than does one heavy spraying.

Cleaning Aerosol Containers

The spray head should be cleaned after each use. Turn the can upside down and spray for a few seconds. When the spray comes out clear, the spray head is clean. Then wipe the spray head and container with a clean cloth. The cloth should be dampened with solvent.

An improperly cleaned spray head should be removed and soaked in lacquer thinner. Use a fine needle to clean the hole in the spray head. With a thin knife, clean the slot in the bottom of the spray head.

New Terms

1. aerosol container
2. banding
3. bristle
4. compressor
5. ferrule
6. fitch brush
7. fluid adjustment screw
8. solvent
9. spray booth
10. spray gun
11. spreader adjustment valve
12. transformer

Study Questions

1. Which finishing materials can be applied with a brush?
2. What is the function of a brush's bristles?
3. Give three reasons why it is important to select the proper brush.
4. Give two ways that the bristles of a quality brush differ from those of an inexpensive brush.
5. What brush shape is best for finishing table legs that have been turned on a lathe?
6. Why would a brush with natural bristles be a poor choice for applying a water-based finish?
7. What kind of brush is best for brushing a glaze?
8. How deep should you dip a brush into the finish?
9. How much pressure should you apply on the brush when brushing a finish?
10. Why should you brush in the direction of edges and grooves?
11. What finishing materials are best applied with spray equipment?
12. Give two purposes of a spray booth.
13. Why should the front and top of a project be sprayed last?
14. How much overlap should there be between spraying strokes?
15. Why should a spray gun be cleaned immediately after each use?
16. How should an aerosol container be cleaned after each use?

Stains and Bleaches

Bleaches and stains are used to change the natural color of wood. Stains darken wood by adding color. Bleaches lighten wood by removing color.

Stains

Stains are solutions of coloring material in solvents. Their purpose is to change the color of wood. They are usually transparent, which means you can see through them. Because stains are transparent, they can darken wood without covering the beauty of the grain. See Fig. 22-1.

Stains are used to change wood color for several reasons.

- **bring out the grain** — By increasing contrasts between light and dark sections, stains enhance the natural beauty of wood.
- **make a surface uniform in color** — Staining will correct unevenness of color.
- **make different woods look the same** — Stains help match the colors in different

kinds of wood. This makes the project look like it is made from one wood.
- **make cheaper woods look expensive** — Furniture is sometimes made of inexpensive wood, then stained to look like expensive woods.
- **create special effects** — Some stains make new pieces look like traditional, "antique" furniture. The application of glazing stains to antique wood is explained in chapter 29.

Types of Stains

There are four types of stains. They are grouped according to their different solvents. The four types are oil, water, spirits (alcohol), and NGR (non-grain-raising). To select the proper stain, you should know the advantages and disadvantages of each.

Oil Stains. Many deep, rich colors can be obtained with oil stains. Oil stains are easy to apply and do not raise the grain. One disadvantage is that the colors tend to fade with age. Another is that the grain pattern loses some of its clearness. Oil stains are suggested for beginners. They are easy to apply, and they provide deep, even coloring. There are two types to choose from: pigmented and penetrating.

Pigmented (wiping) oil stains can be mixed to achieve almost any color tone. They do not penetrate deeply into the surface. They work best on closed-grain wood and are used primarily for blending and retouching colors. Disadvantages are that they cloud the grain and dry slowly.

Penetrating oil stains are more transparent than pigmented stains. They show the grain

Fig. 22-1. One of the first steps in many finishing schedules is the application of a stain. Notice how the stain darkens the color of the wood.

Stain	Advantages	Disadvantages	Application
Pigment (wiping) oil	Easy to apply Does not raise grain	Tends to hide grain pattern Slow drying time	Brush Spray Wipe on
Penetrating oil	Easy to apply Does not raise grain Good color tone and permanence Dries quickly	Tends to bleed into top coat not sealed properly Tends to fade in strong sunlight	Brush Spray Wipe on
Water	Rich, transparent color Excellent color retention Does not bleed	Raises grain, which requires sponging, sizing, and sanding before staining Requires very light sanding after staining	Brush Spray
Spirit	Bright colors Quick drying	Difficult to apply evenly Color fades with exposure to light Slight grain raising Tendency to bleed	Brush Spray
NGR	Rich, transparent color Excellent color retention Does not bleed Does not raise grain Dries quickly	Difficult to apply	Spray

Fig. 22-2. Selecting Stains

better and are easier to apply. They are used mostly with open-grain wood because they penetrate into the pores. One disadvantage is that they tend to bleed into other coats. Another is that they fade when exposed to long periods of direct sunlight.

Water Stains. Fine furniture is often stained with water stains. Water stains are the most transparent stains. They bring out the wood's beauty better than any other stain. They do not fade or bleed. They dry quickly and are inexpensive.

The major disadvantage of water stains is that they raise the grain. This causes a rough surface. Rough surfaces can be avoided by raising the grain before staining. This is done by lightly wetting the wood and then sanding it smooth.

NGR (Non-Grain-Raising) Stains. The NGR stains are made with the same dyes as water stains. However, the NGR solvent does not raise the grain. This gives the NGR stains all the advantages of water stains without the major disadvantage. You need not wet and sand the wood before applying NGR stains. NGR stains are more expensive than water stains, however.

The NGR stains also dry quickly. No waiting is necessary before the next step in the finishing schedule. Because NGR stains dry so fast, they must be sprayed. Only experienced finishers should apply NGR stains.

Spirit (Alcohol) Stains. Bright, beautiful colors in wood can be produced by spirit stains. Spirit stains dry quickly and penetrate into the wood. They do not hold their color, however. They tend to bleed and fade. They are difficult to apply uniformly, and are expensive. They are seldom used for purposes other than repair work and spot finishing.

Applying Stains

Not all stains are applied in the same way. However, a general procedure does apply to all staining operations. Use the following procedures for all stain applications.

1. Prepare the surface. It must be smooth and clean. See section IV for instructions.
2. If the stain needs mixing, mix enough to do the whole project. A slight change in the second mixture can alter the color. Colors also vary from one manufacturer to another. Do not mix the stain too dark. It is easier to darken the stain than lighten it.
3. Check the color on an area that will not show. A scrap piece of the same wood can also be used. If the stain is too dark, lighten it by adding solvent. If it is too light, let the first coat dry. Then apply a second coat.
4. End grain stains darker than the other parts of the wood. You can avoid this by applying a lighter stain to the end grain. Another method is to pre-brush the end grain with the stain's solvent. The solvent will reduce the amount of stain absorbed by the end grain. Use the solvent or the material suggested by the manufacturer.
5. Always stain the parts that show the least first. Then apply stain to the most visible parts.

6. Whenever possible work with the project in a horizontal position. This prevents the stain from running and streaking.
7. If you use a brush, begin each new brush stroke on an unfinished area. This prevents lap marks.
8. Apply the stain WITH the grain when possible.
9. Work small areas at a time.
10. Follow the manufacturer's instructions.

Applying Oil Stains. You can brush, spray, or wipe on oil stains. In most cases a brush works best. Apply a coat of thinned stain, linseed oil, or thinned shellac to the end grain. This prevents the end grain from staining too dark. Apply a full, wet coat of stain. After full penetration (15-20 minutes), wipe with a soft, lint-free cloth. Wipe with the grain. The more you wipe, the lighter the stained effect. Allow about 24 hours to dry.

Applying Water Stains. You can buy water stains by the ounce as dry powders. Mix the powder with a small amount of hot water. Allow the stain to completely dissolve. Add cold water until the desired strength is reached. Generally a mixture of 2 ounces *(57 g)* of stain to 1 gallon *(4 l)* of water is sufficient. Weigh the stain when you mix it with water. This ensures a uniform color if you mix more stain later.

Before applying the stain, you must raise the grain. Do this by wetting the surface with a wet sponge. Let the surface dry overnight. Then sand it with a fine abrasive (6/0 or 220 grit). This keeps the grain from raising when you apply the stain. Remove sanding dust with a clean cloth. Wipe the end grain with clean water or a shellac wash coat. This prevents the end grain from staining too dark.

Spray or brush on water stains. If you use a brush, apply a full, wet coat. This prevents lap marks. Wipe the surface immediately with a dry brush or cloth. This produces an even coat of stain. See Fig. 22-3. Allow 24 hours to dry. Store leftover stain in glass containers since water rusts metal. Mixing only as much stain as you need will save storage space.

Fig. 22-3. Apply water stains by brushing on a wet, heavy coat. Prevent dark spots by immediately brushing out puddles and wet areas with a dry brush. Keep the brush dry by wiping it on a clean cloth.

Fig. 22-4. Applying bleach to a dark wood will lighten the color of the wood.

Bleaches

Bleaches are solutions used to remove color from wood. They contain strong chemicals. They should be used only when nothing else will work. There are three basic reasons for bleaching wood.

- **make a dark wood light**—Bleaching makes dark wood ligher, clearer, and brighter. This brings out the grain and produces a "blond" finish. A light, blond finish might be attractive on your project. If no light-colored wood is available, you can bleach a dark wood. See Fig. 22-4.
- **make the wood uniform in color**—Good finishes do not have light and dark spots. Producing a uniform finish is sometimes difficult, however. The colors in a single board can vary from very light sapwood to dark heartwood. Colors vary even more from one board to another. Matching boards for color can be time-consuming and expensive. It is sometimes easier to

bleach out all of the color. Then a uniform color can be obtained by staining.

- **remove stains**—Bleaching removes natural stains and defects that would show through a clear finish. Acid and mineral stains are the most common stains removed by bleach. If you bleach for this reason, bleach only the stained areas. Bleaching can change the natural wood color of the stained area. This can be corrected by applying stains.

Types of Bleach

Three types of bleach are commonly used in school shops. They are household (laundry) bleach, oxalic acid, and two-solution bleach. Most bleaches can either be mixed in the shop or bought already prepared. All bleaches require a neutralizer. The **neutralizer** stops the chemical action of the bleach. Each bleach has its own neutralizer.

Fig. 22-5. Bleaches range in strength from the weaker household bleaches to the stronger two-solution bleaches. Because they contain toxic materials, all bleaches are potentially harmful.

Fig. 22-6. While applying bleach, wear a face shield to protect your face from splashed bleach. Wear rubber gloves and a rubber apron to protect your body and clothes.

Bleach	Neutralizer
Household bleach (Mix ½ pint bleach to 1 gallon of water.)	Vinegar and water (3 parts vinegar to 4 parts water)
Oxalic acid (Mix 1 part acid to 2 parts water. Add acid to water.)	Borax and water (1 part borax to 4 parts water)
Two-solution bleach (Follow the manufacturer's recommendations.)	Follow the manufacturer's recommendations.

Fig. 22-7. Bleaches and Neutralizers

Household Bleach. Light stains and blemishes can be removed with household bleach. It is the weakest, safest bleach. Because it is weak, you need to make several applications.

You should always dilute household bleach. Mix 1/2 pint *(.25 l)* of bleach to 1 gallon *(4 l)* of water. Neutralize with a mixture of three parts vinegar to four parts water.

Oxalic Acid. For years oxalic acid was the suggested bleaching agent for wood. Two-solution bleach is now used more frequently because it is stronger. Another disadvantage to oxalic acid is that it produces a poisonous dust during sanding. Inhaling this dust can be dangerous.

Mix oxalic acid with hot water (one part acid to two parts water). Be sure to **add** the **acid to the water. Never add water to acid.** Neutralize oxalic acid with a mixture of borax and water (one part borax to four parts water).

Two-Solution Bleach. You can mix two-solution bleach yourself or buy it prepared. Because of the danger in handling bleaches, beginners should use the prepared bleaches. Two-solution bleach is the strongest of the three wood bleaches. It is also the most effective bleach for changing the natural color of wood. Some two-solution bleaches can be combined and applied in one step. Others require two steps. Follow the manufacturer's instructions for applying and neutralizing these bleaches.

Fig. 22-8. While sanding bleached surfaces, wear a filter mask to avoid breathing the sanding dust. Wear goggles to protect your eyes.

Bleaching Safety

You must be careful when you apply bleaches. Bleaches contain chemicals and acids that can be very harmful. It is important to read all bleaching instructions carefully. Practice the following safety rules at all times.

- Always wear goggles, rubber gloves, and a rubber apron when bleaching.
- Before handling a bleach, know its neutralizer. If bleach contacts your skin, immediately flush the area with the proper neutralizer. See Fig. 22-7.
- When mixing bleaches with water, add the acid to the water. Reversing this can cause an explosion.
- Always mix bleaches in glass containers.
- Wear goggles and a filter mask when sanding bleached wood. The dust from bleached wood can be hazardous to your eyes and lungs. See Fig. 22-8.
- If you can, work outdoors. Good ventilation is important, and the sun will aid the bleaching process.

Applying Bleach

You can apply bleach with a brush, sponge, or homemade swab. Brushes and sponges should be synthetic. You can easily make a swab by tying a cloth to the end of a clean, wood stick. To mix bleaches, follow the manufacturer's instructions and see "Types of Bleach" in this chapter.

After application let the bleach dry for about 1 hour. If the surface is still not light enough, apply a second coat. Again, wait 1 hour. Repeat this process until you get the desired color.

Once you have obtained the proper color, apply the correct neutralizer. Unless neutralized, the bleach may continue to lighten the wood or turn it brown. Bubbles and blisters can develop in the finish if the bleach is not neutralized. For proper use of neutralizers, follow the manufacturer's directions and see "Types of Bleach." After neutralizing the bleach, sponge the surface with warm water. Allow the surface to dry for at least 24 hours.

Water raises the grain on wood. This causes a rough surface that must be sanded. Use a fine abrasive (6/0 or 220 grit). Be sure to wear goggles and a filter mask.

New Terms

1. bleach
2. neutralizer
3. oxalic acid
4. stain

Study Questions

1. List five possible reasons for staining wood.
2. How are stains grouped?
3. Name the four types of stain.
4. What type of stain is suggested for beginners?
5. What is the main disadvantage of a water stain?
6. Why must NGR stains be sprayed on?
7. Why is end grain stained differently than the other parts of a project?
8. Why must the stain powders be weighed accurately when mixing stain?
9. Give three reasons for bleaching.
10. List three types of bleach commonly used in a school shop.
11. Which of the three most commonly used bleaches is the strongest?
12. List the three safety items you should wear when bleaching wood.
13. What must you wear when sanding a bleached surface?
14. What can happen if bleaches are not neutralized?

Paste Wood Filler

All wood surfaces have pores (openings). See Fig. 23-1. Open-grain woods such as mahogany, oak, and walnut have large pores. Closed-grain woods such as birch, maple, and cherry have small pores. For a smooth finish on open-grain surfaces, you must fill the pores. You can do this with a paste wood filler.

Paste wood filler consists of silica (ground rock), linseed oil, turpentine, and driers. Wood filler is a thick, heavy paste. It sometimes needs thinning. The proper thickness depends on the size of the wood pores. Woods with large pores, such as mahogany, oak, and walnut, need thick, creamy fillers. Woods with smaller pores such as birch, cherry, and maple are not usually filled. If they are, they need very thin pastes. Turpentine, naphtha, and mineral spirits can be used for thinning. Because some fillers need a special thinner, follow the directions on the filler label.

Fig. 23-1. The pores in closed-grain wood are small and evenly spaced. Open-grain pores are much larger and usually filled.

Paste fillers are available in standard wood colors and in a natural (cream) color. You can also add oil stains to obtain a particular color. You will usually choose a color that matches the wood stain. However, some woodworkers use fillers to create a contrast with the stain. For example, light-colored filler will accent the pores on dark-stained wood.

To match the stain, make the filler slightly darker than the stained wood. If the filler is too light, the wood will have a "washed out," milky look. If too dark, it will draw too much attention to the pores. Test the color of the filler on a scrap piece before applying it.

Wash Coats

Before filling the pores, you must apply a wash coat. Most wash coats are thinned solutions of a sealer. The sealer should be the one recommended for the chosen top coat. Use wash coats for the following reasons.

- They seal any previously applied stain. This prevents the stain from bleeding (seeping and mixing) into the final finish.

Fig. 23-2. Not all woods require filling. When you do fill, the consistency of the filler depends on the size of the pores to be filled.

Closed-grain; not usually filled
Basswood, Cedar, Cypress, Ebony, Fir, Hemlock, Holly, Larch, Pine, Poplar, Spruce, Willow
If filled, require liquid fillers or thin semi-paste types
Beech, Birch, Cherry, Gum, Maple, Sycamore, Redwood
Open-grain; usually filled with thick paste
Ash, Butternut, Chestnut, Elm, Hickory, Locust, Mahogany, Oak, Rosewood, Walnut

Open-grain wood   Closed-grain wood

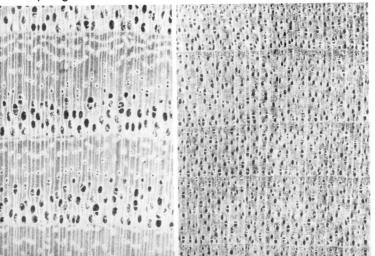

Fig. 23-3. Apply a wash coat before filling pores with a paste wood filler. Most wash coats are thinned solutions of the appropriate sealer. Solutions of shellac and denatured alcohol are also used as wash coats.

- They prevent surfaces from absorbing color and oils from the filler.
- They make surfaces smoother and harder. This makes it easier to apply and remove the filler.

To prepare a wash coat, mix one part sealer with five to seven parts solvent. You can also mix one part shellac with seven parts denatured alcohol. Remember, not all sealers and top coats are compatible. Read the manufacturer's label to make sure.

Apply the wash coat with a brush or spray gun. Cover all surfaces to be filled. After the wash coat dries, sand it lightly with a fine abrasive (280 grit). Then apply the filler.

Applying Fillers

Filling wood pores is a simple operation. However, it must be done carefully to produce good results. The following steps will help you

do a good job. Be sure to apply a wash coat before you start to fill.

1. Do not start with too large an area. You need time to wipe away extra filler before it dries and hardens. Filler that has dried on the surface is difficult to remove.
2. Apply a heavy coat of filler with a stiff brush, as in Fig. 23-4. Brush WITH the grain first, then ACROSS it.
3. Rub the filler into the pores with your hand or a lint-free cloth. Use a circular motion. See Fig. 23-5.
4. Let the filler set (dry) about 10-20 minutes. The time depends on room temperature and ventilation. When the filler loses its wet, shiny appearance, it is ready for the next step. Check this by rubbing your finger across the surface. If the filler slides, let it set a little longer. If the filler rolls up under your finger, you are ready for the next step.

   Do not let the filler dry completely. If it does, you cannot wipe it clean without causing smudges. If the filler does dry completely, remove it. Use a cloth dipped in mineral spirits. Then reapply filler.
5. Remove excess filler by wiping ACROSS the grain with burlap or a coarse cloth. See Fig. 23-6. Apply pressure with the heel of your hand as you wipe. On large, flat surfaces, use a sanding block wrapped

Fig. 23-4. Apply filler by first brushing WITH the grain, then ACROSS the grain.

Fig. 23-5. Rub the filler deeply into the pores using a circular motion.

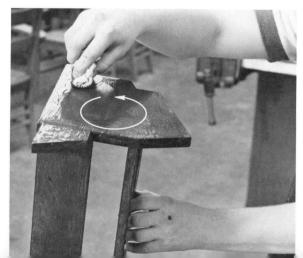

Fig. 23-6. Remove excess filler by wiping ACROSS the grain.

Fig. 23-7. Use a cloth-covered stick to remove excess filler from hard-to-reach places.

with burlap. This helps push the filler into the pores.

6. Make the final cleanup with a clean, soft cloth. Wipe lightly WITH the grain. Be careful not to pull filler out of the pores as you wipe.

7. Wrap a cloth around the end of a pointed stick. Use this stick to remove extra filler from corners, moldings, and carvings. See Fig. 23-7.

8. Check to see that the pores are properly filled. See Fig. 23-8. If not, add another coat of filler. Use the same procedure as before.

9. Allow the filler to dry. Unless the manufacturer gives other instructions, let it dry for 24 hours.

10. After the filler is dry, sand it lightly with a fine abrasive. Wipe the surface clean with a tack rag.

Fig. 23-8. Inspect your work carefully to determine if the pores are properly filled.

11. The surface must now be sealed. See the chapter describing your chosen top coat for instructions.

New Terms

1. closed-grain wood
2. open-grain wood
3. paste wood filler
4. pores
5. wash coat

Study Questions

1. Why are open-grain surfaces often filled with a paste filler before finishing?
2. What determines the proper thickness for paste fillers?
3. What is one reason for using a light-colored filler with a dark-stained wood?
4. Give three reasons for applying a wash coat.
5. When are wash coats usually applied?
6. Why should you apply fillers to a small area first?
7. Which way do you brush when you apply a filler?
8. Describe the method for checking that the filler has set long enough to wipe off the excess.
9. Of what use is a sanding block in filling wood pores?
10. Name three open-grain woods. Name three closed-grain woods.

Oil and Wax Finishes

Oil and wax finishes are the most natural of all finishes. Although almost invisible, they enhance the grain and color of wood. Oils and waxes are also the easiest of all finishes to apply.

Oil Finishes

Oil finishes penetrate (soak) into the wood. Unlike lacquer, shellac, and varnish, penetrating oils are IN the wood, not ON it. Each new coat penetrates deeply into the pores. The oil does not build up on top of the surface. The penetrating oils bring out the warm, natural beauty of the grain. They reveal the true color and texture of the wood. See Fig. 24-2.

Oil finishes are popular for reasons other than their natural beauty. They dry to form a solid layer inside the wood. This gives new life to old, dry wood. It also makes a protective, durable finish that withstands wear. Oil finishes resist alcohol, heat, cuts, scratches, and water.

Fig. 24-1. Penetrating oil finishes are invisible. They produce natural, "close to the wood" finishes. The plans for this project are given in section IX.

SHELLAC, VARNISH, LACQUER

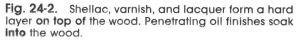

PENETRATING OILS

Fig. 24-2. Shellac, varnish, and lacquer form a hard layer **on top of** the wood. Penetrating oil finishes soak **into** the wood.

Penetrating oils are also popular because they are easy to apply. The work of the stain, filler, sealer, and top coat is often done in one step. The finish can be applied with a cloth. No spray equipment or brushes are needed. Dust is not a problem, so you do not need a special room to finish. Repairing oil finishes is also a simple process.

Over the years woodworkers have developed many different penetrating oil finishes. These mixtures require a great deal of rubbing and take a long time to dry. Today most woodworkers use commercially prepared finishes. Sealacell, Minwax, and Watco Danish Oil are some of the popular brands. These prepared oil finishes dry quickly and require very little rubbing.

Applying Oil Finishes

Procedures for applying commercial oil finishes vary somewhat. For this reason, you should

187

follow the manufacturer's instructions. The following steps provide a basic procedure for applying these finishes.

1. Prepare the wood surface as described in section IV. It is important that the surface be smooth and clean before application.
2. Apply stain if desired.
3. If desired, fill open-grain wood with a paste filler. Some fillers can be mixed with the finish. Follow the manufacturer's instructions.
4. Apply the finish freely with a cloth or brush. Generally, let the oil soak 15 minutes on veneers, 30 minutes on solid wood. Keep the surface wet for 30 minutes. See Fig. 24-3.
5. Polish the surface with a very fine (400 or 600) wet-or-dry abrasive. While polishing, keep the surface wet.
6. Remove excess finish with a clean, dry cloth. Let the surface dry overnight.
7. For best results, repeat steps 4-6. Most manufacturers of prepared finishes suggest two or three coats.
8. Apply wax or polish as desired.

Varnish Wipe-On Finish. You can make a varnish wipe-on finish in the shop or at home. Mix six parts spar varnish, two parts boiled linseed oil, and two parts turpentine or mineral spirits. This finish, although it contains varnish, is used like a penetrating oil finish. To apply varnish wipe-on finishes, follow the procedure for prepared oil finishes.

Mineral Oil Finish. Finishes that do not have poisonous materials in them are **nontoxic finishes.** Projects designed to hold food must be finished with nontoxic finishes. Salad bowls and cutting boards, for example, cannot be finished with the usual finishes. See Fig. 24-4. They are usually finished with mineral oil, which is nontoxic.

Mineral oil is available in most drugstores. Apply it with a brush or clean, lint-free cloth. Apply a full wet coat. Let the oil penetrate for about 20 minutes. Then wipe off the excess with a clean cloth. Wipe with the grain. Allow 24 hours for the oil to dry and apply a second coat. Apply more coats every 3 or 4 months, depending on how often the project is used.

Wax Finishes

In wood finishing, wax is generally used to polish final coats of finish. It is sometimes used, however, as a final finish. It produces a soft, natural appearance and protects the wood from moisture and stains. It also has the advantage of being easy to apply and clean. See Fig. 24-5.

Fig. 24-3. Penetrating oils are easy to apply. Simply brush or wipe on a full wet coat. Continue adding extra oil to dry spots.

Fig. 24-4. These projects were finished with mineral oil, which is nontoxic. Other finishes, such as lacquer and varnish, contaminate (spoil) food.

Fig. 24-5. Paste wax produces a soft, natural finish and protects the wood from moisture and stains. The plans for this project are in section IX.

Fig. 24-6. Use a circular motion to rub several light coats of wax into the wood.

Carnauba wax is the hardest and toughest paste wax. It can be rubbed and polished to a shiny, lusterous finish. It is not used full strength, but mixed with other waxes. The better commercial waxes will contain a high percentage of carnauba wax.

Waxes are available as clear and colored pastes. Generally the clearer waxes are applied to lighter woods. Darker waxes are applied to darker woods. Stains have been added to some waxes. This means that staining and waxing can be done at once.

Use the following procedure to apply a wax finish.

1. Prepare the surface as described in section IV.
2. Stain, if desired.
3. Fill, if desired.
4. Apply a sealer coat. Use thinned shellac, lacquer, or varnish. Let the sealer dry. Then rub it with fine steel wool. Clean the rubbed surface with a tack rag.
5. Apply a coat of wax with a clean cloth. See Fig. 24-6. Be careful not to apply too much wax. A more even finish will result from several light coats than from one heavy coat. Let the wax dry according to the manufacturer's instructions. Wipe away any excess wax. Then polish the surface with a clean cloth or felt pad. Two or three applications provide a satisfactory finish.

New Terms

1. carnauba wax
2. mineral oil
3. nontoxic finish
4. penetrating oil
5. varnish wipe-on finish
6. wax

Study Questions

1. How do penetrating oil finishes differ from the surface finishes such as lacquer and varnish?
2. Describe how a penetrating oil finish affects the appearance of wood.
3. Name at least three reasons for the popularity of penetrating oil finishes.
4. List three factors that make penetrating oils easy to apply.
5. What finish would you select for a salad bowl?
6. How are waxes usually used in wood finishing?
7. Give three advantages of wax as a final finish.

Chapter

25

Shellac

Shellac is made from the gummy resin excreted by the lac insect. The insect deposits the resin (called **lac**) on trees in southeast Asia. The lac is collected, processed, and dried into sheets of shellac.

When dissolved in alcohol, shellac forms a finishing material for wood. For centuries shellac mixtures were the primary wood finishes. Lacquer, however, has replaced shellac as the main wood finish.

Shellac provides a clear, beautiful finish. See Fig. 25-1. It is easy to apply, and it dries quickly. Shellac finishes are also easy to repair.

The main problem with shellac is its inability to resist water. Shellac turns white or develops spots when in contact with water. It also dissolves in alcohol and is not very durable.

Shellac is naturally orange in color. However, most of the shellac used in finishing is bleached white. Orange shellac changes the color of light woods and is used only on darker woods. White shellac does not alter the color of wood. It provides a clear, natural finish.

Fig. 25-1. Shellac produces beautiful finishes for smaller projects such as this bench. To build this bench, see project section of this text.

Shellac is available in 2-, 3-, and 4-pound mixtures called **cuts.** See Fig. 25-2. The 4-pound cut is a frequently used mixture. This mixture contains 4 pounds of shellac in 1 gallon of denatured alcohol. The 2- and 3-pound cuts are also mixed with a gallon of alcohol. A 4-pound cut is, of course, thicker than a 2- or 3-pound cut.

Shellac has a short shelf life. Never buy more than you will use in 60-90 days. Old shellac does not dry after being applied to a surface.

Uses of Shellac

Shellac serves three basic purposes for the wood finisher. It is used as a sealer, a wash coat, and a top coat.

Sealer. A sealer is a mixture that acts as a barrier between coats of finish. It prevents bleeding and mixing of materials that do not work well together. It also seals knots and pitch in softwoods.

Shellac is compatible with most finishing materials, with the exception of some synthetic varnishes. It mixes with both lacquer and oil materials, for example. Therefore, a shellac

Fig. 25-2. Shellac. Never buy more than you can use in 60-90 days.

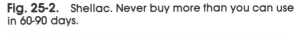

sealer permits lacquer to be used over oil-based finishes. Prepared sealers are manufactured for each kind of top coat. If the manufacturer's recommended sealer is not available, use a mixture of one part shellac (4-pound cut) to two parts alcohol.

Wash Coat. A wash coat is actually a thinned sealer. It prevents bleeding of one finish material into another. Its greatest use is to seal pores before applying a paste filler. The wash coat must be compatible with the top coat material. This is especially important if the top coat is a synthetic varnish. See page 184 for more information on wash coats.

Top Coat. Shellac is still used as a top coat of finish. It dries quickly and produces a beautiful finish. Because it dries quickly, it is especially useful when finishing in dusty areas.

Applying Shellac

You can either spray or brush on shellac. Brushes are used for smaller surfaces. Larger surfaces are usually sprayed. Chapter 21 gives instructions for using spray equipment.

If you use a brush, it should have soft bristles. Brush with long, even strokes. Work quickly, or the shellac will dry unevenly on the surface. Brush in one direction only. Brushing back and forth will also cause an uneven coat.

Apply several thin coats of shellac rather than a few heavy ones. Thin coats are easier to apply. Some woodworkers make later coats thicker than the first few.

All cuts of shellac are thinned with denatured alcohol before application. The general practice is to mix the shellac and alcohol in equal parts. This is not a hard and fast rule, however. Observe the ease or difficulty of application and determine the proper mixture. If you have problems, you probably need to do more thinning. When thinned properly, shellac will flow on smoothly without brush marks. See Fig. 25-3.

To apply a shellac finish, use the following procedure.

Fig. 25-3. Shellac is easy to apply. However, it must be thinned properly to prevent brush marks.

1. Prepare the surface as described in section IV.
2. Apply stain, if desired.
3. Fill, if desired.
4. Apply a sealer coat of shellac. The sealer should be one part shellac to four parts alcohol. Allow about 2 hours to dry.
5. Sand the surface smooth with a very fine abrasive (320). Do this lightly to prevent cutting through the shellac. Clean the surface with a dry cloth.
6. Apply a thin coat of shellac. Allow 2 to 3 hours to dry. Beginners tend to apply shellac too thickly. This produces an uneven finish and makes the finishing process difficult. Remember, it is better to apply several thin coats than a few heavy ones.
7. Repeat step 5.
8. Apply additional coats of shellac as desired. Usually three to five coats will provide an even, glossy finish. Many finishers make each coat thicker than the previous one. Repeat sanding after each coat.
9. After sanding the last coat, polish it with a 3/0 or 4/0 steel wool. Clean with a dry cloth.
10. Apply a coat of wax or polish to protect the finish.
11. Clean the shellac brush in alcohol.

Fig. 25-4. French polishing is done in a figure-eight motion. Never stop rubbing while the pad is on the surface. This will leave an impression of the pad in the finish.

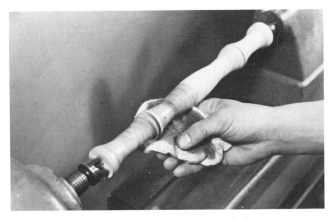

Fig. 25-5. French polishing on the lathe is easy and fast. Hold the pad at the bottom of the project so the project turns away from you.

French Polishing

French polish is a special kind of shellac finish. It has been a popular finish for centuries. Made with shellac and linseed oil, it is hand rubbed into the wood. Rubbed properly, french polishes produce beautiful finishes.

A great deal of skill and effort is needed, however, to apply French polish. It is used mostly for repairing finishes and finishing small projects. It is also used in school shops to finish projects on a lathe. Ready mixed French polishes are now available under various trade names.

To apply French polish, saturate a pear-shaped cloth with shellac (2-pound cut). Lubricate the pad with a few drops of linseed oil or lemon oil. The oil is needed to prevent the pad from sticking. Do not apply too much oil or the finish will eventually lose its luster.

Rub the surface briskly using a figure-eight motion, as shown in Fig. 25-4. Do not stop. When the finish begins to build up, rub back and forth with the grain. Continue applying French polish until the desired finish is reached. To repair a finish, you may need to polish the entire surface. This will produce a uniform luster.

Before using a lathe to apply French polish, remove the tool support. Make sure there are no loose ends on the cloth pad. Loose ends can easily catch in the lathe as the stock turns.

Run the lathe at 900 rpm's. Hold the pad toward the bottom of the stock. See Fig. 25-5. Polish as desired and allow 20 minutes for the finish to dry.

New Terms

1. cut
2. French polish
3. lac
4. sealer
5. shellac

Study Questions

1. From what material is shellac made?
2. What material has replaced shellac as the primary wood finish?
3. List three advantages to using shellac.
4. The major disadvantage of shellac is its inability to resist water. Name two other disadvantages.
5. Why is white shellac used more than the natural orange shellac?
6. If you needed the thinnest possible shellac mixture, would you buy a 2-, 3-, or 4-pound cut?
7. Why is it important to buy only as much shellac as you need?
8. What are the three ways in which shellac is used?
9. Why is shellac used frequently as a sealer?
10. What material is used to thin shellac?
11. Is it better to apply one heavy coat, or several thin coats, of shellac?

Varnish

Varnish is used to form hard, transparent coatings on wood surfaces. Until recently all varnishes consisted of natural gums or resins in oil vehicles. Today, however, many varnishes are made with synthetic materials.

Each type of varnish has advantages and disadvantages. The natural varnishes have a slight amber color. They give wood a deep, rich appearance. Their major disadvantage is their slow drying time. The synthetic varnishes dry much faster and produce very clear finishes. See Fig. 26-1.

Natural Varnish

Natural varnishes produce tough, durable finishes. They resist water, alcohol, grease stains, wear, and temperature changes. A thick, protective film builds up after only a few applications. Natural varnishes are available in gloss and semi-gloss lusters. If desired, they can be polished to a lusterous, shiny finish.

Natural varnish is manufactured with different oil-to-resin ratios. The mixtures with more oil, called **long-oil** varnish, are tough and elastic. Elastic finishes adapt to the expansion and contraction of the wood caused by the weather. **Spar** varnish is a long-oil varnish with a high resistance to water. It is used for exterior purposes.

Varnish made with less oil and more resin is called **short-oil** varnish. Short-oil varnish is not elastic; it is hard and brittle. It can be rubbed and polished to a high luster. It is ideal for interior, decorative pieces that will not be exposed to great temperature changes.

For a general-purpose varnish, oil and resin are mixed to form **medium-oil** varnish. This varnish is used to finish surfaces that must be both hard and elastic. Floors are often finished with medium-oil varnish.

The major drawback to natural varnish is its drying time. It takes 12-48 hours to dry. This means that while the surface is wet, dust and other particles can stick to it. The result is a rough, uneven finish. Rubbing and sanding are needed to make these surfaces smooth. Because they dry so slowly, natural varnishes are being replaced by the newer synthetic varnishes.

Fig. 26-1. Natural varnishes produce deeper, richer appearances than do synthetic varnishes. However, natural varnishes are very difficult to apply because they dry so slowly.

Synthetic Varnish

Synthetic varnishes dry much faster than natural varnishes. Besides this important advantage, they are harder and more durable than natural varnishes. They also resist water, alcohol, grease stains, weather changes, and abrasions. Polyurethane, the most popular synthetic varnish, is used for both interior and exterior applications. It is available in gloss and satin lusters.

Applying Varnish

Apply natural varnish in a dust-free finishing room. Apply synthetic varnish in the cleanest area possible. Use either a brush or spray equipment. If you brush, use a natural or polyester-bristle brush. The brush should be clean, dry, and of good quality. Use a tapered brush if one is available. The following steps provide a general plan for applying varnishes. Always follow the manufacturer's instructions when in doubt.

1. Prepare the surface as described in section IV.
2. Stain, if desired.
3. Fill, if desired.
4. Apply a sealer coat. Follow the manufacturer's suggestions. Use shellac for natural varnishes. For most synthetics use a thinned coat of the varnish.
5. Stir the varnish thoroughly. Do not shake it. This will cause small bubbles to form.

Fig. 26-2. If the varnish has become lumpy in the can, it can be strained clean with a muslin cloth.

The bubbles will make the finish rough and imperfect. If some of the varnish has hardened in the can, it must be strained. See Fig. 26-2.

6. Thin the varnish for the first coat. Follow the manufacturer's instructions. Later coats can be applied full strength.
7. Apply the first coat. Start at the middle and work toward the outside. For inside corners, place the brush in the corner and brush outward. Use a full brush and work as quickly as possible. Cover the entire surface brushing **with** the grain. Then brush **across** the grain. Smooth the finish by making light strokes **with** the grain. Use just the tips of the bristles for this final brushing. See Fig. 26-3.

Fig. 26-3. Apply varnish with a full brush and work quickly. Brush **with, across,** and then lightly **with** the grain.

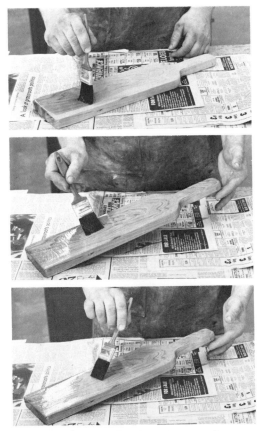

Fig. 26-4. Dust and other particles can settle on slow-drying varnish. Remove large particles while the varnish is still wet.

Fig. 26-5. Varnish stains add color and provide a final finish in one quick step. They tend to build up on the surface and hide the grain, however. They are not used on fine, quality pieces.

8. Remove any small particles on the surface. Use a thin, pointed object. A toothpick or sliver of wood will work well. See Fig. 26-4.
9. Allow the varnish to dry according to the manufacturer's instructions.
10. If you intend to apply another coat, lightly sand the surface with a fine sandpaper (280). Do not sand in the finishing room. Clean the surface with a dry cloth and tack rag.
11. Apply additional coats as desired. As a general rule, three coats of varnish will provide a satisfactory coating. Repeat step 10 after each coat.
12. Rub and polish to the desired luster after the final coat has dried.
13. Clean brushes and other equipment with the recommended solvent. Turpentine works well for most varnishes.

Varnish Stains

Varnish stains consist of clear varnish with color added. These mixtures are used as a combination stain and top coat. Varnish stains do not penetrate into the wood pores as do standard wood stains. If applied unevenly or heavily, they build up on the surface and hide the grain. For this reason varnish stains are never used on quality wood projects. They are used only as a quick method of coloring and finishing. See Fig. 26-5.

New Terms

1. long-oil
2. medium-oil
3. natural varnish
4. polyurethane
5. short-oil
6. spar varnish
7. synthetic varnish
8. varnish stain

Study Questions

1. What is the major disadvantage of natural varnishes?
2. Name two qualities of long-oil varnish.
3. Why is long-oil varnish a good finish for outdoor projects?
4. What type of natural varnish would you use to finish a floor? Why?
5. What problem results from the slow drying time of natural varnishes?
6. Natural and synthetic varnishes are much alike. Name one important way in which they are different.
7. Where must natural varnishes be applied?
8. Give three qualities of the ideal varnish brush.
9. What happens to varnish if you shake it? Why is this a problem?
10. How can you remove small particles stuck to a varnished surface?
11. Give one advantage to using varnish stains. Give one disadvantage.

Lacquer

Lacquer produces deep, rich, clear finishes. It forms a hard, durable finish and resists moisture. It also dries rapidly, eliminating the dust problems that exist with varnishes. For these reasons, most furniture manufactured today is finished with lacquer.

Fig. 27-1. Lacquer is used to finish most of the furniture manufactured today. The plans for this project are in section IX.

Lacquer may not be the best finish for your project, however. Because it dries so fast, it should be applied with spray equipment. If you do not have spray equipment or spraying experience, you should select a different finish. Special brushing lacquers are available, but they are also difficult for beginners to apply. You can use aerosol cans to spray lacquer on small projects. The aerosols are easy to apply but expensive.

Lacquer Materials

Lacquer is not compatible with most finishing materials. Therefore, a wide range of lacquer finishes, sealers, and thinners are manufac-

Fig. 27-2. Be sure to follow the manufacturer's instructions in selecting and matching lacquer materials. Lacquer is not compatible with many finishing materials.

tured. Follow the manufacturer's suggestions for stains and fillers used with lacquer. See Fig. 27-2.

Clear lacquer is available in many forms. The standard type of clear lacquer has a slight amber tint. It has a tendency to yellow with age. A water-white lacquer is also available. It will produce a completely clear top coat. Both of these lacquers are produced in gloss, semi-gloss and flat lusters.

Shading lacquers are clear lacquers with small amounts of color added. Like stains, these lacquers color the wood but let the grain show. They are used primarily to match the colors of different woods. They are also used to darken parts of a project. This creates an antique appearance.

Shading lacquers are applied with standard spray equipment at a low air pressure. They build on top of the surface. This means they will cover the grain if not applied lightly and carefully. Tinting colors are available for mixing with clear lacquer. This way you can produce most desired colors.

Opaque lacquers are also manufactured. They are available in a variety of colors. They are used in place of enamels and paints when quick drying is important.

Brushing lacquer contains materials that slow down the drying process. This makes it possible to brush on the lacquer. You can purchase both clear and colored brushing lacquers.

Lacquer thinners are needed for most lacquer applications. Select the thinners according to the manufacturer's instructions. The thinners must be compatible with the lacquer used as the top coat.

Lacquer sealers are used to seal the finish materials applied before the top coat. This is important because the materials in lacquer are similar to paint remover. Lacquer will mix with and lift fillers and stains that have not been sealed. Sealers also provide a smooth base for the final finish.

Fig. 27-3. Because lacquer dries so quickly, spraying is the best method for applying lacquer.

Spraying Lacquer

The best lacquer finishes are sprayed on rather than brushed on. It is easier to produce a smooth, even finish by spraying. Spraying also reduces the chances of lifting or smearing previous coats. Use the following procedure to spray lacquer. If you use an aerosol, follow the directions on the can.

1. Prepare the surface as described in section IV.
2. Stain, if desired.
3. Fill, if desired.
4. Spray on a coat of lacquer sealer. Thin the sealer as directed by the manufacturer. Follow the step-by-step spraying instructions in chapter 21. Be sure to clean the equipment immediately after each use.
5. Let the sealer dry and sand it lightly with a fine abrasive (280 grit). Then wipe the surface with a clean, dry cloth.

Fig. 27-4. If you brush on lacquer, be sure to use brushing lacquer. Brushing lacquer dries rapidly. Brush it on as quickly as possible.

6. Spray on the desired number of top coats. Thin the lacquer according to the manufacturer's instructions. If necessary, sand lightly between top coats with a fine abrasive. Runs and other imperfections are examples of problems that could require sanding.
7. Rub and polish as desired after the final coat.

Brushing Lacquer

If you apply lacquer with a brush, use a brushing lacquer. Brushing lacquers are manufactured with solvents that slow down the drying process. Brushing lacquer still dries faster than other finishes that are brushed on. See Fig. 27-4.

To brush on lacquer, follow the procedure under "Spraying Lacquer." Use a soft-bristle (fitch) brush. Make long strokes, slightly lapping the previous strokes. Apply a full, wet coat. If you can cover the surface adequately with one coat, do so. Work quickly. Do not go over the surface to brush out the lacquer. Cover the entire surface with the minimum amount of brushing.

New Terms

1. brushing lacquer
2. lacquer
3. lacquer sealer
4. lacquer thinner
5. opaque lacquer
6. shading lacquer

Study Questions

1. Give four reasons why most furniture today is finished with lacquer.
2. For beginners, what is a disadvantage of standard lacquer?
3. Why are so many lacquer materials, such as thinners and sealers, manufactured?
4. What is the difference between the two basic types of clear lacquer?
5. What is one drawback to using shading lacquers?
6. Why must you apply a sealer before a top coat of lacquer?
7. Give two advantages to spraying lacquer rather than brushing it.
8. When do you need to sand between coats of lacquer?

Paint

Paint is an opaque (nontransparent) finish material. Unlike the clear finishes, such as lacquer and varnish, paint hides surfaces entirely. See Fig. 28-1. This makes paint a desirable finish for unattractive surfaces. Paint covers defects and provides a strong, protective coating. Available in thousands of colors, paint also produces colorful, attractive finishes.

Types of Paint

Paint consists of color pigments in a vehicle (liquid). Manufacturers use different kinds and amounts of pigments and vehicles to make paints. By changing the mixtures they produce a wide variety of paints. Some paints work best on wood and plaster. Others are made for concrete and metal. Some are made for exterior use, others for interior use. All paints are divided into two basic groups by their vehicles. The two vehicles are oil and water.

Although they have different vehicles, **enamels** are often grouped with paints. Enamels are also opaque finishes. Most enamels have varnish vehicles. This makes enamel tougher, more durable, and usually glossier than paint. Enamel is, however, more expensive than paint. It also takes longer to dry.

Oil-Based Paints. Compared to water-based paints, oil-based paints are more durable and resist stains better. They take longer to dry, however. For this reason, they should be applied in a dust-free area. They produce an odor and require flammable solvents for thinning and cleaning equipment. Mineral spirits, oleum spirits, and turpentine are used as thinners. Oil-based paints are used when durability and water resistance are needed. Kitchen cabinets, for example, are often painted with oil-based paints.

Water-Based Paints. There are many advantages to water-based paints. They dry quickly and equipment is easily cleaned with soap and water. They are less expensive and easier to apply than oil-based paints. They can be thinned with water, which is cheaper and safer than the oil-based thinners. Water-based paints are also known as latex and rubber-based paints. They are used for interior and exterior walls, and for furniture and trim.

Color

It is both useful and interesting to understand how thousands of paint colors are produced. The following paragraphs briefly explain how the colors are created.

The **primary** colors are red, yellow, and blue. They are intermixed to produce the **secondary** colors: orange, green, and violet. Intermixing the 3 primary and 3 secondary colors produces 6 more colors. This makes up the 12 colors of a color wheel. See Fig. 28-2.

Fig. 28-1. Paint covers the wood and adds color to the surface. You can use paint to beautify your project by hiding unattractive wood.

Adding black to one of these colors produces a **shade.** For example, adding black to red produces maroon, which is a shade of red. Adding white to these colors produces a **tint.** Adding white to red, produces pink, which is a tint of red.

The **compliment** of a color is the opposite color on the color wheel. Notice in Fig. 28-2 that green is opposite red. Green and red are complimentary colors.

You can reduce the brilliance of a color by mixing it with its compliment. Adding green to red, for example, produces a duller red. The more of a complimentary color you add, the duller the color becomes.

These rules for mixing colors apply to all finishing materials. Stains and lacquers, for example, can be changed to almost any desired color. This is why paint stores have so many different colors available. They intermix the primary and secondary colors. They make tints and shades by adding black and white. Finally, they change the brilliance of a color by adding its compliment. Thousands of paint colors result from these simple procedures.

Luster

Paints are available with different amounts of luster (brightness). **Flat, semi-gloss** (eggshell), and **gloss** are the common terms for amount of luster. The three degrees of luster

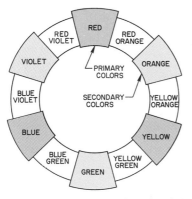

Fig. 28-2. The 12 colors of a color wheel provide the basis for the thousands of paint colors produced.

provide different amounts of protection and durability. You should consider the purpose of the paint when choosing the luster.

Flat paints absorb light, which reduces glare. They are not as durable as semi-gloss and gloss paints. They are most often used for walls and ceilings. Living rooms, halls, bedrooms, and dining rooms are painted with flat paints.

Semi-gloss paints are more durable than flat paints. They can be washed often and are used for bathrooms, kitchens, and children's rooms. They are used for trim around doors and windows. Wood projects such as dressers, boxes, and stools are also painted with semi-gloss paints.

Gloss paints are the most durable paints and the easiest to keep clean. They are used where durability is important. Kitchens, bathrooms, and shop areas are examples. Furniture and small, decorative pieces are also painted with bright, high-gloss paint. The high luster is sometimes undesirable on large wall areas, however. When used sparingly, gloss paints can be very appealing.

Primers

A primer coat is usually applied before a coat of paint. Primers are special mixtures that serve several purposes.

- They prevent previously applied finishes from bleeding into the paint.
- They seal wood pores and stick to surfaces better than paints do. As they seal the pores, they make the surface smooth. The surface is then easier to paint and less absorbent. This saves both time and money.
- Primers also help to preserve the wood. They reduce blistering, peeling, mildew, and rotting.

Primers are always applied over glossy surfaces before flat paints. Follow the paint manufacturer's directions for selection and application of primers.

Applying Paint

Paint can be applied with a brush, spray gun or roller. Large areas are usually rolled. Inside corners, irregular shapes, and small areas are usually brushed. Nylon brushes are used frequently for water-based paints. Brushes with natural bristles are used for oil-based paints. Polyester brushes may be used for either kind of paint. See chapter 21 for more information on selecting brushes.

1. Prepare the surface as described in section IV. It should be smooth and flat. Opaque finishes require less surface preparation than clear finishes, however.
2. Apply a primer coat. Choose a primer that works well with the paint. Follow the manufacturer's instructions for thinning and applying primers.
3. Stir the paint thoroughly. Thin it slightly if necessary.
4. If a brush is used, apply the paint in long, even strokes. Do not apply paint too heavily. See Fig. 28-4.
5. Allow the paint to dry according to the manufacturer's directions.
6. Sand lightly. Use a 280 grit abrasive.
7. Apply additional coats as needed. Sand after each coat. Do not sand the final coat.
8. After you finish painting, clean your equipment immediately. For oil-based paints use turpentine, mineral spirits, or oleum spirits. Use soap and warm water for water-based paints. Chapter 21 has more information on cleaning equipment.

New Terms

1. compliment
2. enamel
3. flat
4. gloss
5. latex
6. luster
7. paint
8. primary colors
9. primer
10. secondary colors
11. semi-gloss
12. shade
13. tint

Study Questions

1. Why is paint a good finish for unattractive surfaces?
2. Paint consists of two basic parts that are mixed differently to produce a variety of paints. What are these two parts?
3. List three differences between paint and enamel.
4. Give two advantages of oil-based paints as compared to water-based paints.
5. List five advantages to water-based paints as compared to oil-based paints.
6. How are the secondary colors produced?
7. How many colors are there on the color wheel described in this chapter?
8. Name the three degrees of luster.
9. Give one advantage of flat paints. Give one disadvantage.
10. Which degree of luster is the most durable?
11. List three purposes of primer coats.
12. When is a primer coat applied, before or after the paint?
13. What are three methods of applying paint?
14. When should you clean your painting equipment?

Fig. 28-3. Rollers are used to paint large surfaces.

Fig. 28-4. Most beginners make the mistake of applying paint too heavily. Dip the brush about halfway and wipe off the excess on the rim of the container.

Fig. 28-5. A properly painted surface is durable and attractive.

Special Finishing Effects

Three special finishing effects are explained in this chapter. Each one can add an extra touch or special look to your project. Each one can increase the beauty of your project. All three effects are easy to produce. By following the procedures in this chapter, you can give your project an antique appearance. You can also decorate it with elaborate designs of your choice.

Glazing

Glazing, sometimes called antiquing, can produce a variety of effects. The most common glazing technique consists of highlighting corners and recessed areas. This is done to produce an aged, antique look. See Fig. 29-1. Commercially prepared glazes are available for most types of finishes. To create an antique effect by highlighting, use the following procedure.

Fig. 29-1. This tissue box was painted and then glazed to produce the antique appearance.

Fig. 29-2. You can vary the glazed effects by using different materials to wipe off the glaze. Experiment with different materials, such as burlap and stiff brushes.

1. Prepare the surface and apply the undercoat material. Most paint and hardware stores sell glazes in kits that include the undercoat. Clear undercoats, such as varnish and lacquer, are available. Undercoats are also available in many different colors. Follow the manufacturer's instructions for applying the undercoat.
2. After the undercoat dries, apply a full, wet coat of glaze. Use a cloth, brush, or spray gun.
3. Let the glaze set for about 10 minutes. It should begin to lose its wet look.
4. Wipe off the excess glaze. Different effects are achieved by wiping with such materials as sponges, burlap, steel wool, and cloths. See Fig. 29-2. You can also vary the effect by leaving more glaze in corners and depressions. Use your imagination to select materials that create the desired effect.

5. When you produce the desired surface appearance, blend the glaze in with a soft fitch brush. Use a clean cloth to wipe off the brush as you work.
6. Allow the glaze to dry according to the manufacturer's instructions.
7. Apply a final top coat of varnish over the glaze. This will provide added protection.

Distressing

Distressing is the process of making new wood projects look like antiques. See Fig. 29-3. There are two methods of distressing: physical and surface. **Physical distressing** actually dents and mars the wood surface. **Surface distressing** produces small marks and spots that look like imperfections.

Physical Distressing. Generally you should physically distress wood before applying any finish. After the final sanding, mark the surface with an ice pick or small nail. The marks should look like worm holes. Then hit the surface randomly with a chain or ring of keys. You can use almost any hard object to physically distress a surface. See Fig. 29-4.

After marking the surface, apply the finish in the usual way. Dark glazes applied over the

finish build up in the marks and dents. This darkens these areas and adds to the aged effect. If you physically distress a painted surface, apply the paint first. Paint would partially fill the distress marks. This would cover up the aged effect.

Surface Distressing. Usually surface distressing is done between top coats. If you are both glazing and distressing, glaze before the first top coat application. Then distress before the second application of finish. This way you can apply distress marks without disturbing the glaze. If the marks are not suitable, you can wipe them off.

Apply surface distress marks with a greaseless crayon or special marking pencil. These markers are available from finishing suppliers.

Fig. 29-3. You can make your project look like an antique by distressing it.

Fig. 29-4. This distressing tool was made by welding together bolts, screws, washers, and chain.

Fig. 29-5. Surface distressing is often done with a greaseless crayon. It is usually done between applications of the top coat.

You can also make distress marks by applying a heavy glaze with a toothpick, pen, or piece of thread. Make crooked lines or small "u's," "l's," or "j's" on the surface. See Fig. 29-5. **Do not** establish a pattern. Scatter the marks randomly across the surface.

You can create splattered, "wormy" effects with a stiff brush and a dark glaze. Barely wet the brush and tap off the excess glaze on a piece of paper. Hold the brush 6 to 8 inches *(150-200 mm)* from the surface. Then flick the brush with a small stick. It is a good idea to practice on a piece of paper first. Adjust the amount of splatter to get the proper effect. You can also distress surfaces with special aerosol sprays. Simply spray on dark brown and black spots. See Fig. 29-6. Then apply a top coat of finish. Follow the manufacturer's instructions for these sprays.

Decoupage

Decoupage is the application of a picture to a piece of wood or a project. See Fig. 29-7. Applied properly, the picture will appear to have been painted on the surface. Sources for pictures to decoupage include wrapping paper, stationary, prints, and greeting cards. Magazine paper is not recommended because the colors bleed. Use the following procedure to decoupage.

Fig. 29-6. You can surface distress your project with special materials available in aerosol cans. Practice on a scrap piece before spraying your project.

Fig. 29-7. Decoupage is used to decorate wood surfaces with pictures.

1. Prepare the surface for a finish, as described in section IV.
2. Apply the desired finish material. If you paint the project, use a flat latex paint.
3. Apply a coat of clear wood sealer over the finish. Finishes and sealers must be compatible. Follow the manufacturer's directions for proper combinations.
4. Lay your design on a clean piece of wax paper. Apply several light coats of clear finish. Allow each to dry before applying the next coat.
5. If you are applying the print whole, you may want to antique it. Do this by tearing the edges so they are uneven. You may even tear into the print itself. After tearing the edges, place the print face down on a piece of scrap. Sand the edges lightly making them thinner and more uneven.
6. Apply glue to the back of the print. The glue should be thinned with water for easy spreading. For delicate, cut-out pictures, spread the glue on the wood surface. Then place the picture in position on the surface.
7. Place a piece of wax paper over the entire surface. Use a rubber roller or a

piece of soft wood to rub the picture flat. See Fig. 29-8. Start at the center and work toward the edges. When the picture is flat and smooth, remove the wax paper. Clean off the excess glue with a clean cloth and water.

8. Allow the glue to dry overnight.
9. Brush or spray on a top coat of the desired finish. Apply the finish to a small area first. Make sure the ink does not bleed into the top coat. If bleeding does occur, apply a thin coat of glue. After the glue dries, apply the top coat. Allow it to dry overnight.
10. Apply five or six coats of finish, allowing each coat to dry before applying the next.
11. Lightly sand the edges of the print. Use a fine abrasive (400 grit silicon carbide). Sand as much as possible without sanding through the finish.
12. Dust with a tack rag or a clean cloth. Dampen the cloth or rag with the solvent for the top coat.
13. Repeat steps 10-12 until the surface is smooth. You should not be able to feel the outline of the print.
14. After you obtain the desired surface, sand it smooth with 400 grit silicon carbide. Then rub with 3/0 steel wool, wax, and polish.

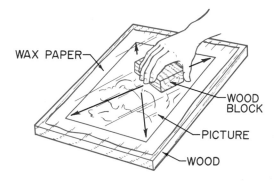

WAX PAPER

WOOD BLOCK

PICTURE

WOOD

Fig. 29-8. Protect the picture with wax paper as you smooth it. Be sure to wipe away all excess glue when you are finished.

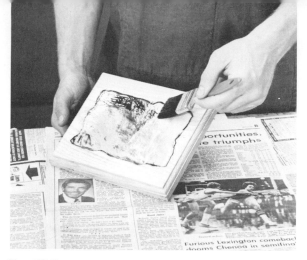

Fig. 29-9. Continue to apply coats of finish over the picture until the surface is completely flat.

Refinishing

Most finishes become dirty and worn over a period of years. They lose their luster as dirt and grime stick to the finish. Sometimes they even crack, dent, or lift away from the wood. Such finishes are often removed, or **stripped,** down to the bare wood. Then a new finish is applied. This process is called refinishing. See Fig. 29-10.

Stripping an old finish is hard, messy, time-consuming work. Before you strip a finish, try to restore it. A good cleaning may be all that is needed. You can fix small dents and scratches with fillers and burn-in sticks (see chapter 19). If these repairs do not work, you can still strip the old finish.

The first step after deciding to refinish is to identify the old finish. This is done by testing small areas with different solvents. Shellac is dissolved by denatured alcohol. Lacquer is dissolved by lacquer thinner. If neither of these solvents dissolves it, the finish is probably varnish. Use the solvent to remove lacquer and shellac. Remove varnish and most other finishes with paint and varnish remover.

To strip the finish, you will need the remover, an old brush, coarse steel wool, a scraper, clean rags, newspapers, a toothbrush, and a metal container. Work outside or in a well-ventilated room. If you work inside, cover everything that could be damaged by the remover. Wear old clothes, rubber gloves, and

Fig. 29-10. Almost all finishes deteriorate with age. If you cannot restore the finish, you will need to refinish it.

Fig. 29-11. As you scrape away the old finish, be careful not to scratch or dent the surface.

safety goggles. Be careful as you work. All removers contain dangerous chemicals and many are flammable. Use the following general procedure to strip a finish. More detailed instructions are usually found on the can of remover.

1. Remove all hardware, knobs, and handles.
2. Brush on a generous amount of remover. Brush in one direction only. Allow time for the remover to lift the finish (usually 15-20 minutes).
3. Gently remove the finish with a scraper as shown in Fig. 29-11. Be careful not to scratch or dent the surface. Apply more remover to hard-to-remove spots. A toothbrush is a handy tool for removing finish from carvings and moldings.
4. Remove the last of the finish with coarse steel wool dipped in the remover.
5. Soak a clean cloth in turpentine and wipe the surface clean. Then, with a clean, dry cloth, wipe the surface dry.
6. Prepare the surface for its new finish. See section IV for instructions on how to prepare a surface.
7. Select and apply the new finish.

New Terms

1. antiquing
2. decoupage
3. glazing
4. physical distressing
5. refinishing
6. stripping
7. surface distressing

Study Questions

1. Describe the most common glazing technique.
2. Name three ways of applying a wet coat of glaze.
3. List four materials that you can use to create different glazing effects.
4. Name the two methods of distressing wood.
5. When do you usually make physical distress marks on wood?
6. Why would you physically distress a painted surface **after** applying the paint?
7. When do you usually make surface distress marks on wood?
8. Give two ways of applying surface distress marks.
9. Describe one method you could use to create a splattered effect when surface distressing.
10. Give three sources for pictures to decoupage.
11. What often happens to finishes, making it necessary to refinish the project?
12. What should you always do before stripping a finish?
13. How do you identify a finish to be stripped?

Rubbing and polishing are the last steps in finishing most lacquer, varnish, and shellac finishes. Rubbing removes imperfections and makes the finish smooth. Polishing restores and adds to the luster of the finish. By rubbing and polishing you can produce the smoothest, most attractive finish possible. Polishing also protects the finish, making it last longer. See Fig. 30-1.

Rubbing a Finish

Even the most carefully applied finish will have imperfections. The slightest brush mark, dust particle, run, or sag can cause a rough finish. Light sanding between coats helps keep the finish smooth. Rubbing the last coat flat and smooth will ensure a beautiful finish.

Different methods and materials are used to rub final finishes. The following information describes the common materials and methods, and their effects on a finish.

Wet-Or-Dry Abrasives. Most rubbing operations begin with light sanding. Use a fine, wet-or-dry abrasive (400 or 600 grit). These abrasives cut rapidly. Be careful not to rub through the finish. Use water as a lubricant. **Lubricants** are liquids used to reduce friction. Lubricants also keep the abrasive clean and prevent scratches. Sand shellac with a dry abrasive. Do not use water with shellac. Use a sanding block for all flat surfaces.

Pumice and Rottenstone. Sanding smooths the finish but leaves it dull and unattractive. The finish is then rubbed to a gloss with abrasive powders. Pumice and rottenstone are common abrasive powders.

Pumice is ground from volcanic ash. It is available in grit sizes from 1-F to 4-F with 4-F being the finest grit.

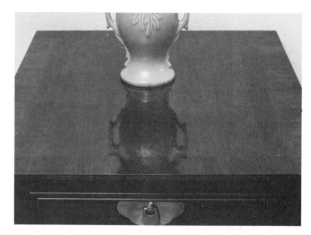

Fig. 30-1. This project was carefully rubbed and polished to make it as smooth and shiny as possible.

Fig. 30-2. Various abrasive materials and lubricants are used to rub final coats of finish.

Rottenstone is similar to pumice. It is made from limestone. It is finer than the finest-grit pumice. Rottenstone is used after pumice for smoother, glossier finishes.

Pumice and rottenstone are mixed with lubricants. Usually a special rubbing oil is used for this purpose. Water can also be used if a higher luster is desired. Do not use water as a lubricant for shellac.

To rub a finish, dampen a cloth or felt pad with the lubricant. Then dip the pad into the pumice or rottenstone. Rub the surface lightly and evenly. Be careful not to rub through the finish. Watch for clogging of dried abrasive on the pad. If the abrasive dries, add more lubricant to the surface. Never add abrasive after you have started rubbing. The new, sharp abrasive will make unwanted scratches.

Continue rubbing until you have a uniformly dull, flat surface. Then clean the surface with a cloth dipped in mineral spirits or naphtha. The finish is now ready for waxing and polishing.

Fig. 30-4. Rubbing with steel wool and wax is a fast way of rubbing and polishing a finish. Steel wool and wax do not produce the best results, however.

Rubbing Compounds. Ready-mixed rubbing compounds are available in paste form. They are used in place of pumice and rottenstone. Rubbing compounds are applied with a damp cloth or felt pad. They come in various grit sizes to control the luster. Choose a fine grit for a high gloss. Different colors are also available. Use a light color on a light finish.

Steel Wool and Wax. A finish can be rubbed to a satin gloss with steel wool and wax. The advantage to this method is that it is fast. Two steps — rubbing and polishing — are done at the same time.

The disadvantage to using steel wool and wax is the less-than-perfect finish. For the smoothest, shiniest finish, use the abrasive powders and then polish.

Use a 3/0 or 4/0 steel wool with a paste wax. The wax serves as both the lubricant and the protective final coat. Dip the steel wool in the wax and rub with the grain. See Fig. 30-4. Check the surface as you rub. When an even, dull surface is produced, buff the wax with a clean, dry cloth. After using a can of wax with steel wool, do not use the wax for any other purpose.

Fig. 30-3. Use a felt pad to apply pumice and rottenstone. For large, flat surfaces, glue or tack the felt to a wooden block.

Polishing a Finish

Polishing is recommended for just about every finish. This is especially true for rubbed finishes. Polishing with waxes and oils gives the finish a soft, attractive luster. Polishing also protects the finish. Just as finishes protect and beautify wood, polishes protect and beautify finishes.

Waxes. Both paste and liquid waxes are used to polish finishes. Both provide good resistance to water and dirt. Liquid waxes are easier to apply, but they are not as durable. The best waxes contain a high percentage of carnauba wax. Select a wax that is about 50% carnauba.

To apply wax, first remove all dust from the surface. Apply a thin coat of wax. Rub it on the surface with a clean, soft cloth. Let the wax dry according to instructions on the label. This is usually 5 to 15 minutes. Then use a clean, dry cloth to buff the wax until it shines. If more protection is needed, apply another coat.

If the project receives hard use, apply more wax as needed. If the wax builds up and turns white, remove it with mineral spirits. Then rewax the surface.

Polishes. Lemon oil polish is the best known of the furniture polishes. Nearly all polishes contain some lemon oil. A good lemon oil polish provides protection from moisture and dirt.

Polishes do not last as long or provide as much protection as waxes. They are applied in much the same way as waxes. Use a clean, dry cloth. Either soak the cloth with polish or pour some polish on the finish. Rub the polish into the finish and wipe off the excess with a dry cloth. You should repolish surfaces at least once a year.

New Terms

1. lubricant
2. polishing
3. pumice
4. rottenstone
5. rubbing
6. rubbing compound
7. wet-or-dry abrasive

Study Questions

1. Name the three finishes that are usually rubbed and polished.
2. Give two reasons why a finish is rubbed.
3. Why is a finish polished?
4. With which finish can you **not** use water as a lubricant?
5. Which abrasive powder has the finest grit — pumice or rottenstone?
6. If you wanted the highest luster possible, would you use water or oil as a lubricant?
7. Name two things to watch for while you rub with pumice or rottenstone.
8. What is the advantage to rubbing a finish with steel wool and wax? What is the disadvantage?
9. Compare liquid and paste waxes. Name one advantage of each.
10. Give two disadvantages of polishes as compared to waxes.

Fig. 30-5. After the wax has dried (usually 10-15 minutes), buff it until it is smooth and shiny.

Section
VI

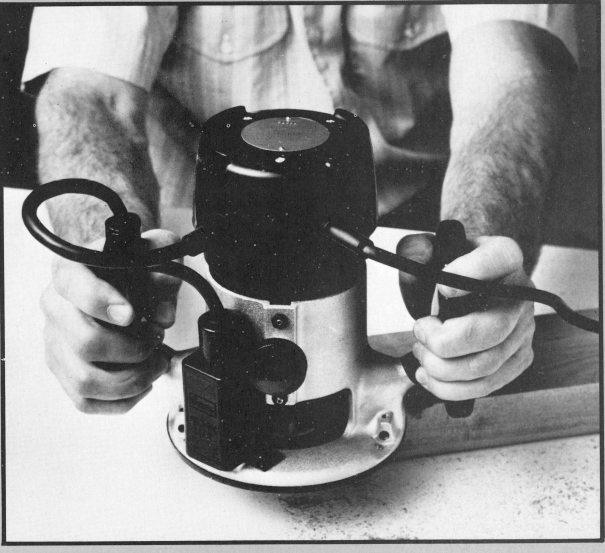

POWER

TOOLS

Power Tool Safety

There are several advantages to working with power tools rather than hand tools. You can do most woodworking operations faster with power tools. Power tools eliminate much of the physical effort in woodworking. Power tools are also easier than hand tools to use accurately. However, power tools can be much more dangerous to operate.

Importance of Safety

Safety is always important. It is especially important when you work with power tools. You should not use any power tools until you understand power tool safety. Machines turn sharp saw blades and cutters at high speeds. Accidents happen so quickly, the operator seldom knows what happened. A board caught in a machine can be thrown from the machine with tremendous force. This is dangerous for everyone in the work area. This is why learning to work safely is important for everyone.

Safety Attitude

Most power tool accidents can be avoided. About eight out of ten are caused by workers without the right safety attitude. These workers do not take safety seriously. Instead of working the "safe way," they work the "fast way." Instead of being safe, they put everyone in danger.

Machine safety is up to you. Develop a "safe way is the best way" attitude. Learn all you can about the safe operation of each machine. Listen and watch closely as your instructor demonstrates how to use a machine. Know all

the safety rules and the steps for operating each tool. Also, make sure you do the steps in the right order. Doing them out of order is often as dangerous as doing them incorrectly.

Machine Know-How

To operate a machine safely, you must know more than just how to turn it on and off. You must know how to do the basic operations. You also need to know how to make simple adjustments. Above all, you must know the machine's limits. Always keep the machine at a safe, steady speed. Never use the machine for a job the machine was not designed to do.

You cannot expect to be an expert on all machines right away. DO NOT EXPERIMENT. If you have a question, ask your instructor. The more you know about a machine, the safer you will be. A machine only does what its operator directs it to do. It can only be as safe as its operator.

As you learn to operate a machine, you will gain confidence. Do not become **too** confident. Overconfidence leads to carelessness, and carelessness causes accidents. This does not mean you should be afraid of machines however. A safe attitude is one of respect — respect for what machines can do.

Safety Rules

Learn the following general safety rules for power tools. Learn them **before** you operate any equipment. Also learn the specific safety rules for each tool. These rules are found in the appropriate chapters.

Fig. 31-1. You can never replace your eyes. Protect them at **all** times.

Fig. 31-3. Do not attempt to clean around a cutting blade that is moving. Make sure the machine is off and the blade completely stopped before you clean.

- Dress appropriately. Remove all ties, scarves, rings, and watches. Roll up long sleeves and tie back long hair. Loose clothing, hair, and jewelry can easily catch in revolving machine parts.
- Always wear approved eye protection in the shop. Some machines require extra eye protection over your safety glasses. See Fig. 31-1.
- Never operate a power tool until your instructor has shown you how. Never use a power tool without your instructor's permission.
- Never operate a power tool when the instructor is out of the shop.
- Make sure all safety guards are in place. See Fig. 31-2. Never remove a safety guard without your instructor's permission. Have your instructor check each setup before you begin working.
- Defects in the wood can be dangerous.

Fig. 31-2. Machine guards are designed to protect the operator. Unless your instructor gives you permission to remove them, the guards should always be in place.

Check the stock carefully for knots, splits, and other defects.
- Keep the machine clean. Remove all tools, lumber, and unnecessary materials. Objects left on the machine can vibrate into revolving cutters. They can then be thrown from the machine with great force. Never clean a machine while it is running. See Fig. 31-3.
- Always work with a plan of procedure. List every step and think through each one ahead of time.
- Before you plug in a machine, make sure the switch is in the "off" position. You do not want the machine to start unexpectedly.
- If you use an extension cord, use the correct wire size. This is determined by the length of cord and size of motor. Using a wire size that is too small will cause the tool to overheat.
- Keep all power cords away from blades and cutters while you work.

Fig. 31-4. Portable power tools are just as dangerous as large machines. All safety rules and attitudes apply to portable tools, as well as large machines.

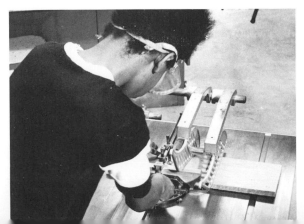

Fig. 31-5. Notice that this worker's hands are **not** in line with the blade. You can avoid putting your hands in a dangerous position if you think through the operation before you start.

Fig. 31-6. Making adjustments on a power tool that is running is extremely dangerous. Unplug the tool if there is a chance of it being turned on accidentally.

- Make sure the power tool is grounded. One with a double-insulated case need not be grounded. If you are unsure about this, check with your instructor.
- Never work in or around water with power tools. Water increases the chances of severe electrical shock.
- Safety zones are areas marked on the floor around machines. Only the operator should be in the Safety Zone.
- Stand in a comfortable, balanced position when working with power tools. Both feet should be firmly on the floor.
- Do not try to handle large, bulky pieces by yourself. Get someone to help you.
- Do not use the machine until it is operating at full speed.

- Always keep your hands a safe distance from cutters and blades. See Fig. 31-5.
- Always keep your eyes on the cutting action. Concentrate on what you are doing at all times.
- Be alert for any odors that might indicate overheating of the machine or stock.
- If anything unusual happens, turn off the machine immediately. If the machine does not sound right, turn it off immediately. As soon as it stops completely, check with your instructor.
- Never make an adjustment unless the power is off. The tool must come to a complete stop. See Fig. 31-6. This does not include speed adjustments on variable speed tools. These adjustments must be made with the machine running.
- Never leave a machine with the power on. The machine should be completely stopped before you leave it.
- Keep the work area clean. Remove all debris when you are finished.
- Never talk to or disturb anyone working with power equipment. If you must talk to an operator, wait until the operator notices you.
- Follow the specific safety rules for each machine.

Study Questions

1. Give three advantages to using power tools rather than hand tools.
2. Give one example of how power tools can be dangerous.
3. Who causes most accidents?
4. Why must you dress appropriately when using power tools?
5. What should you always check just before plugging in a power tool?
6. You should never operate a power tool in or around water. Why?
7. What should you do immediately if you notice something unusual in the operation of a machine?

Drill Press and Portable Electric Drill

The **drill press** is designed to drill and bore round holes. It is also used for mortising, shaping, routing, and sanding. You can make accurate cuts easier with a drill press than with hand tools. This is especially true for angle cuts and large cuts.

Drill presses are made in many sizes. The standard sizes are from 14 to 20 inches. Sizes are determined by the largest circle that the machine can drill through the center. A 15-inch drill press, for example, can drill a hole through the center of a 15-inch (diameter) circle.

The drills and bits used with drill presses to cut round holes are held in the chuck. The chuck is mounted on the end of a spindle. The spindle rotates inside the quill. With the spindle turning, the quill is lowered to make the cut. After the cut is made, a spring raises the quill.

Setting Up the Drill Press

Each job on the drill press requires several preparations. You must choose the correct drill or bit and install it. You must adjust the speed according to hole size. You then need to clamp the table at the correct height and position. Finally, you must set the depth stop for the desired cutting depth.

Drills and Bits. Many different drills and bits are used in the drill press. You need to select the right one for the material and type of job. Some of the more commonly used cutters and their uses are described below.

Machine spur bits are all-purpose bits for making smooth, accurate holes in wood. They are similar to auger bits. However, a machine spur bit has a round shank and brad point. See Fig. 32-2. These bits come in sizes from 3/16 inch to 1-1/4 inches, in steps of 1/32 inch. They have straight, 1/2-inch shanks.

Multi-spur bits are used to bore smooth, accurate, large holes. A multi-spur bit has a

Rockwell International

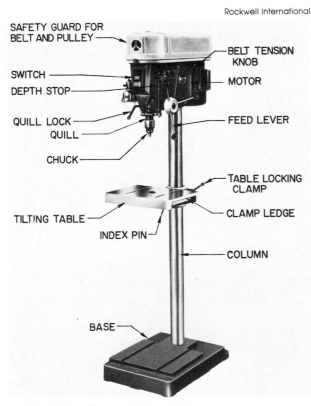

SAFETY GUARD FOR BELT AND PULLEY

SWITCH

DEPTH STOP

QUILL LOCK

QUILL

CHUCK

TILTING TABLE

INDEX PIN

BASE

BELT TENSION KNOB

MOTOR

FEED LEVER

TABLE LOCKING CLAMP

CLAMP LEDGE

COLUMN

Fig. 32-1. The parts of a drill press

Greenlee Tool Company

Fig. 32-2. Machine spur bit

Fig. 32-3. Multi-spur bit

Greenlee Tool Company

Fig. 32-4. Forstner bit.

Connecticut Valley Manufacturing Company

Fig. 32-5. Twist drill

Union Twist Drill Company

Irwin Auger Bit Company

Fig. 32-6. Spade bit

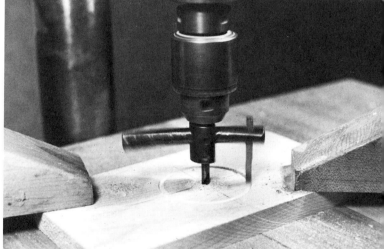

Millers Falls Company

Fig. 32-7. Hole saw

1/2-inch shank and a brad point that will locate the cut. See Fig. 32-3. It will cut plywood without chipping the veneer. It cuts hardwoods and softwoods equally well. It can also be used to make flat-bottomed holes. Common sizes are from 1/2 inch to 2 inches. Larger sizes are available, however.

Forstner bits are guided by their circular cutting rims. See Fig. 32-4. They are used to cut flat-bottomed holes. They range in size from 1/4 inch to 3 inches in diameter. They do not have a lead screw. Those with round shanks are designed for drill presses.

Twist drills are available in sizes ranging from 1/16 to 1/2 inch, by 64ths. They are used in hand drills, power drills, and drill presses. They are used to drill small holes for dowels, bolts, and wood screws. See Fig. 32-5. For 1/4-inch or larger holes, use a machine spur or multi-spur bit. These bits produce cleaner, more accurate large holes.

Spade bits have a flat, spade-shaped end. See Fig. 32-6. They have 1/4-inch shanks. They range in size from 1/4 inch to 1-1/2 inches, by 16ths. Spade bits cut quickly without clogging. They make fairly rough holes, however.

Fig. 32-8. A fly cutter can be used with a drill press to cut large holes. You can adjust the fly cutter to different sizes. Be sure to clamp the stock securely.

Stanley Tools

Fig. 32-9. Power bore bit

Hole saws are used to cut large holes completely through the stock. See Fig. 32-7. The most common diameters are from 1 inch to 3 inches. Larger sizes are available.

Power-bore bits range in size from 3/8 to 1 inch, by 8ths. They cut quickly and smoothly without clogging. See Fig. 32-9.

Installing the Cutter. Cover the table with a piece of scrap wood. This will protect the cutter and the table while you install the bit. Insert the shank all the way into the chuck. The standard drill press chuck holds shank diameters of 1/2 inch or less. Tighten the chuck jaws around the cutter with a chuck wrench as shown in Fig. 32-10. Make sure you **remove the wrench from the chuck**. If not removed, the wrench could be thrown from the chuck at a high speed.

Setting Speeds. For woodworking, drill presses run at speeds from 450 to 4700 rpm's. Set the speed according to the hole size and hardness of the wood. For large holes (1/2 inch or more) and hard wood, use the lowest speeds. Use higher speeds for small holes.

On some drill presses speeds are adjusted with **belt drives** and **step pulleys**. Other models change speeds with **variable-speed controls**. With step pulleys, change the speed by moving the belt to a different position. See Fig. 32-11. (**Caution:** Always disconnect the power when changing the belt positions.) Placing the belt on the smallest motor pulley and the largest spindle pulley produces the slowest speed. With variable-speed controls, the machine must be running while you change the speed. Speeds are adjusted by simply turning a lever.

Fig. 32-10. Chuck wrenches are used to loosen and tighten the jaws of the chuck. Be sure to remove the wrench immediately after use.

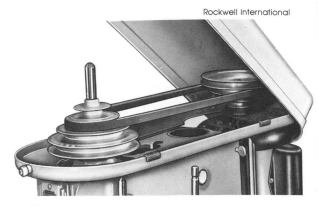

Fig. 32-11. On some drill presses, the speed is changed by moving the belt on the pulleys. The power should be disconnected before making this adjustment.

Adjusting the Table. Place the stock on the table. Loosen the clamp that locks the table in place. Raise or lower the table as needed. There should be about 1/2 inch *(12 mm)* between the cutter and the stock. Make sure the hole in the table is directly under the cutter. Also be sure the table is perpendicular to the bit for straight cuts. When the table is positioned correctly, reclamp it.

If you are cutting completely through the stock, place a scrap piece under it. This will help prevent splintering. It will also protect the cutter and the table. Put the scrap piece under the stock before you adjust the table.

Setting the Depth Gauge. You can cut holes to certain depths by adjusting the depth gauge. To do this, draw a line on the stock at the desired depth. Then place the stock on the table. Make sure the power is off. Pull the feed lever down until the cutter is even with the depth line. Clamp the quill to hold the cutter in this position. Set the depth gauge to the proper depth. See Fig. 32-12. Then release the quill clamp and make a test cut.

Drill Press Safety

- Know and follow the general safety rules for operating power tools on page 211.

- **Never** leave the chuck wrench in the chuck. Remove the chuck wrench **immediately** after installing or removing a cutting tool.
- Clamp small pieces of stock. Also clamp the stock when you cut large holes. The cutter could pull the stock from your hand. If you are not sure you can hold the stock, **clamp it**.
- Keep your fingers away from the rotating cutters.
- Use only straight-shanked cutters in the drill press chuck. Never use an auger bit with a tapered tang.
- When using a sanding, routing, shaping, or mortising attachment, know and follow the safety rules for the corresponding machine.
- Use the correct speed for the job. Drilling large holes requires **low** speeds. Drilling in hard stock also requires low speeds.
- Disconnect the power when changing belt speeds.
- If a cutter catches in the wood, turn the machine off and step back. Wait until the machine stops completely before removing the stock.
- Never leave a machine until it has come to a complete stop.

Fig. 32-12. To drill a certain depth, lock the quill at the desired depth. Then adjust the depth gauge.

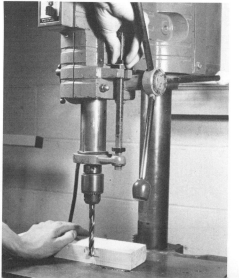

Fig. 32-13. The table must be perpendicular to the cutter to drill a straight hole. You can check this with a try square.

Drilling and Boring

In all drilling and boring operations you need to lay out the locations of the holes. Use a scratch awl to mark the locations. Chapter 11 has more information on how to lay out the holes.

Always guard against splintering when cutting through the stock. One method is to put a scrap piece under the stock. Another method is to stop drilling just as the cutter point breaks through the second side. Then turn the stock over and finish the cut. Reducing the feed rate will also decrease the chances of splintering.

Making Straight Holes. You cannot make straight holes unless the table is perpendicular to the bit. Use a try square as shown in Fig. 32-13 to check squareness. You can usually hold the stock by hand. Use one hand to hold the stock. Use the other hand to pull the feed lever down. Always keep your fingers away from the cutter. If you are not sure you can hold the stock, clamp it. For example, small stock and pieces with large holes are often difficult to hold and should be clamped.

Line up the center of the hole and the bit. Then feed the bit into the wood slowly. See Fig. 32-14. For large and deep holes, occasionally raise the bit. Let the bit cool. Then remove cuttings that could clog the cut.

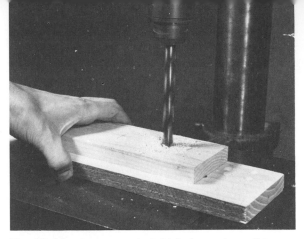

Fig. 32-14. Boring a straight hole such as this one does not require clamping. Notice the scrap piece. It prevents splintering and protects the cutter and table.

Fig. 32-15. You can cut straight holes on the end of stock by turning the table. Make sure the table is parallel to the cutter and that the stock is well clamped.

Making Holes at an Angle. Legs of a stool or table are often attached at an angle. Cutting angled holes is fairly easy on a drill press. This is because the table is adjustable. To set up an angle cut, set a T-bevel to the desired angle. Then loosen the table. Hold the T-bevel as shown in Fig. 32-16. Tilt the table to the proper angle and tighten it.

Always clamp the stock when cutting at an angle. Cutters tend to move the stock when the table is angled. Clamping a scrap block to the stock will help guide the cutter. This is especially helpful if the scrap block is cut at the same angle. See Fig. 32-17. Make a hole through the block and into the stock. You can use the same scrap block to cut other holes the same size.

You can also cut compound angles on a drill press. To do this, tilt the table and angle the stock (usually 45°). The chart in Fig. 32-18 gives the proper tilt for the most common compound angles.

Making Holes in Round and Irregular Shapes. Special methods are used to clamp and support round and irregular stock. Use a V-block to hold round stock and dowel rods. See Figs. 32-19 and 32-20. Each irregular piece requires its own clamping setup. See Figs. 32-21 and 32-22 for some drilling methods used with irregular stock.

Fig. 32-16. To cut holes at an angle, use a T-bevel to set the table at the desired angle.

Fig. 32-17. Always clamp the stock securely when making an angle cut. Clamp a scrap piece on top of the stock to ensure a smooth hole.

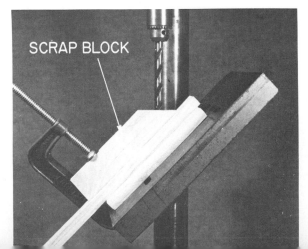

SCRAP BLOCK

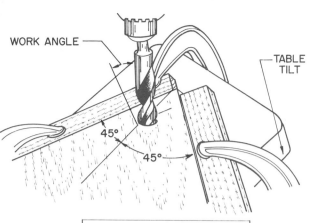

WORK ANGLE

TABLE TILT

45°

45°

Equal Compound Angles			
Work Angle	Table Tilt	Work Angle	Table Tilt
2 °	2-3/4 °	12 °	16-3/4 °
3 °	4-1/4 °	13 °	18-1/4 °
4 °	5-1/2 °	14 °	19-1/2 °
5 °	7 °	15 °	21 °
6 °	8-1/4 °	17-1/2 °	24-1/4 °
7 °	9-1/2 °	20 °	27 °
8 °	11 °	22-1/2 °	30-1/4 °
9 °	12-1/2 °	25 °	33 °
10 °	13-3/4 °	27-1/2 °	36 °
11 °	15-1/4 °	30 °	39 °

Fig. 32-18. This is the proper setup for drilling a compound angle. Use the chart to tilt the table to the correct angle.

Other Operations

You can use the drill press for more than just drilling and boring. With the right attachments you can sand, shape, rout, and mortise on the drill press.

Fig. 32-22. In this method of drilling dowel holes for miter joints, the wood fence is clamped at a 45° angle.

Sanding. Various diameters of **sanding drums** are available for the drill press. See Fig. 32-23. **Abrasive sleeves** are manufactured to fit the drums. Some drums have 1/2-inch shafts that fit in the drill press chuck. Others have tapered sleeves that fit the tapered spindle. The drill press speed should be set at about 1200 rpm's for sanding.

Fig. 32-19. Use a V-block to hold dowel rods and other cylindrical stock. Line up the cutter with the center of the "V."

Fig. 32-20. You can use a V-block to hold cylindrical stock being cut on an end.

Fig. 32-21. Drilling and boring irregular-shaped stock often requires unique clamping arrangements. Two hand screws are being used here.

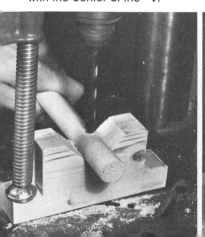

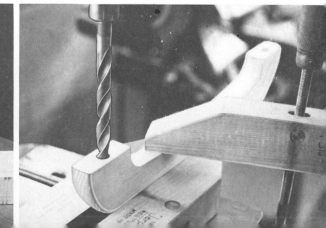

Make a small table to support the stock. Position it on the drill press table as shown in Fig. 32-23. The hole in the sanding table lets you use the drum at different heights. This way you can use all of the abrasive sleeve.

Lock the sleeve in place by tightening the nut at the bottom of the drum. Always feed the stock against the drum's rotation. Review all safety rules for the operation of sanders in chapter 44.

Shaping. You can also use the drill press to shape stock. An **arbor attachment** holds the cutters, and a special table guides the stock. The table has a fence similar to a standard shaper fence. See Fig. 32-24. You can adjust the fence in two parts. Run the drill press close to 5,000 rpm's for best shaping results. Review the safety rules and operating instructions in chapter 43.

Routing. Whenever possible, use a standard router for routing operations. Some routing jobs, however, are easier on the drill press. See

Fig. 32-25. Routing on the drill press requires a **routing attachment**. Never use the standard drill press chuck. It is not designed for this type of work. If used for routing, the chuck could loosen and release the cutter. For best results, run the drill press at about 5,000 rpm's. Always feed against the rotation of the cutter. Review the safety rules and the operating instructions in chapter 42.

Mortising. Special machines are built just for the purpose of mortising. You can also cut a mortise on a drill press. To do this you need a **mortising attachment** and a **mortising bit and chisel**. See Fig. 32-26. The bit turns inside the chisel, which remains stationary. The rotating bit removes most of the stock. The chisel makes the hole square by cutting away the corners. No two mortising attachments are installed the same way. Follow the instructions in the manufacturer's manual. For more information on the different types of mortise-and-tenon joints, see chapter 12.

When making a mortise-and-tenon joint, cut the mortise first. Lay out the mortise as explained in chapter 13. Select the mortising attachment with the proper size chisel. The mortise length results from making a series of square cuts end to end.

1. Position and clamp the fence. The mortising attachment should line up with the mortise to be cut. Make sure the sides of the chisel are perpendicular to the fence.
2. Set and clamp the depth gauge for the desired depth. Set the gauge about 1/8

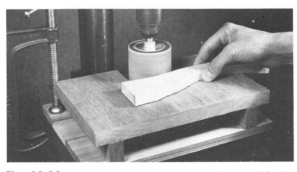

Fig. 32-23. A sanding drum makes it possible to sand on a drill press. The special sanding table lets you adjust the drum to different heights.

Fig. 32-24. You can shape wood with a drill press by using a shaping attachment.

Fig. 32-25. Use a special router chuck to do routing operations on a drill press. Run the machine at 5,000 rpm's for best results.

inch deeper than the length of the tenon. This provides for excess glue.

3. Cut a spacer block out of a scrap piece. Make it the exact length of the mortise. Lay it on the table next to the fence. Locate the mortise from the end of the stock by clamping a stop block on the fence. See Fig. 32-27.

4. Place the spacer block between the stop block and the end of the stock. Make one end cut.

5. Remove the spacer block and make the other end cut. Remove the material in between by making additional cuts.

You must sometimes cut two mortises into adjoining sides of a leg. To do this, make the first cut deep enough to meet the first side of the second mortise. Cut the second mortise the full depth. Then miter the ends of the tenons on the rails to meet in the corner.

Electric Drill

Portable electric drills make hand drilling easy and quick. They are often used in place of the drill press. Many large projects cannot be moved to the drill press. For these jobs electric drills are much handier than the drill press. Common sizes of electric drills are 1/4, 3/8, and 1/2 inch. Their sizes are determined by the capacity of their chucks. See Fig. 32-28.

Electric drill motors run at speeds between 750 and 4,000 rpm's. Use slower speeds to cut large holes in wood. Also use slower speeds for metal working. Some electric drills have variable-speed controls. The chucks on these drills turn faster as you apply more pressure to the trigger. Some drills also have reversing switches. You can use variable-speed drills with reversing switches as power screwdrivers. Special screwdriver bits are made for this purpose. See Fig. 32-29.

Electric Drill Safety

• Know and follow the general safety rules for operating power tools on page 211.

Fig. 32-26. A mortising attachment is needed to mortise with a drill press.

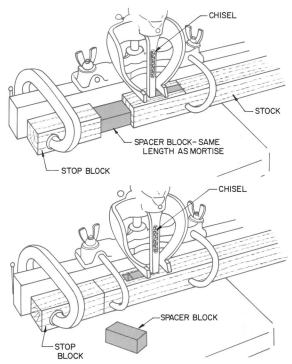

Fig. 32-27. Make the end cuts of the mortise first. If you are mortising several identical pieces, use a spacer block.

Fig. 32-28. Portable electric drill (3/8 inch) and chuck wrench

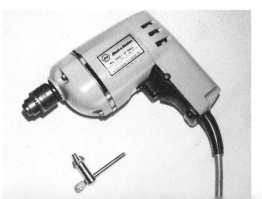

PHILLIPS   **STANDARD**

Rockwell International

Fig. 32-29. You can use the electric drill with screw-driver bits to drive and remove screws.

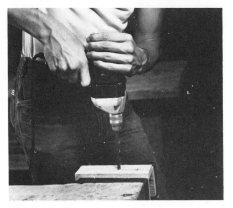

Fig. 32-30. Be sure you hold the portable drill at the desired angle.

- Remove the chuck wrench from the chuck after installing the cutter.
- Do not lay the drill down until it has completely stopped.
- Make sure you are not standing in or around water when you use an electric drill. This increases the chances of severe electrical shock.

Using Electric Drills

Electric drills use the same drills and bits as drill presses and hand drills. To install a cutter, open the chuck and insert the shank. Tighten the chuck by turning the outside of the chuck clockwise. Be sure the cutter is centered in the chuck. Then tighten the chuck with a chuck wrench. **Do not forget to remove the chuck wrench**.

Lay out and mark the location of the hole with a scratch awl. Place the center of the cutter on the mark. Hold the drill at the desired angle and pull the trigger. Apply enough pressure to feed the cutter into the stock. Do not force the drill. Let the cutter make a smooth, clean hole. See Fig. 32-30.

New Terms

1. abrasive sleeve
2. arbor attachment
3. drill press
4. hole saw
5. machine spur bit
6. mortising attachment
7. mortising bit and chisel
8. multi-spur bit
9. portable electric drill
10. power bore bit
11. routing attachment
12. sanding drum
13. spade bit
14. variable speed control
15. V-block

Study Questions

1. List four operations in addition to drilling and boring that you can do on a drill press.
2. How are the sizes of drill presses determined?
3. List the four steps in setting up a drill press.
4. What is an all-purpose bit used in drill presses to make holes in wood?
5. Give two reasons why you should cover the drill press table with a piece of wood before installing a cutter.
6. What is the chuck capacity on most drill presses?
7. Should you adjust the drill press to a high, or a low speed to cut large holes in hard wood?
8. Give three reasons for placing a scrap piece under stock that will be drilled all the way through.
9. What should you do immediately after installing a cutting tool in a drill press?
10. Give two examples of situations in which you would clamp the stock being drilled.
11. What layout tool do you need to adjust a drill press table for an angle cut?
12. Explain why you should use an extra table when sanding on a drill press.
13. What tool must you have for routing operations done on a drill press?
14. What types of jobs are often easier to do with a portable electric drill than with a drill press? Explain.

Jigsaw and Saber Saw

Jigsaws and saber saws are used to make curved and irregular cuts. Both saws are **reciprocating saws.** This means that the saw blades move up and down. This up-and-down sawing action is the same action used in hand sawing. Jigsaws are like large, power-operated coping saws. Saber saws are like power compass or keyhole saws.

Jigsaws

Jigsaws are sometimes called scroll saws. See Fig. 33-1. They are used mainly to make fine, detailed cuts on thin stock. Jigsaw blades are very small. For this reason jigsaws can cut sharp corners and small designs. Jigsaws also have the advantage of being able to make inside cuts. They make these cuts without cutting through the outside stock. See Fig. 33-2.

The main parts of a jigsaw include the over arm, table, and motor. These parts are mounted on a base. The motor drives a mechanism that creates the up and down cutting action. The lower blade chuck is attached to this mechanism. The upper blade chuck is attached to the tension sleeve. Blades are in-

Rockwell International

Fig. 33-1. This is a 24-inch jigsaw (also called scroll saw). The size is determined by the distance from the blade to the back of the over arm.

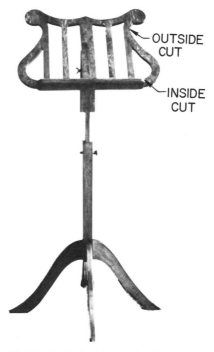

Fig. 33-2. Making both inside and outside cuts was necessary to construct this music stand. You will find the plans for this project in section IX.

Material or Operation	General Features of Blade	Operating Speed CSM
HARDWOOD ¾ in. stock	Medium temper, set teeth. Not over 15 teeth per inch.	1000 to 1750
HARDWOOD ¼ in. stock	Medium temper. Teeth need not be set.	1750
SOFTWOOD ¾ in. stock	Medium temper, set or wide-spaced teeth. Not over 10 teeth per inch.	1750
SOFTWOOD ¼ in. stock	Teeth need not be tempered or set.	1300 to 1750
PUZZLES, INLAYS, MARQUETRY	Not tempered; not set. Blade must be thin.	1300 to 1750
PLASTIC, BONE, IVORY (rough cut)...	Medium temper, set teeth.	1000 to 1300
PLASTIC, BONE, IVORY (finish cut)...	Medium temper, with or without set.	1000 to 1750

Fig. 33-3. Jigsaw Blades and Cutting Speeds

serted through a hole in the table and clamped into both chucks.

At the base of the guide post is the upper guide assembly. This assembly supports the blade above the table. The lower guide supports the blade below the table. The hold down helps keep the stock flat on the table. A tilt scale under the table tilts the table to one side or the other. This makes it possible to cut bevels up to 45°.

Jigsaw sizes are determined by the distance from the blade to the back of the over arm. Standard sizes for school shops are the 18- and 24-inch models. A smaller 12-inch model is sometimes used for light work.

Jigsaws make between 600 and 1700 cutting strokes per minute (csm). The methods of adjusting speeds vary from model to model. Generally the higher speeds are used for soft materials. Lower speeds are used for harder materials. Recommended cutting speeds for different situations are given in Fig. 33-3.

Jigsaw Blades

A standard jigsaw blade for cutting wood is .11 inch wide and .02 inch thick. It has 15 teeth per inch. Other sizes, with more or less teeth, are also available. Three factors determine the best blade for a particular job.

- thickness of stock
- hardness of stock
- sharpness of curves

Thin, narrow blades make it easier to cut sharp curves. Finer (more teeth per inch) blades are needed for thick, hard stock. As a general rule, you should use the widest, coarsest blade that will make the desired cut. The chart in Fig. 33-3 gives recommended blades for different situations.

Fig. 33-4. There are three basic steps for inserting a jigsaw blade: 1) clamping the blade in the lower chuck, 2) clamping it in the upper chuck, 3) adjusting the guide assembly.

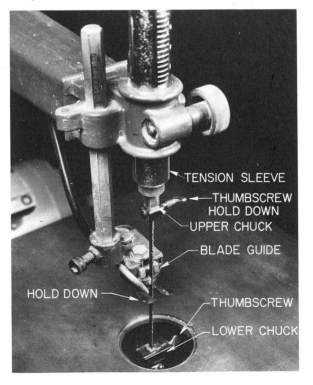

To insert the blade, place it (teeth down) in the lower chuck. Make sure the blade is perpendicular to the table. Tighten the thumbscrew on the lower chuck. Then loosen the tension sleeve clamp. Bring the upper chuck down to the blade and clamp the blade securely. Pull the tension sleeve up and tighten the clamp. Thin blades require less tension than thick blades. Using the minimum amount of tension will make the blade last longer. If the blade buckles on the upstroke, more tension is needed.

Once the blade is secure, adjust the blade guide. Adjust it according to the correct blade thickness. Set the guide just behind the gullets (notches) in the blade. Do not allow the teeth to run in the guide. This will dull the teeth.

Now place the stock against the blade. Set the hold down on top of the stock. The hold down should apply a little pressure to the stock. When it does, clamp it in position.

Jigsaw Safety

- Know and follow the general safety rules for operating power tools on page 211.
- Make all setups and adjustments with the power off.
- Use the correct blade for the stock (thickness) and curve (sharpness) being cut.
- Never try to turn a small radius with a wide blade. The radius should not be more than three times the blade width.
- Clamp the blade securely in both chucks with the teeth pointing down.
- Adjust the guides so they properly support the blade.
- Adjust the hold down so that it applies light pressure to the stock.
- Rotate the motor by hand to check that all adjustments have been made properly.
- Plan cuts to avoid backing out of curves.
- Do not force the work into the blade. This can cause the blade to bend and break.
- Keep your fingers out of line with the saw.

Using a Jigsaw

Trace the pattern to be cut onto the stock. You can either sit or stand to operate a jigsaw. The important thing is to be comfortable. Cut with the blade on the waste side of the cutting line. Feed the work into the blade at a constant speed. Do not force it.

Think through all your cuts before you start. Planning your cuts will save time and help you avoid problems. For example, the over arm often gets in the way of large pieces. You can sometimes avoid this problem by feeding from the side rather than the front. When you make several cuts, it is sometimes helpful to number them. Getting into difficult spots is easy; getting out is not.

Curved Cuts. It is important to be patient when cutting curves. Allow yourself time to guide your work along the pattern line. If you hurry, you will spend more time filing and sanding later. It is easier to let the machine do the work. Relief cuts, as shown in Fig. 33-5, will make it easier to cut complex patterns. **Relief cuts** eliminate backing out of long cuts and forcing sharp turns.

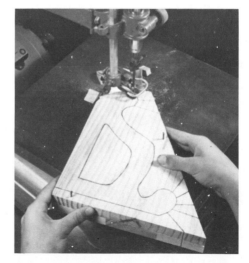

Fig. 33-5. Relief cuts make it possible to cut sharp outside curves. Notice the two boards nailed together. Cutting them at the same time ensures that they are the same size and shape.

Inside Cuts. A major advantage of the jigsaw is its ability to make inside cuts. Inside cuts are cuts that cannot be started from the outside of a board. See Fig. 33-6. To make an inside cut, drill a hole within the design. The hole should be large enough to pass the blade through. Sometimes the inside design includes a true circle. If it does, drill the hole the same size as the circle.

Disconnect the jigsaw power supply to set up the job. Release the blade from the upper chuck. Then raise the tension sleeve out of the way. Also loosen and raise the upper guide assembly. Then lower the bottom chuck to its lowest position. Slip the stock over the top of the blade. Readjust the upper guide assembly and replace the blade in the upper chuck. Apply the needed tension and connect the power. To remove the stock after the cut, simply reverse this procedure.

Beveled Cuts. Because you can tilt the table, beveled cuts are fairly easy on a jigsaw. Simply loosen the table clamp and tilt the table to the angle desired on the tilt scale. Work on only one side of the blade when making beveled cuts. See Fig. 33-7. Cutting on both sides will result in reversed bevels. Most woodworkers position the stock so the waste is above the blade.

Fig. 33-6. The first step in making an inside cut is drilling a hole. The blade is then inserted through the hole. Drill extra holes to help turn the blade around sharp corners.

Marquetry. A decorative arrangement of wood pieces is called marquetry. Many different types and colors of wood are used. The small wood pieces are carefully cut on a jigsaw. This produces beautiful pictures and designs in wood, such as the one in Fig. 33-8. The steps in making a simple marquetry are shown in Fig. 33-9. The pieces of wood are cut from veneers. This is generally done with a thin blade at a slight angle. The angle cut helps hide the kerf. See Fig. 33-10.

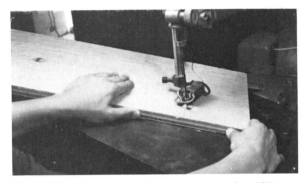

Fig. 33-7. You can make angle cuts by tilting a jigsaw table. This worker must make all cuts with the waste side to the left of the blade. Working around the blade would result in reversed bevels.

Silas Kopf

Fig. 33-8. This picture, made from small pieces of wood, is an example of marquetry.

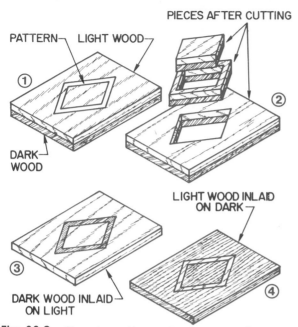

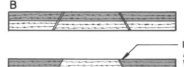

A

IF THE CUTS ARE MADE STRAIGHT THE KERFS WILL SHOW WHEN THE PIECES ARE ASSEMBLED.

B

IF THE CUTS ARE MADE AT A SLIGHT ANGLE, NO KERF WILL SHOW WHEN THE PIECES ARE ASSEMBLED.

Fig. 33-10. Cut the wood pieces used in marquetry at a slight angle. They will then fit tighter and the saw kerfs will be less visible.

PATTERN — LIGHT WOOD — PIECES AFTER CUTTING

DARK WOOD

① ②

LIGHT WOOD INLAID ON DARK

③ ④

DARK WOOD INLAID ON LIGHT

Fig. 33-9. Steps in making a simple marquetry

Saber Saws

Saber saws are also called bayonet saws. They are used as portable jigsaws. See Fig. 33-11. They are available in several sizes and shapes. Saber saw blades are attached on only one end. This lets you make inside cuts without disconnecting the blade. Saber saws cut on the upstroke rather than the downstroke.

Saber Saw Blades

Saber saw blades for cutting wood have 6 to 12 teeth per inch. Other blades are available for cutting leather, cardboard, rubber, plastic, and metal. Wide blades are used for straight cuts. Narrow blades are available for cutting curves. To cut a circle, use a blade no wider than one-third the circle's radius. For example, the widest blade for cutting a circle with a 3/4-inch radius would be 1/4 inch wide.

Each saber saw manufacturer makes a different blade chuck. Some universal blades fit several different chucks. Be sure the blade fits the saw you are using. The chart in Fig. 33-12 will help you select the best blade.

Rockwell International

ON-OFF SWITCH — HANDLE

GUIDE KNOB

BLADE SCREW

TILTING BASE

BLADE

Rockwell

Fig. 33-11. Saber saws are available in various sizes for light-, medium-, and heavy-duty work.

Before you install a blade, make sure the saw is unplugged. Loosen the set screw on the chuck. Insert the blade into the chuck as far as it will go. Then tighten the set screw securely.

Length	Teeth Per 1"	Use
3-1/2"	7	Fast-ripping woods, plywood to 2-1/2"
3-1/2"	10	Medium cuts woods, plywood to 2-1/2"
3"	10	Finish cuts woods, plywood to 2-1/2"
6"	7	Fast-ripping woods, up to 4"
3-1/2"	14	Heavy metals over 3/8" thick
3"	24	Metals 1/8" to 5/8" thick
3"	32	Metals 1/16" to 3/8" thick

Fig. 33-12. Selection of Saber Saw Blades

Saber Saw Safety

- Know and follow the general safety rules for operating power tools on page 211.
- Make sure the switch is in the OFF position before connecting the power.
- Never raise the saw from a cut while it is operating. The saw could kick out of your hand and cause an injury.
- Wait until the blade completely stops before putting the saw down.

Fig. 33-13. Although saber saws are often used freehand, you can use them with ripping guides to make straight cuts.

Using a Saber Saw

Saber saws are usually guided freehand along a pattern or outline. Ripping guides are sometimes used for straight cuts. See Fig. 33-13. The ripping guide is adjustable. It is clamped in place with a thumbscrew or machine screw.

You can adapt the ripping guide to cut accurate circles. Set the guide to the desired radius. Locate the center of the circle. Then drive a nail through the hole in the rip guide. The saw will pivot on the nail and cut a true circle. See Fig. 33-14.

You can also make bevel cuts with a saber saw. You can do this by tilting the base. Disconnect the power and loosen the base clamp. Then set the scale to the desired angle.

Fig. 33-14. By using a ripping guide as shown, you can easily cut a true circle with a saber saw.

New Terms

1. inside cut
2. marquetry
3. reciprocating saw
4. relief cut

Study Questions

1. What is the main use of jigsaws?
2. Jigsaws have the advantage of being able to make a certain kind of cut. What kind?
3. How is the size of a jigsaw determined?
4. Would you set the jigsaw at a high, or a low speed to cut a hard material?
5. Give three factors that determine the best jigsaw blade for a particular job.
6. What is the advantage of using the minimum amount of tension that will hold a blade in place.
7. When should you number your cuts? Why should you number them?
8. Why is it necessary to cut on only one side of the jigsaw blade when making beveled cuts?
9. Name two ways that saber saws differ from jigsaws.
10. If a circle has a radius of 3/8 inch, what is the widest saber saw blade that can be used to cut that circle?

Band Saw

Band saws are used for many different cutting operations. They are used primarily to make outside, irregular cuts. Band saws are not generally used to make straight cuts. This is because greater accuracy is possible with table saws. Band saws are also used to cut materials other than wood. Abrasive belts are used on a band saw to sand curved cuts.

All band saws have two wheels, one above and one below the table. See Fig. 34-1. The saw blade, a continuous steel band, rides around these wheels. The blade moves through adjustable guides above and below the table. The guides keep the blade from twisting when cutting curves. The upper guide is raised and lowered for different thicknesses of stock. On most models the table can be tilted 10° to the left and 45° to the right. This makes it easy to cut bevels with a band saw. Many band saws

are also equipped with a rip fence and miter gauge.

The size of a band saw is determined by the diameter of its wheels. The most common sizes in school shops are 12, 14, 18, and 20 inches. Most of these machines will cut stock up to 6 inches *(150 mm)* thick. Larger machines will cut thicker stock.

Band Saw Blades

Blades for standard band saws are available in widths from 3/16 to 1 inch. They are sold in lengths and thicknesses that fit various models. Smaller thicknesses and narrower widths are used to cut sharper curves.

Different types of teeth are manufactured for band saw blades. The **hook tooth** with a **raker set** is considered best for wood. This blade will also cut plastics. See Fig. 34-2. For most work, blades with four to six teeth per inch work well. Blades with more teeth per inch make smoother cuts. They do not cut as fast, however.

Changing Blades. Before you change band saw blades, disconnect the power. Then remove the upper and lower wheel guards. Also remove the throat plate and the blade slot set screw. Lower the upper wheel by turning the blade tension handle. Then remove the old blade.

Rockwell International

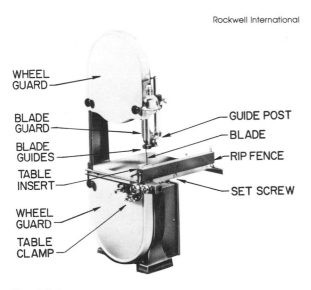

WHEEL
GUARD

BLADE
GUARD

BLADE
GUIDES

TABLE
INSERT

WHEEL
GUARD

TABLE
CLAMP

GUIDE POST

BLADE

RIP FENCE

SET SCREW

Fig. 34-1. Parts of a band saw

Fig. 34-2. A hook tooth with a raker set is the best type of band saw blade for cutting wood. The teeth tilt alternately to the left, to the right, and then point straight up.

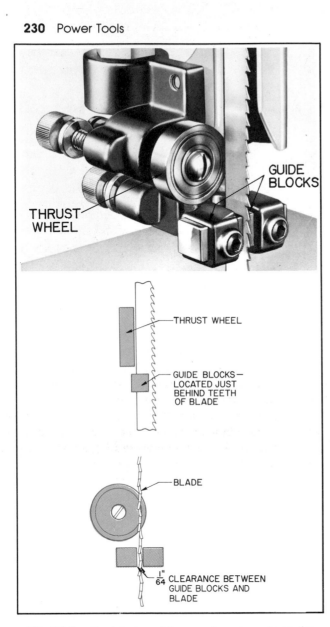

Fig. 34-3. The blade guides on a band saw keep the blade from twisting. These diagrams show how to adjust the blade in the guides.

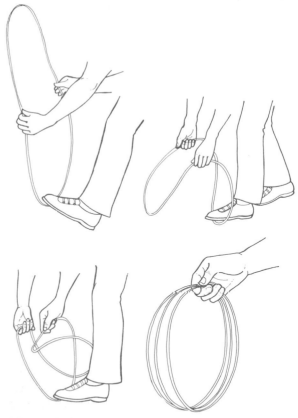

Fig. 34-4. Use this procedure to fold a band saw blade for storage.

The teeth of the new blade should point down and toward you as you hold the blade in front of you. If the teeth point up, turn the blade inside out. Install the blade on the wheels. Apply slight tension by raising the upper wheel. Turn the bottom wheel by hand. The blade should stay in the center of the wheel rim. If it does not, adjust the tilt of the upper wheel. When the blade is centered, adjust the wheel to the right tension. The correct tension depends on the width of blade being used.

Adjust both blade guides. See Fig. 34-3. Position the guide blocks just back of the blade's teeth. Then adjust the blade clearance. Use a small piece of paper on each side of the blade. Adjust the blocks until they just touch the paper. This will leave about 1/64 inch (.4 mm) clearance between the blade and the blocks. Finish the adjustments by setting the thrust wheels. They should be about 1/64 inch behind the blade. Make a final check by turning the wheel. Then have your instructor inspect your adjustments.

Folding Blades. Band saw blades are large and awkward to handle. A blade for a 20-inch band saw, for example, is over 12 feet (360 cm) long. To fold and store a blade, hold it in front of you. See Fig. 34-4. Twist the blade in toward the center. As you do this, force the top of the loop away and down. This will form three loops, making the blade easier to store. Tie the loops together with string so they do not come apart.

Band Saw Safety

- Know and follow the general safety rules for operating power tools on page 211.
- Adjust the upper guide so it is from 1/8 to 1/4 inch *(3 to 6 mm)* above the stock.
- Keep your hands out of line with the blade. Keep your fingers at least 2 inches *(50 mm)* from the blade at all times. Planning your cuts will help you avoid unsafe positioning.
- Never stand on the right side of a band saw. If the blade breaks, this is a dangerous area.

Fig. 34-5. The proper position for operating a band saw is in front of the machine. Never stand to the right of the blade.

- Do not start cutting until the machine has reached full running speed.
- Avoid backing out of long cuts and curves. Plan your cuts and make relief cuts. When you must back out of a long cut, turn off the machine. Wait until the blade stops to back out.
- If the machine is making unusual noises, turn it off. If it is not running properly, turn it off. Wait until it completely stops. Then immediately ask your instructor for help.
- If the blade breaks, turn off the machine. Then ask your instructor for help.
- If you cut round or cylindrical stock, clamp the stock securely. This will keep it from rotating while you cut.
- When making compound cuts, be sure the stock is properly supported on the table.

Using a Band Saw

The worker in Fig. 34-5 is in the right position to operate a band saw. If you are right-handed, stand slightly to the left of the table. Use your right hand to feed the stock. Use your left hand to guide it. Apply even, forward pressure. Try to keep your right hand about 15 inches *(375 mm)* from the blade. This will give you the best possible control.

Cutting Curves. You can easily cut fairly sharp curves with a band saw. Select a blade the correct width for the desired curve. The chart in Fig. 34-6 gives the sharpest curve a

Width of Saw Blade	Minimum Radius of Circle
1/8″	1/2
3/16″	3/4
1/4″	1
3/8″	1-1/4
1/2″	1-1/2
5/8″	1-3/4

Note: The saw must be sharp and properly set in order to make cuts of the diameter given.

Fig. 34-6. Band Saw Blade Widths for Curves

Fig. 34-7. For complex cuts, it is a good idea to "rough out" the design. It is then easier to make the detailed cuts.

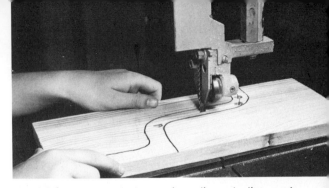

Fig. 34-9. Making holes such as these in the waste stock will help you turn the blade through sharp curves.

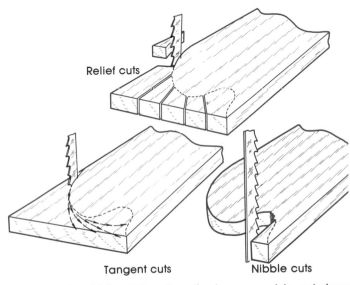

Relief cuts

Tangent cuts

Nibble cuts

Fig. 34-8. Different methods are used to cut sharp curves

blade can cut. Guide the stock carefully along the waste side of the pattern. Think through complex curves ahead of time. It is often helpful to number the cuts. Remember, you want to avoid backing out of all cuts, especially curves.

Cutting sharp curves can cause blades to bind, and possibly break. You can use several methods to avoid binding. One is to "rough out" a complex cut before following the pattern lines. See Fig. 34-7. Another method is to break a long cut into a series of short cuts. You can make **relief, tangent**, and **nibble** cuts, as shown in Fig. 34-8. You can also drill turning holes, as shown in Fig. 34-9. These holes will let you move the blade in tight spots. You can then continue cutting.

Cutting Circles. Before you cut a circle, measure the radius. Then use the chart in Fig. 34-6 to select a blade. Select the widest blade that will make the cut. Always start circle cuts on end grain. This makes it easier to follow the cutting line. Cutting with the grain, blades tend to follow the grain line.

If you are cutting several true circles the same size, use a circle jig. See Fig. 34-10. Fasten the circle jig to the table. The pivot point should be at a right angle to the blade. Otherwise the saw will not cut a true circle.

Making Compound Cuts. A compound cut is a cut made from two or more sides of the stock. Compound cuts are used primarily to make rough shapes for carving and decorative parts for furniture. See Fig. 34-11. To make a compound cut, trace the pattern on two adjoining sides of the stock. Then cut along the lines on one side. Use small nails or masking tape to reattach the waste pieces. Drive the nails in the waste material, away from the cutting line. Saw along the pattern on the second side. Then remove all waste pieces.

Making Straight Cuts. Band saws are not as accurate as table saws for making straight cuts. You can use a band saw, however, to crosscut, rip, resaw, and miter. You can use rip fences and miter gauges. You can also make straight cuts freehand. Make sure the blade is sharp. If the cuts should be square, use a try square to check the table angle. Make sure the machine is off. Then place the square on the table next to the blade. Adjust the table as needed.

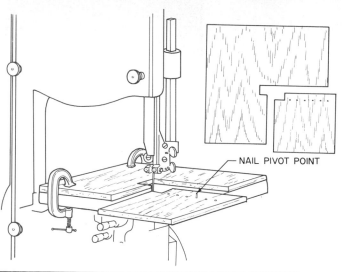

NAIL PIVOT POINT

Fig. 34-10. A circle-cutting jig can be used to cut circles easily with a band saw. You can make a simple jig like the one shown here. Make sure the pivot point is even with the cutting edge of the blade.

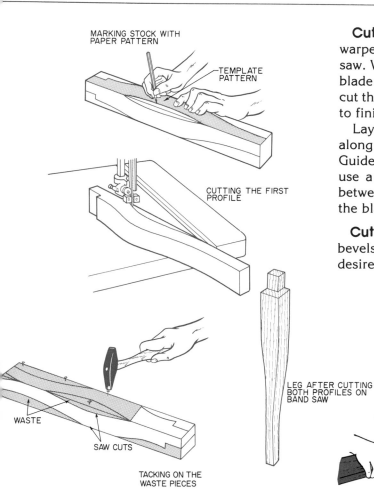

MARKING STOCK WITH PAPER PATTERN

TEMPLATE PATTERN

CUTTING THE FIRST PROFILE

LEG AFTER CUTTING BOTH PROFILES ON BAND SAW

WASTE

SAW CUTS

TACKING ON THE WASTE PIECES

Fig. 34-11. Compound cuts can be made on a band saw by following these steps.

Cutting Warped Stock. It is safer to cut warped stock on a band saw than it is a table saw. With a band saw there is no chance of the blade kicking the stock back. You can rough cut the stock on the band saw. Then machine it to finish size with the jointer and table saw.

Lay out the cutting line. Support the stock along the cutting line as shown in Fig. 34-12. Guide the stock into the saw freehand. Do not use a fence. Warped stock can easily wedge between the fence and blade. This can cause the blade to break.

Cutting Angles. You can cut chamfers and bevels on the band saw. Tilt the table to the desired angle. See Fig. 34-13. This setup is

Fig. 34-12. Cutting warped stock is safer on the band saw than the table saw. Do not use a fence. Support the stock directly under the cut.

Fig. 34-13. Bevels and chamfers can be cut on a band saw by tilting the table.

Fig. 34-14. You can resaw boards by using both a table saw and a band saw. Use a pivot block or rip fence to guide the stock.

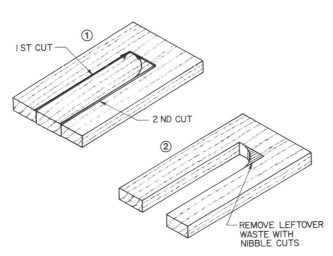

Fig. 34-15. Use this procedure to cut inside corners with a band saw.

useful in cutting corners from stock. Corners are often cut from stock that will be turned on a lathe. You can also use the band saw to cut bevels and chamfers on irregular or curved stock.

Resawing. Thick boards can be cut into thinner pieces by resawing. To resaw a board on a band saw, use a sharp, 3/4- or 1-inch blade. Resawing is much easier if you first cut each edge with a table saw. Then guide the band saw blade through the cuts. Feed the stock slowly. Use a pivot block or rip fence as a guide. See Fig. 34-14.

Cutting Inside Square Corners. You can cut inside square corners faster with a band saw than with a jigsaw or saber saw. Cut along one side until you reach the corner. Then back

the blade out. Make the second cut along the other side. Before you reach the second corner, curve the cut toward the first corner. Then cut out the remaining stock. See Fig. 35-15.

New Terms

1. band saw
2. compound cuts
3. hook tooth with a raker set
4. nibble cuts
5. resawing
6. tangent cuts

Study Questions

1. What is the primary use of band saws?
2. What type of band saw blade is best for cutting wood?
3. About how many teeth per inch are there on an all-purpose band saw blade?
4. How much space should there be between a band saw blade and the upper guide blocks?
5. Why should you never stand to the right of a band saw that is running?
6. How far should your guiding hand be from a band saw blade for the best possible control?
7. What is the widest band saw blade you can use to cut out a 3-inch diameter disk?
8. List four methods that help to avoid binding in sharp cuts.
9. Why should you always start circle cuts on end grain?
10. Why is it safer to cut warped stock on a band saw than a table saw?

Table Saw

Table saws are also called circular saws and variety saws. They are used for many basic operations. They are also used to cut several kinds of joints. Ripping, crosscutting, mitering, and tapering can all be done on table saws. Table saws are probably the most useful, versatile power tools used in woodworking.

A typical table saw is shown in Fig. 35-1. Below the table is a saw **arbor** that holds the circular saw blade. On different sides of the frame are raising and tilting wheels. The wheels are used to raise, lower, and tilt the saw arbor and blade. The safety guard and splitter cover the blade and protect the operator. Tables are equipped with a miter gauge for crosscutting and a rip fence for ripping. Table saw sizes are determined by the largest blade diameter recommended for a machine. Most saws hold blades up to 10 inches in diameter.

Rockwell International

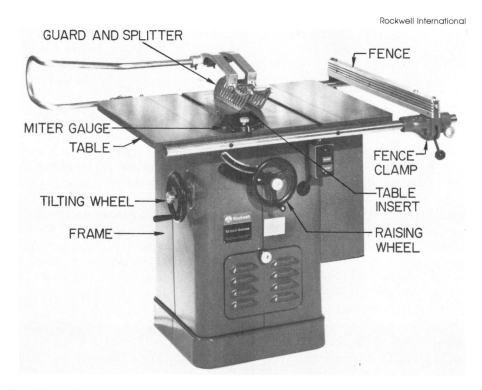

GUARD AND SPLITTER

FENCE

MITER GAUGE

TABLE

TILTING WHEEL

FRAME

FENCE CLAMP

TABLE INSERT

RAISING WHEEL

Fig. 35-1. The table (circular) saw is probably the most versatile and useful power tool in the woodworking shop.

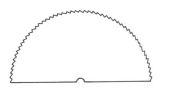

Crosscut (Cutoff) — fine teeth for fast, smooth cutting **across** the grain of hard and soft wood, sheeting, flooring, and wood molding

Planer (Hollow-Ground) Combination — fast-cutting teeth, hollow ground for clearance; excellent blade for all furniture and cabinet work

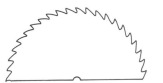

Ripsaw Blade — designed to cut hard and soft wood **with** the grain

Carbide-Tip Blades — premium blades for faster fine cutting, mitering, and finishing; also last longer than conventional blades.

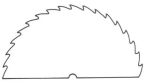

Combination Blade — designed for all-purpose work; smooth cutting in any direction, through all types of wood

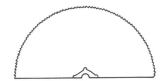

Plywood Blade — small, fine teeth for smooth, economical cutting of paneling, plywood, and laminates.

Fig. 35-2. Circular Saw Blades

Circular Saw Blades

Circular saw blades are made in different sizes. They are also made with different kinds of teeth. Figure 35-2 shows the common types for cutting wood. Combination blades are all-purpose blades. They can be used for both crosscutting and ripping. Crosscut blades work best for crosscutting. Ripsaw blades work best for ripping.

Some crosscut, ripsaw, and combination blades have **carbide tips**. The small pieces of carbide make these blades harder than standard blades. Because they are harder, they stay sharp much longer. Carbide-tip blades are more expensive than standard blades, however.

A **dado head** is a set of several blades. Dado heads are used to make cuts wider than those made by a single blade. Such cuts are neces-sary to make dado, groove and rabbet joints. A standard set contains outside and inside cutters. See Fig. 35-3. The two outside cutters look like regular saw blades. Each of these makes a cut 1/8 inch wide. The inside cutters have only two cutting edges. These edges are 1/16, 1/8 and 1/4 inch wide. The inside cutters serve as spacers between the outside cutters. Different combinations of inside and outside cutters make cuts wider than 1/4 inch, in 1/16-inch steps. Adjustable dado heads, such as the one in Fig. 35-4, are also available.

Before you change a blade, disconnect the power. Then remove the guard and the table insert. Raise the blade to its highest position. Wedge a scrap piece between the blade and table to secure the blade. Use a wrench to remove the arbor nut and washer. (The nut will

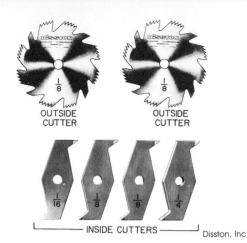

Fig. 35-3. Dado heads are used to make cuts wider than those made by a single saw blade. Wide cuts are necessary to make dadoes, grooves, and rabbets.

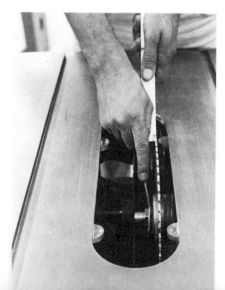

Rockwell International

Fig. 35-4. This is an adjustable dado head. The head is adjusted to different widths by turning the center portion of the blade.

Fig. 35-5. Use a scrap piece to wedge the blade while you tighten or loosen the arbor nut. Make sure the power has been disconnected before you do this.

loosen in the direction of rotation.) See Fig. 35-5. Install the new blade so the teeth point in the direction the blade rotates. This will be toward the front of the saw. Use the scrap piece to hold the blade as you replace and tighten the arbor nut. Then replace the table insert and guard.

Table Saw Safety

SAFETY

- Know and follow the general safety rules for operating power tools on page 211.
- You cannot use the guard for all operations. Have your instructor check any setup that does not include the guard. Special setups should also be checked by your instructor.
- Never cut freehand on the table saw. Use the rip fence for ripping and the miter gauge for crosscutting.
- Always maintain control of the stock between the fence and the blade. Use your hand to push the stock away from the blade. Use a push stick for narrow stock. This will prevent a kickback.
- Never stand directly behind the blade.
- Never place your hands in line with the cut.
- Use a sharp blade. Dull blades are dangerous. They are more likely to cause kickbacks. Dull blades also require more pushing. This increases the chances of your hands slipping.
- The stock must lie flat on the table. Never cut warped or twisted stock on a table saw. Edges placed against the rip fence must be straight.
- Helpers should only support and hold stock. They should never pull or push the stock through the blade. The operator should always be in control.
- Never remove scrap cuttings from around the blade unless the machine has been turned off and has come to a complete stop.

- Never use the fence as a guide if the distance between the blade and the fence will be greater than the length of stock against the fence.
- Clamp a clearance block to the fence when you use the fence as a stop for cutting short pieces to length.
- Table saw blades should project no more than 1/8 inch *(3 mm)* above the surface of the stock.
- Lower the blade below the table when you finish with the saw. Do not leave the machine until the blade comes to a complete stop.

Ripping

Before you rip a board, make sure it has been properly prepared. It must have one straight edge. The bottom face must be flat. Use either a ripsaw or combination blade. Adjust the blade to project 1/8 inch *(3 mm)* above the stock's surface.

Set the fence the desired distance from the blade. Most machines have a ripping scale on the front edge of the table. With the machine off, check the distance. Measure from the fence to a blade tooth set toward the fence. See Fig. 35-6. Allow an extra 1/16 inch *(1.5 mm)* if you must later plane the sawed edge smooth. Never rip stock that is shorter than the distance between the blade and the fence.

Fig. 35-6. To set the rip fence for ripping, measure from the fence to a blade tooth bent toward the fence. Be sure the machine is turned off.

Do not stand directly behind the blade when ripping. Most operators stand slightly to the left. Put the straight edge of the board against the fence. The flat face should be down. Start the motor. Push the stock firmly into the blade with your right hand. Use your left hand to hold the stock against the fence. Always keep your left hand away from the blade. See Fig. 35-7.

If you rip a board less than 4 inches *(100 mm)* wide, use a **push stick**. See Figs. 35-8 and 35-9. The push stick will protect your hands as you feed the stock. To hold long, narrow stock,

Fig. 35-7. When you rip a board, stand slightly to the left of the blade. Push with your right hand and hold the board against the fence with your left. Keep both hands away from the blade. **(The guard has been removed to show the operation.)**

Fig. 35-8. To rip narrow boards less than 4 inches (100 mm) wide use a push stick. For some narrow pieces it is necessary to remove the guard. **(The guard has been removed to show the operation.)**

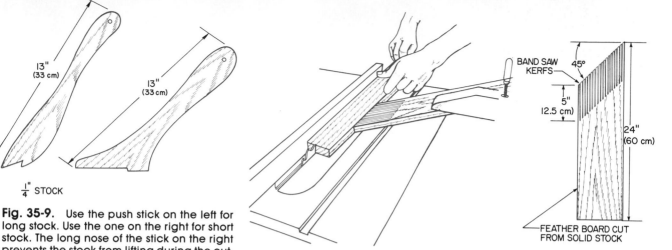

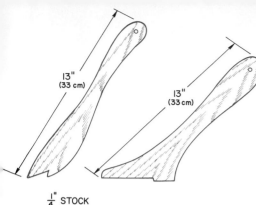

Fig. 35-9. Use the push stick on the left for long stock. Use the one on the right for short stock. The long nose of the stick on the right prevents the stock from lifting during the cut.

Fig. 35-10. Feather boards are useful in holding long, narrow boards against the rip fence. Apply moderate pressure in front of the blade.

Fig. 35-11. Have someone help you or use a roller stand to support long stock.

Fig. 35-12. To resaw a board, make cuts on each edge with a table saw. Use a band saw for finishing cuts on wide boards.

you can also use a **feather board**. As you push the stock through the saw, the feather board holds the stock against the fence. See Fig. 35-10. Have a helper support the stock as it comes through the saw. If there is no helper available, use a roller stand. See Fig. 35-11.

You can make a thick board thinner by **resawing** it. Set up the saw as shown in Fig. 35-12. Set the blade about 1/8 inch *(3 mm)* higher than half the board's width. Make a cut. Use a feather board to help you hold the stock. Then turn the board over and make another cut. Make sure the same face is against the fence for both cuts. Use a band saw to resaw boards too wide for the table saw.

Crosscutting and Squaring Ends

To crosscut or square an end, use either a crosscut or combination blade. Adjust the blade to 1/8 inch *(3 mm)* above the stock. Set the miter gauge at 90°. Use a steel square to check that the gauge and blade are perpendicular. Make sure the guard and splitter are in place.

To cut only one or two pieces, remove the rip fence. Prepare the stock by making one edge straight and the bottom face flat. Mark the cutting length across the face and edge of the stock. Place the straight edge of the stock against the miter gauge. The flat face should be down. Align the stock so it will be cut on the waste side of the line. Start the motor and stand to the left of the blade. Hold the stock firmly against the miter gauge with your left

Fig. 35-13. When crosscutting stock, hold the stock against the miter gauge with your left hand and push with your right hand. Cut on the waste side of the line. **(The guard has been removed to show the operation.)**

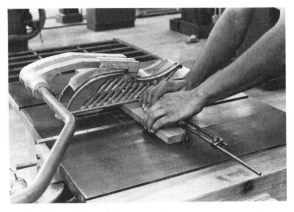

Fig. 35-14. Use a stop rod to crosscut several long pieces to the same length. Insert the rod into the miter gauge. Set it the desired distance from the blade.

hand. With your right hand push the stock into the blade. See Fig. 35-13. Turn the saw off. Wait until the blade stops. Then remove any waste from around the blade.

To cut several long pieces the same length, use a **stop rod**. See Fig. 35-14. Insert the rod into the miter gauge. Set it to the desired length. Measure from a tooth set to the left, to the rod. Make sure the rod is not in line with the blade. Square one end of the stock. Place that end against the stop rod. The bottom face of the stock should be flat. Turn on the motor and slide the stock through the saw.

You can also cut several short pieces to the same length with a **clearance block**. See Fig. 35-15. Use a thick piece for the block. This reduces the chance of the stock becoming lodged between the fence and blade. Lodged pieces can be kicked back at you.

Fig. 35-15. Cutting several short pieces to the same length is often done with a clearance block. **(The guard has been removed to show the operation.)**

Place the block against the fence. Adjust the fence for the desired cutting length. Measure from the block to a tooth set toward the fence. Then move the block in front of the blade. The block should be at least the width of the stock in front of the blade. When the block is positioned, clamp it to the fence.

Make sure the guard and splitter are in place. Place the stock against the miter gauge. One end of the stock should be square. The flat face should be down. Butt the squared end against the clearance block. Start the motor. Holding the stock firmly against the miter gauge, push it through the cut. Cut the desired number of pieces. Do not remove the pieces until the blade stops completely.

Cutting Sheet Stock

Sheet stock includes such materials as plywood, hardboard, and particle board. These materials are usually large and difficult to handle. This makes cutting them on a table saw awkward and dangerous. Cut large pieces into smaller pieces with a handsaw or portable saw. Then cut to finish size on the table saw. If needed, have a helper support the stock while you cut. Use a roller stand if there are no helpers available.

Use a plywood, fine crosscut, or planer blade to cut plywood. Hardboard and particle board are harder than plywood. They should be cut with a carbide-tip blade. To reduce splitting, always cut plywood with the good side up. Putting masking tape over the cutting line will also help eliminate splitting. To cut sheet stock, use the ripping and crosscutting methods described earlier.

Cutting Miters, Chamfers, and Bevels

To cut a miter, set the miter gauge to the desired angle. Then follow the same cutting method used for crosscutting. Hold the stock tightly against the gauge. Feed it slowly into the blade. Stock held at an angle tends to "creep" along the miter gauge. Use a stop rod or wooden fence to hold the stock stationary. See Fig. 35-16. The fence will also help prevent splintering. To cut several pieces the same length, clamp a stop block to the fence.

Cut chamfers and bevels by tilting the blade to the desired angle. Use the rip fence as a guide to cut long pieces. See Fig. 35-17. Use the miter gauge to make shorter end cuts.

Fig. 35-16. Clamping a wooden fence to the miter gauge will reduce "creeping" and splintering when cutting miters. Glue a piece of fine abrasive paper to the fence. **(The guard has been removed to show the operation.)**

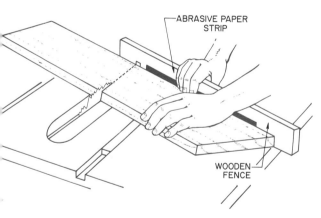

Fig. 35-17. To cut a bevel, tilt the blade to the desired angle. Notice that the blade is tilted away from the fence for the safest possible operation. **(The guard has been removed to show the operation.)**

Cutting Dadoes and Grooves

You will usually cut dadoes and grooves with a dado head. However, joints of 1/4 inch *(6 mm)*, or less, can be cut with a single blade. Using a single blade is also faster for cutting only one or two joints.

Lay out the cuts. Adjust the blade to cut the correct depth. Use the miter gauge for dadoes and the rip fence for grooves. Make a series of cuts as shown in Fig. 35-18.

To cut several identical dadoes and grooves and those wider than 1/4 inch *(6 mm)*, use a dado head. In these cases, the dado head is quicker and more accurate than a single blade. Use the combination of blades and cutters that will cut the desired width. Mount the blades on the arbor. The teeth should point toward the front of the table. This is the same direction in which the blade rotates.

You may need to use two outside blades without the inside cutters. If you do this, be sure to align the teeth properly. The set of the teeth should be in the same direction for both blades. The sharp edges should not be tightened against each other. Position the inside cutters with their cutting edges in the gullets of the outside cutters. Also space the inside cutters equally to balance the weight. Install the special table insert for the dado head. Then place the guard in position. The dado head removes

Fig. 35-18. You can sometimes cut dadoes and grooves faster with a single blade than with a dado head. Make a series of cuts to remove the waste material. **(The guard has been removed to show the operation.)**

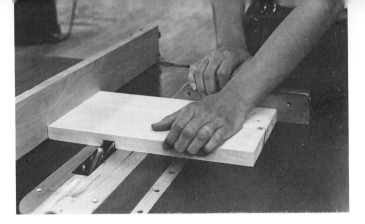

Fig. 35-19. To cut a dado with a dado head, you can use both the miter gauge and the fence. The fence serves as a stop. **(The guard has been removed to show the operation.)**

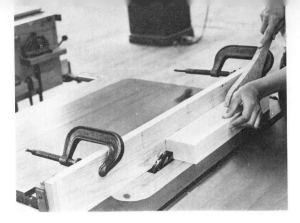

Fig. 35-21. When cutting a rabbet with a dado head, clamp a board to the rip fence to protect the dado head. Raise the dado head into the board until the desired depth is reached.

more stock than a single saw blade. Be sure to hold the stock securely and feed it slowly. See Fig. 35-19.

Cutting Rabbets

If you are cutting only one or two rabbets, use a single blade. This will be quicker than installing the dado head. Lay out the rabbet on the end of the stock. Set the saw at a height just less than the depth of the rabbet. Adjust the fence to the width of the rabbet. Measure from the fence to a blade tooth set away from the fence. Make the first cut with the stock face down. See Fig. 35-20. Then set the blade at a height equal to the rabbet's width. Set the fence so the blade cuts just inside the layout line. Make the second cut.

To cut several rabbets, install a dado head. Use a dado head that is equal to the rabbet's width, or slightly wider. Set the dado head below the table. Clamp a wood fence to the rip fence. This prevents the dado head from rubbing against the metal rip fence. See Fig. 35-21.

Fig. 35-20. Cutting a rabbet with a single blade

It also helps adjust the width of the rabbet. Turn on the power and raise the dado head slowly. Cut into the wood fence until you reach the depth of the rabbet. Turn the power off. Adjust the fence to the width of the rabbet. Then move the stock through the cut.

Cutting Tenons

Carefully lay out the tenon. Make it about 1/8 inch *(3 mm)* shorter than the mortise depth. This provides space for excess glue. The most important tenon dimensions are the width and thickness.

To cut a tenon with a dado head, set up the saw as shown in Fig. 35-22. Use the widest dado head possible. The fence should serve as a stop block. Adjust it according to the length of the tenon. Adjust the height of the blade to cut the proper thickness. Push the stock through the saw until you remove all the waste. Cut both faces. Then set the blade height to cut the width of the tenon.

Fig. 35-22. Cutting a tenon with a dado head. Slide the stock away from the fence before each pass to remove waste stock.

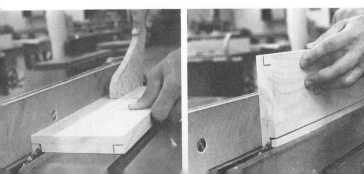

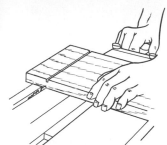

Fig. 35-23. Cutting a tenon with a tenoning attachment. Make the shoulder cuts first. Then use the tenoning attachment for the remaining cuts. Keep both hands on the attachment.

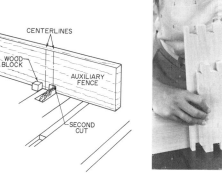

Fig. 35-24. An auxiliary fence makes cutting finger joints easy. Make the distance between the first and second cuts equal to the width of the dado head.

To cut a tenon with a tenoning attachment, use a combination blade. Set the miter gauge at 90°. Make the shoulder cuts as shown in Fig. 35-23. Do not make the cuts deeper than the layout lines. After making the shoulder cuts, clamp the stock in the tenoning attachment. See again Fig. 35-23. Adjust the attachment so the blade cuts on the waste side of the line. Set the blade height so it just meets the shoulder cut. Never cut a tenon this way without a tenoning attachment.

Cutting Finger Joints

Finger joints are strong, attractive corner joints. They are used primarily in making boxes. Finger joints are difficult to cut by hand. However, they are easy to make on a table saw. See Fig. 35-24.

Install a dado head the same width as the desired finger width. The fingers should be about the same width as the thickness of the stock. Adjust the saw depth to cut slightly deeper (1/32 inch, .8 mm) than the stock thickness. This allows for sanding the end grain after assembly. Cut a wooden auxiliary fence for the miter gauge. Line up the center of the fence with the dado head. Then make a cut in the fence.

Lay out the second cut. Make the distance between the first and second cuts equal to the width of the first cut. Draw a line on the fence halfway between the first and the second cuts. Then draw a line through the center of the layout for the second cut. Glue a small block of wood into the first cut. It should project from the fence a distance equal to twice the stock's thickness. Line up the second cut with the dado head. Then screw the wooden fence to the miter gauge. Position the edge of one piece to be cut even with one line. Position the other piece even with the second line. Turn the power on and make a cut. Place this cut over the block and make the second cut. Continue this way until the joint is complete.

Cutting Tapers

You can cut tapers on a table saw with a tapering jig. If the stock will have both a joint and a taper, cut the joint first. Then lay out the starting point and the amount of taper. See the instructions on page 72 for laying out tapers.

An adjustable tapering jig is shown in Fig. 35-25. To set the jig, mark the length of the taper. Measure the length from the hinge. Then measure the amount of taper between the two pivoting parts. Tighten the wing nut and place the stock in the jig. Position the jig next to the fence. Place the wide end of the stock next to the front edge of the saw blade. Then adjust and secure the fence. Start the cut just below the starting point line. This leaves extra material for planing the edge smooth. Hold the stock against the jig and the jig against the fence while cutting.

You can taper two adjoining sides with one setup. If you are tapering opposite sides, you must reset the jig. For the second cut, set the jig at double the amount of taper. Reposition the fence and make the cut as before.

Cutting Coves

Coves (concave shapes) can be cut in wood with a table saw. This is done by cutting at an angle across the side of the blade. Using this method does not produce a true radius, however. If a true radius is needed, the cuts must be sanded true.

Use a board with a straight edge as a guide fence. The angle of the fence determines the

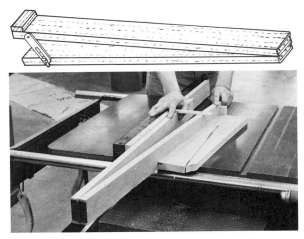

Fig. 35-25. An adjustable tapering jig can be used to cut tapers. **(The guard has been removed to show the operation.)**

Fig. 35-26. To cut coves, make each cut about 1/16 inch (1.5 mm) deep.

width of the cove. The height of the blade determines the depth of the cove. Clamp the fence at the desired distance and angle. See Fig. 35-26. Lower the blade for the first cut. Hold the stock against the guide fence. Feed the stock as you would for ripping. Make several light cuts. Do not cut more than 1/16 inch (1.5 mm) at a time. Use a thick blade with a carbide tip if possible.

New Terms

1. arbor
2. carbide tip
3. clearance block
4. cove
5. dado head
6. feather board
7. push stick
8. stop rod
9. table saw

Study Questions

1. How are table saw sizes determined?
2. What is one advantage of carbide-tip blades? What is one disadvantage?
3. What is the purpose of a dado head?
4. To what height should a circular saw blade be set for a ripping operation?
5. When should a push stick be used for ripping operations on a table saw?
6. At what angle would you set the miter gauge to crosscut a board?
7. For what operations is a stop rod most useful?
8. Why should a clearance block be as thick as possible?
9. What are two things you can do to reduce splitting when cutting plywood?
10. When should you use a single blade to cut dadoes and grooves?
11. Why must a wood fence be clamped to the rip fence when cutting rabbets with a dado head?
12. In making finger joints, how wide should you make the fingers?
13. What must be used to cut tapers on a table saw?
14. What is the maximum depth of a single cut when cutting a cove?

Radial Arm Saw

Radial arm saw blades move back and forth on an arm. See Fig. 36-1. The stock stays in place while you pull the saw through it. This makes the radial saw perfect for cutting long boards. These boards are hard to handle on a table saw.

You can use the radial saw for several other operations. You can use it to rip stock and cut bevels. You can cut angles and joints, such as dadoes, grooves, and miters. With attachments, you can also sand, rout, and shape on a radial arm saw.

The parts of a radial saw are labeled in Fig. 36-1. The arm pivots on the column. The arm also moves up and down. The motor and blade arbor are suspended from the **yoke**. The yoke pivots under the track of the arm. The saw's size is determined by the largest blade diameter suggested for the saw. The same blades used in table saws are used in radial saws.

Changing Blades

To change blades, disconnect the power and remove the guard. Raise the blade high enough to clear the table. Hold the saw arbor stationary. The proper method for holding the arbor depends on the saw. See Fig. 36-2. **Do Not** try holding the saw arbor with a wedge between the blade and table. This could force the saw out of adjustment and affect its accuracy. While holding the arbor, remove the nut with a wrench. Turn the nut in the same direction the blade rotates. Then slide the saw from the arbor.

Make sure you install the new blade properly. The bottom teeth should point towards the back of the machine. This is the same direction the blade rotates. Put the blade on

the arbor. Replace the flange (washer) and the arbor nut. Tighten the arbor nut securely. Then replace the guard and connect the power.

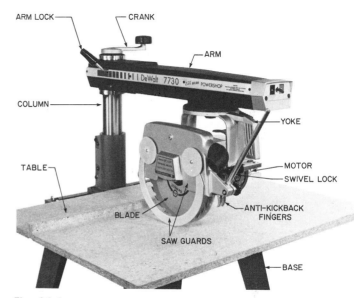

Fig. 36-1. Radial arm saws can be used for many operations. They are ideal for cutting long stock.

Fig. 36-2. To change blades on a radial saw, you must hold the arbor stationary. On this model a wrench is being used to hold the arbor while the nut is loosened with another wrench.

Radial Arm Saw Safety

- Know and follow the general safety rules for operating power tools on page 211.
- Make all adjustments while the machine is turned off.
- Never reach across the path of the blade. When the machine is running, always keep your hands at least 6 inches *(150 mm)* from the blade.
- Wait until the blade is running full speed to start a cut.
- Never stand in line with the blade. If you pull the blade with your right hand, stand to the left. If you pull the blade with your left hand, stand to the right.
- Use one hand to pull the saw through the stock. Use the other hand to hold the stock against the fence. Keep both hands away from the cutting line.
- Cut only one piece of wood at a time.
- Feed the blade slowly. Some materials cut too fast. With these materials you may need to hold the saw back.
- Never use the radial saw for ripping without your instructor's permission.
- When ripping, adjust the anti-kickback fingers to 1/8 inch *(3 mm)* below the surface of the stock.
- Always feed the stock against the rotation of the blade when ripping.
- Use a push stick to move narrow pieces through the blade when ripping.
- Return the saw to the rear position after each cut.

Crosscutting

Use a crosscut or combination blade for crosscutting operations. Adjust the arm so it is perpendicular to the fence. Make sure the arm locks in this position. Set the arm elevation. The blade should cut about 1/8 inch *(3 mm)* below the table's surface. Position the anti-kickback fingers about 1/8 inch above the stock. Then cut a scrap piece. Use a square to check the cutting angles.

Place the stock against the fence and align the cut. Hold the stock in position with one hand. Grasp the saw handle with the other. When the blade is turning full speed, pull the saw through the stock. The blade's rotation forces the stock against the fence. See Fig. 36-3. For this reason, you must feed the saw slowly.

To cut several pieces the same length, use a **stop block**. See Fig. 36-4. Measure the desired distance from the blade. Clamp the stop block to the fence at that distance. Push the stock against the block. Hold the stock with one hand. Pull the saw with the other hand. To cut long pieces, clamp an extension on the fence. Then clamp the stop block to the extension.

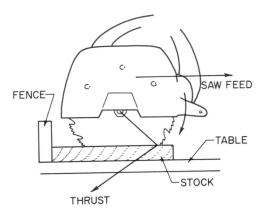

Fig. 36-3. When crosscutting, the radial saw blade rotates down and away from the operator. Because the stock is forced into the fence, the saw should be pulled slowly through the cut.

Fig. 36-4. To crosscut several pieces the same length, clamp a stop block to the fence. Raise the block above the table. This will prevent trapped sawdust from causing inaccurate cuts.

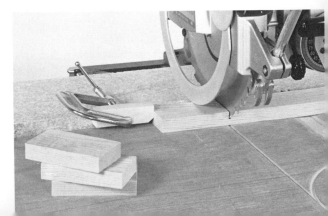

Ripping

To rip a board, use a ripping or combination blade. Make sure the arm is perpendicular to the fence. Then turn the yoke so the blade is parallel to the fence. See Fig. 36-5. The locking pin should snap in place when the blade and fence are parallel. Turn the motor **outboard** (away from the rear column and fence). This position is used for most ripping operations. See Fig. 36-5 again. You sometimes need to turn the motor **inboard** (toward the fence) to rip wide pieces. See Fig. 36-6. Outboard ripping is the safest method. It allows more room for pushing the stock through the cut.

Position the yoke at the desired cutting width. Lock the yoke in position. Turn on the power. Lower the blade about 1/8 inch *(3 mm)* below the table surface. The guard should be just above the stock at the infeed end. The anti-kickback fingers should be 1/8 inch *(3 mm)* below the top of the stock. Hold the stock against the fence. Feed it against the rotation of the blade. See Fig. 36-7. Use a push stick and keep your hands away from the blade.

Cutting Dadoes and Grooves

Before cutting dadoes and grooves, make the stock flat and uniformly thick. Remember, the blade cuts from the top. Any variation in thickness will affect the cutting depth. Cutting warped stock will also produce uneven dadoes and grooves.

Cutting Dadoes. To cut a dado, position and lock the arm perpendicular to the fence. Set the yoke so the blade is also perpendicular to the fence. Install a dado head of the desired width. To set the cutting depth, put the stock under the blade. Then lower the blade until it touches the stock. Remove the stock and lower the blade to the desired depth. Each turn of the elevating crank moves the blade about 1/8 inch *(3 mm)*. Cut a scrap piece to check the cutting angle and depth. Use a stop block to cut similar dadoes on two or more pieces. This ensures that the cuts will be located accurately.

Fig. 36-5. The common ripping procedure (outboard ripping) for radial saws is to turn the motor away from the rear column and fence. The operator then stands to the right.

Fig. 36-6. Inboard ripping (shown here) is not as safe as outboard ripping. Use inboard ripping only when necessary. Always stand to the left when you use this method.

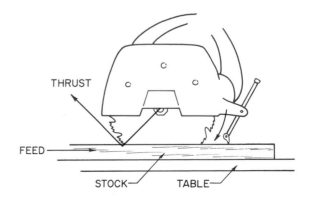

Fig. 36-7. In ripping operations, the blade rotates against the direction of feed. Compare this to Fig. 36-3.

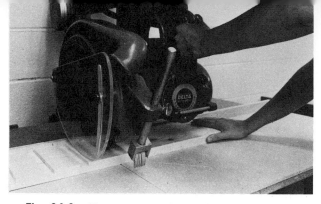

Fig. 36-8. You can cut dadoes with a radial arm saw.

Hold the stock against the fence with one hand. Slowly pull the saw through the cut with your other hand. Be sure to grasp the saw handle firmly. A dado head removes more wood than a standard blade. This means that a dado head will cut faster than a regular blade. Always keep your hands out of line with and away from the dado head.

Cutting Grooves. You can cut some short grooves by pulling the saw along the track. Most grooves, however, are longer than the track. You must cut these grooves with a ripping setup.

Position and lock the arm and yoke so the blade is parallel to the fence. Install a dado head. Set the cutting depth as described for cutting dadoes. Make a test cut on a scrap piece. Be sure the guard and anti-kickback fingers are set properly. Feed the stock against the rotation of the blade. See Fig. 36-9. Keep your hands out of line with the cut. Also keep them away from the blade.

Fig. 36-9. Cutting grooves on a radial arm saw is similar to ripping operations.

Fig. 36-10. You can both crosscut and rip bevels with a radial arm saw.

Cutting Bevels

You can cut bevels on a radial saw by tilting the motor and blade. Raise the blade about 2 inches *(50 mm)* above the table. Release the tension on the swivel lock and pull the locking pin. Tilt the blade to the desired angle. Then lock it in position. The locking pin will accurately lock the blade at common angles, such as 30° and 45°.

You can either crosscut or rip a bevel. See Fig. 36-10. Follow the directions in this chapter for crosscutting and ripping. Be sure to adjust the guards and anti-kickback fingers.

Cutting Miters

To cut a miter, set the arm at the desired angle. Make sure the blade is above the table. Release the tension on the arm lock handle. Pull the locking pin. Swing the arm to the desired angle. Then lock it in position. The locking pin will accurately position the arm at common angles, such as 30° and 45°.

Cutting miters is a crosscut operation. Use a crosscut or combination blade. Lower the blade to about 1/8 inch *(3 mm)* below the table surface. Hold the stock against the fence. Keep your hands away from the blade and out of the cutting line. Pull the saw slowly into the cut. See Fig. 36-11.

DeWalt

Fig. 36-11. Miters can be cut on a radial saw by turning the arm to the desired angle. (The guard has been removed to show the operation.)

Picture frames and boxes with tapered sides are often made with **compound miters**. A compound miter is a double angle. It is a miter and bevel made in one cut. To cut a compound miter, you must turn the arm and tilt the blade. See Fig. 36-12. The chart in Fig. 36-13 gives the needed adjustments for common four-sided frames.

Cutting Plywood

Cutting plywood can sometimes be a problem. Thin face veneers tend to chip and tear while being cut. Use special plywood blades to cut plywood. These blades have many small teeth per inch. This produces the smoothest possible cut. If you do not have a plywood blade, use the blade with the most teeth. Try to use the blade with the least amount of set. Make all cuts with the finished side face up. Put a piece of masking tape over the cutting line to reduce chipping and tearing.

Fig. 36-12. To cut compound miters you must turn the arm and tilt the yoke.

New Terms

1. anti-kickback fingers
2. compound miter
3. inboard
4. outboard
5. radial arm saw
6. stop block
7. yoke

Study Questions

1. Why is the radial arm saw better than the table saw for cutting long stock?
2. If you properly install a blade on a radial arm saw, in which direction will the bottom teeth point?
3. For which operation — ripping or crosscutting — do you need a push stick?
4. Describe the correct arm elevation for a crosscut operation.
5. With which radial arm saw operations would you probably use a stop block?
6. Which ripping method is safest — outboard or inboard?
7. Why is it important that the stock be of uniform thickness when cutting dadoes and grooves with a radial saw?
8. What adjustment needs to be made to make bevel cuts on a radial arm saw?
9. What is a common problem in cutting plywood?
10. Describe two features of the blade you would use in place of a plywood blade.

Fig. 36-13. Compound Miter Adjustments

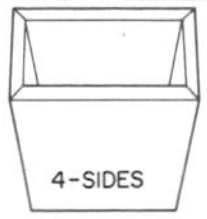

Work Angle (Degrees)	Blade Tilt (Degrees)	Arm Setting (Degrees)
5	44¾	5
10	44¼	9¾
15	43¼	14½
20	41¾	18¾
25	40	23
30	37¾	26½
35	35¼	29¾
40	32½	32¾
45	30	35¼
50	27	37½
55	24	39¼
60	21	41

Portable Circular Saw and Motorized Miter Box

Portable circular saws are used to cut stock that is hard to handle on other machines. They are very useful when cutting large stock. For example, a large, 4 x 8 foot plywood sheet is difficult to cut on table saws and radial arm saws. These sheets are easy to cut with portable circular saws, however. Carpenters use portable power saws frequently.

The parts of a portable circular saw are shown in Fig. 37-1. The blades are similar to those used in table saws and radial arm saws. The blades are powered by an electric motor. A trigger switch in the handle operates the motor. The motor, blade and handle assembly are mounted on a base.

The blade projects below the bottom of the base. Adjusting the distance the blade projects, changes the cutting depth. Angle cuts can be made by tilting the base from 90° to 45°. Two factors determine the size of a portable circular saw. One is the largest blade diameter suggested by the manufacturer. The other is the horse power rating of the motor.

Changing Portable Saw Blades

Be sure the power has been disconnected before you change a blade. To remove the blade, hold it stationary. Put a nail in the small hole in the blade. Hold the nail against the saw base. If there is not a hole, wedge a scrap piece of wood between the saw teeth and the base. Then use a wrench to remove the arbor nut and washer. The nut will loosen the same way the blade rotates. See Fig. 37-2.

Move the guard out of the way. Remove the blade. Clean the arbor and the washers. This helps the new blade lie flat and run true. Install the new blade. The teeth should point the way the blade rotates. (The bottom teeth should point toward the front of the saw.) Replace the washer. Then tighten the arbor nut holding the blade as before.

Fig. 37-2. A block of wood can be used to hold a portable saw blade in place while the arbor nut is loosened.

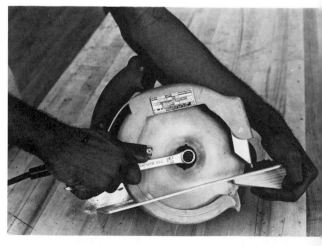

Fig. 37-1. Portable circular saw

Rockwell International

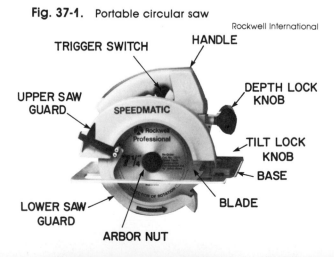

TRIGGER SWITCH

HANDLE

UPPER SAW GUARD

SPEEDMATIC

DEPTH LOCK KNOB

TILT LOCK KNOB

BASE

LOWER SAW GUARD

BLADE

ARBOR NUT

Portable Circular Saw Safety

- Know and follow the general safety rules for operating power tools on page 211.
- Make sure the bottom saw guard operates properly.
- Always disconnect the power before making adjustments and changing blades.
- Never set the blade to project more than 1/8 inch *(3 mm)* deeper than the thickness of the stock.
- Support the stock firmly on a bench or sawhorse.
- Never place your hand in line with the cut. This applies to both the front and rear of the saw.
- Never stand directly behind the saw. If the saw kicks back, you could be hurt.
- Keep your balance as you use the saw. Do not reach too far or overextend yourself.
- Never remove the saw from a cut until the blade has completely stopped.
- Keep the power cord away from the saw blade.
- Never use the rip fence for pieces shorter than 20 inches *(500 mm)*. Short pieces may become wedged between the fence and blade. The pieces can then be kicked back.

Using the Portable Circular Saw

You can use the portable saw for crosscutting, ripping, cutting bevels, and cutting plywood. The portable saw's main advantage is that it can be easily moved. You can take it to

Fig. 37-3. A protractor attachment is used to make accurate square and angle cuts with a portable circular saw.

Fig. 37-4. A straightedge can be clamped along the cutting line to make accurate cuts.

the stock. You need not move the stock to the saw.

You will use some basic procedures for all cuts. First adjust the angle and depth of cut. Set the front edge of the base on the stock. Align the blade on the waste side of the layout line. Do not let the blade touch the stock. Start the saw. Wait until the blade reaches full speed. Then start the cut. Push the saw slowly along the layout line. Do not force the cut. This will bind the blade and cause a rough cut.

Crosscutting. Probably the most common use of the portable saw is cutting stock to length. Generally you can guide the saw freehand. For more accurate cuts, use a protractor attachment. See Fig. 37-3. You can set this attachment at any angle. If a protractor is unavailable, use a straightedge. Clamp the straightedge to the stock at the desired angle. Be sure to allow for the width of the saw base. Do this by adding space between the layout line and the straightedge. Hold the saw base against the straightedge as you cut. See Fig. 37-4.

Ripping. A rip fence makes ripping easy. See Fig. 37-5. Simply set the fence the desired width from the blade. Keep the fence firmly

Fig. 37-5. A rip fence can be used to make fast, accurate ripping cuts. The fence keeps the saw a uniform distance from the edge.

Fig. 37-6. Tilting the base of the portable saw makes it possible to cut bevels and miters.

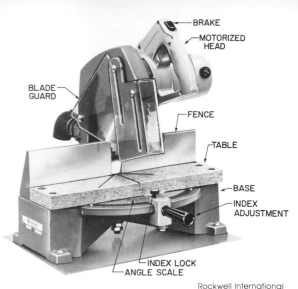

Fig. 37-7. Motorized miter box

Rockwell International

against the edge of the stock as you cut. Be sure the edge is straight. An irregular edge will cause an irregular cut. Do not use the fence for pieces shorter than 20 inches *(500 mm)*. Most rip fences have a maximum cutting width of 6 inches *(150 mm)*. For wider pieces, use a straightedge as described for crosscutting. If accuracy is not important, use the saw freehand.

Cutting Bevels. To cut bevels, tilt the base to the proper angle. The tilting scale indicates the degree of bevel. Tighten the lock knob to secure the base. Adjust the cutting depth. Use the saw as described for crosscutting and ripping. See Fig. 37-6.

Cutting Plywood. You can cut plywood easily with a portable saw. For best results, use a plywood blade. You can also use combination and crosscut blades. Cut the panel with the good side down. This produces the smoothest possible cut on the good side. Make cuts as described for crosscutting and ripping. Make all your measurements from the factory edges.

Motorized Miter Box

The motorized miter box makes fast, accurate cuts. It works like an adjustable miter box to make finished crosscuts and miter cuts. It is used mostly to cut small pieces for close-fitting joints. Moldings, trim, and frames are some examples.

The motorized miter box looks like a portable saw mounted on a miter box. See Fig. 37-7. The saw pivots at the rear of the box. A trigger

switch in the handle turns the saw on. The saw is then pulled down in a chopping motion to make cuts. The blade and motor can be clamped at any angle between 90° and 45°. They can be stopped automatically at the common settings of 90° and 45°. Motorized miter boxes use circular saw blades similar to those used with table saws. Planer and fine crosscut blades are preferred.

Changing Miter Saw Blades

Before changing a blade, disconnect the power. Then lift the guard. Use the two special wrenches supplied with the saw. Insert the hexagon wrench into the end of the arbor. This keeps the blade from turning. Use the other wrench to loosen the arbor nut. See Fig. 37-8.

Fig. 37-8. Always disconnect the power before changing a blade on a motorized miter box.

Rockwell International

Remove the arbor nut, washer, and blade. Clean all surfaces and install the new blade. Replace the washer and arbor nut. The recessed side of the washer should be next to the blade. Then tighten the nut securely.

Motorized Miter Box Safety

- Know and follow the general safety rules for operating power tools on page 211.
- Hold the stock tightly against the fence. The saw will throw stock not held against the fence.
- Never remove scrap stock from around the blade while the blade is moving.
- Always keep your hands at least 4 inches *(100 mm)* from the blade.
- Always disconnect the power before making adjustments and changing blades.
- Make sure the blade has completely stopped before you leave the machine.

Using the Motorized Miter Box

To use the motorized miter box, first set the cutting angle. Loosen the index lock. Pull back on the index adjustment handle. Move the handle to the desired angle, as shown on the angle scale. Then tighten the index lock. For cuts of 90° and 45°, there are positive stops. This lets you adjust the cutting angle quickly.

Fig. 37-9. This worker is making an angle cut with the motorized miter box. Notice that the board is held firmly against the table and fence.

Rockwell International

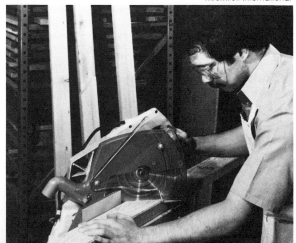

After the desired angle is set, place the stock on the table. Align the blade and the cutting line. Use a stop block to cut several pieces the same length. Clamp the stop block to the fence. For pieces longer than the fence, use an extension. Clamp the extension to the fence. Then clamp the stop block to the extension. When using a stop block, hold the stock between the blade and the block. This will prevent possible binding and kickbacks.

Use one hand to hold the stock. Hold it firmly on the table. Also hold it firmly against the fence. Keep your hand at least 4 inches *(100 mm)* from the cutting line. With the other hand, grasp the handle. Then start the saw. Let the blade reach full speed. Pull it down and make the cut. See Fig. 37-9. Lift the saw out of the cut. Then release the switch and press the brake button. After the blade stops completely, remove the stock.

New Terms

1. motorized miter box
2. portable circular saw

Study Questions

1. When would you use a portable circular saw rather than a table saw or radial arm saw?
2. Briefly describe two methods of holding a portable saw blade stationary while changing the blade.
3. List three sawing operations for which you can use the portable circular saw.
4. Name two tools that are used with the portable saw to make the most accurate crosscuts.
5. What is the shortest piece that should be ripped with a portable circular saw and a rip fence? What is usually the widest piece that can be ripped with a rip fence?
6. For what types of sawing is the motorized miter box most often used?
7. What two types of blades are preferred for the motorized miter box?

38

Jointer and Power Plane

Jointers are machines that do the work of a hand plane. Jointers are used mainly to make edges straight and square. They are also used to smooth surfaces. Rabbets, tongues, chamfers, bevels, and tapers are sometimes cut on jointers.

The parts of a jointer are shown in Fig. 38-1. The cutting is done with knives mounted in the cutterhead. The **cutterhead** holds three knives

and turns at a high speed. See Fig. 38-2. The length of the knives determines the jointer's size. This length also determines the widest board the jointer will plane. An 8-inch jointer, for example, has knives 8 inches *(200 mm)* long. It will plane surfaces up to 8 inches wide.

Jointers have two tables — the infeed and the outfeed. Both tables are raised and lowered with handwheels. Adjusting the **infeed table** controls the cutting depth. The lower the infeed table sits below the knives, the deeper the cut. A depth scale on the machine shows the cutting depth. The **outfeed table** is always set at the same height as the knives. The outfeed table holds the stock level as it comes through the cut.

The fence runs along the length of the tables. For most operations it is perpendicular to the tables. It can be tilted from 90° to 45° for cutting bevels and chamfers. The angle of tilt is shown on the tilt scale.

You can also clamp the fence at different locations across the tables. This is done for rabbeting. It is also done to make use of sharp areas on the knives. Simply loosen the fence clamp and slide it to the desired location. Then reclamp it.

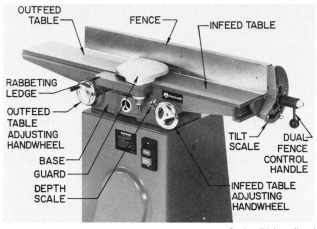

Rockwell International

Fig. 38-1. The parts of a jointer. The cutterhead is located under the guard.

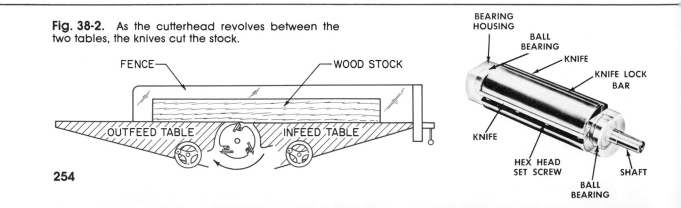

Fig. 38-2. As the cutterhead revolves between the two tables, the knives cut the stock.

Jointer Safety

- Know and follow the general safety rules for operating power tools on page 211.
- Never joint a board less than 10 inches *(250 mm)* long. Short stock can tip down into the cutterhead. Then the stock could be thrown back with tremendous force.
- Always use a push stick when planing a face. This protects your fingers as the end crosses the cutterhead.
- Never stand directly behind the jointer. This is a dangerous position if the stock kicks back.
- Keep your fingers away from the front of the stock. While jointing a face, keep your fingers at least 6 inches *(150 mm)* from the front end.
- Never apply pressure with your hands directly over the cutterhead. Always keep your hands at least 4 inches *(100 mm)* from the cutterhead.
- Always feed the stock **with** the grain. This reduces vibration and produces a smoother cut.
- Get your instructor's approval when making special setups.
- Do not leave the machine until the cutterhead has completely stopped.

Planing a Face

Boards often need to be cut to finish size. The first step is usually planing a face flat. This can be done on a jointer. To plane a face flat on a jointer, adjust the cutting depth. The depth will depend on the width and hardness of the stock. Make shallow cuts on wide or hard stock. You can make deeper cuts on narrow or soft stock. Generally, the cutting depth should not be more than 1/8 inch *(3 mm)* for soft or narrow stock. It should not be more than 1/16 inch *(1.5 mm)* for hard or wide stock.

Do not remove any more material than is necessary. When possible, make a few heavy cuts. Making many light cuts will usually produce an unwanted taper. Feed the stock so it

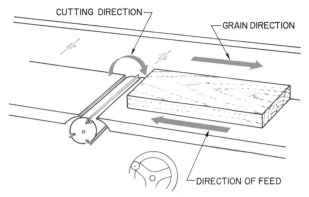

Fig. 38-3. Feed the stock so the knives cut in the same direction as the grain. This will prevent chipping.

will be cut **with** the grain. See Fig. 38-3. Cutting **against** the grain can cause the wood to chip. If the stock is warped, place the concave side down.

Always use a push block. See Figs. 38-4 and 38-5. Hold the push block with your right hand. Hold the center of the stock with your left hand. Keep your fingers away from the ends of the board. Push the stock into the cutter at a slow, steady rate. Apply even downward pressure. Feeding the stock too fast will produce a rough cut.

Jointing an Edge

For many operations, you must make an edge straight and square with a face. Doing

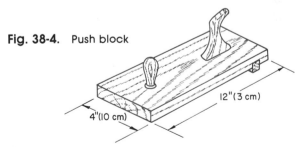

Fig. 38-4. Push block

Fig. 38-5. Using a push block to plane a face

this on a jointer is called **jointing**. Before you joint an edge, check that the fence is perpendicular to the table. Use a try square as shown in Fig. 38-6. Then adjust the infeed table to the cutting depth. Usually this will be less than 1/8 inch *(3 mm)*.

Hold the already planed face firmly against the fence. Feed the stock so it will be cut **with** the grain. Push the end of the board with your right hand. Use a push stick for narrow boards. With your left hand hold the stock against the table and fence. As your left hand approaches the cutterhead, move it to the rear table. See Fig. 38-7. Never apply pressure to the board directly over the cutterhead.

Do not try jointing extremely rough or irregular edges. Use a handsaw or band saw to make the edges straight. Then run the edges through the jointer.

Planing End Grain

You can usually cut end grain smoothly and accurately with a sharp saw. You can, however, trim end grain on a jointer when necessary. The board must be at least 10 inches *(250 mm)* wide to do this.

Fig. 38-6. Use a try square to check that the fence is square with the table.

Fig. 38-7. Edge jointing a board. **Never** place your hand directly over the cutterhead. **(The guard has been removed to show the operation.)**

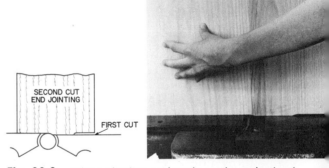

Fig. 38-8. When planing end grain, make a short cut from one end. Then complete the cut from the other end. This will prevent splintering. **(The guard has been removed to show the operation.)**

Adjust the infeed table for light cuts. Make a short cut from one edge of the end grain. See Fig. 38-8. Then turn the piece around. Feed from the second edge. Feed the stock until it meets the first cut. This will prevent the back edge from chipping.

If you are planing both ends and both edges, plane the ends first. Then plane the edges. This way you can smooth any chipped end grain when you plane the edges.

Planing Bevels and Chamfers

To cut a bevel or chamfer, adjust the fence to the desired angle. Check the tilt of the fence with a T-bevel. You can tilt the fence in or out. Greater accuracy is possible with the fence tilted over the table. See Fig. 38-9. If you must

Fig. 38-9. You can tilt the fence either in or out to cut bevels and chamfers on a jointer. Use a block to hold the stock against the fence when the fence is tilted away from the table (bottom photo).

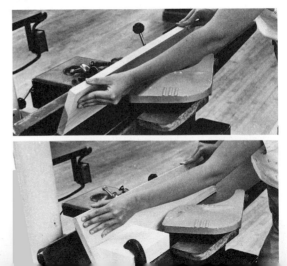

tilt the fence out, clamp a scrap piece to the outfeed table. This will prevent the stock from sliding away from the fence. Make light cuts until the desired depth is reached.

Planing a Rabbet

You can cut a rabbet quickly and easily on a jointer. Position the fence for the width of the rabbet. Measure from the outside edge of the knife to the fence. Adjust the infeed table for the depth of the rabbet. To cut deep rabbets, you may need to reset the infeed table and make additional cuts. On many jointers you must remove the guard to cut a rabbet. Always check with your instructor before removing a guard. Clamping a piece of wood to the fence will cover the exposed cutters. See Fig. 38-10.

Planing a Taper

To cut a taper, first mark the stock where the taper should start. Then move the guard out of the way. Lay the stock on the infeed table. Position the stock so the mark is on the edge of the outfeed table. Clamp a stop block against the stock on the infeed table. See Fig. 38-11. Set the infeed table for the amount of taper. For deep tapers plan to make two or three equal cuts.

Turn on the jointer. Butt the end to be tapered against the stop block. Pull the guard back so the board can sit on the outfeed table. Lower the stock onto the cutterhead as shown in Fig. 38-12. Feed the stock slowly with a push stick or push block.

Fig. 38-10. When cutting a rabbet, you may need to remove the guard. If you remove the guard, clamp a scrap piece to the fence to cover the cutterhead.

The jointer will cut a little deeper at the beginning of the cut. Smooth this area with a thin cut after completing the taper. Cut along the entire board from the wide end to the narrow end. This will avoid tear-out and produce a smoother cut.

Portable Power Planes

Portable power planes are like small hand-held jointers. See Fig. 38-13. They have cutterheads similar to jointers. They are also adjusted the same way jointers are. Power planes are used to plane surfaces. They are also used to make ends and edges straight. Stock too heavy, large, or awkward for jointers is often cut with a power plane. The most common use of power planes is fitting doors and paneling.

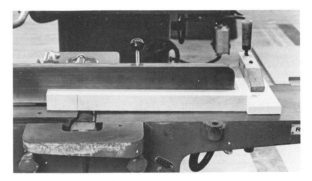

Fig. 38-11. This is a setup for planing a taper on a jointer. Position the stop block so the layout line is even with the edge of the outfeed table.

Fig. 38-12. To cut a taper, carefully lower the stock onto the revolving cutterhead. Use either a push stick or push block to push the stock through the cut. **(The guard has been removed to show the operation.)**

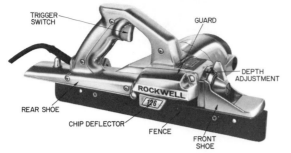

Fig. 38-13. Portable power plane

Rockwell International

Black and Decker

Fig. 38-14. Use a power plane as you would a hand plane. Shift the pressure from the front to the back as you move through the cut.

Power Plane Safety

- Know and follow the general safety rules for operating power tools on page 211.
- Before you plug in the plane, be sure the switch is in the "off" position.
- Keep your hands and fingers out of line with and away from the cutterhead.
- Never set the plane down until the cutters come to a complete stop.
- Keep the power cord away from the cutterhead.

Using a Power Plane

To plane a face with a power plane, you must remove the fence. Adjust the front shoe for the depth of cut. Raise the shoe for a deep cut. Lower it for a light cut. Make the thinnest cut possible to smooth the surface.

Clamp the stock securely. Place the front shoe on the stock. The cutter should be just off the end. Start the cut, applying firm pressure to the front shoe. Through the middle of the cut, apply equal pressure to the front and rear

shoes. Transfer pressure to the rear shoe as you finish the cut. Push the plane at a smooth, even rate for the best cut. You must make more than one pass on stock wider than the width of the plane.

The fence on a power plane is adjustable from 90° to 45°. To plane an edge, set the fence at the desired angle. Set the front shoe for the proper depth. Make sure the stock is securely clamped. Push the plane at a slow, steady speed. Apply pressure as described for planing a face. See Fig. 38-14. You may need to make two or three passes to complete an angle cut.

New Terms

1. cutterhead
2. infeed table
3. jointer
4. jointing
5. outfeed table
6. portable power plane

Study Questions

1. What are the primary uses of the jointer?
2. Which of the two jointer tables regulates the cutting depth?
3. What is usually the first step in cutting a board to finish size?
4. What is the result of making many light cuts on a jointer?
5. When planing a warped face on a jointer, which side should be turned down?
6. How should you prepare extremely rough or irregular edges for jointing?
7. Why should you make cuts from each edge when planing end grain on a jointer?
8. When cutting bevels and chamfers on a jointer, is it best to turn the fence in or out? Why?
9. The jointer will make a deep cut at the beginning of a taper. Describe the method for smoothing this area.
10. For what kinds of stock would you use a portable power plane rather than a jointer?

Surfacers are also called **planers** and **thickness planers**. They are used to cut boards to a desired thickness. They are not used for any other purpose. A standard surfacer is shown in Fig. 39-1.

Surfacers, like jointers, have a rotating cutterhead. The cutterhead contains either three or four knives. Unlike jointers, surfacers cut from the top rather than the bottom. They are also **self-feeding**. This means that the machine pulls the stock through the cut.

The diagram in Fig. 39-2 shows how a surfacer works. The **infeed rolls** feed the stock into the cutterhead. They feed the stock at a steady rate. Notice that the top roll is corrugated. This gives the roll a better grip on the stock. The chip breaker prevents kickbacks and chipping. The pressure bar holds the stock down as it comes through the cut. The stock then passes between the two **outfeed rolls**. These rolls continue the self-feeding process.

Surfacers are manufactured in various sizes. Sizes are determined by the widest, thickest board a machine can surface. The 18 x 6 inch and 24 x 8 inch machines are commonly found in school shops.

Surfacer Safety

- Know and follow the general safety rules for operating power tools on page 211.
- Remove all loose knots from the stock before surfacing.
- Do not surface stock shorter than the distance between the centers of the infeed and outfeed rolls. This is usually 12 inches *(300 mm)*, or less.
- Never stand directly behind a board being surfaced. The stock could kick back and cause an injury.
- Never look into the surfacer while the cutterhead is rotating.

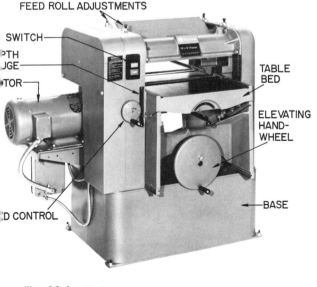

Fig. 39-1. Surfacer

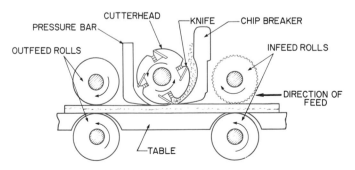

Fig. 39-2. Surfacers are self-feeding. The infeed and outfeed rolls move the stock at a steady rate. The table adjusts up and down to control the cutting depth.

- Make sure one face is flat before you surface a board. Place the flat face against the table.
- If a board does not feed through the surfacer, turn off the power. Wait until the cutterhead stops completely. Then lower the table and remove the board.
- Keep your hands away from the areas around the feed rolls. You could easily pinch your fingers in these areas.
- Feed the stock **with** the grain. Otherwise, the stock can chip and break. The pieces can then be thrown from the surfacer.

Surfacing Stock

Do not surface a board unless it has a flat face. If necessary, plane a face flat on a jointer. Then measure the board at its thickest part. Subtract the desired cutting depth from this measurement. Adjust the table to this setting with the elevating handwheel.

The cutting depth depends on the board's width and hardness. Generally 1/16 inch *(1.5 mm)* is the maximum cut. Always plan the cuts. Try to remove an equal amount of stock from each side of the board. This will reduce warpage.

Place the flat surface down on the table. Turn the board so it will be cut **with** the grain. See Fig. 39-3. Start the machine. Slide the board forward until the infeed rolls begin

Fig. 39-4. Stand to one side of the board as you feed stock into the surfacer.

feeding it. See Fig. 39-4. Then move around the machine. Support the long pieces as they come through the machine. Make additional cuts as needed.

When surfacing boards of various thicknesses, plane the thickest boards first. Plane the boards until they are all the same thickness. You can then surface them without resetting the machine for every board.

Some surfacers have a variable-speed feed control. You can use the faster feed rates for rough cuts. Use the slowest feed rate for finish cuts.

Short Stock. Some boards are too short for a surfacer to feed. To be surfaced, a board must be as long as the distance between the centers of the infeed and outfeed rolls. This distance depends on the manufacturer and the size of the machine. It is usually about 12 inches *(300 mm)*. Do not put boards shorter than 12 inches in the surfacer.

If you are surfacing several short boards, butt them end to end. See Fig. 39-5. This will produce a more uniform thickness for each board. It will also keep the boards moving steadily through the machine. To use this procedure you must first make the boards the same thickness.

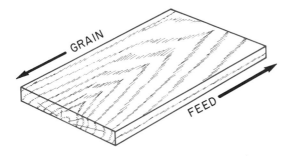

Fig. 39-3. Feed stock into surfacers so the cut will be made **with** the grain. This will produce a smoother cut.

Fig. 39-5. Butt short pieces end to end to feed them through the surfacer. This produces a more uniform thickness and keeps the boards moving. Never put a board less than 12 inches (300 mm) long in a surfacer.

Fig. 39-6. To surface stock less than 1/4 inch (6 mm) thick, place it on a backing board. The backing board must be of uniform thickness. It must also be longer and wider than the stock.

Thin Stock. Surfacers can break up stock less than 1/4 inch *(6 mm)* thick. You can avoid this by placing thin stock on a backing board. A **backing board** is a scrap piece of uniform thickness. The backing board must be longer than the stock to be surfaced. It should also be wider than the stock. See Fig. 39-6. To set the depth of cut, measure the total thickness of both pieces. Then subtract the amount to be cut off. Set the surfacer for the resulting thickness. Feed the thin stock as you would a single board.

Squaring Stock

You often need to square stock while cutting it to finish size. To square stock you must do a sequence of operations. You can use the following sequence for most jobs.

1. Plane the best face flat and true on a jointer. If the stock is too wide, use a hand plane.
2. With the planed face against the fence, joint the best edge. If grain direction makes this impossible, do this step after step 3.
3. On the surfacer, cut the board to its finish thickness. Surface the board with the planed face down. This will make the second face flat and parallel to the first.
4. Rip the board to the desired width on the table saw. Make sure the jointed edge is against the fence.
5. On the table saw, square one end of the board. Then cut the board to length.

You can also use the surfacer to size square parts such as furniture legs. Simply joint one face and edge. Set the surfacer for the desired cutting depth. Then surface the two opposite sides with the same setting.

New Terms

1. backing board
2. infeed roll
3. outfeed roll
4. self-feeding
5. surfacer

Study Questions

1. For what one purpose are surfacers used?
2. What is the length of the shortest board that should be surfaced on most surfacers?
3. What is the maximum cutting depth for most cuts made on a surfacer?
4. On surfacers with variable-speed feed controls, would you use the fastest rate for rough, or for finish cuts?
5. List the basic steps in squaring stock with power tools.
6. What are three necessary features of a backing board?

Rotary Jointer Surfacer

Rotary jointer surfacers are planing machines. They are often referred to as Uniplanes. They are used mainly for planing small stock and end grain. They are also used to plane faces and edges and cut miters, bevels, and chamfers.

A Uniplane is shown in Fig. 40-1. The round cutterhead holds a series of cutters. The cutterhead is mounted vertically. It rotates behind an opening in the fence. The cutters extend through the opening. They cut the stock as it passes the opening. Because the opening is so narrow, small pieces can be planed safely.

The Uniplane can make cuts up to 1/8 inch *(3 mm)* thick. It can plane stock as wide as 6 inches *(150 mm)*. The table tilts up to 45° for bevel and angle cuts. It also has a miter gauge.

Rotary Jointer Surfacer Safety

- Know and follow the general safety rules for operating power tools on page 211.
- Make sure all guards are in place and properly adjusted.
- Before making an adjustment, turn the machine off and wait for the cutterhead to stop completely.
- Hold the stock firmly on the table when making a cut. Also hold it firmly against the fence.
- Never let your hand pass over the cutters. As it comes close to the cutterhead, remove your hand from the stock. Then move your hand to the outfeed side of the cutterhead.
- Use a push stick to push small stock past the cutters. Use a push block when planing faces and edges. This protects your fingers.

Using the Rotary Jointer Surfacer

The rotary jointer surfacer works much like a jointer. There is an important difference, however. The jointer cuts stock **with** the grain. This produces the smoothest possible surface. The Uniplane cuts stock **across** the grain. This type of cutting does not produce as smooth a surface.

To use a Uniplane, first set the cutting depth. Do this by turning the depth-of-cut control. Make most cuts about 1/16 inch *(1.5 mm)* deep.

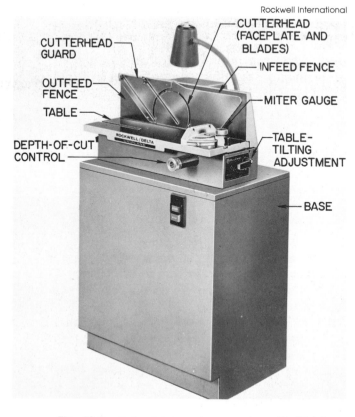

Rockwell International

CUTTERHEAD GUARD

CUTTERHEAD (FACEPLATE AND BLADES)

INFEED FENCE

OUTFEED FENCE

TABLE

MITER GAUGE

DEPTH-OF-CUT CONTROL

TABLE-TILTING ADJUSTMENT

BASE

Fig. 40-1. Rotary jointer surfacer — also called Uniplane

The only other parts needing adjustment are the table and miter gauge. For straight cuts these are set at 90°. You can use a square to check these angles.

Planing Faces and Edges. To plane faces and edges, first set the cutting depth. Then place the surface to be planed against the fence. Hold the stock firmly. Use a push block as shown in Fig. 40-2 to feed the stock. Hold the push block in one hand. Hold the stock against the fence with your other hand. Remember, do not let your hand pass directly over the cutters.

Fig. 40-2. Use a push block to plane the face of a board.

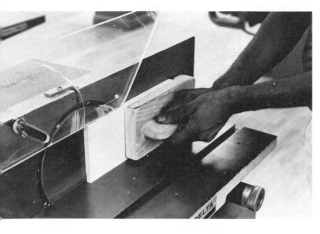

Fig. 40-3. Planing an edge

Rockwell International

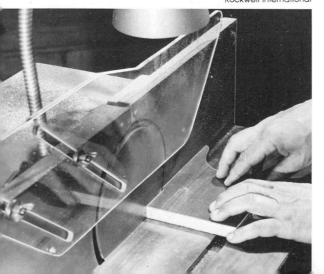

When your hand gets close, move it to the stock on the outfeed side of the cutterhead. Continue feeding the stock with the push block.

Planing End Grain. The Uniplane planes end grain cleaner and safer than does any other machine. This is due to the downward shearing action of the cutters. To plane end grain, adjust the cutting depth for a light cut. Light cuts produce the smoothest possible surfaces on end grain.

Cut boards wider than 8 inches *(200 mm)* the same way you cut edge grain. Support stock less than 8 inches wide with the miter gauge. Also support stock longer than 20 inches *(500 mm)* with a miter gauge. Place the miter gauge in the table groove. Hold the stock against the miter gauge as shown in Fig. 40-4. Hold the end to be planed against the infeed fence. Then push the miter gauge and stock past the cutters.

Cutting Bevels and Chamfers. To cut bevels and chamfers, tilt the table to the proper angle. Do this by loosening both the front and rear locking handles. Set the table as desired and tighten the handles. Then adjust the cutting depth. Try to make two or three equal cuts to produce the desired depth. Make test cuts on a scrap piece the same thickness as your stock.

Fig. 40-4. Use the miter gauge when cutting end grain on boards less than 8 inches (200 mm) wide.

Place the stock on the table. Hold it firmly against the fence. Push the stock past the cutter. See Fig. 40-5. Keep your fingers away from the cutterhead at all times. Use push sticks if necessary. To make cuts on narrow pieces, hold the stock against the miter gauge.

Planing Small Stock. On a Uniplane there is only a small gap between the cutterhead and the fence. This means there is little room for stock to tip into the cutters. For this reason, you can plane small pieces safely on a Uniplane.

Make very light cuts when planing small stock. Use push sticks to move the stock past the cutters. See Fig. 40-6. Do not try holding small pieces with your fingers. Keep your fingers away from the cutters at all times.

Fig. 40-5. When cutting a bevel, try to make two or three equal cuts to produce the desired depth.

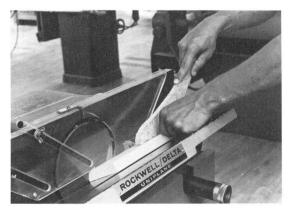

Fig. 40-6. Use push sticks to push small stock through the rotary jointer surfacer.

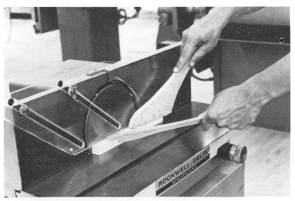

Cutting Compound Miters. Most compound miters are cut on table saws and radial arm saws. These cuts can be trimmed on a Uniplane. See Fig. 40-7. To do this, you must tilt the table and adjust the miter gauge. The proper adjustments for four-sided objects are given in Fig. 36-13, page 249. Make compound miter cuts the same way you cut end grain with a miter gauge.

Fig. 40-7. To trim a compound miter you must angle both the table and the miter gauge.
Rockwell International

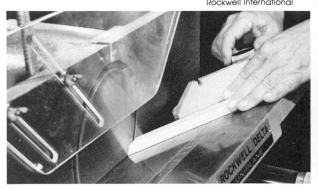

New Terms

1. rotary jointer surfacer
2. Uniplane

Study Questions

1. What are the main uses of rotary jointer surfacers?
2. What is the deepest cut a Uniplane can make? What is the widest cut a Uniplane can make?
3. What is the major difference in the way Uniplanes and jointers cut?
4. How deep should most cuts be with a Uniplane?
5. Why is the Uniplane the best machine for planing end grain?
6. When would you use the miter gauge to plane end grain on a rotary jointer surfacer?
7. Why is the Uniplane the best machine for planing small stock?

Chapter

Lathe

41

Wood lathes are used to turn pieces of wood. While the wood rotates, it can be cut to the desired shape. This is done by holding special lathe tools against the spinning wood. Anything from a wooden bowl to a baseball bat can be shaped on a lathe.

The lathe is a fairly simple machine. It does not have any cutters. It consists basically of a **bed**, a **headstock**, and a **tailstock**. A standard lathe is shown in Fig. 41-1.

One end of the stock is mounted on the headstock spindle. The motor, which adjusts to various speeds, turns the spindle. The tailstock moves along the bed and is clamped at different positions. The tailstock supports the other end of the turning stock. A **tool support** is clamped at different positions along the bed. It supports the lathe tools during the cutting.

The size of a wood lathe is determined by two factors. One is the longest piece of stock the lathe can turn. The other factor is the swing. The **swing** is the largest diameter of stock that can be turned over the bed. A 12 by 38-inch lathe will turn stock up to 38 inches *(950 mm)* long and 12 inches *(300 mm)* in diameter. Some lathes have a gap bed. A **gap bed** permits the turning of larger diameters next to the headstock.

Lathe Tools

Lathe tools have long handles and heavy blades. They are actually chisels and gouges designed specifically for lathe work. There are six basic kinds. See Fig. 41-3. Each is designed for a certain type of cut.

Gouges are used for rough cutting. They are usually the first tools used to shape the stock

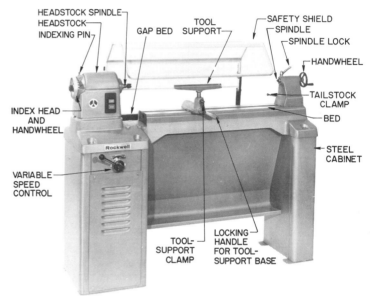

Rockwell International

Fig. 41-1. Wood lathe. This model has a variable speed control and a gap bed for large faceplate turning.

Fig. 41-2. Common set of lathe tools

Woodcraft Supply Corporation

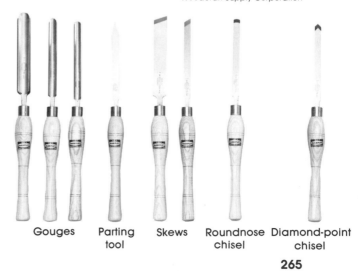

Gouges   Parting tool   Skews   Roundnose chisel   Diamond-point chisel

to basic dimensions. Gouges should not be used for faceplate turning, however.

Skews are used to make smooth cuts, V-cuts, and shoulder cuts. They are also used to round outside edges and cut beads.

Roundnose chisels are used to shape concave surfaces. They can be used for both rough and smooth cuts.

Squarenose chisels are used to make straight, flat-bottomed cuts.

Diamond-point chisels are used to make V-cuts. They are also used to cut corners and beads.

Parting tools are used to make narrow, deep cuts. They are used to make depth cuts and to trim ends.

Selecting Stock

Almost any board can be shaped on a lathe. This depends, of course, on having sharp tools and using the lathe properly. Generally hardwoods are easier to shape than softwoods. Walnut is especially suitable for lathe turning. Plywood and particle board, however, should never be turned on a lathe. Weak areas in these materials can separate. This can be dangerous for everyone in the shop.

You should carefully inspect all stock before turning it on a lathe. The stock must be free of splits, checks, knots, and other defects. While the wood turns at high speeds, splits and checks may open. They can then break loose and be thrown from the lathe. Pressure from the lathe tools increases the chances of this

happening. You must also check that all glue joints are tight.

Laying Out the Stock

The layout of stock to be turned is very important. The stock must be measured and clearly marked before any cuts are made. The layout marks will guide you and help you avoid mistakes.

Rules, calipers, and dividers are the most useful measuring tools for lathe work. See Fig. 41-4. **Calipers** are used to measure lengths and diameters. Rules are used to set the calipers and measure lengths. Dividers are used mainly to scribe diameters for faceplate work. Dividers are also used to lay out equal distances.

Follow a plan or pattern to lay out a piece for turning. It is best to draw the pattern full size. This will help you visualize the turning. A full-size pattern also makes it easier to transfer measurements to the stock.

You may want to make a template from your pattern. See Fig. 41-5. Making a template will reduce the number of measurements needed. Templates are especially helpful when you are making duplicate parts. A set of table legs would be an example of this. Make your templates with either cardboard or hardboard.

Lathe Speeds

Lathe speed must be carefully regulated. Turning stock too fast is dangerous. Turning stock too slowly will result in poor-quality

Fig. 41-3. These are the shapes of the basic lathe tools.

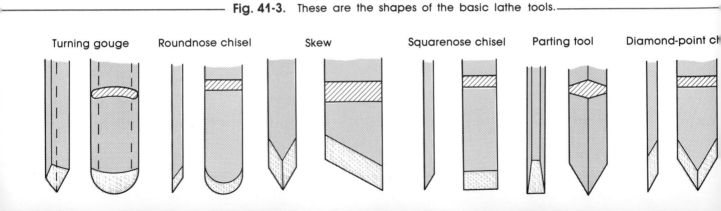

Turning gouge | Roundnose chisel | Skew | Squarenose chisel | Parting tool | Diamond-point ch

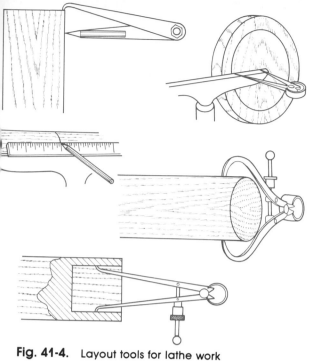

Fig. 41-4. Layout tools for lathe work

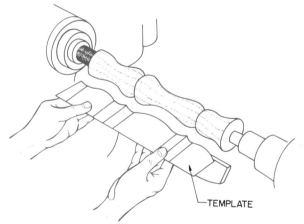

—TEMPLATE

Fig. 41-5. A template such as the one shown here can save you time when shaping many identical parts. Use the template to check your progress as you work.

work. The proper speed depends on the kind of cut and the diameter of the stock. Generally the larger the stock, the slower the speed. Three kinds of cuts are made on a lathe: rough, general, and finish.

Rough cutting is done after the stock is first mounted. During rough cutting, all the corners are removed. The stock is also cut to rough size.

Fig. 41-6. Lathe Speed Chart

DANGER

DO NOT EXCEED THESE RECOMMENDED SPEEDS. SERIOUS INJURY CAN RESULT IF PARTS BEING TURNED ARE THROWN FROM THE LATHE.

Dia. of Stock (in inches)	Roughing R.P.M.	Gen. Cutting R.P.M.	Finishing R.P.M.
Under 2	1520	3000	3000
2 TO 4	760	1600	2480
4 TO 6	510	1080	1650
6 TO 8	380	810	1240
8 TO 10	300	650	1000
10 TO 12	255	540	830
12 TO 14	220	460	710
14 TO 16	190	400	620

General cutting follows the rough cutting. It is a shaping and smoothing operation. Most designs are cut during general cutting. **Finish cutting** is the final smoothing of the stock. It includes fine, detail cutting, as well as sanding. Figure 41-6 gives the proper speeds according to stock diameters and types of cuts.

Most lathes have a variable speed control. Adjust the speed on these lathes while the lathe is running. Set the speed before you mount the stock.

Some lathes have a four-step pulley system. To change speeds on these lathes, you must stop the machine. Disconnect the power first. Then move the belt to the desired pulleys. Placing the belt on the smallest motor pulley produces the slowest speed.

Lathe Safety

SAFETY

- Know and follow the general safety rules for operating power tools on page 211.
- Wear a face shield or safety goggles when using a lathe. If you wear a face shield, you must also wear safety glasses.
- Do not use a lathe unless you have permission from your instructor.
- Make sure the stock is free of knots, splits, and other defects. Loose pieces are easily thrown from lathes.

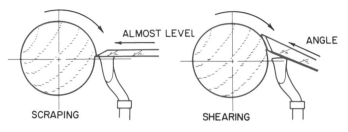

Fig. 41-7. Two methods are used to shape stock on a lathe.

- Keep your tools sharp. Dull tools are more dangerous than sharp ones.
- Do not use your hands to touch the turning stock.
- Never wear loose clothing when using a lathe. Always tie back long hair. It is easy to catch hair and clothing in the lathe.
- Always turn the stock by hand before starting the lathe.
- Check the speed setting before turning on the lathe. Turning stock too fast is dangerous.
- On a variable speed lathe, adjust the speed before mounting the stock. Set the speed control at its lowest setting.
- Always keep the tool support as close to the stock as possible. This is usually less than 1/8 inch *(3 mm)*. As the stock becomes smaller, reposition the tool support. Stop the machine before adjusting the support.
- Keep the tool support and the tailstock clamped securely.
- Lubricate the cup center to reduce friction. This will help prevent burning. You need not lubricate ball bearing centers.
- Hold the tools securely. Keep one hand near the tool support. Place the other hand on the end of the tool's handle.
- When faceplate turning, use only the scraping method of cutting. Do not use a gouge.
- Always remove the tool support when sanding on the lathe. Otherwise, you can pinch your hands between the stock and the support.

- Always remove the centers after you finish turning. They are sharp. If brushed against, they can cause injuries.
- Let the stock come to a stop by itself. Never grab the stock to slow it down.

Cutting Methods

Two cutting methods are used to shape stock on the lathe. See Fig. 41-7. **Scraping** is the easiest and most used method. You can use any of the lathe tools for scraping. Hold the tool flat on the tool support. Move the tool horizontally into the turning stock. The tool scrapes away the wood fibers and leaves a rough surface. You can, however, produce a fairly smooth surface by taking light cuts. Be sure to use the proper lathe speed.

Shearing cuts are more difficult to make than scraping cuts. Shearing cuts remove the stock much faster, however. They also produce a smoother surface, which requires less sanding. Use only gouges and skews to make shearing cuts. Hold the tool at an angle to the stock. Roll the tool as you cut the desired shape. To do this successfully you must practice a great deal.

Spindle Turning

Spindle turning is also called **turning between centers**. This is because the stock is supported between the two centers. See Fig. 41-8. The **spur (live) center** rotates in the headstock spindle. This rotation turns the stock. The **cup (dead) center** is located in the tailstock. It remains stationary and holds the stock in position. Spindle turning is used to shape table legs, tool handles, baseball bats, and other similar items.

Preparing the Stock. First select the stock. It should be about 1 inch *(25 mm)* longer than the finish length. It should also be a little larger than the finish diameter. The ends of the stock should be cut square.

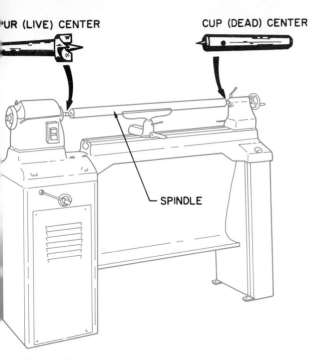

SPUR (LIVE) CENTER   CUP (DEAD) CENTER

SPINDLE

Fig. 41-8. This is the basic setup for spindle turning.

Find the center on each end of the stock. Use one of the methods shown in Fig. 41-9. Mark the center by making a deep indention with a scratch awl. This end will receive the cup center. On the other end make two saw kerfs 1/8 inch (3 mm) deep. Use a backsaw or band saw. Make the kerfs through the center at right angles to each other. Drive the spur center into these kerfs as shown in Fig. 41-10. Use only a soft-

Fig. 41-9. Use either of these methods to locate the center of the stock.

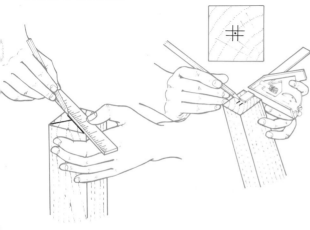

faced mallet. The kerfs will prevent the stock from splitting.

Set the lathe speed for rough cuts. See the chart in Fig. 41-6. You must do this before mounting the stock. Turning large diameter stock too fast could throw it from the lathe. This could cause severe injuries.

To mount the stock, hold it horizontally. Slide the shank of the spur center into the headstock spindle. Then slide the tailstock against the other end of the stock. Lock the tailstock in place. Turn the tailstock hand-wheel until the cup center is firmly set in the stock. Then tighten the spindle lock and turn on the lathe. Force the cup center into the end of the stock about 1/8 inch *(3 mm)*. Turn off the lathe. Then loosen the spindle lock and move the center back. Put a few drops of oil into the depression made by the center. Put the end of the stock back on the center. Then tighten the spindle lock.

Fig. 41-10. Driving a spur center. You need not make saw kerfs when driving spur centers into softwood.

Fig. 41-11. This drawing shows the proper way of setting up the tool support.

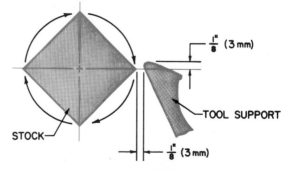

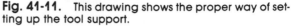

$\frac{1}{8}$" (3 mm)

TOOL SUPPORT

STOCK

$\frac{1}{8}$" (3 mm)

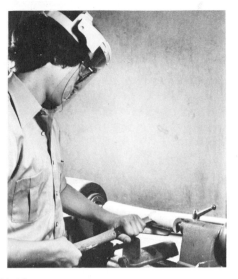

Fig. 41-12. For rough turning, hold the tool as shown here. Be sure you have a firm stance and are wearing the proper eye protection.

Fig. 41-13. Depth cuts are made with a parting tool and calipers.

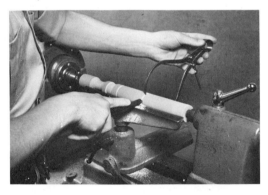

Fig. 41-14. For shaping and finishing cuts, hold the tool as shown.

Move the tool support 1/8 inch *(3 mm)* above the stock's center line. Also move it 1/8 inch from the stock. See Fig. 41-11. Rotate the stock with the handwheel on the headstock. Check that the stock turns freely, but is not loose between centers.

Rough Turning. Use a gouge to make rough cuts. If you are right handed, place your right hand on the end of the handle. Hold the blade with your left hand. Your wrist should be next to the tool support. See Fig. 41-12. Take light cuts to reduce tear-out and chipping. Once the stock has a round shape, increase the lathe speed. Adjust the speed for general cutting. See the chart in Fig. 41-6.

To cut the stock to its basic shape, make several depth cuts. **Depth cuts** are cuts made to show how much stock needs removing. These cuts are made with a parting tool and calipers. See Fig. 41-13. When making depth cuts, always set the calipers 1/16 inch *(1.5 mm)* over finish size. This allows for finishing cuts. Use a gouge to cut the stock even with the depth cuts.

Defects in the stock are hard to see while the stock is turning. You should frequently stop the lathe and remove the stock. Then check it for defects. This is especially important if turned stock has not been worked for a day or two. Splits and checks could have developed during this time.

Finish Turning. After cutting the stock to its basic shape, increase the lathe speed. Adjust the speed for finish cutting. See the chart in Fig. 41-6. Use a skew, squarenose chisel, or diamond-point chisel. Make light cuts to produce a smooth surface. See Fig. 41-14. Readjust the calipers to the exact finish diameter. Once the finishing cut is complete, the surface is ready for sanding.

To remove the stock from the lathe, loosen the spindle lock. Back off the spindle with the handwheel. Then remove the cup center. To do this, turn the handwheel until the spindle backs completely into the tailstock. This will force the cup center out of the spindle. Remove the spur center with a knockout bar. Push the bar through the opening for the headstock spindle. Hold the center as you lightly tap it loose with the bar.

Turning Decorative Shapes

You can use the lathe to make many decorative shapes in wood. The most common are tapers, shoulders, V-cuts, beads, and coves. See Fig. 41-15. These shapes are sometimes used separately. They are also used together to form interesting designs. To cut decorative shapes, set the lathe at general cutting speeds. See the chart in Fig. 41-6.

Cutting Tapers. Baseball bats are examples of long tapers made on lathes. Tapers are also used to shape table legs, pedestals, and the sides of bowls.

To lay out a taper, first measure several diameters along the pattern. Then mark corresponding points on the stock. Make a depth cut at each of these points. Use a parting tool and calipers, as shown in Fig. 41-13. Make each cut so the stock is 1/16 inch *(1.5 mm)* larger than the marked diameters. See Fig. 41-16.

When cutting a taper, always move the cutting tool from the wide to the narrow end. This will produce a smoother surface. Cut only as deep as the depth cuts indicate. Use a gouge for rough cuts. Use a skew for the finish cut. When faceplate turning, use a roundnose chisel for rough cuts. Use a skew for the final cut.

Cutting Shoulders. Shoulder cuts are made at right angles to the turned surface. They are usually made at the ends of the stock and between other cuts. To cut a shoulder, first lay out its location and width. Then rough out the shoulder with a parting tool. Make finish cuts with a skew, squarenose chisel, or diamond-point chisel. See Fig. 41-17.

V-Cuts. To make a V-cut, first lay out the width and center line. You can use either of the

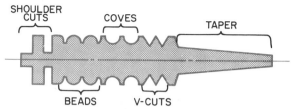

Fig. 41-15. These are the most common decorative cuts.

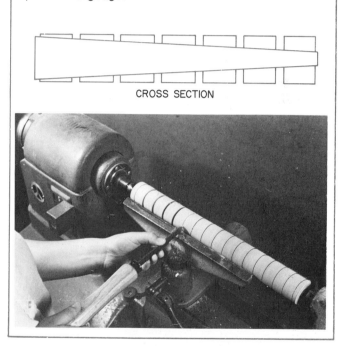

Fig. 41-16. Depth cuts indicate the amount of stock to be removed to produce the desired taper. Cut tapers with a gouge.

CROSS SECTION

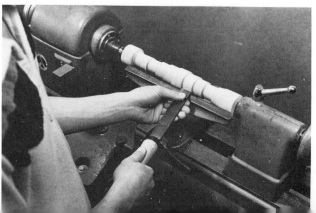

Fig. 41-17. This worker is shaping a shoulder with a skew.

two cutting methods to shape the V. If you scrape the V, use a diamond-point chisel. Simply move the chisel straight into the stock. Start the cut at the center line. Push the chisel inward until you reach the width lines. See Fig. 41-18.

If you make shearing cuts, use a skew. Place the skew on edge with the heel down. Cut into the stock at the center line with the heel. Slowly pivot the skew to one side. This will cut one-half of the V. Then pivot the skew to the other side. This will cut the other half. See Fig. 41-19.

Cutting Beads. Beads are rounded, convex-shaped cuts. To lay out a bead, mark its width and center. Then make depth cuts on each side. You can use either cutting method to shape a bead. If you scrape the bead, use a diamond-point chisel. Pivot the chisel toward the center of the bead, as shown in Fig. 41-20.

It is more difficult to shape a bead by shearing. Use a skew to make a shearing cut. Start the cut at the center of the bead. Tip the skew up and at an angle to the stock. The heel of the skew should be tilted downward. Slowly twist the skew as you reduce the cutting angle. See Fig. 41-21. Repeat this procedure on the other side of the center line.

Fig. 41-18. Scraping a V-cut with a diamond-point chisel

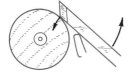

Fig. 41-19. V-cuts can be made by shearing with a skew.

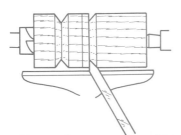

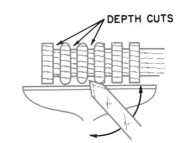

Fig. 41-20. Beads can be made by scraping with a diamond-point chisel.

Fig. 41-21. You can also cut beads by shearing with a skew.

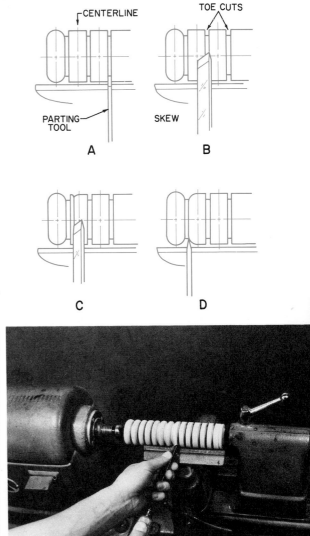

Cutting Coves. Coves are rounded, concave-shaped cuts. To lay out a cove, mark its width and center line. Make a depth cut at the center line. Cut to about 1/8 inch *(3 mm)* of the cove's finish diameter. Use a roundnose chisel to scrape a cove. See Fig. 41-22. Pivot the chisel back and forth to cut the desired shape.

To shear a cove, use a gouge. Start the cut at one edge of the cove. Tilt the gouge almost on edge. Twist the gouge as you move toward the center line. See Fig. 41-23. Repeat this operation on the other side of the cove.

Faceplate Turning

Faceplate turning is used to make many objects. Bowls, plates, round boxes, and lamp bases are just a few examples. In faceplate turning only one end of the stock is attached to the lathe. See Fig. 41-24. Wood screws are usually used to attach the stock to the faceplate. The faceplate is attached to the headstock spindle. The spindle then turns the stock.

Preparing the Stock. Be sure the stock is large enough to make the project. Make one end of the stock flat and square. Find and mark the center of the stock. Then lay out the rough diameter. Remove the excess material with a band saw. Make the stock as round as possible as you do this. Be sure to leave the stock at least 1/4 inch *(6 mm)* over finish size.

Fig. 41-23. This worker is shearing coves with a gouge.

Fig. 41-24. This is a typical setup for faceplate turning.

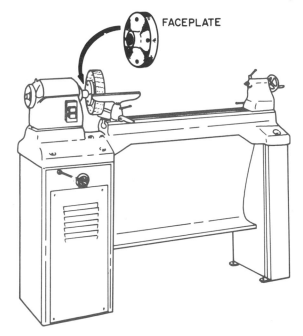

FACEPLATE

Fig. 41-22. This is how coves are scraped with a roundnose chisel.

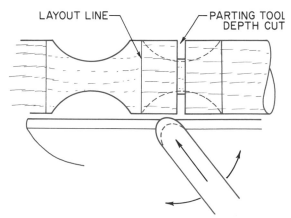

LAYOUT LINE

PARTING TOOL DEPTH CUT

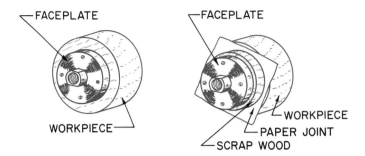

Fig. 41-25. These are the most common methods of attaching stock to a faceplate.

Fig. 41-27. When cutting the edge of a faceplate turning, you can use the tailstock for added support.

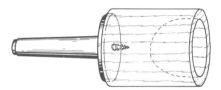

Fig. 41-26. A screw center can be used to hold small stock for faceplate turning.

Set the lathe speed for rough cuts. See the chart in Fig. 41-6. It is important to set the speed before mounting the stock. Be sure to use the correct speed for the stock's diameter. Starting large diameter stock at too high a speed could throw it from the lathe. This could cause severe injuries.

Attach the stock to the faceplate. Two methods are used most frequently. See Fig. 41-25. The easiest method is to use wood screws. You should use the largest screws possible. The larger the stock, the larger the screws should be. Screws do leave holes in the stock. Only use this method if the holes will not show.

The other method of attaching the stock is to use a **paper joint**. To use a paper joint, apply glue to the stock and a piece of scrap. (Never use plywood for the scrap piece.) Place a piece of bond or kraft paper between the two surfaces. Clamp them together and allow the glue to dry. Then use screws to attach the scrap piece to the faceplate.

Screw the faceplate on the headstock spindle. Tighten the faceplate with firm hand pressure.

Do not turn the lathe on to help tighten the faceplate. This will make it very hard to get the faceplate off.

After turning the stock, separate it from the scrap piece. First remove the faceplate from the lathe. Then remove the two pieces from the faceplate. Place a chisel at the glue line. Point the chisel in the direction of the stock's grain with the bevel facing the scrap piece. Strike the chisel with a mallet. This will force the chisel between the two pieces.

Rough Turning. Use the scraping method for all faceplate turning. Use a roundnose chisel rather than a gouge. The edge of the gouge can dig into the rotating stock. This can cause the stock to break loose from its mounting. The stock can then be thrown from the lathe.

Make your first cuts on the edge of the stock. See Fig. 41-27. Position the tool support even with, or slightly above, the center of the stock. For added support, use the tailstock. Clamp it so that the cup center is against the stock. Cut the stock to rough size as described for spindle turning.

After roughing the edges to shape, slide the tailstock away. Position the tool support for face cutting. See Fig. 41-28. Place the tool's cutting edge exactly at the center of the face. Always cut on the side of the stock that is turning down.

Fig. 41-28. You can cut the inside of a bowl by scraping with a roundnose chisel. Always cut on the side rotating downward.

Fig. 41-30. Duplicators are used to shape identical pieces. Notice the template used as a guide.

If you are cutting a concave shape, such as the inside of a bowl, drill a depth hole. Drill the hole near the center of the stock. Drill it to the desired depth. You can then cut to the bottom of the hole. This method eliminates the chance of cutting too deeply. It also eliminates repeated measurements to check the depth.

Finish Turning. Make finish cuts on faceplate turnings the same way you would on spindle turnings. Set the lathe speed for finish cuts. Use a roundnose chisel or a skew. Make light, smooth cuts to reduce the need for sanding.

Sharpening Lathe Tools

To grind lathe tools, follow the instructions on page 75. Be careful not to change the bevel angles. The correct angle for each tool is shown in Fig. 41-29. Hone only those tools used for shearing cuts (skews and gouges). Do not hone tools used for scraping. The burr (wire edge) formed by grinding helps remove stock.

Duplicators

A duplicator is a lathe attachment used to make many identical parts. Several models of duplicators are available. They all work on basically the same principle. A template is made to match the desired turning. The template is then attached to the duplicator. The stock is turned to the shape of a cylinder. The regular lathe tools are used for this. The cutter on the duplicator then follows the template to produce the desired pattern. See Fig. 41-30. The result is usually a rough cut. Finishing cuts with regular lathe tools will probably be needed. Therefore, the duplicator should be set to cut slightly over finish size.

Fig. 41-29. Recommended Angles for Sharpening Lathe Tools.

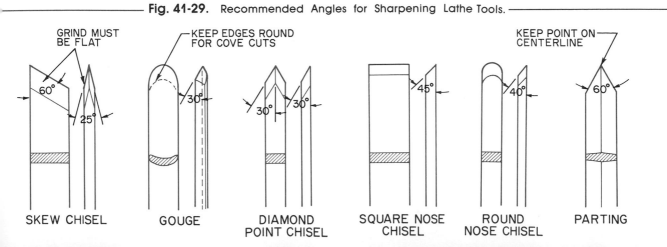

SKEW CHISEL   GOUGE   DIAMOND POINT CHISEL   SQUARE NOSE CHISEL   ROUND NOSE CHISEL   PARTING

Drilling and Boring on the Lathe

You can drill and bore stock on a lathe. To do these operations, you need a drill chuck. The drill chuck is mounted in one of the spindles. For some operations the chuck is mounted in the headstock spindle. For others, it is mounted in the tailstock spindle.

The lathe is sometimes used to drill holes in faceplate turnings. For these operations, install the drill chuck in the tailstock spindle. Then insert the cutter in the chuck. Turn the faceplate at a slow speed. Use the handwheel to move the cutter into the turning stock. See Fig. 41-31.

To drill holes in long stock, install the chuck in the headstock spindle. Make sure the tapered shank is firmly placed in the spindle. Then install the cutter in the chuck. Run the lathe at a very slow speed. Align the stock with the cutter as shown in Fig. 41-32. Clamp the tailstock spindle at the end of the stock. Turn on the lathe. Use the tailstock handwheel to feed the stock into the rotating cutter.

Fig. 41-31. To bore a faceplate turning, mount a drill chuck in the tailstock.

Fig. 41-32. To drill a hole in the end of a spindle, mount a drill chuck in the headstock.

Sanding on the Lathe

You can sand round stock while it is mounted on the lathe. See Fig. 41-33. Before sanding, clamp the tool support safely out of the way. Otherwise your fingers could be pinched between the tool support and the stock. Choose the correct abrasive for the kind of wood and condition of the surface. See chapter 17 for information on abrasives and grit sizes.

As the stock turns, hold the abrasive against it. Your fingers should point in the direction the stock rotates. Move the abrasive back and forth perpendicular to the rotation. Do not hold the abrasive stationary. Remove all tool marks with the coarse abrasive. Then use finer abrasives.

For spindle turnings, turn off the lathe to do the final sanding. You can final sand most faceplate turnings with the lathe on. Use a fine abrasive. Sand in the direction of the wood grain.

Finishing on the Lathe

You can finish your project while it is mounted on the lathe. This type of finishing is especially useful for one-piece projects. Bowls, candle holders, and salt and pepper shakers are some examples. French polish is very popular for lathe finishing. See chapter 25 for information on applying French polish on a lathe.

Wax finishes are also easy to apply on a lathe. To apply a wax finish, first brush on the sealer. Allow the sealer to dry. Then sand it smooth.

Fig. 41-33. This is the correct method of sanding a concave surface on a faceplate.

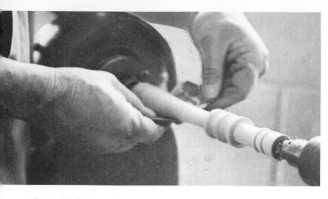

Fig. 41-34. Sanding a spindle turning. The tool support should be moved well away from the turning.

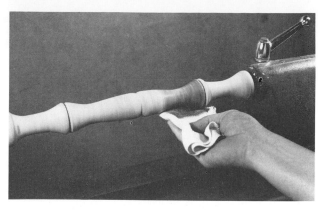

Fig. 41-35. Applying French polish on a lathe

Turn the lathe on at a slow speed. Apply the wax with a clean cloth. Then increase the speed to the finishing speed for the stock's diameter. This will dry the wax faster. Do not leave the lathe while the project is drying.

After the wax has dried, slow down the lathe. Buff the wax with a clean, soft cloth. Repeat waxing and buffing until the desired finish is achieved. Always buff at a slow speed. Faster speeds will heat the wax and melt it. The cloth will then remove the wax rather than buff it.

New Terms

1. bed
2. calipers
3. cup center
4. diamond-point chisel
5. depth cut
6. duplicator
7. faceplate turning
8. finish cutting
9. general cutting
10. headstock
11. paper joint
12. rough cutting
13. roundnose chisel
14. scraping
15. shearing
16. skew
17. spindle turning
18. spur center
19. squarenose chisel
20. swing
21. tailstock
22. tool support
23. wood lathe

Study Questions

1. What are the three basic parts of a wood lathe?
2. What two factors determine the size of a lathe?
3. List the six basic tools used for shaping wood on a lathe.
4. Why should plywood and particle board never be turned on a lathe?
5. List the three tools most useful for laying out stock to be turned on a lathe.
6. In what cases are templates especially useful?
7. Which of the two cutting methods used in lathe work produces the smoothest surfaces? Which method is the most difficult to do?
8. Describe the position of the tool support for spindle turning.
9. How much larger than finish size should the stock be after depth cuts are made?
10. What are the five most common decorative cuts made on a lathe?
11. In which direction should the cutting tool be moved when shaping a taper?
12. What is the basic difference between faceplate turning and spindle turning?
13. What two methods are used most frequently to attach stock to a faceplate?
14. On which side of the stock do you always cut during faceplate turning?
15. Which lathe tools should not be honed? Why?
16. Why should duplicators be set to cut slightly over finish size?
17. What speeds are used for drilling and boring operations on a lathe?
18. Describe the sanding technique for rough sanding on a lathe.
19. What two finishes are frequently applied on a lathe?

42

Router

Routers are used mainly to cut joints and decorative shapes in wood. They are also used to trim the edges of plastic laminates and veneers. A typical router is shown in Fig. 42-1. Many different styles are manufactured. All routers work on the same principle, however.

A router is basically a motor mounted in a base. The base adjusts to the desired cutting depth. A chuck on the motor holds the router bit. The router bit turns at high speeds to make the cut.

The size of a router is determined by two factors. One is the horsepower of the motor. The other is the size of the chuck. Most routers have from 1/2 to 2-1/2 horsepower. Small routers have a chuck capacity of 1/4 inch. These routers hold bits with shanks up to 1/4 inch in diameter. Larger routers can hold 3/8-inch and even 1/2-inch shanks.

Router Bits

The size and shape of a router cut is determined by the bit. There are many sizes and shapes of router bits available. The outline of the bit shows the design it will cut. See Fig. 42-2. Most bits are made of high-speed steel. They are ground to a keen cutting edge. Many bits have carbide cutting edges. These bits are more expensive, but they stay sharp longer.

Stanley Tools

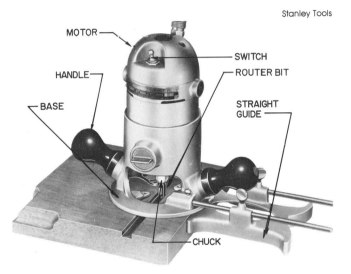

Fig. 42-1. Router

Fig. 42-2. The cuts that can be made with a router are determined by the types of bits used.

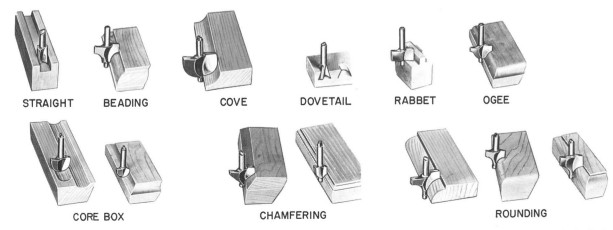

STRAIGHT   BEADING   COVE   DOVETAIL   RABBET   OGEE

CORE BOX   CHAMFERING   ROUNDING

Stanley Tools

Selecting a Router Bit. Select a router bit by looking at its profile. This shows the design the bit will cut. To get a certain design, it is sometimes necessary to use two different bits. See Fig. 42-3.

Some router bits have a cylinder-shaped guide on the bottom of the bit. See Fig. 42-4. This guide is called a **pilot**. The purpose of the pilot is to guide the bit along the edge of the stock. This holds the bit a uniform distance from the edge. The cut can only be as smooth and even as the edge. A nicked edge, for example, will cause an uneven cut.

Other router bits have small **ball-bearing guides**. These guides produce less friction than pilot guides do. With less friction there is less chance of burning the stock. Ball bearing guides are especially useful for trimming plastic laminates and veneers.

Installing a Router Bit. Before you install a bit, disconnect the power. Then lock the router shaft. Different methods are used for different routers. Loosen the chuck by turning the nut counterclockwise. See Fig. 42-5. Insert the bit.

Put the shank at least 1/2 inch *(12 mm)* into the chuck. Tighten the chuck securely.

When the bit is secure, adjust the cutting depth. This is done by moving the motor in the base. The distance the bit extends from the base will be the cutting depth. Use a ruler to measure the distance. Lower the motor to increase the cutting depth. Raise the motor to decrease it. When you have the correct setting, clamp the base securely to the motor. Check the setting by placing the stock next to the cutter. See Fig. 42-6. Make a test cut on a piece of scrap stock.

Router Safety

* Know and follow the general safety rules for operating power tools on page 211.
* Disconnect the power before changing router bits.
* Clamp router bits securely in the chuck. At least 1/2 inch *(12 mm)* of the shank should be inserted.

SAFETY

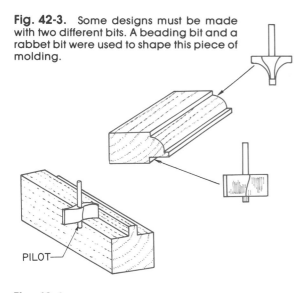

Fig. 42-3. Some designs must be made with two different bits. A beading bit and a rabbet bit were used to shape this piece of molding.

PILOT

Fig. 42-4. Pilot guides keep router bits in line with the edge of the stock. For the cut to be straight, the edge must be straight.

Fig. 42-5. This worker is using two wrenches to loosen the chuck.

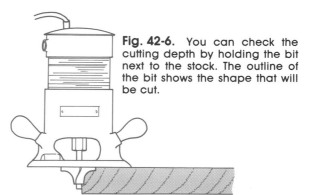

Fig. 42-6. You can check the cutting depth by holding the bit next to the stock. The outline of the bit shows the shape that will be cut.

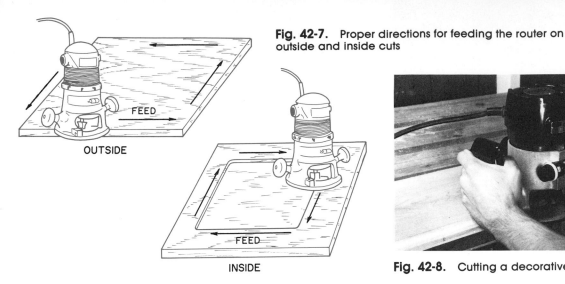

Fig. 42-7. Proper directions for feeding the router on outside and inside cuts

OUTSIDE

FEED

FEED

INSIDE

Fig. 42-8. Cutting a decorative edge

- Make sure the router switch is in the "off" position before connecting the power.
- Do not make any router cuts unless the stock is securely clamped. The router can throw loose stock with great force.
- Before you start cutting, make sure nothing is in the router's path.
- Hold the router tightly when starting the motor.
- Always feed the router **against** the rotation of the bit. If you feed **with** the rotation, the bit can dig into the stock. This can cause the router to kick back or throw the stock.
- After finishing a cut, wait for the router to completely stop. Then lay the router down. The bit should point away from you.

Using a Router

Do not plug the router in unless the switch is off. Turn the switch on when you have a firm grip on the handle. Be sure the stock is securely clamped to the workbench. Feed the router opposite the direction the bit rotates. Feed the router counterclockwise when cutting outside edges. Feed it clockwise when cutting inside edges. See Fig. 42-7.

Feed the router at a steady speed. Feeding too fast will make a rough cut and overwork the motor. Feeding too slowly will overheat the bit. This can burn the wood and produce marks that are hard to remove. Experiment on a scrap

piece. The rate of feed will vary, depending on the bit size and type of wood.

Routing Decorative Edges. Many router bits are designed to cut decorative edges in wood. Most of these bits have a pilot guide. The stock must be clamped securely before you begin routing. Rout end grain first. Then rout along the edges as shown in Fig. 42-8. This will prevent splintering at the corners during the final cuts.

Making Straight Cuts. Routers are excellent tools for making many straight cuts. Joints such as dadoes, rabbets, and grooves can be cut with a router. Straight router bits are used with either an edge guide or straightedge. See Figs. 42-9 and 42-10. Edge guides are useful when cutting close to an edge. A straightedge can be used almost anywhere on the stock. You can easily make a straightedge with shop materials. All you need is a straight piece of wood or metal.

Fig. 42-9. An edge guide can be used to make rabbet cuts. This guide can be used for most straight cuts close to an edge.

Fig. 42-10. A wooden straightedge can be used to guide a router through dado cuts. Make sure the straightedge is securely clamped to the stock.

Routing Freehand. Routers are used freehand to cut irregular designs in wood. **Core box** bits are usually used for this type of routing. To make accurate freehand cuts, you must have steady hands. Make sure your design is clearly marked before you start cutting.

Routing with a Template. Irregular designs are also cut with a template and guide. Templates are especially useful when making several identical cuts. You can buy many special templates. You can also make your own as shown in Fig. 42-11.

Fig. 42-11. You can make a template in the shop for routing irregular designs. A special guide follows the curves of the design as you cut.

Cutting Dovetails. Dovetails are difficult to cut by hand. They are easy to cut, however, with a router and dovetail attachments. To do this you need a **dovetail jig, dovetail template, template guide,** and **dovetail bit.** Use the following procedure to cut dovetails for the front and sides of a drawer.

1. Attach the template guide to the router base.
2. Install the dovetail bit through the template guide.
3. Adjust the cutting depth. The cutter should project 19/32 inch *(15 mm)* beyond the router base.
4. Attach the dovetail jig to the bench. The front edge of the jig should project slightly beyond the edge of the bench.
5. Clamp the drawer side vertically at the front of the jig. See Fig. 42-12 (A). The side that will be the inside of the drawer should face out.
6. Clamp the drawer front horizontally at the top of the jig. See Fig. 42-12 (B). The side that will be the inside of the drawer should face up. The edge of the stock should be against the locating pins. The end of the stock should be tight against the surface of the drawer side. When the stock is positioned correctly, clamp it.
7. Clamp the template to the jig as shown in Fig. 42-12 (C).
8. Cut the dovetails. Follow the template with the router. Make sure the router base stays flat on the template. Feed from left to right as you face the setup.

Fig. 42-12. This illustration shows the steps in setting up a jig and template to cut dovetails for a drawer (front and side).

Fig. 42-13. Cutting dovetails

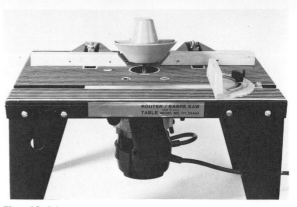

Fig. 42-14. With a router table you can convert a router into a small shaper. This setup is especially useful for cutting small stock.

See Fig. 42-13. Do not lift the router from the template when you finish cutting. Slide it out of the cut to remove it.

9. Remove the pieces from the jig. Then put them together to check the joint. If the joint is too loose, lower the motor in the base about 1/64 inch *(.4 mm)*. If it is too tight, raise the motor 1/64 inch. If the joint is not flush, you need to adjust the fingers of the template. Move the template in or out as needed. Then make another cut as described in step 8. Continue cutting until you get the proper fit.

10. Cut the other side of the drawer. You must cut the second drawer side on the opposite side of the jig. The piece cut on the left side becomes the right side of the drawer. The piece cut on the right becomes the left side of the drawer. When making a box, cut two diagonal corners on one side of the jig. Cut the other two corners on the other side of the jig.

Using a Router Table. A router is sometimes used like a small shaper. For these operations, the router is attached upside down to a router table. This setup makes it easier to rout small pieces. It also increases the accuracy of the cuts.

Commercial router tables have a miter gauge and adjustable guide fence. See Fig. 42-14. A simple router table can be made with a piece of plywood. The table may or may not have legs. Without legs it could be clamped between two bench tops. A fence can be used as a guide. It could either be bolted or clamped to the table.

New Terms

1. ball bearing guide
2. core box bit
3. dovetail bit
4. dovetail jig
5. dovetail template
6. pilot
7. router
8. router bit
9. router table
10. template guide

Study Questions

1. What is the main use of routers?
2. What is the chuck capacity of a small router?
3. Give one advantage and one disadvantage of bits with carbide edges.
4. Some router bits have a pilot. What is the purpose of the pilot?
5. For what router operations are ball bearing guides especially useful?
6. How is the cutting depth of a router adjusted?
7. In which direction should you feed a router?
8. What can happen if you feed a router too fast? What can happen if you feed a router too slowly?
9. When routing decoratives edges, why should you cut the end grain first?
10. To cut dovetails with a router, what four pieces of equipment do you need besides the router?
11. Describe the setup in which a router can be used like a shaper.

Shapers are used to make decorative cuts in wood. They are also used to cut several types of joints. Shaper cuts are limited only by the types of cutters available.

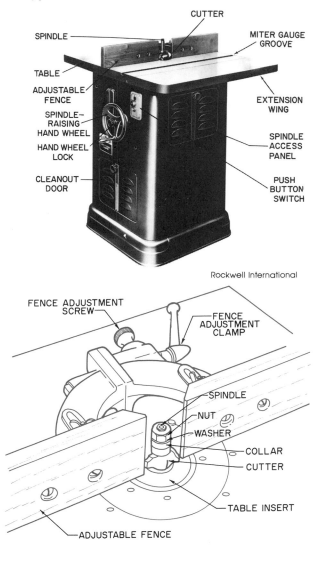

CUTTER

SPINDLE

MITER GAUGE GROOVE

TABLE

ADJUSTABLE FENCE

EXTENSION WING

SPINDLE-RAISING HAND WHEEL

SPINDLE ACCESS PANEL

HAND WHEEL LOCK

CLEANOUT DOOR

PUSH BUTTON SWITCH

Rockwell International

FENCE ADJUSTMENT SCREW

FENCE ADJUSTMENT CLAMP

SPINDLE

NUT

WASHER

COLLAR

CUTTER

TABLE INSERT

ADJUSTABLE FENCE

Fig. 43-1. Floor-model shaper

A shaper is basically a vertical spindle mounted on a table. See Fig. 43-1. Cutters are installed on the spindle, which rotates. The cutters can be rotated at speeds ranging from 5,000 to 10,000 rpm's. The spindle size determines which cutter sizes can be used. The most common spindles have 1/2-inch diameters.

The spindle adjusts up and down to control the cutting depth. The motors on most shapers are reversible. They can rotate the spindle in either direction. This means the cutters can be turned over. A greater variety of cuts can be made this way. Cuts on straight stock are guided with a fence or miter gauge. Cuts on irregular stock are guided against a **depth collar**. The collar is attached to the spindle.

Shaper Cutters

Many different sizes and shapes of shaper cutters are available. See Fig. 43-2. The cutters are made out of high-speed steel. They also

Fig. 43-2. Profiles of shaper cutters   Rockwell International

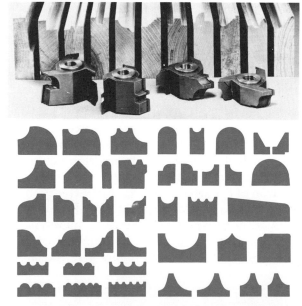

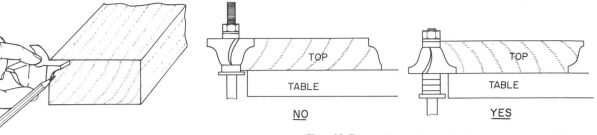

Fig. 43-3. Make a line with a pencil to show the shape and depth of the desired cut. This line will help you set up the cut.

Fig. 43-5. Position the cutter to cut on the bottom of the stock whenever possible. Place the collars below the cutter if possible. This way only a few spindle threads will be exposed.

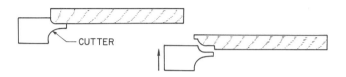

Fig. 43-4. One cutter can be used to make several types of cuts. Changing the cutting depth produces variations in the type of cut. Turning the cutter upside down produces even more variations.

have sharply ground cutting edges. Many are available with carbide tips for heavy-duty use. Three-lip, solid cutters are the safest and most commonly used.

Selecting the Cutter. To make a particular shape, select a cutter with a matching shape. Hold the cutter against the end of the stock as shown in Fig. 43-3. Try the cutter in different positions to determine the cutting depth. Do not forget that the cutting depth will affect the resulting shape. See Fig. 43-4.

When the cutter is correctly positioned, mark along its edge with a pencil. The mark shows how the cut will appear on the stock. It also helps you adjust the cutting depth on the shaper.

Installing the Cutter. Before you install the cutter, disconnect the power. Make sure the spindle and cutter are clean. Wipe away all foreign materials, such as dirt and wood chips.

If possible, install the cutter so it cuts the bottom of the stock. See Fig. 43-5. This is safer than cutting the top of the stock. The unused part of the cutter is not exposed this way.

Cutting on the bottom also makes a more uniform cut. This is especially true for large

stock and warped stock. If large stock tips, with the cutter on top, a deeper cut results. If the cutter tips on the bottom, a shallower cut results. The deep cut cannot be corrected. The shallow cut can still be cut to the desired depth.

Use **collars** as spacers to correctly position the cutter. See again Fig. 43-5. Place most of the collars **under** the cutter. Then place the cutter on top of the collars. Put one collar above the cutter. Over this collar, place a safety washer. Then tighten the nut securely. See Fig. 43-6.

Placing collars under the cutter will cover the threads. Exposed threads can be dangerous since hair and clothing can catch in them. A few threads should be exposed above the nut, however. This is necessary to make sure the cutter and collars stay tightened. The rotating spindle can also be dangerous. Do not let it project above the table any higher than is necessary.

Cutter Rotation. After installing the cutter, check the rotation of the spindle. First make sure there is nothing on the table. You do not want the cutter to hit any tools or attachments. Turn the motor on and off quickly to observe the rotation. The cutter should rotate toward its flat side. If necessary, reverse the motor direction.

The cutter rotation determines the direction of feed. You must always feed **against** the rotation. When the cutter turns counterclockwise, feed from right to left. When the cutter turns clockwise, feed from left to right. See Fig. 43-7. Feeding stock the wrong way is dangerous. It could cause a serious injury.

Shaper Safety

- Know and follow the general safety rules for operating power tools on page 211.
- Make sure the power has been disconnected before making any adjustments.
- If possible, position the cutter at the bottom of the stock.
- Always place a safety washer under the nut to secure the cutter.
- Do not turn the machine on until you are sure the cutter turns freely. Rotate the spindle by hand with a scrap piece to check the clearance.
- Before cutting, turn the machine on and off quickly. Make sure the spindle rotates in the right direction.
- Always feed **against** the cutter rotation. Continue all the way through the cut. Never back up. Feeding **with** the rotation can throw the stock from the shaper.
- Make sure the cutter has completely stopped before cleaning materials from the table.
- When using the fence as a guide, be sure it is fastened securely.
- Use a ring guard when shaping against a collar.
- Always keep your hands at least 6 inches *(150 mm)* from rotating cutters.
- Never leave the machine until the cutter comes to a complete stop.

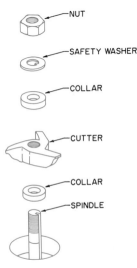

Fig. 43-6. Typical cutter assembly. Always install the safety washer. The washer keeps the nut tight.

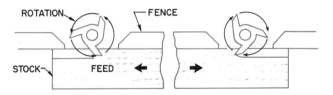

Fig. 43-7. Always feed the stock opposite the cutter rotation.

Straight Shaping

Use the fence as a guide to shape straight edges and ends. Locate the fence to regulate the cutting width. Regulate the cutting depth by raising and lowering the spindle. This is done with the spindle-raising handwheel. Always cut end grain before cutting edges. This way the edge cuts will remove splinters made by the end cuts.

To shape part of an edge, use the uncut area as a guide. Push this area along the fence. See Fig. 43-8. The fences should be in a straight line. Feed against the cutter rotation. Keep your hands at least 6 inches *(150 mm)* from the cutter. If possible, use a guard. You can use a wood block to help guard the cutters. See Fig. 43-9. When necessary, use a push stick.

To shape an entire edge you must offset the fences. This means adjusting the second fence for the amount of cut. See Fig. 43-10. To do this, start making a cut. Make it long enough for the shaped area to reach the second fence. Then stop the shaper. Adjust the second fence to make contact with the cut area. The fence will then support the stock along its complete length. This will produce a smooth cut.

Fig. 43-8. When straight shaping part of an edge, align the fences. **(The guard has been removed to show the operation.)**

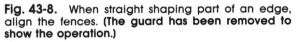

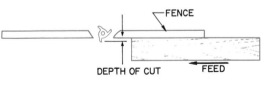

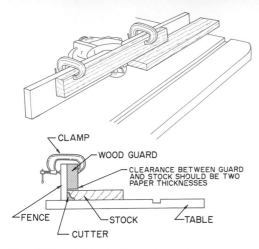

Fig. 43-9. A block of wood can be used as a guard. The wood block will also help hold the stock on the table. If the fences are offset, clamp the block to the outfeed fence only.

Contour Shaping

When shaping a contoured edge, install a ring guard. The ring guard provides added safety. See Fig. 43-11. Use a depth collar as a guide to regulate the cutting width. Depth collars are available in many sizes for a variety of cuts. You may use them either above or below the cutter. How you use them depends on the shape being cut. See Fig. 43-12. The collars with large diameters hold the stock away from the cutter. This produces a light cut. Collars with smaller diameters let the stock closer to the cutter. This produces deeper cuts.

Using a depth collar as a guide requires a starting pin. The tapered **starting pin** starts the cut. Holes are provided in the table for the pin. If the cutter will rotate counterclockwise, place the pin to the right. See Fig. 43-13. If the cutter will rotate clockwise, place the pin to the left.

Place the stock against the starting pin to start the cut. Pivot the stock even with the outside edge of the collar. After starting the cut,

Fig. 43-11. This is a typical shaper setup for cutting irregular stock.

Rockwell International

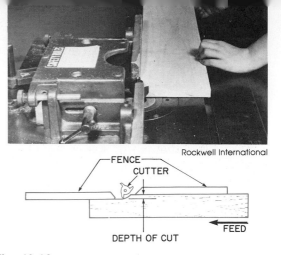

Rockwell International

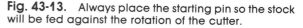

Fig. 43-10. When straight shaping an entire edge, offset the fences. This is necessary to support the stock during the cut. **(The guard has been removed to show the operation.)**

Fig. 43-12. You can place the collar either above or below the cutter. Whenever possible, place the collar above the cutter. Then the cutter will not be exposed during use.

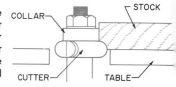

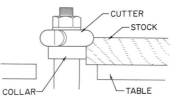

Fig. 43-13. Always place the starting pin so the stock will be fed against the rotation of the cutter.

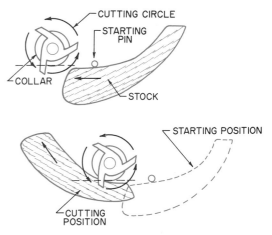

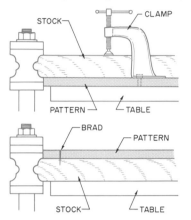

Rockwell International

Fig. 43-14. Shaping an edge with a template

Fig. 43-15. Different setups are used to shape stock with a template. Whenever possible, place the template on top of the stock. This is the safest setup.

you need not keep the stock against the pin. Guide the stock against the depth collar. Feed at a smooth, even rate. Apply only enough pressure to keep the stock against the collar. Too much pressure causes the collar to wear into the stock.

When shaping a contoured edge, the uncut part of the edge serves as a guide. It guides the stock as it rides against the depth collar. Therefore, you must sand the edge before shaping. Sand the edge smooth to the exact edge desired. Any defect in the edge will produce the same defect in the cut. Also make sure the uncut edge is large enough. It must bear against the collar easily. The collar will wear down a small area (less than 1/4 inch, *6 mm*, wide). Because soft wood wears quickly, it may need more than a 1/4-inch bearing surface.

Shaping with a Template

You can use a template to shape irregular stock. This is done by guiding the template

against the depth collar. See Fig. 43-14. To make a template, use stock from 1/2 to 3/4 inch *(12 to 18 mm)* thick. Use hard wood if possible. Hard wood will withstand wear against the depth collar better than soft wood will. The edges of the template must be carefully shaped and smoothed. Any defects on these edges will produce the same defects on the stock. Handles can be attached to templates to provide safe hand holds. See again Fig. 14-14.

Prepare the stock by rough cutting it with a band saw. Cut the stock just over finish size. This will leave enough stock for a complete shaper cut.

Place the template either on top of or under the stock. The nature of the cut will determine which is best. See Fig. 43-15. For heavy cuts, the template is usually clamped to the bottom of the stock. For light cuts, the template is usually placed on top. It is attached to the stock with wood screws or brads. See Fig. 43-15.

New Terms

1. collar
2. depth collar
3. shaper
4. starting pin

Study Questions

1. Give two uses of shapers.
2. What is the advantage of being able to reverse the rotation of a shaper cutter?
3. Is it more desirable to make shaper cuts on the bottom, or the top of the stock?
4. What factor determines the direction of feed on a shaper? Describe the proper feeding direction.
5. Why should you shape end grain before shaping edges?
6. What will happen if you apply too much pressure to the stock as it rides against a depth collar?
7. Why should templates be made from hard wood whenever possible?
8. Is the template placed above, or below the stock when making light cuts?

Sanding Machines

Sanding machines make sanding fast and easy. Used properly, they can save you much time. Used improperly, they can do more damage than good.

There are many types and styles of sanders. They can be divided into two groups: stationary and portable. **Stationary sanders** are large shop machines designed for heavy-duty work. Belt sanders, disc sanders, belt-stroke sanders, spindle sanders, and sander-grinders are some examples. **Portable sanders** are small, hand-held machines. Portable belt and finishing sanders are the two most commonly used for woodworking.

SAFETY Sanding Safety

- Know and follow the general safety rules for operating power tools on page 211.

Fig. 44-1. Stationary belt sander (6-inch model) in the vertical position

Rockwell International

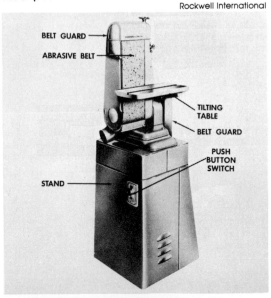

BELT GUARD

ABRASIVE BELT

TILTING TABLE

BELT GUARD

PUSH BUTTON SWITCH

STAND

- Do not operate a sander with a torn belt or loose disc.
- Disconnect the power before changing abrasives.
- On a portable sander, be sure the switch is off before connecting the power.
- Always clamp or hold the stock securely when using portable electric sanders.
- Keep your fingers away from the abrasive. The abrasive can quickly remove skin.
- Always let portable sanders reach full speed before setting them on the stock.
- Always lift portable sanders from the stock before turning them off.
- Wait until portable sanders come to a complete stop before setting them down.

Stationary Belt Sander

Belt sanders turn an abrasive belt at high speeds. See Fig. 44-1. The width of the belt determines the machine's size. The most common belts are 6 inches wide.

The belts are turned around two pulleys. Between the pulleys is a flat surface called a **platen** or **shoe**. The platen supports the stock as pressure is applied against the belt. The bottom pulley is connected to the motor. This pulley is rubber coated to help grip the belt. The top pulley is adjustable. It provides tension and keeps the belt in the center of the platen.

The table supports the stock while the stock is being sanded. The table can be tilted to various angles. This is done to sand bevels, chamfers, and angles. The table also has a groove for a miter gauge. The miter gauge is used for both straight and miter sanding.

Rockwell International

Fig. 44-2. Stationary belt sanders are used horizontally to sand faces flat.

Rockwell International

Fig. 44-3. You can sand a miter on a belt sander. Notice that both the table and the sander have been tilted for this operation.

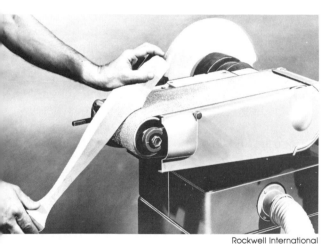

Rockwell International

Fig. 44-4. This worker is sanding a concave shape with a belt sander. The machine is usually positioned horizontally for these operations.

Using a Stationary Belt Sander. You can use stationary belt sanders vertically and horizontally. See Fig. 44-2. Use the table to sand both straight and convex surfaces. See Fig. 44-3. Apply just enough pressure to sand the surface without slowing the motor. Use a V-block to

sand cylinders or dowel rods. Do not sand short or thin pieces. They could lodge between the table and belt.

To sand concave surfaces, remove the upper guard. Set the machine in a horizontal position. See Fig. 44-4. Sand directly over the top pulley. Hold the stock tightly.

Portable Belt Sander

Portable belt sanders are very useful just before finish sanding. They work like stationary belt sanders. They sand on a much smaller scale, however. The belts used on most portable sanders are 3 or 4 inches wide.

Using a Portable Belt Sander. You must use portable belt sanders with extreme care. Otherwise, you can easily tip them into the stock. This could gouge and mark the surface of your project. These marks are difficult to remove.

Clamp the stock securely to a bench. Hold the sander over the area to be sanded. Place the electric cord over your shoulder. This keeps the cord out of your way. It also helps prevent damage to the cord. Turn on the machine and wait until it reaches full speed. Then set the belt on the surface of the stock. Keep the platen flat against the surface. See Fig. 44-5. Do not apply added pressure. The machine's weight will be enough.

Move the sander back and forth along the stock. Each stroke should overlap the previous

Fig. 44-5. Using a portable belt sander. This sander has a dust bag that collects the sanding dust.

one by half the belt's width. Sand in the direction of the grain. Extend each stroke beyond the stock about half the platen's length. Do not allow the sander to tip. This will cause an uneven surface. Keep the sander moving at all times. Any hesitation will make a low spot in the surface.

Remove the sander from the surface before turning the sander off. Letting the sander come to a stop on the surface is dangerous. It will also scratch the surface. Wait for the belt to stop completely before setting the sander down.

Changing Belts. Before changing belts, disconnect the power. Release the belt tension by pushing in the front pulley. Install the new belt. Make sure it runs in the right direction. It

Fig. 44-6. Replacing a belt on a portable belt sander

Fig. 44-7. Belt-stroke sander

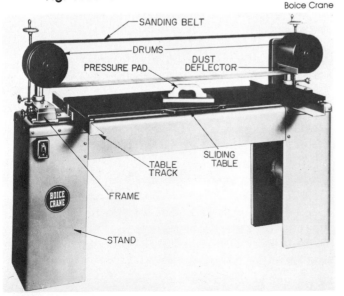

should run from front to back on the bottom of the machine. See Fig. 44-6. Usually an arrow on the machine indicates which way the belt turns. There is also an arrow on the inside of the belt. Position the belt so the two arrows point in the same direction.

Once the belt is positioned, release the front pulley. Set the machine on end. Make sure the belt turns in the center of the platen. Turn the power on and off quickly to check the belt. If necessary, adjust the front pulley until the belt is centered. Be sure the edge of the belt does not cut into the metal housing.

Belt-Stroke Sander

Belt-stroke sanders are large, industrial sanders. See Fig. 44-7. They are used mostly to finish sand large, flat surfaces. They are sometimes used to remove surface defects, tear-out, and chipping.

On most machines, the distance from pulley to pulley is 5 feet *(1.5 m)*, or more. The belts must be more than twice this length. A large table under the belt supports the stock. The table is mounted on rollers. This way it can be easily moved back and forth. The table adjusts up and down to handle various stock thicknesses.

To sand finishes with a belt-stroke sander, place the stock on the table. The side to be sanded should be turned up. Position the stock against the stop at the drive pulley end of the table. Adjust the table height. The belt should just clear the stock.

With one hand, hold the table handle. Hold the pressure pad (wood block) in the other hand. Move the stock back and forth under the belt. Apply pressure to the back of the belt with the pressure pad. Slowly move the pad along the length of the stock. Do not stop or hesitate. This could cause a low spot. When you apply the finish, the low spot will be magnified.

Stationary Disc Sander

Stationary disc sanders are the most accurate sanders in the shop. The abrasive disc is

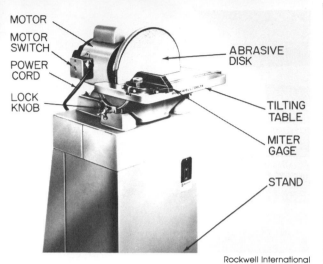

Fig. 44-8. Stationary disc sander. This model has a 12-inch disc.

Rockwell International

Fig. 44-9. Notice that the worker is sanding only on the side of the disc moving down toward the table.

glued directly to a flat, metal disc. See Fig. 44-8. There is no "give" or flexing around pulleys and over platens. For this reason, disc sanders are used frequently for precision work.

Stationary disc sanders are used to sand edges and ends. The stock is supported on a table. The table can be tilted to sand bevels and chamfers. It also has a groove for a miter gauge. The sander's size is determined by the disc diameter. The most common size is 12 inches.

Using the Stationary Disc Sander. Do not use the disc sander until it reaches full speed. Always work on the side of the disc that is turning down. See Fig. 44-9. Hold the stock firmly on the table. Apply light pressure against the rotating disc. Reduce the pressure if the disc starts to slow down.

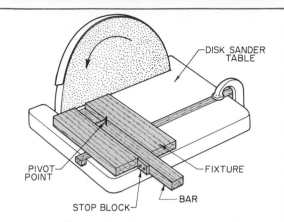

The stock will be mounted on the pivot point. Reposition the stop block or move the pivot point to sand circles of different sizes.

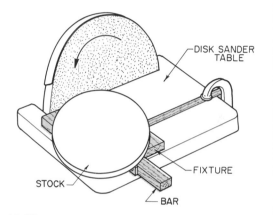

Fig. 44-10. A circle-cutting fixture can be used to sand perfect circles on a disc sander. This fixture can also be used on a belt sander.

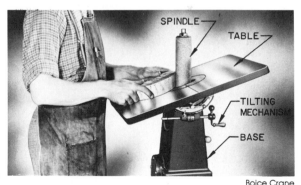

Boice Crane

Fig. 44-11. Spindle sander

Spindle Sander

Spindle sanders are used to sand curved edges. See Fig. 44-11. An abrasive sleeve is attached to the spindle. The spindle rotates and moves up and down. Both spindles and abrasive sleeves come in various diameters. This makes it possible to sand curves of different sizes. The table can be adjusted to sand angles.

Using the Spindle Sander. To use the spindle sander, adjust the table to the desired angle. Install the correct spindle and sleeve for the radius to be sanded. Different methods are used to hold spindles. Release the nut on top of the spindle to replace sleeves. Hold the stock firmly on the table. Apply smooth, even pressure against the spindle. Always move the stock **against** the spindle rotation. This is usually from right to left. Keep the stock moving at a steady rate.

Portable Finishing Sander

Finishing sanders remove small scratches and defects. They are used to make wood as smooth as possible. This is done just before the project is finished. Finishing sanders are also used to sand between coats of finish. There are two basic types of finishing sanders: orbital and oscillating.

Orbital sanders turn the abrasive in a circular motion. They remove material quickly. They may, however, make small, circular scratches. The faster the abrasive turns, the fewer scratches there will be. Some orbital sanders operate between 10,000 and 12,000 opm's (orbits per minute). Sanders with high opm's and a fine abrasive (100 grit, or finer) produce smooth, scratch-free surfaces.

Oscillating sanders move the abrasive back and forth in a straight line. They do not remove

Fig. 44-12. Finishing sanders

Black and Decker

Rockwell International

Fig. 44-13. Move the finish sander **with** the grain, as shown by the arrows.

material as quickly as orbital sanders do. They produce smooth, scratch-free surfaces.

Installing Abrasive Sheets. Before you install an abrasive sheet, disconnect the power. Both ends of the abrasive sheet are clamped to a pad. Loosen the clamps and remove the old abrasive sheet. Cut a new abrasive sheet to fit the pad. One-half or one-third of a standard 9 x 11 sheet will fit most pads. Clamp the new sheet with the front clamp. Pull the sheet tightly along the bottom of the sander. Then fasten it in the rear clamp.

Using the Finishing Sander. When using a finishing sander, clamp the stock securely to a bench. Hold the sander firmly. Do not apply downward pressure. The machine's weight will keep the machine against the surface. Start the sander and let it reach full speed. Then guide it over the surface. Let the machine do the work. Move the sander back and forth **with** the grain. See Fig. 44-13. Avoid sanding **across** the grain. When finished, lift the sander from the surface before turning it off. Wait until it stops completely to set it down.

When sanding coats of finish, hold the stock firmly. Clamping the stock could mar the finish. Use a very fine abrasive. In most cases, you should use a 320- or 400-grit silicon carbide. Do not use water as a lubricant. Using power tools near water increases the chances of electrical shock.

Sander Grinder

Sander grinders are similar to belt sanders, but use narrow belts. Most belts are 1 inch wide. See Fig. 44-14. These machines are used to sand small, hard-to-reach areas. They are used

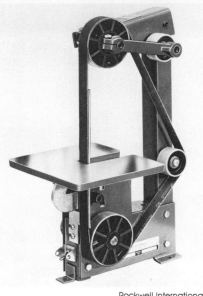

Fig. 44-14. Sander grinder

Rockwell International

Fig. 44-15. Sanding drums such as these can be purchased separately and used on drill presses and lathes.

Fig. 44-16. Small sanding drums can be inserted in portable electric drills to sand curves.

to sand wood, metal, and plastic. They can also be used to sharpen edge tools.

Use a sander grinder like a small stationary belt sander. Sand straight stock against the platen. Remove the platen to sand convex edges on stock. This lets the belt conform to the edges.

Sanding with Other Machines

Machines other than sanding machines can be used for sanding. This is made possible by the many sanding attachments available. Sanding drums are used in drill presses and lathes. See Fig. 44-15. Smaller drums are available for use with portable electric drills. See Fig. 44-16. Flap wheels and brush-backed sanding wheels are also used in electric drills. See Fig. 44-17. Disc and table attachments make it possible to disc sand on the lathe.

New Terms

1. belt-stroke sander
2. brush-backed wheels
3. flap wheels
4. orbital sander
5. oscillating sander
6. platen
7. portable belt sander
8. portable finishing sander
9. pressure pad
10. sander grinder
11. sanding drum
12. spindle sander
13. stationary belt sander
14. stationary disc sander

Fig. 44-17. Brush-backed sanding wheels can be used to sand irregular shapes.

Merit Abrasive Products, Inc.

Study Questions

1. Sanders can be divided into two groups. Name the two groups.
2. On a stationary belt sander, which pulley adjusts the tension on the belt?
3. Compare the most common belt widths for stationary and portable belt sanders.
4. How much overlap should there be between strokes with portable belt sanders?
5. What is the major use of belt-stroke sanders?
6. Which type of sander used in the shop is the most accurate?
7. How are abrasive discs attached to the metal discs on disc sanders?
8. For what types of jobs are spindle sanders used?
9. In what direction should you move the stock when using a spindle sander?
10. Name the two types of portable finishing sanders.
11. Which type of finishing sander removes material quickly?
12. List three power tools besides sanding machines that can be used for sanding.

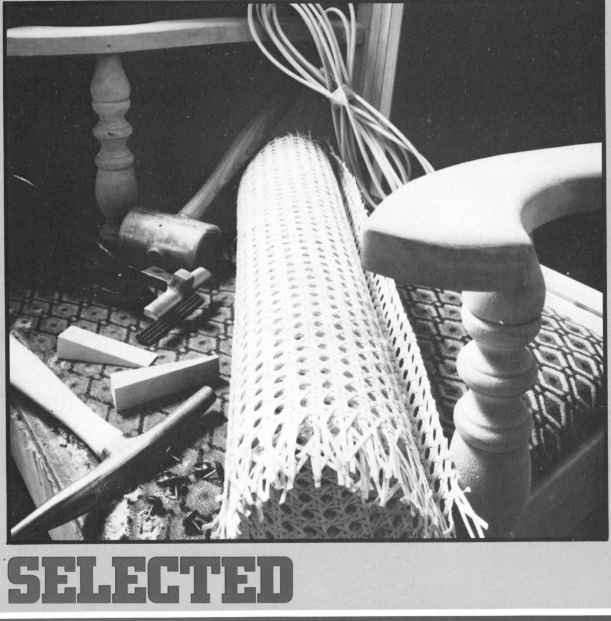

SELECTED

WOODWORKING TOPICS

Cabinetmaking

Cabinetmaking is a general term for making fine wood objects. Furniture and cabinets, for example, are major products of cabinetmaking. In the past, skilled woodworkers, called **cabinetmakers,** hand built most wood furniture. Today most of our wood furnishings are mass produced in large factories. Furniture produced this way can be made quickly and economically. However, most factory-made furniture lacks the originality and quality of hand-made furniture.

Fine cabinetmaking has not completely vanished. A few skilled woodworkers still specialize in making quality wood products. These cabinetmakers generally make their products by special order. They design and build furniture to fit the customer's needs. They use their skills and experience to select, cut, shape, and join the wood. It may take days, weeks, or even months to complete the job. Even for an experienced cabinetmaker, quality takes time.

It takes years of experience to become a skilled cabinetmaker. However, anyone with enough motivation and a few tools can succeed at cabinetmaking. This chapter will provide the information you need to make basic cabinets and furniture.

Tables

Tables are one of the most basic forms of furniture. All tables have a top and legs. Most tables have **rails,** which provide added strength and stability. See Fig. 45-2.

Most tabletops are made from edge-joined solid wood, or plywood. The tops are fastened to the rails, which connect the top to the legs. The legs support the table the desired distance above the floor.

Fig. 45-1. Professional cabinetmakers specialize in making quality wood products.

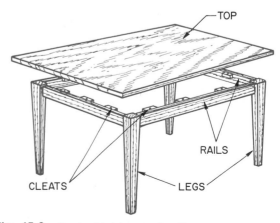

Fig. 45-2. Typical table construction

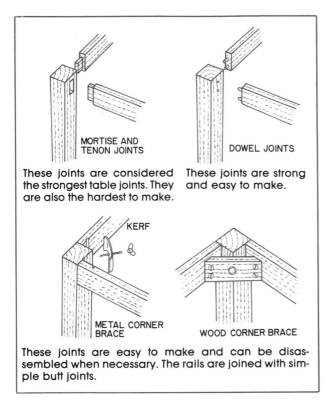

These joints are considered the strongest table joints. They are also the hardest to make.

These joints are strong and easy to make.

These joints are easy to make and can be disassembled when necessary. The rails are joined with simple butt joints.

Fig. 45-3. Joints used to attach table legs to rails

Fig. 45-4. Hardware and legs that can be attached directly to tabletops are available.

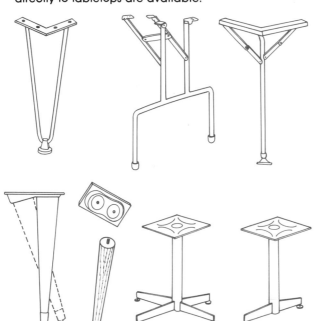

In designing a table, there are two considerations. They are the height of the table and size of the top. These dimensions are largely determined by how the table is used. A ping pong table, for example, must be taller, wider and longer than a coffee table. Basic tables are fairly easy to make. Construction becomes more difficult as tables become fancier.

Attaching Table Legs. There are several ways of attaching table legs to rails. Unfortunately, the strongest methods are also the most difficult. The most common methods are shown in Fig. 45-3. In some cases legs can be attached directly to the table. This eliminates the need for rails. Special manufactured legs and brackets are used instead. See Fig. 45-4.

Fastening Tabletops. Attaching tabletops to the rails can present problems. Tops made of solid wood expand and contract as the humidity changes. The wood may split if fastened improperly to the rails. The larger the tabletop, the more it will fluctuate. Small tops, less than 12 inches *(300 mm)* square, do not fluctuate enough to cause problems.

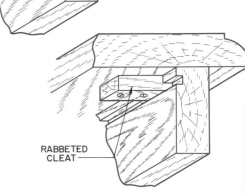

Fig. 45-5. These tabletop fasteners allow for expansion.

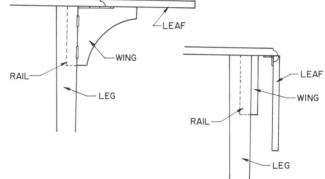

Fig. 45-6. Methods of fastening tabletops to frames

Fig. 45-8. Drop-leaf tables are usually made with rule joints. These joints are attractive when the leaf is down. They are hidden from view when the leaf is raised.

Fig. 45-7. Drop-leaf table

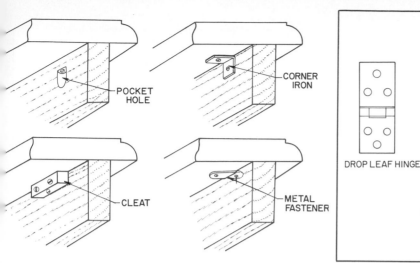

Fig. 45-9. A wing is often attached to a drop-leaf rail to support the leaf. The wing is attached with hinges so it can be swung out of the way when the leaf is lowered.

To attach solid tabletops, use one of the methods shown in Fig. 45-5. Either method will fasten the top firmly to the rails and prevent warping. The top will still be able to fluctuate laterally (sideways).

Like small tops, plywood and particle board tops fluctuate very little. This makes them much easier to attach to their rails. You can attach them solidly with one of the methods shown in Fig. 45-6.

A **drop-leaf table** has leaves (sections) that "drop" (fold down) when not in use. See Fig. 45-7. The stationary part of the tabletop is attached to the rails. This is done with one of the methods described above. The table's leaves are attached to the stationary table with hinges. Special drop-leaf hinges are required. Drop-leaf hinges are longer than normal hinges. Being longer, they allow extra room for a rule joint.

A **rule joint** is designed to be attractive when the leaf is down. It is also designed to be invisible when the leaf is in use. See Fig. 45-8. Rule joints are made with a router or shaper. The stationary top is shaped with a convex bit. The drop leaf is shaped with a matching concave bit. Matching bits must be used for the joint to mesh properly. Although less attractive, a regular butt joint can be used instead of a rule joint.

There are many ways to support the leaf when it is in use. One of the most common methods is to use a **wing.** See Fig. 45-9. The wing is hinged to the rail. It folds out of the way so the leaf can be lowered. Metal drop-leaf supports are also available. See Fig. 45-10.

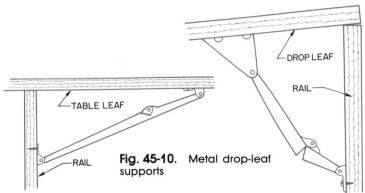

Fig. 45-10. Metal drop-leaf supports

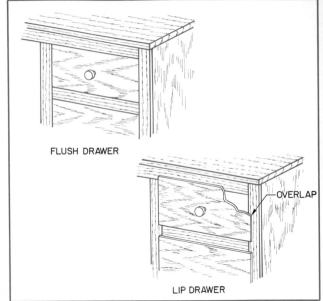

Fig. 45-12. The two basic kinds of drawers are flush and lip drawers.

Drawers

Drawers provide convenient, attractive storage areas. They consist of five parts: a front, two sides, a back, and a bottom. See Fig. 45-11. There are two kinds of drawers: flush and lip. See Fig. 45-12.

A **flush** drawer fits even with the front of the cabinet frame. It must fit with about 1/16 inch (1.5 mm) clearance on all sides. If the drawer fits too tightly, it will bind in the cabinet frame. If it fits too loosely, it will look sloppy.

A **lip** drawer has a rabbet cut around the back of the drawer front. The rabbet (lip) hides the space between the drawer and the cabinet frame. This type of drawer need not fit as precisely as flush drawers.

Various materials are used to make drawers. Drawer fronts are usually made of attractive materials. They are most often made from the same material used for the cabinet frame. The sides and back of the drawer are rarely visible.

Fig. 45-11. Common drawer construction showing parts

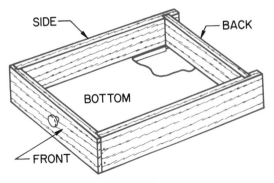

They can be made of less expensive woods. In high-quality drawers these parts are made from woods such as oak and maple. Drawer bottoms are generally made of 1/4-inch plywood or hardboard.

Many different joints are used to make drawers. See Fig. 45-13. Dovetails are considered the best joints for attaching the sides to the front. Rabbet joints, however, are much easier to make. If reinforced with nails, screws, or dowels, rabbet joints are also strong.

The sides are usually attached to the back with butt joints or dado joints. Dadoes provide plenty of strength and are easy to make. The drawer bottom is attached to the sides and front with groove joints. Rabbet joints are also used for this purpose. However, they are not as strong or durable as groove joints for this purpose.

Making a Drawer. Use the following procedure to make a drawer.

1. Select the material to be used for the drawer front.
2. Cut the front to size. Allow 1/16 inch (1.5 mm) clearance between the frame and the front on all sides. The clearance will compensate for wood expansion in

humid weather. For a lip drawer, add the width of the lip to each side.

3. Select the joints you will use. See Fig. 45-13. Chapters 12 and 13 have detailed information about the various joints.

4. Cut the sides and the back. Be sure to allow for the joints. Do not use plywood for these parts.

5. Cut the drawer bottom. In most cases, 1/4-inch plywood or hardboard works well.

6. Cut the grooves for the bottom in the front and sides. The grooves should be at least 1/4 inch *(6 mm)* deep.

7. Cut the joints to attach the sides to the front. For quality construction, use a dovetail (chapter 42) or rabbet joint.

8. Cut the joints to attach the sides and back. This is usually done with dadoes or rabbets.

9. Dry assemble the drawer to check the fit.

10. If the drawer fits properly, sand the parts. Round the top edges of the sides.

11. Apply glue to the front and back joints. Reassemble the drawer. Do not glue the bottom piece in the grooves. Clamp or tack the drawer together until the glue dries.

12. After the glue has dried, tack the bottom to the back. Use small nails.

13. If making more than one drawer, mark each drawer for identification.

Drawer Guides. Tracks for easy opening and closing of drawers are provided by drawer guides. If made and installed properly, drawer guides support the drawer. They also prevent the drawer from binding. Four kinds of drawer guides are commonly used. They are center guides, side guides, corner guides, and manufactured guides. All but the manufactured guides can be made with shop materials.

The type of drawer guide used could change the project design. You should select your guides before you start your project. Many working drawings identify the drawer guides to be used.

Center guides are probably the most trouble-free guides. They are most often used for wide drawers. This is because wide drawers are more likely to bind. Center guides allow easy sliding and are simple to construct. See Fig. 45-15.

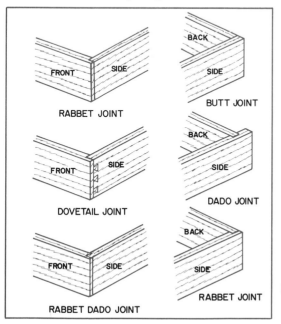

Fig. 45-13. Many joints can be used to attach the parts of a drawer.

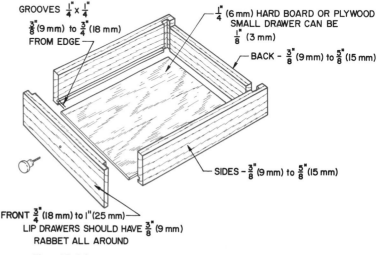

Fig. 45-14. Assembly view of a drawer. This shows typical thicknesses of drawer parts.

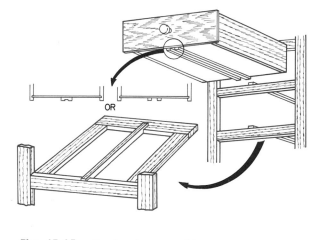

Fig. 45-15. Center drawer guides

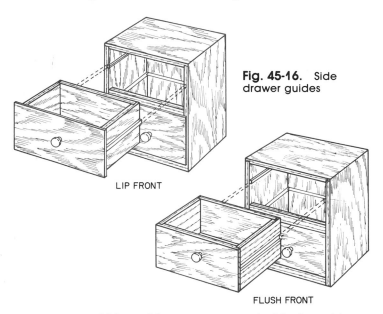

LIP FRONT

FLUSH FRONT

Fig. 45-16. Side drawer guides

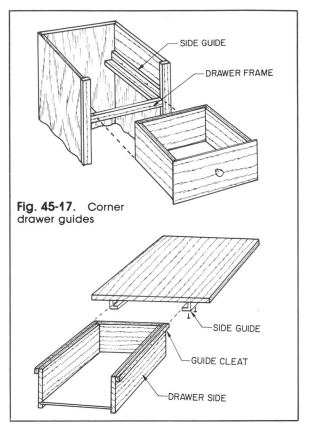

Fig. 45-17. Corner drawer guides

Side guides are most suitable in cabinets with solid sides. These sides provide good surfaces for cutting dadoes or attaching guide cleats. See Fig. 45-16. For flush drawers, attach the cleats to the cabinet sides. Then cut the dadoes in the drawer sides. For lip drawers, cut the dadoes in the cabinet sides. Then attach the cleats to the drawers.

Corner guides usually support drawers at the bottom corners. Attach L-shaped wood pieces to the bottom of the frame, as shown in Fig. 45-17.

You can also use corner guides to support the top of a drawer. Do this when the drawer will hang from a flat surface. Attach the cleats to the drawer sides when using this method.

Manufactured guides come in many styles. See Fig. 45-18. These guides are strong. This makes them good choices for drawers that will hold heavy items.

Other Drawer Parts. Several parts besides drawer guides are used in drawer construction. They are necessary parts of an attractive, easy-to-use drawer.

Kickers are designed to prevent drawers from tipping when pulled out. Make a kicker out of a wood strip. Attach the kicker to the center of the cabinet frame. See Fig. 45-19. If this is not possible, use two kickers. Then place one kicker on each side of the drawer.

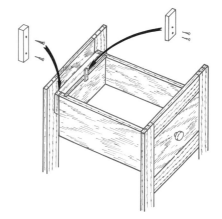

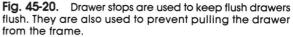

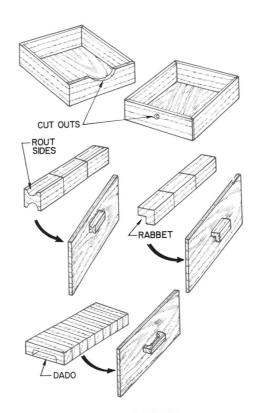

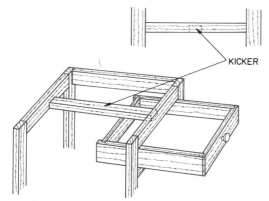

Pulls and handles provide handholds for pulling drawers (and doors) open. A wide variety of types and styles are available commercially. You can also make your own out of wood. See Fig. 45-21.

Fig. 45-18. Manufactured drawer guides

Fig. 45-20. Drawer stops are used to keep flush drawers flush. They are also used to prevent pulling the drawer from the frame.

Fig. 45-21. These are a few methods of making your own drawer or door pulls.

KICKER

Fig. 45-19. Kickers keep drawers from tipping down while open.

Drawer stops are usually made from small wood blocks. They are attached to the back of the frame and drawer. Those attached to the frame prevent flush drawers from being pushed in too far. Lip drawers do not need these stops. The lip on the drawer serves as a stop. Stops attached to drawer backs prevent drawers from being pulled from their frames. See Fig. 45-20.

CUT OUTS

ROUT SIDES

RABBET

DADO

Cabinet Doors

Two basic methods are used to put doors on cabinets. One method is to use hinges. Hinges let the doors swing open and closed. The other method is to use sliding doors. These doors slide in grooves built into the cabinet. Whichever method is used, the cabinet frame should be made before the doors are fitted.

Hinged Doors. You can make hinged doors in different styles. The most common styles are frame, panel, and solid doors. See Fig. 45-22. You can use different methods to mount any of these doors. These methods are flush mounting, surface mounting, and insetting with a lip. See Fig. 45-23.

A wide variety of hinges work well for attaching cabinet doors. **Butt** or **scissor** hinges are used for flush-and surface-mounted doors. **Semi-concealed** hinges are used for lip doors. Select the hinges before you make the door. You will usually need two for each door.

Attaching cabinet doors with hinges requires careful layout and cutting. Poorly attached hinges will not work well. They will also detract from the cabinet's appearance. Take your time when attaching hinges.

Butt hinges are commonly used to install flush- and surface-mounted doors. Use the following procedure to attach a door with butt hinges. Also see Fig. 45-24.

1. Fit the door properly to the frame. For a flush door, leave a gap, about 1/16 inch *(1.5 mm),* on all sides of the door.
2. Lay out the location of each hinge. Do this on the edge of the door. Space the hinges equally from the ends of the door. Common distances are 1 to 2 inches *(25 to 50 mm)* from each end.
3. Position the hinges on the edge of the door. The knuckle should just extend over the corner. Mark the outline of each hinge.
4. Set a marking gauge to the exact hinge thickness. Mark this thickness on the face of the door. Mark it between the

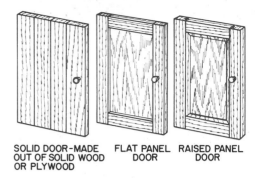

SOLID DOOR-MADE OUT OF SOLID WOOD OR PLYWOOD   FLAT PANEL DOOR   RAISED PANEL DOOR

Fig. 45-22. Common types of hinged doors

layout lines for the hinges. These marks indicate the cutting depth for the gain (recessed area for hinge).

5. Cut along the outline of the gains. Use a sharp knife and a try square.
6. Clean out the gains with a chisel and mallet. Guide the chisel with the bevel side down. Tap it lightly with the mallet. Be careful not to cut any deeper than the thickness of the hinge.
7. Install the hinges in the gains. Use one screw in the center of each hinge.
8. Center the door in the cabinet frame. Use thin wood pieces at the bottom and sides to position the door correctly. Then mark the hinge positions on the frame.
9. Remove the door. Lay out the gains on the frame. Use a square to mark the tops and bottoms. Use a marking gauge to mark the depths and widths.
10. Cut the gains in the frame as described in steps 5 and 6.
11. When the gains are complete, attach the door. Hold the door open and insert one screw in each hinge.
12. Make sure the door works properly before installing the remaining screws. The hinges may need adjusting. The most common problem is gains that are too deep. This prevents the door from closing. To fix this, place thin pieces of paper or veneer in the gains.
13. When the door works properly, attach the door knob. Use a manufactured knob or make your own. See Fig. 45-21.

14. Attach the door catch. **Door catches** prevent doors from swinging open when not in use. They also prevent flush doors from closing too far. Several types are available. See Fig. 45-25. Most catches are either spring loaded or magnetic.

Semi-concealed hinges are used to install lip doors. These hinges are easy to install. They do not require the cutting of gains. One section of the hinge is attached to the frame. The other section fits the lip in the door. See Fig. 45-26. Select the hinge before making the door. The lip in the door must fit the offset in the hinge. Fit the hinge on the door first. Then align and attach the door to the frame.

Sliding Doors. Doors installed with hinges need room to swing open and shut. In some cases there is not enough room for this. Sliding doors are installed in these cases. Most sliding cabinet doors are made of plywood and hardboard. Some are even made of glass. Solid wood is rarely used to make sliding doors. It could warp and become stuck in the sliding door tracks.

There are many different types of tracks for sliding doors. You can make your own or buy a

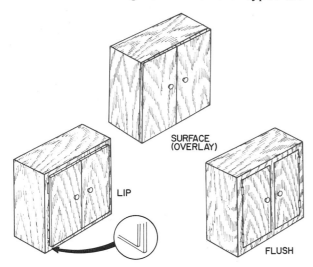

Fig. 45-23. Methods of mounting a hinged door

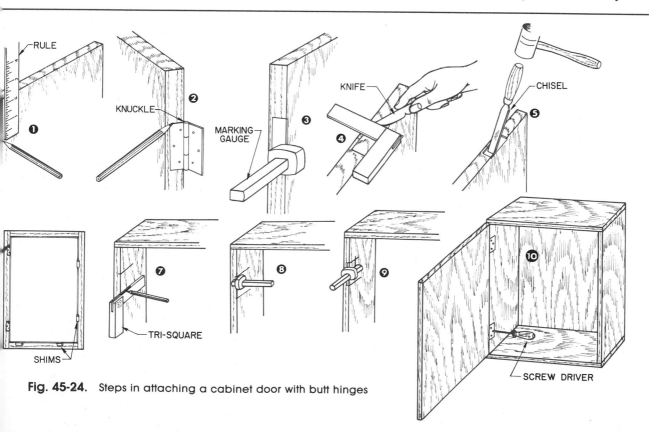

Fig. 45-24. Steps in attaching a cabinet door with butt hinges

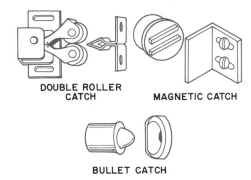

Fig. 45-25. Catches such as these are used on cabinet doors to make sure they stay shut.

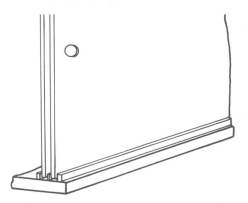

Fig. 45-28. These sliding doors were made by installing wood strips inside the cabinet.

Fig. 45-26. This is how a lip door is attached to a frame with a semi-concealed hinge.

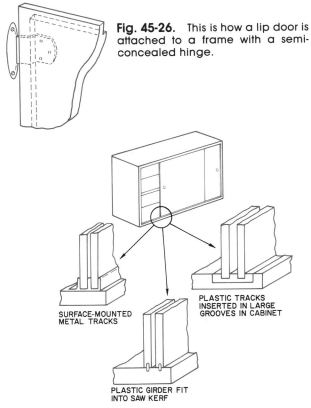

Fig. 45-27. Manufactured sliding door tracks

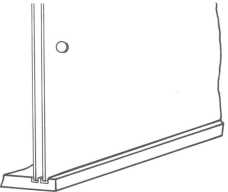

Fig. 45-29. Another method of making sliding door tracks is to cut grooves into the cabinet. This must be done before the cabinet is constructed.

This will let the doors slide freely. It will keep them from binding in the track.

You can also make tracks by cutting grooves near the front of the cabinet. Do this before assembling the cabinet. Cut the top grooves twice as deep as the bottom grooves. This gives you room to insert the doors. See Fig. 45-29. Space the grooves about 1/16 inch *(1.5 mm)* wider than the thickness of the doors. This will keep the doors from binding.

Tambour Doors. Tambours are flexible sliding doors. Roll-top desks are examples of furniture with tambour doors. Tambours are made by gluing narrow strips of wood to canvas. The strips of wood provide strength and beauty. The canvas provides flexibility. With this flexibility the door can be opened by curving it out of the way. See Fig. 45-30. Use the following steps to make tambour doors.

manufactured track. Manufactured tracks are made of metal or plastic. Choose the track before cutting the doors to size. See Fig. 45-27.

You can easily make a track out of wood strips. See Fig. 45-28. You can use wood strips and decorative molding, such as quarter round. Glue or screw the wood strips to the cabinet. In spacing the strips, allow an extra 1/16 inch *(1.5 mm)*.

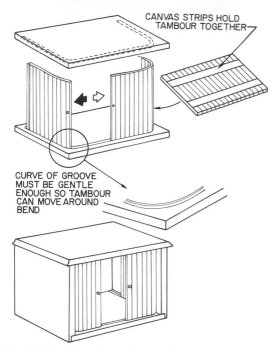

CANVAS STRIPS HOLD
TAMBOUR TOGETHER

CURVE OF GROOVE
MUST BE GENTLE
ENOUGH SO TAMBOUR
CAN MOVE AROUND
BEND

Fig. 45-30. Tambour doors, with their unique, attractive design, could add to the beauty of your project.

1. Cut a piece of solid wood to the thickness and length of the desired tambours. Shape the strips if desired. See Fig. 45-31. If the tambours will be thick, rout a rabbet on the ends of the stock. This will reduce the size of the groove needed in the cabinet. Make the top rabbet twice as wide as the bottom rabbet.
2. Cut the stock into narrow strips of equal width. Make one strip (for each door) slightly wider than the rest. This provides room to attach a handle.
3. Assemble the strips on a bench. Turn the back side up and align the ends.
4. Apply glue to two pieces of canvas. Let the glue become tacky (almost dry). Then stick the canvas pieces across the backs of the wood strips. Put a piece of canvas near each end. The canvas should not cover the ends, however. These ends must fit into the cabinet grooves. Be careful no glue seeps between the strips. Adhesive-backed felt can be used in place of canvas and glue.
5. Construct the tracks by routing grooves in the cabinet. Use a router and template.

See Fig. 45-32. Make the curves as gradual as possible. The top and bottom curves must match exactly. Make the grooves 1/16 inch *(1.5 mm)* wider than the thickness of the strips. This will allow enough clearance to slide the tambours. Rout the top grooves twice as deep as the bottom grooves. This will let you insert the tambour in the grooves.

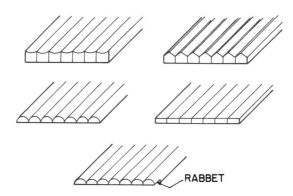

RABBET

Fig. 45-31. Common shapes of tambours. In most cases it is easier to shape the tambours before they are cut into strips. You can also use preshaped wood molding as ready-made strips.

The ends of tambours are often rabbeted to reduce the width of the grooves that must be made.

Fig. 45-32. The most accurate way to cut grooves for tambours is to make a template. Then cut the grooves with a router.

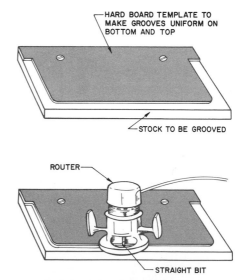

HARD BOARD TEMPLATE TO
MAKE GROOVES UNIFORM ON
BOTTOM AND TOP

STOCK TO BE GROOVED

ROUTER

STRAIGHT BIT

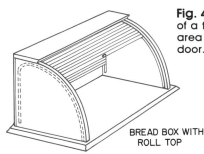

Fig. 45-33. One advantage of a tambour is that a curved area can be covered with a door.

BREAD BOX WITH ROLL TOP

Shelves

There are three important considerations when making shelves. They are shelf width, the distance between shelves, and fastening methods.

The first two considerations depend on what the shelves will hold. For example, some books are as narrow as 8 inches *(200 mm)*. Others are as wide as 12 inches *(300 mm)*. The proper width for making bookshelves would depend on the books.

Shelves are rarely less than 9-1/2 inches *(237 mm)* apart. Bottom shelves are often farther apart than top shelves. Shelves for knickknacks would not need to be as wide as bookshelves.

Fig. 45-34. Methods of making fixed (permanent) shelves

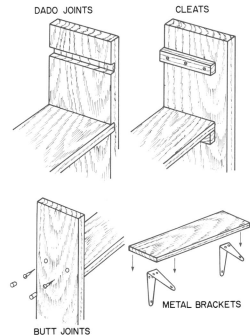

DADO JOINTS   CLEATS

BUTT JOINTS   METAL BRACKETS

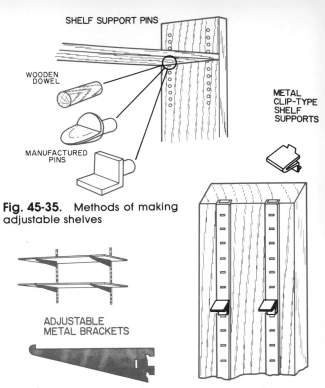

SHELF SUPPORT PINS

WOODEN DOWEL

MANUFACTURED PINS

METAL CLIP-TYPE SHELF SUPPORTS

Fig. 45-35. Methods of making adjustable shelves

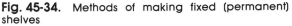

ADJUSTABLE METAL BRACKETS

Shelving for record albums must be at least 12-1/2 x 12-1/2 inches *(312 x 312 mm)*. Measure the objects carefully before laying out and building the shelf.

Different fastening methods are used to hold shelves to cabinets. Which method is best depends on the type of shelf. The two basic types are fixed (stationary) and adjustable. Fixed shelving is permanently fastened to the cabinet sides. Several methods are used. See Fig. 45-34.

Adjustable shelves can be adjusted to fit various needs. See Fig. 45-35. The most common way to support adjustable shelving is to use metal shelf-support holders. Fasten the metal track in a groove on the inside of the cabinet. Then insert the metal clips at the desired height.

Building with Plywood

Plywood makes an excellent building material for furniture and cabinets. It is available with attractive surface veneers. It is also more dimensionally stable than solid wood. This means that plywood pieces do not warp or expand and contract as much as solid wood.

The major problem with plywood is that it has unattractive edges. These edges must be hidden with edge material. Several ways of doing

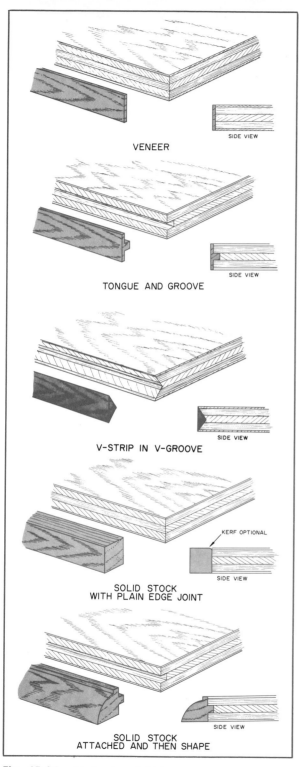

VENEER

TONGUE AND GROOVE

V-STRIP IN V-GROOVE

SOLID STOCK
WITH PLAIN EDGE JOINT

KERF OPTIONAL

SOLID STOCK
ATTACHED AND THEN SHAPE

Fig. 45-36. Methods of hiding exposed plywood edges

this are shown in Fig. 45-36. Regardless of the method, select material that matches the plywood face veneer.

New Terms

1. butt hinge
2. cabinetmaking
3. door catch
4. drawer guide
5. drop-leaf table
6. flush drawer
7. kicker
8. lip drawer
9. pull
10. rail
11. rule joint
12. scissor hinge
13. semi-concealed hinge
14. stop
15. tambour
16. wing

Study Questions

1. What are the two major considerations in designing a table?
2. Fastening solid wood tabletops to rails can be a problem. Why is it important to fasten them properly?
3. List the five parts of a drawer.
4. List five types of joints used to construct drawers.
5. Give three functions of drawer guides.
6. What type of drawer guide is the easiest to make?
7. What two purposes do drawer stops serve?
8. Give the two basic methods of attaching doors to cabinets.
9. List three kinds of hinges used to attach cabinet doors.
10. What is the purpose of a marking gauge in laying out the position of a butt hinge?
11. How can you fix a gain that has been cut too deep?
12. Why is solid wood rarely used to construct sliding doors?
13. In cutting grooves for sliding door tracks, why are the top grooves cut twice as deep as the bottom grooves?
14. What problem would result from placing the canvas pieces at the ends of the wood strips when making tambour doors?
15. What are the three important considerations when making shelves?

Chapter 46

Veneers and Plastic Laminates

Veneers and plastic laminates are made in thin sheets. These sheets are generally used to cover unattractive base materials. Veneers are used mainly for decoration. Plastic laminates are used mainly for protection.

Veneers

Veneers are thin sheets of wood. They are usually only 1/28 inch thick. Veneers are used to construct plywood. They are also used to decorate unattractive surfaces. See Fig. 46-1. A table, for example, could be made with inexpensive fir plywood. It could then be covered with an expensive teak veneer. It would then look like solid teak at about a quarter the price.

Veneers are made by first cutting logs into sections. These sections are called **flitches.** One of five methods is then used to cut veneers from the flitches. See Fig. 46-3. In each method, a long, razor-sharp knife cuts the veneer. Which

method is used largely determines the veneer's grain pattern.

Rotary cutting is the most common method of cutting softwood veneers. This method produces a long, continuous veneer. It does not produce the most attractive grain patterns for cabinet work, however.

Hardwood veneers are usually cut with one of the other methods. Plain slicing produces attractive patterns on most woods. Quarter slicing and rift cutting are commonly used on oak to produce straight grain patterns.

Selecting Veneers. Veneers are generally selected by the type of wood and the grain pat-

Fig. 46-1. This side table looks as though it is made of solid wood. However, it was made with particle board and then covered with veneers.

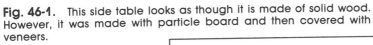

Fig. 46-2. Veneers are used to make plywood. Changing the directions of each layer of veneer makes the plywood strong.

CORE

FACE VENEERS

CROSS-BANDING

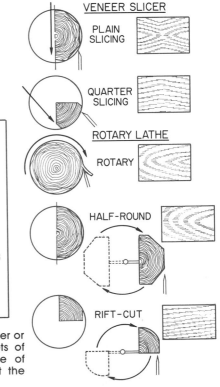

VENEER SLICER

PLAIN SLICING

QUARTER SLICING

ROTARY LATHE

ROTARY

HALF-ROUND

RIFT-CUT

Fig. 46-3. In most cases a veneer slicer or rotary lathe is used to cut thin sheets of veneers. You can see that the type of machine and direction of cut affect the grain pattern of the veneer.

tern. The various cutting methods affect the grain pattern. The part of the tree producing the veneer also affects the grain pattern. See Fig. 46-4. The more unusual the pattern, the more expensive the veneer. Generally, **burl** veneers are the most desirable. This is due to the irregular and beautiful swirl of burl grain patterns.

Matching Veneers. Special grain patterns can be produced by matching different veneers. See Fig. 46-5. The veneers are cut so they can be placed in the desired patterns. Success at matching veneers depends on how carefully they are cut. Poor joints and misaligned pieces can ruin an otherwise attractive surface.

Applying Veneers

Veneers can be applied to plywood, particle board, and solid wood surfaces. The surfaces should be smooth and flat. The veneers should

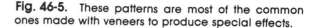

Fig. 46-5. These patterns are most of the common ones made with veneers to produce special effects.

be applied on both sides of the base material. This prevents warping. The veneer should also be applied so the veneer and base grains are

Fig. 46-4. Veneers cut from different parts of a tree produce different grain patterns.

Fine Hardwoods-American Walnut Association

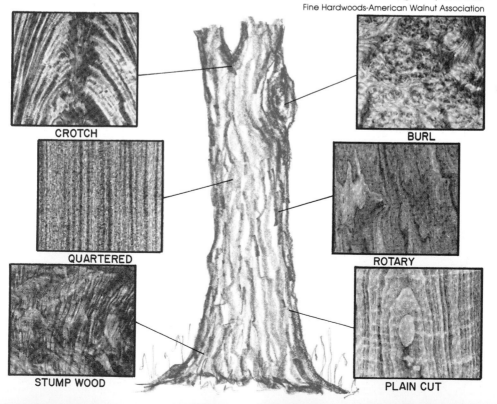

Fig. 46-6. Veneer saw

The Woodworkers' Store

Fig. 46-9. After fitting the joints accurately, tape them in place with veneer or masking tape. Be sure to tape on the side of the veneer that will face up.

Fig. 46-7. Trim the edges of veneer joints by holding them between two straightedges. Then plane them with a hand plane.

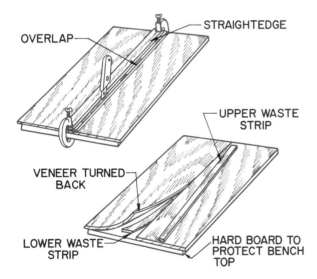

STRAIGHTEDGE

OVERLAP

UPPER WASTE STRIP

VENEER TURNED BACK

LOWER WASTE STRIP

HARD BOARD TO PROTECT BENCH TOP

Fig. 46-8. Cut joining veneers to match. Overlap the veneers and make one stroke with a knife. Since the veneers are shaped with the same cut, they should match perfectly.

perpendicular. This reduces the chance of the veneer splitting as the base material expands and contracts.

Cutting Veneers. Lay out veneers with a pencil and straightedge. Cut them about 1/8 to 1/4 inch *(3 to 6 mm)* over finish size. This allows for trimming to make an exact fit.

Veneers are very thin and delicate. You should usually cut them with hand tools. Use a sharp knife such as an X-acto or sloyd knife. You can also use a veneer saw or dovetail saw. See Fig. 46-6. Hold a hardwood straightedge on the veneer. Saw or cut along the edge. Protect the bench surface by placing hardboard, or a similar material, under the veneer.

Trimming Veneers. You must trim the edges of veneers to make perfect joints. Gaps make the surface less attractive. To trim joining veneers, clamp them between two straight pieces of wood. The layout lines should just show above the wood pieces. Then plane the veneers flush with the wood pieces. Use a hand plane for this operation. See Fig. 46-7.

Another method of fitting veneers together is to overlap and then cut them. See Fig. 46-8. Overlap the veneers about 1 inch *(25 mm).* Guide a sharp knife along a straightedge to make a straight cut. Make sure you cut through both pieces with a single cut.

Joining Veneers. After making all cuts, arrange the veneers in the desired pattern. The edges should fit tightly together. If light shows through a joint, trim the pieces until the joint is tight.

Tape the joints together on the sides that will face up. See Fig. 46-9. Use masking tape or veneer tape. Then double check the fit. Retrim any problem areas.

When the fit is perfect, glue the veneers together. Fold the veneers back and apply glue to the exposed edges. See Fig. 46-10. Use white glue. Then lay the sheet flat. Tape the bottom face of each joint. This will help hold the joints together while the glue dries. After the glue has dried, remove the tape on the bottom face.

Fig. 46-10. After the joints are taped, fold the edges back and apply glue as shown. Then lay the veneer flat and tape the other side.

The veneer sheet is now ready to apply to the base surface. Remember, you should apply veneer to both sides of the base surface. This will prevent warping. Use a cheaper veneer for the bottom side.

Gluing Veneers. Glue the veneer to the base surface with contact cement. Apply an even coat to the back of the veneer and top of the base. Use a brush or roller. Wait until the cement dries to the touch. This usually takes about 10 to 15 minutes. Check the label on the can of cement. Apply a second coat to dull areas to ensure a good bond.

When all areas are dry, put the veneer and the base together. The two surfaces will bond instantly. Once they touch, they cannot be moved. This means you must align the surfaces carefully before touching them together.

With small veneer sheets you can insert a piece of paper between the surfaces. The paper prevents the adhesive from bonding. This gives you more time to align the surfaces. Once they are aligned, slide the paper out to make the bond. See Fig. 46-11.

A different method can be used to align large surfaces. Place wood strips or dowel rod every 15 inches (375 mm) along the length. When the surfaces are aligned, slide out the strips. Start in the middle and work outward. Firmly press the veneer in place as you go. Rub the veneer with a roller or wood block wrapped in cloth. See Fig. 46-12. This will make sure the veneer has bonded. Start in the middle and rub outward. Areas that are blistered should be

wet slightly with warm water. This will make the areas fexible. Then roll these areas until the veneer bonds to the surface. Clamp any areas that are not sticking well.

Sanding Veneers. After the glue dries, trim and sand the veneer carefully. Remember that the veneer is very thin. Do not use coarse abrasives. Be very careful on the edges. It is easy to round the edges too much. This makes them unattractive.

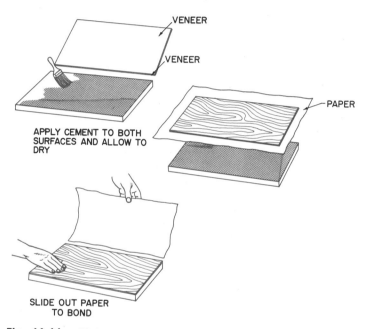

Fig. 46-11. Gluing veneer using contact cement. The paper prevents the two surfaces from bonding while you align them.

Fig. 46-12. Using a veneer roller to make sure the veneer is securely bonded to the base material. Pay particular attention to the veneer joints.

Miller Desk, Inc.
Fig. 46-13. The top of this file cabinet is covered with plastic laminates.

Plastic Laminates

Plastic laminates are thin sheets of hard plastic. They are bonded to other materials to form durable, attractive surfaces. They are used because of their strong resistance to water, stains, and wear. Kitchen and vanity countertops, tabletops, and many other surfaces are covered with plastic laminates. See Fig. 46-13.

Plastic laminates come in a wide variety of colors, textures, and patterns. The color and grain pattern of many plastic laminates closely resemble wood. Laminates such as these will not ruin the natural appearance of your project.

Plastic laminates consist of nylon, cotton, and cellulose or fiberglass. A resin adhesive is used to bond these materials in layers. This is done under high pressure and heat in large presses. The finished laminate is lightweight, hard, and brittle. It resists high temperatures, scratching, denting, and normal household chemicals. It is easily cleaned with detergent and water.

Most plastic laminates are sold by the sheet. The sheets are usually 1/16 inch thick. However, they range in thickness from 1/10 inch to 1/32 inch. They are usually sold in widths of 24, 30, 36, 48, and 60 inches. Although they

Fig. 46-14. Using a circular saw to cut plastic laminate. Be sure the laminate is well supported, with the bad side facing up. Use a straightedge to guide the saw.

can be purchased in any length, standard lengths are 6, 8, 10, and 12 feet.

Cutting Laminates. Table saws and portable circular saws are usually used to cut laminates. Because plastic laminates are so hard, they dull cutting tools quickly. For this reason, carbide-tip blades are generally installed in the saws. See Fig. 46-14. Plastic laminates can also be cut with saber saws, keyhole saws, and hacksaws.

Where you lay out your cuts depends on the saw you use. If you use a table saw, hacksaw, or keyhole saw, make the layout lines on the good side of the laminate. If you use a portable circular saw or saber saw, lay out the laminate on the bad side. The cutting action of the blade should always be against the good side.

Use a pencil to lay out the cutting lines. There should be at least 1/4 inch (6 mm) extra material on each side. This allows for trimming after the laminate has been glued to the project. Avoid making joints in the laminate. It is hard to match these joints so they will not show. Also be sure to support the laminate as you cut it. This will prevent it from breaking during the cut.

Gluing Laminates. Use contact cement to glue plastic laminates to the base material. Use the same procedure described for gluing veneers.

When the laminate forms outside corners, bond the vertical piece first. Trim that piece carefully. Then bond the horizontal piece. On inside corners, bond the horizontal piece first. Then bond the vertical piece. Try to bond all

Fig. 46-15. Laminate trimmers are designed especially for trimming the edges of plastic laminates.

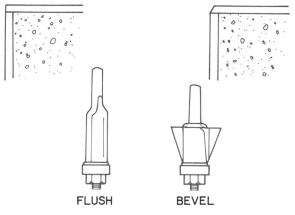

FLUSH   BEVEL

Fig. 46-16. Laminate trimming bits for use in laminate trimmers and routers

other pieces so as few edges as possible show from the front of the project.

Trimming Laminates. The best way to trim plastic laminates is with a special laminate trimmer. See Fig. 46-15. Routers also produce excellent results. Special carbide-tip trimming bits are available to cut flush or beveled edges. See Fig. 46-16.

Let the router or trimmer reach full speed. Guide it along the edges of the project. See Fig. 46-17. The pilot on the bit will keep the cut even with the edge. Be sure to keep the machine base flat against the surface. If it tips,

Fig. 46-17. Using a router and laminate bit to trim a plastic laminate. Move the router at a steady speed while keeping the base flat on the stock.

it will gouge the edge. Always cut in the direction opposite the rotation of the bit.

You can also use hand planes to trim laminates. Keep the blade sharp. Take shallow cuts.

After trimming, smooth and slightly bevel the edges. Use a smooth mill file. This will improve the appearance of the edges and reduce their sharpness.

New Terms

1. burl
2. flitch
3. laminate trimmer
4. plain slicing
5. plastic laminate
6. quarter slicing
7. rift cutting
8. rotary cutting
9. veneer

Study Questions

1. How thick are most veneer sheets?
2. Give two uses of veneers.
3. List four methods for cutting veneers.
4. What type of tools are used to cut veneers?
5. Why should veneers be glued to both sides of the base surface?
6. Explain the purpose of a piece of paper in bonding a veneer to a surface.
7. How thick are most plastic laminates?
8. Why are carbide-tip blades used to cut plastic laminates?
9. When laminating an outside corner, should you bond the vertical, or the horizontal piece first?

Chapter

47

Upholstering

An **upholsterer** installs and repairs the soft coverings on furniture. We usually think of upholstery as completely covering furniture. Materials such as springs, padding, and cloth are used. However, covering simple chairs and stools with foam, cane, and splint materials is also a form of upholstery. Procedures for making these seats are provided in this chapter.

Upholstery Tools

An upholsterer's tools vary from one job to the next. Which ones are needed depend on the project and the materials. A basic upholstery kit usually contains the following tools.

Upholsterer's hammers are magnetized on one face of one end of the head. The magnet makes it possible to pick up tacks quickly. It also helps drive them in place.

Webbing stretchers are used to stretch webbing tightly across a frame. They have wooden

handles with steel points on one end. The sharp points grip the webbing. The other end of the stretcher is placed against the furniture frame. The webbing can then be stretched.

Staplers are used in place of a hammer and tacks. They are used when many fasteners must be driven into a frame. Staplers fasten material to the frame quickly and neatly.

Ripping chisels are used to remove tacks and staples from frames. Ripping chisels have a tapered end. This end can be forced under the head of the tack. Then the tack can be pried loose.

Steel tapes are used to measure upholstery materials and furniture parts. Flexible tapes are best since they can bend around curved surfaces.

Straight and curved needles are used to sew buttons, borders, and corners.

Regulators are used to smooth rough areas in pads after the covering has been applied.

Fig. 47-1. These are some of the common tools used by upholsterers. Many more specialized tools are also used by professional upholsterers.

C.S. Osborne

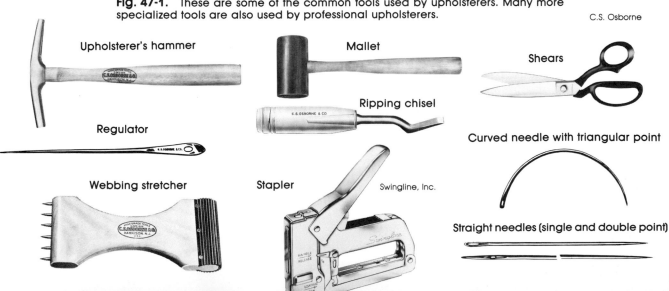

Upholsterer's hammer

Mallet

Shears

Regulator

Ripping chisel

Curved needle with triangular point

Webbing stretcher

Stapler

Swingline, Inc.

Straight needles (single and double point)

Upholsterer's shears work much like regular scissors. They are heavier than scissors, however. Because they are heavy, they can cut thick cloth.

Upholstery Materials

Several types of upholstery materials are used to make seats, backs, and cushions. These materials are usually combined to produce the desired coverings.

Webbing is an important part of some upholstered furniture. It supports materials such as springs and padding. It must be fastened to the frame tightly and correctly to work right. See Fig. 47-2. Modern furniture is often made of rubber and plastic webbing. Such webbings resist moisture and decay. Some webbings are exposed; others are covered with loose cushions.

Padding is used to provide comfort. Many different types of padding materials are used. Foam rubber and plastic foams are the most common. See Fig. 47-3. These materials are lightweight and flexible. They also resist moisture and tearing, and are noncombustible.

Upholstery tacks are used to attach upholstery to frameworks. See Fig. 47-4. They are coated to resist rust. Some upholstery tacks are decorative. These tacks are used where the

tacks will show. **Webbing tacks** have barbed ends that hold tightly in wood frames. **Gimp tacks** are used to fasten **gimp,** a decorative edging material. Gimp is used to cover seams and exposed tacks. See Fig. 47-5.

Tacking tape is a special adhesive tape for attaching foam pads to bases. One side of the tape sticks to the pad. The other side is then tacked to the base.

Fig. 47-3. Foam materials make exceptionally good padding. This foam piece has been cored to increase its cushion effect.

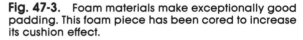

Fig. 47-2. The webbing on this chair supports the springs and padding. A fabric covering will be added later to produce an attractive, comfortable chair.

Fig. 47-4. Types of upholstery tacks

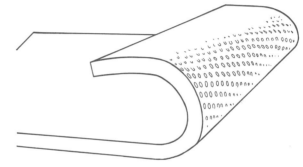

FANCY TACKS

UPHOLSTERERS'
TACKS

GIMP TACKS

Fig. 47-5. Gimp

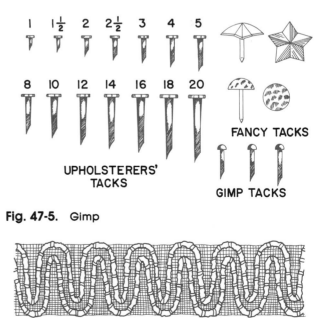

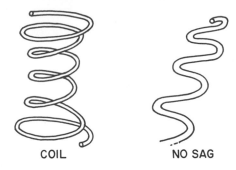

COIL   NO SAG

Fig. 47-6. Springs are often used in couches and large easy chairs. Upholstering with springs is more difficult than simple pad upholstery.

Springs are used in many types of upholstery. They come in many styles and shapes. They are used to add comfort and support to a seat. See Fig. 47-6.

Cane, splint, and rush are materials made from various plants and trees. They have long been used to make comfortable chair and stool seats. Many antique chairs were originally upholstered with these materials. Cane, splint, and rush are still popular today and provide attractive alternatives to pad seats. Procedures for making cane and splint seats are provided later in this chapter.

Making a Pad Seat

The simplest upholstered seat is a pad seat. A pad seat consists of a foam pad covered with fabric, leather, or vinyl. The pad is usually attached to a plywood base. The base is then attached to the chair frame. Padded seats are most often used on dining room chairs, side chairs, and simple stools. See Fig. 47-7. To make a pad seat you need the following tools and materials.

- plywood, 1/2 to 3/4 inch thick
- saw for plywood
- foam rubber, 1-1/2 to 2 inches thick
- tacking tape, 3 to 4 inches wide (or muslin strip)
- rubber cement
- upholsterer's tacks #6 (or hand stapler)
- scissors
- bowl of water
- upholsterer's hammer
- drill and 1/4 inch twist drill

Fig. 47-7. The seat of this chair is made of plywood. It has been covered with padding and fabric.

Fig. 47-8. This plywood seat base is ready for upholstering.

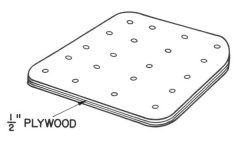

1/2" PLYWOOD

1. First cut the plywood base for the seat. Use 1/2 inch plywood on most applications. Cut the base to fit about 1/4 inch *(6 mm)* from the inside of the frame on all sides. Then drill 1/4-inch holes in the plywood. This lets the foam "breathe." Space the holes about 3 inches *(75 mm)* apart. See Fig. 47-8. When reupholstering a chair, you can usually use the old base. However, if the old base does not seem sturdy, cut a new one.

2. Determine the kind of edge you want for your seat. Three basic shapes are used for the edges of padded seats. They are **cushioned** edges, **feathered** edges, and **squared** edges. Cushioned edges are formed by tucking under excess foam. See Fig. 47-9.

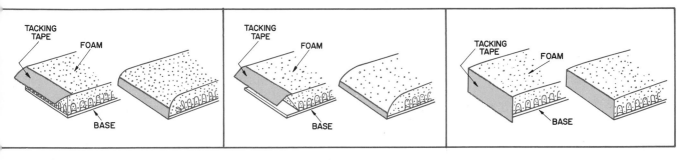

Fig. 47-9. Making a cushioned edge (cutaway view)

Fig. 47-10. Making a feathered edge (cutaway view)

Fig. 47-11. Making a squared edge (cutaway view)

Feathered edges are gently rounded. See Fig. 47-10. Squared edges are, of course, straight and square. See Fig. 47-11.

3. Use the plywood base as a pattern to cut the foam. Lay the base on the foam rubber. Then trace around the base with a felt-tip pen. For cushioned edges, add 3/4 inch *(18 mm)* on all sides. For feathered and square edges, add 1/4 inch *(6 mm)* on all sides. Bevel the underside of the foam for feathered edges.

Cut the foam rubber with scissors. Dip the scissors in water as you cut. This lubrication will make the cutting easier.

4. Apply tacking tape to the foam pad. For cushioned and feathered edges, put the tape on the top surface around the edges. See Figs. 47-9 and 47-10. For squared edges, put the tape on each edge of the pad. See Fig. 47-11. You can also use muslin and rubber cement to attach the foam pad. Glue the muslin to the pad with the rubber cement. Position the muslin as you would tacking tape.

5. After the tape has stuck tightly to the foam, pull the tape under the base. Then tack the tape down on all sides. See Fig. 47-12. This process varies according to the type of edge. See again Figs. 47-9, 47-10, and 47-11.

On squared edges, glue the pad to the plywood for extra holding power. This will prevent the pad from shifting. Apply rubber cement to the top of the plywood in a large X. Also apply it to the bottom of the foam. Position the pad on the plywood. Then tack down the tacking tape.

6. Apply the final cover. Use an undercover of muslin if your top fabric is loosely woven or thin. Strong fabric and fabric-backed materials can be put directly over the foam.

Use the seat as a pattern to cut the fabric to shape. Allow an extra 2 inches all around the shape.

7. Place the cover fabric on a firm, clean surface. The top side should face down. Center the seat (bottom up) in the middle of the fabric. Pull the fabric around the seat. Tack it in the center of each side of the seat. Then slip tack (tack just enough to hold) the fabric every inch *(25 mm)*. Make sure the cover is pulled tight and even all around. If the surface wrinkles,

Fig. 47-12. Tacking the tacking tape to the base

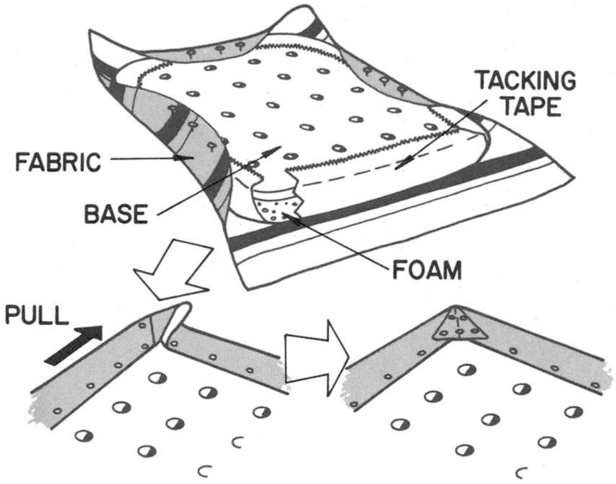

Fig. 47-13. When applying fabric to a seat, fold and tack the corners last.

remove the necessary tacks. Then repull the fabric tight. When the cover is tight and even, finish driving the tacks. Tack the corners last. See Fig. 47-13.

8. Place the covered seat in the chair. Attach the seat with wood screws. This is usually done by counterboring through the seat rails or corner blocks. Four screws will usually hold the seat firmly.

Making A Pressed Cane Seat

Cane seats are comfortable and attractive. They were used in some of the first American-made furniture and are still popular today. Early furniture makers wove the cane directly on the chair. Although this is still done, **pressed** (machine woven) cane is now available. It is much easier and faster to apply. See Fig. 47-14. To make a pressed caned seat you need the following tools and materials.

- five or more hard-wood wedges
- pressed cane
- router and veiner bit (1/16 inch larger than size of spline)
- spline (thin reed strip to insert into groove)
- rubber mallet
- utility knife
- glycerin
- water container (large enough to cover the webbing)
- scissors
- chisel
- white glue
- towel

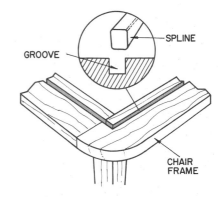

Fig. 47-14. The seat of this chair has been covered with pressed cane.

Fig. 47-15. A groove must be cut in the chair frame to attach the cane and spline.

1. The first step in applying cane is to rout a groove for the spline. See Fig. 47-15. (If you are recovering an old seat, simply clean out the old groove.) The most accurate way to rout a groove is to first make a hardboard template. Make the template the desired shape for the chair seat. The groove should be at least 3/4 inch *(18 mm)* from the inside edge of the frame.

Rout the groove with a bit 1/16 inch larger than the spline. Standard splines are 1/4 inch thick. For these splines, use a 3/16-inch veining bit. Set the router depth to 1/4 inch *(6 mm)*.

2. Choose the desired type of cane. Pressed cane is available in many different weave styles and sizes. See Fig. 47-16. It comes in widths of 12 and 24 inches. It

is sold by the running foot. Get enough to overlap the groove by at least 1 inch *(25 mm)* on all sides. Also purchase enough spline to go completely around the groove, plus 1 inch *(25 mm)*.

3. Make a paper pattern in the shape of the desired seat. Check your pattern by laying it over the seat opening. It should overlap the groove 1 inch *(25 mm)*. See Fig. 47-17A.

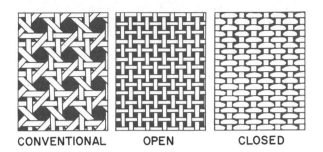

Fig. 47-16. These are only a few of the many cane weaves.

CONVENTIONAL   OPEN   CLOSED

Fig. 47-17. Steps in making a cane chair seat

A. The paper pattern should overlap the groove by an inch (25 mm).

B. Install the cane in the groove by forcing the cane with a wedge. Do not damage the cane.

C. You can use a chisel to carefully trim the cane below the edge of the groove. Do not drive the chisel so hard that you damage the groove.

D. Squeeze a thin line of glue inside the groove. You can also use an artist's brush to spread the glue.

E. Hold the wedge over the spline. Tap the wedge to drive the spline into the groove.

F. Use a utility knife to cut the last part of the spline to length. Protect the chair with a scrap piece.

4. Lay the cane flat on a level surface. Place the pattern on the cane. The cane webbing should be parallel and square with the sides of the pattern. Then use scissors to cut the cane along the pattern.

5. Measure the spline length by laying the spline in the groove. The spline should overlap itself by an inch *(25 mm)*.

   For square grooves, cut each side length slightly longer than needed. Use tin snips or a utility knife. Then lay each length into the groove and mark the corners. Cut each end at an angle. The strips will then form mitered joints at the corners.

6. Put the spline into warm water for 2 minutes. Then remove it and wrap it in a towel.

7. Prepare enough glycerin solution to cover the cane. Use 1-1/2 tablespoons of glycerin to 1 cup of water. Soak the cane about 20 minutes, or until it is pliable. Do not soak the cane too long. This can cause the cane to darken.

8. Apply a thin line of glue inside the groove. Remove the cane from the water. Place it over the opening. Position it so the webbing is square and parallel with the sides of the opening.

9. Use the hardwood wedges to drive the cane into the groove. See Fig. 47-17B. Drive a wedge in the center of each side with a mallet. Leave these wedges in place. Be careful not to cut the cane. If it is not pliable enough, resoak it.

10. Use another wedge to drive the rest of the cane into the groove. If there are corners, do them last. They require special care.

11. Use a sharp utility knife or chisel to cut off the excess cane. Cut the cane slightly below the top of the groove. See Fig. 47-17C.

12. Apply a thin line of glue inside the groove, above the cane. See Fig. 47-17D. Spread the glue evenly. An artist's brush works well for this purpose. Then lay the spline in the groove. For a continuous spline, begin at the least noticeable place. Begin pressing the spline in by hand. Tap down on the flat side of a hardwood wedge to finish driving the spline. See Fig. 47-17E. Cut the spline to length just before tapping down the final section. See Fig. 47-17F.

For a square seat, lay the pieces in the grooves loosely. Make sure the corners are properly mitered. Then tap the splines into the grooves as described above.

Making a Splint Seat

Early American woodworkers made splint from the inner bark of hickory and ash trees. They hand cut this material into strips. Then they used it to make seats for chairs and stools. See Fig. 47-18.

Today most splint is cut by machine. Ash wood is still used to make splint for attractive, rustic-looking seats. However, most splint is now made from a palm wood called **rattan.**

Splint is sold by the pound. It is available in widths of 1/2, 3/8, and 3/4 inch. Splint is generally sold in one-chair bundles. It takes about 80 feet *(24 m)* of splint to make a 15 x 15 inch *(375 x 375 mm)* seat.

Fig. 47-18. The seat of this chair was made with splint.

Cohasset Colonials, Cohasset, MA

The frames required for splint seats are simple. All that is needed are four rails. These rails are made of 3/4- to 1-inch dowel rod. They are connected to four legs. To make the splint seat, you need the following tools and materials.

- sharp knife (or tin snips)
- bucket of water
- masking tape
- stapler
- sponge
- glycerin
- strong string (or heavy thread)
- clothespins (three or four)
- carpenter's square
- tung oil
- bundle of splint
- teaspoon

1. To make a splint chair, first select several long, straight pieces of splint. Check the pieces for cracks and breaks. Then determine which is the top side. Do this by flexing the splint. The top side will remain smooth when flexed. The bottom side will splinter. The splint also has a grain direction. You should weave the splint with the top side up in the direction of the grain.

2. Roll several pieces of splint into small rolls. The top sides should be on the outside. Clip each roll with a clothespin. Then put the rolls in a bucket of water. Add 1-1/2 tablespoons of glycerin for every cup of water. This will help soften the splint. Allow the splint to soak about 30 minutes. As you use a roll, put another in to soak. This will keep you supplied with soft splint as you work.

3. If your seat is not rectangular, mark off the excess on the front rail. Use a carpenter's square to measure the excess. See Fig. 47-19.

4. Begin installing the splint from back to front. This process is called **warping**. Tape or staple one end of a splint roll inside the left rail. See the enlarged view in Fig. 47-20A. The rough side of the splint should be turned away from the rail. Then work the splint under the back rail and over the top. See again Fig. 47-20A. The top side will now be up. Position the

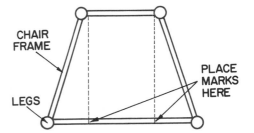

Fig. 47-19. On seats that are not rectangular, mark the front rail as shown. You will warp your first splints just inside these marks.

splint next to the left rear leg. Now pull the splint strip across the seat opening, around the front rail, and over the rear rail again. Continue this warping until the back rail is completely filled. If the seat frame is rectangular, both rails will now be filled. If it is not, small side triangles should remain uncovered. You will fill these spaces later.

Do not pull the splint tight. It needs some give (slack) to allow for weaving. Keep the rows of splint close together and parallel to each other. Fasten the loose end under the seat with a clothespin.

You will need to splice (join by overlapping) the splints. To do this, overlap the pieces about 2 inches *(50 mm)*. Make sure the grains run in the same direction. Then staple the splints together. Use pliers to bend over the ends of the staples. Always make the splice under the seat. This way the splice will not show. Another method of splicing is to cut notches in the splint. Then the splints are tied as shown in Fig. 47-20B.

5. Select a weaving pattern. Herringbone is a simple and popular pattern. The pattern in Fig. 47-20C was made by weaving two over and three under. Many variations of this pattern can be used. You can also make up your own pattern. Make a paper model of original patterns to check the effect. The size of the seat and splint will

Fig. 47-20. Steps in making a splint chair seat.

A. Begin warping the splint from back to front.

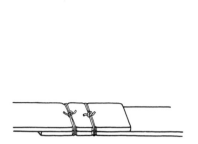

B. For this notching method of splicing splints, string is used to tie the splints together.

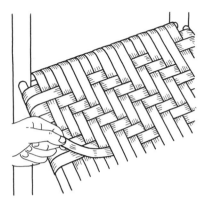

C. This pattern was created by weaving two over and three under.

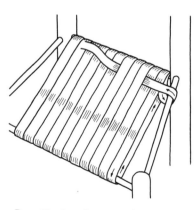

D. Starting the weaving

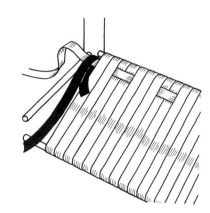

E. Starting the later warping for chairs that are not rectangular

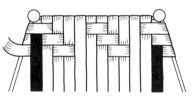

F. Do additional warping as you weave toward the front of chairs that are not rectangular.

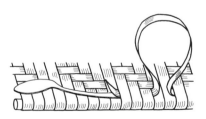

G. Use a spoon handle to thread the last splint.

From **Step-By-Step Furniture Finishing** by Nancy Howell-Koehler
© 1975 Western Publishing Company, Inc.
Reprinted by permission

influence your choice of a pattern. More variety is possible with large seats and small splints.

6. Before weaving, sponge the warped splints with water. This will make them flexible for weaving.

7. Unfasten the loose end of your warped splint. Splice this end to a new piece of splint. Make the splice under the seat so it does not show. Be sure the grain directions match. Bring the splint around the back rail. Then pull it around and over the right rail. See Fig. 47-20D. You are now ready to weave.

8. Weave your first row as close to the back rail as possible. Weave across to the opposite rail. Then check the row to be sure you followed the pattern. You may need to adjust your pattern next to the side rails. This will keep the pattern correct in the center of the seat. After weaving the first row across the top, turn the chair over. Continue the row across the bottom. Follow the same procedure that you used on the top.

9. As you continue weaving, you will need to splice new pieces. Attach them as you did before. Always splice on the underside of your chair. Make sure the grains match and the splint slides easily.

10. If the seat frame is not rectangular, you must do additional warping. This is necessary to cover the side openings and support the weaving strips. Wet a piece of splint two and one-fourth times the length of the opening. Fold one end back several inches and crease it. Then hook this end over the weaving strip. See Fig. 47-20E. Warp this splint around and under the front rail. Pull the splint back to meet itself and splice the ends. Then continue weaving. Warp new splints on each side as you come to unsupported areas. See Fig. 47-20F. For an average chair you may need to do this four times on each side.

11. Keep the splint moist at all times during the weaving process. Dry splint will break easier and make weaving harder. Check each row after weaving it. Make sure the splints are straight and parallel.

    The weaving becomes more difficult as you approach the front rail. This is because most of the slack has been removed. The last row is especially difficult. You must work on top of the front rail to weave this row. Use a screwdriver or the handle of a teaspoon to pry the splints apart. See Fig. 47-20G. Weave the last splint across the bottom until it ends.

12. Trim any rough edges as the chair begins to dry. Allow 24 hours to dry. Then lightly sand the surface. You can leave the seat bare or seal it with transparent tung oil. Apply the tung oil to the top and bottom of the seat. Several coats are needed to keep out moisture and dirt. Allow each coat to dry thoroughly before applying the next one.

New Terms

1. cane	13. tacking tape
2. cushioned edges	14. upholsterer
3. feathered edges	15. upholsterer's hammer
4. gimp	
5. gimp tacks	16. upholsterer's shears
6. padding	17. upholstery
7. pressed cane	18. upholstery tacks
8. rattan	19. warping
9. ripping chisel	20. webbing
10. rush	21. webbing stretcher
11. splint	22. webbing tacks
12. squared edges	

Study Questions

1. List five tools used by upholsterers.
2. List five materials used by upholsterers.
3. What is the simplest type of upholstered seat?
4. Give the three shapes used for padded seats.
5. In what cases should a padded seat have an undercover?
6. Why are cane seats easier to make now than they were 200 years ago?
7. What can happen to cane that is soaked too long in a glycerin solution?
8. Name two woods from which splint is made.
9. How can you determine which side of a piece of splint is the top side?
10. Give two reasons for keeping splint moist while weaving it.

Chapter 48

Carpentry

Carpentry is the craft of shaping and assembling wood structures. It includes the building of wooden frameworks for structures such as houses and bridges. It also includes filling in and covering these frameworks. Stairs, shingles, cabinets, and countless other items must be built.

To do so many jobs, carpenters must possess a great deal of knowledge. They must know about such subjects as wood, architecture, geometry, and modern construction methods. They must also possess the physical ability to perform many different tasks.

The type of work done by most carpenters has changed in recent years. More large structures are now being built with materials such as steel and concrete. This has led to specialization within carpentry. Many carpenters work on just one part of a structure. For example, some carpenters do nothing but build roofs.

Fig. 48-1. Besides a great deal of knowledge, carpentry demands physical endurance and coordination.

Others specialize in building forms for concrete. The "all-around," complete carpenters work mostly on smaller structures, such as houses and garages. With the trend toward specialization, the number of these carpenters is dwindling.

A career in carpentry can be rewarding in several ways. There are many good-paying jobs available. More carpenters are employed than any other type of tradesperson (bricklayers, painters, plumbers, etc.). There is also a great deal of satisfaction in being an accomplished carpenter. Building houses for example, is a useful, satisfying occupation.

This chapter briefly describes the step-by-step process of building a house. The descriptions are very general and not at all complete. This will, however, give you a basic idea of what carpenters need to know and do. It will show you how they use skill, knowledge, and raw materials to build a modern home.

Reading Plans

Carpenters must be able to read the architect's plans. These plans, or **blueprints**, show how and to what dimensions a structure will be built. A blueprint is similar to the working drawings used to build woodworking projects. Blueprints are much more complex, however.

A complete set of house plans contains several pages of individual plans. Carpenters are mainly concerned with the floor plan. The **floor plan** shows the outline of the structure. It also provides interior dimensions needed by the carpenter. See Fig. 48-2.

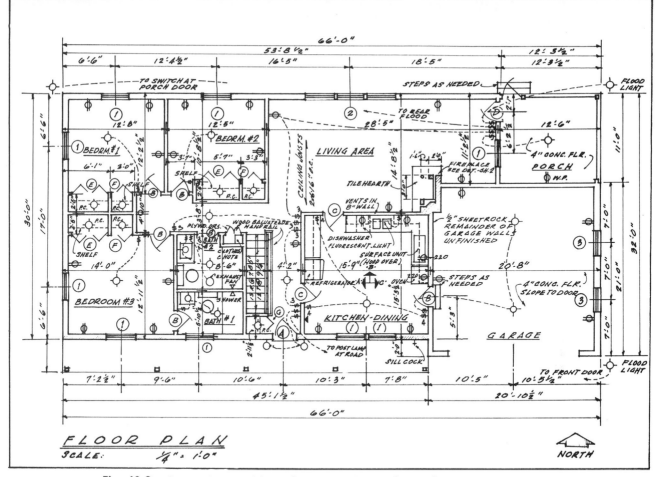

Fig. 48-2. Carpenters must know how to read complex architectural drawings. These drawings provide the measurements needed for construction.

Rough Framing

Most of the work done by carpenters falls into two categories. One is rough framing, the other is finish carpentry. Rough framing includes the building of floors, walls, and roofs. The rough framing is usually completed before any of the finish carpentry begins.

The two common types of rough framing are platform and balloon framing. **Platform framing** means that each floor, or story, is built separately, one on top of the other. See Fig. 48-3. **Balloon framing** means that the floors are connected by wall supports (studs) that run from the floor to the rafters. See Fig. 48-4. Platform framing is easier to build because each story provides a working base for the next. It is used for most houses built today.

Fig. 48-3. Platform framing is the most common type of house framing. It provides a subfloor to stand on while framing walls for the next story.

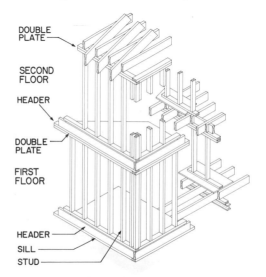

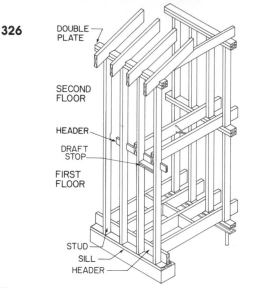

DOUBLE PLATE

SECOND FLOOR

HEADER

DRAFT STOP

FIRST FLOOR

STUD
SILL
HEADER

Fig. 48-4. Traditional balloon framing has the advantage of being vertically stable.

Footings and Foundations. The construction of any building begins with the footings and foundation. See Fig. 48-5. They provide the strong, sturdy base that will hold the structure. Without this base the house's weight would cause the house to shift and settle unevenly.

Footings are usually made of concrete. Foundation walls are made of poured concrete, blocks, or bricks. Carpenters often lay out and build the necessary forms. Most of the work is then done by bricklayers and concrete workers. The major part of the carpenter's work begins after the foundation is set.

Fig. 48-5. Footings and foundations provide a secure base for the structure.

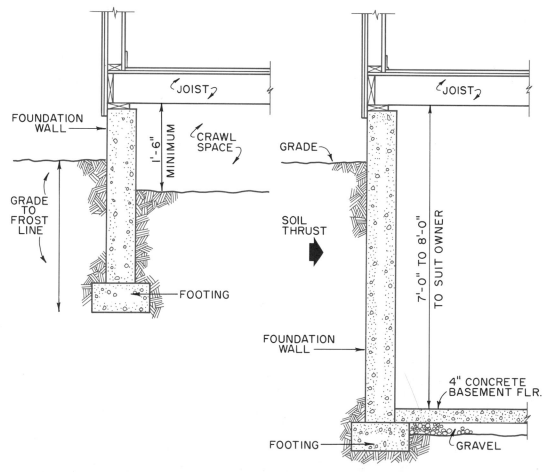

JOIST

FOUNDATION WALL

1'-6" MINIMUM

CRAWL SPACE

GRADE TO FROST LINE

FOOTING

JOIST

GRADE

SOIL THRUST

7'-0" TO 8'-0" TO SUIT OWNER

FOUNDATION WALL

4" CONCRETE BASEMENT FLR.

FOOTING

GRAVEL

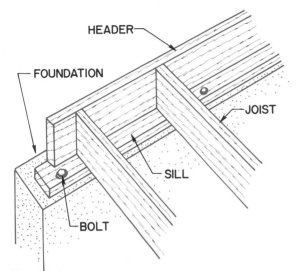

Fig. 48-6. The sills are bolted to the top of the foundation walls. Then the headers are toenailed along the outside edges of the sills. The headers provide a framework for the joists.

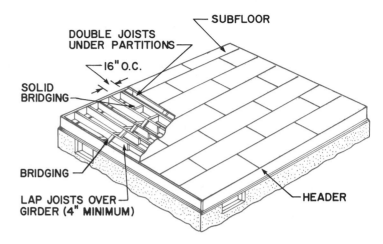

Fig. 48-7. Plywood subfloors are usually laid at right angles to the joists.

Floor Framing. The first step in floor framing is bolting the **sills** to the top of the foundation walls. See Fig. 48-6. **Headers**, usually 2 x 10 boards, are then toenailed on top of the sills. The **joists**, which support much of the building's weight, extend across the foundation walls. They are usually 16 inches apart o.c. (on center).

When the joists need more support, **girders** are set midway between the walls. To prevent the joists from twisting, carpenters install **bridging** between the joists. The bridging also helps distribute the weight. Then the carpenters lay the subfloor over the joists. Plywood or solid boards are usually used for subfloors. See Fig. 48-7.

Wall Framing. Once the subfloor is in place, the wall frame is constructed. Wall frames are usually assembled and then raised into position. The parts of a typical wall frame are shown in Fig. 48-8.

The lowest member is called the **sole plate**. The highest member is called the **top plate** (later doubled). **Studs** run from the sole plate to the top plate. Both interior and exterior wall coverings will later be nailed to the studs. The

Fig. 48-8. Studs and plates are usually made from 2 x 4 boards. Studs are usually spaced 16 or 24 inches (400 to 600 mm) apart o.c. (on center).

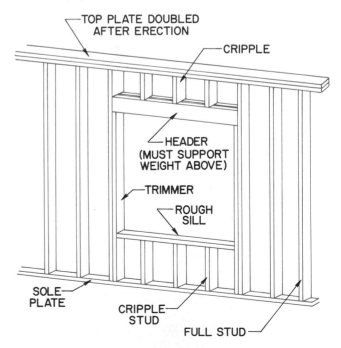

Fig. 48-9. Several workers are needed to raise and brace wall frames. After the frame is placed according to the plans, it is nailed to the floor frame.

Fig. 48-10. Plywood and various types of fiberboard are commonly used for wall sheathing. These materials are available in large sheets for easy application.

correct stud positions are marked on both the top and sole plates. They are then nailed in place.

Most wall frames have openings for doors and windows. The **trimmer** studs frame each side of the opening. They run from the sole plate to the header. The **header** frames the top of the opening and supports the weight above the opening. The bottom of the opening is framed by the **sill**, which is sometimes doubled. **Cripple** studs run from the top and sole plates to the header and sill respectively.

After wall frames are assembled, they are raised, braced, and nailed to the floor frame. See Fig. 48-9. The corners are constructed

Fig. 48-11. There are many kinds of roof trusses, which are easy to install. They are simply nailed to the top plate.

when joining walls are raised. Then **sheathing** (rough covering) is nailed to the exterior side of the frame. See Fig. 48-10. The sheathing strengthens and insulates the wall. Later it will provide a nailing base for shingles or siding.

Ceiling and Truss Framing. After the wall frames are raised and nailed, the double top plate is added. Once this is done, the ceiling frame can be constructed. Ceiling frames are much like floor frames without headers. Their main purpose is to support the finished ceiling. As with floors, the main members are called joists. The joists are usually made with 2 x 6 or 2 x 8 boards.

The ceiling framework is sometimes part of a truss. A **truss** is a triangular framework that supports both the ceiling and the roof. See Fig. 48-11. Trusses are extremely strong. They do not require interior support. Trusses are usually assembled in factories as complete units. They are then shipped to job sites.

Roof Framing. Carpenters must know several construction methods to build the many different roof frames. See Fig. 48-12. Each type has advantages and disadvantages. Flat roofs are the cheapest and easiest to make. However, flat roofs are not easy to insulate and do not shed water well. This makes them poor choices for cold, damp climates. Hip roofs are more difficult and expensive to build than gable roofs. However, the overhang of a hip roof provides shade and protection on each end of the house. The mansard and gambrel

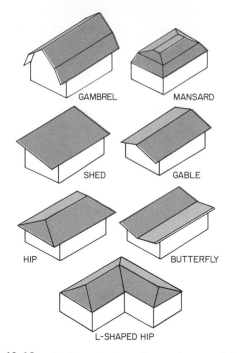

Fig. 48-12. Besides being decorative roof frames must be strong and rigid to withstand the weather and support roofing materials.

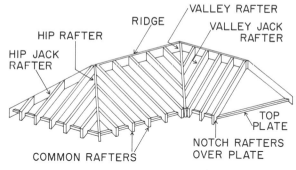

Fig. 48-13. Roof framing members

roofs are also costly, but they allow for more living space on the top floor. Owners and architects usually determine the roof style. The carpenter then follows the plans to build the roof.

Most roofs are sloped. The basic parts of a sloped roof are labeled in Fig. 48-13. The **ridge** is the highest member. It runs horizontally through the middle of the roof. The **common rafters** run from the ridge to the top plate. A notch called a **bird's mouth** is cut in each rafter. It allows the top plate to support the rafter.

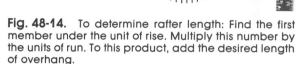

Fig. 48-14. To determine rafter length: Find the first member under the unit of rise. Multiply this number by the units of run. To this product, add the desired length of overhang.
Length of rafter: 13.42" x 7-1/4 = 97.3" = 8' 1-1/4" + 2' = 10' 1-1/4"

The carpenter's main concerns in roof framing are the overhang and slope. **Overhang** is the part of each rafter extending beyond the top plate. **Slope** is the amount of incline the roof has in a certain distance.

Carpenters know that the length of the rafters will determine the slope. Making the rafters a certain length produces the desired slope and overhang. Most carpenters determine rafter length with the rafter tables on framing squares. Fig. 48-14 is an example of how carpenters use the framing square. This is, of course, a simple example for a gable roof. Carpenters must use more complicated methods and tables for other roof styles.

Once the roof is framed, carpenters apply the sheathing. Sheathing provides a nailing surface for the final roof covering. It also adds to the strength and rigidity of the roof frame. Today most sheathing is made of plywood. The face grain is nailed at right angles to the rafters for additional strength. See Fig. 48-15.

Fig. 48-15. Plywood roof sheathing is easy to apply, does not shrink or swell like wood sheathing, and is rigid.

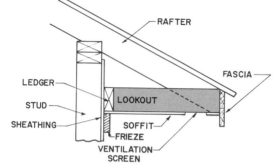

Fig. 48-16. Building cornices is an important task of finish carpenters.

Finish Carpentry

Most finish carpentry is done after the rough framing. Finish capentry includes such tasks as adding final coverings to floors, walls, and roofs. It includes the installation of doors, windows, and insulation. It also includes the framing and building of stairs, cabinets, and interior trim. Some of the jobs done by finish carpenters are briefly described here.

Exterior Walls. Carpenters measure, cut, and nail siding materials for outside walls. Many different materials are used. Carpenters apply wood, plastic, and metal materials. Bricklayers and stone masons apply masonry materials (brick and stone). Wood coverings are available in a variety of shapes and sizes.

Exterior Trim. Carpenters usually install the trim around windows and doors. They also frame and build the cornice, or eave. The **cornice** provides a finish trim for the connection of the walls and roof. The cornice usually covers the rafters. A typical style of cornice and its parts are shown in Fig. 48-16.

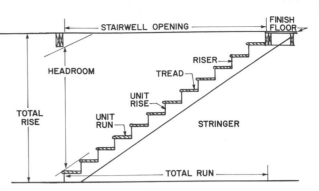

Fig. 48-17. Parts of a stairway

Stairs. Some carpenters specialize in building stairs. These carpenters must know how to build many types of stairs. Stairways can be open, closed, circular, straight, or L-shaped. The parts of a stair are shown in Fig. 48-17.

Many dimensions must be figured and measured accurately to build a stairs. The stringers, for example, must be built to a certain length. To be as safe as possible, they should have a certain number of risers and treads. Riser and tread dimensions must be properly balanced with each other. Special problems, such as allowing enough headroom in confined areas, must also be solved.

To build a safe, attractive stairway, carpenters need much skill and knowledge. Besides the usual carpentry skills, they must use many different formulas. Many of these formulas are found in trade books. Others are learned through experience.

Interior Trim. One of the last jobs in finish carpentry is adding interior trim. This includes wood trim, or molding, around doors and windows. It also includes **baseboards**, which cover the wall-floor joints at the base of walls. Applying trim is a delicate job that demands skill and patience. The final appearance of the house is often judged by the quality of its interior trim.

Specialization. Many carpenters specialize in one or more types of finish work. Some devote all their time to building and installing cabinets and interior trim. Others concentrate

Fig. 48-18. Building and installing attractive door and window moldings and baseboards requires a great deal of skill. Interior trim such as this adds to the value of a house.

on building stairways or attaching siding to houses.

Many of the finishing jobs are no longer done by carpenters. Many floors are covered with carpets applied by carpet layers. Interior walls are covered by plasterers and dry wallers. Roofers attach the final covering of shingles to roofs. These specialized workers need never master the skills of an "all-around" carpenter. They can, however, work with bricklayers, painters, electricians, and plumbers to finish the carpenter's work.

New Terms

1. balloon framing
2. baseboard
3. bird's mouth
4. bridging
5. carpentry
6. common rafter
7. cornice
8. cripple
9. finish carpentry
10. floor plans
11. footing
12. foundation
13. girder
14. header
15. joists
16. overhang
17. platform framing
18. ridge
19. rough framing
20. sheathing
21. sill
22. slope
23. sole plate
24. stud
25. top plate
26. trimmer
27. truss

Study Questions

1. List four jobs a carpenter might do.
2. Name three subjects that a carpenter must know about.
3. Explain how the work done by most carpenters has changed in recent years.
4. Give two ways in which a career in carpentry can be rewarding.
5. How does a set of architect's house plans differ from the working drawings for a woodworking project?
6. With which part of the architect's plans is the carpenter most concerned?
7. Name the two types of rough framing. Which is used most often?
8. What are the first two steps in the actual construction of a house?
9. What is the first step in framing a floor?
10. How far apart are floor joists usually placed?
11. What additional support is needed for the joists when the foundation walls are far apart?
12. When is the wall frame constructed?
13. Which type of roof is the cheapest and easiest to make? Why is this type of roof built less often than other types?
14. What are the carpenter's two major concerns in building a roof frame?
15. What tool do most carpenter's use to determine the proper lengths of rafters?
16. Most roof sheathing is made of what material?
17. List three concerns of the carpenter in building stairs.
18. Name at least four kinds of tradespeople, other than carpenters, involved in the construction of houses.

Careers

This chapter is about **careers.** Do you know what a career is? It is really many things. First of all it's a job, and, like any job, it means working. It also means being paid for the work you do.

But a career is more than just a job. It includes a series of jobs, one after another. Career jobs are not chosen at random, however. They are all related. In a career, all jobs are in one area of work, such as construction, medicine, forestry, or education.

Careers also last much longer than jobs. A job may last a day, a month, or even a summer.

But a career can last for many years. In fact, a career often lasts all of a person's adult life.

You should now begin to understand how important a career is. When you are older, you will devote most of your time to your career. Your career will determine the kind of work you do. It will determine how much money you make. Where you live and work will be influenced by your career. In other words, your lifestyle and happiness will depend a great deal on the career you choose.

Your career choices are exactly that — your choices. No one stamped an occupation on your birth certificate. No one is going to force you into a career you don't want. There are an unlimited number of careers to choose from. You can pick whichever one you want.

You can start making career decisions now. This doesn't mean that you should plan your entire future today or tomorrow. Choosing a

Fig. 49-1. Workers from over a dozen different careers are needed to construct a building such as this one. Many of these careers are related to wood and wood materials.

Fig. 49-2. Career opportunities can change radically from one generation to the next. This computer terminal may not have existed when your parents were in school. It might very well be replaced with something else twenty-five years from now.

career is not one big decision. It's a series of decisions, each one bringing you closer to your most desirable career.

Many people do not choose a career until they are over 20 years old. It takes time to become aware of and explore the different career opportunities. It takes time to find out what kind of person you are. It also takes time to discover the things you like to do best.

There are lots of things you can do to help yourself make career decisions. Many of them you can do now. Others will come later. This chapter offers some tips on making the right career decisions. It also includes some general descriptions of careers related to woodworking. Finally, it provides some short biographies as examples of different careers. Read the chapter and get started with your own career.

Basic Skills

Without knowing it, you have already made some career decisions. For example, deciding to attend school was a career decision. While attending school, you are learning some basic skills that will help you all through your life. These skills will help you continue your self-education. They will keep the door open to a greater variety of careers. Without these skills you will be limiting your opportunities in the years ahead. These skills can be divided into the following four groups.

- Communication — the ability to read, write, listen, and speak.
- Mathematics — the ability to use numbers to solve problems.
- Research — the ability to find answers on your own.

Juan Rodriquez — Lumberyard Manager

Juan's only concern while attending school was getting out of school. Almost all of the local factories required at least a high school diploma. So Juan stayed in school. He took the courses that he thought would help him get a job when he graduated. Most of these courses were in the industrial arts department.

During his senior year Juan was forced to get a job to support his new car. His first job was helping a masonry contractor lay blocks. The work was hard. There were many days that Juan did not go to work. He quit this job and got another frying hamburgers at the local fast food restaurant. After two weeks he couldn't stand being inside all day, so he quit.

Then near the end of his senior year, Juan got a job in a local lumberyard. Juan spent his days loading and unloading heavy building materials. Although the work was hard, Juan came to work every day.

After graduation Juan continued to work on a full-time basis at the lumberyard. He learned a great deal about the lumber business from his boss. As the years passed and he learned more and more, Juan became a valuable employee.

He learned the standard sizes of lumber. He learned to cut lumber to specification. He learned about fasteners, pulls, and other hardware items — what was best to use and how much each cost. Most of all he learned how to advise the "Saturday Mr. Fixits."

Soon Juan was training other workers. He was eventually made responsible for receiving and shipping materials. Juan found his work satisfying and financially rewarding. He had no need of formal education beyond high school.

Fig. 49-3. This photograph illustrates three of the four basic skills. Can you name them? How might it represent the fourth skill?

- Self-motivation — the ability to "get going" on your own without needing encouragement from others.

Work on these four areas while you explore and select career possibilities. It's just like picking out a new bike or car. The more you have to choose from, the better chance there is of finding one you like. There will be more careers to choose from if you have mastered these skills.

Personal Characteristics

You have interests, skills, and a personality that are unique to you. If you haven't already, you need to discover these things about yourself. You need to analyze and examine what kind of person you are. You need to know if you are suited to certain kinds of work.

Self-analysis is important to career selection. It is not uncommon to find people who have never taken the time to learn about themselves. As a result, they drift from job to job. They never seem to be satisfied with their work, or life in general. Don't be one of these unhappy people. Consider the following questions and ideas and find out about yourself.

Interests. Stop and think for a few minutes about the following questions. How do you spend your free time? Do you like being indoors, or outdoors? What are your favorite subjects in school? What areas of work would you like to try? Do you like working with tools? Do you like reading and writing? Answer these questions and any others that will help you identify your interests.

Fig. 49-4. Your hobbies can tell you a lot about your interests. This boy enjoys building model airplanes. Can you think of any careers that he might find interesting?

Prepare a list of ten work areas in your order of preference. Put the list aside for several days. Then read it again. Would you still put them in the same order? Would you eliminate some and add others? Those careers at the top of your list are worth exploring further. See page 337 for ways of gathering information about a particular career.

Abilities. Your successes and failures in school will play an important role in your career selection. The same is true of your successes and failures in work and social experiences. Through

Fig. 49-5. This girl enjoys drawing sketches for her art class and has won several awards. Her artistic talents would be very helpful in such careers as industrial design, drafting, and graphic arts.

Fig. 49-6. A profitable newspaper route requires a great deal of self-motivation and self-discipline. This girl might someday use these qualities to develop her own successful business.

Fig. 49-7. This camp counselor enjoys working with children and is usually patient and understanding. He should consider these personality traits when making his career decisions.

these experiences you have gained some knowledge about your skills and abilities. It is only natural to take advantage of these talents. If you were 7 feet tall and could make nine out of ten baskets from 20 feet, your career choice would probably be easy.

What are you good at? Make a list of five areas in which you have at least average abilities. How could you transform these abilities into a successful career?

Personality. Give careful consideration to the following personality questions. Can you work with others, or do you like to work alone? Do you like competition? Can you take orders? Can you accept criticism? Are you a "self-starter"? Are you quiet and shy? Do you demonstrate good self-control when frustrated?

These are only a few questions to answer when reviewing your personality. Having the wrong personality for a job can make you very unhappy. If you are quiet and shy, you probably wouldn't be successful as a salesperson. If you are independent and daring, you might try starting a business of your own. Being honest with yourself about your own personality, can be difficult. It can also be very rewarding in terms of career decisions.

Fig. 49-8. Some people actually enjoy reading and studying hour after hour. Do you? If so, you may want to go on to college and prepare for a career in a specialized area.

Physical Makeup. Physical characteristics may limit you to certain career choices. If you have a vision problem, you would not enjoy a career in drafting. If you have a respiratory problem, you may find working outdoors impossible. Some construction jobs require great physical strength. Others do not. Jobs in some

Fig. 49-9. Consider your physical makeup when making career decisions. Although some careers may be physically impossible for you, there will still be many that suit your talents and interests.

careers, such as law enforcement, set specific physical standards.

It may be difficult for you to speak, walk, or reach. If it is, remember that you are not the only one with such a condition. Thousands of people are now working at their chosen jobs because work areas have been changed to meet the workers' needs. This can not always be done, however. It is therefore wise to know about a number of careers. Then you will truly have a choice.

Financial Need. Money is more important to some people than others. How much money will you need? How many expensive items are needed to make you happy? Will your career choice provide high enough salaries? Some careers are more financially rewarding than others.

Money questions are probably the most difficult to answer now. Perhaps they are the least important. Just remember, rewards differ from career to career. The important question is, "How important is money to me?" People are happy in the many thousands of different-paying jobs.

Fig. 49-10. If you like fancy sports cars, trips to Hawaii, and "the best things money can buy," financial need will be an important part of your career decisions. Decide how important money is to you and then examine the financial possibilities of various careers.

Alan Johnson — Home Builder

Alan took all the required courses in junior high. He found many of them dull and boring. He was convinced that he did not want to go to college. He enjoyed being outdoors and working with his hands.

At the urging of his parents and counselor, he took some vocational courses. His first course in industrial arts led to a second. In high school he took basic drafting and wood and metal courses, all of which he enjoyed. A beginning course in electricity later proved to be helpful in his career decision.

While a junior in high school, Alan enrolled in the vocational building-trades course. The class project that year was to remodel an old house. The students were required to read blueprints, do rewiring, and replace many sections of the house. Alan enjoyed his job assignment more than any of his other school subjects. He also had a long talk with his uncle who worked as a construction foreman. The job sounded interesting to Alan.

Alan was offered a position with a local construction firm upon graduation from high school. This firm specialized in preparing preconstructed rafter sections for homes. After three months of building the same rafter section, Alan was bored with his work. Even the excellent pay could not relieve his boredom.

His building trades background in high school had shown Alan many different kinds of job opportunities. He realized now that he enjoyed the variety of tasks. He also realized that it took more than money to make him happy. He got a position as an apprentice carpenter. The pay was much less at the start, but Alan enjoyed the work. Although he never mentioned it, Alan was thankful that his parents had suggested that he take some vocational courses. He couldn't imagine what sort of a career he would have had otherwise.

Career Evaluation

You cannot make wise career choices unless you know what choices are available. You should do everything possible to learn about career opportunities. The following information offers some tips on how to do this.

Exploring in School. You already know that attending school will help you learn important basic skills. Going to school will also help you explore career areas. Taking different courses you find out what basic subjects you like best. You also find out which areas you don't like. This helps you narrow down the broad field of careers.

Try to take as many courses as possible. Develop a broad background. Take both academic and vocational courses. Take all the extra courses you can, such as art and music. Get a taste of everything. You never know until you try whether or not you will like something.

Work Experiences. If you have had a job, you have been introduced to a career area. Each future job will also expose you to a new career. Initially you will see a career from the lowest rung of the career ladder. Nevertheless, you will have a chance to see several different jobs within that area. For example, by helping a mason, the laborer gets a good idea of what a career in masonry is like. The laborer will also have some contact with the contractor. This might lead to an interest in general contracting. The more different kinds of jobs you have, the more career areas you can discover and evaluate.

338

Fig. 49-11. Your library Career Information Center contains many publications that will guide you in gathering career information.

Fig. 49-12. A planned visit to a work site may reveal much new information about a career area.

Research. Obviously you cannot get all your career knowledge through work experience and school. Researching careers is a good way to add to your career knowledge. Send for business literature, government publications, and career manuals. The career center or guidance office in your school has career information. The public library also has career information. Make use of all these materials. Researching careers is one of the fastest and surest ways of obtaining career information.

Visits to Work Sites. You have probably taken many field trips. Many of these trips were planned to acquaint you with different kinds of workers. Before finishing school you will make several more visits. Try to identify different kinds of jobs on each visit. Watch the workers and try to imagine yourself doing their jobs. Ask yourself how you would like these jobs. You might very well find a career this way.

Discussions with Workers. Many adults spend much time talking about their jobs. You can take advantage of this in your career search. Talking to people is a good source of information about careers. Most people will gladly answer questions about their work. Remember, however, some workers are not happy with their jobs. They have not made wise career decisions. Get all the information you can. Then picture yourself in that job.

Careers Related to Woodworking

There are many careers related to woodworking. They range from botany professor to lumberjack, from carpenter to forest ranger. Positions in woodworking careers are available from Maine to California. Over 1.7 million people are employed in wood-related careers. Some of the more common careers are described here.

Forestry. In the early years of our country, trees were cut down randomly. Only parts of the trees were actually used. Today, forestry is much more complex. Trees are grown as a crop. **Botanists** (plant specialists) select trees

Fig. 49-13. Forest managers must carefully inspect and care for the young trees that will produce tomorrow's lumber. This forester is checking the growth of cottonwood seedlings on a Kentucky plantation.

Westvaco

Lisa Thompson — Furniture Salesperson

Lisa was interested in all of her junior high courses. She was often asked what she was going to take when she went to college. It was a hard question to answer. Science, math, and foreign languages were all favorites.

In high school Lisa enrolled in a general drafting course. Drafting came easy for Lisa. She liked working with precise measurements. She was soon working far ahead of her classmates on more advanced drafting projects. Drafting II followed Drafting I and Lisa enrolled in a woodworking class. Lisa continued to take all the math, science, and foreign language she could.

General biology was required. In this class Lisa became aware of the career opportunities in forestry. The woodworking instructor also told her a lot about his forestry experiences in Oregon. It seemed there was no limit to the number of jobs in this field.

Lisa entered college still not certain of her career choice. After courses in history, English, and foreign languages, she began to take engineering courses. During her junior year in college she was offered an internship with a large furniture manufacturing company. This company was recognized throughout the world for its quality furniture. The internship gave Lisa an opportunity to see manufacturing operations first hand. Lisa also worked closely with a variety of supervisors to learn about several different areas of the business.

When Lisa graduated from college she was asked to join the company full time. They believed her broad academic and vocational training would make her a valuable addition to the company. Since the company did business on an international level, they knew her training in Spanish and French would be useful. Her first assignment with the company was to work with the international sales department.

Lisa was unable to decide on a career because of her varied interests. She was smart enough to develop her basic skills while trying to decide. She also used high school and college to explore different career areas. Lisa was rewarded with an interesting, happy career.

for breeding. The goal of botanists is to develop trees that grow fast, have quality wood, and resist diseases. **Entomologists** (insect specialists) work to control insect damage to trees. **Forestry managers** plan the cutting of the trees. They try to protect the various parts of the tree. This produces a wider variety of wood products.

All of these workers are highly trained. They use knowledge, skill, and hard work to develop tree crops. To plant, care for, and protect the trees is rewarding work.

Lumbering. One of the oldest industries in the United States is lumbering. In the 1600's logs from the east coast were sent to England. There they were used in that country's shipbuilding industry. Lumbering is still an important industry in this country. Trees are cut down from the pine forests of Georgia to the Douglas fir forests of Washington and Oregon. Thousands of workers are employed in cutting the trees and transporting them to mills. Thousands more process the raw lumber into boards and wood materials for the construction industry. For more detailed information on lumbering, see chapter 51.

Throughout the lumbering industry there is a common concern for trees. Everyone in the

Fig. 49-14. A career as a lumberjack means lots of rugged, outdoor work. This lumberjack is cutting a cedar tree in the state of Washington.

industry is concerned about a continuing supply of trees. Great efforts are being made toward the maximum use of trees in producing lumber. For example, specialized businesses on the Olympic Peninsula of Washington State produce shingles from cedar trees. Fir and hemlock trees are cut into heavy lumber or processed into plywood.

Making plywood is even being done at sea in floating factories. Ships pick up lumber at northern ports on the west coast. While sailing south, the lumber is processed aboard ship. It is made into finished plywood for sale at other U.S. ports.

The lumbering industry will continue to search for new uses for wood products. As these uses are discovered, new career opportunities will develop. Being part of these new and expanding operations would be exciting and rewarding.

Papermaking. The process of using plant products to make paper is called **papermaking.** This process began with the Egyptians' use of papyrus over 5,000 years ago. Obviously the paper industry has changed a great deal in

Fig. 49-15. Papermaking has changed a great deal in the 5,000 years since it began in Egypt. For example, papermakers now use computers to control the winding of finished paper rolls.

5,000 years. Paper is still used primarily for writing and printing purposes, however. Today it is also used for construction and for making containers. It is even used to make clothing. Every year the number of products made from paper increases. This means more and more jobs will be added to the thousands already in existence.

Manufacturing. The lumbering industry gave birth to one of our first manufacturing industries. Products such as tar and turpentine were manufactured from American lumber. These products were used by the shipbuilding industry in England, and later by colonial shipyards. Wood products were also being produced in small woodworking shops. Wagons, furniture, and other wood products were made in large numbers.

Over the years the manufacturing of wood products has changed. Many products once made of wood are now made of metal and plastic. However, wood has become an important material in making patterns for these products. Wooden kitchen utensils, window blinds, and crates are examples of other wood products still in demand.

As you can imagine, consumer demand for wood products has increased with the population. This has reduced the number of one-man

Fig. 49-16. One of the many jobs in a furniture factory is finishing the furniture parts as they come off the assembly line.

woodworking shops. Machines have gradually taken over the work of these woodworkers. Mass production has increased the consistency of quality work. It has kept costs low and supplies plentiful. As a result, thousands of people work to manufacture wood products.

Cabinetmaking. In the early days of our country only wealthy people could import furniture from Europe. Our vast forests encouraged settlers to make their own benches, cupboards, tables, and cradles. Soon there were woodworking shops in the growing towns and cities. Chippendale, Hepplewhite, and Sheraton were English designers whose furniture was later copied in this country. Today American-made furniture is respected all over the world. Americans such as Duncan Phyfe, John Henry Belter, and Frank Lloyd Wright developed designs that are uniquely American.

New technology has changed the cabinet-making industry. Machinery and assembly line techniques are now used to make furniture. Designers, cutters, shapers, turners, finishers, and polishers are still needed, however. Some of the furniture is made entirely by hand. Other pieces are only finished with hand tools. Industrial equipment is similar to the power machines you use in your school shop.

Fig. 49-17. Not all furniture is mass produced. This cabinetmaker has his own shop where he produces custom-made furniture.

White Furniture

In addition to furniture factories, there are many small shops that do made-to-order work. These cabinetmakers often specialize in using local materials and following regional designs. There might very well be such a furniture factory or shop in your community.

Have you enjoyed working with the tools, materials, and machines in this course? If so, you might enjoy a career in cabinetmaking. Changes in consumer demands and available materials might change careers in cabinetmaking. The necessary skills will not change, however.

Construction. The construction industry has recently undergone a period of rapid growth. One reason for this is that buildings always wear out. Another reason is that the population has been increasing. There will probably always be a need for construction. As new housing costs increase, remodeling of existing housing also increases.

The construction industry employs many different kinds of workers. Skilled carpenters, architects, and electricians are needed. Thousands of unskilled laborers are also needed. Many of these jobs require apprenticeships. An **apprentice** is a person who learns by working. This on-the-job training usually requires some "book work" as well. Construction jobs in all of these categories can be found anywhere in the country. Generally, the salaries are good and much of the work is outdoors.

Fig. 49-18. Skilled framing carpenters such as this one are just a few of the many important workers in the construction industry.

Paslode Corporation

Wood Science. Wood scientists play a valuable role in the wood industry. They identify woods according to the needs of a particular industry. They inform the botanists of the qualities needed in woods. For example, there may be a need for trees with a high resin content to produce turpentine. Or rapidly growing trees may be needed for the paper and packaging industries. It is the job of the scientist to determine which trees will best fit the needs. The wood scientists combine academic knowledge with management skills. They use their abilities to keep the lumbering industry supplied with wood.

Fig. 49-19. Science is continually increasing the efficiency of wood industries. This scientist is recording information that will eventually help speed the growth of pine trees.

Westvaco

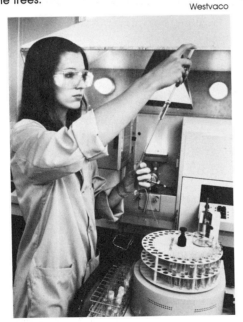

Teaching. There are many teaching opportunities in wood-related areas. Woods teachers are needed in junior highs, high schools, and colleges. Maybe you would enjoy teaching others how to work with wood.

Teaching others usually requires a college education, depending on the subject. The best teachers are often those who have the most

Fig. 49-20. If you enjoy working with wood, you might someday enjoy a career as a woodworking teacher.

work experience. Apprentice carpenters, for example, are often taught by experienced carpenters on the job.

Toward Career Selection

Earlier in this chapter you were provided with a list of personal characteristics to consider. You were also asked to list ten career choices. Now it is time to compare your personal characteristics with your career choices.

First, under your top career choice, list the requirements for success in that career. Use your own knowledge to list several requirements. Research that career through reading and interviews to discover more requirements. If you have an opportunity, talk to workers and visit job sites.

Next, beside each requirement, write a personal characteristic that compares with the required one. Read the story of Eric Bates. Then fill out your own chart like the ones in Figs. 49-21 and 49-22. After completing the chart, compare the required characteristics with your own. How do they match up? Are you well suited for this career? Finding the ideal career is not always easy. But remember, there is a career that is best for you.

Eric Bates — Student

As Eric neared the end of the eighth grade, he was not sure what he liked most. His junior high school had provided a good foundation in math, science, language arts, and social studies. He had been required to take economics, music, and art. Junior high had given him a chance to explore different subjects and develop basic skills. He prepared a list of ten interesting jobs.

1. Forestry
2. Drafting
3. Teaching
4. Photography
5. Art
6. Carpentry
7. Business
8. Biology-Environment
9. Sports-Basketball/Track
10. Travel

He selected his top two choices. Then he completed the comparison chart. See Figs. 49-21 and 49-22.

Eric discovered that there were many different courses important to his career choice. He planned his high school schedule to fit his general needs. He planned to take as much English and math as possible. This would further develop his basic skills. He also planned to take science courses, such as biology and physics. Metals, drafting, and electronics courses would make up his vocational study.

Eric felt that he knew where he was going with his education. He had a direction. The work study program in his senior year would give him an opportunity to put his talents to work.

During high school, he would visit different colleges and technical schools. He would read help-wanted ads and career literature at the library. He would also meet with employers and counselors. These people could help him find jobs in his areas of interest.

Fig. 49-21. Forestry — Eric's Comparisons

	Career Requirements	My Personal Characteristics
Interests	Forestry workers must be interested in trees, wildlife, biology, and natural environments. They must be interested enough in these subjects to take four years of college forestry or biology, and to continue their educations throughout their lives.	I like to walk in the forest and see the plants and animals. I also like to draw and photograph them. I want to go on to school after high school but I'm not sure I want to study just about trees or animals.
Abilities	Forestry workers must be able to make accurate short and long range decisions. They must have a broad background in math and science, and be able to apply this and other knowledge.	I can make both short and long range plans. I'm not sure I like science that much.
Personality	Forestry workers must have good self-confidence, self-reliability, and self-motivation. They must be able to work long periods of time alone, and keep careful, accurate records.	I feel pretty good about what I do. I like to work on my own much of the time. I like precision. I'm a pretty good self-starter.
Physical Makeup	Forestry workers must be able to physically endure extended out-of-doors work in all kinds of weather, hike long distances while carrying equipment, and they should not suffer from allergies.	I'm in pretty good physical condition. I play basketball and run the mile in track. No allergies.
Financial Need	Some forestry jobs pay better than others. Training and responsibility often determine the level of pay.	I'm not that sure how much everything costs so it's kind of hard to know how much I will need.

Fig. 49-22. Drafting — Eric's Comparisons

	Career Requirements	My Personal Characteristics
Interests	Drafters must be interested in drawing, details, and precision. They should also be interested in the training needed to make technical drawings.	I like to draw. I'm interested in how things fit together and work. I want to go to school after high school but not for too many years. I want to go to work as soon as I can.
Abilities	Drafters must be able to completely visualize the object to be drawn and know how the parts fit together and work. They must have a good general background in the subjects to be illustrated.	I often take things apart and put them together. I am particularly interested in motors, gears, and machines.
Personality	Drafters must be precise and willing to represent this precision in each illustration. They must have the patience to work in isolation at one location and for extended periods of time. They should be independent enough not to require constant supervision.	I think it's neat how things can be designed to fit together. I would like to learn how to design my own machines. I like to work on my own. Once I know what I'm going to do, I get started and finish it on my own.
Physical Makeup	Drafters must have good vision and a steady hand.	My vision is pretty good even though I wear glasses. Everybody tells me my drawings are pretty good. My friends think I should become an artist.
Financial Need	Some drafting jobs pay more than others. Training, speed, and quality will help to determine levels of income.	I'm not that sure how much everything costs so it's hard to know how much I will need. Maybe when I get older I will know this.

New Terms

1. apprentice
2. botanist
3. career
4. entomologist
5. forestry manager

Study Questions

1. List the four basic skills mentioned in this chapter.
2. How can learning the four basic skills affect your career choices?
3. What often happens with the careers of people who never do a self-analysis?
4. Answer the first seven questions under "Personality." Study your answers and then name one career for which you would be well suited. Name one for which you would not be suited. Explain.
5. When considering your financial needs, what is the most important question to ask yourself?
6. Name two places you can go to obtain literature about career opportunities.
7. List the five ways mentioned in this chapter of gathering information about careers.
8. Name three specific careers within the general area of forestry.
9. List the eight general career areas having to do with woods.
10. Pick the one wood-related career that you would like to know more about. Why do you think you might like this type of career?

Section

VIII

WOOD
TECHNOLOGY

Tree Parts and Identification

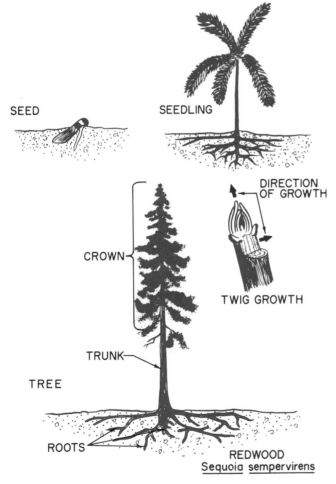

SEED

SEEDLING

DIRECTION OF GROWTH

CROWN

TWIG GROWTH

TRUNK

TREE

ROOTS

REDWOOD
Sequoia sempervirens

Fig. 50-1. Most trees grow from seeds. The largest American tree (redwood) is produced by a very small seed.

Most trees develop from seeds. Trees produce countless numbers of seeds each year. See Fig. 50-1. One tree produces enough seeds in ten years to cover the entire earth with trees. However, not all seeds survive to produce a tree. Unfavorable growing conditions, diseases, and animals destroy many seeds. Of those that begin growth, less than 1% actually grow into commercially valuable trees.

Each kind of tree needs certain conditions to grow. Some seeds, for example, need a wintering period. During this period the seeds create chemicals for germination. **Germination** is the initial growth of a seed into a plant. As the seeds continue to grow, small **seedlings** (young trees) develop.

Trees show a general growth pattern of **up** and **out.** The trees become taller as new buds produce growth. This growth takes place at the tip of each branch. Such growth accounts for the expansion of the upper, branching portions of the tree.

Several factors affect the continued growth of trees. Moisture, light, temperature, minerals, gases, and gravity are important factors. Together these factors make up the tree's total environment.

Environments differ greatly throughout the world. This makes the forests different. Zebrawood, for example, grows only in parts of Africa. Giant redwoods can be grown only in northern California and Oregon. Even within the boundaries of the United States, the forests are quite different. The forests of the Northwest, for example, are not at all like those of the South. See Fig. 50-2.

Fig. 50-2.   Many kinds of trees will grow wherever they are planted. Some trees, however, grow more widely in certain sections of our country.

Forest researchers are constantly looking for ways to increase the production of wood. In some cases they have actually developed new kinds of trees. See Fig. 50-3. These trees sometimes grow more rapidly than trees native to the region.

The Inside of a Tree

Like all living things, a tree is composed of cells. As the tree grows, it constantly produces new cells. When the cells die, they become the woody mass of the tree.

Leaf cells contain **chloroplasts**, where sunlight is converted into chemical energy. This process is called **photosynthesis**. During this process, carbon dioxide is taken from the air. The carbon dioxide is combined with water and minerals from the root system. With proper sunlight these materials are converted into

Fig. 50-3.   This small seedling is being tested to determine its hardiness. Tests like these help researchers identify better, faster-growing trees.

Weyerhaeuser

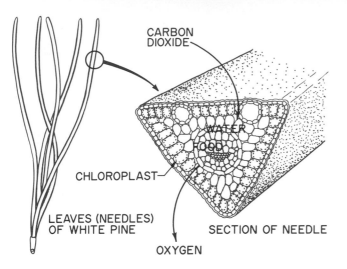

CARBON DIOXIDE

CHLOROPLAST

LEAVES (NEEDLES)
OF WHITE PINE

SECTION OF NEEDLE

OXYGEN

Fig. 50-4. Leaf cells can be likened to miniature factories. Raw materials (water and minerals) are processed (photosynthesis). The product (food) nourishes the tree.

food for the tree. See Fig. 50-4. This food is needed to keep the tree alive and growing. In addition, the leaves give off oxygen as a by-product of photosynthesis. This benefits other living things that depend on oxygen for life.

Water, gases, and nutrients (nourishing ingredients) flow throughout the tree. They flow through a thin layer of living cells called the **cambium**. The cambium surrounds the tree and is the only living part of the trunk. See Fig. 50-5.

The cambium layer is vital to the tree's life. Damaging the cambium can interrupt the flow of water, gases, and nutrients. If this happens, the cells above the damaged area soon die. This can result in the death of either part, or all of the tree. Stripping bark from a tree often destroys the cambium. Lightning, disease, and insects can also damage the cambium.

The cambium is made up of two types of cells. They are **xylem** and **phloem**. Xylem cells are formed on the inside of the cambium. They transport water and minerals from the root system up through the tree.

Old xylem cells become wood as they are replaced by new cells. This freshly made wood is called **sapwood**. See again Fig. 50-5. Sapwood is generally light in color. It is also fairly porous (contains holes).

As the tree grows older, new layers of sapwood are added. They slowly compress the old wood in the center of the tree. As the wood is compressed, it dries out. This dry, dense wood is called **heartwood**. Heartwood is usually darker in color than sapwood.

Phloem cells are formed on the outside of the cambium. They transport food manufactured in the leaves throughout the tree. When

Fig. 50-5. Cutaway view of a tree trunk

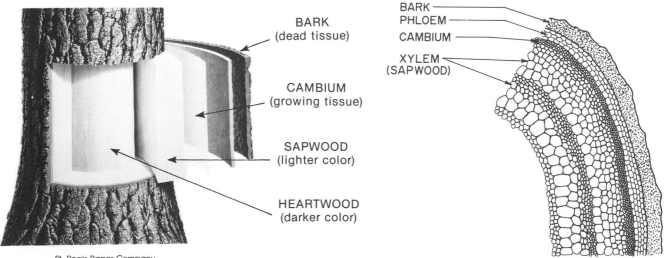

BARK
(dead tissue)

CAMBIUM
(growing tissue)

SAPWOOD
(lighter color)

HEARTWOOD
(darker color)

BARK
PHLOEM
CAMBIUM
XYLEM
(SAPWOOD)

Fig. 50-6. Springwood cells are larger than summerwood cells. Springwood cells also form larger bands.
Forest Products Laboratories

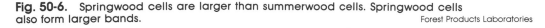

| Springwood | Summerwood | Cambium | Bark |

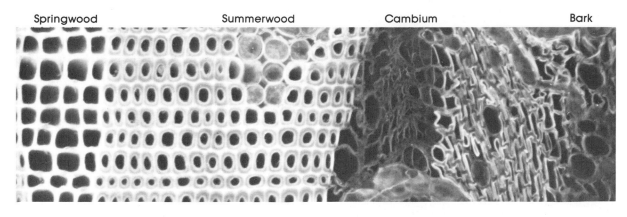

phloem cells die, they are forced outward. They then become the tree's new bark. Bark must be produced constantly to protect the tree's outward growth.

Tree Growth

Xylem cells produced during peak growing seasons are large. The wood made from this growth is called **springwood**. Cells produced during less favorable conditions are smaller, with thicker walls. Wood made from this growth is called **summerwood**. See Fig. 50-6. Because summerwood is denser than springwood, summerwood usually appears darker.

The different growth rates produce a series of rings called **annual rings**. See Fig. 50-7. The age of a tree can be determined by counting these rings. Forest managers do this by cutting a small plug. See Fig. 50-8. The plug is taken from the center of the tree. Then the growth rings on the plug are counted. The hole from which the plug came is treated to prevent disease.

Physical conditions greatly affect the growth of xylem cells. The widths of the annual rings can vary from year to year. Even two points in the same ring can vary in width.

Different kinds of trees also grow at different rates. Trees that grow very rapidly generally have widely spaced annual rings. Slow-growing trees have narrow rings.

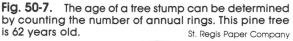

Fig. 50-7. The age of a tree stump can be determined by counting the number of annual rings. This pine tree is 62 years old. St. Regis Paper Company

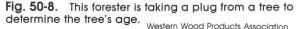

Fig. 50-8. This forester is taking a plug from a tree to determine the tree's age. Western Wood Products Association

LEAVES

LEAF

CONE

FRUIT
(ACORN)

CONIFEROUS TREE
(BALSAM FIR)

DECIDUOUS TREE
(BLACK OAK)

Fig. 50-9. All trees can be divided into two groups: coniferous and deciduous.

Types of Trees

There are many species (kinds) of trees. They can be divided into two basic groups. These groups are **deciduous** trees and **coniferous** trees. See Fig. 50-9. Deciduous trees are broad-leaf trees. Most deciduous trees lose their leaves in the winter. Coniferous trees, also called evergreen trees, have needle-shaped leaves. Most of these trees keep their leaves all year.

Wood is labeled according to the type of tree from which it is cut. Wood from coniferous trees is called **softwood**. Wood from deciduous trees is called **hardwood**. These terms do not always indicate a wood's hardness or softness. Many softwoods are harder than some hardwoods. Balsa wood, for example, is a hardwood, but is much softer than pine (softwood).

Hardwoods and softwoods have different grain structures. All softwoods are closed grain. **Closed grain** woods have small, hard-to-see pores. Their surfaces are smooth and nonporous. Examples are pine and spruce.

Most hardwoods are open grain. **Open grain** woods have large, noticeable pores. Their surfaces are generally rough and porous. Examples include oak, hickory, and mahogany. Some hardwoods do have small enough pores to be considered closed grain. Maple, willow, and cherry are some examples.

Tree Identification

You can identify different kinds of trees by studying and comparing their parts. The flower parts of trees are quite different. So are the leaves and buds. Branch patterns and wood textures differ from tree to tree. Look at the leaf and fruit differences between the trees in Fig. 50-11. These differences will help identify some living trees.

Trees are also identified by the colors and grain patterns of their wood. The "Wood Species" part of section VIII identifies many types of woods. Full-color photos are provided for easy identification. Possible applications for these woods are also provided.

Fig. 50-10. The different pore sizes of open and closed grain woods can be seen in these magnified views.

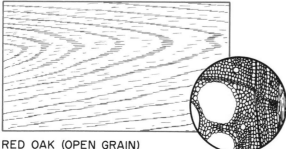

RED OAK (OPEN GRAIN)

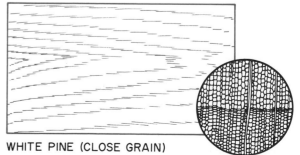

WHITE PINE (CLOSE GRAIN)

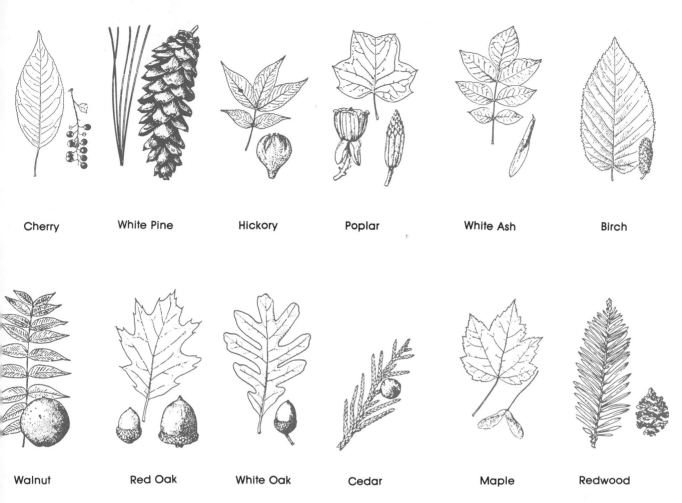

Fig. 50-11. Each type of tree has its own leaf shape and type of seed. If you recognize these parts, it is easy to identify grown trees.

New Terms

1. annual rings
2. cambium
3. chloroplast
4. coniferous
5. deciduous
6. germination
7. heartwood
8. phloem
9. photosynthesis
10. sapwood
11. seedling
12. springwood
13. summerwood
14. xylem

Study Questions

1. Name three things that destroy seeds.
2. Describe the general growing pattern of trees.
3. List six factors that affect the growth of a tree.
4. Give a reason why damage to the cambium might kill a tree.
5. What is the function of xylem cells? of phloem cells?
6. Name two differences between coniferous and deciduous trees.
7. Name three parts of trees that help to identify different kinds of trees.

Forestry and Lumber

Forests cover about 30% of the earth's land area. In the United States there are over 750 million acres of forest lands. Almost all parts of the United States have some forest area. See Fig. 51-1.

Large companies and private citizens own more than half of this country's forests. The companies develop their forests for commercial purposes. This process takes many years. Finally the trees can be cut. They are then milled into lumber, which is used in construction and making wood products. Most individuals use their forests for recreational purposes.

The United States government owns about 200 million acres of forest lands. It develops many of its forests into national parks, such as Yosemite and Yellowstone. It also establishes large forest areas to preserve the natural beauty of the land. These areas provide homes and shelter for wildlife.

Fig. 51-1. Most regions of the United States have large forest areas.

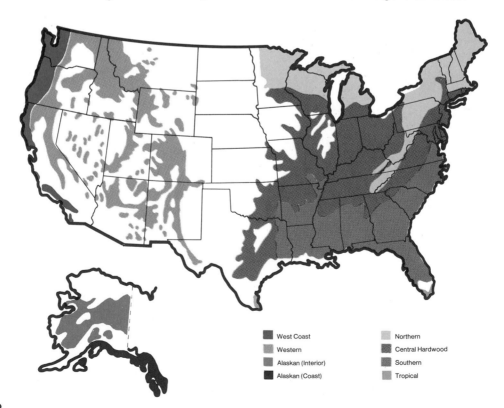

West Coast

Western

Alaskan (Interior)

Alaskan (Coast)

Northern

Central Hardwood

Southern

Tropical

Fig. 51-2. Forests like this one provide lumber for building homes and making other wood products.

The Value of Forests

Forests are important for several different reasons. They provide homes, shelter, and protection for deer, bears, and other animals. The roots of the trees and other plants hold the soil in place. This way the forests prevent the soil from washing away. Forests also serve as recreational sites for millions of campers, hunters, and hikers.

Forests are perhaps most important as resources for lumber. Of all the plants found in forests, trees are the most remarkable. They are the tallest and strongest of all the plants. They also produce the enormous amount of wood used to build countless objects.

Unlike other resources, such as coal and copper, forests can be renewed. They can be replanted with new young trees, called seedlings. For this reason, **forestry** (using and maintaining forests) is an important occupation today. The foresters are trying to manage the forests wisely. This means the forests will still be full of trees 100 years from now. The forests will be just as valuable then as they are today. See Fig. 51-3.

Protecting Forests

To get the greatest possible value from our forests, we must protect them. The dangers are many. As the demand for wood increases, protecting the forests becomes more and more important.

Fig. 51-3. These small seedlings will develop into the forests that supply future generations with valuable wood materials.

People are the greatest threats to the safety of forests. Careless people start fires. A fire can destroy a forest in only a few hours. Each year fires destroy thousands of acres of forest. It is true that lightning causes some fires. People cause most of them, however.

Greedy people also endanger forests. Because wood is valuable, some people overcut forests. They do not plant enough seedlings to replace the old trees. Through our laws we must protect forests from this type of poor management.

Insects can destroy thousands of acres of forest lands in just a few days. Foresters must check trees for insect damage frequently. They sometimes spray forests to prevent insect damage.

Foresters must also protect forests from diseases and animals. Diseases can cause great numbers of trees to die. Animals often eat seeds and small seedlings before the trees reach maturity.

Harvesting Forests

Cutting trees to make wood products is called **harvesting.** Harvesting must be carefully planned. The long range use of the land must be determined. If future forest crops are desired, a plan for renewing the forest must be developed.

Masonite Corporation

Fig. 51-4. Trees are harvested with large chain saws. They are then cut into smaller logs for transporting.

Potlach Corporation

Fig. 51-5. The unobstructed path through the air is often the most efficient way to move timber into a clearing.

The actual harvest begins with cutting down the trees. See Fig. 51-4. After the trees are cut down, each one is measured. The measurements tell the number of board feet in each tree. Then the trees are cut into the needed lengths.

The intended use of the tree determines how the tree will be cut into lengths. Telephone poles, for example, are made from logs as long as 75 feet (22.5 m). Wood used to make paper can be cut much shorter. It may be cut in lengths as short as 48 inches (1.22 m).

Fig. 51-6. Timber is transported from the forest to the mill in many different ways.

Weyerhaeuser

International Paper

After the trees are cut to length, the limbs are removed. Very little of the tree is left unused. As much of the tree as possible is used in the manufacturing of wood products.

Transporting Timber

Having been cut for shipment, the logs are dragged, rolled, slid, or carried to a clearing. Sometimes hot-air balloons and helicopters are used to move logs to a clearing. See Fig. 51-5.

The logs are then transported to the mill. Trucks, railroads, and waterways are the major means of transportation. See Fig. 51-6. In some areas, all three means of transportation are needed to get a log to the mill.

The Sawmill

Logs are processed into lumber and wood products at a sawmill. Some large mills employ hundreds of people. Smaller mills employ as few as two or three people. In the larger mills, machines do much of the work. In some cases computers are used to control these machines.

Whether the mill is small or large, several steps are involved in processing logs into lumber. Each log must be debarked, cut, graded, stacked, dried, and surfaced. Different procedures are used to accomplish these tasks. Which methods are used will depend on the size of the operation. The available equipment is also a factor in determining methods.

Debarking. The first step in processing a log is usually debarking. The bark is often removed with mechanical chippers and rollers. See Fig. 51-7. Sometimes it is blasted from the log with water under high pressure. The bark will be used for decorative ground cover and insulation.

Cutting. After debarking, the log is moved to the headsaw. The headsaw operator, the **head-rig sawyer,** decides how to cut the log. See Fig. 51-8. This decision depends on the quality of wood and the lumber sizes needed. The sawyer's job is to cut the wood to make the best use of it. He looks for defects to determine how much quality lumber the log will yield.

The sawyer controls a saw-and-hoist system. This system moves the log about so certain cuts can be made. See Fig. 51-9 for different ways the sawyer can saw the log. These different cuts yield various sizes of lumber.

Fig. 51-7. A mechanical cutter strips bark from a log.

Fig. 51-8. The headrig sawyer controls the cutting of logs into lumber. He determines the best way to cut each log to get the most high-quality lumber.

Western Wood Products Association

Edgers, Trimmers, and Chippers. As the boards are cut from the log by the sawyer, they are moved to the edgers and trimmers. Either conveyors or rollers are used to move the logs. The **edger saw** trims the rough edges and cuts boards to width. The **trimmer saw** cuts the boards to final length. The trimmer saw also removes defects from the boards.

Each of these cutting steps produces waste material. This waste is sent to the chipper. The **chipper** cuts the waste into small pieces. These pieces are used to make various products. Paper and particle board are two important products. The processes used to make these products are described later in this chapter.

Grading

Every board cut from the log must be graded. This means the boards need to be inspected for defects. The size, location, and type of defects are determined. Then the percentage of clear wood is calculated. This information is used to grade boards according to standards established by lumber manufacturers.

Different standards are used to grade hardwoods and softwoods. Hardwoods are graded mainly on clear area. Softwoods are graded primarily on strength. The different grades are usually listed at the lumber yard. This lets you choose the quality of lumber you need for the job. Just remember — the better the grade, the fewer the defects and the stronger the board. Of course, higher grades are more expensive.

Fig. 51-9. Different parts of the log yield different cuttings. Smaller logs may be cut into 2 x 4's, 2 x 8's, and 1 x 6's. A larger log may yield 4 x 4's and other heavier boards.

St. Regis Paper Company

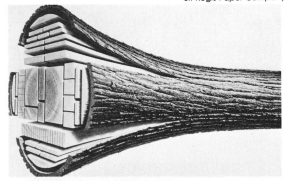

Drying

All lumber was once part of a living organism. Like other living things, trees contain a large amount of water. Twigs and buds may be 90% water. The trunk can be as much as 50% water. The water must be removed from lumber to prevent cracking and splitting. This is done by drying.

Two methods are used to dry lumber. One method is called **air drying**. In this method wood is stacked in an area exposed to the weather. Small sticks called **stickers** are placed between each layer of wood. The stickers let the air circulate freely through the stack. A simple shed protects the top of the stack from rain. Air drying can take months or years depending on the wood, the amount of water, and the climate.

A faster, more thorough method of drying wood is **kiln drying**. The stacked lumber is placed in a large building, called a kiln. See Fig. 51-10. Inside these kilns, the air temperature and humidity are carefully controlled. Temperatures are raised while the humidity is lowered. This causes the wood to lose its excess moisture. The process can take from several days to several months. Kiln drying reduces the moisture content much faster than air drying. The kiln method can also remove more moisture than air drying can. For this reason, kiln-dried lumber should always be used for indoor projects.

Fig. 51-10. In kiln drying lumber is stacked on flat cars and rolled into large kilns.

Weyerhaeuser

Surfacing

What happens to lumber after it dries, depends on how it will be used. Most hardwoods, and some softwoods, are sold as rough lumber. Rough lumber is shipped from the mill without being surfaced.

Most lumber is either dressed or shaped at the mill. **Dressed** lumber is surfaced on any combination of sides and edges. The different combinations, such as S4S and S2S, are specified by the buyer. **Worked** lumber is dressed and then shaped. This means that the lumber is cut to a particular design. Tongue-and-groove boards and moldings are examples of worked lumber.

The Lumber Industry

In this chapter, and in chapter 4, you have read about how wood is processed. You also read about wood being prepared for various consumer uses. Because of its many uses, wood is processed in a variety of ways. No warehouse contains more than a fraction of the many processed forms of wood. Heavy timbers for dock pilings, railroad ties, and telephone poles may be stored in one yard. Fine moldings, panels, and other interior woods may be found elsewhere. The vast differences in these wood forms suggest the variety of businesses in the lumber industry.

All the lumber used in American industries comes from the sawmills. The mills are located near the forests that supply the logs. Most mills saw only a few kinds of lumber. The lumber is then sent to different parts of the country. Building materials for bridges and docks, for example, are needed all over the land. Because of this, these materials must be shipped great distances. Other industries, such as the furniture industry, are generally located closer to the forests and mills. North Carolina, for example, has many furniture-making companies. Much of the wood for these factories comes from nearby forests.

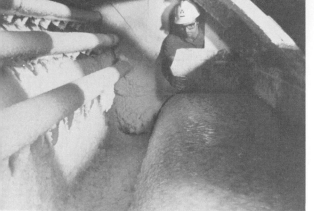

Fig. 51-11. This mixture of water and wood pulp is rolled and dried into paper.

Weyerhaeuser

Pulp and Paper

Wood that has been ground or chemically treated to form a soft mass is called **pulp.** Pulp processing plants are located near the sawmills. At the mills, unused wood is cut up in chipping machines. It is then sent to the pulp plant for grinding or chemical processing. Mechanical cutters and grinders are used to smash ground pulp. This pulp is used to manufacture magazines and newspapers. Chemically treated pulp is used to make fine paper for textbooks and typewriter use. Many paper and cardboard plants are close to the pulp factories.

A water and pulp mixture that has been ground several times is called **slurry.** The slurry is placed on a moving belt. The water is then evaporated from the mixture. The fibers that remain are pressed through rollers. They are then dried as paper. The process varies depending upon the kind of paper being made.

Processed Lumber

Efforts are made to use all parts of the tree. Even sawdust and scrap pieces are used. They are added to the fibrous material coming from the chipper. This material is added to the waste from plywood manufacturing (See chapter 4.) These materials are then processed into valuable products such as particle board and hardboard.

Both particle board and hardboard are made by pressing the waste particles together. This is done with tremendous heat and pressure.

Special resins are used to bond the particles in particle board. Hardboard fibers are bonded together with their own natural adhesives. Both materials are manufactured into sheets similar to plywood. Some particle board and hardboard is manufactured into other shapes. Some examples of this are chairbacks, toilet seats, and sporting goods.

Many new uses for wood have been discovered over the years. As the world's population has grown, so has the need for wood. But amazingly, the harvesting of lumber has increased little in the past century. This is due to the wiser use of wood. It is the result of increased efforts to use every bit of the tree. Such careful use is the first law of conservation. Another important law is replacement.

Fig. 51-12. These furniture parts look like solid wood. They were actually made by compressing fibers into the desired shapes and textures. Fiberboard materials such as these provide economic alternatives to solid wood.

Masonite Corporation

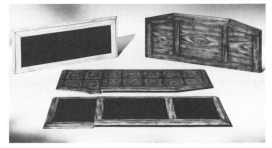

Fig. 51-13. Seventy trees were needed to build a typical log cabin (320 sq. ft.). Today seventy trees would provide enough lumber to build a home of 3500 sq. ft., plus enough tissue and paper to last the average family 30 years.

Georgia-Pacific Corporation

Westvaco

Fig. 51-14. This large forest is being harvested in small sections. The surrounding forest area will serve to reseed the cut area.

Reforestation

Perhaps the most important activity in forestry is reforestation. This is the process of reseeding an area that has been cut. Selecting individual trees or whole areas for cutting must be done carefully. When an area is stripped of its trees, seedlings must be planted. Then the area must be left alone for many years. Trees can take from 40 to 100 years to grow to maturity. Because the time span is so great, the importance of replanting is sometimes overlooked.

Sometimes a few healthy trees are left standing in a cut area. These trees are left to reseed the area. This is not a guaranteed method of providing for tomorrow's forests. Reseeding with nursery-bred seedlings is more reliable.

Fig. 51-15. Planting seedlings after the forest has been harvested is the best way of ensuring our future wood supplies.

Southern Forest Products Association

The number of seedlings planted must be greater than the number of trees expected to survive. Ten times as many seedlings as trees to be harvested are usually planted. Many seedlings will be eaten by deer. Others will be choked by weeds or washed away in storms.

After the seedlings take root, they grow into saplings and small trees. Then they are thinned out and cut. These small trees are used for fencing and light construction materials. The thinning opens the area to more sunlight. It also allows fewer trees to draw nutrients from the soil and air. In time the trees will develop into a forest. An area that was without trees will have become a valuable forest area.

New Terms

1. chipper
2. debarking
3. dressed lumber
4. edger saw
5. forestry
6. harvesting
7. headrig sawyer
8. pulp
9. reforestation
10. slurry
11. sticker
12. trimmer saw
13. worked lumber

Study Questions

1. Give three reasons why forests are important.
2. What are two dangers to forests?
3. What two factors determine the lengths into which a tree is cut?
4. Name three ways logs may be moved to a clearing.
5. List the six steps used in processing logs into lumber.
6. Why must wood be dried?
7. What three factors determine the time needed for drying?
8. Name two industries that use a large quantity of wood products.
9. How does slurry become paper?
10. What are three uses of particle board and hardboard?
11. What is the most reliable way of reseeding a forest?

Selected Wood Species

Larger wood species photographs were provided by the Fine Hardwoods/American Walnut Association; smaller wood species photographs were provided by the Frank Paxton Company.

Modern desk made of birch and goncalo alves.

Tom Wessells, Newport News, VA

Alder

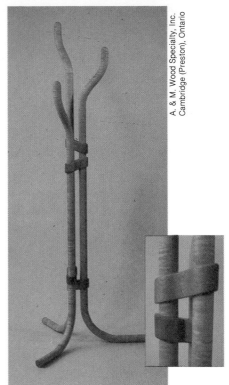

A. & M. Wood Specialty, Inc.
Cambridge (Preston), Ontario

"Cactus" coat tree made of curly maple, cherry, and zebrawood.

Ash, White (Brown Heart)

Ash, White (White Heart)

Alder. Origin: Pacific coast. Lightweight, fine texture, good impact resistance. Good machining and finishing qualities. Often stained to blend with walnut, mahogany, or cherry veneer. Used mainly for furniture frames.

Ash. Origin: Eastern, central U.S. Straight, open grain, moderate workability. Hard, shock-resistant. Used for tool handles, cabinets, furniture, doors, sports equipment.

Mahogany bowl.

Rob Russell, Joliet, IL

Banak. Origin: Central and South America. Medium weight; soft. Easily worked. Used for furniture, cabinets, veneer, and plywood.

Basswood. Origin: Eastern U.S. Lightweight, close grain; soft, fine texture. Easily worked with hand tools; resists warpage. Very stable. Used for patterns, templates, drawing boards, and core stock in veneered panel.

Beech. Origin: Eastern U.S. Moderately hard; even textured. Straight, close grain. White sapwood; reddish brown to white heartwood. Excellent tensile strength and nail- and screw-holding power. Moderately workable. Used for flooring, furniture, crates, dowels, musical instruments, veneers.

Birch. Origin: Eastern U.S., Canada. Close-grained, uniform texture, often curly or wavy figure. Sapwood white; heartwood reddish brown. Strong, hard. Machines and finishes well. Many uses, including furniture, cabinets, dowels, instruments, flooring.

Banak   **Basswood**

Biplane made of cherry, maple, and walnut.

Beech, American   **Birch**   **Birch (Rotary Sliced)**

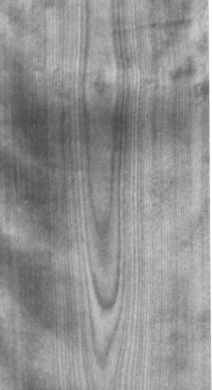

Bubinga
(Quarter Sliced — Figured)

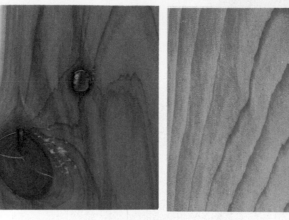

Cedar, Aromatic Red

Cedar, Western

Stuff Box, made of cherry and rosewood.

Cherry

Cherry (Gummy)

Bubinga. Origin: West Africa. Fine-textured, hard. Sometimes has a purplish cast. Dark, uniform stripe pattern. Easily worked. Used for cabinetwork and decorative plywood.

Cedar, Aromatic Red. Origin: Southern, eastern U.S. Actually not a cedar, but a member of the juniper family. Medium-density softwood. Non-porous, close grained, knotty. Sapwood white; heartwood red. Highly fragrant. Easily worked. Used for chests, closet linings, novelty items.

Cedar, Western. Origin: Northern Pacific coast. Lightweight, fragrant. Straight, close grain. Very durable under a variety of weather conditions. Stains well; machines, seasons easily. Used for shingles, exterior construction, interior construction and trim.

Cherry. Origin: Eastern U.S. Moderately heavy, hard, and strong. Must be carefully worked to avoid knots. Close-grained, very stable. Machines and sands well. Not easily worked with hand tools. Used for furniture, interior trim, gunstocks, paneling.

Cocobolo

Chestnut (Wormy)

Cypress

Cottonwood

Ebony, Macassar

Philip Sayles, Woodstock, IL

Candlestick made of cocobolo.

Chestnut. Origin: Eastern U.S. Coarse texture, wormy. Very stable and durable. Works and machines easily. Once plentiful but most destroyed by blight. Used for paneling, chests to give rustic effect. Also used for plywood core stock.

Cocobolo. Origin: Central America. A rainbow-streaked rosewood, oily and very hard. Red when cut but darkens quickly. Difficult to work due to interwoven grain. Decorative uses such as small boxes, knife handles. Only heartwood used.

Cottonwood. Origin: Eastern U.S. Lightweight; small pores. Excellent nailing properties, hard to split. Machines easily but dulls cutting edges. Does not finish well. Best worked when very dry. Used for boxes, crates; crossbanding, cores for plywood.

Cypress. Origin: SE U.S. coast. Medium to coarse grain. Lightweight. Heartwood strong and very durable, termite and decay resistant. Easily worked. Superior paint-holding qualities. Used for exterior applications, paneling.

Ebony, Macassar. Origin: Macassar. Extremely hard, dense. Black and brown streaks, very patterned. Difficult to work. Larger work likely to check. Used for wall paneling, inlay, marquetry, ornamental work.

Freight train made of red oak, koa, and cherry.

R. J. Ostrowski
Toledo, OH

362

HANDS ON! Magazine (Shopsmith, Inc.) Jim Lombard

Drafting table. See the project section of this text.

Elm, Gray

Elm, Red

Gum, Red (Figured)

Gum, Tupelo

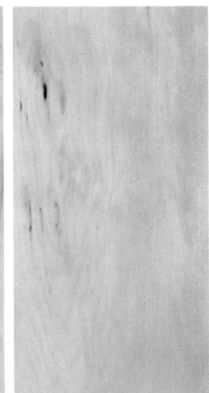

Elm, Gray. Origin: Eastern U.S., SE Canada. Also called "white elm" or "American elm." Strong, shock resistant. Excellent bending properties. Machines well but somewhat difficult to season. Finishes well. Used for veneer, paneling, handles.

Elm, Red. Origin: Eastern U.S., SE Canada. Heartwood reddish to dark brown; sapwood light grayish brown. Hard, strong, durable, and shock resistant. Excellent bending properties; machines and finishes well. Used for cabinetwork and paneling. Often marketed as "northern gray elm."

Gum, Red. Origin: SE U.S. Also called "sweet gum." Close-grained, uniform texture. Medium hardness, density, strength. Excellent turning and finishing properties. Can be stained to match more valuable woods such as maple or walnut. Used in cabinetwork, furniture, plywood, veneer, doors.

Gum Tupelo. Origin: SE U.S. Often referred to as "tupelo." Fine, uniform texture. Interlocked grain; low stability. Has good machining and finishing properties. Requires careful seasoning to prevent warpage. Used for furniture structures, crates, cabinetry, and novelties.

Cherry, maple, and walnut scoops. Lathe-turned and hand-carved.

Hackberry. Origin: Eastern U.S. A member of the elm family. Medium density and strength. Machines, turns, finishes well; excellent gluing properties. High resistance to shrinking and warpage. Excellent bending properties. Used for furniture frames, tables and chairs, crates.

Hickory. Origin: Eastern U.S. Member of walnut family, very close resemblance to pecan. Very heavy, hard, and shock resistant. Elastic but strong. Heartwood reddish brown; sapwood white. Very durable if kept dry. Machines, turns, bends well. Used for handles of striking tools, ladder rungs, skis.

Koa. Origin: Hawaii. Fine texture, similar to walnut but not as hard. Easily worked; finishes extremely well. Requires moderate care to avoid lifting grain. Used for musical instruments, art objects, furniture, and paneling.

Hackberry

Hickory (Narrow Heart)

Hickory (Character Marked)

Koa

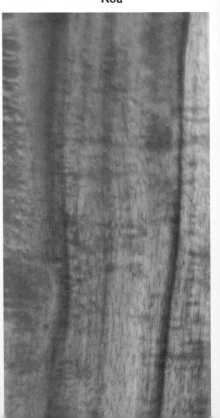

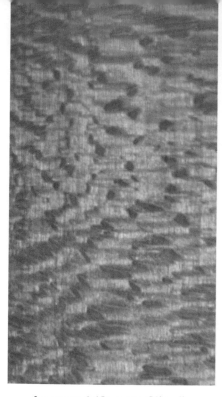

Lacewood (Quarter Sliced)

Lacewood. Origin: Australia. Silvery hue; small, flaky grain due to large rays. Coarse texture. Usually quartered to produce attractive pattern. Used for decorative work on small areas of furniture and paneling.

Limba. Origin: Congo. Often sold under tradename, Korina®. Fine-textured blond wood. Few pores but large enough to give interesting grain. Easily worked with hand or machine tools. Used for furniture and paneling.

Locust, Honey. Origin: East central U.S. Fairly coarse, heavy. Bends well and has high compression strength and shock resistance. Somewhat difficult to work and will check if not carefully seasoned. Used for furniture frames, containers, and structures.

Prairie Woodworks
Bloomington, IL

Dining table and benches.

Limba (Quarter Sliced)

Locust, Honey

Wood sculptures.

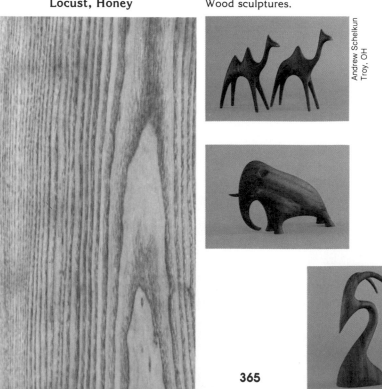

Andrew Schelkun
Troy, OH

365

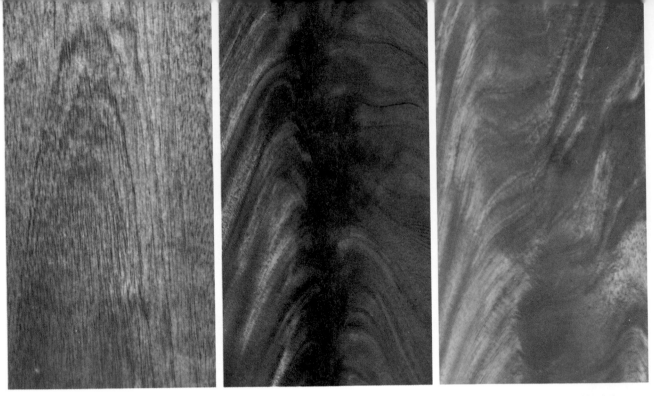

Mahogany, African

Mahogany, African (Crotch)

Mahogany, African (Swirl)

Mahogany, African. Origin: West Africa. Medium weight and hardness. Open-grain pore structure. Very stable. Available in a variety of attractive grain patterns and figures. Excellent workability and finishing qualities. Good turning and carving properties. Considered the ideal cabinet wood. Used for fine furniture and cabinetry and in boat building.

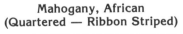

Mahogany, African
(Quartered — Ribbon Striped)

Mahogany, African
(Quartered — Mottled)

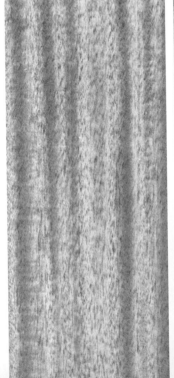

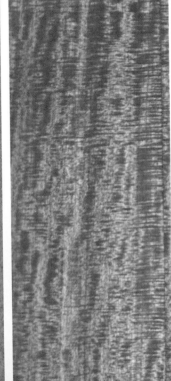

Swing.

Mitchell Azoff, Waukesha, WI
Mindscape Gallery and Studio, Evanston, IL

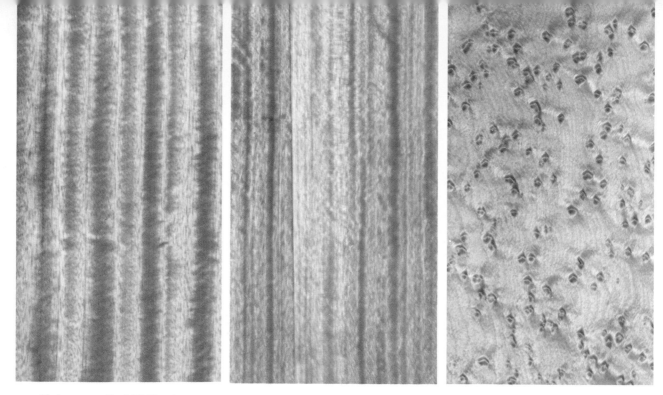

**Mahogany, Red Philippine
(Quarter Sliced)**

**Mahogany, White Philippine
(Quarter Sliced)**

Maple (Bird's-eye — Half Round)

Maple (Half Round — Plain)

Maple (Figured)

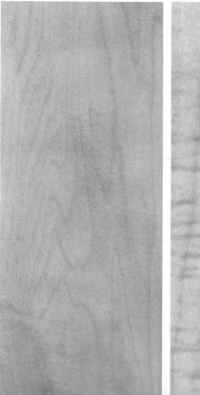

Mahogany, Philippine. Origin: Philippine Islands. Not a true mahogany; also called "lauan." Strong and elastic. Has a ribbon-stripe interlocking grain structure; coarse in texture. Works well and resists decay and warpage. Used for furniture, doors, cabinetmaking, paneling, and boats.

Maple, Hard. Origin: Eastern U.S. and Canada. Heavy, strong, and hard. Very fine grain, often figured as in curly or bird's-eye maple. Has high shock resistance and wears very well. Moderate workability; tends to split when nails or screws are applied. Turns well and takes a high polish. Used for furniture, flooring, cutting boards, workbenches, bowling pins.

Cabinetmaking bench, made of hard maple.

Glenn Gordon, Chicago, IL

Oak pie safe.

Prairie Woodworks, Bloomington, IL

Red oak and zebrawood mirror.

Steve Loar, Lemont, IL

Oak, Red. Origin: Eastern U.S. Heavy, hard, open-grained wood. Has a reddish hue, distinguishing it from white oak. Very strong, and has great wear resistance. Has moderate workability and excellent bending and turning characteristics. Finishes well, but pores must be paste filled. Used for flooring, paneling, house trim, and furniture.

Oak, White. Origin: Eastern U.S. and California. Same characteristics as red oak, except wood is lighter in color, and has greater resistance to decay and water. Pores of white oak are filled with a substance called **tyloses,** which imparts water resistance to the wood. Used in all areas of woodworking. Examples of uses are barrels, shipbuilding, flooring, furniture, and house trim.

Oak, Red	Oak, White	Oak, White (Rift Cut)

Padauk, Burma (Quarter Sliced)

Dining table made of cherry and padauk.

Mark Levin, Chicago, IL

Michael S. Chinn, Long Beach, CA

American Crafts Council

Chest, made of cherry, padauk, rosewood, and birch.

Padauk. Origin: Burma. Also called "vermillion." Hard, firm texture. Very stable and durable. Seasons well but difficult to work because of interlocked grain. Used for art objects and novelty items.

Pecan. Origin: Eastern and Southern U.S. Heavy close-grained wood; hard and strong. Bends, finishes, and machines well, but has poor gluing and nailing characteristics. Used for furniture, flooring, wall paneling, and novelties.

Pecan   **Pecan (Pecky)**

Musical birdcage of walnut.

Roger E. Egan
Bloomington, IL

Pine, Southern Yellow. Origin: SE U.S. Includes many species of southern-grown pines. Heavy and coarse in texture. Close-grained. Strong and hard. Moderate workability. Used for furniture, structures, paneling, telephone poles, and crates.

Pine, White. Origin: Western U.S. A soft, dimensionally stable wood. Fine, uniform texture. Heartwood tan or brown; sapwood white. Easily worked and can be carved to intricate detail. Used for light construction, patternmaking, interior trim work, and Colonial furniture.

Primavera. Origin: Mexico, Northern South America. Also inaccurately called "white mahogany." Very stable. Medium density; moderately lightweight. Has excellent finishing properties and is used for fine cabinetwork.

Redwood. Origin: N. California to Oregon. Lightweight, close-grained, soft, and moderately strong. Highly resistant to decay and fire. Contains no pitch. Easily worked and stable. Used for exterior trim, shingles, siding, fences, structural timbers, and lawn furniture.

Rosewood, Brazilian. Origin: Brazil. Very stable, hard, and durable. Fairly workable, finishes very smoothly and has a high natural polish. Used for furniture, musical instruments, paneling, art objects. Only heartwood used.

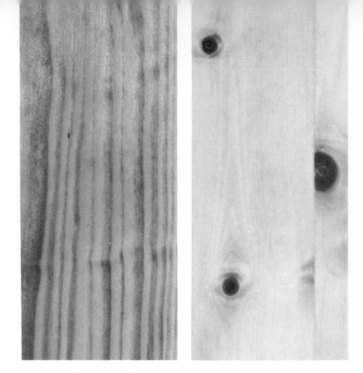

Pine, Southern Yellow   **Pine, White (Knotty)**

Primavera

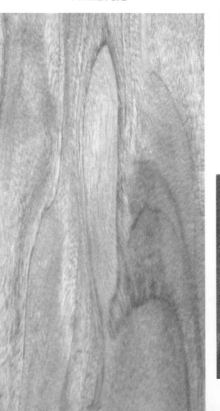

Mark Lindquist, Henniker, NH

Container turned from cherry burl.

Rosewood, Brazilian

Redwood

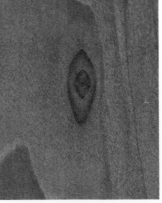

370

Sapele
(Quarter Sliced — Figured)

Canopy bed.

Sassafras

Satinwood, East Indian
(Quartered — Figured)

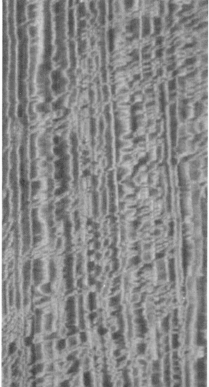

Sapele. Origin: West Africa. Resembles African mahogany though harder, heavier, and not as dimensionally stable. Medium durability and stability. Works quite well with hand and machine tools. Used for furniture and cabinetwork.

Sassafras. Origin: Central to eastern U.S., southern Ontario. Soft and brittle, light, nonporous. Stable and durable. Quite workable but care must be taken in planing not to lift grain. Used for paneling, boats, novelty furniture.

Satinwood, East Indian. Origin: East Indies, Ceylon. Also called "Ceylon satinwood." Hard, dense; interlocking grain. Oily and fine-textured. Fairly workable but inclined to check. Used primarily for furniture.

Pelican.

Spruce, Sitka

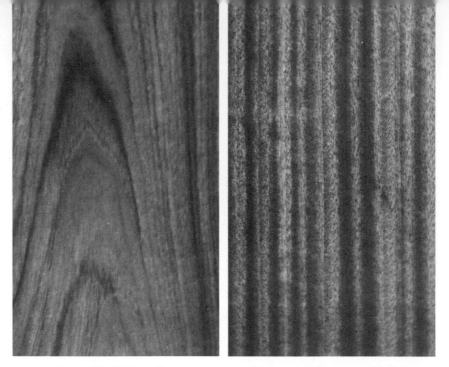

Teak (Half Round)   **Tigerwood (Quarter Sliced)**

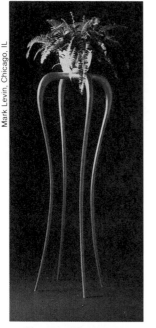

Mark Levin, Chicago, IL

Plant stand, made of cherry and walnut.

Spruce, Sitka. Origin: Alaska to N. California. Lightweight, soft, close-grained. Has highest strength-to-weight ratio of any wood in the world. Does not machine well. Used for general carpentry, ladders, scaffolding, and sail masts.

Teak. Origin: Burma, India, Thailand, Java. Hard, strong, and extremely durable. Dimensionally stable. Has an oily appearance. Fairly workable but dulls tools quickly. Relatively rare and expensive. Used for fine furniture, paneling, ship and boat building.

Tigerwood. Origin: West Africa. Member of the mahogany family. Sometimes called "African walnut." Has a ribbon-stripe pattern; irregular, scattered pores. Good stability when properly seasoned. Easily worked, good finishing qualities. Used for cabinet-work and paneling.

Padauk lamp.

Bert Lustig
Mindscape Gallery & Studio
Evanston, IL

Rob Russell, Joliet, IL

Walnut bowls.

372

Walnut (Narrow Heart)   **Walnut (Wide Heart)**   **Walnut (Character Marked)**

Walnut. Origin: Eastern U.S. Also called "American walnut" or "black walnut." Medium heavy, strong, very stable. Has fine texture and open grain. Heartwood chocolate brown, often with purple cast. Sapwood white. Easily worked and has excellent finishing and carving qualities. Most valuable U.S. furniture wood. Yields a wide variety of grain and figure patterns. Primary uses include fine furniture and cabinets, gunstocks, musical instruments, paneling, and veneers.

Mark Levin, Chicago, IL

Walnut lamp tables.

Walnut (Quarter Sliced — Pin Knotty)   **Walnut (Butt)**   **Walnut (Figured)**

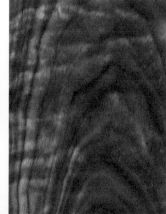

373

Jim Davis, Hoffman Estates, IL

Marquetry.

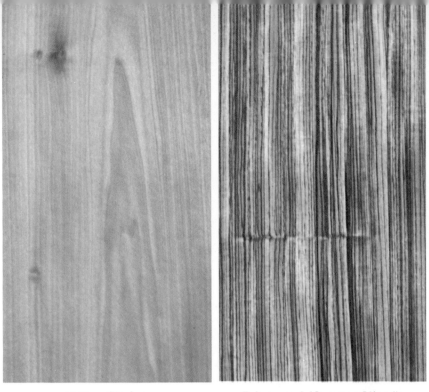

Yellow Poplar

Zebrawood (Quarter Sliced)

Yellow Poplar. Origin: SE U.S. Not actually a poplar but a member of the magnolia family. Straight, soft, even-textured. Close-grained. Lightweight but moderately strong. Works and finishes well. Used for furniture construction, siding, interior molding, doors, and novelties.

Zebrawood. Origin: Central, West Africa. Also called "zebrano." Heavy, hard, and coarse. Highly decorative grain pattern. Can be polished to a high luster. Used as quartered veneer for decorative effect as wall paneling, inlay.

Mark Levin
Chicago, IL

Sling chair, white oak/leather construction.

Bowl, turned from laminated walnut and maple.

John Fossum, Allston, MA
American Crafts Council

R. J. Ostrowski, Toledo, OH

Butterfly puzzle made of pine.

The following projects have been designed for a variety of skill levels. For your first project pick one that is relatively easy to build. As you gain skill, select tougher projects. A metric chart has been included for each project. If you decide to build your project with metric measurements, simply use the chart to change the customary measurements into metrics.

PROJECTS

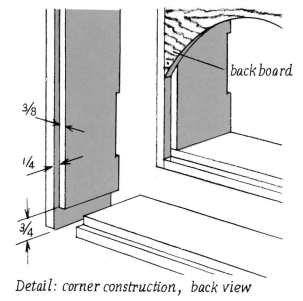

Detail: corner construction, back view

3/8

1/4

3/4

back board

alternate treatment of door top

scale: 1" squares

cleat

radius 4 1/4

1/2

radius 1"

radius 7

door
7 15/16

Materials (Dart Board)

No. pcs.	Part	Dimensions
2	sides	3/4 x 2-1/4 x 17-1/2
1	top	3/4 x 2-1/4 x 15-1/4
1	bottom	3/4 x 2-1/4 x 15-1/4
2	doors	3/4 x 7-15/16 x 22-1/2
4	cleats	1/2 x 1-1/2 x 6
1	backboard	1/4 x 15-1/4 x 16-3/4
1	target disc	1/2 x 14 diameter Homosote or ceiling tile
4	hinges	3/4 x 1-1/2 butt
12	screws	1 x 7 flat head (cleats)
8	nails	4d finish (corner joints)
quant.	brads	3/4 x 17 (backboard)
2	door catches	optional

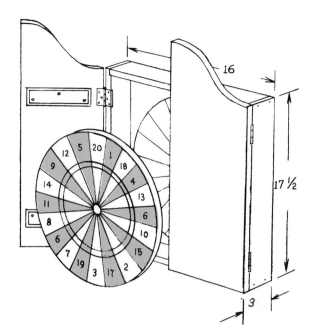

Metric Measurements

"	cm	"	cm	"	cm
1/4 =	.6	2-1/4 =	5.6	14 =	35.0
3/8 =	.9	3 =	7.5	15-1/4 =	38.1
1/2 =	1.2	4-1/4 =	10.6	16 =	40.0
3/4 =	1.8	6 =	15.0	16-3/4 =	41.8
1 =	2.5	7 =	17.5	17-1/2 =	43.7
1-1/2 =	3.7	7-15/16 =	19.85	22-1/2 =	56.2

Construction Note
Drill slight angle holes in bottom cleat to hold darts.

Designed by Kelley Mixon

TISSUE BOX HOLDER

Metric Measurements

"	cm
1/2 =	1.2
3-1/8 =	7.8
5-7/8 =	14.7
10-1/2 =	26.2

HAND MIRROR

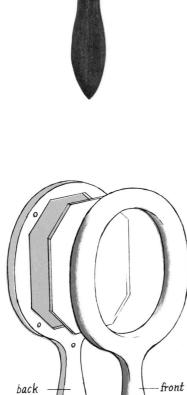

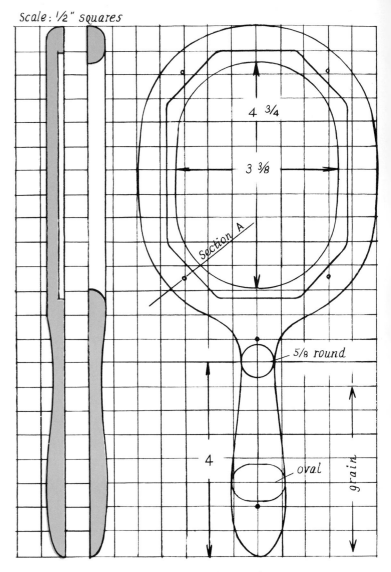

Scale: 1/2" squares

4 3/4

3 3/8

Section A

5/8 round

oval

grain

4

back — front

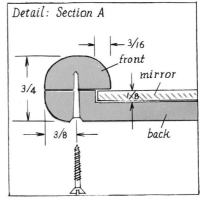

Detail: Section A

3/16

front

mirror

3/4

1/8

3/8

back

378

Materials (Hand Mirror)

No. pcs.	Part	Dimensions
1	front	3/8 x 5-1/2 x 11-1/2*
1	back	3/8 x 5-1/2 x 11-1/2*
1	mirror	1/8 x 3-3/4 x 5
1	mirror padding	3-5/8 x 4-7/8
6	screws	5/8 x 4 flat head brass

*1 pc 7 x 18-1/2 will make both.

Metric Measurements

"	cm	"	cm	"	cm
1/8	= .3	3-3/8	= 8.4	5	= 12.5
3/16	= .45	3-5/8	= 9	5-1/2	= 13.7
3/8	= .9	3-3/4	= 9.3	7	= 17.5
1/2	= 1.2	4	= 10.0	11-1/2	= 28.7
5/8	= 1.5	4-3/4	= 11.8	18-1/2	= 46.2
3/4	= 1.8	4-7/8	= 12.2		

Construction Notes

1) Use closed-grain wood such as maple, beech, cherry, or two different woods for color contrast.
2) Front: Rough-shape handle and outside before cutting out oval.
3) Back: Rout mirror recess before shaping outside. Check combined thickness of mirror glass and padding; padding is to prevent glass from rattling.
4) Make and fit paper cutting pattern for glass.
5) Make trial pilot holes and countersinks for screws, using scrap wood.
6) Screw back to front for final shaping and sanding.

CORNER SHELF

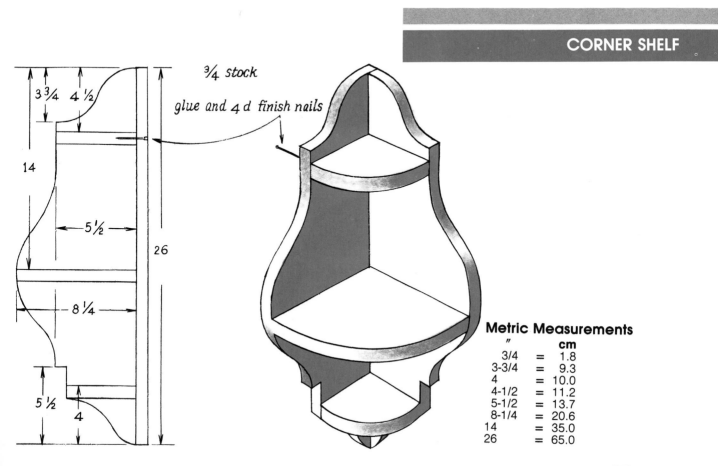

3/4 stock

glue and 4 d finish nails

Metric Measurements

"		cm
3/4	=	1.8
3-3/4	=	9.3
4	=	10.0
4-1/2	=	11.2
5-1/2	=	13.7
8-1/4	=	20.6
14	=	35.0
26	=	65.0

PIE TIN CABINET

Materials

No. pcs.	Part	Dimensions
1	top	3/4 x 11-1/4 x 23-1/4
3	shelves	3/4 x 11 x 23-1/4
1	bottom	3/4 x 11 x 23-1/4
1	backboard	1/4 x 23-1/4 x 29-3/4
4	door stiles	3/4 x 2 x 30
4	door rails	3/4 x 2 x 11-15/16
2	door panels	8-11/16 x 26-3/4 24 gauge sheet metal
4	butt hinges	3/4 x 2-1/2
24	screws	5/8 x 6 flat head
2	drawer pulls	3/4 diameter wood or brass
2	door catches	

Metric Measurements

"	cm	"	cm	"	cm
1/4 =	.6	3-1/4 =	8.1	11-15/16 =	29.85
3/8 =	.9	6 =	15.0	23-1/4 =	58.1
5/8 =	1.5	6-1/2 =	16.2	24 =	60.00
3/4 =	1.8	6-9/16 =	16.35	26-3/4 =	66.8
1 =	2.5	8-11/16 =	21.65	29-3/4 =	74.3
2 =	5.0	11 =	27.5	30 =	75.0
2-1/2 =	6.2	11-1/4 =	28.1		

Construction Notes

1) If the 3 shelves are to be fitted loose for cleaning removal, install door catches on underside of top.
2) Alter size of cupboard to fit your own needs.

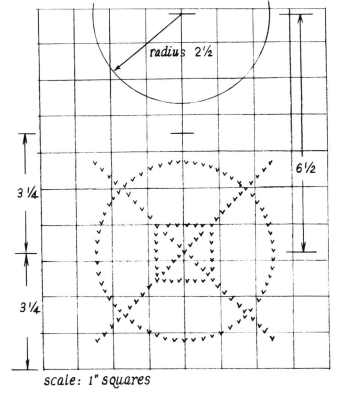

radius 2½

6½

3¼

3¼

scale: 1" squares

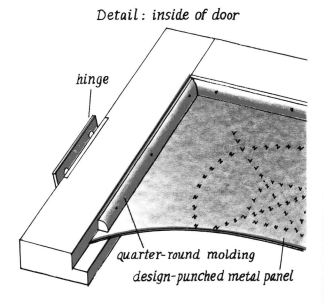

Detail: inside of door

hinge

quarter-round molding

design-punched metal panel

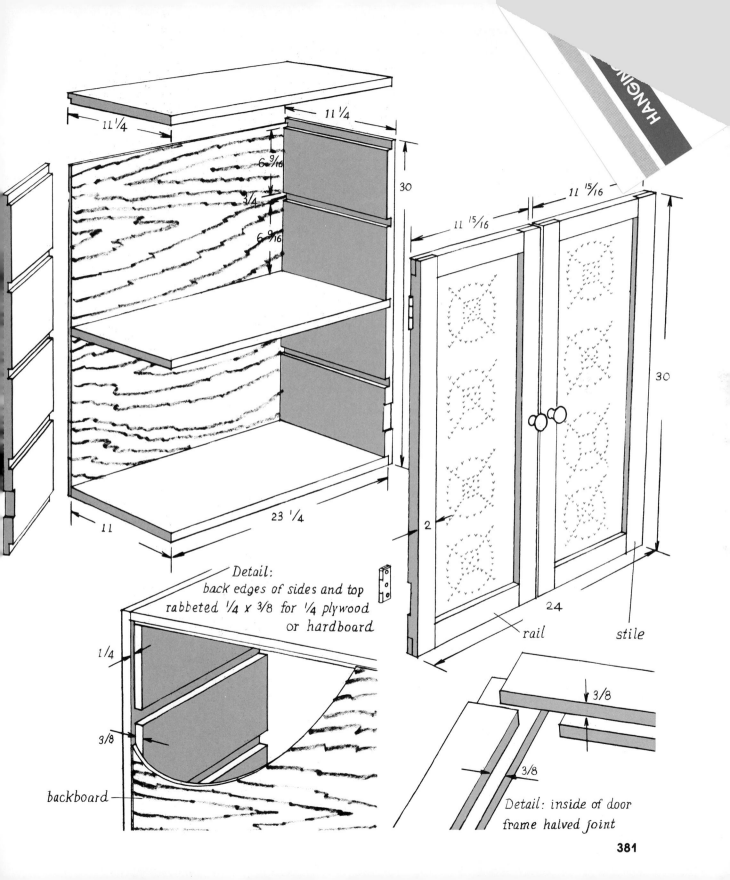

11 1/4

11 1/4

6 9/16

3/4

6 9/16

30

11 15/16

11 15/16

30

2

23 1/4

11

24

rail

stile

Detail:
back edges of sides and top
rabbeted 1/4 x 3/8 for 1/4 plywood
or hardboard

1/4

3/8

backboard

3/8

3/8

Detail: inside of door
frame halved joint

Materials

No. pcs.	Part	Dimensions
2	ends	5/8 x 7-1/2 x 30
1	top shelf	5/8 x 4-3/4 x 29-1/4
1	middle shelf	5/8 x 6 x 29-1/4
1	bottom shelf	5/8 x 7-1/2 x 29-1/4
1	bottom	5/8 x 7-1/4 x 29-1/4
1	center muntin	5/8 x 2-3/4 x 7-1/4
1	backboard	1/4 x 3-1/8 x 29-1/4
2	drawer fronts	5/8 x 2-1/4 x 14
2	drawer backs	5/8 x 2-1/4 x 14
4	drawer sides	3/8 x 2-1/4 x 6-5/8
2	drawer bottoms	1/4 x 6-5/8 x 13-5/8
2	drawer pulls	
3	screws	1-1/4 x 7 flat head
24	wire nails	1-1/4 x 17

Metric Measurements

"	cm	"	cm	"	cm
3/16 =	.45	3-1/8 =	7.8	8-1/2 =	21.2
1/4 =	.6	4 =	10.0	9 =	22.5
3/8 =	.9	4-3/4 =	11.8	9-1/4 =	23.1
5/8 =	1.5	6 =	15	13-5/8 =	34
3/4 =	1.8	6-5/8 =	16.5	14 =	35
1 =	2.5	7 =	17.5	17 =	42.5
1-1/4 =	3.1	7-1/4 =	18.1	18 =	45
1-3/4 =	4.3	7-1/2 =	18.7	29-1/4 =	73.1
2-1/4 =	5.6	7-3/4 =	19.3	30 =	75
2-3/4 =	6.8	8 =	20.00		

Construction Notes

1) Cut dado joints before cutting scroll work.
2) Glue dado joints, clamp shut, drive and set 3 spiral nails into each shelf-end while clamps are on.
3) Glue drawer joints, fasten with 1-1/4 x 17 wire nails, three per joint.
4) Drill pilot holes, countersink, and drive 3 screws through bottom up into center muntin.

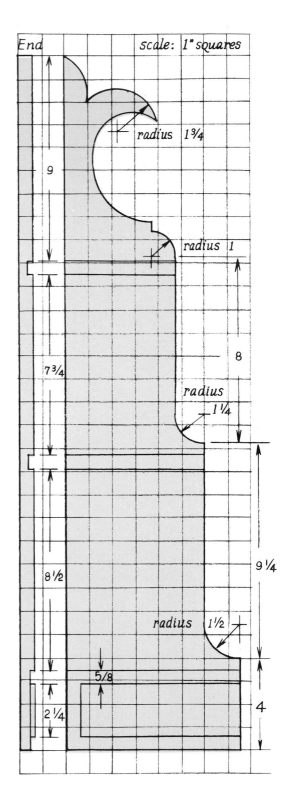

End   scale: 1" squares

radius 1¾

9

radius 1

8

7¾

radius 1¼

8½

9¼

radius 1½

5/8

2¼

4

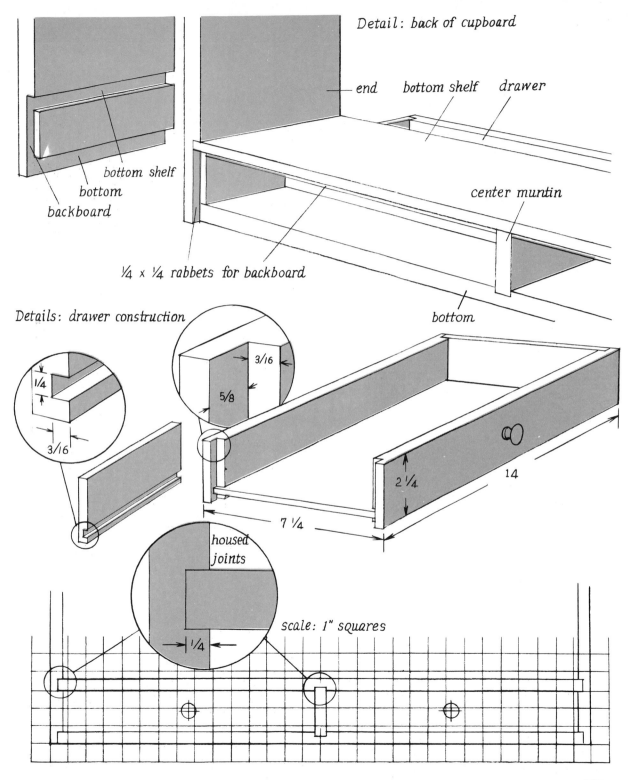

Detail: back of cupboard

end   bottom shelf   drawer

bottom shelf

bottom

backboard

center muntin

¼ × ¼ rabbets for backboard

bottom

Details: drawer construction

¼

3/16

3/16

5/8

14

2 ¼

7 ¼

housed
joints

scale: 1" squares

¼

BACKGAMMON BOARD

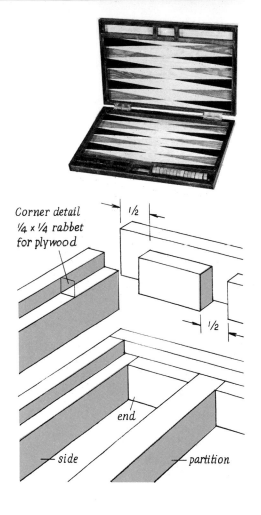

Corner detail
¼ x ¼ rabbet
for plywood

½

½

end

side

partition

Materials

No. pcs.	Part	Dimensions
4	ends	1/2 x 13/16 x 10-1/16
4	sides	1/2 x 13/16 x 15
2	partitions	1/2 x 9/16 x 15
4	(dice) partitions	3/8 x 9/16 x 1-9/16
2	bottoms	1/4 x 9-9/16 x 15
4	hinges	1/2 x 2 butt
24	screws	3/8 x 3 flat head
30	players	3/8 x 1 diameter dowel
1	clasp	optional
1	handle	optional

Metric Measurements

"	cm	"	cm	"	cm
1/16	= .15	1	= 2.5	5-7/8	= 14.7
1/8	= .3	1-1/16	= 2.65	7-1/2	= 18.7
1/4	= .6	1-1/4	= 3.1	7-3/4	= 19.3
3/8	= .9	1-1/2	= 3.7	9-9/16	= 23.85
1/2	= 1.2	1-9/16	= 3.85	10-1/16	= 25.15
9/16	= 1.35	2	= 5.0	15	= 37.5
5/8	= 1.5	2-1/16	= 5.15		
13/16	= 1.95	3	= 7.50		

Construction Notes

1) Hardwood is recommended throughout.
2) Paint design on bottom before making saw kerfs to obtain sharp, clean edges.
3) All joints glued only for neat appearance. Optional: Use glue and 3/4 brads in four corner joints.

Alternate Design

Use smooth-bottom board (no saw kerfs), pre-painted with design.

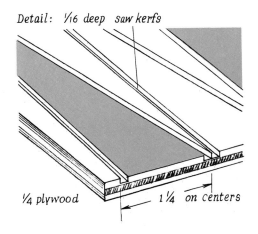

Detail: ¹⁄₁₆ deep saw kerfs

¼ plywood   1 ¼ on centers

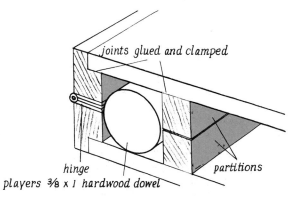

Detail: section through two halves of box

joints glued and clamped

hinge

partitions

players ⅜ x 1 hardwood dowel

384

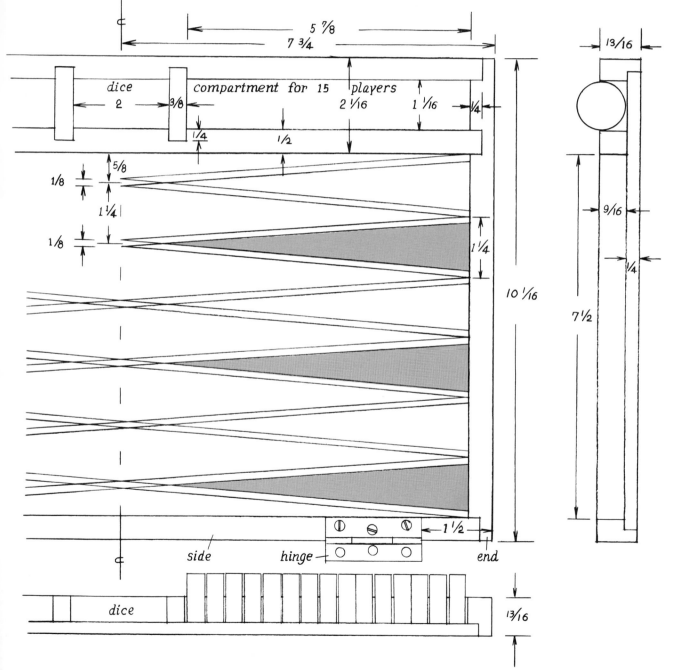

Half plan: 10 1/16 x 15 1/2 when folded shut

5 7/8

7 3/4

dice 2   3/8   compartment for 15 players   2 1/16   1 1/16   1/4

1/4   1/2

5/8

1/8

1 1/4

1/8

1 1/4

10 1/16

side   hinge   1 1/2   end

dice

13/16

13/16

9/16

1/4

7 1/2

385

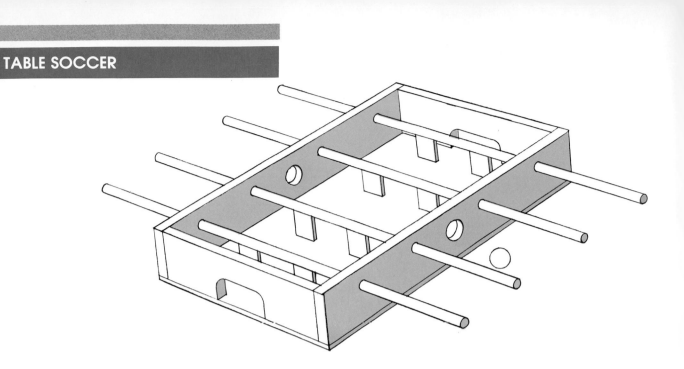

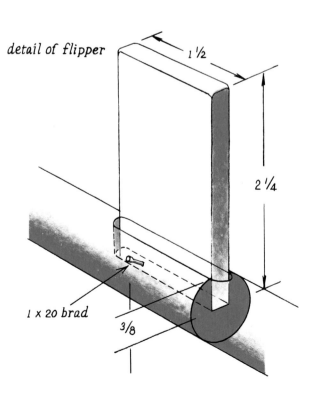

detail of flipper

1 1/2

2 1/4

3/8

1 x 20 brad

Materials

No. pcs.	Part	Dimensions
2	sides	3/4 x 3-3/4 x 23
2	ends	3/4 x 3-3/4 x 12-1/2
1	bottom	1/4 x 14 x 23
4	dowel rods	3/4 x 28-1/4
8	flippers	1/4 x 1-1/2 x 2-1/4
8	nails	8d finish
quant.	wire nails	1-1/4 x 16
8	brads	1/2 x 20
1	ball	standard ping pong (1-15/32 diam)

Metric Measurements

"	cm	"	cm	"	cm
1/4	= .6	2-1/4 =	5.6	12-1/2 =	31.2
3/8	= .9	3 =	7.5	14 =	35.0
3/4	= 1.8	3-1/2 =	8.7	18 =	45.0
1-3/16	= 1.95	3-3/4 =	9.3	23 =	57.5
1-1/4	= 3.1	4 =	10.0	28-1/4 =	70.6
1-1/2	= 3.7	4-3/4 =	11.8	40-1/2 =	101.2
1-7/8	= 4.7	8-1/4 =	20.6		

Construction Notes

1) Cut 3/8-deep mortises for flippers with drill press, 1/4 router bit and V-block.
2) Glue flippers into mortises; secure each with one 1/2 x 20 brad.
3) Attach bottom with 1-1/4 x 16 wire nails.
4) Optional: Staple cloth pocket over goal openings. Dip handles in plastisol.

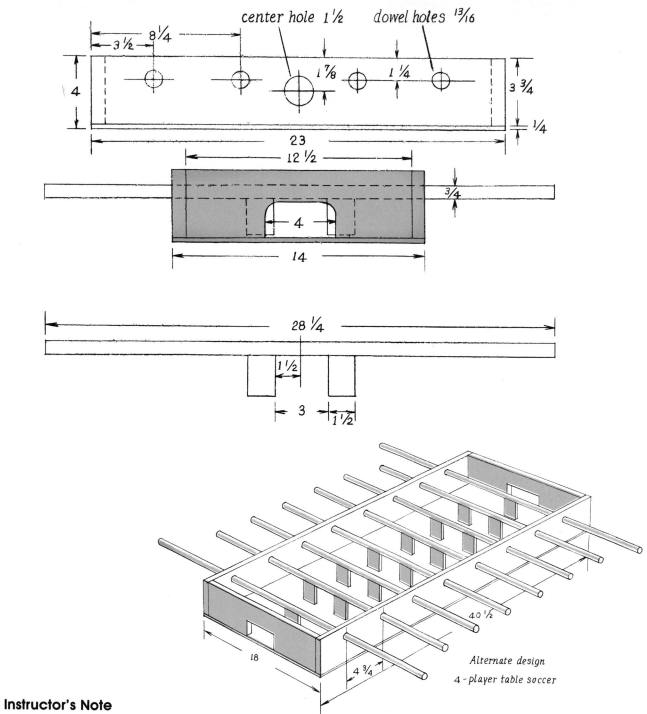

center hole 1½   dowel holes ¹³⁄₁₆

8¼
3½
4
1⅞
1¼
3¾
¼
23

12½
¾
4
14

28¼
1½
3
1½

4.0½
18
4¾

Alternate design
4 - player table soccer

Instructor's Note
12 bottom pieces can be cut from one sheet of 4 x 8 ft.
1/4 plywood or tempered masonite.

Alternate Design
full-sized table soccer for 4 or 8 players

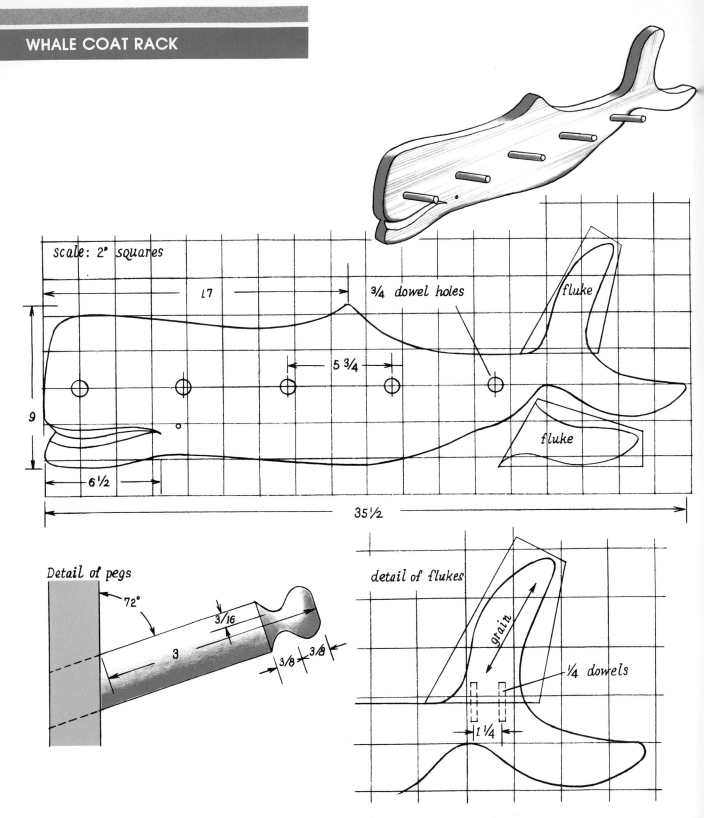

scale: 2" squares

17

¾ dowel holes

fluke

5 ¾

fluke

9

6½

35½

Detail of pegs

72°

3/16

3

3/8 — 3/8

detail of flukes

grain

¼ dowels

1 ¼

Materials (Whale Coat Rack)

No. pcs.	Part	Dimensions
1	whale body	7/8 x 9 x 35-1/2
5	coat pegs	3/4 x 4-1/8

Metric Measurements

"	cm	"	cm	"	cm
3/16 =	.45	1-1/4 =	3.1	6-1/2 =	16.2
1/4 =	.6	2 =	5.0	9 =	22.5
3/8 =	.9	3 =	7.5	17 =	42.5
3/4 =	1.8	4-1/8 =	10.3	35-1/2 =	88.7
7/8 =	2.2	5-3/4 =	14.3		

Construction Notes

1) Join upper fluke to tail before cutting whale to shape.
2) Optional: chamfer edges around whale body; turn knobs on ends of coat pegs
3) Glue pegs in place.

MIRROR WALL SCONCE

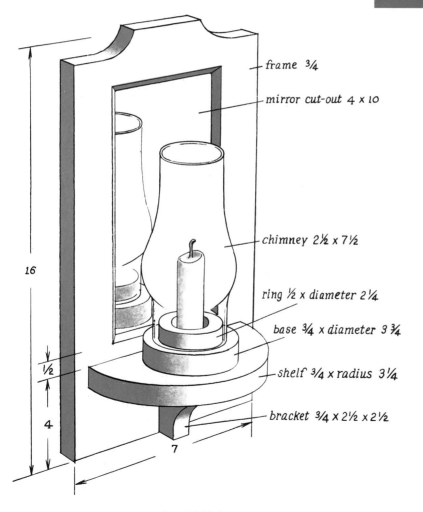

frame 3/4

mirror cut-out 4 x 10

chimney 2½ x 7½

ring ½ x diameter 2¼

base 3/4 x diameter 3 3/4

shelf 3/4 x radius 3¼

bracket 3/4 x 2½ x 2½

16

½

4

7

Designed by Jack P. Weisenborn and Gerald Peinkofer

Metric Measurements

"		cm
1/2	=	1.2
3/4	=	1.8
2-1/4	=	5.6
2-1/2	=	6.2
3-1/4	=	8.1
3-3/4	=	9.3
4	=	10.0
7	=	17.5
7-1/2	=	18.7
10	=	25.0
16	=	40.0

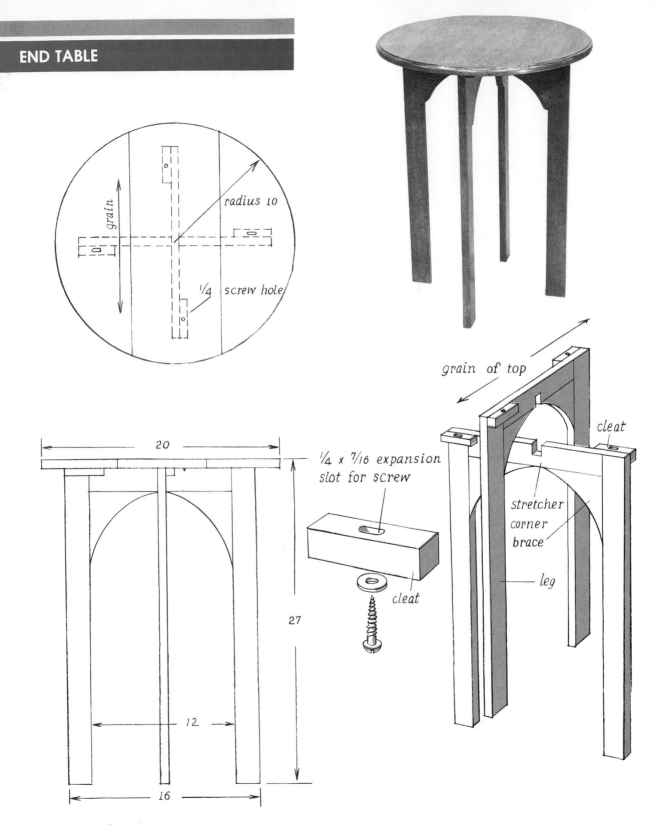

radius 10

grain

¼ screw hole

grain of top

cleat

stretcher

corner
brace

leg

20

¼ x ⁷⁄₁₆ expansion
slot for screw

cleat

27

12

16

Materials

No. pcs.	Part	Dimensions
1	top	3/4 x 20 x 20
4	cleats	3/4 x 3/4 x 3
4	legs	3/4 x 2 x 26-1/4
2	stretchers	3/4 x 2 x 20
4	corner braces	3/4 x 3-1/2 x 7 (1 pc 4-1/4 x 19-1/4 makes 4 braces, 4 cleats)
8	dowel pins	3/8 x 1-1/2
8	splines	1/4 x 3/8 x 3-3/4
4	screws	1-1/4 x 9 round head
4	flat washers	to fit

Metric Measurements

"	cm	"	cm	"	cm
3/16	= .45	2	= 5.0	8	= 20.0
1/4	= .6	3	= 7.5	12	= 30.0
3/8	= .9	3-1/2	= 8.7	16	= 40.0
7/16	= 1.05	3-3/4	= 9.3	19-1/4	= 48.1
3/4	= 1.8	4-1/4	= 10.6	20	= 50.0
7/8	= 2.2	6	= 15.0	26-1/4	= 65.6
1-1/8	= 2.8	7	= 17.5	27	= 67.5
1-1/2	= 3.7	7-1/4	= 18.1		

Construction Notes

1) Sequence for assembling base: Glue corner braces with splines to stretchers; glue dowels into stretcher ends; attach legs.
2) Rout rim of table top as desired, or leave plain.

Alternate Design

Modify proportions and dimensions for: (1) night table, (2) end table, (3) plant stand.

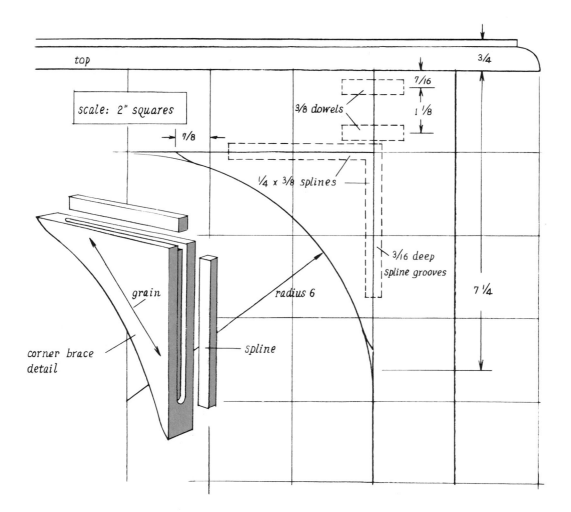

top

scale: 2" squares

7/8

3/8 dowels

7/16

1 1/8

3/4

1/4 x 3/8 splines

grain

radius 6

3/16 deep spline grooves

7 1/4

corner brace detail

spline

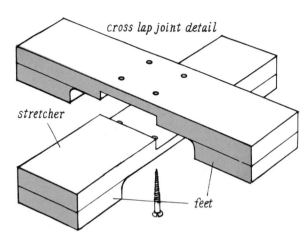

cross lap joint detail

stretcher

feet

Designed by Russell Hutchings

scale: 1" squares

top cleat

2 ¾

1 ½

3 ½

½

1

¼

3 ¼

8

3 ½

3 ½

Materials (Pedestal Table)

No. pcs.	Part	Dimensions
1	top	1-1/4 x 16 x 16
1	top cleat	3/4 x 5-1/2 x 5-1/2
1	spindle	3-1/2 x 3-1/2 x 13
2	stretchers	3/4 x 3-1/2 x 3-1/2
4	feet	3/4 x 3-1/2 x 4
4	screws	2 x 10 flat head (base)
4	screws	1-1/2 x 9 flat head (top)

Metric Measurements

"	cm	"	cm	"	cm
1/4 =	.6	2 =	5.0	9 =	22.5
1/2 =	1.2	2-3/4 =	6.8	10 =	25
3/4 =	1.8	3-1/4 =	8.1	13 =	32.5
1 =	2.5	3-1/2 =	8.7	16 =	40
1-1/4 =	3.1	5-1/2 =	13.7		
1-1/2 =	3.7	8 =	20		

WHALE TABLE

Metric Measurements

"		cm
3/4	=	1.8
1	=	2.5
1-1/2	=	3.7
2	=	5.0
2-3/8	=	5.9
3	=	7.5
3-3/4	=	9.3
5	=	12.5
12	=	30.0
19	=	47.5
54	=	135

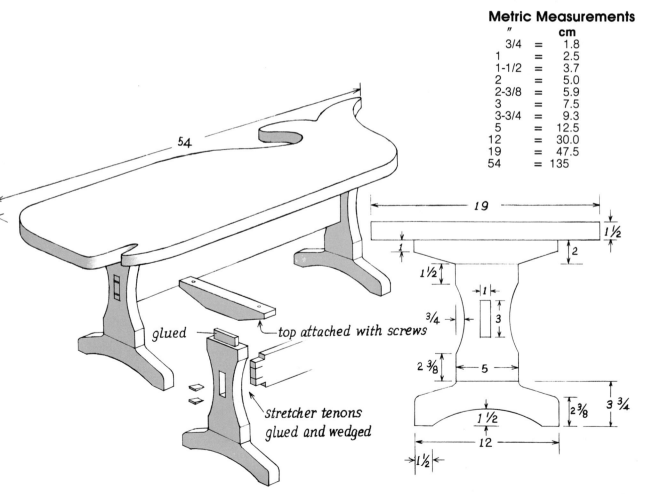

glued

top attached with screws

stretcher tenons glued and wedged

393

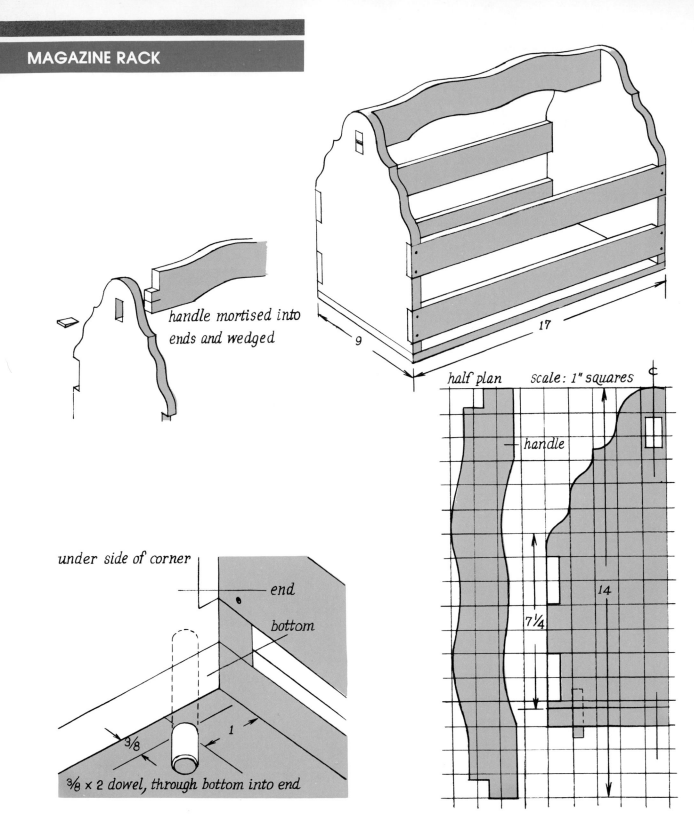

handle mortised into
ends and wedged

9

17

half plan   scale: 1" squares

handle

14

7¼

under side of corner

end

bottom

3/8

1

3/8 × 2 dowel, through bottom into end

Materials (Magazine Rack)

No. pcs.	Part	Dimensions
2	ends	3/4 x 9 x 13-1/4
1	bottom	3/4 x 9 x 17
4	slats	1/2 x 2 x 17
1	handle	3/4 x 2-5/8 x 17
2	wedges	3/4 x 1 x 0-1/8
4	legs	3/8 x 2 dowel
16	nails	4d finish (slats)

Metric Measurements

"	cm	"	cm	"	cm
1/8 =	.3	1 =	2.5	9 =	22.5
3/8 =	.9	2 =	5.0	13-1/4 =	33.1
1/2 =	1.2	2-5/8 =	6.5	14 =	35.0
3/4 =	1.8	7-1/4 =	18.1	17 =	42.5

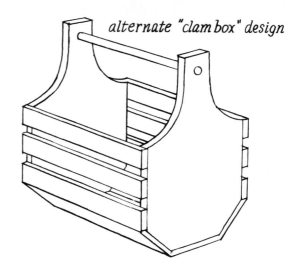

alternate "clam box" design

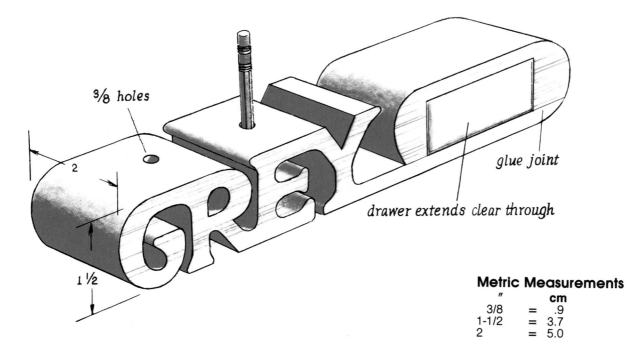

3/8 holes

2

1 1/2

glue joint

drawer extends clear through

Metric Measurements

"		cm
3/8	=	.9
1-1/2	=	3.7
2	=	5.0

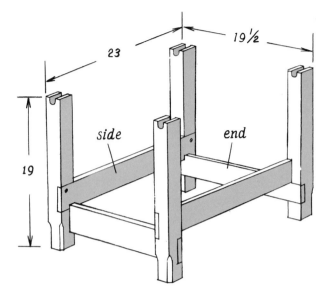

23

19½

19

side

end

scale: 1" squares

side

end

3½

Detail: notches in tops of legs

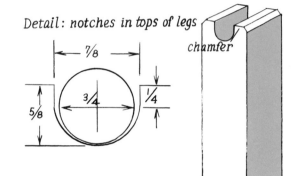

⅞

¾

⅝

¼

chamfer

Detail: corner construction

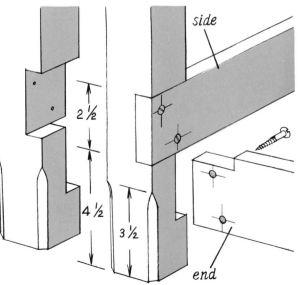

2½

4½

3½

side

end

Materials

No. pcs.	Part	Dimensions
2	sides	3/4 x 2-1/2 x 23
2	ends	3/4 x 3 x 19-1/2
4	legs	2 x 2 x 19
2	dowels	3/4 x 25
1	canvas carrier	18-1/2 x 40
2	carrier handles	1 x 18 webbed strap
16	screws	1-1/2 x 9 flat head
16	rivets	copper belt type with roves, length gauged for 4 thicknesses of canvas

Metric Measurements

″	cm	″	cm	″	cm
1/4 =	.6	3 =	7.5	19 =	47.5
5/8 =	1.5	3-3/8 =	8.4	19-1/2 =	48.7
3/4 =	1.8	3-1/2 =	8.7	23 =	57.5
7/8 =	2.2	4 =	10.0	25 =	62.5
1 =	2.5	4-1/2 =	11.2	40 =	100
2 =	5.0	8-1/2 =	21.2		
2-1/2 =	6.2	18-1/2 =	46.2		

Construction Notes

1) Glue and attach sides to legs first, with 1-1/2 x 9 screws.
2) Canvas Carrier: After turning in and stitching hem on all four edges, wrap one end around dowel and rivet. Then check overall length of carrier before doing other end. Bottom of carrier, when in place, should be higher than top edges of frame-ends.

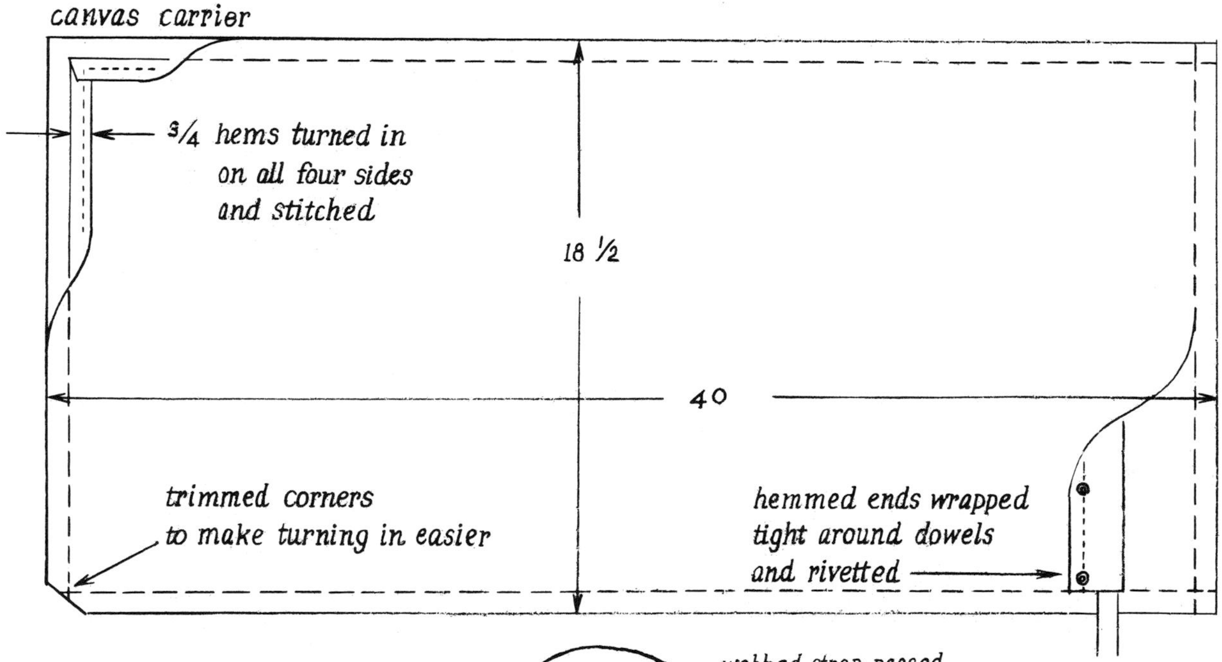

canvas carrier

3/4 hems turned in on all four sides and stitched

18 1/2

40

trimmed corners to make turning in easier

hemmed ends wrapped tight around dowels and rivetted

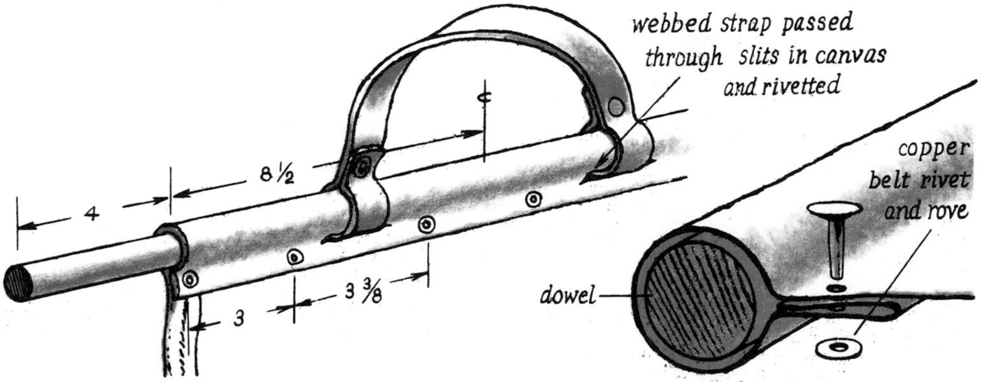

webbed strap passed through slits in canvas and rivetted

8 1/2

4

3 3/8

3

copper belt rivet and rove

dowel

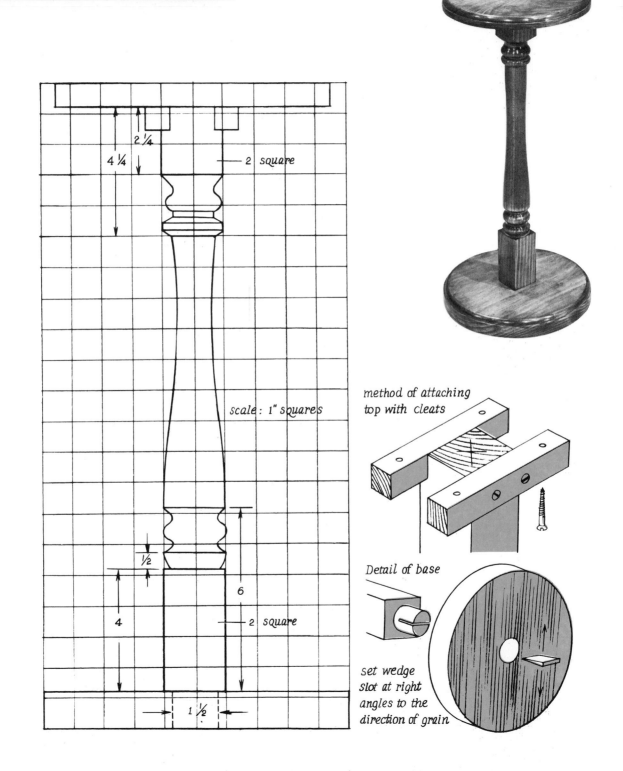

2 ¼

4 ¼

— 2 square

scale: 1" squares

½

6

4

— 2 square

1 ½

method of attaching
top with cleats

Detail of base

set wedge
slot at right
angles to the
direction of grain

Materials (Pedestal Fern Stand)

No. pcs.	Part	Dimensions
1	top	3/4 x 9 round
1	base	1-1/4 x 10 round
2	cleats	3/4 x 3/4 x 5
1	spindle	2 x 2 x 20-1/4
8	screws	1-1/2 x 8 flat head
1	wedge	1 x 1-1/4 tapered 0 to 1/8

Metric Measurements

"	cm	"	cm	"	cm
1/8 =	.3	1-1/2 =	3.7	5 =	12.5
1/2 =	1.2	2 =	5.0	6 =	15.0
3/4 =	1.8	2-1/4 =	5.6	9 =	22.5
1 =	2.5	4 =	10.0	10 =	25.0
1-1/4 =	3.1	4-1/4 =	10.6	20-1/4 =	50.6

Construction Notes

1) Attach top with direction of grain at right angles to 5″ length of cleats.
2) Rout rim of top and base or leave plain.

Alternate Design

Turn the bottom 4″ of the spindle round instead of leaving square.

BASEBALL HOLDER

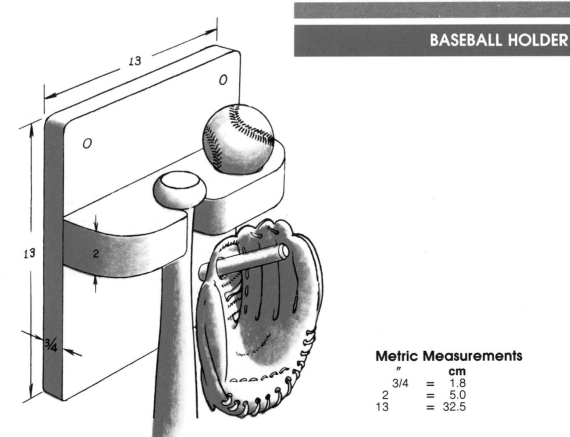

Metric Measurements

"	cm
3/4 =	1.8
2 =	5.0
13 =	32.5

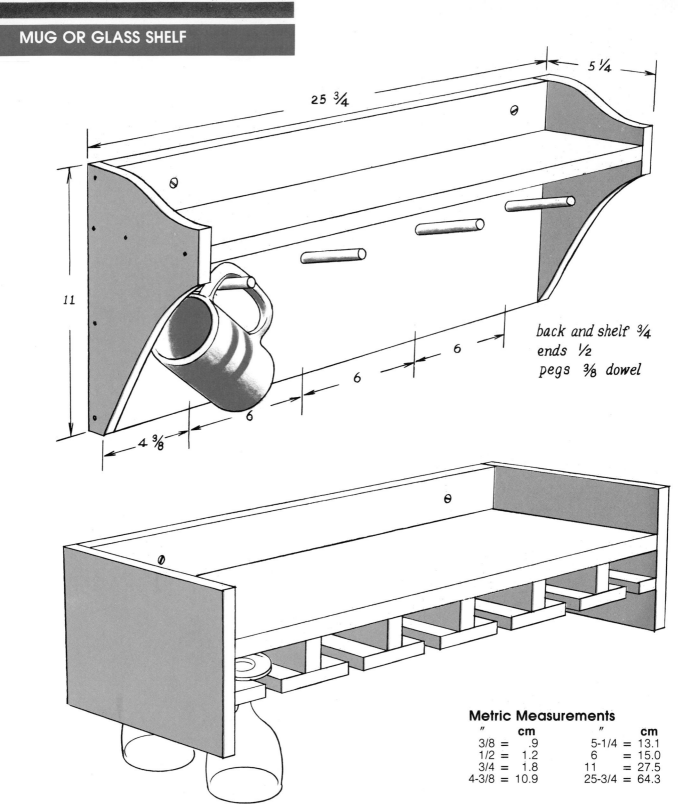

25 ¾

5 ¼

11

4 ⅜

6

6

6

6

back and shelf ¾
ends ½
pegs ⅜ dowel

Metric Measurements

"	cm	"	cm
3/8 =	.9	5-1/4 =	13.1
1/2 =	1.2	6 =	15.0
3/4 =	1.8	11 =	27.5
4-3/8 =	10.9	25-3/4 =	64.3

CUTTING BOARDS

Materials

No. pcs.	Part	Dimensions
ONION		
1		3/4 x 6-5/8 x 11-5/8
CAT	one-piece version	
1		3/4 x 5 x 12-1/2
FISH	one-piece version	
1		3/4 x 3-1/2 x 14
	rack	
1	R	3/4 x 1 x 4-5/8
1	L	3/4 x 3/4 x 3-5/8
1	back	1/4 x 3 x 4-5/8

Metric Measurements

″	cm	″	cm	″	cm
1/4	= .6	3-1/2	= 8.7	11-5/8	= 29.0
1/2	= 1.2	3-5/8	= 9.0	12-1/2	= 31.2
3/4	= 1.8	4-5/8	= 11.5	14	= 35.0
1	= 2.5	5	= 12.5		
3	= 7.5	6-5/8	= 16.5		

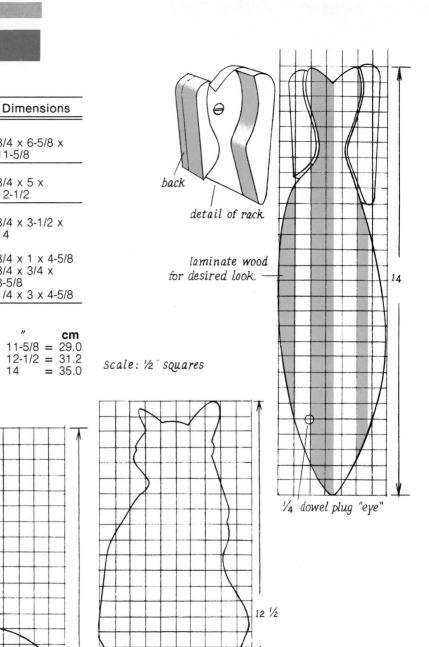

back

detail of rack

laminate wood for desired look.

14

scale: ½" squares

¼ dowel plug "eye"

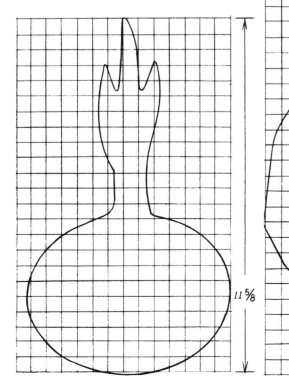

11 ⅝

12 ½

401

COASTER SET

Designed by John R. Lindbeck

Materials

No. pcs.	Part	Dimensions
COASTERS		
8	rings	1/4 x 3-7/8 x 3-7/8
8	discs	1/16 cork, 2-7/8 diameter
8	backs	1/8 veneer 3-7/8 x 3-7/8
HOLDER A		
1	base	1 x 4 x 8-1/2
2	sides	1/4 x 1 x 8-1/2
HOLDER B		
1	base	3/4 x 5-1/2 x 8-1/8
1	end	3/4 x 5-1/2 x 6-1/2
1	hanger rod	3/8 x 8-1/2 dowel

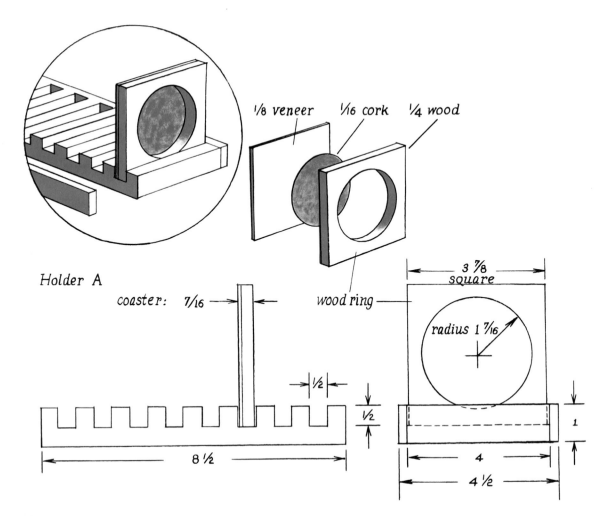

⅛ veneer   ⅟₁₆ cork   ¼ wood

wood ring

Holder A

coaster: 7/16

3 ⅞ square

radius 1 7/16

1/2

1/2

8 1/2

4

4 1/2

1

Metric Measurements

"	cm	"		cm	"		cm
1/16 =	.15	1	=	2.5	4-1/2	=	11.2
1/8 =	.3	1-7/16	=	3.55	5-1/2	=	13.7
1/4 =	.6	2	=	5.0	6	=	15.0
3/8 =	.9	2-7/8	=	7.2	6-1/2	=	16.2
7/16 =	1.05	3-1/2	=	8.7	7-3/4	=	19.3
1/2 =	1.2	3-3/4	=	9.3	8-1/8	=	20.3
9/16 =	1.35	3-7/8	=	9.7	8-1/2	=	21.2
3/4 =	1.8	4	=	10.0	11-1/2	=	28.7

Construction Notes

Make coasters before making either holder. The actual thickness of cork and veneer may vary and will require adjustments in the width of slots in Holder A, as well as lengthwise dimensions of both holders.

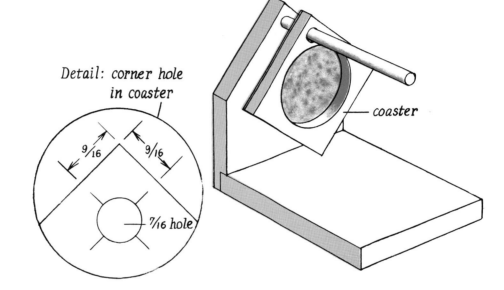

Detail: corner hole in coaster

9/16   9/16

7/16 hole

coaster

Holder B

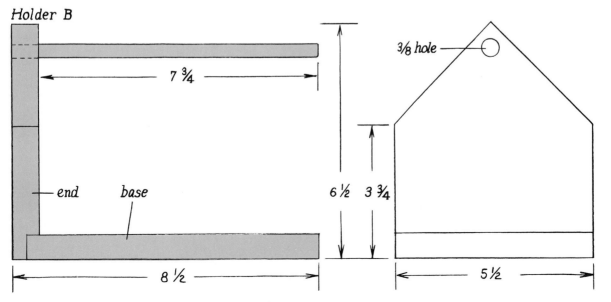

7 ¾

end   base

8 ½

3/8 hole

6 ½   3 ¾

5 ½

403

SEWING/TOOL BOX

Materials

No. pcs.	Part	Dimensions
2	sides	3/8 x 3 x 11-1/4
2	ends	3/8 x 3 x 9-1/2
1	partition/handle	3/8 x 5-1/2 x 11-1/4
1	bottom	1/4 x 9-1/2 x 12
quant	nails	1-1/4 x 18 brads

Metric Measurements

"	cm	"	cm	"	cm
1/4 =	.6	3 =	7.5	5-3/4 =	14.3
3/8 =	.9	3-1/4 =	8.1	9-1/2 =	23.7
1 =	2.5	3-7/8 =	9.7	11-1/4 =	28.1
1-1/2 =	3.7	5-1/2 =	13.7	12 =	30.0

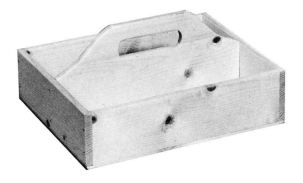

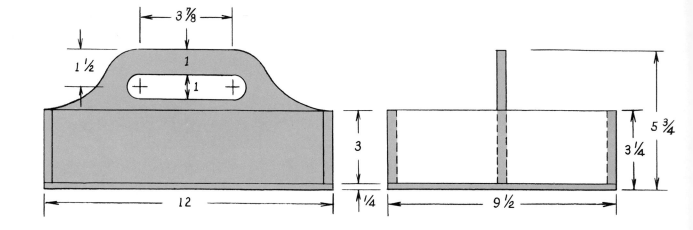

FRUIT TRAY

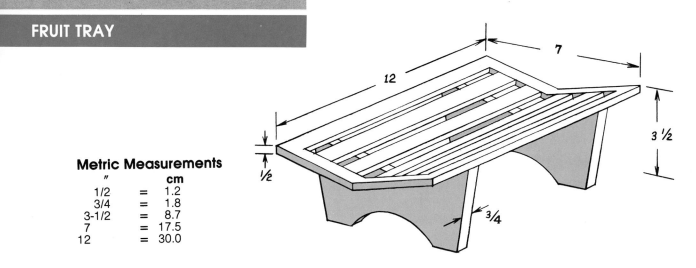

Metric Measurements

"		cm
1/2	=	1.2
3/4	=	1.8
3-1/2	=	8.7
7	=	17.5
12	=	30.0

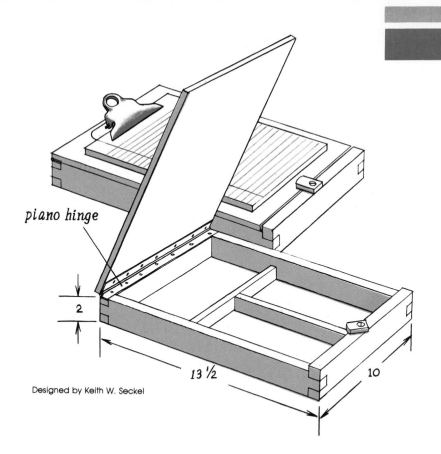

piano hinge

2

13 ½

10

Designed by Keith W. Seckel

Metric Measurements
"		cm
2	=	5.0
10	=	25.0
13-1/2	=	33.7

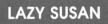

LAZY SUSAN

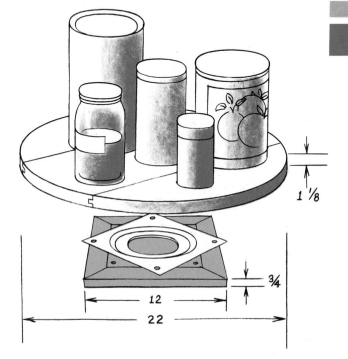

1 ⅛

¾

12

22

Metric Measurements
"		cm
3/4	=	1.8
1-1/8	=	2.8
12	=	30.0
22	=	55.0

Materials

No. pcs.	Part	Dimensions
2	ends	3/4 x 11-1/2 x 17-1/4
1	bottom	3/4 x 10 x 26-1/2
1	front	3/4 x 11-3/4 x 26-1/2
1	back	3/4 x 11-3/4 x 26-1/2
1	lid	3/4 x 10-1/4 x 29
1	back lip	3/4 x 1-3/4 x 29
26	nails	6d square cut
8	screws	1-1/4 x 7 flat head
8	dowel plugs	3/8 x 3/8 + trimmed flush
1	pair hinges	antique butterfly

Metric Measurements

"	cm	"	cm	"	cm
3/8 =	.9	10	= 25.0	18	= 45.0
3/4 =	1.8	10-1/4	= 25.6	26-1/2	= 66.2
1 =	2.5	11-1/2	= 28.7	28	= 70.0
1-3/4 =	4.3	11-3/4	= 29.3	29	= 72.5
5-1/2 =	13.7	12	= 30.0		
6 =	15.0	17-1/4	= 43.1		

Construction Notes

1) Back lip is fastened to top edge of back with nails.
2) Bore 3/8 holes for plugs; then drill 1/16 pilot holes.
3) Attach butterfly hinges flat on the top and back lip.
4) Optional 2" butt hinges can be set into edges of top and lip.
5) If square cut nails are not available, grind or file the heads of box nails so they look like square nails.

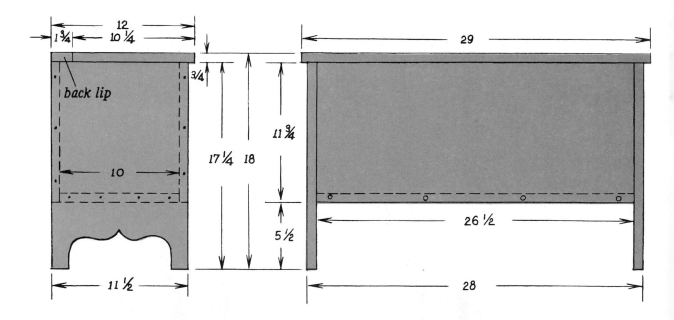

scale: 1" squares

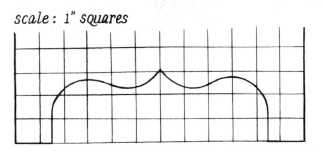

ends fastened with
6d square cut nails

front and back fastened
with 1¼ x 7 screws

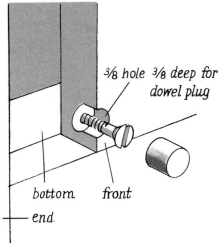

3/8 hole 3/8 deep for
dowel plug

bottom   front

— end

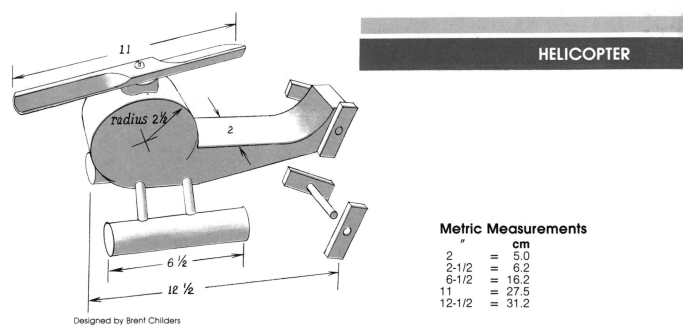

11

radius 2½

2

6 ½

12 ½

Designed by Brent Childers

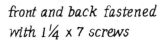

HELICOPTER

Metric Measurements

"		cm
2	=	5.0
2-1/2	=	6.2
6-1/2	=	16.2
11	=	27.5
12-1/2	=	31.2

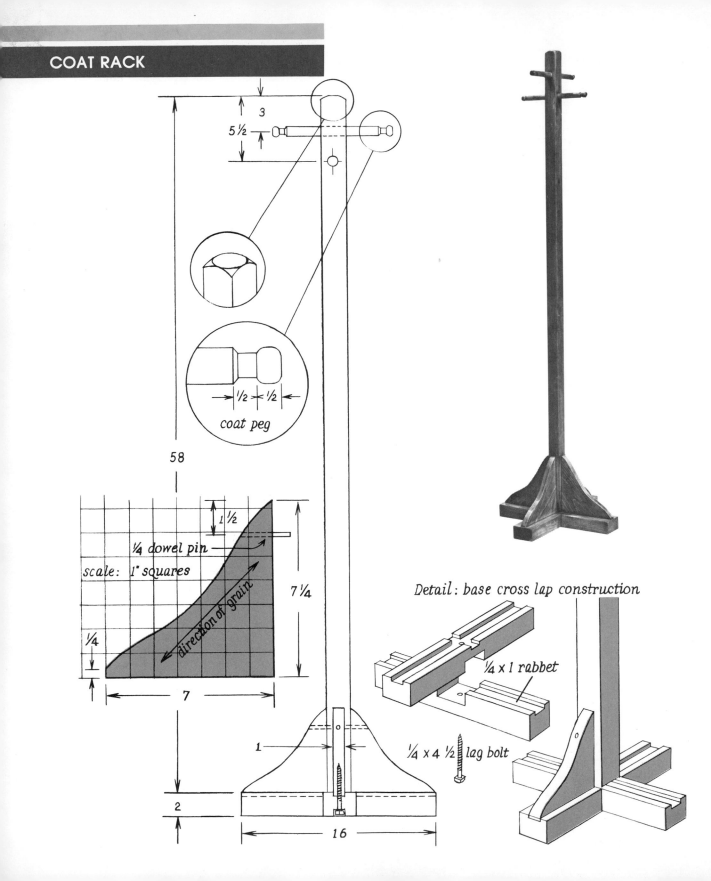

3

5 ½

coat peg

½ ½

58

1 ½

¼ dowel pin

scale: 1" squares

direction of grain

7 ¼

¼

7

1

2

16

Detail: base cross lap construction

¼ x 1 rabbet

¼ x 4 ½ lag bolt

Materials (Coat Rack)

No. pcs.	Part	Dimensions
1	post	2 x 2 x 58
2	base stretchers	2 x 2-3/4 x 16
4	base braces	1 x 5-1/4 x 10-1/4
4	dowel pins	1/4 x 2-1/2
2	coat pegs	3/4 x 10 dowel
1	lag bolt & lock washer	1/4 x 4-1/2

Metric Measurements

"	cm	"	cm	"	cm
1/4 =	.6	2-1/2 =	6.2	7 =	17.5
1/2 =	1.2	2-3/4 =	6.8	7-1/4 =	18.1
3/4 =	1.8	3 =	7.5	10 =	25.0
1 =	2.5	4-1/2 =	11.2	10-1/4 =	25.6
1-1/2 =	3.7	5-1/4 =	13.1	16 =	40.0
2 =	5.0	5-1/2 =	13.7		

KITCHEN POT AND PAN RACK

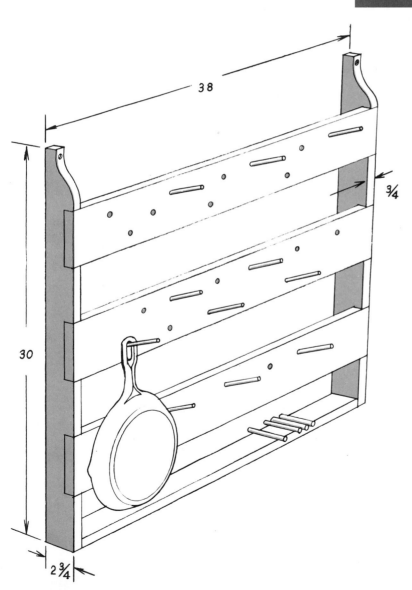

Metric Measurements

"		cm
3/4	=	1.8
2-3/4	=	6.8
30	=	75.0
38	=	95.0

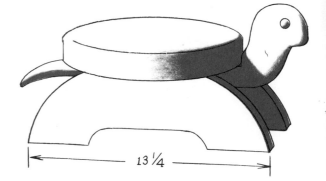

13 ¼

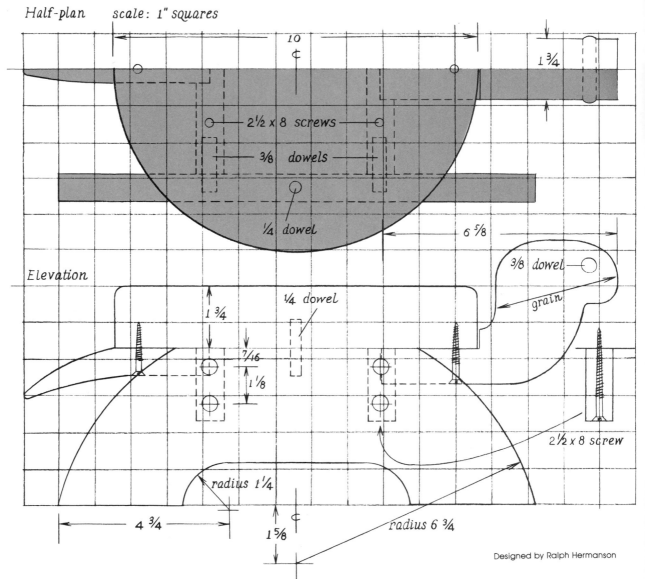

Half-plan   scale: 1" squares

10
¢

1 ¾

2½ x 8 screws

3/8 dowels

¼ dowel

6 ⅝

3/8 dowel

grain

Elevation

1 ¾

¼ dowel

7/16

1 ⅛

2½ x 8 screw

radius 1¼

4 ¾

radius 6 ¾

1 ⅝

Designed by Ralph Hermanson

410

Materials (Turtle Stool)

No. pcs.	Part	Dimensions
1	seat	1-3/4 x 10 diameter
2	sides	3/4 x 4-1/4 x 13-1/4
1	head	1-3/4 x 4 x 6-5/8
1	tail	3/4 x 1-1/2 x 5-1/4
2	cross braces	3/4 x 2 x 5-3/4
8	dowel pins	3/8 x 6-3/4 (sides)
2	dowel pins	1/4 x 1-1/2 (seat)
1	dowel pin	3/8 x 2 (eyes)
1	screw	1-1/2 x 7 flat head (tail)
1	screw	1-3/4 x 7 flat head (head)
4	screws	2-1/2 x 8 (seat)

Metric Measurements

"	cm	"	cm	"	cm
1/4	= .6	1-5/8	= 4.0	5-3/4	= 14.3
3/8	= .9	1-3/4	= 4.3	6-5/8	= 16.5
7/16	= 1.05	2	= 5.0	6-3/4	= 16.8
3/4	= 1.8	2-1/2	= 6.2	7	= 17.5
1	= 2.5	4	= 10.0	8	= 20.0
1-1/8	= 2.8	4-1/4	= 10.6	10	= 25.0
1-1/4	= 3.1	4-3/4	= 11.8	13-1/4	= 33.1
1-1/2	= 3.7	5-1/4	= 13.1		

KNIFE BLOCK

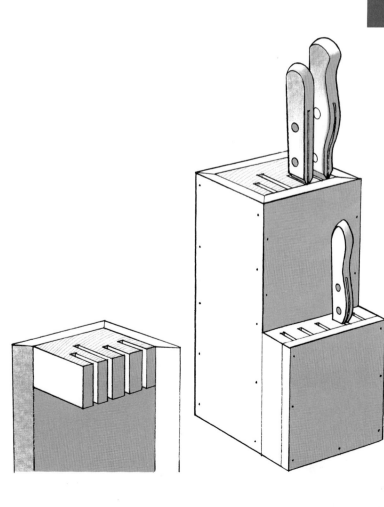

BOOK STAND

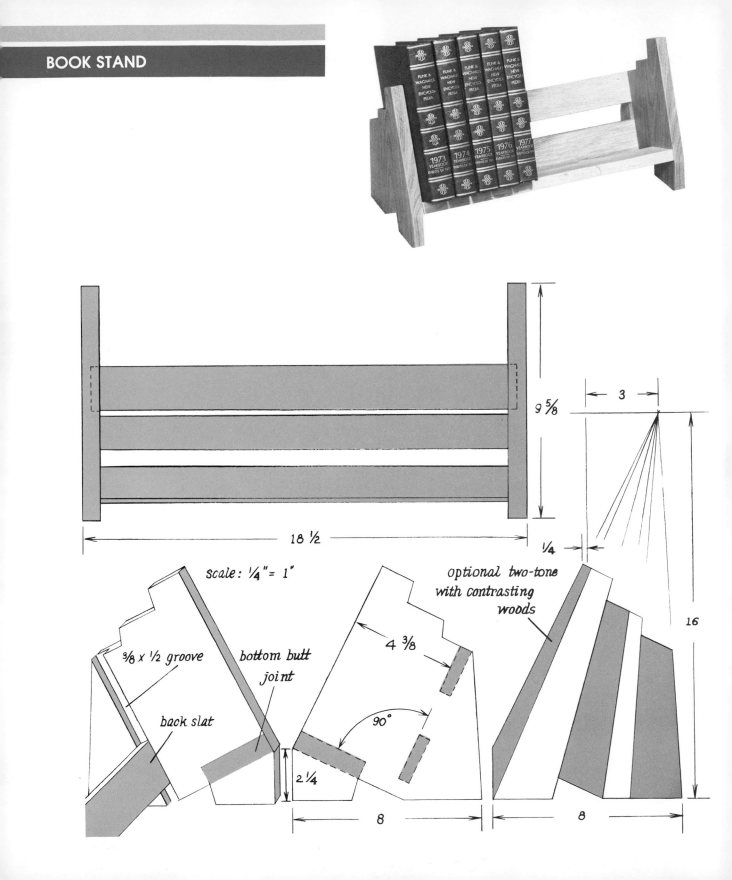

9 5/8

3

1/4

16

18 1/2

scale: 1/4" = 1"

3/8 x 1/2 groove

bottom butt joint

back slat

4 3/8

optional two-tone with contrasting woods

90°

2 1/4

8

8

Materials (Book Stand)

No. pcs.	Part	Dimensions
2	ends	3/4 x 8 x 9-5/8
1	bottom	3/4 x 3 x 17
2	back slats	1/2 x 2 x 17

Metric Measurements

"	cm	"	cm
1/4 =	.6	3 =	7.5
3/8 =	.9	4-3/8 =	10.9
1/2 =	1.2	8 =	20.0
3/4 =	1.8	9-5/8 =	24.0
1 =	2.5	16 =	40.0
2 =	5.0	17 =	42.5
2-1/4 =	5.6	18-1/2 =	46.2

TIC TAC TOE

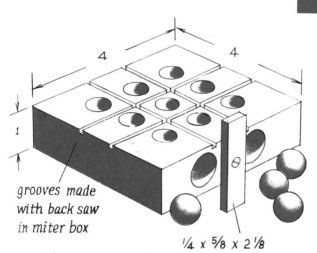

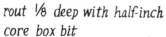

grooves made
with back saw
in miter box

1/4 x 5/8 x 2 1/8

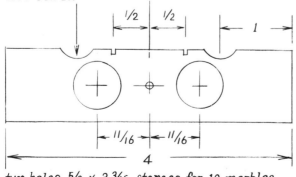

rout 1/8 deep with half-inch
core box bit

two holes 5/8 x 3 3/16, storage for 10 marbles

Metric Measurements

"		cm
1/8	=	.3
1/4	=	.6
1/2	=	1.2
5/8	=	1.5
11/16	=	1.65
1	=	2.5
2-1/8	=	5.3
3-3/16	=	7.95
4	=	10.0

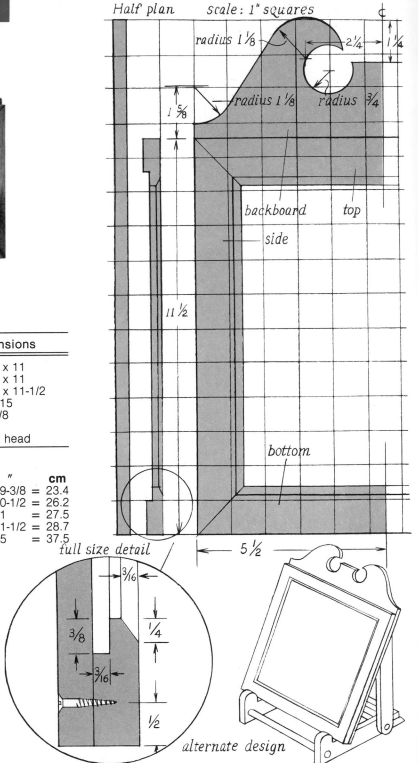

Half plan   scale: 1" squares

radius 1⅛ — 2¼ — 1¼

radius 1⅛   radius ¾

1⅝

backboard   top

side

11½

bottom

5½

full size detail

3/16

3/8   ¼

3/16

½

alternate design

Materials

No. pcs.	Part	Dimensions
1	top	1/2 x 1-3/8 x 11
1	bottom	1/2 x 1-3/8 x 11
2	sides	1/2 x 1-3/8 x 11-1/2
1	backboard	3/8 x 11 x 15
1	glass	8-7/8 x 9-3/8
	padding	9 x 10-1/2
10	screws	5/8 x 6 flat head

Metric Measurements

″	cm	″	cm	″	cm
3/16 =	.45	1-1/4 =	3.1	9-3/8 =	23.4
1/4 =	.6	1-3/8 =	3.4	10-1/2 =	26.2
3/8 =	.9	1-5/8 =	4.0	11 =	27.5
1/2 =	1.2	2-1/4 =	5.6	11-1/2 =	28.7
3/4 =	1.8	5-1/2 =	13.7	15 =	37.5
1 =	2.5	8-7/8 =	22.2		
1-1/8 =	2.8	9 =	22.5		

Construction Notes

1) Glue and assemble 4 pieces of mirror frame; clamp up square and let dry.
2) Insert glass and only enough padding (blotting or newspaper) to prevent rattling.
3) Attach backboard: 3 screws top and bottom, 2 on each side.

Alternate Design

Use same dimensions or reduce for portable dresser-top mirror and folding stand.

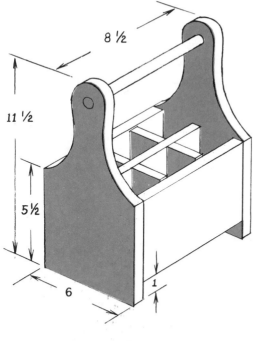

8 ½

11 ½

5 ½

6

1

each partition is 2 x 2

ends and sides ¾
partitions ½
handle ½ dowel

loose-fit removable
partition unit

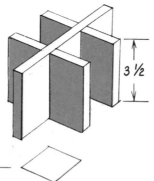

3 ½

Metric Measurements

"		cm
1/2	=	1.2
3/4	=	1.8
1	=	2.5
2	=	5.0
3-1/2	=	8.7
5-1/2	=	13.7
6	=	15.0
8-1/2	=	21.2
11-1/2	=	28.7

PLASTIC LAMINATE CUTTING BOARD

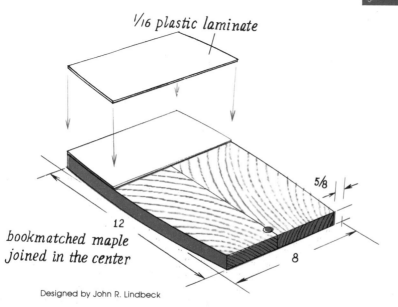

1/16 plastic laminate

5/8

12

bookmatched maple
joined in the center

8

Designed by John R. Lindbeck

Metric Measurements

"		cm
1/16	=	.15
5/8	=	1.5
8	=	20.0
12	=	30.0

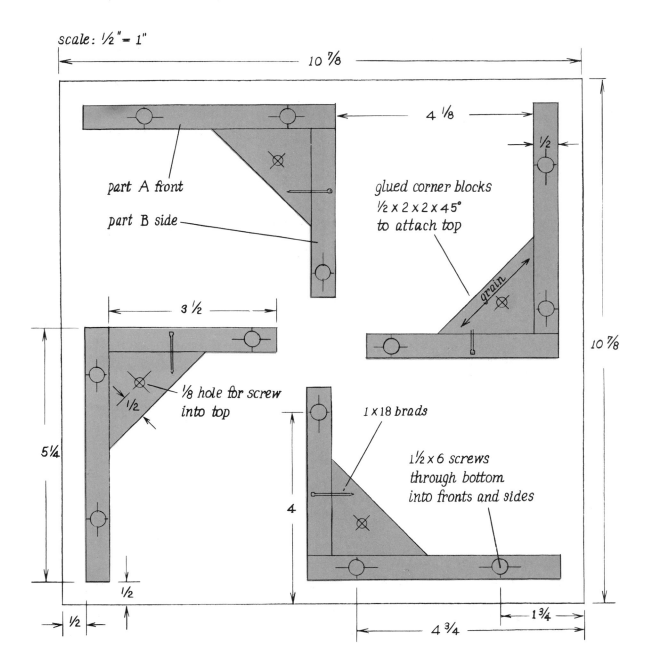

scale: ½" = 1"

10 ⅞

4 ⅛

½

part A front

part B side

glued corner blocks
½ x 2 x 2 x 45°
to attach top

grain

10 ⅞

3 ½

⅛ hole for screw
into top

½

1 x 18 brads

1½ x 6 screws
through bottom
into fronts and sides

5¼

4

½

½

4 ¾

1 ¾

Rockwell International
Power Tool Division

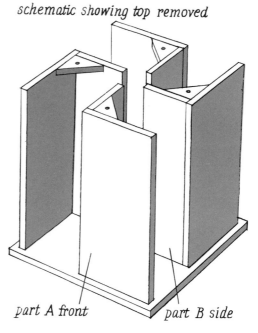

schematic showing top removed

part A front   part B side

Materials

No. pcs.	Part	Dimensions
2	top & bottom	1/2 x 10-7/8 x 10-7/8
4	part A front	1/2 x 5-1/4 x 11-1/4
4	part B side	1/2 x 3-1/2 x 11-1/4
4	corner blocks	1/2 x 2 x 2 x 45°
1	swivel base	1/2 x 8-1/4 x 8-1/4
1	swivel unit	4" or 6" diameter
12	screws	1-1/2 x 6 flat head (bottom)
4	screws	3/4 x 6 flat head (top)
4	brads	1 x 18 (into corner blocks)
8	screws	1/4 x 3 (swivel unit)

Metric Measurements

"	cm	"	cm	"	cm
1/8	= .3	3-1/2	= 8.7	6	= 15.0
1/2	= 1.2	4	= 10.0	8-1/4	= 20.6
1	= 2.5	4-1/8	= 10.3	10-7/8	= 27.2
1-3/4	= 4.3	4-3/4	= 11.8	11-1/4	= 28.1
2	= 5.0	5-1/4	= 13.1	12-1/4	= 30.6

Construction Notes

1) Construction sequence: a) Glue fronts and sides together. b) Attach to bottom. c) Glue in corner blocks. d) Attach optional handle to top. e) Attach top. f) Attach swivel unit.

2) Optional: Omit swivel unit and its wood base.

Alternate Design

A holder can be built to fit smaller tapes by changing dimensions to match actual tapes.

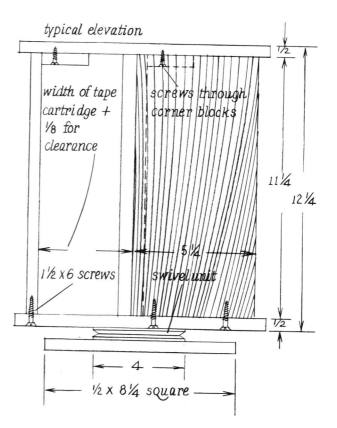

typical elevation

width of tape cartridge + 1/8 for clearance

screws through corner blocks

1/2 x 6 screws

swivel unit

5 1/4

11 1/4

12 1/4

1/2

1/2

4

1/2 x 8 1/4 square

417

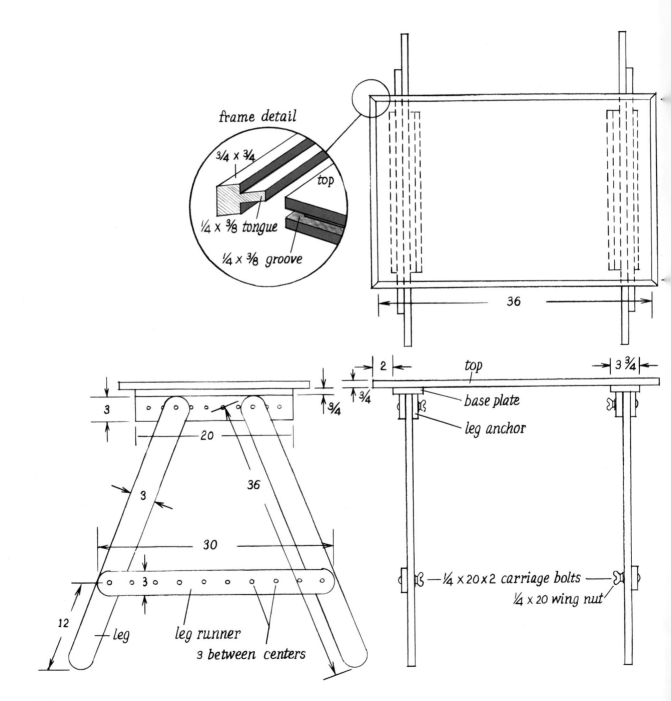

frame detail

3/4 x 3/4

top

1/4 x 3/8 tongue

1/4 x 3/8 groove

36

2

3/4

top

3 3/4

base plate

leg anchor

3

20

36

3

30

3

12

leg

leg runner

3 between centers

1/4 x 20 x 2 carriage bolts

1/4 x 20 wing nut

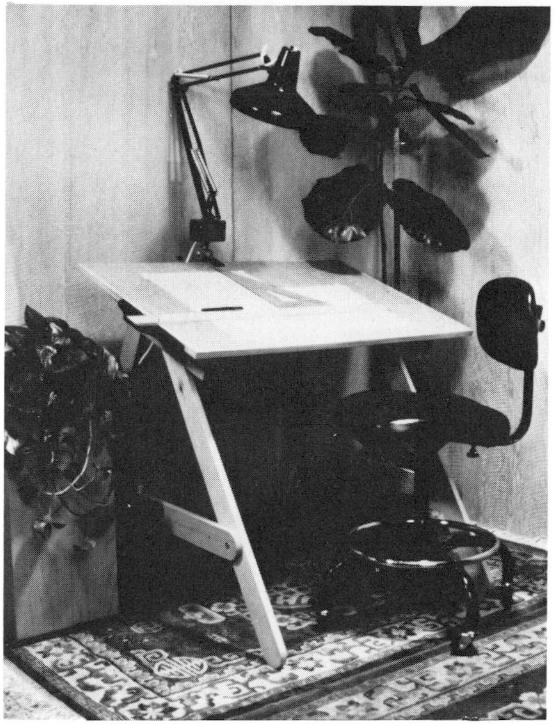

HANDS ON! Magazine (Shopsmith Inc.)
Designed by Jim Lombard

Materials

No. pcs.	Part	Dimensions
1	top	3/4 x 24 x 36 plywood
2	frame ends	3/4 x 3/4 x 25-1/2
2	frame sides	3/4 x 3/4 x 37-1/2
4	legs	3/4 x 3 x 36
2	leg runners	3/4 x 3 x 30
4	leg anchors	3/4 x 3 x 20
2	base plates	3/4 x 3-3/4 x 20
4	carriage bolts	1/4 x 20 x 2
4	carriage bolts	1/4 x 20 x 2-1/2
8	wing nuts	1/4 x 20 and flat washers
20	screws	1-1/4 x 8 flat head

Metric Measurements

"	cm	"	cm	"	cm
1/4	= .6	3	= 7.5	25-1/2	= 63.7
3/8	= .9	3-1/4	= 8.1	30	= 75.0
3/4	= 1.8	3-3/8	= 8.4	36	= 90.0
1-1/8	= 2.8	3-3/4	= 9.3	37-1/2	= 93.7
1-13/16	= 4.45	12	= 30.0		
2	= 5.0	24	= 60.0		

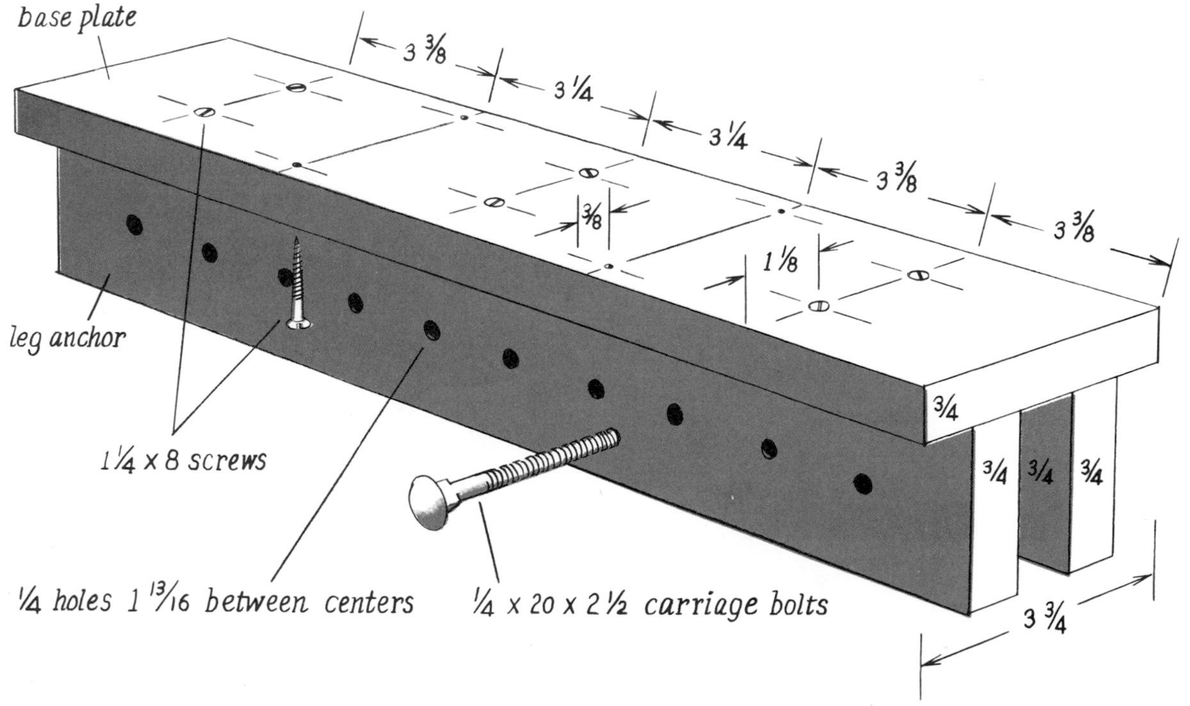
base plate
3 3/8
3 1/4
3 1/4
3 3/8
3 3/8
3/8
1 1/8
leg anchor
3/4
3/4
3/4
3/4
1 1/4 x 8 screws
1/4 holes 1 13/16 between centers
1/4 x 20 x 2 1/2 carriage bolts
3 3/4

MUSIC STAND

Materials

No. pcs.	Part	Dimensions
1	lyre	1/2 x 14 x 20 plywood
1	lyre lip	1 x 1 x 20
1	bracket	3/4 x 4 x 8
4	screws	1 x 6 flat head brass (lip)
2	screws	1-1/4 x 6 flat head brass (bracket)
4	legs	3/4 x 3-3/4 x 16-3/4
4	screws	1-1/2 x 7 flat head (attach legs A)

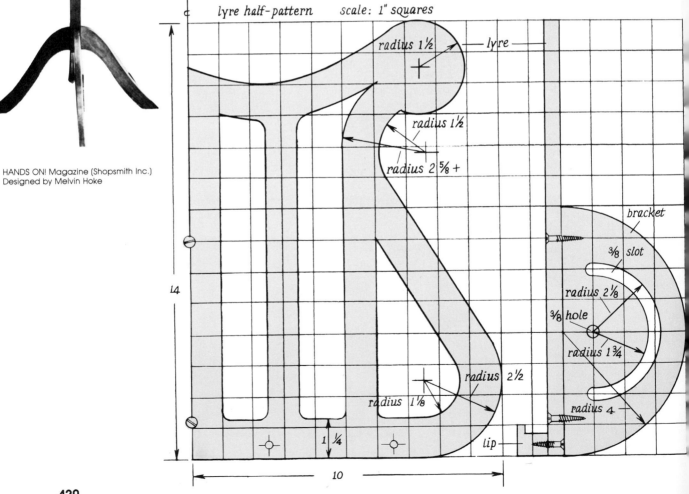

HANDS ON! Magazine (Shopsmith Inc.)
Designed by Melvin Hoke

Materials (Music Stand, cont'd.)

No. pcs.	Part	Dimensions
1	stem	3/4 x 2 x 30
2	stem heads	3/4 x 2 x 9
2	stem box halves	3/4 x 3 x 18
1	dowel	3/8 x 4 (bracket swivel & lock pin)
1	dowel length	1/4 x 18 (joints)
1	carriage bolt	1/4 x 2-1/2 with flat washer & wing nut
1	drawer pull	1″ round

Metric Measurements

″	cm	″	cm	″	cm
1/4 =	.6	1-3/4 =	4.3	9 =	22.5
3/8 =	.9	2 =	5.0	10 =	25.0
1/2 =	1.2	2-1/8 =	5.3	14 =	35.0
3/4 =	1.8	2-1/2 =	6.2	16-3/4 =	41.8
1 =	2.5	2-5/8 =	6.5	18 =	45.0
1-1/8 =	2.8	3 =	7.5	20 =	50.0
1-1/4 =	3.1	3-3/4 =	9.3	30 =	75.0
1-1/2 =	3.7	4 =	10.0		
1-5/8 =	4.0	8 =	20.0		

Construction Note

1) Attach legs A to stem box halves before gluing box together.

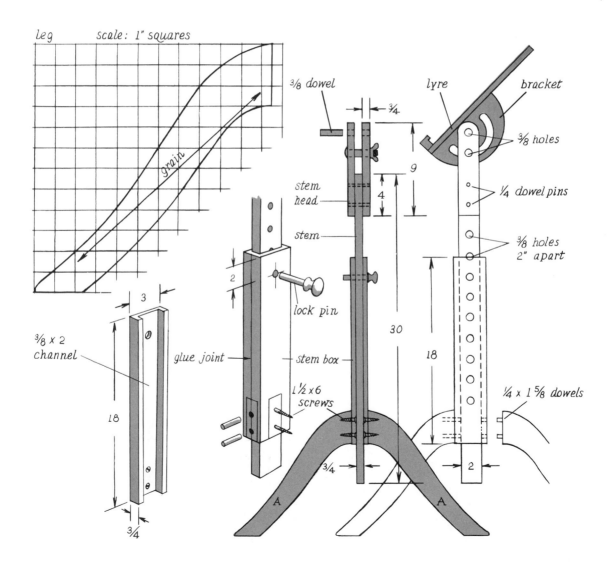

leg   scale: 1″ squares

grain

3/8 dowel

lyre   bracket

3/4

3/8 holes

stem head

9

4

1/4 dowel pins

stem

3/8 holes 2″ apart

lock pin

30

18

3/8 x 2 channel

glue joint

stem box

1 1/2 x 6 screws

3

18

A

3/4

A

2

1/4 x 1 5/8 dowels

3/4

2

421

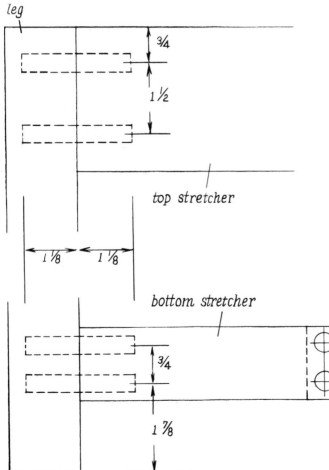

leg

3/4

1 1/2

top stretcher

1 1/8   1 1/8

bottom stretcher

3/4

1 7/8

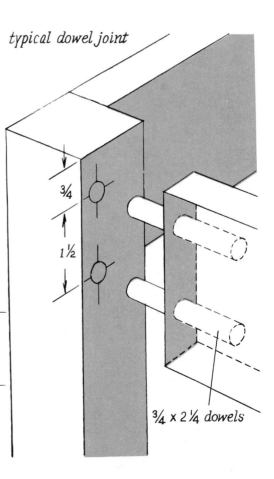

typical dowel joint

3/4

1 1/2

3/4 x 2 1/4 dowels

Materials

No. pcs.	Part	Dimensions
4	legs	1-1/2 x 1-1/2 x 17-1/2
2	top stretchers	3/4 x 3 x 15
2	top end stretchers	3/4 x 3 x 10
2	bottom end stretchers	3/4 x 1-1/2 x 10
1	center stretcher	3/4 x 1-1/2 x 16-1/2
4	cleats	3/4 x 3/4 x 2-1/2
1	seat	3/8 x 12-1/8 x 17
1	length dowel	3/8 x 36

Metric Measurements

"	cm	"	cm	"	cm
1/8	= .3	1-7/8	= 4.7	16-1/2	= 41.2
3/16	= .45	2-1/4	= 5.6	17	= 42.5
3/8	= .9	3	= 7.5	17-1/2	= 43.7
3/4	= 1.8	10	= 25.0	18	= 45.0
1	= 2.5	12-1/8	= 30.3	36	= 90.0
1-1/8	= 2.8	13	= 32.5		
1-1/2	= 3.7	15	= 37.5		

Construction Note

For instructions on upholstery see chapter 47.

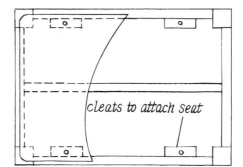

cleats to attach seat

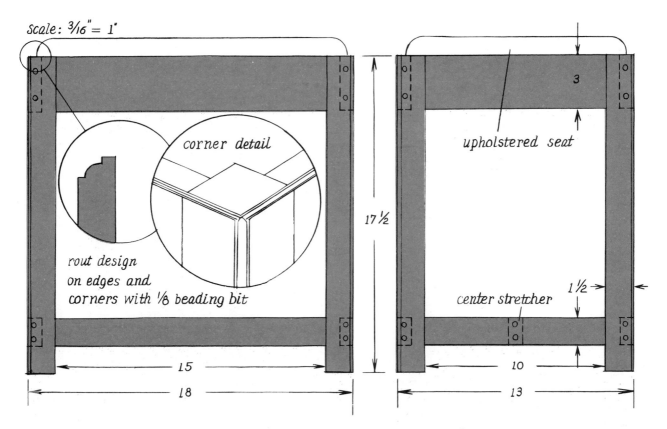

scale: 3/16" = 1"

corner detail

rout design on edges and corners with 1/8 beading bit

upholstered seat

center stretcher

RECORD RACK

Materials

No. pcs.	Part	Dimensions
4	legs	1-1/4 x 1-1/4 x 16-3/4 hardwood
4	rails	3/4 x 19 hardwood dowel
2	top braces	3/4 x 9-1/4 hardwood dowel
2	bottom braces	3/4 x 11-1/2 hardwood dowel
6	vertical rods	3/16 x 14-7/8
1	back rod	3/16 x 19-7/8

Metric Measurements

"		cm	"		cm
3/16	=	.45	9-1/4	=	23.1
5/8	=	1.5	11-1/2	=	28.7
3/4	=	1.8	12	=	30.0
1-1/4	=	3.1	14-7/8	=	37.2
1-5/8	=	4.0	16-3/4	=	41.8
1-13/16	=	4.45	19	=	47.5
3-1/2	=	8.7	19-7/8	=	49.7
4	=	10.0	20	=	50.0

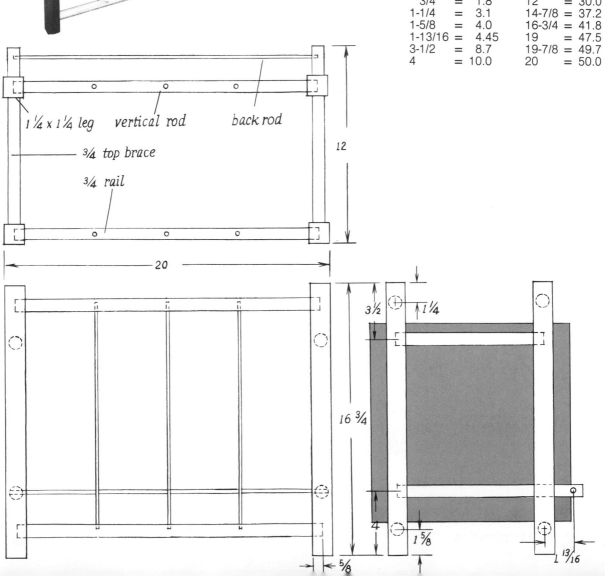

1¼ x 1¼ leg   vertical rod   back rod

¾ top brace

¾ rail

12

20

3½   1¼

16¾

4   1⅝

⅝

1 13/16

Materials

No. pcs.	Part	Dimensions
1	top	1-1/2 x 12 x 18
2	legs	2 x 3-1/2 x 12
2	feet	2 x 5-1/2 x 12
8	dowel pins	1/2 x 2-1/2

Metric Measurements

"	cm	"	cm
1/8 =	.3	2-1/2 =	6.2
1/2 =	1.2	3-1/2 =	8.7
1 =	2.5	5-1/2 =	13.7
1-1/4 =	3.1	6-1/2 =	16.2
1-1/2 =	3.7	12 =	30.0
2 =	5.0	18 =	45.0

HANDS ON! Magazine (Shopsmith Inc.)
Designed by Warren Hoit

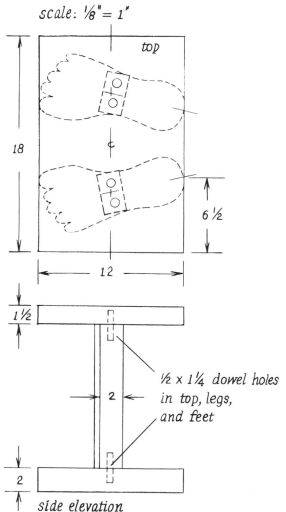

scale: 1/8" = 1"

top

18

6 1/2

12

1 1/2

2

1/2 x 1 1/4 dowel holes
in top, legs,
and feet

2

side elevation

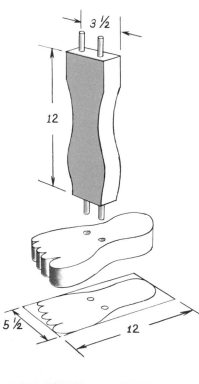

3 1/2

12

5 1/2

12

425

Glossary

abrasive — a rough substance, such as garnet, flint, aluminum oxide, and silicon carbide used to smooth and polish surfaces

adhesive — a sticky substance used to hold parts tightly together

air drying — the natural drying of wood by the sun and wind; used to dry wood for outdoor uses

annual rings — a series of rings formed by the growth of springwood and summerwood in a tree trunk; can be counted to determine the tree's age

antiquing — technique of using glazes to highlight corners and recessed areas; produces aged, antique look

apprentice — a person who learns a profession through on-the-job training

auger bit — a cutting tool designed for use in bit braces

automatic (push) drill — a small hand drill operated by pushing down on the handle

backing board — a flat board used to carry thin stock through a surfacer

backsaw — a saw named for the metal spine that stiffens the saw's thin blade; used to make accurate cuts for wood joints

balloon framing — a type of building frame in which the studs run from the sill plate to the rafters

band clamp — a clamp with a canvas band and tightening device for clamping round and oddly shaped objects

bar clamp — a clamp with a steel bar and two jaws; often used to clamp narrow boards into wide panels

baseboard — a piece of trim nailed to the base of a wall to cover the wall-floor joint

bench hook — a board with a block at one end; used to hold wood in place for sawing

bench rule — a basic measuring rule in 1-, 2-, and 3- foot lengths

bevel — an angle cut across an entire edge or end

bill of materials — a list of all the materials required to complete a project

bird's mouth — a notch cut in a rafter to fit over the top plate

bit brace — a hand boring tool used with boring bits to make holes

blind hole — a hole that does not extend completely through the wood

block plane — a small hand plane ideal for planing end grain and fitting furniture parts and interior trim

board foot — measurement used in buying solid lumber; equals 1 inch thick, 12 inches wide, 12 inches long

boring — the process of making a hole (usually larger than 1/4 inch) with a boring bit

box nail — a nail thinner and lighter than a common nail; used to make boxes and crates

bridging — pieces inserted between floor joists to prevent twisting and to help distribute weight evenly

brushing lacquer — a slow drying lacquer that can be applied with a brush

burl — an abnormal growth on a tree trunk; desirable for veneers because of its swirling grain pattern

burn-in stick — a material used to fill holes in wood; usually made of shellac

burnisher — a tool used to form new edges on scrapers

butt chisel — a short, beveled chisel used primarily to cut gains for door hinges

butt hinge — a square or rectangular hinge used for flush- and surface-mounted doors

butt joint — a simple joint made by butting two surfaces

buttons — small wood pieces used to cover screw heads in counterbored holes

cabinetmaking — the making of fine wood objects, including furniture and cabinets

cabinet scraper — a scraper resembling a spokeshave and used to smooth surfaces; often replaces rough and intermediate sanding

calipers — a measuring tool used mainly to measure round stock

cambium — the thin layer of living cells that surrounds a tree and through which water, gases, and nutrients flow

cane — long, slender stems (usually from rattan palms) used to make seats and backs for chairs; now mostly machine-woven (pressed)

carbide steel — extra hard steel used on the tips of saw teeth and other cutters; stays sharp for extended use

career — a series of related jobs forming a profession; extensive training and education often required

carpentry — the craft of shaping and assembling structures

carriage bolt — an oval-headed bolt used in construction and for joints not visible

casing nail — a nail with a cone-shaped head that can be set below the surface; used for installing windows, door frames, flooring, and trim

C-clamp — a C-shaped clamp used mainly for small pieces

centi — prefix meaning 1/100

chalk line — marking tool that is stretched and snapped to mark a long, thin line

check — crack across the annual growth rings on the end of a board

chuck — the part of a machine or tool that holds the bit or attachment, such as the three-jawed chuck of a hand drill

circular plane — a plane with a flexible frame; ideal for smoothing curved surfaces

claw hammer — a hammer with a claw for removing nails

clearance block — a thick piece of stock used as a gauge in cutting pieces to the same length

clinching — the process of bending over nails driven completely through two boards to strengthen the joint

closed coat — a type of coated abrasive with no spaces between the grains

closed-grain — term for describing wood with small, close-knit pores

coated abrasives — abrasive materials bonded to a backing; "sandpaper"

combination square — a square with an adjustable head used to draw lines and angles, check for squareness, and measure distance

common nail — a large, flat-headed nail ranging in size from 2d to 60d; used mainly in building construction

compass saw — a saw with narrow, tapered blade; used to cut large curves and irregular shapes

compliment — an opposite color on a color wheel

compound cut — cut made on two or more sides of the stock; used mainly to make rough shapes for carving and decorative parts of furniture

compressor — an air pump that provides the compressed air needed to operate a spray gun

coniferous — a classification of trees; keep needle-shaped leaves all year; wood is called softwood

contact cement — an adhesive used primarily to bond plastic laminates, veneers, and metal to wood

coping saw — a saw with a thin blade fastened to a metal frame; used to make fine, irregular shapes and inside cuts

cornice — exterior trim that connects the walls and roof; usually covers the rafters

corrugated fastener — a small ribbed strip of steel with teeth used to quickly join pieces of stock

counterboring — the process of making a hole so a screw can be set below the surface

countersinking — the process of cutting a cone-shaped hole for a flat or oval screw head to be set level with the surface

cove — a concave shape cut in wood

cripple — a short stud used to frame openings in wall frames

crossbands — the veneer sheets on either side of a plywood core

crosscut saw — a saw with small, sharp teeth for cutting across the grain; used to cut wood to length

cup (dead) center — a metal projection that attaches stock to the tailstock of a lathe; does not turn

customary system — a system of measurement used in the United States; being replaced by the metric system

dado head — a set of two saw blades and several chippers used to make cuts wider than those made by a single blade

dado joint — a joint made by cutting a recess across the grain in one board and fitting the end of another board into the recess

deciduous — a classification of trees; lose broad leaves in fall and winter; wood is called hardwood

decimal system — a number system in which all units and prefixes are multiples of 10

decoupage — the application of a picture to a wood surface so the picture appears painted on

depth gauge — a guide for making cuts to a certain depth, such as the gauge attached to auger bits when drilling blind holes

diamond-point chisel — a lathe cutting tool designed to make V-cuts; also used to cut corners and beads

dimensionally stable — term describing materials that do not expand or contract with weather changes

distressing — the process of making a new wood surface look old, by denting and marring it (physical), or by marking it with crayons or pencils (surface)

divider — a marking tool used to make perfect arcs and circles and mark off equal spaces

double-edge scraper — a scraper with a double-edged blade; used primarily to remove dried glue spots, paint, and old finishes

double plane iron — plane iron and plane iron cap held together with a screw in a hand plane; performs the actual cutting

dovetail jig — a metal attachment used as a guide to cut dovetails with a router

dovetail joint — a strong, interlocking joint of alternating notches (the shape of dovetails)

dovetail saw — a thin-bladed saw strengthened with a metal spine; designed to cut dovetail joints

dowel — a cylindrical piece of wood usually used to reinforce butt joints

dowel bit — a bit used to bore dowel holes

dowel center — small metal point used to mark the location of dowel holes

doweling jig — a device for holding drills or bits perpendicular when cutting dowel holes

dowel joint — a joint reinforced with dowels

drawer guide — a track on which a drawer slides; provides smooth, easy movement and support

draw filing — the process of pulling a file across a surface; often used for sharpening scrapers

dressed lumber — lumber that is surfaced on any combination of sides and edges

drilling — the process of making holes (usually less than 1/4 inch) with a drilling tool

drill points — cutting tools used in automatic drills

drop-leaf table — a table with leaves that can be folded down when not in use

duplicator — a lathe attachment used to make identical parts

enamel — an opaque finish much like paint

expansive bit — a bit with two adjustable cutters; used with bit braces to bore large holes

extension rule — a small, sliding ruler at the end of a zig-zag rule; used to measure inside distances

faceplate turning — a lathe turning method in which only one end of the stock is attached to the lathe

face veneer — an outside veneer of plywood

feather board — a wood piece with a series of kerfs cut in one end for flexibility; used to hold stock against a table saw fence

file — a steel blade covered with rows of small cutting edges (teeth) for cutting and smoothing

file card — a wire brush used to clean files and rasps

finger joint — a joint of interlocking, square notches

finishing nail — a nail with a small head that can be set below the surface; used for cabinets, furniture, and moldings

finishing schedule — a list of finish materials and techniques in the order in which they will be used in the finishing process

firmer chisel — an all-purpose chisel ranging in width from 1/8 inch to 2 inches; edges are not usually beveled

fitch brush — a brush made with skunk hair; ideal for applying brushing lacquer and glazes

flitch — a log section from which veneers are cut

floor plan — a drawing of a structure's outline; includes interior dimensions needed by carpenters

footing — the concrete base on which a wall is built; provides a sturdy base for the structure

fore plane — an 18-inch plane used to plane long boards and edges

forestry — the science of developing and caring for forests

Forstner bit — a bit used to make flat-bottomed holes and to hollow out large cavities

foundation — the concrete, brick, or block base of a structure; prevents lifting and uneven settling

framing square — a large steel square with special scales and tables for carpenters

French polish — a finish made of shellac and linseed oil that is hand rubbed into wood

gauge number — a number that indicates the diameter of a nail or screw

gimp — a decorative braided edging tacked to an upholstered seat to cover seams and exposed tacks

girder — a heavy post placed midway between foundation walls to support floor joists

glazing — see *antiquing*

Good 1 side (G1S) — term designating a sheet of plywood with one face veneer of a good grade

Good 2 sides (G2S) — term designating a sheet of plywood with both face veneers of a good grade

gouge — a chisel with a curved blade used to hollow out cavities for bowls and similar projects

grade — a term designating the quality of a material

gram — a weight measurement in the metric system

grid — a pattern of crossing lines drawn to scale; used to transfer irregular designs during layout

groove joint — a joint made by cutting a recess with the grain in one board and fitting the end of another board into the recess

half lap joint — a joint made by cutting away half the thickness of each member, making the joint the same thickness as the rest of the stock

hand drill — a hand tool operated with a handle and crank for drilling small holes

hand scraper — a tool consisting of a steel blade; used to shave off thin layers of wood

hand screw — a versatile, commonly used clamp with two handles and two wooden jaws

hardboard — thin sheets of processed wood; hard, moisture resistent, and mold-proof

hardwood — wood from deciduous (broad-leaf) trees, such as maple, walnut, and cherry

header — 1) a piece of lumber (usually 2 x 10) used in floor framing; 2) board used to support weight over an opening, such as a window

heartwood — the dry, dense wood at the tree's core

hole saw — a cutting tool used to cut large holes completely through stock

honing — the process of sharpening a cutting edge by rubbing it on a stone

inside cut — a cut that cannot be started from the outside of the stock

jack plane — an all-purpose plane with a 14- or 15-inch frame; used for rough and final cuts

jointer plane — the longest available plane; used to plane long surfaces

jointing — the process of using a jointer to make an edge straight and square with a face

joist — a long structural member that extends across foundation walls to support a floor or ceiling

kerf — the groove made by a saw cut

keyhole saw — a narrow-bladed, tapered saw used to cut curves and intricate shapes

kicker — a wood piece attached to a cabinet frame to prevent a drawer from tipping when pulled out

kiln drying — the process of drying lumber in ovens; dries wood enough to be used indoors

kilo — prefix meaning 1,000

knot — wood defect that occurs at the base of a limb or branch

lacquer — a clear finishing material made from various substances, usually synthetic

lag screw — a screw with a square head that provides extra holding power in places that do not show

latex — water-based paint

layout — the measuring and marking of materials to be cut and shaped

lineal foot — the measurement used in buying moldings and preshaped wood; equals 12 inches long

luster — the brightness or sheen (such as semi-gloss and gloss) of a finish material

machine spur bit — an all-purpose bit for making smooth, accurate holes in wood with a drill press

mallet — a soft-faced hammering tool used to drive chisels, gouges, and carving tools

marking gauge — a layout tool for marking lines parallel to edges; useful in marking thicknesses

marquetry — a decorative arrangement of wood pieces

mending plate — a flat piece of steel used to reinforce and repair broken or weakened joints

meter — the base unit for measuring length in the metric system

metric system — a decimal system of measurement used throughout the world

milli — prefix meaning 1/1,000

mill marks — small, arc-shaped marks in wood left by power planing and jointing machines

miter box — a U-shaped box with slots for making accurate angle and straight cuts with a backsaw

miter clamp — a clamp for holding miter joints in place during gluing

miter joint — a joint made by cutting two pieces at an angle (usually 45°) and joining them together

miter saw — a large backsaw used in an adjustable miter box

mock-up — a model built from a sketch to show how a project will look after it is built

molding — a piece of wood used for decoration

mortise-and-tenon joint — a strong joint in which the finger (tenon) of one member fits into the notch (mortise) of the other member

multiview drawing — a drawing that includes three views of a project (front, top, side)

nail claw — a small steel bar with a curved slot at one end for pulling nails

nail set — a small steel punch with a cupped end used to set nails below a surface

neutralizer — an agent that stops the chemical action of a bleach

oilstone — an abrasive stone used to sharpen cutting edges on tools

open coat — a type of coated abrasive with spaces between the abrasive grains

open-grain — term for describing wood with large, open pores

OSHA — the Occupational Safety and Health Act of 1970; set safety standards for industries to protect workers from injury

paint — an opaque finish of color pigments in oil or water vehicles

panel saw — a small (20-inch) crosscut saw

particle board — a processed board made by combining wood wastes, vegetable fibers, petroleum wax, and adhesive under pressure

parting tool — 1) a V-shaped carving tool used to make lines in wood; 2) lathe cutting tool used to make deep, narrow cuts

paste filler — thick paste used to fill the pores in open-grain wood; makes rough surfaces smooth

penetrating oil — an oil finish that penetrates the wood rather than building up on the surface

penny — the term (abbreviated "d") referring to the size of a nail

Phillips-head screw — a wood screw with a cross-shaped slot on its head

phloem — cells formed on the outside of the cambium; transport food manufactured in the leaves to all parts of the tree

photosynthesis — the process in which plants convert sunlight and raw materials into food for growth

pictorial drawing — a drawing that shows three views of a project by picturing it at an angle

pilot hole — a hole drilled into a piece of wood to receive the threaded part of a screw

pipe clamp — a clamp made of pipe; used to clamp materials of various lengths

pitch pockets — small cavities in the surface of a board that often contain sap (pitch) or bark

plain sawing — a sawing method in which the wood is cut tangent to the annual growth rings

plain slicing — a method used to cut hardwood veneers; produces attractive patterns on most woods

plan of procedure — a list of the necessary steps in building a project

plastic laminate — a thin sheet of hard plastic used to cover base materials

plastic wood — a wood-like plastic used to fill holes

platform framing — a type of structural framework in which each floor is built first; walls are then attached to the floor

plugs — see *buttons*

plumb bob — a weight on the end of a string; used to determine if something stands vertically

plywood — a construction material made by gluing together thin layers of wood at right angles

pocket chisel — a short-bladed chisel with beveled edges

polyurethane — a very durable type of synthetic varnish

primary colors — red, yellow, and blue

primer — a finishing mixture applied to a surface to prepare the surface for painting

pumice — an abrasive powder used to rub a final coat of finish to a gloss

push stick — a wood piece used to push narrow stock through a machine cut

quarter sawing — a method of sawing in which the wood is cut perpendicular to the annual growth rings

quarter slicing — a method of cutting oak veneers; produces straight grain patterns

rabbet-dado joint — a joint in which a dado is cut in one piece and a rabbet in the other

rabbet joint — a joint made by cutting a recess along the edge or end of one piece and fitting the end of another piece into the recess

rabbet plane — a plane designed to cut rabbet joints

rafter (common) — the roof supports that slope from the ridge to the top plate

rail — a horizontal piece connecting different vertical members, such as table legs; provides strength and stability

raising the grain — the process of wetting wood surfaces to raise the fibers for sanding; ensures a smooth, even surface

rasp — a hardened steel blade covered with small cutting edges; used to remove large amounts of stock

relief cut — a preliminary cut that eliminates backing out of long cuts and forcing sharp turns

resawing — the process of cutting thick boards into thinner boards

ridge — the horizontal beam running through the middle of a sloped roof at the roof's highest point

rift cutting — a method of cutting wood, usually oak; produces straight grain patterns

ripping bar — a strong steel tool with a curved slot at one end for pulling firmly embedded nails

ripping chisel — a chisel used to remove tacks and staples from a chair frame

ripsaw — a saw with large, rough teeth for cutting with the grain; used to cut wood to width

rotary cutting — a method of cutting softwood veneers; produces a long, continuous veneer

rottenstone — an abrasive powder used to rub a final coat of finish to a high gloss

roundnose chisel — a lathe cutting tool used to shape concave surfaces

router plane — a plane used to clean out the bottoms of dadoes, grooves, and other recessed areas

rubbing compound — a ready-made paste of various grit sizes and colors for rubbing a final coat of finish

rule joint — a special joint for drop-leaf tables; attractive when the leaf is down, invisible when the leaf is up

rush — a variety of wet land plants with long fiberous stems; used to weave rush seats

safety zone — an area marked on the floor around a machine indicating a danger area

sanding block — a device used to hold coated abrasives; ensures smooth, level sanding

sanding drum — a cylinder covered with an abrasive sleeve; attaches to lathes, drill presses, and electric drills

sapwood — the freshly formed wood toward the outside of a tree, consisting of old xylem cells

scale — a measuring tool used to make drawings to scale (according to a proportional relationship between two sets of dimensions)

scissor hinge — a hinge used for flush- and surface-mounted doors

scratch awl — a layout tool for making light scratches on stock; often used to mark locations for holes

Screw Mate — a tool used in a drill to make a shank hole, pilot hole, and countersink, in one operation

Screw Sink — a tool used in a drill to make a shank hole, pilot hole, and a counterbore, in one operation

scribe — to mark by scratching

sealer — a mixture that acts as a barrier between coats of finish to prevent bleeding and mixing

secondary colors — the colors orange, green, and violet; produced by intermixing the primary colors

seedling — a young tree

semi-concealed hinge — a hinge used for lip doors; only the jamb leaf is visible when hung properly

set — the alternating of saw teeth to the left and right; makes kerf wider than the blade to prevent binding

shade — a color produced by adding black to one of the twelve colors on the color wheel

shakes — cracks between the annual growth rings on the end of a board

shank hole — a hole drilled in the first of two pieces to receive a screw

sheathing — the covering material (usually plywood) nailed to the framing members of a building

sheet metal screw — a screw that is threaded along its entire length; useful for attaching plastic or sheet metal to wood

shellac — a clear finishing material made from lac and denatured alcohol

sill — 1) the bottom member of an opening in a wall frame; 2) first structural member bolted to the top of the foundation walls

sketch — a freehand drawing used to solve problems in designing a project

skew — a lathe cutting tool used to make smooth cuts, V-cuts, and shoulder cuts

sliding T-bevel — a tool that can be adjusted to any angle from 0 to 180°; used to check and transfer angles

slipstone — a small, fine oilstone used to sharpen curved and V-shaped blades

slope — the amount of incline a roof has in a certain distance

sloyd knife — a marking tool used to scribe precise layout lines

smooth plane — the shortest bench plane; used primarily for final smoothing and planing, and trimming short stock

softwood — wood from coniferous trees, such as spruce, pine, and redwood

sole plate — the bottom member of a wall frame

solvent — a liquid in which a solid dissolves

spindle turning — a method of lathe turning in which the stock is turned between the two spindles

spiral ratchet screwdriver — a screwdriver that installs and removes screws very quickly; used with changeable blades

spline joint — a joint made strong by inserting a thin piece of wood (spline) into a groove in the joint

splint — a long strip of wood or bark used to make seats for chairs

spokeshave — a cutting tool used to form and shape irregular designs

spray booth — a well-ventilated, enclosed area for spraying finishes

spray gun — the device that regulates the pattern and flow of finish during spraying

spring clamp — a clamp resembling a large clothespin; used to clamp small work

springwood — light, porous wood produced during peak growing seasons

spur (live) center — a spiked, rotating steel projection that attaches the stock to the headstock spindle of a lathe

square foot — the measurement used in purchasing plywood, particle board, and hardboard; equals 12 inches wide and 12 inches long

squarenose chisel — a lathe cutting tool designed to make straight, flat-bottomed cuts

squeeze-out — the glue squeezed from a joint when pressure is applied

stain — a finish material that adds color without hiding the grain

starved joint — a joint from which too much glue has been squeezed

stating the problem — the listing of problems to which the design of a project is the solution

steel square — a large, L-shaped square used to lay out lines and angles and check squareness

stop block — a block used as a gauge in cutting several pieces the same length

straightedge — any tool with at least one straight edge; used to make straight lines between measured points

stretcher — horizontal member that fastens between furniture legs; provides reinforcement

stud — a vertical board (usually a 2 x 4) in a wall frame, to which wall coverings are nailed

subassembly — a small part of a complex assembly

summerwood — dense wood produced during the summer growing season

Surfaced 4 Sides (S4S) — term designating a board planed smooth and flat on both faces and edges

Surfaced 2 Sides (S2S) — term designating a board planed smooth and flat on both faces

Surform Tools — forming tools used to quickly shape and remove wood, plastic, and soft metals

sweep — 1) the amount of curve in a gouge; 2) circle made by turning the handle of a bit brace

tacking tape — a tape used by upholsterers to tack foam pads to their bases

tack rag — a cloth moistened with varnish and turpentine to wipe sanded surfaces clean

tambour — a flexible sliding door such as those used on roll-top desks

tang — a long, narrow point or shaft on one end of a cutting tool; inserted into handles or machine chucks

tape measure — a flexible steel measuring blade coiled in a protective case

taper — an angle cut running the length of a board; becomes narrower towards one end

template — a pattern of cardboard or thin wood; used to lay out and cut curved, identical parts

tint — a color produced by adding white to one of the twelve colors on the color wheel

toenailing — a method of nailing an end of one board to the face of another by driving the nails at a 30° angle

tongue-and-groove joint — a joint made by fitting the tongue of one piece into the groove of another

top plate — the long board that forms the horizontal top of a wall frame

trammel points — a marking tool with two points attached to a bar; used to scribe large arcs and circles

transformer — the device in a spray setup that removes dirt, water, and oil from the compressed air and regulates the air pressure

trimmer — a stud that frames the side of an opening in a wall frame

truss — a strong, triangular framework (usually factory assembled) that supports the ceiling and roof of a structure

try square — small square consisting of a blade and wooden handle; used to check squareness and measure and lay out widths and lengths

twist drills — cutting tools used in hand and electric drills and drill presses to make holes in wood, metal, and plastic

upholsterer's hammer — a special hammer with a magnetized face for picking up tacks and driving them into place

upholstering — the process of installing soft coverings on furniture

upholstery tacks — special, rust-resistant tacks used in upholstering

varnish — a clear finishing material made of natural gums and resins, and oil vehicles

varnish stain — a finish material of clear varnish and color used to stain and seal at the same time

V-block — a device used to hold round stock during drilling operations

veneer — thin layer of wood used to construct plywood and cover unattractive surfaces

wane — an undesirable, rounded edge on a board

warp — an unwanted twist or bend in a board

wash coat — a thinned solution of the appropriate sealer; usually applied before fillers

wax — a finish material used as a polish and sometimes as a final finish

webbing — a rubber, cloth, or plastic upholstery material that supports springs and padding

webbing stretcher — an upholstery tool for stretching webbing across a frame

wet-or-dry abrasive — abrasive used with lubricant to sand final coats of finish

whittling — a carving method using knives and saws to produce three-dimensional objects

wood putty — a doughy substance used to repair small defects in wood

worked lumber — lumber that is cut to a particular design at the sawmill

working drawing — a detailed drawing that shows the size, shape, and dimensions of a project and its parts

xylem — cells formed on the inside of the cambium that transport minerals and water from the root system throughout the tree

zigzag rule — a rule that can be folded and unfolded with a zigzag motion; usually in 4-, 6-, and 8-foot lengths

Index